A Great Plains

D0834514

A Great Plains Reader

Edited by

Diane D. Quantic

and P. Jane Hafen

University of
Nebraska Press
Lincoln and London

Acknowledgments for the use of previously
published material appear on pages 723–28,
which constitute an extension of the copyright page.

978
G

∞

Library of Congress
Cataloging-in-Publication Data
A Great Plains reader / edited by Diane D. Quantic
and P. Jane Hafen.
p. cm.
Includes bibliographical references and index.
ISBN 0-8032-3802-9 (cl.: alk. paper) –
ISBN 0-8032-8853-0 (pbk.: alk. paper)
1. Great Plains–History–Sources. 2. Frontier and
pioneer life–Great Plains–Sources. 3. Great Plains–
Description and travel–Sources. 4. Great Plains–
Biography. 5. Natural history–Great Plains–Sources.
I. Quantic, Diane Dufva. II. Hafen, P. Jane.
F591 .G763 2003
978—dc21
2002031968

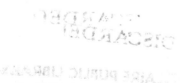

Contents

Foreword: What Is in This Reader, *xi*
Introduction: Toward a Definition of the Great Plains, *xvii*

PART I. THE LAY OF THE LAND

The Nature of the Plains: Impressions, *3*
N. Scott Momaday, *4*
  Excerpt from *The Names*, *4*
Ian Frazier, *15*
  Excerpt from *Great Plains*, *15*
Sharon Butala, *24*
  The Subtlety of Land, *24*
Loren Eiseley, *37*
  The Flow of the River, *37*
William Least Heat-Moon, *44*
  Atop the Mound, *44*

Plains Nature: Natural Histories, *49*
John Madson, *50*
  The Lawns of God, *50*
William Stafford, *68*
  In Response to a Question, *68*
Greg Kuzma, *70*
  Songs, *70*
Dan O'Brien, *73*
  Excerpt from *The Rites of Autumn*, *73*
Paul A. Johnsgard, *82*
  Seasons of the Sandhill Crane, *82*
Paul Gruchow, *88*
  Spring 4, *88*
Bruce Cutler, *93*
  From a Naturalist's Notebook, *93*
Linda Hasselstrom, *95*
  Coffee Cup Cafe, *95*
  Red Glow in the Western Sky, *97*
William Least Heat-Moon, *100*
  Under Old Nell's Skirt, *100*
Denise Low, *105*
  Another Tornado Dream, *105*

Wallace Stegner, *107*
  The Question Mark in the Circle, *107*

PART 2. NATIVES AND NEWCOMERS ON THE GREAT PLAINS

First Stories: Native American Accounts, *123*
Zitkala-Ša, *125*
  When the Buffalo Herd Went West, *125*
Charles Eastman, *130*
  A Legend of Devil's Lake, *130*
John G. Neihardt, *136*
  The Great Vision, *136*
Luther Standing Bear, *150*
  Crow Butte, *151*
  The Holy Dog, *152*
Ella Cara Deloria, *154*
  Excerpt from *Waterlily*, *154*
Zitkala-Ša, *166*
  Impressions of an Indian Childhood, *166*
Louise Erdrich, *179*
  Father's Milk, *179*
Joy Harjo, *193*
  Grace, *193*
  Deer Dancer, *194*
  For Anna Mae Pictou Aquash . . . , *196*
  Deer Ghost, *197*

Stories of Exploration and Travel: Newcomers' Accounts, *199*
Pedro de Castaneda, *201*
  Excerpts from "The Narrative of the Expedition of Coronado," *202*
Meriwether Lewis and William Clark, *206*
  Excerpt from *The Lewis and Clark Journals*, *207*
Edwin James, *218*
  Excerpt from *From Pittsburgh to the Rocky Mountains*, *218*
Josiah Gregg, *231*
  On the Trail, *231*
Diane Glancy, *241*
  October \ From the Back Screen of the Country, *241*
Susan Shelby Magoffin, *243*
  Excerpts from *Down the Santa Fe Trail and into Mexico*, *244*
Washington Irving, *251*
  The Grand Prairie—A Buffalo Hunt, *251*
Francis Parkman, *258*
  The Platte and the Desert, *258*

Preface to *The Oregon Trail,* 4th ed., *266*
Preface to *The Oregon Trail,* illustrated ed., *268*
Kenneth Porter, *270*
   Land of the Crippled Snake, *270*
Mark Twain, *273*
   Excerpts from *Roughing It, 273*

PART 3. ARRIVING AND SETTLING IN

Pioneers, *285*
James Fenimore Cooper, *287*
   Ishmael Bush's Camp, *288*
Robert J. C. Stead, *297*
   Prairie Land, *297*

Settlers, *305*
Linda Hogan, *307*
   Calling Myself Home, *307*
   Red Clay, *308*
   Heritage, *309*
   Return: Buffalo, *310*
   Crossings, *312*
Hamlin Garland, *314*
   Among the Corn Rows, *315*
William Allen White, *333*
   A Story of the Highlands, *334*
Diane Glancy, *339*
   September \ Peru, Kansas, *339*
O. E. Rølvaag, *341*
   Home-founding, *342*
John Ise, *368*
   A New Homestead, *369*
William Stafford, *374*
   The Farm on the Great Plains, *374*
Era Bell Thompson, *376*
   God's Country, *376*
James Welch, *389*
   Excerpt from *Killing Custer, 389*
Louise Erdrich, *407*
   Dear John Wayne, *407*

PART 4. ADAPTING TO A NEW COUNTRY

Surviving Nature's Storms, *411*
Ron Hansen, *413*
   Wickedness, *413*

Sinclair Ross, *426*
   A Field of Wheat, *426*
May Williams Ward, *434*
   Dust Bowl (A Sequence), *434*
Lois Phillips Hudson, *437*
   The Water Witch, *437*

Creating Communities in America, *445*
Willa Cather, *447*
   Neighbour Rosicky, *447*
O. E. Rølvaag, *471*
   Excerpt from *Peder Victorious*, *471*
Mari Sandoz, *480*
   The Christmas of the Phonograph Records, *481*
Will Weaver, *491*
   A Gravestone Made of Wheat, *491*
Luther Standing Bear, *504*
   What the Indian Means to America, *504*
Zitkala-Ša, *507*
   Americanize the First American, *507*
Elizabeth Cook-Lynn, *512*
   End of the Failed Metaphor, *512*
Linda Hogan, *520*
   Oklahoma, 1922, *520*

PART 5. THE GREAT PLAINS COMMUNITY

The Great Plains Community, *529*
William Allen White, *531*
   The Passing of Priscilla Winthrop, *531*
Langston Hughes, *541*
   Dance, *542*
   Carnival, *552*
Larry Woiwode, *560*
   The Old Halvorson Place, *560*
Greg Kuzma, *574*
   A Person in My Life, *574*
Frederick Manfred, *581*
   Wild Land, *581*
Wright Morris, *609*
   Excerpt from *The Home Place*, *611*
Robert Kroetsch, *621*
   Excerpt from *Badlands*, *622*
Douglas Unger, *629*
   Excerpt from *Leaving the Land*, *629*

Sharon Butala, *641*
　A Tropical Holiday, *641*
Garrison Keillor, *650*
　Collection, *651*
　Life Is Good, *654*
John Janovy Jr., *659*
　Home on the Range, *659*
Ron Hansen, *669*
　Red-Letter Days, *669*
Louise Erdrich, *678*
　The Tomahawk Factory, *678*
Linda Hasselstrom, *694*
　Going to the Post Office, *694*
William Stafford, *698*
　The Rescued Year, *698*

EPILOGUE

Sustaining America's Grasslands, *703*
Kathleen Norris, *705*
　Sea Change, *706*
Wes Jackson, *712*
　Matfield Green, *713*

Source Acknowledgments, *723*
Index of Works by Author, *729*

Foreword: What Is in This Reader

Selections in this reader reflect historical and contemporary experiences of life on the Great Plains. Stories by Hamlin Garland, Willa Cather, O. E. Rølvaag, Mari Sandoz, and Black Elk are classics of Great Plains literature. Other selections are included because they are especially good accounts of common Great Plains experiences that, over the years, have become embedded in our mental store-houses as typical stories of the Great Plains. Selections by contemporary writers represent reworkings of classic themes and indicate new directions for the region's literature. Native American writers remind us of traditional values. Although some of these authors and works may prove ephemeral, they nevertheless reflect the region's accumulated characteristics at the beginning of the twenty-first century.

We hope that readers familiar with the Great Plains will find selections that confirm or illuminate their own observations and experiences. Readers who have not read widely of the region's literature should find a variety here that will introduce them to the region.

The parts of *A Great Plains Reader* are organized around common topics. We invite you, the reader, to browse and enjoy the changes of place and time rather than to head straight through the volume bent on an inexorable survey of Great Plains literature. For the curious reader and the student of literature there are suggestions for further readings. A few footnotes for unfamiliar terms and references are provided. We hope you will gain from these readings a deeper appreciation for the grand sweep of space we have confidently labeled the Great Plains.

In part 1, "The Lay of the Land," writers consider the ways that travelers and residents have attempted to record the imprint that the deceptively simple landscape leaves on the observer. The first section there, "The Nature of the Plains: Impressions," focuses on the psychological impact that the physical landscape has on observers. As William Least Heat-Moon says, "people connect themselves to the land as the imaginations allow." N. Scott Momaday recounts his earliest memories of his family's historical and mythical Kiowa past. Ian Frazier guides the contemporary traveler's first visual and visceral experience coming onto the plains. Sharon Butala has a keen eye for the hidden flower or creature on her husband's Canadian ranch, and Loren Eiseley, an equally keen observer of the plains' imaginative dimension, literally connects himself with the breadth of the Platte River by floating over the sands of geologic time. Heat-Moon describes the mirage of distance that defines his walk toward a high point in the Kansas Flint Hills.

"Plains Nature: Natural Histories," the second section, includes the careful observations of residents who have learned the language necessary to recreate on paper the region's physical landscape: the weather and, more especially, the flora and fauna that is apparent to anyone who looks carefully at the "empty" grasslands. John Madson's careful catalog of prairie grasses reflects a naturalist's attention to the complex relationships hidden in the grasses' intricate networks. William Stafford and Greg Kuzma record their poetic perspectives of plains nature. Dan O'Brien, following the falcon's invisible sky-path, describes the region's grasslands as he travels south with his falcon, Dolly. Paul Johnsgard creates word pictures of the graceful sandhill crane. Paul Gruchow describes wind, a constant in the life of any plains resident. Linda Hasselstrom provides an account of a plains social hour; she and Bruce Cutler record their reactions to the prairie fires that still elicit terror among prairie dwellers. Heat-Moon relates his discovery of an old house, a foundation for his reading of the history of the place. Denise Low presents a poet's imaginative perspective on the plains' tornadic character. In "The Question Mark in the Circle," Wallace Stegner contrasts a child's excited perspective with the grim reality that confronts his parents.

Part 2, "Natives and Newcomers on the Great Plains," focuses on Indian accounts and reports of the first European explorers. These selections written by Indians include legends and experiences that describe the intricate network of social customs and religious beliefs that guided the tribes' ways of living on the Great Plains. Zitkala-Ša and Charles Eastman relate traditional Sioux stories. John Neihardt records the stories and visions of the Lakota elder Black Elk. Luther Standing Bear (Dakota), Ella Deloria (Dakota), and Zitkala-Ša recount their childhood introductions to white society. Two contemporary Indian authors, Joy Harjo (Muscogee Creek) and Louise Erdrich (Ojibwe), use traditional stories and tribal histories in their poetry and fiction.

In the second section of part 2 we provide passages from the reports of explorers who searched for money and space to ensure the wealth and ambition of Europeans and eastern Americans. Accounts of the expeditions led by Coronado, Lewis and Clark, and Stephen Long stirred the interest of traders who established trails across the plains and were followed by people anxious to improve their social and economic situations by going to a "new" country. Edited accounts of these first expeditions began to appear in the early 1800s, and they captured the imagination of Americans who persisted in regarding the West in mythic dimensions. The land looked empty, and despite the absence of a water passage to the rich trade with China, the nation's Manifest Destiny clearly called for westward expansion to the very edge of Oregon's rugged coast without regard to the impact on the area's indigenous inhabitants.

In an excerpt from *Commerce on the Prairies*, Josiah Gregg provides a vivid account of the journey on the Santa Fe Trail across Kansas to New Mexico, while Susan Shelby Magoffin provides a parallel view to Gregg's. As a young woman of seventeen she kept a journal of the adventures and hardships she encountered traveling the Santa Fe Trail with her husband, a seasoned Santa Fe trader. Inevitably, literary travelers added reports of their journeys on the prairies. Washington Irving toured the Oklahoma prairies in 1832, anxious to see the "great Indian tribes" before they disappeared or became "amalgamated." Already an established writer, Irving undertook his trip west as a way to reacquaint himself with America after spending almost two decades in Europe. Frances Parkman's *The Oregon Trail,* another literary account of prairie travels and adventure, has remained in print almost continuously since it was first published in 1849, including editions illustrated by Frederic Remington and Thomas Hart Benton. In *Roughing It* Mark Twain reported on his travels across the region bound—like thousands of others—for the Nevada gold fields. Twain's contribution added to plains lore his distinctively satirical account of his encounters on the trail. These and many other less-memorable reports added to the amalgam of fact and imagination—with the noted absence of Native voices—that was forming the standards for popular tales of the Great Plains.

Part 3, "Arriving and Settling In," includes stories of the first white settlers who came onto the plains without any real knowledge of the land. Carrying with them supplies and expectations not always suited to the tasks they faced, some stayed only long enough to realize failure. In James Fenimore Cooper's *The Prairie,* the settler Ishmael Bush assumes that the absence of topographical landmarks means that they are beyond the "marks" of civilization as well: he assumes that everything he sees is his for the taking. Natty Bumppo, in contrast, lives a simple, nomadic life and finds peace and comfort among his Indian friends (the "noble savage" prototype that still exists) under the great dome of sky: he dies facing a blazing prairie sunset. Even in this early imaginative work Cooper recognizes the ambiguity of the pioneers' presence in a place that they can either respect or exploit.

Newcomers who stayed had to learn to adapt to the land, creating homes from the sod itself and adjusting to the capricious weather and the isolation dictated by the Homestead Act, which required settlers to live on their 160-acre claims. The stories of this period reflect the authors' ambivalence about a place that demanded hard work and isolation but promised security and abundance.

Canadian writers have contributed to Great Plains lore accounts of settlers coming onto the prairies of Manitoba, Saskatchewan, and Alberta. Their stories are similar to ones written about the more southern Great Plains, with a few notable differences. Canadians did not share the myth of the Wild West: white settlers spread across the Canadian prairie somewhat later than in the United States and the rule of law was more firmly established before they came. Nevertheless, the hardships of the place and the grim purposefulness of those who sacrificed family and themselves to survive on it are evident in Canadian fiction. Robert J. C. Stead, in his novel *The Homesteaders,* recounts the histories of families whose contrasting values became evident on the frontier. The passage from

Stead's work included in this volume is an account of the selection of a homesite that will, in large measure, determine a family's success or failure.

Some of the settlers who came to stay on the Great Plains homesteaded, but others took over farms abandoned by those who moved further west or gave up and backtrailed to the east. Linda Hogan's poems remind us of the deep ties Indians have to the land claimed by these newcomers and that some Indians were involuntarily displaced to the Great Plains as well. Hamlin Garland's story "Among the Corn Rows" relates the determination of a young man to be an equal in the community of fellow homesteaders and to become a successful farmer with a wife equal to the task of helping him establish his own place on the land. Some came and stayed only because they were too poor or too dispirited to leave. William Allen White's piece "A Story of the Highlands" is an account of a woman's steady decline into isolation and madness, trapped on the dry and desolate high plains. Diane Glancy's poetic wordplay establishes a kind of balance for those who long ago "settled in."

Rølvaag's classic novel *Giants in the Earth,* the story of a small community of Norwegians who move to the very edge of Euro-American settlement in Dakota territory, is one of many novels that relate the experiences of immigrants who had to adapt to a new culture as well as to an unfamiliar landscape. Rølvaag tells the story of Per Hansa, the heroic yeoman farmer fully confident of his success, and his reluctant wife who feels threatened and intimidated by the prairie landscape. John Ise recounts the experiences of his parents who arrived on the plains and stayed long enough to assure their children's success, and Stafford remembers his summers as a boy on a Saskatchewan wheat farm while his father tried, and failed, to be a wheat farmer.

Among the settlers on the Great Plains were exodusters, freed slaves who with thousands of European immigrants flooded onto the plains in the years immediately following the Civil War. Era Bell Thompson's autobiography is one of only a few accounts of the efforts of African Americans to establish farms on the Great Plains. James Welch's accounts of his Blackfeet ancestors' fate and Erdrich's poetic address to John Wayne remind us that the settlers who were intent on transforming the plains into farmland displaced the native tribes who had lived on those grasslands for hundreds of years.

Readers can trace the development of the Great Plains in the region's literature. Writers do not simply retell the pioneers' stories: they create their own variations of the repetitive story of the struggle to survive physical and economic hard times. The stories in part 4, "Adapting to a New Country," recount the various difficulties that later arrivals faced in the effort to establish stable farms, families, and communities. The section includes accounts of survival: those who faced social and cultural isolation or confronted the vagaries of weather—blizzard, dust, or drought—and those who persisted until they had familiar communities around them. Ron Hansen, Sinclair Ross, and Lois Phillips Hudson retell the survival story: physical and psychological deprivation persist, especially among women left isolated and vulnerable by forces that can still destroy crops and lives. Hansen titles his story of a Nebraska blizzard "Wickedness," summing up the apparently conscious determination of the storm to annihilate the people trapped in its grip. Ross's farmer survives a hailstorm that destroys his promising crop, but more destructive than pounding hail is the farmer's breakdown, witnessed by his wife. May Williams Ward lived in western Kansas in the 1930s. Her poem "Dust Bowl (A Sequence)" is her memory of those stormy years. Hudson sums up the effects of long-term drought and depression, stating, in effect, that one exacerbates the other.

The stories in the section "Creating Communities in America" explore the various barriers that Indians, immigrants, and newcomers face as they work to establish their own communities or adapt to communities that have already determined social and cultural norms. Cather's Anton Rosicky spends his last months retelling his story of immigration to assure himself that his children understand the importance of having a place on the land. In *Peder Victorious,* the second volume of his trilogy of Norwegian immigration and acculturation presented here, Rølvaag examines the cultural conflicts that separate immigrant parents and their Americanized children. Sandoz recounts the arrival of a phonograph that brings a community together, and Will Weaver counters with a contemporary retelling of a community's rejection of a latter-day immigrant.

For almost two hundred years American Indians have faced seizure of their lands and forced attempts at assimilation. Indifference, prejudice, abandonment, hostility, and even sympathy from the white majority have prohibited Indian nations from determining their own futures and from telling their own stories. Many of the writers in this volume have constructed their own ideas of Indians based on stereotyped and imaginative objectifications. Other writers simply have forgotten about the original inhabitants of the Great Plains so that the absence of Natives and the silence of their voices are conspicuous. In the 1920s various groups, both Indian and white, advocated fuller inclusion of Native Americans in the decision-making processes that would guarantee protection of rights and property. Zitkala-Ša and Standing Bear wrote declarations concerning these issues. Elizabeth Cook-Lynn provides a contemporary commentary on Indians' continuing struggle for recognition on their own terms. In the opening chapter of her novel *Mean Spirit,* Linda Hogan focuses on the exploitation of the Oklahoma Indians' oil and land.

The final part of this compilation, "The Great Plains Community," includes accounts of change in the social order, in families, in generations, and in communities. The stories included reflect the conflicting impulses that people and towns contend with: optimism versus fatalism, individualism versus community interdependence. White presents a humorous account of the forces of democratization at work in a small-town women's club. Langston Hughes writes of a young black boy's introduction to the wider world through jazz and a traveling carnival in a small Kansas town. In "The Old Halvorson Place" Larry Woiwode encapsulates the subtle changes that result from gradual out-migration when new tenants of a house come upon evidence of the former owners. Kuzma focuses on one person, his father, in his poem about the persistence of memory. In a story by Frederick Manfred an unbroken piece of land becomes a connection to ghosts of the past. Canadian Robert Kroetsch, in his novel *Badlands,* considers William Dawe, who attempts to slip from time and history by floating down Alberta's Red Deer River to prehistoric bedrock. Butala recounts a woman's brief but idyllic escape in "A Tropical Holiday." Douglas Unger's story *Leaving the Land* recounts the losses, personal and corporate, in a fading western South Dakota town, and in "Red-Letter Days" Hansen chronicles the enervating lassitude that characterizes some of those who grow old in isolated small towns. Erdrich recounts the efforts of the stubborn entrepreneur Lyman Lamartine to bring economic success to his tribe's reservation. John Janovy and Hasselstrom recount activities that fill the days of people who elect to stay on isolated ranches and towns because they cannot imagine living any place else. Garrison Keillor, like White, adds humor to his account of life in a town where even the simplest act can become a story.

The epilogue focuses on the future of the American Great Plains. Kathleen Norris and Wes Jackson, writing from quite different perspectives, suggest changes in attitude and social structure that could enable people on the Great Plains to live well in places they have learned to value.

The stories, essays, excerpts, and poems in *A Great Plains Reader* reflect the intricate and complex relationships of land and people in the Great Plains. We hope they enable you to explore your own Great Plains experience.

Introduction: *Toward a Definition of the Great Plains*

Transcontinental travelers who fly over the Great Plains are puzzled at the geometry below them: fencelines and roads outline pastures and fields at sharp right angles, and towns look like counted cross-stitch squares of orderly trees and lines of lights at night. Only along waterways does the high-flying observer see the meandering lines of trees that mark creeks or rivers following their own courses across the apparently flat land. Travelers on the arrow-straight interstates find the trip across the region monotonous. They do not understand how anyone can see a landscape where they see nothing but a flat line. Such a perspective belies a rich and varied place of ancient stories and constant change.

Most residents of the Great Plains learn to appreciate the immensity of a far horizon under a great sky dome. They see the groves of trees, the grain elevators, and the water towers as pinpoints that signal human presence between the sharp grids of roads and sections lines. Those who have patience and a sharp eye learn to look around their feet for the bravura color of the prairie flowers and the carefully hidden eggs of grassland birds. Great Plains dwellers know that what lies beneath the surface determines success or failure. The intricate networks of pasture grasses and dark brown fields signal fertile soils. The Ogallala aquifer, an ocean trapped thousands of feet below the high plains of Kansas and Nebraska, supplies water to the center pivot sprinklers that water the round fields of corn that feed the cattle that support the beef industry that brings prosperity to the plains. All of this activity is invisible on the flat surface that retreats into the rearview mirror of the traveler headed somewhere else.

Most books about the Great Plains begin with an effort to pin down the region geographically, to make one simple definition apply to one definite place. But the fact is, every map of the Great Plains differs from every other map. Although most residents and travelers believe they know just where the Great Plains begin and end, specific all-purpose boundaries soon become problematic. To consider the region's literature, for example, the definition must encompass a complex network of factors: not only the setting, the political boundaries, the geography, and the ecology, but more elusive qualities too. Recurrent themes in the literature center on the efforts of Natives and newcomers to adapt to the land itself and to transform not only the land but their own lives as well.

Oklahoma, Kansas, Nebraska, South Dakota, North Dakota, and, in Canada, the southern reaches of Alberta and Saskatchewan form the core for any definition of the Great Plains. The region is characterized by open grasslands, cash crops such as wheat and cattle, and fluctuating extremes in population density and climate. The contiguous regions of Texas, Colorado, Wyoming, Montana, Minnesota, Iowa, and Manitoba share some features with the Great Plains states so that the map bends in and bulges out, amoeba-like, along the region's borders. Ecologically the region can be subdivided into the tallgrass prairie, a transitional mixed-grass central plain, and shortgrass high plains. The one-hundredth meridian marks the border between the tallgrass prairie's rich soils and adequate rainfall and the high plains with their short grasses, sandy soils, and drier climate that is less suited to farming and more dependent upon the finite water supply that lies thousands of feet below ground.[1] Within these regions there are subregions based on a veritable maze of biological and social considerations.

For thousands of years people have ventured onto the Great Plains. The movement among seasonal camps that was a way of life for the Plains Indians is expressed in contemporary history as patterns of mobility; ironically, movement is one constant in the region. Each wave of expanding white settlement and Indian displacement contributed to cultural, economic, and social differences still evident across the region. The histories of the various indigenous and immigrating Indian tribes vary considerably by region and time, just as the history of European and non-Native American migration varies across the region. For example, the borderland Civil War battles in "bleeding Kansas" and the transcontinental trails to Oregon and California remain defining features of these states' histories. Oklahoma remained "Indian territory," at least officially, until the 1890s. The last waves of homesteading in the early years of the twentieth century lured settlers onto the marginal lands of Nebraska and the Dakotas, pushing the Indians onto steadily diminishing-in-size reservations. On the Canadian prairies the presence of the Royal Canadian Mounted Police made the settlement of the prairies by whites a more sedate affair, although the Métis resistance of Louis Riel left a lasting legacy of conflict. As each region was opened to settlement, events in Europe determined to some extent who would immigrate to these new lands and what the social and cultural norms of their communities would be.

The Spaniards left behind horses that profoundly transformed native cultures, giving them mobility but also adding responsibility for supporting the animals and the larger communities that followed the buffalo over wide expanses of the plains. When other tribes arrived, displaced by the expanding white populations, competition for space and resources, bison and grass, forced all of the tribes on the plains to transform their traditional tribal structures in order to accommodate change. For many this meant moving to unfamiliar territories.

All of these migrating populations soon realized that the weather would be extreme in a region where storms could sweep in from the north or the south, building in intensity as they crossed great expanses of grassland without any topographic interruptions for thousands of miles. How to live without trees for fuel and for building houses was a primary challenge for all of the migrants. Many Plains Indians abandoned their villages, their commodious lodges, and their cultivated fields, and developed the tipi—a movable dwelling their horses could carry—in their wide sweeps across the plains in search of the buffalo. White settlers devised ways to create homes out of sod, either cutting it into building blocks or digging into the earth itself. With reluctance, we assume, they followed the lead of the Indians and learned to use dried buffalo and then dried cow chips for fuel.

The white settlers set out to transform the Great Plains into the Nation's Breadbasket, the Garden of the World. Wheat, a cash crop, would be the means for accomplishing this "Manifest Destiny." Immigrants from the steppes of Russia brought new, hardy varieties of winter wheat with them that flourished on the high plains. The homesteader in many a Great Plains story sets his plow into the soil and drops in his seed, transforming the landscape into ordered fields even before he turns his attention to providing a dwelling for his family.

Social adaptation followed these ecological and economic adaptations and transformations. Indians worked with varying success to preserve their own cultures when white authorities imposed their own educational, religious, and social standards on the tribes, mandating fundamental changes in education, social organization, and cultural practices. Despite some notable successes, many Indians and Indian tribes became the victims of whites who used the laws to appropriate their land as they attempted to eradicate Native cultures. Adaptation is not always a positive gain. Nevertheless, indigenous peoples survive with a strong sense of identity and remain a continuing presence on the plains.

Each wave of settlers who came west discovered that they had to adopt new standards to create a proper community on the Great Plains. Farm families were separated from their neighbors by distances that often made it difficult to sustain the close-knit clusters of farm homes like those in Europe or the networks of small farms and villages in the states along the eastern seaboard. Most plains towns were located along the railroad lines, built at regular intervals along the tracks as shipping and trading points. Even today many plains towns line up across the region's maps at twenty- or thirty-mile intervals, thinning out as the roads climb onto the high plains. In those early towns the farmers sold their wheat and bought needed items at prices determined by the merchants, the railroads, and the markets in faraway cities. As a result, the towns often became places of tension and conflict rather than social interaction. Farmers were isolated by geography, economy, and social class. This does not mean, however, that there was no social interaction or viable culture on the Great Plains. Indeed, as the readings in this collection demonstrate, over the years those who stayed developed lively social settings and a distinct cultural identification.

European immigrants had to overcome many of the same barriers as American settlers, but in addition they had to learn English and adapt to American cultural norms. For many this meant abandoning cultures deeply rooted in their own native languages. They had to replace social and religious practices tied to their European homes with unfamiliar customs in their efforts to enter mainstream

American society. For many the transformation into "Americans" was a painful and sometimes tragic process.

Despite—or perhaps because of—the popular perception of the Great Plains as a place of unpleasant extremes, the region has become a topic of conversation among economists, ecologists, historians, conservationists, and students of the region's literature, as well as the butt of quips that equate open spaces with empty lives. Some of the more serious conversations concern the steady decrease in rural populations and the decline of the family farm, the coming crisis in the water supply, the persistent erosion of the soil, the pollution of the region's streams, or the disappearance of the few remnants of the original plains ecosystems that signal the death of the land itself and the collapse of the region's economy. Scholars in various disciplines study the effects of drought, erosion, fire, and grazing on the region's pastureland, looking for alternatives to an economy based on a finite supply of underground water and fluctuating market prices that are often below the cost of growing the crop or feeding the cattle. Economists consider farm and ranch production, market variables, trade routes, the financial viability of the small towns and cities that dot the region, and the rise and fall of industries that are tied to the continuing productivity of the land. Ecologists note the succession and decline of native plants and animals on the prairies and high plains, and document the region's fragile ecosystems. Historians reconsider the relationships between the Native peoples and those who came later. Chambers of Commerce explore the possibilities of eco-tourism, a modern twist on the Wild West myth.

Although popular commentators are still apt to refer to the place they are reporting from as "the last frontier," thinking it a rather quaint phrase, the frontier persists on the Great Plains not only as a geographic location but also as a symbolic margin in American life, the point of uncertainty where disaster or success can be the unpredictable outcome. The frontier mentality left a legacy of displaced native peoples and the eradication of plains animals and ecosystems. Nevertheless, the frontier belief in unlimited promise is also part of the perseverance that is, to some extent, still a necessity on the Great Plains. On the most elemental level the region's weather is a continual study in extremes. The temperature might read eighty degrees one day—or hour—and thirty degrees the next. A false spring may lure gardeners outdoors in March to plant rows of vegetables that later flash freeze under April ice. Sudden, torrential rains can break a drought and hailstones can pulverize a wheat field in minutes. Blizzards strike with unexpected suddenness. Even in a time of Nexrad radar, tornadoes, the region's weather icon, can strike without warning, leaving behind a wake of capricious destruction that seems especially malevolent.

Farmers on the Great Plains do indeed feed the nation's people and its export economy. In the solid-rock Flint Hills of Kansas and Oklahoma and the Sandhills of the high plains the native grasses provide renewable food for cattle and a growing number of herds of the region's ancient natives, the bison. For farmers and residents of small towns, communication by phone, fax, and e-mail provides links to the rest of the world, and satellite television brings the world to their living rooms—but physical distance still isolates the farms and small towns. Hope sometimes surrenders to economic reality. If a farmer with a few hundred acres sells out to his neighbor and moves away, the rural community is diminished: the school loses a few more pupils so that the rest of the children must board the bus to a consolidated school miles away, banks consolidate their small-town branches, mom and pop grocery stores and cafes close, and the post office shuts its doors. In the Sandhills of the high plains, when a rancher sells his thousands of acres to a corporation, it hires a professional manager who in turn replaces people with more efficient machines and computers. In that case it is not a small town but an entire region that is diminished. For the Indians on reservations scattered across the region, despite steady increases in population the struggle to survive is often complicated by the psychological, economic, and geographic marginal status these people endure.

Some scholars and observers, rather than talk about the Great Plains as a geographic place, focus on the frontier character. Protagonists in early Great Plains stories are likely to be people who came west because they believed in the myth of the garden of the world or a democratic utopia: they believed that on the frontier they would realize their dreams of owning land and would be part of a community based on the equality of hard work and personal character rather than family wealth or social class. These mythic assumptions provide a persistent point of conflict in Great Plains fiction. Authors of contemporary fiction often draw upon the remnants of these earlier myths, knowing their readers will recognize the familiar patterns. Indigenous writers chronicle conflicts with displacement and racism, yet these writers maintain a sense of identity in contemporary cultures while keeping tenuous connections to enduring tribal traditions.

Any definition of the Great Plains must be, to say the least, long. The definer must consider geographic boundaries; ecological and historical commonalities and subtle variants that do not always conform to geographic or political boundaries; the transformation of the land into fields and pastures that produce cash crops; the adaptation of countless people to the climate; and isolation, dictated in large measure by the ecology and topography of the land itself. And, perhaps most important, the definer must consider the Great Plains as a state of mind: the ineffable quality of the region that results in a cautious approach to any act or decision, evident in the conservation of words and actions that comes from the ironic combination of the hard lessons of failure and a kind of perverse optimism based on a deep commitment to the land.

The stories, essays, excerpts, and poems in *A Great Plains Reader* consider these qualities of the Great Plains, but it is this last quality—frame of mind—that interests writers the most. Wright Morris carved out a forty-year career writing novels and essays and photographing abandoned objects across the plains in his attempt to come to terms with the plains character. He concluded it was a matter of opinion. Willa Cather wrote about the "thing not named," the indefinable quality of a piece of writing that the reader must feel on the page. Hamlin Garland, O. E. Rølvaag, Wallace Stegner, Louise Erdrich, Ron Hansen, and Douglas Unger, poets William Stafford and Joy Harjo, essayists John Janovy, Kathleen Norris, and Sharon Butala, and countless other Great Plains writers examine themselves and create characters who spend their lives trying to explain what about the Great Plains pulls them back when they want to leave. *A Great Plains Reader* provides a sampling of their explorations into the Great Plains as a place and a state of mind.

Notes

1. Some commentators put this dividing line at the ninety-eighth meridian, or describe it as an invisible continuum, but the one-hundredth serves as a neat round number–dividing line.

1. The Lay of the Land

The Nature of the Plains: *Impressions*

In this section are contemplative observations about the prairie and the plains. The writers record feelings that many Great Plains residents find difficult to express as words. Metaphorically, those who have lived on the plains cannot get the smoke, the dust, the present, or the past of the place out of their lives. The writers in the following pages experience the Great Plains as something more than simple topography. The maps of words they create are multiple overlays that provide frames of reference for their personal and often emotional responses to the land.

The Great Plains, a landscape without apparent boundaries, may confound the casual sojourner, but most people who live in this region—where there is little to see—learn to see even more. These writers are aware of the land's subtle effect on their powers of observation. They use close observation and metaphor to convey the sense of place, often mystical in nature, that they have felt. As Sharon Butala says, "sky and land, that is all, and grass, and what Nature leaves bare the human psyche fills."

Further Reading

Anderson, Robert. *From the Hidewood: Memories of a Dakota Neighborhood*. St. Paul: Minnesota Historical Society, 1996.

Critchfield, Richard. *Those Days: An American Album*. New York: Anchor Doubleday, 1986.

Duncan, Dayton. *Miles from Nowhere: Tales from America's Contemporary Frontier*. 1993; rpt. Lincoln: University of Nebraska Press, 2000.

——. *Out West: A Journey through Lewis and Clark's America*. 1987; rpt. Lincoln: University of Nebraska Press, 2000.

Gilfillan, Merrill. *Magpie Rising: Sketches from the Great Plains*. Boulder CO: Pruett, 1988.

Knopp, Lisa. *Field of Vision*. Iowa City: University of Iowa Press, 1996.

——. *The Nature of Home*. Lincoln: University of Nebraska Press, 2002.

N. Scott Momaday (b. 1934)

In this passage from *The Names,* N. Scott Momaday links memory, history, and the present of his Kiowa people through the Pohd-lohk, who keeps the past alive by reviewing the tribe's century-old calendar book. This tribal history is a reminder to his reader that behind the two hundred years of traditionally reported Great Plains history lies the unknown, "a kind of prehistoric genius and impenetrable genesis" that inextricably links tribal identity to place as well as time.

Momaday (Kiowa Cherokee) was born in Lawton, Oklahoma. His parents taught school on the Navajo, Jemez, and San Carlos Apache Reservations in New Mexico and Oklahoma. He received his bachelor's degree from the University of New Mexico and his master's and Ph.D. degrees in English Literature at Stanford University. Momaday taught at Stanford and the University of California at Berkeley before returning to the Southwest as a distinguished professor at the University of Arizona. He became the first American Indian author to win the Pulitzer Prize, for his novel *House Made of Dawn* (1968). Like most American Indian authors he has published in a variety of genres—novels, poetry, and essays. He is also an accomplished painter.

Excerpt from *The Names* (1976)

The arbor is a square frame building, cool and dark within. Two timbers, like telegraph poles, support the high, pitched roof, which is made of rafters and shingles, warped and weather-stained. Inside, on such a day as this, there are innumerable points of light at the roof, like stars, too small to admit of beams or reflections. The arbor is a place from which the sun is excluded at midday, a room that is like dawn or dusk at noon, and always there is a particular weather inside, an air that is cooler and more fluent than that of the plain, like wind in a culvert, and a deeper, more congenial shade. At times you can hear the wind, for it runs upon the walls and moans, but you cannot know it truly until you are old and have lived with it many years; so they say, who are old. It is the same wind that brings about the chinooks in the old homeland of the Kiowas to the north, the bleak winters and black springs of the whole Great Plains. It is at once the most violent and placid motion in the universe.

There is a clapboard siding to the framework. At the base it is low, rising some three feet or so from the red, earthen floor and giving way to a wide latticework and screens, an open window that encircles the great room. Here and there are certain amenities; an icebox, a cupboard, a low shelf upon which there are metal boxes and basins, shaving mugs and a mirror, a kerosene lamp and a lantern. Adjacent to the northwest corner of the room there is another, smaller block of space, the kitchen, in which there are a stone fireplace and a chimney, a grill, a cutting board, and various implements for cooking. Just now, after the noon meal, there are fragrances of spice, of boiled meat and fried bread, melons, and warm, sweet milk. Here, at this hour, in this season, you do not expect that something extraordinary will happen, only that a bird will call out in a moment, and a low wind arise, carry, and descend.

On this August day, 1934, the old man Pohd-lohk awoke before dawn. For a time he lay still in the darkness beside his wife, Tsomah, not listening to the slow, persistent sound of her breathing in sleep, but leading his mind out and away towards the center of the day. He arose quietly and drew the light, cotton blanket about his naked body, taking up his clothes, which he carried outside and placed on the edge of the porch. At the corner of the house a dog appeared, a rangy, overgrown pup, short-haired and liver-colored, wagging its tail. It seemed a vague epitome of the darkness; he regarded it for a moment, then let it go.

The first light appeared among the trees like smoke and crept upon the hard, bare ground at his feet, blushed upon the skyline to the north and east, where the river made a great bend and the trees grew up in a thicket in a deep crease of the bank. He peered into the dark wall of the grove in the middle distance and saw that it drew slowly upon him in the light and wavered, so it seemed, then settled back into the depths. He thought at such times that the world was centered upon him, that everything near and far must refer to him, drawing close from every quarter upon the very place where he stood. Always he loved to be out and alone in the early morning.

He shivered and huddled over upon himself, bunching the long muscles of his arms and shoulders in the blanket. He had good use of his body still, though now he moved about slowly in his age. He was a good-looking man, having been lively in his youth and closely disciplined in his prime. His body was hard and thick and grew supple in the sun; his eyes were clear and his vision keen. In his face there was reflected all the force of will and intelligence that truly defined him. His sunburned hands were fine and fluent, and with them he could still perform the intricate work of fixing beads and feathers to buckskin, and he made arrows that were precisely delicate and true.

In a moment the sun appeared, and he held his head back and closed his eyes, praying, the long, loose white hair gathering up in the peak and fold of the blanket at his neck.

A rooster crowed among the trees. It was a shrill and vibrant sound, like a cry, that carried for long moments and held like heat on the air. He opened his eyes suddenly and looked after it, but he could not determine where the creature was, and he thought of hunting, of waiting long ago in the same light (or was it a harder, bleaker light, a midwinter dawn?) and listening for such a sound, a thin cry in the distance. Once as a young man he had heard in a high wind the whimper of young wolves, hectic and hollow, and he had known at once, instinctively, where and what they were, and he went to them quietly, directly, so that there should be almost no fear on either side, singing lowly to them. They lay huddled among the rocks, three of them, shuddering with cold, their eyes closed and their fine blue fur gaping in the wind. And he shielded them for a time with his hands and wanted so much to touch them, to hold the soft warm shapes close against him, but he dared not touch them, for fear that he should leave a scent like doom upon them, and after a while he left them alone, as he had found them.

Pohd-lohk, old wolf.

He was awake now and restless. He stepped down from the porch and crossed the yard to the place where he must purify himself, a small, hide-covered framework of eighteen willows, that which is called *seidl-ku-toh*. It stood no higher than his waist, and he entered it on his hands and knees, leaving the blanket outside, and made a fire in the pit. Then, while the stones were heating, he went out again—he felt the sun flaring upon him—to get water and to breathe the last cold air of the night into his lungs.

Later in the bath, while the stones sizzled and steam rose up around him, Pohd-lohk combed out his long hair and braided it. He thought of the dead, of Kau-au-ointy, the mother of his wives, and of Mammedaty, his stepson, of others. Already indistinct in his mind, they happened upon him often now and without substance, like sudden soft winds and shadows in his dreaming, and he imagined who they were and what had happened to them, that they should have been there and then gone forever, and he thought it a strange thing, their going, sad and imponderable at the center. But at the same time the thought of it filled him with wonder, and he saw what it was to be alive. Then, always, his spirit wheeled and ran away with him, out upon an endless, sunlit plain.

Afterwards: the sun was high and the air already heavy and hot. The light was not yet flat, but nearly golden in the yard, where it was broken upon the limbs and leaves of an elm and scattered on the grass and ground. Through a window he saw a magpie drop down among the shadows, gleaming as it settled in the mottled light.

Pohd-lohk began to deal with time, his old age, a restlessness. He went into his room, the room where he and Tsomah slept, and closed the door. He opened a bureau drawer and stood for a moment before it. In it were his best possessions, including a human bone, the forearm of a Crow whose name was Two Whistles. He placed the fingers of his right hand upon it—it was hard and smooth as the stones he heated for his bath—and he caught his breath, as if the bone had quickened to his touch. He removed a book and spectacles; these he kept always together, wrapped round with a red kerchief. The book, a ledgerbook which he had obtained from the Supply Office at Fort Sill, had been in his possession for many years, from the time he was a private in L Troop, Seventh Cavalry, under the command of Hugh Scott, and it meant a great deal to him. He laid his hands to it in a certain way, with precise, familiar care. It was a calendar history of the Kiowa people from 1833.

He could not remember how it was that he came to his special regard for history, or to his resolve that he, Pohd-lohk, should set it down in pictures on a page, but the book had become a serious affair in his life. In it he indicated at first events that had been recorded on an older calendar, a painted hide, then things that had been told to him by his elders or that fell within the range of his own memory. Now that he was old, Pohd-lohk liked to look backwards in time, and although he could neither read nor write, this book was his means. It was an instrument with which he could reckon his place in the world; it was as if he could see in its yellow, brittle leaves the long swath of his coming to old age and sense in the very nature of it— the continuity of rude images in which the meaning of his racial life inhered—a force that had been set in motion at the Beginning. The calendar was a story, or the seed of a story, and it began a hundred years in the past. Beyond that, beyond the notion of a moment in 1833, there was only the unknown, a kind of prehistoric and impenetrable genesis, a realm of no particular shape, duration, or meaning. It was an older, larger story, a story of another people, another reality at last. He believed in it, but he could not take hold of it and set it down. The Kiowas had entered the world through a hollow log; they had known good things and bad, triumph and defeat; and they had journeyed a long way from the mouth of the log. But it was all one moment to Pohd-lohk, as if everything, the whole world, had been created on an afternoon in 1830 or 1832.

He opened the book to the first page, and it was *Da-pegya-de Sai*, November, 1833, and the stars were falling. He closed his eyes, the better to see them. They were everywhere in the darkness, so numerous and bright indeed that the night was shattered. They flew like sparks, he thought, and he thought also of slender, pointed leaves turning in the sun, and of pure light glittering upon water. But as he watched, dreaming, the stars were at last like nothing he had ever seen or should ever see beyond this, the havoc he imagined and remembered in his blood. Truly they were not like sparks or leaves or facets of light upon water. In some older and more nearly perfect synthesis of motion and light the stars wheeled across the vision of his mind's eye. They swung and veered; they drew near and loomed; and they fell slowly and silently away in the void. Silently. Men, women, and children were running here and there in the flashing light, their eyes wide and their mouths twisted with fear, but he could not hear their running, nor even the sound of their cries. And yet it did not seem strange to him that there should be no sound upon the scene. It was as if the earth—or even so much of it as he knew—had fallen off into the still, black depths. Even as this bright catastrophe was somehow the element of his perception just now, in his dreaming, so was silence the element in which the stars moved inexorably. They fell in long arcs and traces, bright delineations of time and space, describing eternity. He looked after them with strange exhilaration, straining to see.

Or it was *Ta'dalkop Sai*, 1839–40, and the designation before him was the crude figure of a man covered with red spots. This was in commemoration of the great smallpox epidemic which began on the upper Missouri in the summer of 1837 and which, in the course of three years, is estimated to have destroyed fully one third of the native inhabitants of the Great Plains.

Always when he thought of it Pohd-lohk could see the bodies of the dead, not their faces, but only their faceless forms, the abstractions of some hideous reality that was a shade beyond his comprehension. More real to him by far were the survivors, those whose grief, he thought, must have been a plague in itself, whose wailing must have been like the drone of locusts in the fields. In his own lifetime, 1892, he had seen a woman kneeling over the body of her child, who had succumbed to measles. She had inflicted bloody wounds upon her arms and shoulders with a knife; she had cut her hair so that it lay close to the scalp and ragged. And all the while that he watched, his rage and shame having come together in a kind of helpless fascination, she emitted cries, hollow, thin, full of wild, incomprehensible grief.

Again, it was 1851–52. That winter there was a hard thing for the coming-out people to bear. A Pawnee boy who had been captured the year before by Setangya, the great warrior chief of the Kaitsenko society, escaped and took with him the best horse in the tribe, a bay hunter known as Guadal-tseyu, "Little Red." Pohd-lohk had turned this matter over in his mind a thousand times. It might have been a different story among the Pawnees, the story of the boy. But in his own terms, which comprised Pohd-lohk's particular idea of history, it was the story of the horse—and incidentally of the Kiowas at a given moment in time. Moreover, it was a tragic story—nearly as much so from his point of view as was that of the plague, which he imagined no more vividly—inasmuch as it centered upon a whole and crucial deprivation, the loss of a horse, a hunting horse, a loss that involved the very life's blood of the culture. Once upon a time, as he thought of it, there was a horse, and never before had there been such a horse, and it was lost, and with it was lost something of the coming-out people, too, a splinter from the bone. It was a simple story in the telling, but there were many implications, many shadows on the grass. He imagined Guadal-tseyu. Now and then it seemed to him that he had got hold of it, that he could feel the horse under him, the whole strength and whole motion of it. It was hard to hold and half wild in its spirit, but it was all the more congenial to his mind for that, all the more appropriate to the landscape from which it had sprung like a gust of wind. He thought he could see it, the red hunting horse, but it was fleeting. He saw the ghost, the sheer energy of it. Perhaps when it stood still, he thought, it was the ordinary image of a horse, neither more nor less, standing away in the whole hollow of the plain, or away on a ridge, the sky all around it, small and alone, lonely. But when it wheeled and broke into a run, as it did always in his dreaming, it seemed to concentrate the wind and the stars, to gather the splinters of the sun to itself. And someone in his lineage, a man long ago in the Yellowstone, had seen such a thing, a fish flashing at a waterfall in the late afternoon, hurtling high above a dark rainbow on the spray.

Or it was the summer of 1883, in which Sampt'e was killed. Pohd-lohk had known this man and had seen fit to commemorate him, to fix him forever in the scheme of remembered time. But now, as he thought back to that green summer, it was the sun dance that stood out in his mind. It was called *A 'dalk'atoi K'ado,* "Nez Percé sun dance." Pohd-lohk was in his twenties at the time. He was then, as he thought of it now, at the end of his youth, as vital and strong as he should ever be, and scarcely concerned to admit of age or illness. *A 'dalk'atoi K'ado.* He thought of it as the one time in his life to which he would willingly return from any and all other times; it was simply the best of his memories. The place of the sun dance was pasture land by that time, owned and enclosed by a white cattleman whom the Kiowas called Map'odal, "Split-nose." The lodge was erected on a low rise of dark, rich land on the Washita River where two dense groves of pecan trees grew in a large semicircle. It was a bright, hot summer, a summer of the plains, and it followed upon a hard winter. The camps were gleaming against the dark, shimmering backdrop of the groves, and the arbors, faceted with bright leaves, shone like fire, and there were pennants of red and blue and yellow cloth everywhere, moving in the breeze.

That summer the Nez Percés came. It was then five years since they had been released from imprisonment at Fort Leavenworth and two before they should be allowed to return to their northern homeland. They seemed a regal people, as tall as the Kiowas, as slow to reveal themselves. There was an excitement about them, something of legendary calm and courage. It was common knowledge that, under their great chief Joseph, they had fought brilliantly against the United States and had come very close to victory. It was the first time that Pohd-lohk had seen them, but he had known of them all his life. The Kiowas remembered that, long ago, they had come upon these imposing people, "people with hair cut off across the forehead," in the highlands on the edge of the Northern Plains. This was a part of that larger story in which Pohd-lohk believed. It was a good thing to have the Nez Percés; they were worthy guests, worthy of him, he thought, of his youthful vigor and good looks. For their benefit he strutted about and set his mouth just so, in the attitude of a warrior.

And there were Tsomah and Keahdinekeah, whom he would take for his wives. Keahdinekeah was then twenty-five years old and the mother of the child Mammedaty. She was slender and straight, and she had inherited her mother Kau-au-ointy's strength of will and character. She carried herself with remarkable dignity and grace, so much so indeed that these traits should be apparent even to a child, her great-grandson, sixty years later.

Pohd-lohk sang, for a man sings of such a woman. His dreaming came to an end in the song, and he put the book and spectacles away. His mind turned and drew upon something else now, something that had run through his thoughts for several days, a serious matter. It was time to go, and he set out, walking easily in the heat, towards the trees that grew on Rainy Mountain Creek.

There, in a wide clearing above the bank, Keahdinekeah sat on the edge of the bed in her room. It was late morning, almost noon, and she had been sitting there alone for a long time. It was very hot; even though the window was wide open, the air was heavy and stale in the room. The room smelled of old, settled things, curios and keepsakes that were Keahdinekeah's, having no essence but that of belonging to her. She nodded from time to time, dozing, her eyes closed and her small, crooked hand folded in her lap. She was very small, as if in her waning and weariness all of her little, aged bones had collapsed within her. She was seventy-six years old now, and nearly blind. Unlike Pohd-lohk, she showed her age, seemed even older than she was. Since the death of Mammedaty, her firstborn and favorite son, she had withdrawn into herself—in grief at first, but then as a matter of preference. She had finished with the things that enabled her to live well in the ordinary world; they had passed away from her one by one; and now she was herself waiting to pass away into the darkness that had come upon her and lay like evening at her eyes. It was a long wait—and it would go on for more than a decade—but she kept it with trust and good will. And she was glad to have visitors when they came.

Without knocking, Pohd-lohk opened the door to her room. She looked up, but he knew that she could not see who was there.

Old woman.
  Old man!

He paused for a moment in the doorway, wiping the sweat from his forehead.

It is hot.
  Yes?
  Hot.

There was a dull luster upon the objects in the room, the knobs of metal and hollows of wood, the blocks and wedges of a patchwork quilt, bits of carnival glass. There was a very low amber brilliance, a soft, nearly vibrant glowing, upon the whole setting. The air was close, stifling.

Come, old woman, let's sit outside, in the arbor.

She held out her hand to him, and he helped her to stand and walk. They went out of the house and across the yard, where a speckled hen scratched in the dirt beside a shallow cistern at the well. It raised its head and regarded them sideways. Keah-dinekeah walked very softly, in moccasins, on Pohd-lohk's arm.

The arbor was a makeshift affair, nothing but a lean-to, made out of poles and branches. The poles were many years old, smooth and gray, with long, gaping cracks here and there. The branches had been placed on the framework in May or June; the leaves had long since wilted, and most of them were shriveled now and brittle, in spite of the very humid heat. Even so, the arbor afforded them a little shade, and it was soothing. They sat down on a bench at the long table, over the top of which a heavy red oilcloth had been stretched and tacked down. It was ragged and badly faded, but it was cool to the touch. Flies buzzed about them, slowly, as if they were moving against a wind.

How is my sister Tsomah?
  Oh, she is all right, very well, in fact. She said to tell you that she is drying some meat, that you ought to come and pay her a visit.
  Yes? Well, it may be so, but I don't get out much, you know. I can't see very well at all now.

She looked straight ahead, her eyes open, and he could see in them the milky film of her blindness. A silence fell between them, and she reached for his hand, held it tight, smiling.

Well, Pohd-lohk, it is good to have you here; I am glad that you came.
  So, I must go on about my business.

Yes?
It is very important.
Yes?
Oh, yes.
Well, then.
I am on my way to see your great-grandson.
Eh neh neh neh neh!

She clasped her hands together, laughing. And after a moment she was lost in thought, and again there was a silence between them.

And afterwards, when Pohd-lohk had gone, Keahdinekeah sat again on the edge of her bed and thought of Tsoai and of her great-grandson. Neither had she ever seen, but of Tsoai she knew an old story.

Eight children were there at play, seven sisters and their brother. Suddenly the boy was struck dumb; he trembled and began to run upon his hands and feet. His fingers became claws, and his body was covered with fur. There was a bear where the boy had been. The sisters were terrified; they ran, and the bear after them. They came to the stump of a great tree, and the tree spoke to them. It bade them climb upon it, and as they did so it began to rise into the air. The bear came to kill them, but they were just beyond its reach. It reared against the tree and scored the bark all around with its claws. The seven sisters were borne into the sky, and they became the stars of the Big Dipper.

Tsoai loomed in her mind; nor could she have imagined it more awesome than it is, the great black igneous monolith that rises out of the Black Hills of Wyoming to a height of twelve hundred feet above the Belle Fourche River. Many generations before, the Kiowas had come upon Tsoai, had been obliged in their soul to explain it to themselves. And they imagined that it stood in some strange and meaningful relation to them and to the stars. It was therefore a sacred thing, Keahdinekeah knew. And her grandson Huan-toa had taken his child to be in Tsoai's presence even before the child could understand what it was, so that by means of the child the memory of Tsoai should be renewed in the blood of the coming-out people. Of this she thought, and she said to herself: Yes, old man, I see; I see now what your errand is.

Pohd-lohk crossed Rainy Mountain Creek on a log, a walnut that he himself had felled the year before. The trees were thick along the creek, the foliage dense. There were shafts of sunlight all about, smoking, so many planes of bright light on the dark shadows of the creek. Birds fluttered up here and there, flashing across the planes and angles of light in the tunnel of trees. Insects made minute, hectic motions on the brown water, which bore up a long, crooked drift, the most fragile mesh of silt and webs. Small white butterflies glittered and bobbed in the humid air, moving in their own way, rising and falling in time to a rhythm too intricate for the old man to follow with his eyes. It was like a dance. He picked his way along a dim, narrow path that led upwards through brier and berry thickets to the top of the land.

Ahead on the highest knoll was the house where Mammedaty had lived in his last years, the arbor and the barn. These, from where he walked now on the first wave of the plain above the creek, stood up against the sky, as if they were the only landmarks in a hundred miles. In the conjugation of distance and light at this house of the day they might have been little or large, near or far away. It seemed to him that he was forever coming upon them.

In the arbor Pohd-lohk entered among the members of his dead stepson's family and was full of good humor and at ease. He took up the child in his hands and held it high, and he cradled it in his arms, singing to it and rocking it to and fro. With the others he passed the time of day, exchanged customary talk, scattered small exclamations on the air: Yes, yes. Quite so. So it is with us. But with the child he was deliberate, intent. And after a time all the other voices fell away, and his own grew up in their wake. It became monotonous and incessant, like a long running of the wind. The whole of the afternoon was caught up in it and carried along. Pohd-lohk spoke, as if telling a story, of the coming-out people, of their long journey. He spoke of how it was that everything began, of Tsoai, and of the stars falling or holding fast in strange patterns on the sky. And in this, at last, Pohd-lohk affirmed the whole life of the child in a name, saying: Now you are, Tsoai-talee.

I am. It is when I am most conscious of being that wonder comes upon my blood, and I want to live forever, and it is no matter that I must die.

Further Reading

The Ancient Child. 1990.
In the Presence of the Sun: Stories and Poems. 1993.
The Man Made of Words: Essays, Stories, Passages. 1997.
The Way to Rainy Mountain. 1976.

Reading about N. Scott Momaday

Allen, Paula Gunn. "Whose Dream Is This Anyway? Remythologizing and Self-definition in Contemporary Indian Fiction." *The Sacred Hoop: Recovering the Feminine in American Indian Traditions.* Boston: Beacon Press, 1986. 76–101.

Gish, Robert. "N. Scott Momaday." *Updating the Literary West*. Fort Worth: Texas Christian University Press, 1997.

Roemer, Kenneth M., ed. *Approaches to Teaching Momaday's* The Way to Rainy Mountain. New York: Modern Languages Association, 1988. 537–40.

Scarberry-Garcia, Susan. *Landmarks of Healing: A Study of House Made of Dawn*. Albuquerque: University of New Mexico Press, 1990.

Schubnell, Matthias. *N. Scott Momaday: The Cultural and Literary Background*. Norman: University of Oklahoma Press, 1985.

Trimble, Martha Scott. *N. Scott Momaday*. Western Writers Series. Boise ID: Boise State University, 1973.

Woodward, Charles. *Ancestral Voice: Conversations with N. Scott Momaday*. Lincoln: University of Nebraska Press, 1989.

Ian Frazier *(b. 1951)*

Ian Frazier approaches the Great Plains as many Americans do—first as a tourist gliding west in a jet high above the patchwork plains, and then as a naive—no, innocent—Montana nova-resident lured by Hollywood movies to the prairie's rim. Frazier good-naturedly admits that he is an urban voyeur, someone who would never deliberately move to the Great Plains, but for three years he ventured onto the high plains, driving thousands of miles up and down and back and forth, from his temporary Montana home. "I didn't pass a single place that looked as if it was in any way expecting me," Frazier confides, reflecting the feeling that other "strangers" may feel when stumbling into a small town just off the superhighway. As Frazier begins to become part of the Great Plains, he introduces his reader to the region's geographic and cultural landscapes. The result is *Great Plains*, a kind of newcomer's guide to the grasslands.

Known for the mix of irony and affection in his various works, Frazier grew up in Ohio and graduated from Harvard University where he served on the staff of the *National Lampoon*. A frequent contributor to the *New Yorker* and other magazines, he lives most of the time in the wilds of New York City.

Excerpt from *Great Plains* (1987)

Away to the Great Plains of America, to that immense Western short-grass prairie now mostly plowed under! Away to the still-empty land beyond newsstands and malls and velvet restaurant ropes! Away to the headwaters of the Missouri, now quelled by many impoundment dams, and to the headwaters of the Platte, and to the almost invisible headwaters of the slurped-up Arkansas! Away to the land where TV used to set its most popular dramas, but not anymore! Away to the land beyond the hundredth meridian of longitude, where sometimes it rains and sometimes it doesn't, where agriculture stops and does a double take! Away to the skies of sparrow hawks sitting on telephone wires, thinking of mice and flaring their tail feathers suddenly, like a card trick! Away to the air shaft of the continent, where weather fronts from two hemispheres meet, and the wind blows almost all the time! Away to the fields of wheat and milo and sudan grass and flax and alfalfa and nothing! Away to parts of Montana and North Dakota and South Dakota and Wyoming and Nebraska and Kansas and Colorado and New Mexico and Oklahoma and Texas! Away to the high plains rolling in waves to the rising final chord of the Rocky Mountains!

A discount airplane ticket from New York City to the middle of the Great Plains—to Dodge City, Kansas, say, which once called itself Queen of the Cow-towns—costs about $420, round trip. A discount ticket over the plains—to the mountains, to Salt Lake City, to Seattle, to Los Angeles—is much cheaper. Today, most travellers who see the plains do it from thirty thousand feet. A person who wanted to go from New York to California overland in 1849, with the Gold Rush, could take a passenger ship to Baltimore, the B & O Railroad to Cumberland, Maryland, a stagecoach over the Allegheny Mountains to the Monongahela River, a steamboat to Pittsburgh, another steamboat down the Ohio to the Mississippi to St. Louis, another from St. Louis up the Missouri to Independence or St. Joseph or Council Bluffs, and an ox-drawn wagon west from there. If you left the East in early April, you might be on the plains by mid-May, and across by the Fourth of July. Today, if you leave Kennedy Airport in a 747 for Los Angeles just after breakfast, you will be over the plains by lunch. If you lean across the orthopedist from Beverly Hills who specializes in break-dancing injuries and who is in the window seat returning from his appearance on *Good Morning America,* you will see that the regular squares of cropland below you have begun to falter, that the country is for great distances bare and puckered by dry watercourses, that big green circles have begun to appear, and that often long, narrow rectangles of green alternate with equal rectangles of brown.

Chances are, nothing in the seat pocket in front of you will mention that those green circles are fields watered by central-pivot irrigation, where a wheeled span of irrigation pipe as much as a quarter mile long makes a slow circuit, like the hand of a clock. If you ask the flight attendant about those green and brown rectangles, chances are he or she will not say that in the spring of 1885 a wheat farmer on the Canadian plains named Angus Mackay was unable to plant a field which had already been plowed when his hands left to help suppress a rebellion of frontiers-men of French and Indian ancestry against the Dominion of Canada, and so he left the field fallow, cultivating it occasionally to kill the weeds; that when he planted it the following year, it weathered a drought to produce thirty-five bushels of wheat per acre, thirty-three bushels more than continuously cropped land; that the practice he had initiated, called summer fallow, was an effective way to con-serve moisture in the soil in a semi-arid climate, and many other farmers adopted it; that the one problem with summer fallow was the tendency of fields with no crop cover sometimes to dry up and blow away; that in 1918 two other Canadian farmers, Leonard and Arie Koole, experimented successfully with crops planted in narrow sections at right angles to the prevailing winds, to protect sections of fallow ground in between; and that this refinement, called strip farming, turned out to be the best way to raise wheat on the northern plains.

Crossing high and fast above the plains, headed elsewhere, you are doing what rain clouds tend to do. You are in a sky which farmers have cursed and blasted with dynamite barrages and prodded with hydrogen balloons and seeded with silver-iodide crystals and prayed to in churches every day for months at a time, for rain. Usually the clouds wait to rain until they are farther west or east—over the Rockies, or the Midwest. Probably, as you look out the airplane window, you will see the sun. On the plains, sunshine is dependable. Most of the buildings on the plains have roofs of galvanized metal. As dawn comes up, and the line of sunlight crosses the land, the roofs of barns and equipment sheds and grain silos and Department of Agriculture extension stations and grain elevators and Air Force barracks and house trailers and pipe warehouses and cafes and roadside-table shelters start to tick and pop in scattered unison, all the way from Canada to Texas.

The Great Plains are about 2,500 miles long, and about 600 miles across at their widest point. The area they cover roughly parallels the Rocky Mountains, which make their western boundary. Although they extend from the Southwestern United States well into Canada, no single state or province lies entirely within them. North to south, the states of the Great Plains are:

Montana	North Dakota
	South Dakota
Wyoming	Nebraska
Colorado	Kansas
New Mexico	Oklahoma
Texas	

The Great Plains include the eastern part of the first column, the western part of the second column, some of west Texas, and all of the Texas panhandle. In Canada, they include southern Alberta, Saskatchewan, and Manitoba. They are five hundred to a thousand miles inland from the Pacific Ocean, and over a thousand miles inland from the Atlantic. The Texas plains are about five hundred miles from the Gulf of Mexico.

Just where the Great Plains begin and end is not always certain. To the west, they sometimes continue past the Rocky Mountain front through gentle foothills all the way to the Continental Divide. To the north, flatlands stretch past the Arctic Circle, but the open prairie has given way to boreal pine forests long before that. In the Southwest, a change from semi-arid grassland to true desert is sudden in some places, slow in others. Of all the Great Plains boundaries, the eastern one is the hardest to fix. Many geographers and botanists have said that the Great Plains begin at the hundredth meridian, because that is the approximate limit of twenty-inch annual rainfall. Before Europeans came, it was more or less where the tall grasses of the East stopped and the Western short grasses started. (The hundredth meridian is the eastern line of the Texas panhandle; a map of the lower forty-eight states folds in half a little bit to the right of it.) Since the same amount of rain never falls two years in a row, this eastern boundary always changes. Sometimes it happens to coincide at certain points with the Missouri River; the eastern side of the river will be green and lush, and the western side will be a tan and dusty cowboy-movie set. Farmers can't grow corn, or raise dairy cattle, or do much European-style agriculture at all on sub-twenty-inch rainfall, and when they first moved out onto the Great Plains, they sometimes had difficulty borrowing money. Many banks and insurance companies had a policy of not lending money for the purposes of agriculture west of the hundredth meridian. So, whether or not the rain stopped exactly at the hundredth meridian, at one time lots of Eastern loan officers did. If you were beyond their help, you knew you were on the Great Plains.

It makes sense that traditional finance would balk there, because the Great Plains don't exactly qualify as real estate. In fact, the Great Plains are probably better described in terms of the many things they aren't. They aren't woodlands; their subsoil doesn't have enough moisture for tree roots. You can go a long way out there without seeing a single tree. They aren't mountains (although they contain the Black Hills in South Dakota and the Bearpaw Mountains in Montana and the Cypress Hills in Canada), and they aren't Land of a Thousand Lakes (although they used to have many sweetwater springs, and hundreds of rivers and streams, and an underground aquifer the volume of Lake Huron), and they aren't standard farmland (although they export two-thirds of the world's wheat, and could export more). And although they have suffered droughts about every twenty years since white people first settled there, and millions of acres have gone to blowing sand, and although Zebulon Pike, who happened to pick a route that led through the sandhills region when he explored for the government in 1806–7, compared the Great Plains to the deserts of Africa, and although the members of a later expedition, in 1819–20, agreed with Pike, and published a map with the words "Great Desert" across the southern plains, and although a popular atlas of 1822 extended the label over more territory and in another edition changed it to "Great American Desert," and although that appeared in the middle of North America on maps and globes for fifty years afterwards, and generations of geography students wondered about it and dreamed of going there, the Great Plains are not a desert.

White people did not consider moving onto the Great Plains in any numbers until after the Civil War. When they did, railroad promoters, governors of empty Western states, syndicates with land to sell, emigration societies, scientists, pretend scientists, politicians in crowded Eastern states, U.S. Geological Survey officials, Walt Whitman, *The New York Times, The New York Tribune,* all loudly advertised the Great Plains as a garden spot. The idea of the Great American Desert came in for much scoffing and debunking. Strangely, the Great Plains greened up with good rains several times just as another wave of homeseekers was about to go there. People thought they'd harvest a couple of good crops and pay off their starting costs and be in business. In the 1870s and '90s, and in 1918–24, and, most spectacularly, in the 1930s, drought knocked parts of these waves back. Since their days as a Great Desert, the Great Plains have also been the Frontier (supposedly of such importance in the formation of the American character), the "newer garden of creation" (Whitman's phrase), the Breadbasket of the World, the Dust Bowl, Vanishing Rural America. The Great Plains are like a sheet Americans screened their dreams on for a while and then largely forgot about. Since 1930, two-thirds of the counties on the Great Plains have lost population. About fifteen years ago, the Great Plains reappeared, briefly, as part of the New Energy Frontier. The Great Plains contain more than fifty percent of America's coal reserves. When we finally do run out of oil, somebody will probably think up yet another name for the Great Plains.

In the fall of 1982, I moved from New York to Montana. I sublet my apartment to my sister, packed my van, and headed west. On the way, I stopped in Cleveland to usher at my other sister's wedding. At the reception, to entertain the bridesmaids, I ate a black cricket the size of my thumb. Later, I was driving around the city's west side by myself singing "Jerusalem" with the windows open, tears streaming down my face. The next morning I wanted to call the hangover ambulance and go to the hangover hospital. The singing, and the feel of the cricket's toothpicky legs between my teeth, replayed in my mind on a tight tape loop. I took my van to Mike's Sohio Service Center for a tune-up, and when they were done I drove to Chicago. I stayed with friends there for one night, and then I drove on through Wisconsin, Minnesota, South Dakota, and didn't really stop until I crossed the Montana state line. At the edge of a little town, I pulled off the road, took off my shoes, moved some stuff from the mattress, and fell asleep, the gasoline still sloshing back and forth gently in the tank.

America is like a wave of higher and higher frequency toward each end, and lowest frequency in the middle. When the ticking of the car roof in the sun woke me, I looked out the windshield and saw nothing. A Hefty trash bag against a barbed-wire fence, maybe, torn to pennants by the wind; a metal prefab building in the distance; bunch grass blowing; a road as straight as a string. I started the car and went on. I didn't pass a single place that looked as if it was in any way expecting me: no landscaped residential communities, no specialty sporting-goods stores, no gourmet delis offering many kinds of imported beers. Just grain silos, and flat brown fields with one cow on them, and wheat fields, and telephone poles, and towns with four or six buildings and a "No U-Turn" sign at each end. In the larger town of Shelby, Montana, I went to a cafe called Ma's, and people looked at me. I bought a newspaper to see about houses for rent, and from a picture at the top of a column recognized the columnist, a man with a large waxed mustache, sitting one table away. I continued west, across the Blackfeet Indian Reservation, into the foothills of the Rocky Mountains, and then up through the mountain canyons. All at once a low-slung '67 Pontiac full of long-haired Indians passed me, going about ninety. Then a Montana state highway cop, with no sirens going. Then several more cars of Indians, then another highway cop, then more Indians. Just across the Flathead River and inside the boundary of Glacier National Park, I came upon the cars again. They were now pulled every which way off the road; policemen and Indians, both, were just standing there, hands in pockets. Some were looking off into the brush. Nobody's mouth was moving.

On the other side of the mountains, in the city of Kalispell, Montana, I finally saw a few people who looked kind of like me. I parked my van and took a $15-a-week room in the Kalispell Hotel. The bathroom was down the hall; the walls were thin. I spent several hours listening to a man in the next room trying to persuade another man to trade him five dollars for five dollars' worth of food stamps. Daily, I looked at houses to rent—shotgun cottages by the rail yards, ski chalets with circular fireplaces, and a house that was built under a small hill, for energy reasons. Finally I found one I liked, a cedar A-frame cabin with a wood stove and a sleeping loft and a flower box with marigolds. The house was on a long road that went from pavement to dirt and back to pavement. Beyond the road were foothills, clear-cut of timber in patches, like heads shaved for surgery, and beyond the hills were mountains. At the rental agency, I overheard a secretary giving someone else directions to the house. I mentioned to the agent that I could pay a two- or three-month security deposit in cash. The next morning, the agent left a message for me at the Kalispell Hotel and I called her back and she said I had the house.

I did not know one person in Montana. I sat in the house and tried to write a novel about high school; I went for walks, drank quarts of Coors beer, listened to the radio. At night, a neighbor's horse shifted his weight from hoof to hoof out in the trees, and sometimes cropped grass so near I could hear him chew. The first snowstorm blew in from the north, and crows crossed the sky before it like thrown black socks. For years in New York I had dreamed of Montana. Actually, I had also dreamed of joining the Army, going to truck-driving school in New Jersey, building a wooden sailboat, playing the great golf courses of the world, and moving to Fiji. I had examined all those ideas and then rejected them. Montana made the most sense to me. I saw the movie *Rancho Deluxe* (filmed in Livingston, Montana) eight or nine times. At parties, I told people, "Well, I'm going to be moving to Montana soon." Now here I was. Suddenly I no longer had any place to dream about.

So I started to dream about the Great Plains. For fantasies, the Great Plains are in many respects the perfect place. They're so big that you could never know all there is to know about them—your fantasies could never wear them out. Even the plural in their name seems to make them extend farther into a distant romantic haze. Also, they are a place where I will probably never live. This is important, because anyplace I move, I ruin. Look at the north side of Chicago. Look at SoHo.

I move in, the rents go up, coffee shops become French restaurants, useful stores close. Don't ask me how I do it—it's just a talent I have. A hundred years ago, it was not unusual to hear of single men and women and young couples with families moving out to start farms on the Great Plains. Today you hear of people my age being urban pioneers in some neglected neighborhood, or moving to the suburbs, or moving to Northern California or Washington or northwest Montana, like me. You never hear of us moving to the Great Plains.

Whenever money and the weather allowed, I would cross the mountains and drive around on the plains. A friend came to visit in the spring, and the first thing I did was take her there. My friend is from the West Indies; she had never seen the American West, except for California. We followed U.S. Highway 2 to Glacier National Park, and then we went up the Going-to-the-Sun Highway, past the standing dead trees burned in the lightning fire of 1967, through tunnels in the rock, past precipitous drops on the passenger side, past cliffs dripping water, past old snowdrifts with graffiti scratched on them, past our own chilled breath blowing out the car windows, past mountains with white, sharp tops, and then across Logan Pass, on the Continental Divide. I kept telling my friend I wanted her to see the Great Plains. The road began to descend, and at the turn of each switchback another mountain range would disappear, like scenery withdrawn into the wings, while the sky that replaced it grew larger and larger. We left the park and turned onto U.S. Highway 89. A driver coming down this road gets the most dramatic first glimpse of the Great Plains I've ever seen. For some miles, pine trees and foothills are all around; then, suddenly, there is nothing across the road but sky, and a sign says HILL TRUCKS GEAR DOWN, and you come over a little rise, and the horizon jumps a hundred miles away in an instant. My friend's jaw—her whole face, really—fell, and she said, "I had no idea!"

We came through the lower foothills, with vertebrae of rock sticking through their brown backs, and soon we were driving on a straight dirt road through unfenced wheat fields. We stopped the car and got out. The wheat—of a short-stemmed variety bred to mature at a height convenient for harvesting machinery—stretched in rows for half a mile in either direction. Through the million bearded spikes the wind made an "s" sound bigger than we could hear. We drove on, and birds with long, curved bills (Hudsonian godwits, the bird book said) flew just above us, like gulls following a ship. The sky was 360 degrees of clouds, a gift assortment of mares' tails and cumulus and cirrus, with an occasional dark storm cloud resting on a silvery-gray pedestal of rain. We could see the shadows of the clouds sliding along beneath them far into the distance. I said that when early travellers on the plains came through a big herd of buffalo, they could watch the human scent move through it on the wind, frightening animals eight and ten miles away. Suddenly we crossed the path of one of the rainclouds, and the hard dirt road turned to glue. Mud began to thump in the wheel wells, and the car skidded sideways, went off the road, and stuck. We got out in cement-colored mud over our ankles. Two pieces of harvesting machinery sat in a field nearby; other than that, there was no sign of people anywhere. I tried to drive while my friend pushed, then she drove while I pushed, then I left it in gear and we both pushed. We whipped the mud to peaks. It clotted on the wheels until they became useless mudballs. Finally I took a flat rock and got down on all fours and scraped the mud off each wheel. Then my friend drove carefully in reverse for one wheel turn until the wheels were covered again. Then I scraped the mud off again, and we drove another revolution. We kept doing this over and over until we made it back to dry ground. It took about two hours. Another event early travellers mentioned in their diaries was miring their wagons in the gumbo mud of the Great Plains. Now I knew what they meant. When I got back in the car, I was all-over mud and my fingernails were broken. From her purse, my friend produced a freshly laundered white cotton handkerchief.

For hours we drove on roads which Rand McNally & Company considers unworthy of notice. A moth glanced off the edge of the windshield, and in the sunset the dust its wings left sparkled like mascara. That night, my friend said on a gas-station pay phone, "I'm on the Great Plains! It's amazing here! The sky is like a person yawned and never stopped!"

Eventually, over several summers, I drove maybe 25,000 miles on the plains—from Montana to Texas and back twice, as well as many shorter distances. I went to every Great Plains state, dozens of museums, scores of historic sites, numerous cafes. When I couldn't travel, I borrowed books about the plains from the Kalispell Public Library—*Curse Not His Curls,* by Robert J. Ege (a ringing defense of General Custer), and *Crow Killer: The Saga of Liver-Eating Johnson.* I also watched the local newspapers for items about the plains, and finally I learned why the Indians and policemen I had seen by the road the day I first arrived were standing that way. They were at the place where the bodies of two missing Blackfeet Indians, Thomas Running Rabbit and Harvey Mad Man, had been found earlier in the afternoon.

Police in Eureka, California, had arrested two Canadians for robbing a convenience store, and had discovered that the Canadians' car was the same one the young Blackfeet men were driving when they disappeared. In custody, one of the Canadians, a nineteen-year-old named André Fontaine, said that they and another man had hitchhiked down from Red Deer, Alberta, to West Glacier, Montana; that there the three met two Indians in a bar; that they drove west with them in the Indians' car; that the Indians stopped the car; that his companions took the Indians into the woods; that he heard two shots; that his companions came running from the woods; that the three then drove away. Aided by this information, police soon caught the third man, a Canadian named Ronald Smith, in Wyoming. All three were returned to Montana and held in the Flathead County Jail. At first, they pleaded not guilty, but then Ronald Smith confessed to shooting both the young men. Smith was twenty-four, and he said he had always wanted to see what it felt like to kill somebody. He said that it felt like nothing. While awaiting trial as an accomplice, André Fontaine was asked to appear as a guest on F. Lee Bailey's television show, *Lie Detector*. The Flathead County Attorney, a county sheriff's detective, a local police detective, and a court-appointed defense attorney accompanied André Fontaine back to California for the taping. The show put them up in North Hollywood at the Beverly Garland Hotel, except for the prisoner, who stayed in the Los Angeles County Jail. When Ronald Smith confessed, he had requested the death penalty. He had said that he felt he was beyond rehabilitation, and that the Indians in the Montana prisons would probably kill him anyway. Shortly before his execution date, he changed his mind. Lawyers took his appeal through the county and state courts, which denied it, and to the U.S. Supreme Court, which refused to hear it. Then they filed another appeal in the federal courts challenging the constitutionality of the death penalty. Three years after the crime, while the appeal was still at the state level, I moved from Montana back to New York.

Further Reading

Coyote vs. Acme. 1996.
Dating Your Mom. 1986.
Family. 1994.
Lamentations of the Father. 2000.
Nobody Better, Better Than Nobody. 1989.
On the Rez. 2000.

Sharon Butala *(b. 1940)*

In this passage from her memoir, *The Perfection of the Morning*, Sharon Butala, a modern immigrant to the high plains, considers the land and people she came to know when she left her academic life in 1976 and moved to her husband's ranch in southern Saskatchewan, the same area around East End that Wallace Stegner writes about in *Wolf Willow* (1962). It is a life fraught with challenges, as she explains in *The Perfection of the Morning*: "Returning to my old life was no longer possible, but when I looked around and told myself, 'This is my home; this is my home till I die' that, too, seemed equally unimaginable. . . . if I walked every day and studied the landscape, the weather, the animals, trying to fit them into a life-scheme I could live with, I was also learning about Nature and, thus, about rural life." Like other plains residents, she recognizes the power of nature to change the lives of humans who respond both consciously and subconsciously to the natural world. "The Subtlety of Land" is Butala's chronicle of her own adaptation to the Great Plains, a place that is, she says, "geology stripped bare" but also a place where dreaming becomes an integral part of living.

When Butala first arrived on the unfamiliar prairie, she approached it as a visual artist, accustomed to careful observation. Journal writing led her to find words to respond to her new prairie life until prairie life itself became a constant presence in the novels, stories, and nonfiction she began to write. Sharon Butala was born in Nipawin, Saskatchewan, in the region north of the Great Plains, and was educated at the University of Saskatchewan. Her first nonfiction work, *The Perfection of the Morning*, was nominated for the Governor General's Award in 1994.

The Subtlety of Land (1994)

Some years later, when I was an established author, I said to a Toronto reporter who had asked me a question about him, "My husband is a true rural man."

"What does that mean?" the reporter asked, his voice full of skepticism.

"It means," I said, "that he understands the world in terms of wild things." I was a little surprised myself at my answer, having been called upon to explain something that until that moment had seemed self-evident, and realizing that, caught off guard, I had hit on the heart of the matter.

The reporter's pencil stopped moving, his eyes shifted away from me, he reflected, his eyes shifted back to me, and without writing anything down he changed the subject. When I told this story to a writer-naturalist friend, he said, laughing, that for the reporter my answer "does not compute."

A true rural person must be somebody born and raised on the land, outside of towns, and far from most other people. That being a given, then it follows that such life experience must result in an intrinsic understanding of the world different from that of someone raised in the cement, asphalt, glass and crowds of the city. Peter's thinking about the world was different from mine in ways that went beyond our different sexes or our different lifestyles. Where I had been trained to understand human nature from Freud and pop psychology, and the functioning of the world from classes in political economy and in history, that is, from formal education, Peter's starting point was what he had all his life lived in the midst of—it was Nature.

As years on the ranch passed, though, I began to learn from Nature too; I began to catch a glimpse of the world as he saw it through my own life in Nature. When that began to happen, a new understanding slowly, very slowly, began to dawn on me about what a life in Nature teaches one. I began to see that there might be more at the root of this difference in understanding of how the world works than I had guessed at, thinking it had to do only with simple, surface matters, like understanding cattle behavior well enough to predict their next move, or knowing the habits of antelope, or reading the sky with accuracy. I didn't yet have any idea what this deeper knowledge might be, but I watched Peter closely and tried to see what he saw.

While he was doing the spring irrigation at the hay farm, he would sometimes come across fawns only a few days old lying in the hay where they'd been left by their mothers who had gone off to forage. More than once he came to the house to get me so I could see the little spotted creature for myself.

"Watch," he would say. "When they're this young they don't even move when you come near them." Then he would bend down, pick up the trusting fawn in his arms, carry it to the closest grass-covered dike, and place it gently down where the irrigation water couldn't reach it. I worried about the mother locating her baby, but he said, with the confidence born of experience, "Don't worry. It won't take her a minute to find him." When we went back hours later the fawn would always be gone. These and other incidents reminded me over and over again that Peter, and other rural people who knew no other landscape, had formed his attitude to the prairie and his understanding of its weather, its growth patterns and its animals by a lifetime of immersion in it.

In my reading and occasionally in conversation with urban visitors, I read or hear people either saying directly or implying indirectly that *true rural* people don't notice or appreciate the beauty in which they live. Although I don't say so, the arrogance and ignorance of such remarks always makes me angry, implying as it does that rural people lack humanity, are somehow an inferior branch of the human species, that beauty is beyond their ken. It is one thing to come from the city and be overwhelmed by the beauty of Nature and to speak of it, and another thing entirely to have lived in it so long that it has seeped into your bones and your blood and is inseparable from your own being, so that it is part of you and requires no mention or hymns of praise.

Peter preferred to do our annual spring and fall cattle drives on horseback, a trek which took three days. Bringing the cattle down to the valley around Christmastime could be very unpleasant and then it was often hard to get help, so that we sometimes made that move with only Peter, me and one other person. But three days out on the prairie during a warm spring were paradise; we never had any trouble rounding up enough riders then. If the spring move was usually a joy, the best part of it was the eight to ten miles of unbroken prairie without even any true roads through it that we used to cross each time.

I knew the first time Peter took me across those miles of prairie that I loved to be there far from towns or even houses, on native shortgrass that had never been broken, where the grass hadn't been overgrazed and was full of birds' nests in the spring, and long-eared jackrabbits as big as small dogs, antelope in the distance, and coyotes that often followed us singing all the way.

Of course, unless she's a dyed-in-the-wool, bona fide horse-and-cattlewoman herself, when it's time to move cattle, and especially if there are adolescent sons on the place, the rancher's wife usually gets stuck driving the truck. The rancher is the one with the understanding of the cattle, knowledge of the route, and the cattle-management skills. As boss and owner, he has to ride. If there are adolescents along, it's taken for granted that they'll ride because they have to learn, which has a high priority on Saskatchewan ranches, and because it's so much fun and nobody wants to deprive kids of a little harmless fun.

The rancher's wife packs the meals, stows them in the truck, serves them when the time comes and packs up after. She carries drinking water and coffee and the extra jackets or the ones taken off when the day gets too warm. She carries tack, fencing pliers and other tools, and sometimes, if the move is just before calving begins, she'll have a newborn in the back of the truck and often several of them, each one marked in some way—maybe a colored string around its neck—so it can be returned to the right mother every few hours. As the drive wears on, she's likely to have exhausted adolescents in the cab with her, while their horses are either driven ahead or led by one of the men from his own horse. Usually, at some point, somebody will take pity on her and spell her off for an hour or so, so that she can get out into the fresh air and ride a little herself.

When you move cattle you move, depending on the weather, at the leisurely pace of about two miles an hour. For long stretches you don't need to speak at all, and you can ride a mile or more away from any other rider if you want to. As you ride, the prairie slowly seeps into you. I have never felt such pure, unadulterated joy in simple existence as I have felt at moments out on the prairie during the spring move.

Ordinarily I wouldn't get to ride until we were close to the ranch and our helpers went home. Then Peter and I changed our headquarters from the hay farm to the ranch house and we'd ride horses out to the cattle to bring them the rest of the way home. Occasionally, he'd have someone along who didn't ride and who would drive the truck so that I could ride. Most of the time, though, I reluctantly drove the truck and kept my fingers crossed for a chance either to ride or, as I sometimes did, to walk leading Peter's horse—for me to ride him was unthinkable, the very thought making my stomach turn over and my knees quake—while Peter spelled me off in the driver's seat.

Nowadays we calve at the hay farm instead of at the ranch, mostly because it's easier to keep an eye on the cows, but also because there's shelter for them here during the inevitable calf-killing spring storms. Often, too, in spring there is no water in the ditches or fields along the way and, of course, the cattle must have water each day, moving or not. If we calve at the hay farm—Peter not being a believer in early calving—by the time we're ready to move in late April most of the farmers along the route have seeded their crops. The traditional mistrust between farmers and ranchers being what it is, it would be dangerous if one cow strayed one foot from the road allowances, those which, usually without bothering to get permission from the municipality, farmers haven't plowed up and seeded to wheat. And cows being what they are, you never know when one might take it into her head to head out, calf at her side, racing for Alaska or Mexico across a newly seeded field with a couple of cowboys in hot pursuit. Guns have been pointed on such occasions. Nowadays, it hardly seems worth the risk.

During one of the last spring moves we made, Peter had had more people along than he'd expected and before we'd gone very far he'd given one of the kids my horse, which he'd been leading, to ride. Not long after that, he'd put my saddle— the only one with stirrups that could be shortened enough for small people—to another teenager to use. I had reconciled myself to not being able to ride on this move. I could still look at the landscape, I could roll down the window and smell the sweet air and feel the breeze and the sun on my face, and occasionally I could stop, get out, and stroll around a bit in the grass.

We always made it a practice to stop for a meal when we reached that stretch of pure unbroken prairie. The riders would dismount and hobble their horses or tie them to the fence, I'd park the truck, Peter would throw down a couple of hay bales for a table or for people to sit on, and I'd put out the lunch. We'd sit in the sun and eat sandwiches, and his mother's baked beans, the pot wrapped in layers of newspapers to keep it warm, and drink coffee from thermoses. Long before we reached there I'd have begun to look forward to that moment.

I discovered what the annual day spent crossing these acres of prairie meant to me when, as we were about to begin that part of the trip, a circumstance arose—I don't even remember what it was—that meant somebody had to drive one of the men the twenty or so miles around the fields, down the roads and wait with him there at the corrals for the riders and cattle to arrive. Since Peter could hardly order anybody else to do it, and nobody volunteered, it was taken for granted that as his wife I would leave the drive and take this man where he needed to go.

I wanted to protest, but I couldn't bring myself to do it in front of so many people, especially since arguing or complaining are just not done on a trip like that. It would be a little like a sailor telling the captain of a ship that he didn't feel like taking the watch that night. My true feelings were too private to speak out loud, and I couldn't come up with any practical reason why I shouldn't have to that didn't hint of adolescent pique or, not knowing how the others felt about the prairie—but the fact that nobody volunteered to go should have given me a hint— that I could be sure anybody but Peter would understand. And everyone else was a volunteer; I was official staff. I knew I wouldn't be able to go back and catch up with the drive, either. For me, for that year, the drive was over.

I got back in the truck and started driving, trying to smile, trying to make conversation, while all the time I was fighting back tears. I wanted so badly to spend that last few hours on the prairie, the only time we ever went through those fields, that I had an actual pain in my chest as I drove away and that stayed with me till I went to bed that night.

I said about that incident much later to a friend, "If everything happens to teach you something, why was that taken away from me? What was I supposed to learn from that?" and answered myself, "To teach me how much the wild prairie means to me." Years later, I was able to go further: to understand how precious it is, how unique, how deeply it might affect one, changing even one's understanding of life.

Sometimes I think I'm still not over that loss. Especially since, during the good times, farmers bought all that land the rest of the gang traveled over on horseback that day, and plowed it up to turn it into a farm. Now, ten years later, the farming operation is failing, but you can't turn plowed-up shortgrass prairie back into the original terrain. It's gone forever, or given a human life span, as good as forever, along with the wildlife that lived on it.

It occurs to me now to wonder if perhaps the very real—and surprising even to me—sorrow I felt that day as I drove away, and all the rest of the day and for days afterward, wasn't perhaps intuitive, if perhaps a part of me knew that I would never again experience the sweetness of that air, the sun warm on my face and hands, the view so vast the soul felt free, because by the next spring or the spring after that it would be gone forever.

As the years passed, I felt more and more that the best comfort I had was in being in the landscape. I was only mildly curious about how the prairie was formed, and when and how it was evolving, and I certainly had none of the interests of ecologists or environmentalists. I was merely looking at the prairie as a human being, savoring it for its beauty which engaged all the senses and brought with it a feeling of well-being, contentment and often even joy.

My approach was to simply wander in it with no particular destination, to lie in the sun and bury my nose in the sweet-smelling grasses and forbs such as sage, to admire the colors and textures of the sedges, shrubs and succulents which make up the mixed grass prairie, or to sit on a slope looking out across miles of prairie to the horizon, watching the shifting of shadows and lights across it, thinking no thoughts that, a moment later, I would remember. I was there only to enjoy the prairie. I asked for nothing more, not thinking there was anything more.

I had only the most cursory interest in the names of the plants, although Peter's mother taught me a few of those which flowered: scarlet mallow, three-flowered avens, gumbo primrose, golden bean, which she called "buffalo bean," and which someone else told me she knew as the wild sweet pea. I could hardly miss the wild rose or the prairie sunflower, and I knew a few others such as the wild licorice and the wild morning glory and anemones which grow along the riverbank, from my childhood in the north. Peter showed me the greasewood, badger bush and club moss and pointed out the two species of cactus—the prickly pear and the pin-cushion—and much later I learned from a rancher's wife (herself a rancher and also a poet) that if you had the patience to gather the berries, you could make cactus-berry jelly. I taught myself a few: the many types of cinquefoil and sage, and milkweed, and the Canada thistle with its purple flower that a saddle horse—"Watch this," Peter said—would clip tidily off with its bared teeth, never touching a barb. I longed to see a field of wild prairie lilies as I had in my childhood in the north, but I never have, not even a single flower growing wild in the grass.

Because we had a hay farm, I learned to identify a number of grasses—timothy, bromegrass, foxtail—and legumes—clover, alfalfa—which I saw every day, some of which were imported species, crested wheat grass, Russian wild rye, and many of which, like reed canary grass, were very beautiful. I attended three daylong range schools with Peter, one in the Bears Paw Mountains of Montana, but I did so chiefly for the adventure and to spend an entire day on the prairie instead of only a few hours. At these schools I learned to identify death camas when I saw it, and a few of the many native species of grass—needle-and-thread grass, June grass, blue grama or buffalo grass—and a forb or two.

Other seasons brought different pleasures. All one snowy winter I walked a mile down the riverbed every morning with the dog trotting ahead, flushing out cattle from the banks or far back around the last curve where the fenceline crossed and stopped them, then chasing them up to the feed-grounds where Peter and his hired man were throwing out hay, grain bales and grain itself. For two winters the snow was so deep that it muffled sound so that the cattle which had sought shelter in these snug places couldn't hear the tractor and didn't come out for feed. Or sometimes, looking back, I think Peter came and got me each morning to make that walk out of understanding that I needed to feel useful, a part of the operation, and that if I spent all of each day inside that tiny log house I would soon be "bushed," develop cabin fever, be impossible to live with—that I might leave.

I remember those walks each morning as among the best of my life. I would head down the riverbed, following in the tracks of the cattle where the snow was too deep to walk comfortably in. The banks of the river are high and steep, and the winds had pushed the snow into deep banks that overhung the edges of the cliffsides in fat lips of snow that looked like waves on the ocean and from which long icicles sometimes hung. Looking up from the snowy riverbed, I saw white walls of snow and then the snowy billows and beyond them the brilliant sky. I saw the places where partridges snuggled up for the night to keep warm and followed the tracks of coyotes and foxes and animals whose tracks I didn't recognize. I was picking up knowledge, hardly even noticing that was what I was doing. Running to cut off a cow, I fell headlong in the snow and, with no one watching me, lay there laughing, blinking up at the sky, losing myself in its blue depths.

For most people the worse the weather is, the more likely they are to stay indoors; not so for old-fashioned ranchers—for them the worse the weather, the more likely the rancher is to be out in it, in the midst of blizzards searching for cattle out on the prairie and chasing them down into the shelter of deep coulees, or home to the windbreaks and corrals. On such days I went along with Peter and learned again that the human limits of endurance are much greater than day-to-day life has us believe; that is, I became less afraid of the weather at the same time as I became a good deal more respectful of it.

One of the first Christmas gifts Peter gave me was a pair of cross-country skis, and as long as there was enough snow, which there usually isn't in this desert country, I'd be out on the prairie in the winter, too, skiing. I began to take my skis and go out into the hills during storms, having discovered that I liked storms for the way they changed the appearance of familiar places and for the sense of mystery they brought to them.

Memories of my childhood came back to me: playing in the bush with my friends, with my sisters and cousins in our grandmother's garden, skating on frozen sloughs in winter till the pain from the cold became so bad even we kids couldn't stand it anymore and went home, the winter we had built a snow fort that lasted for months as we added on and made it more and more substantial so that it stood well into spring. I felt like a child again, had fleeting moments when I remembered how wonderful the world itself had once seemed, and how it was to be cared for, worry-free, and living in the body again and not just the mind.

And I was recreating myself as a writer. I not only was meditative by nature, this having been developed in me as the result of being an extremely shy and retiring child in a big family, I had also developed in me the seeds of the observer. It was a lucky thing, although I'd never have admitted it then, to have arrived a stranger in a strange land, when I was no longer young, with a touch of the observer's cold eye already in my makeup.

I found myself observing the very people with whom I seemed to have so little in common. I saw the people of my new community as different from those of the rest of the province, and I was surprised to discover that they themselves seemed to define themselves as different, although nobody ever explicitly said so, in that they often had closer links both in terms of lifestyle and in family ties to Alberta and to Montana than they did to Saskatchewan. Many of the families had begun as Americans and had close relatives on the farms and ranches over the border and in Alberta, and when young people went off to higher education or trades schools or to jobs, when I first came here, they were much more likely to go to Alberta than to Saskatoon or even Regina. As a group they seemed to me often to think more like western Americans or like Albertans, with that essentially conservative, independent cast of mind, than they did like the good-old-Tommy-Douglas-prairie-socialist school of thought to which I belonged and which had always seemed to me to define Saskatchewan.[1]

I soon discovered, in my attempt to tell the story of these people and this place, that my fund of facts, of precise knowledge, was inadequate to the task I'd set myself. Each story, each book, each play would become an exercise in information gathering. When Peter couldn't answer my questions I turned to books. Peter took me to meet old people, old men who'd pioneered in the area, and I listened to their stories and made notes, and where it was possible, which was practically never, I tried to match their memories to the scant written history I could find.

I carried a notebook everywhere. Chasing cows home on bitter winter days, I'd stop the truck, get out, draw a little diagram of the way an animal had pushed away the snow from a sage bush, write a description of the bush and the snow and the droppings the animal had left, the colors, the place where the sun was in the sky on that day at that time and how the cattle looked. I wrote the last few pages of *The Gates of the Sun* sitting on a straw bale in the back of the pickup in a neighbor's field while I waited for Peter to finish baling the straw, pausing in my scribbling only to ask questions of Peter and the neighbor, when they stopped for coffee, about what was a native species, whether bird, animal or plant, and what wasn't. It constantly amazed me how much the men knew.

With every story and every book I was forced to search out new information. My fund of information, of facts, obtained in all these ways—my own observations, Peter's answers to my incessant questions, the stories of old people, books— was growing. Without intending to or even really wanting to, I was becoming knowledgeable about the history of the area and its plant and animal life. Although I will never know all there is to know—Peter still knows a thousand times more than I do—having begun by being transported by its beauty, and then being overwhelmed by my sense of loneliness and purposelessness, I was at last starting to feel at home in the terrain, at home in the landscape. Of course, I didn't see this as it was happening, but by learning to name things in my new environment, by discovering the scheme of the place and the way the parts fit together, I was making them my own, and by this I was slowly healing myself.

Years later when I was the expert instead of the neophyte, a friend and I were out walking in the rain. In this semiarid country where rain is rare and precious, walking in it is exhilarating, imbued even with a touch of magic. We came to a place where a pair of great horned owls sat watching us, and as my friend went closer to see them better, I sat in the grass in my leaky boots and a borrowed yellow rain jacket which came to my knees, not minding the wet, looking out over the misty fields, noticing how everything smelled different because of the moisture, how colors had changed and intensified.

I thought of how my friend and I had moved over the wet ground, where we had gone and not gone, what we had found ourselves doing, and suddenly I realized that it was the land—Nature—that had guided our steps, made our choices for us, and not the other way around. That is, because we were friends and rambling in the countryside for the pleasure of each other's company and for the pleasure of being out-of-doors, having no set plan or goal, we had gone where the shape of the land had suggested itself to us; we had done what the land had made available to us. If it was too muddy or wet in one place, we went somewhere else; if a hill was too steep, we went around; there was no way to cross the river without swimming and it was too cold to swim, so we followed its course instead and sat on its bank.

I thought, then said, "This land makes Crees of us all." By this, I meant that it appeared to me that the Crees, for example, developed the culture they developed because it was the best fit between themselves and the land. And it was the *land* that taught them that. They adapted to the land, and not the other way around as we Europeans so stupidly did, trying to force this arid western land to be, as government propaganda had for seventy-five years and more put it, "the bread-basket of the world."

I began to think about the ways in which land affects the individual, or at least this particular landscape, the Great Plains of North America. I began to see that in our human arrogance we assume we can affect the land but it can't affect us— except in practical ways: hurricanes, floods, drought—when there are plenty of ways we might find that the land—Nature—is affecting us without our being aware of it. In considering the differences between Peter and myself, I had not imagined or considered the possibility that he had been shaped by the land, by Nature, that in subtle ways we've never identified nor even really talked about, his psyche itself had been shaped by Nature not merely by *his* observations of *it* but by its subtle, never described or even consciously realized, influence on *him*.

The Great Plains landscape is an elemental one. There is little natural water in the form of flakes or rivers or even ponds, no forests, no mountains—just miles and miles of land and a sky across which weather visibly, majestically, passes. One winter visitor to this place said it reminded him of the high Arctic where he had once lived, and several others, Wallace Stegner included, spoke of the plains of Africa. The landscape is so huge that our imaginations can't contain it or outstrip it, and the climate is concomitantly arbitrary and severe.

It is geology stripped bare, leaving behind only a vast sky and land stretched out in long, sweeping lines that blend into the distant horizon with a line that is sometimes so clear and sharp it is surreal, and sometimes exists at the edge of metaphysics, oscillating in heat waves or, summer or winter, blending into mirages and the realm of dreams and visions which wavers just the other side of the horizon. The Great Plains are a land for visionaries, they induce visions, they are themselves visions, the line between the fact and dream is so blurred. What other landscape around the world produces the mystic psyche so powerfully? Sky and land, that is all, and grass, and what Nature leaves bare the human psyche fills.

It was not until I moved into the country to live that my significant dreaming really began. I did not think about this fact, but if I had, I am sure I would have explained it as a by-product of the radical change in my way of life. Eventually it was suggested to me by an eminent western Canadian writer in whom I had confided that perhaps living in this ancient, skeletal landscape had brought on these dreams. At the time I reserved judgment, but a few years later, in another context, another western Canadian writer told me how she had, after years of living in the city where she didn't believe she had dreamt at all, moved out into the country and suddenly began having vivid, meaningful dreams. She attributed these to the influence of the landscape in which she now made her home.

In the context of these remarks it seems to me very significant that dreams have always held an important place in Aboriginal cultures of the Great Plains of North America, as they have in many other such cultures around the world. Aboriginal people take the content of their dreams as simply another source of information about the world, a guide for action, and as prophecy, either in their individual lives or as directives to their communities. In these cultures it is considered extremely foolish, a great insult, even a sin, to ignore an important dream.

Prophetic dreams are accepted at face value and are used as a basis for action. A South Dakota writer living near Rapid City told me that a few years ago Chief Crazy Horse—whose name I'm told should more accurately be translated as "Enchanted Horse," or "Vision Horse"—appeared in dreams to the elders of his nation to warn them about an imminent flood on a branch of the Cheyenne River. The flood did occur and it killed more than a hundred of his people who lived along the banks. Hugh Brody, in *Maps and Dreams,* describes a hunting culture, the Beaver Indians of northeastern British Columbia, where the best hunters are guided by dreams to their kill; the very best hunter-dreamers have even dreamt the way to heaven and then, awaking, have drawn the map.

Although I sometimes go for long stretches without any dreams that seem important to me, a few years ago I began to have the occasional prophetic dream myself. I dreamt the San Francisco earthquake a couple of weeks before it happened. Since I'd never been to San Francisco, I thought the city in the dream was Vancouver and the broken bridge, the Lions' Gate. Although it was a powerful enough dream to tell people about it, I certainly never took it as prophecy until I saw the broken span of the bridge on television. It was identical to the one in my dream where it had been the main icon. I dreamt of the Japanese airplane that lost its rudder and, after weaving drunkenly through the air for half an hour, crashed into a mountain. I was in bed dreaming it as it was happening. When I got up the first thing Peter did was to tell me about this terrible event that had just happened in Japan. I even dreamt of the death of one of the Russian Communist leaders a few days before he died. It may be that I've had more prophetic dreams than I know but simply haven't remembered. Actually I think this may be true of everyone, but most people don't record their dreams as I usually do, and so forget them.

I have described the dream I had in which a giant eagle and a giant owl appeared to me. It became for me a life-dream, a significant dream that launched me on a journey through comparative religion, mythology, the study of dreams, psychoanalysis, and finally into the study of the nature of the female. At an archetypal level, it is a dream about masculine power, symbolized by the soaring eagle, and feminine power, symbolized by the owl standing near me on the ground. In beauty and power they are exactly equal, but I, a woman, had spent my life to this point following the eagle—that is, accepting masculine interpretations of life in general and, of my own life, accepting masculine goals and taking masculine desires for my own—instead of cleaving to the owl, searching out and coming to terms with my own feminine soul.

My search for understanding of the dream led me into and through my novel *Luna*—the story of the lives of contemporary ranch and farm women and how they live, feel about, and understand their rural, agricultural, traditional lives—and from there into my short story collection *Fever*, a much more personal and urbanized study of the same issues. It's been a good dozen years since I had that dream and I still run across further ways to interpret it. Not only have I accepted it as guidance in the direction my life has taken, it is, to a degree, the foundation on which I have built the rest of my life.

I think that significant dreaming is one way in which Nature influences and changes the individual, developing in her/him an awareness of Nature as more than mere locale, or a setting, a context, as more than beauty, as more than something that is merely Other.

It was in Joseph Campbell's *Primitive Mythology* that I first heard of Aboriginal dreamtime, and not long after, in a much more firsthand and compelling way in *The Lost World of the Kalahari* by Laurens van der Post. All peoples of the earth have creation stories of one kind or another. The stories of prescientific peoples tell variously of a time when the world was in the process of being created along with the creatures on it. This was a timeless time, a time before time, when animals, plants and people could become one another and the formations of the earth were taking shape. It is called, in mythologies around the world, dreamtime, and out of it springs stories and legends about archetypal creatures, sometimes gods, whose manifestations remain now in the fallen time.

It seems, too, that on some level this timeless time still exists in another realm, and those people peculiarly blessed—including, but never exclusively, shamans— may still go there. In this realm many strange things can happen: animals can

converse with humans and vice versa; the dead may appear and speak, or creatures from the dreamtime thought by some of us to be merely metaphoric. The
earth becomes more beautiful, approaches, even achieves, perfection, and everything in it and on it is imbued with meaning. And especially the sense of the ticking
of time vanishes.

I believe that since Aboriginal people around the world have nontechnological
cultures and live in and by Nature—or at least, once did when their cultures were
developing—and these cultures had developed the concept of dreamtime and took
dreaming very seriously whether in New Zealand, Australia, the Kalahari Desert
of Africa, or the Great Plains of North America, that surely it was Nature which,
whether with will and intention or not, taught, allowed, gave them dreams as an
instrument of knowledge.

I began to see from my own experience living in it that the land and the wild
creatures who live in it and on it, and the turning of the earth, the rising and setting
of the sun and the moon, and the constant passing of weather across its surface—
that is, Nature—influenced rural people to make them what they are, more than
even they knew.

Close proximity to a natural environment—being in Nature—alters all of us in
ways which remain pretty much unexplored, even undescribed in our culture. I
am suggesting that these ways in which such a closeness affects us, from dreams to
more subtle and less describable phenomena, are real, and that we should stop
thinking, with our inflated human egos, that all the influence is the other way
around. We might try to shift our thinking in this direction so that we stop blithely
improving the natural world around us, and begin to learn, as Aboriginal people
have, what Nature in her subtle but powerful manner has to teach us about how
to live.

More and more I am coming to believe that our alienation from the natural
world is at root of much that has gone so wrong in the modern world, and that if
Nature has anything to teach us at all, her first lesson is in humility.

Notes

1. Tommy Douglas was premier of Saskatchewan for seventeen years. A democratic social-
ist, he introduced pension plans, central banking, and unemployment insurance and is best
known for establishing medicare in Canada.—Eds.

Further Reading

Coyote's Morning Cry: Meditations and Dreams from a Life in Nature. 1995.
Fever. 1990.
The Fourth Archangel. 1992.

The Garden of Eden. 1998.
Gates of the Sun. 1986.
Luna. 1988.
Queen of the Headaches. 1989.
Real Life. 2002.

Reading about Sharon Butala

Hillis, Doris. "Interview with Sharon Butala." *Wascana Review* 22 (1987): 37–53.
Quantic, Diane. "Women's Response to the Great Plains Landscape as Spiritual Domain: Kathleen Norris and Sharon Butala." *Literature and Belief* 21.3 (spring 2003): 57–79.

Loren Eiseley (1907–1977)

Like Sharon Butala, Loren Eiseley sees more than meets the eye on the Great Plains expanse. Imagining the river and surrounding plains as a place rooted in time, Eiseley sees in the sandbars of the Platte, the river that drains much of the central Great Plains, evidence of the deep links between ice age bedrock and the shifting sands of the present river channels.

Eiseley was born in Lincoln, Nebraska. While he lived in Lincoln the population doubled, but Eiseley always lived on the edge of town. He had easy access to the pond, the creekbank, and other landscapes that appear and reappear in his writings. These early explorations became the basis for his lifelong study of natural history, especially prehistory. From 1931 to 1933 Eiseley participated in the University of Nebraska's Morrill Paleontological Expedition in northwest Nebraska. In 1934 he left Nebraska to earn his master's and Ph.D. degrees in anthropology at the University of Pennsylvania. He taught at the University of Kansas and Oberlin College before returning to the University of Pennsylvania in 1947.

The Immense Journey (1957) established Eiseley as an accessible interpreter of the intersection between science and humanism. This selection reflects his firm belief in the need for man not only to reason but to imagine as well.

The Flow of the River (1957)

If there is magic on this planet, it is contained in water. Its least stir even, as now in a rain pond on a flat roof opposite my office, is enough to bring me searching to the window. A wind ripple may be translating itself into life. I have a constant feeling that some time I may witness that momentous miracle on a city roof, see life veritably and suddenly boiling out of a heap of rusted pipes and old television aerials. I marvel at how suddenly a water beetle has come and is submarining there in a spatter of green algae. Thin vapors, rust, wet tar and sun are an alembic remarkably like the mind; they throw off odorous shadows that threaten to take real shape when no one is looking.

Once in a lifetime, perhaps, one escapes the actual confines of the flesh. Once in a lifetime, if one is lucky, one so merges with sunlight and air and running water that whole eons, the eons that mountains and deserts know, might pass in a single afternoon without discomfort. The mind has sunk away into its beginnings among old roots and the obscure tricklings and movings that stir inanimate things. Like the charmed fairy circle into which a man once stepped, and upon emergence learned that a whole century had passed in a single night, one can never quite define this secret; but it has something to do, I am sure, with common water. Its substance reaches everywhere; it touches the past and prepares the future; it moves under the poles and wanders thinly in the heights of air. It can assume forms of exquisite perfection in a snowflake, or strip the living to a single shining bone cast up by the sea.

Many years ago, in the course of some scientific investigations in a remote western county, I experienced, by chance, precisely the sort of curious absorption by water—the extension of shape by osmosis—at which I have been hinting. You have probably never experienced in yourself the meandering roots of a whole watershed or felt your outstretched fingers touching, by some kind of clairvoyant extension, the brooks of snow-line glaciers at the same time that you were flowing toward the Gulf over the eroded debris of worn-down mountains. A poet, Mac-Knight Black, has spoken of being "limbed. . . . with waters gripping pole and pole." He had the idea, all right, and it is obvious that these sensations are not unique, but they are hard to come by; and the sort of extension of the senses that people will accept when they put their ear against a sea shell, they will smile at in the confessions of a bookish professor. What makes it worse is the fact that because of a traumatic experience in childhood, I am not a swimmer, and am inclined to be timid before any large body of water. Perhaps it was just this, in a way, that contributed to my experience.

As it leaves the Rockies and moves downward over the high plains towards the Missouri, the Platte River is a curious stream. In the spring floods, on occasion, it can be a mile-wide roaring torrent of destruction, gulping farms and bridges. Normally, however, it is a rambling, dispersed series of streamlets flowing erratically over great sand and gravel fans that are, in part, the remnants of a mightier Ice Age stream bed. Quicksands and shifting islands haunt its waters. Over it the prairie suns beat mercilessly throughout the summer. The Platte, "a mile wide and an inch deep," is a refuge for any heat-weary pilgrim along its shores. This is particularly true on the high plains before its long march by the cities begins.

The reason that I came upon it when I did, breaking through a willow thicket and stumbling out through ankle-deep water to a dune in the shade, is of no concern to this narrative. On various purposes of science I have ranged over a good bit of that country on foot, and I know the kinds of bones that come gurgling up through the gravel pumps, and the arrowheads of shining chalcedony that occasionally spill out of water-loosened sand. On that day, however, the sight of sky and willows and the weaving net of water murmuring a little in the shallows on its way to the Gulf stirred me, parched as I was with miles of walking, with a new idea: I was going to float. I was going to undergo a tremendous adventure.

The notion came to me, I suppose, by degrees. I had shed my clothes and was floundering pleasantly in a hole among some reeds when a great desire to stretch out and go with this gently insistent water began to pluck at me. Now to this bronzed, bold, modern generation, the struggle I waged with timidity while standing there in knee-deep water can only seem farcical; yet actually for me it was not so. A near-drowning accident in childhood had scarred my reactions; in addition to the fact that I was a nonswimmer, this "inch-deep river" was treacherous with holes and quicksands. Death was not precisely infrequent along its wandering and illusory channels. Like all broad wastes of this kind, where neither water nor land quite prevails, its thickets were lonely and untraversed. A man in trouble would cry out in vain.

I thought of all this, standing quietly in the water, feeling the sand shifting away under my toes. Then I lay back in the floating position that left my face to the sky, and shoved off. The sky wheeled over me. For an instant, as I bobbed into the main channel, I had the sensation of sliding down the vast tilted face of the continent. It was then that I felt the cold needles of the alpine springs at my fingertips, and the warmth of the Gulf pulling me southward. Moving with me, leaving its taste upon my mouth and spouting under me in dancing springs of sand, was the immense body of the continent itself, flowing like the river was flowing, grain by grain, mountain by mountain, down to the sea. I was streaming over ancient sea beds thrust aloft where giant reptiles had once sported; I was wearing down the face of time and trundling cloud-wreathed ranges into oblivion. I touched my margins with the delicacy of a crayfish's antennae, and felt great fishes glide about their work.

I drifted by stranded timber cut by beaver in mountain fastnesses; I slid over shallows that had buried the broken axles of prairie schooners and the mired bones of mammoth. I was streaming alive through the hot and working ferment of the sun, or oozing secretively through shady thickets. I *was* water and the unspeakable alchemies that gestate and take shape in water, the slimy jellies that under the enormous magnification of the sun writhe and whip upward as great barbeled fish mouths, or sink indistinctly back into the murk out of which they arose. Turtle and fish and the pinpoint chirpings of individual frogs are all watery projections, concentrations—as man himself is a concentration—of that indescribable and liquid brew which is compounded in varying proportions of salt and sun and time. It has appearances, but at its heart lies water, and as I was finally edged gently against a sandbar and dropped like any log, I tottered as I rose. I knew once more the body's revolt against emergence into the harsh and unsupporting air, its reluctance to break contact with that mother element which still, at this late point in time, shelters and brings into being nine tenths of everything alive.

As for men, those myriad little detached ponds with their own swarming corpuscular life, what were they but a way that water has of going about beyond the reach of rivers? I, too, was a microcosm of pouring rivulets and floating driftwood gnawed by the mysterious animalcules of my own creation. I was three fourths water, rising and subsiding according to the hollow knocking in my veins: a minute pulse like the eternal pulse that lifts Himalayas and which, in the following systole, will carry them away.

Thoreau, peering at the emerald pickerel in Walden Pond, called them "animalized water" in one of his moments of strange insight. If he had been possessed of the geological knowledge so laboriously accumulated since his time, he might have gone further and amusedly detected in the planetary rumblings and eructations which so delighted him in the gross habits of certain frogs, signs of that dark interior stress which has reared sea bottoms up to mountainous heights. He might have developed an acute inner ear for the sound of the surf on Cretaceous beaches where now the wheat of Kansas rolls. In any case, he would have seen, as the long trail of life was unfolded by the fossil hunters, that his animalized water had changed its shapes eon by eon to the beating of the earth's dark millennial heart. In the swamps of the low continents, the amphibians had flourished and had their day; and as the long skyward swing—the isostatic response of the crust—had come about, the era of the cooling grasslands and mammalian life had come into being.

A few winters ago, clothed heavily against the weather, I wandered several miles along one of the tributaries of that same Platte I had floated down years before. The land was stark and ice-locked. The rivulets were frozen, and over the marshlands the willow thickets made such an array of vertical lines against the snow that tramping through them produced strange optical illusions and dizziness. On the edge of a frozen backwater, I stopped and rubbed my eyes. At my feet a raw prairie wind had swept the ice clean of snow. A peculiar green object caught my eye; there was no mistaking it.

Staring up at me with all his barbels spread pathetically, frozen solidly in the wind-ruffled ice, was a huge familiar face. It was one of those catfish of the twisting channels, those dwellers in the yellow murk, who had been about me and beneath me on the day of my great voyage. Whatever sunny dream had kept him paddling there while the mercury plummeted downward and that Cheshire smile froze slowly, it would be hard to say. Or perhaps he was trapped in a blocked channel and had simply kept swimming until the ice contracted around him. At any rate, there he would lie till the spring thaw.

At that moment I started to turn away, but something in the bleak, whiskered face reproached me, or perhaps it was the river calling to her children. I termed it science, however—a convenient rational phrase I reserve for such occasions—and decided that I would cut the fish out of the ice and take him home. I had no intention of eating him. I was merely struck by a sudden impulse to test the survival qualities of high-plains fishes, particularly fishes of this type who get themselves immured in oxygenless ponds or in cut-off oxbows buried in winter drifts. I blocked him out as gently as possible and dropped him, ice and all, into a collecting can in the car. Then we set out for home.

Unfortunately, the first stages of what was to prove a remarkable resurrection escaped me. Cold and tired after a long drive, I deposited the can with its melting water and ice in the basement. The accompanying corpse I anticipated I would either dispose of or dissect on the following day. A hurried glance had revealed no signs of life.

To my astonishment, however, upon descending into the basement several hours later, I heard stirrings in the receptable and peered in. The ice had melted. A vast pouting mouth ringed with sensitive feelers confronted me, and the creature's gills labored slowly. A thin stream of silver bubbles rose to the surface and popped. A fishy eye gazed up at me protestingly.

"A tank," it said. This was no Walden pickerel. This was a yellow-green, mud-grubbing, evil-tempered inhabitant of floods and droughts and cyclones. It was the selective product of the high continent and the waters that pour across it. It had outlasted prairie blizzards that left cattle standing frozen upright in the drifts.

"I'll get the tank," I said respectfully.

He lived with me all that winter, and his departure was totally in keeping with his sturdy, independent character. In the spring a migratory impulse or perhaps sheer boredom struck him. Maybe, in some little lost corner of his brain, he felt, far off, the pouring of the mountain waters through the sandy coverts of the Platte. Anyhow, something called to him, and he went. One night when no one was about, he simply jumped out of his tank. I found him dead on the floor next morning. He had made his gamble like a man—or, I should say, a fish. In the proper place it would not have been a fool's gamble. Fishes in the drying shallows of intermittent prairie streams who feel their confinement and have the impulse to leap while there is yet time may regain the main channel and survive. A million ancestral years had gone into that jump, I thought as I looked at him, a million years of climbing through prairie sunflowers and twining in and out through the pillared legs of drinking mammoth.

"Some of your close relatives have been experimenting with air breathing," I remarked, apropos of nothing, as I gathered him up. "Suppose we meet again up there in the cottonwoods in a million years or so."

I missed him a little as I said it. He had for me the kind of lost archaic glory that comes from the water brotherhood. We were both projections out of that timeless ferment and locked as well in some greater unity that lay incalculably beyond us. In many a fin and reptile foot I have seen myself passing by—some part of myself, that is, some part that lies unrealized in the momentary shape I inhabit. People have occasionally written me harsh letters and castigated me for a lack of faith in man when I have ventured to speak of this matter in print. They distrust, it would seem, all shapes and thoughts but their own. They would bring God into the compass of a shopkeeper's understanding and confine Him to those limits, lest He proceed to some unimaginable and shocking act—create perhaps, as a casual afterthought, a being more beautiful than man. As for me, I believe nature capable of this, and having been part of the flow of the river, I feel no envy—any more than the frog envies the reptile or an ancestral ape should envy man.

Every spring in the wet meadows and ditches I hear a little shrilling chorus which sounds for all the world like an endlessly reiterated "We're here, we're here, we're here." And so they are, as frogs, of course. Confident little fellows. I suspect that to some greater ear than ours, man's optimistic pronouncements about his role and destiny may make a similar little ringing sound that travels a small way out into the night. It is only its nearness that is offensive. From the heights of a mountain, or a marsh at evening, it blends, not too badly, with all the other sleepy voices that, in croaks or chirrups, are saying the same thing.

After a while the skilled listener can distinguish man's noise from the katydid's rhythmic assertion, allow for the offbeat of a rabbit's thumping, pick up the autumnal monotone of crickets, and find in all of them a grave pleasure without admitting any to a place of preëminence in his thoughts. It is when all these voices cease and the waters are still, when along the frozen river nothing cries, screams or howls, that the enormous mindlessness of space settles down upon the soul. Somewhere out in that waste of crushed ice and reflected stars, the black waters may be running, but they appear to be running without life toward a destiny in which the whole of space may be locked in some silvery winter of dispersed radiation.

It is then, when the wind comes straitly across the barren marshes and the snow rises and beats in endless waves against the traveler, that I remember best, by some trick of the imagination, my summer voyage on the river. I remember my green extensions, my catfish nuzzlings and minnow wrigglings, my gelatinous material-izations out of the mother ooze. And as I walk on through the white smother, it is the magic of water that leaves me a final sign.

Men talk much of matter and energy, of the struggle for existence that molds the shape of life. These things exist, it is true; but more delicate, elusive, quicker than the fins in water, is that mysterious principle known as "organization," which leaves all other mysteries concerned with life stale and insignificant by com-parison. For that without organization life does not persist is obvious. Yet this organization itself is not strictly the product of life, nor of selection. Like some dark and passing shadow within matter, it cups out the eyes' small windows or spaces the notes of a meadow lark's song in the interior of a mottled egg. That principle—I am beginning to suspect—was there before the living in the deeps of water.

The temperature has risen. The little stinging needles have given way to huge flakes floating in like white leaves blown from some great tree in open space. In the car, switching on the lights, I examine one intricate crystal on my sleeve before it melts. No utilitarian philosophy explains a snow crystal, no doctrine of use or disuse. Water has merely leapt out of vapor and thin nothingness in the night sky to array itself in form. There is no logical reason for the existence of a snowflake any more than there is for evolution. It is an apparition from that mysterious shadow world beyond nature, that final world which contains—if anything contains—the explanation of men and catfish and green leaves.

Further Reading
Darwin's Century. 1958.
The Unexpected Universe. 1979.

William Least Heat-Moon *(b. 1939)*

William Least Heat-Moon is a sojourner, one who pauses in his travels to delve deeply into a place, exploring every aspect of his subject. Critics have put him in the company of travel writers as dissimilar as Mark Twain and Henry David Thoreau. His first book, *Blue Highways* (1982), recounted a trip across America on the back roads, a record of his encounters with the places and people that define America's extra-ordinariness. His latest book, *River Horse* (1999), is an account of his cross-country journey by water.

In *PrairyErth* he explores Chase County in the Kansas Flint Hills. Most of the county is pastureland, one of the last stretches of virgin native tallgrass prairie in North America. Part of this land is the ten-thousand-acre Tallgrass Prairie National Preserve. Heat-Moon creates a "deep map," an exhaustive catalog of the county. He methodically dissects it into grids, a simple task since the area is almost square and uninterrupted by rivers or towns that could cut across his cartographic metaphor. Heat-Moon explores what interests him within each grid—geologic formations, signs of Indians' presence, cottonwood trees, pack rats, cafe owners, cattlemen, and villagers. "Atop the Mound" is Heat-Moon's description of the art of walking in the prairie.

Heat-Moon has helped readers focus on the necessity of overlooked places— back roads, small towns, empty cemeteries, and rivers and streams that provide the "runoff" for our superhighways, urban sprawl, and mighty rivers. He was born William Trogdon in Kansas City, Missouri. He earned bachelor's and master's degrees in English and a Ph.D. in photojournalism from the University of Missouri.

Atop the Mound (1991)

What I cherish I've come to slowly, usually blindly, not seeing it for some time, and that's just how I discovered Jacobs' Mound, a truncated cone sitting close to the center of the Gladstone quadrangle. This most obvious old travelers' marker shows up clearly from two of the three highways, yet I was here several days before I noticed it, this isolated frustum so distinct. I must have been looking too closely and narrowly, but once I saw its volcano-cone symmetry (at night in the fire season, its top can flame and smolder) I was drawn to it as western travelers have always been to lone protuberances—Independence Rock, Pompey's Pillar, Chimney Rock—and within a day I headed down the Bloody Creek Road until the lane played out in a grassed vale. Some two aerial miles west of the mound, I climbed a ridge and sat down and watched it as if it might disappear like a flock of rare birds. That morning four people told me four things, one of them, the last, accurate: the regular sides and flattened top of the knob prove Indians built it for a burial mound; Colorado prospectors hid gold in it; an oil dome lay beneath it; and, none of those notions was true.

I walked down the hawk-harried ridge and struck out toward the mound, seemingly near enough to reach before sunset. Its sea-level elevation is fifteen hundred feet, but it rises only about a hundred from its base and three hundred above the surrounding humped terrain. In places the October grasses, russet-colored like low flames as if revealing their union with fire, reached to my belt and stunted my strides, and there were also aromatic asters and false indigo, both now dried to scratching stiffness. From the tall heads of Indian grass and the brown stalks of gayfeather, gossamer strung out in the slow wind like pennants ten and twelve feet long and silver in the sun, and these web lines snagged my trousers and chest and head until, after a mile, I was bestrung and on my way to becoming cocooned. Gray flittings rose from the ground like winged stones and threw themselves immediately into invisibility—I think they were vesper sparrows. Twice, prairie chickens broke noisily and did their sweet, dihedral-winged glides to new cover (Audubon said their bent-down wings enable the birds to turn their heads to see behind as they fly). I stopped to watch small events but never for long because the mound was drawing me as if it were a stone vortex in a petrified sea.

There are several ways not to walk in the prairie, and one of them is with your eye on a far goal, because you then begin to believe you're not closing the distance any more than you would with a mirage. My woodland sense of scale and time didn't fit this country, and I started wondering whether I could reach the summit before dark. On the prairie, distance and the miles of air turn movement to stasis and openness to a wall, a thing as difficult to penetrate as dense forest. I was hiking in a chamber of absences where the near was the same as the far, and it seemed every time I raised a step the earth rotated under me so that my foot fell just where it had lifted from. Limits and markers make travel possible for people: circumscribe our lines of sight and we can really get somewhere. Before me lay the Kansas of popular conception from Coronado on—that place you have to get through, that purgatory of mileage.

But I kept walking, and, when I dropped into hollows and the mound disappeared, I focused on a rock or a tuft of grass to keep from convoluting my track. Hiking in woods allows a traveler to imagine comforting enclosures, one leading to the next, and the walker can possess those little encompassed spaces, but the prairie and plains permit no such possession. Whatever else prairie is—grass, sky, wind—it is most of all a paradigm of infinity, a clearing full of many things except boundaries, and its power comes from its apparent limitlessness; there is no such thing as a small prairie any more than there is a little ocean, and the consequence of both is this challenge: try to take yourself seriously out here, you bipedal plodder, you complacent cartoon.

I came up out of a hollow, Jacobs' Mound big now on the horizon, and I could feel its swell in my legs, and then I was in the steep climb up its slope, and: I was on top. From the highway I'd guessed the summit to be the size of a city block, but it was less than a baseball infield, its elliptical perimeter just a hundred strides. So, its power lay not in size but rather in shape and dominion and its thrust into the imagination.

I sat and looked. The thousands of acres that lay encircled around the knob I really didn't see, not at first. I saw air, and I said, good god, look at all this air, and I recalled a woman saying, *Seems the air here hasn't ever been used before.* From a plane you look down, and from a mountain you look down, but from Jacobs' Mound you look out, out into. You're not up in the sky and you're not on the ground: you're nicely in between, at the altitude of those who fly in their dreams and skim roofs and treetops. Jacobs' Mound is thrush-flight high.

And then I understood: I like this prairie county because of its illusion of being away, out of, and I like how its unpopulousness seems to isolate it. Seventy percent of Americans live on two percent of the land, but in front of me, no percentage of them lived. Yet, in the far southeast, I could see trucks inching out the turnpike miles, the turbulence of their passage silenced by distance. And I could see fence lines, transmission towers, and dug ponds, things the pioneers would have viewed as marks of a progressive civilization but which to me, a grousing neo-primitivist, were signs of the continuing onslaught. The view I had homesteaders would have loved, and the one they had of unbroken vegetation and its diversities I would cherish. On top of the mound, insects whirred steadily, and the wind blew in easy continuousness, a drone like that in a seashell at the ear. In the nineteenth century, the Kansas clergyman and author William Quayle (who once wrote, *In a purely metaphorical sense I am a turnip*) traded his autograph for an acre of prairie, and, yesterday, I thought him a thief, but now, seeing the paltriness of an acre, I figured he was the one swindled.

On his great western expedition of 1806, Zebulon Pike crossed the Flint Hills just south of the big knob, and he surely couldn't have resisted climbing this rise for a good look around. In later years, perpendicular to his course ran an old freighter road and stage line that cut between here and Phenis Mound across the county line and five miles east. Near its base, a century ago, farmer John Buckingham plowed up a small redwood chest, took it home, pried it open, and found some old parchments, one marked in crude characters of eccentric orthography advising that nearby a buried sword pointed to the spot on Phenis Mound where lay a cache of golden nuggets. Buckingham thought it a prank until he remembered plowing up a rusted saber the year before; but his and others' diggings yielded only what the inland sea put down a quarter billion years ago.

People connect themselves to the land as their imaginations allow. The links of Chase countians to Jacobs' Mound, at least in an earlier time, were more calligraphic than auricular, and at my feet lay proof: a piece of limestone, palm-sized and flattened like a slate and cut into it a reversed J surmounted by an upside-down V: perhaps a cattle brand. In the days of first white settlement, people rode out here in buggies and hayracks, filled their jugs at one of the springs below the mound, picnicked on the summit, and scratched their names into the broken stones. I looked for more: nothing. Then I turned over a small rock and there, in faint relief under the low sunlight, JOHNY, and on another, MAE, and then I began turning stones, their hardness against one another striking out a strange and musical ringing, and I found more intaglios weathered to near invisibility but the letters uncommonly adroit. The mound was so covered with bits of alphabet it was as if Moses had here thrown down his tablets.

And then from the dark, granular soil I turned one that froze me: WAKONDA. In several variants, Wakonda is a Plains Indian name for the Great Mysterious, the Four-Winds-Source-of-All. Then my sense returned: an ancient Indian writing in Roman characters? I looked closely and could barely make out W KENDA running to the fractured right edge. Perhaps once: W. KENDALL. I put it again face-down so that it might continue its transfer into the mound.

Across America, lone risings have been sacred places to tribal Americans, places to reach out for the infinite. Where whites saw this knob and dreamed gold, aboriginal peoples (it's my guess) found it and dreamed God, and it must have belonged to their legends and gramarye, and they surely came to this erosional ellipse as leaves to the eddy.

Plains Nature: *Natural Histories*

It is a truism among Great Plains observers that there are two ways to look at the landscape: at the far horizon or at one's feet. While writers presented in the last section, "The Nature of the Plains," focus on the metaphysical landscape imposed on the observer's imagination, the writers included here explore the biological, ecological, and botanical meanings of the more immediate Great Plains experience. They compel the reader to consider the visible nature of the Great Plains. Some focus diligently on the ground underfoot so that every flower and grass stem becomes a distinct, named segment of the landscape. Others provide links to the destructive vagaries of weather and wide-angle views of the region's topography and history, while still others ask the reader to regard prairie fire and wind as very real personal threats. Whatever form their observations take, these writers represent plains residents who note the details.

The source of conflict in much Great Plains fiction is the need to know the nature of the place itself: its topography, ecology, climate, and history, that is, its promise or its threat. Writers must know the lay of the land in order to acknowledge its subtle effect on human inhabitants.

Further Reading

Flores, Dan. *The Natural West: Environmental History in the Great Plains and Rocky Mountains.* Norman: University of Oklahoma, 2001.
Jackson, Wes. *New Roots for Agriculture.* Lincoln: University of Nebraska Press, 1980.
Kraenzel, Carl Frederick. *The Great Plains in Transition.* Norman: University of Oklahoma Press, 1955.
Manning, Richard. *Grassland: History, Biology, Politics and Promise of the American Prairie.* New York: Viking Penguin, 1995.
Webb, Walter Prescott. *The Great Plains.* Boston: Ginn, 1931.

John Madson (1923–1995)

John Madson literally gets down to the grass roots in this selection from his book *Where the Sky Began* (1982). The essay is a veritable geography of prairie grasses. His patch of tallgrass prairie is an anomaly in a region where the rich prairie soil was long ago transformed into cropland. Madson's fascination with detail places him in the same class as Annie Dillard, Anne Zwinger, and, in this volume, Paul A. Johnsgard, all naturalists who create careful portraits of the natural world. Their writing differs from that of nature writers who respond more philosophically and emotionally to the landscape before them, as Henry David Thoreau did in *Walden* and as Sharon Butala does in this volume.

Madson was a conservationist and writer who published widely in newspapers and magazines. He served on the boards of the National Wildlife Federation and Outdoor Writers' Association of America. He graduated from Iowa State University with a degree in wildlife biology. He also pursued graduate studies in fisheries biology.

The Lawns of God (1982)

Long ago, the prairie grasses taught me that I have more in common with Rip Van Winkle than with Leather-Stocking.

Oh, I'll rush around through the boondocks if the occasion demands. But even then I keep an eye peeled for prime loafing areas—especially through midday when most of the action is slow, anyway. Maybe I'll shut down beside a sandbar log by a creek riffle, dozing to water music and the rattle of kingfishers. And there's a favored place under a bur oak at the edge of a clay bluff where I can stretch out and look past the toes of my boots and down over the bends of my home river.

But the best loafing place of all, come high summer, is in the deep grasses of a certain quarter-section of original prairie.

It is just below a swell of ground between the tallgrasses of the low flats and the midgrasses at the crest of the rise, a place where bunch-forming prairie dropseed grows in solid clumps a few feet apart. The intervals between these little hassocks are heavily matted with dried grasses in a resilient bed, slightly curved and conforming perfectly to a horizontal man. The mat of last summer's grasses is springy and firm; beneath it is the deep bed of fluffy prairie loam that is wholly unlike the solid black soils of adjacent croplands. There are no clods, stones, sticks, or roots in this bed. With one of those firm sods of prairie dropseed as a pillow, it makes for as fine an afternooning as any loafer could want.

I lie there just under the wind, the grasses harping and singing faintly, their tones rising and falling, the prairie world washing over me. There is no point in moving; with a little time, the wind will bring the world to me in a steady and varied traffic. Watching under the brim of my hat I see a dragonfly, alias devil's darning needle, darting downwind to the slough off below. Next comes a squadron of monarch butterflies on their way to some crimson patch of butterfly milkweed. A male bobolink arrives twenty feet above me, hanging on the wind and stating his territorial claims with a flow of bubbling song, and then slides off to the east. His departure reveals the red-tailed hawk that he had eclipsed—a mote that swings and drifts, too high to be hunting and too late to be migrating, and plainly soaring just for the sheer exuberant hell of it, exulting in the prairie thermals that cushion his pinions from below and the prairie sun that beats on them from above. The hawk appears to be busily occupied, but he doesn't fool me. He's just another loafer. It takes one to know one.

Thoughts while loafing:

Not even Rip Van Winkle could have slept for twenty years on a prairie. The place for that is a deep glen that encloses a man in a snug vessel of trees and hills, insulating him from the sky and wind. A grassland crackles and flows with stimuli, charging a man to get on with something. A prairie never rests for long, nor does it permit anything else to rest. It has barriers to neither men nor wind and encourages them to run together, which may be why grasslands men are notorious travelers and hard-goers, driven by wind and running with it, fierce and free.

Forests have surely housed many free and fierce people, but I somehow imagine them as being preoccupied with laying ambushes in thickets, worshiping oak trees, and painting their bellies blue. I could never take Druids seriously. They're not in the same class as Cossacks, Zulus, Masai, Mongols, Comanches, Sioux, the highland clans of treeless moors, and trail drovers tearing up Front Street. Grasslanders, all.

There was a vein of wild exultation in such men. It wasn't just the high-protein diet, nor even that some of those men were mounted—although the horse people were among the wildest of all. I have a hunch that it was the mood of the land, stimulating its people with openness, hyperventilating them with freedom in a world of open skylines and few secrets. Such grasslanders never seemed to harbor the nasty little superstitions that flourish in fetid jungles and dank forests. Their superstitions were taller, their sagas and legends more airy and broad, and running through their cultures was a level conviction that they were the elite. While some forest people retreated into the shadowlands, men of the open had no choice but to breast the fuller world—and often came to do so with pride and even arrogance. It was a sense that was transferred almost intact when men left the land

and took to the open seas, or learned to fly. They were all part of the same—
wanderers beyond horizons, children of the wind who belonged more to sky than
to earth, conscious of being under the Great Eye . . .

High above the red-tailed hawk are the steady ranks of cloud, coasting down
the westerlies. When I first lay down here they were dragging their shadows across
me; now they are driving their shadows ahead of them, telling me that the afternoon is wearing on. Which is as much clock as anyone needs. The hawk, not
occupied with loafing thoughts, has already heeded his clock. He is losing altitude and returning to work. It's time that I did the same. Loafing done, I stand up
in the wind.

I see each oncoming gust before I feel it—advancing swiftly across the prairie in
a long wave of motion, sometimes escorted by patches of cloud shadow that
change the tone and color of the grassland as the wind changes the shape. More
than in forest, and even more than on sea or lake, it is here that the wind is most
visible. The ripening grasses bend and winnow, the waves of our air ocean rolling
over the wild meadows until, as Willa Cather put it: "The whole country seems to
be running."[1]

The wind will enter the distant grove of trees with a roar, for it resents the oaken
strength of trees and shouts and growls as it wrestles them, tossing their crowns
furiously. But out here on the open prairie that wind only sighs and whispers,
passing over the grasses with little resistance. The grasses bow to the wind's force,
acquiescing to its passage and letting it go unchallenged and undiminished.

Tallgrasses are adjusted to their lives with wind; their tough stems are resilient
and slender, strong without weight or broad dimension, and slipping easily out of
the wind's grasp. Much of this sinewy strength is provided by the outer rind of the
grass stem, which is reinforced by an oxide of silicon—a sort of primitive fi-
berglass. This is the stuff that gives a glossy, polished appearance to maturing
grasses and may comprise 70 percent of a grass's ash content. Certain bamboos
contain so much silica that a knife can be whetted on their stems, and the hollow
interiors of those stems may contain white residues of hydrous silica called *ta-
bishir*—almost identical with the hydropane variety of mineral opal. Traces of
biogenic opal in old soils may remain for thousands of years—fossil evidence that
grasslands once existed in regions that have long been forested.

Silicon apparently serves grass as lignin serves trees; both reinforce the cel-
lulose of cell walls and allow those plants to attain heights that they could never
reach if they relied solely on the turgor pressure of their cells and were tightly
inflated with their own juices. My favorite belt knife testifies to the mineral tough-
ness of ripe grass stems. It is good steel, and kept very sharp, but cutting a few
armfuls of ripe Indian grass will dull the knife almost as much as dressing a
bull elk.

A lot of creative engineering has been lavished on grasses. The stems, or
"culms," have joints called "nodes," which are solid partitions that reinforce the

tubular stems at regular intervals and provide rigid anchor points for the base of each leaf. The internodes between these joints are usually hollow, although they may be filled with pith, as in corn. In all cases, the internodes of the culms are thin-walled, light, flexible, and remarkably strong.

At each joint of the grass stem is a leaf whose lower part is a split sheath wrapped tightly around the stem. At the summit of this sheath the grass leaf flattens, departing from culm in a long, narrow blade. The junction of leaf sheath and blade may have a small "ligule"—a stiff little membrane in some grasses—that reduces the amount of water that might flow down the leaf blade and into the sheath, promoting the growth of fungi. Some grasses have semicircular auricles at the juncture of blade and sheath, tightly grasping the stem with pincers that reinforce the grip of the sheath and resist tearing by wind.

The leaves of many prairie grasses have special structures for adjusting to drought. Canada wild rye, the bluestems, and Indian grass have leaves of nearly uniform thickness, with groups of large "hinge-line" cells in the upper epidermis of the leaf tissue. These hinge cells lose water rapidly, contract, and cause the leaf to roll up in a long tube. The pores through which water vapor is normally trans-pired are on the inside of this tube, and the exposed lower surface of the leaf is highly impervious to water and allows no loss of precious water vapor during drought periods.

Grass leaves are also neatly adapted to withstand grazing by animals. These leaves grow from their bases on the stems, and not from the tips. If a grass blade is eaten, it continues to grow; if the stem itself is eaten, new shoots are produced by old stem bases near the surface of the ground. When such stem bases are nu-merous, the grass forms a characteristic tuft or bunch.

The flowers of grasses are insignificant little structures, lacking fragrance, nec-tar, and bright colors. There's no spectacular floral envelope, or corolla, but only two or three delicate scales. Grass flowers are wind-pollinated, with no need to attract insects. The grass fruits themselves are usually small—but are amazing little packages of superbly balanced nutrition that are infinitely important to man. All of our tame cereals, of course, have been bred from wild grasses. Yet the wild grasses continue to be of immense value in their original form—anchoring and building soils, and producing meat and wool. And there may always be outdoor purists who insist that wild rice is the only acceptable stuffing for roast wild turkey and Canada goose, and that the split-bamboo flyrod and citronella mosquito lotion are hallmarks of the ultimate trout fisherman.

As grasses depend on wind for pollination and fertile seed production, most also depend on wind for the spread of those seeds. Some tiny grass seeds float for great distances on wind; the little spikelets of Vasseygrass, *Vaseyochloa multiner-vosa*, have been recovered by research planes at 4,000 feet. This grass, introduced into Louisiana from South America a century ago, has been wind-spread from Virginia to Southern California.

Other grass seeds are transported by animals. I have discarded wool socks (that I foolishly wore with low moccasins in late summer) rather than pick out the barbed spears of some needlegrasses and wild barleys that turned the socks into bristling masses that were torture to wear. Such seeds can be maddening to sheep and other heavy-coated animals. Equipped with long bristles or "awns" that twist and untwist with changes in humidity and temperature, they can literally screw their barbed points through fur and into flesh to cause painful sores and infection. And during those barefoot summers of boyhood, we learned to dread the spiked fruits of another grass, *Cenchrus pauciflorus,* the sandbur.

For spreading out of place, the grasses depend on transport of seed by wind or animal. For spreading in place, they rely on special stems that creep underground or just above the surface. The underground stems, or rhizomes, are jointed culms that extend laterally below the earth's surface and produce new stems and rootlets from the tip of the rhizome or from its nodes. A stolon is a reproductive stem that grows along the surface of the ground, putting down rootlets from its growing tip. A perennial grass may form a dense sod, a mass of individual stems, by either rhizomes or stolons. All of which are anchored and nourished by a dense crowd of fibrous roots and rootlets that extend deep into the prairie loam and may support a clump of tallgrass for half a century.

Each stem of prairie grass stands straight, a slender antenna between the flood of solar energy and the deep banks of stored energy within the soil. Unlike the miserly trees, a grass does not hoard that energy by tying it up in woody structure. The grass spends itself freely and annually, deepening and fattening the black soils below and pouring strength into the animal biomass above. Climax prairie is the product bought with all this spending, an investment of energy that compounds itself. Each creature of the prairie community, from bison to corn farmer, has shared the dividends of the grass. Each, in its own way, has proclaimed that "all flesh is grass."

My loafing prairie has most of the main components of any tallgrass prairie, allowing for the fact that it's rather flat and poorly drained country of the type most recently glaciated—a sort of child land whose face hasn't really jelled into mature features.

Still, the lay of the land is modestly varied—with little swells and swales and enough physical relief to encourage some plants that like their feet moist and others that like their feet comparatively dry.

Off below me is a rank belt of sloughgrass, marking a wet swale of the kind that early wagoners learned to avoid by watching for "black grass." Although slough-grass is a rather serious green, it can hardly be regarded as "black." But the sedges just beyond it are a somber conifer-green that shows dark against the vivid tones of the upslope grasses.

Sloughgrass is the most hydric of the tallgrasses, loving deep, moist, poorly aerated soils that other prairie grasses would never tolerate. It marks the last low advance of the prairie grasses to the edge of marsh and slough. Just beyond it begin the sedges, grading into cattails and bulrush. With time, sloughgrass will fill a swale of low land, raising it above its former cattail and sedge vegetations and converting the place to rich prairie soil that will be occupied by tall grasses that require slightly drier conditions. Almost transcontinental in its range, sloughgrass is a common land-builder at the edges of water—from the brackish marshes of the Atlantic coast to wet swales in the Far East.

Also called "prairie cord grass" (presumably because of its tough leaves and stems), its Sunday name is *Spartina pectinata*. Some call it "ripgut," and you need only run your hand along the edge of a leaf to see why. The leaf-edge is finely serrate, with a stiff wire edge like a good butcher knife. Before I learned to wear gloves while cutting mature sloughgrass for dog bedding, I used to wonder who was harvesting whom.

That's a prosperous stand of ripgut down there; it's doing well, and by late summer the wiry floral stalks may rise nine feet above the boggy soil. It comes on rather late, often in mid-April, but then grows faster than any other prairie grass. The root system is tough and dense—a tangled mass of coarse, gnarled, woody rhizomes and rootlets that form a sod as solid as a floor. In a woodless country, such a plant was put to special uses. Twisted faggots of tough sloughgrass leaves and stems made pretty good fuel, and sloughgrass sod was probably the best of any for building sod houses. The Mandans and other prairie Indians used the leaves to thatch their permanent lodges, covering that thatching with several inches of soil. Prairie settlers adopted this, and often used sloughgrass to thatch haystacks and outbuildings. If cut early in the summer, before it toughened, sloughgrass made good hay—but the leaves had a way of tangling so badly that it took a good man to pitch a great forkful up onto a hayrack. Even when loaded, the hay was still a problem. Old-timers have told me that entire loads of fresh-cut cord grass hay had an enraging habit of slipping off a wagon—and then the heavy work of pitching the hay began all over again.

In spring and early summer, sloughgrass is one of the preferred grasses for grazing, but by late summer it is much too coarse and tough for forage. When cured, however, it's useful for livestock bedding because it doesn't break down easily. I've never found anything better for a dog kennel. All in all, useful stuff.

The prairie around me appears to be a rather uniform, sunswept grassfield that varies somewhat in tone and texture. At a closer look, these grass patterns begin to resolve into rather distinct communities that are graded according to elevation and drainage. The lushest, tallest grasses occur lower down, through the poorly drained swales and flats. These are the hydric grasses such as ripgut, requiring plenty of moisture. Just beyond them are more mesic grasses, still in well-watered soils but farther from the slough edge and extending up the gentle slopes. Even farther up are the shorter xeric, or "dry-loving," grasses on the relatively exposed, well-drained crests of the prairie swells. Height classes of these wild grasses express water supply, just as trees do. The early settlers confused the picture by referring to "low prairie" and "high prairie"—an allusion to elevations of the land and not to the height of the grasses. Generally, low prairie has high grasses and high prairie has low grasses.

Downslope from where I stand, just this side of the dark swale of sloughgrass, is a lighter-colored, less dense grass with strong glossy leaves and upper parts with a rather lacy, open look. This is switch grass, *Panicum virgatum,* another excellent hay and livestock food. It lacks the dense, jungly appearance of the sloughgrass; the ground beneath it appears to be more open, and its midsummer seed heads are opening into broad spangles up to two feet wide. The plants are not as tall as the cord grass, nor even as tall as some grasses farther up the slope, but some of the panicled seed heads may stand six feet high. Here and there among the patches of switch grass are the heavy, bearded heads of a wild grain—the Canada wild rye, *Elymus canadensis,* its green, heavy seed heads already nodding on the slender four-foot stems. Greenish-blue, and up to nine inches long, the heavy spikes of wild rye were used as food by some Indians.

Closer toward me—stretching up the lower and middle contours of the long gentle slope where I am standing—is an old friend. The symbolic grass of tall prairie, an official stamp of prairie authenticity, the big bluestem or *Andropogon gerardi.*

This is one of the great dominants of true prairie, the most universal of the prairie's tallgrasses and a marvel to the early settlers who plunged into it and left accounts of big bluestem so tall that it could be tied in knots across the pommel of a saddle. That, and the stories of bluestem pastures so dense and deep that cattle vanished in them and could be found only if a herdsman went to high ground or stood in his saddle to watch for telltale movement in the sea of towering grasses. Such anecdotes are so common that they are trite; yet there's no reason to doubt them. In my home county in central Iowa, early settlers carved routes through the big bluestem prairie by dragging heavy logs chained to teams of oxen. Big bluestem sod, with its coarse rootstocks and rhizomes, was a favorite for building sod houses. Almost as good as sloughgrass sod, it was far easier to cut.

The big bluestem association—the singular community of grasses and flowers commanded by big bluestem—has been called "the true prairie, *the* prairie." Big bluestem covered the secondary flood plains of broad stream valleys, advancing upslope along gentle hillsides and benches. In old Illinois, it was the climax grass of uplands as well as lowlands, and in Wisconsin and Iowa entire townships were covered with big bluestem—a reflection of the generous rainfall and gentle drainage of those regions. On some Kansas prairies, big bluestem apparently hid cattle even on some of the uplands, and the Flint Hills of eastern Kansas are still called "The Bluestem Hills" by some ranchers. Farther out in the drier prairies, this lofty grass retreated down into protected swales and ravines. But it reigned wherever good moisture levels prevailed—from the low valleys of Lake Winnipeg south, down through the alluvial flats of prairie rivers and well-watered uplands with gentle drainage gradients, all the way to the Gulf Coast of Texas.

It is a mighty grass. The leaf growth may stand three feet above the ground, and the strong seed stems often rise over six feet high. In my little patch of backyard prairie, well-watered and fertile, the culms of big bluestem extend higher than I can reach—at least nine feet tall.

It has other names, such as "bluejoint," which confuses it with similar grasses. One of the common names is "turkey foot," or "bluejoint turkey foot," because of the distinctive three-branched seed head that is unmistakable. It takes its most common name from the bluish-purple bloom of the main stem.

Although it is generally a lowland grass, big bluestem avoids the moist, heavy, poorly aerated soils in which cord grass thrives. Big bluestem wants plenty of moisture, but occupies a middle ground between the wet and dry, between the hydric and xeric. It is *mesic* in its moisture needs—an ecological analog of domestic corn. The finest corn habitat today is that in which big bluestem reigned yesterday.

For some obscure reasons, big bluestem tended to move up the slopes following settlement—giving rise to the old saying that "bluestem followed the settler." The well-drained prairie uplands were usually the ones first broken and planted to crops, and the typical midgrasses of those uplands were the first of the wild prairie grasses to be wiped out by cultivation. If those plowed fields were left fallow, big bluestem and other tallgrasses often moved in and the growth of midgrasses was not renewed. Today, big bluestem is likely to occur in prairie relicts that were originally occupied by midgrasses, which is not to say that big bluestem was immune to the ravages of cultivation. Like other tallgrasses, it was a magnificent hay and pasture grass—although it had to be mowed for hay early in the season before it became tough and sinewy. But the upper parts of the prairie were usually the first to be broken and cultivated, giving the lower stands of big bluestem a slight reprieve—and a limited opportunity to replace midgrasses that the pioneers had found somewhat easier to plow.

The stands of big bluestem below and around me are an almost closed community as far as other grasses are concerned. Forming dense sod and thick foliage, turkey foot greatly reduces light penetration to the soil and discourages most shorter species. This apparently doesn't deter its own shaded seedlings; the leaves of big bluestem seedlings can synthesize food under light values that may be only five percent that of full sunlight. It is a tall, strong, vigorous "dominant"—in the sense that its influence largely dictates the conditions under which other plants in its community must develop. Even where there may be some open ground between the sods of big bluestem, the overwhelming influence of this mighty grass prevents occupation of that soil by lesser types. In the lushest parts of the tall prairie region, the *Andropogon gerardi* community is a terminal association that has maintained its integrity for thousands of years.

But there is something that I miss on this northern Iowa prairie—or know that I'll miss when the tall grasses are fully mature.

There is little Indian grass here, the *Sorghastrum nutans* so familiar farther south in my section of southwestern Illinois and more southerly parts of the tallgrass prairie country. It is almost identical with big bluestem in size and requirements, but isn't as happy on the northern prairies. There's quite a bit of it in the Flint Hills and points south, but even in its best range it isn't as abundant as big bluestem. It has a relatively weak spot in its life history—an inability to tiller and form underground rhizomes under tough competition, and it is unable to spread as strongly as big bluestem.

Yet it's a spectacular grass—every bit as tall and showy as turkey foot, with leaves that branch off the stem at a 45° angle instead of drooping and spreading as widely as big bluestem's. Ripe Indian grass is a golden lance that is usually a bit more erect than bluestem and is somewhat more likely to be found at all levels of the prairie—on certain uplands as well as slopes and bottom ground. The leaves are usually broader and a bit lighter in color than big bluestem's, and long before its plumelike seed head appears, Indian grass can be identified by a distinct little clawlike ligule on the upper surface of the leaf blade where it joins the sheath. (In their early stages of growth, before any floral parts appear, several features identify the tallgrasses. Sloughgrass has its finely serrated leaf edges; Indian grass has that special ligule. Big bluestem has a slightly flattened lower stem and usually has hairy lower leaves, and switch grass has a dense nest of fine, silvery hairs where the leaf blade joins the sheath. Of these wild grasses, Canada wild rye is the only one that has strong, pincerike auricles tightly clasping the stem at the base of the leaf blade.)

Although Indian grass is less likely than big bluestem to be found in broad, dense stands, there is a four-acre patch of pure Indian grass on an open hillside in the woods near my home. This lies along the route of my Saturday morning excursions with Cub Scouts and Girl Scouts—which still mix like oil and water in spite of the unisex trend. I've often led these yelling emulsions of boys and girls to that stand of *Sorghastrum*—priming them with a couple of suitable Indian yarns and then sending some of them into the tallgrass as ambushers, to be followed by the main wad of ambushees while I lounge on the hilltop. The rich yellow depths of the Indian grass—it's called "goldstem" by some—undergo a wracking convulsion. It seems a rather modest adventure, I know, but being an Indian four feet tall who's lost in a fastness of eight-foot grass is about as much as you could ask of a September morning. And there's always a kid or two who gets lost in there. A search party is organized, solemnly charged with a sense of mission, and sent to the rescue—giving me another half-hour of idleness.

A big patch of all *Sorghastrum* is the ultimate playground. The kids are safely lost in deep grass that soaks up their noise and energy, finally spewing them out tired, quieter, and almost human. Another plus for prairie.

Upslope from the big bluestem and Indian grass, the midgrasses begin—less rank, more finely foliaged, and standing little more than waist-high at maturity.

Of all these (and there are more midgrasses than tallgrasses), the little bluestem *Andropogon scoparius* is the greatest dominant—as much the master of its upland realm as its tall cousin is of the lower ground. Together, the two bluestems constituted nearly three fourths of the cover on original tallgrass prairie. In some transition zones, as in the western parts of the Flint Hills and lower reaches of Nebraska's Sand Hills, big and little bluestem may grow in mixed stands of almost equal proportions. But farther west, in the mixed prairies lying between the tallgrass country and Great Plains, little bluestem may represent 90 percent of the grassy vegetation.

It is a shorter, finer, more delicate grass than big bluestem, without the characteristic turkey-foot seed head. The flower stalks of little bluestem rarely grow more than three feet tall—the ripening seeds equipped with fluffy plumes that named the plant "prairie beardgrass." Like big bluestem, it is superb forage for tame and wild grazers, and the weight gains of cattle on well-managed bluestem pastures can be phenomenal. For over a century the vast bluestem pastures in the Flint Hill of eastern Kansas have been prized for their spring and summer forage, and are historic finishing range for Texas cattle.

Little bluestem leaves are more slender and wiry than those of big bluestem, and until they mature the leaves are light green. Then they begin developing a distinctive reddish cast that deepens in autumn into rich russet, bronze, and maroons. An autumn ridge of little bluestem is unmistakable—the prairie's reply to the hard maples and sumacs of the forest. Big bluestem also develops a winey shade in late fall, but never matches that of its little cousin.

To see both bluestems in late summer is to see prairie. Especially under what Wallace Stegner called "the grassy, green, exciting wind, with the smell of distance in it."[2] As you stand on a long prairie swell in summer fields of little bluestem, wind is apparent not only in waves of motion but in shades of varying green. Pressed downwind away from you, the little bluestem prairie is the light green of upper leaf surfaces. Turn and look behind you—there, upwind, the prairie is darkened with deeper underleaf tones and shadow. A puff of wind runs past not just as visible shape and motion, but as a shifting wave of color distinct from the whole, something like the undercurl of a tall ocean comber just before it topples.

By comparison to little bluestem, other midgrasses are rather minor characters in most portions of the prairie. However, my loafing prairie—a rather flat, poorly drained place with no uplands worth mentioning—has no little bluestem that I know of. The dominant "upland" grass here is prairie dropseed, a midgrass that is apparently tolerant of poor drainage because I can see it growing on some of the flats below. All around me are the distinctive sods of prairie dropseed. Early this spring, when part of the prairie was burned, these dropseed bunches emerged as firm little hassocks on the prairie soil—straight-sided and rather cylindrical, up to six inches high and a foot across. At such times, my khaki-clad posterior has a chronically charred appearance, for a dropseed sod is a perfect place to sit and take notes. Each of these sods becomes a dense clump of yellow-green, gracefully drooping leaves that may be as much as eighteen inches high. By late summer the seed stems will be three feet tall, each terminating in a broad, spreading panicle that bears the rather large seed heads.

Farther north, little bluestem is increasingly mingled with needlegrass, June grass, porcupine grass (*Stipa spartea*) and the wheatgrasses. Yet, even in south-western Manitoba, two of the commonest prairie species are big and little blue-stem. And farther south and west, in warmer and drier regions, it's no contest. Little bluestem is king.

Needlegrass, one of the midgrass dominants of the northern prairies, once reigned over thousands of square miles of uplands. It is a grass of the sandy prairie rises, with long tapering leaves that are finely corrugated above and shining green beneath. No grass is more graceful in the wind, the shoulder-high, heavily fruited stems bending and nodding in rippling fields. Unlike other prairie grasses that cure in shades of tan, yellow, or russet, needlegrass stems and leaves usually become dead white, and from a long distance the late autumn prairie appears to be drifted with snow.

Sideoats grama (*Bouteloua curtipendula*) is a common and more southerly mid-grass with leaves that can be identified by fine leaf-edge hairs with swollen bases, and flower stalks that zigzag up through the seed heads. Like the other common midgrasses, it is excellent livestock forage.

There are transitions among prairie grasses, from north to south as well as east to west. In the easterly, well-watered portions of the tall prairie, big bluestem may be the dominant grass even on uplands—but farther west it tends to retreat into lower parts of the prairie, leaving the exposed, well-drained uplands occupied by the little bluestem community. There are always exceptions to this; a certain upland prairie, by virtue of poor drainage, may wear tall grasses that are normally found farther down in well-watered flats. It is conceivable that a stand of slough-grass might exist in a high, "hanging" swale well above some lower slopes that are better drained and are dominated by little bluestem.

Latitude has a strong effect on the distribution of wild grasses, for some are of northern origin while others hail from southerly regions. Prairie grasses are gener-ally classed as "cool-season" and "warm-season" types. During the xerothermic postglacial period when grasses began to replace trees in drying, warming parts of what would be prairie country, certain grasses moved east out of dry western regions, and others moved north out of the southeast and southwest. The two types mingled freely, for their requirements had considerable overlap. But as the climate again cooled and moistened, some western species of grasses tended to shrink back toward the drier ranges from which they had come. The grasses of southern origin remained, for the general climate was still within acceptable limits for grasses that had evolved in more southerly climates. The most important grasses in the tallgrass prairie—big and little bluestem, Indian grass, and slough-grass—are all of southeasterly origin and still occur today in forest openings and savannahs of the east and southeast. Prairie dropseed and switch grass are also warm-season grasses that originated south of their modern ranges.

On the other hand, some prairie grasses are of northern origin: the cool-season grasses such as June grass, needlegrass, Canada wild rye, and slender wheatgrass. Such grasses typically renew their growth in early spring and have usually reached maximum development from early April to early June. By late spring or early summer they have matured and produced their seed—usually becoming semi-dormant during the hot months and resuming growth during the cool autumn months. By contrast, the warm-season grasses commence annual growth later in the spring—growing continuously all summer long and producing seed from late summer into early fall. After that there is no growth, and these grasses invariably "ripen" and lose their green tones after seed production. Big bluestem is a prime example of a warm-season grass of southerly origin, growing continuously from April until mid-August or early September—when its job of seed production is finished. A typical and familiar cool-season grass is Kentucky bluegrass, which produces shoots, leaves, and seed heads in early spring, is dormant during the hot, dry summer, renews growth in the cooler, wetter days of fall, and may remain green until the first hard frost.

These traits are reflected in prairie latitude. Needlegrass is of little importance from Kansas south, and Indian grass shows decreasing importance in the more northerly prairie ranges. To the North Dakota prairie farmer, needlegrass and June grass are familiar parts of the homeland; to the Oklahoma farmer, Indian grass and broomsedge are just as familiar. Both farmers know big bluestem, for turkey foot is a universal component of tallgrass prairie.

There are about 150 kinds of grasses in tallgrass prairie, but probably no more than ten of these ever achieve any real dominance in their own special parts of the prairie. Most of the grasses are of minor importance, also-rans in terms of total prairie cover but genuine prairie components nonetheless. In terms of total range, and density within that range, nothing can compare with the two bluestems. They are succeeded in rank by Indian grass, sloughgrass, switch grass, prairie dropseed, and sideoats grama—followed by dwindling proportions of Canada wild rye, June grass, porcupine grass, the wheatgrasses, needle-and-thread, the needlegrasses, and others.

In the smooth, undulating sweep of my loafing prairie there are no angular interruptions, no sharp gradients. Any breaks in the land are masked and smoothed by the summer waves of high grasses. But a few yards away from me, crowned by a mass of blue milk-vetch, is an odd mound about twelve feet in diameter and two feet higher than the surrounding level. Forty yards away there is another. All in all, there are over a hundred of these strange mounds on the Kalsow Prairie.

Called "Mima mounds," they take their name from the Mima Prairie south of Olympia, Washington—a place that's studded with the little hillocks. They resemble burial mounds as much as anything, and were once thought to be Indian gravesites—although digging always fails to produce any bones or artifacts. Here at Kalsow these mounds range in diameter from six to seventy-two feet, and some rise several feet above the prairie. They are most obvious in late winter when the prairie vegetation is flattened and the slightest relief in the landscape is revealed, but even in midsummer the strange, alien mounds are distinct because they support different plants than the prairie around them.

No one is sure how these Mima mounds are formed. The most common theory is that they were begun by animal digging—certain ants or perhaps pocket gophers—and enlarged by frost heaves and differential contraction and expansion of the soil, growing larger as they caught dust blown in from adjacent farmlands. There is no doubt that they attract animals; they often show signs of digging, and the mounds often are soft and friable, with the consistency of a new gopher mound, although gophers alone would never raise mounds as large as these.

The mound itself is a loose column of earth that may be six feet deep. It lacks any sort of soil profile, and is obviously created by a digging, heaving, and mixing action of some sort. Back in the late 1950s, a young graduate student named John Tester grew interested in Mima mounds in Minnesota's Waubun Prairie. He dug into the subject in late autumn and winter, and found large numbers of toads hibernating in the loose soil of the mounds, evidently moving up or down in relation to temperature and staying just under the frost line. One mound less than thirty feet in diameter held 3,276 toads that had burrowed an average of three feet deep—moving nearly four tons of soil in one year. Toads may not have caused those Mima mounds, but they certainly helped maintain them. Other diggers did their part, too, and so did frost and soil expansion.

Whatever their cause, the Mima mounds are a broken thread in the native fabric of the prairie. They are intense, isolated foci of disturbance that are exploited by plants that otherwise would not invade the unbroken prairie. Some of the Mima mounds here are crowned with thick little stands of Kentucky bluegrass—a foreign invader that may occur nowhere else in the heart of this native prairie. The mounds often host weed species whose seeds were blown in or carried in from the surrounding farmlands: lamb's quarters, bedstraw, bitter-weed, and bindweed. At the same time, the mounds seem to repel such prairie natives as rattlesnake-master, leadplant, blazing-star, and wild indigo. Each Mima mound is a microenvironment occupied by nonprairie—a beachhead of invasion, a sort of Ellis Island of the prairie world that accommodates foreigners. There may be a few prairie species that tolerate such disturbance: wild rose, sloughgrass, Canada wild rye, and a couple of native sunflowers may be found on or beside the mounds. But most of the originals seem to shun the mounds, and refuse to occupy them.

With some tactical support by man, those foreign invaders on their Mima mound beachheads could end up dominating a prairieland.

Original prairie plants are classed as "decreasers" or "increasers," according to their response to human land use. Most are decreasers, fading swiftly and vanishing in the course of heavy grazing, mowing, and plowing. Rugged and successful as they are in their climate habitat, they are often pathetically vulnerable to land-use pressures—especially those wild legumes and grasses that are eagerly sought by livestock and are sensitive to the overgrazing and trampling that occurs in most modern pastures.

As the prime native plants are weakened by such intensive use, their dominant grip on the prairie is also weakened, and the increasers are released by this lessening of dominance. In most of the tall prairie, such forage grasses as big and little bluestem were simply unable to support the relentless pressures of cattle, horses, sheep, and mowing, and native grasses were replaced by Kentucky bluegrass—a type that can withstand almost unlimited grazing.

It isn't just a matter of livestock grazing on the grass leaves, for a grass leaf grows from the base and if the leaf tip is bitten off or cut, the leaf continues to grow. The critical factor is whether or not the growing point of the leaves is repeatedly removed.

A bluestem grass shoot is a succulent cylinder of leaf sheaths—the older ones outside, the younger leaves within. The first new leaves develop from the growing point of the individual grass plant, which remains in the surface soil. When the foliage of big bluestem is about two feet high, the growing point that produces the leaves may be several inches above the soil. If that growing point is far enough out of the soil so that it can be grazed by livestock, no new leaves will be produced. Switchgrass, one of the most sensitive "decreasers," extends its growing point far out of the soil as early as May, and is readily "grazed out" early in the growing season. And although a grass plant may survive without developing seed, it cannot survive long without foliage and root development. By contrast, such "increaser" grasses as Kentucky bluegrass maintain their growing points at a level with the soil surface, where they are protected from grazing and continue to produce leaves indefinitely.

Prairie grasses are rugged individuals that have adapted through millennia of heat, drought, fire, and competition. But as "decreasers," their growing points must be conserved and allowed to replace any leaf growth that has been lost. Light grazing that is limited to leaves has no serious effect. But heavy grazing and close, frequent mowing can tip the balance in favor of bluegrass, which is highly tolerant of close cropping—as every suburban lawnkeeper knows.

Under normal prairie conditions, Kentucky bluegrass has hardly a chance. For one thing, prairie is most combustible in early spring and fall when a maximum dry plant debris is present—periods when bluegrass is green and growing but when the native warm-season grasses have either not begun their annual growth or have completed it. Bluegrass will be killed by fires that have no effect on big or little bluestem, and during the summer heyday of the native grasses shading is so intense that bluegrass could not thrive even if that was the bluegrass's strong growing season—which it is not.

But let the ancient continuum be repeatedly broken so that the native sod is weakened—decreasing plant detritus and fire, and increasing light intensity under the thinning native grasses—and bluegrass quickly gains mastery. Continually aided by its allies of overgrazing and trampling, it triumphs over the disadvantaged native species. Now the tables are turned, and even if the bluegrass pasture is left fallow indefinitely, a successful retaking of that lost ground by the full community of prairie plants is a painfully slow process that may require two hundred years.

Kentucky bluegrass, let it be said, isn't a "bad" grass. It is usually a highly valued grass. Generally regarded as a native of Europe that was introduced with other seeds by the early colonists, it can't even be condemned as an alien invader—for there is evidence that it is native in southern Canada. But as a strong increaser, it is bad in the sense that it almost irreversibly replaces native grasses when the latter are weakened. Welcome or not, bluegrass takes over.

Today, tall prairie in its vast original form has vanished. All the components are still there, but they have been fragmented and scattered, surviving in little outposts that are beleaguered and besieged by the trained armies of domestic plants. The original prairie plants no longer are joined in the great climax association in which they thrived for thousands of years. So it goes—for now.

And we drive along interstate highways through what was once tall prairie, past roadsides of brome, through landscapes of bluegrass pastures and neat fields of pampered grains, with woodlots and groves thriving where trees scarcely existed for fifteen thousand years. But up there in a neglected fence corner are a few towering culms of big bluestem. The wild grasses are waiting. The originals, bred and conditioned by a particular climate in special ways. Let those fields be abandoned by man—as they will all be, someday—and the tame grasses and interloper weeds will lose their strongest ally. The ancient war of selection and adjustment will be renewed more furiously than ever. For years, perhaps centuries, a riot of strong exotics may dominate the land. But sooner or later the old stocks will reassert themselves, and native prairie will reclaim its ancient holdings—with man beyond any point of rejoicing or interference.

I am asked, now and then, how one can know native prairie when he sees it. How does genuine prairie emerge from the landscape—what sets it apart from fallow pasture, or from cultivated land gone wild and weedy?

Most prairie relicts are small, lingering as scraps and edges in a tame landscape, and it takes a practiced eye to spot such little remnants. But there should be no question if the surviving prairie has enough size to retain something of its old character and integrity, for it is strikingly different from the fields and pastures around it.

Several years ago I was hunting for a small prairie preserve in Iowa that I'd never seen, and I was having a devil of a time finding it. The place had an area of only twenty acres, had just been bought by the state, and hadn't exactly been heralded as the newest thrill center of the Cornbelt. No one seemed to know much about it, or care, although one old farmer voiced the unsolicited opinion that it must be a waste of good corn ground. So I just moseyed around through that March countryside of spring plowing, brushy creek bottoms, and overgrazed bluegrass pastures, looking. Some of the pastures were greening up, and there were a few fields of vivid winter wheat; otherwise, the farmscape was a drab pattern of deep black and dull grays that lay in geometric blocks and strips.

Then I turned a corner and saw it, a half-mile east of me, spread across two low hillsides that sloped down to a little creek lined with ash and box-elder.

My first impression of Sheeder Prairie was of badly worn and weathered canvas, somewhat ragged and patched, and bleached into soft grays, off-whites, and faded duns. It was entirely different in tone and texture from anything else in that landscape, with an indefinable shaggy, fierce look that drew one's eyes from the tame lands around it. From any angle it occupied stage center, fixing attention with that strange magnetic quality that can always be felt but never explained, that sure quality of wildness. The surrounding fields lay about like stolid domestic animals, passive and bland, awaiting the pleasure of their masters. The little prairie crouched on its hillsides, still its own master in a wholly mastered land, aloof and brooding and ordered by no commands save those of sun and rain. Once, long ago, I saw a buffalo bull in a small herd of domestic cows. This was the same. There was the same effect of surprise, and then the sharp sense of contrast between a wild original and its spiritless descendants.

As a game biologist and hunter, my second impression of Sheeder Prairie was that of a place worth going to and being in—a feeling that I found to be shared by a coyote, several pheasants, a couple of quail coveys, and the first upland plovers of the year.

At any season, there is *variety* in the prairie aspect. This is most apparent in original prairie with marked changes in elevation and varied communities of grasses—each different from all others at any time of year, and each lending its distinctive shade, pattern, and texture to the whole. In midspring and early summer, the varying greens and height classes all respond differently to wind and light. In late summer a prairie's tallgrasses are like nothing else, and there's no mistaking a stand of nine-foot big bluestem that gives way to the midgrasses of the upper slopes, the whole scene shot with vivid flashes of color that vanish and reappear as the wind shifts the grassy screens before myriad flowers.

In winter, there is a differential weathering and bleaching that never occurs in monocultured fields and pastures. A prairie's cool-season grasses tend to cure in tones of gray, white, and pale yellows, while the warm-season grasses turn golden, tan, russet, and bronze. You'll see this in fall and winter, driving west of Topeka on Interstate 70 approaching the Flint Hills. It isn't just that the sky opens up, or that the land suddenly rises in tall ranks toward the West, but the hills are a winey russet with a richer tone than the croplands behind—and you know that you're looking into leagues of treeless bluestem pasture.

Those are the long looks. A closer look at a patch of native prairie will reveal a number of plants that you may seem to know from somewhere, with a sense of having seen them from the corner of your eye in some field edge long ago. Here in prairie they are all brought together, and reassembled in original community. But there are likely to be strange, spectacular plants that are new to you. In all my ramblings through the Midwest, I can't recall ever seeing wild indigo or rattlesnake-master that wasn't growing in a prairie relict of some kind. That's the only place you'll find them—they just aren't the sort to volunteer in a lawn or at the edge of a garden, and once you see them you'll never forget them.

Some tracts regarded as "prairies" are simply old pastures that have been neglected for a long time, and now contain a few native flowers and grasses and a number of foreign invaders. They invariably have a long record of plowing, mowing, or heavy grazing; and the marks of such practices may linger indefinitely. Such a history will usually disqualify a particular area as "native" prairie, although some light grazing and mowing won't seriously affect a prairie's pedigree.

There are certain prairie indicators that are quite accurate, for such plants do not occur in concert if the land has been intensively used. Well-drained uplands of original prairie will invariably be occupied by stands of little bluestem, prairie dropseed, sideoats grama, and other native midgrasses. Farther downhill, of course, there will be vigorous stands of the tall stuff: big bluestem, Indian grass, sloughgrass, and airy patches of tall *panicum*. Depending on the season, there will be such forbs (any nonwoody plant that is not a grass) as compass-plant, rattlesnake-master, blazing-star, yellow star-grass, blue-eyed grass, black samson (also called purple coneflower), yellow coneflower, bottle gentian, wood betony, penstemon, and many others. Wild legumes such as leadplant, purple prairie clover, and wild indigo are usually sure signs of genuine prairie, for they are among the first to vanish from tamed land and are often the last to return. Conversely, a closed community of old-stand prairie isn't like to include such familiar invaders as purple vervain, Canada thistle, dandelion, ragweed, Kentucky bluegrass, red clover, or brome.

There are only a few tall prairies left today, but they are worth seeking—worth going to and being in. They are the last lingering scraps of the old time, fragments of original wealth and beauty, cloaked with plants that you may never have seen before and may never see again. If you are a man, stand in such a place and imagine that you hold your land warrant as a veteran of the War with Mexico, looking out over fields of lofty grasses on your own place at last, your own free-and-clear quarter-section share of the richest loam in the world. If you are a woman, watch your children at play in wild gardens of strange flowers, and imagine your nearest neighbor twenty miles away.

If you are a child, lie in a patch of blazing-star and dream of Indians.

Notes

1. The complete quote, from Willa Cather's *My Ántonia,* spoken by the narrator, Jim Burden, is: "As I looked about me I felt that the grass was the country as the water is the sea. The red of the grass made all the great prairie the color of water-stains, or of certain seaweeds when they are first washed up. And there was so much motion in it; the whole country seemed, somehow, to be running."—Eds.

2. The complete quote from Wallace Stegner in *Wolf Willow* is: "Across its empty miles pours the pushing and shouldering wind, a thing you tighten into as a trout tightens into fast water. It is a grassy, clean, exciting wind, with the smell of distance in it, and in its search for whatever it is looking for it turns over every wheat blade and head, every pale primrose, even the ground-hugging grass."—Eds.

Further Reading

Out Home. 1980.
Stories from Under the Sky. 1961.

William Stafford *(1913–1993)*

A native of Hutchinson, Kansas, William Stafford recorded the natural world from the Great Plains to Oregon, where he was known as the state's poet laureate. In Kansas he worked various jobs in construction and at an oil refinery and pursued his education at community colleges before receiving his bachelor's and master's degrees from the University of Kansas. During World War II he was a conscientious objector and lived in California and Arkansas work camps. Stafford taught at Lewis and Clark College in Portland, Oregon, from 1948 until his retirement in 1980, taking time off to teach occasionally at other colleges and to earn his Ph.D. from the University of Iowa in 1954. He won the 1963 National Book Award for *Traveling Through the Dark* and wrote sixty-six other books. He spent much of his later years traveling, giving readings throughout the world.

Like Willa Cather, Stafford has turned to the Great Plains he left behind for many of his poems. His close observation of western places enables him to "invest the western scene and the western manner with universal meaning," as the critic John Russell Roberts put it.

In Response to a Question (1998)

The earth says have a place, be what that place
requires; hear the sound the birds imply
and see as deep as ridges go behind
each other. (Some people call their scenery flat,
their only picture framed by what they know:
I think around them rise a riches and a loss
too equal for their chart—but absolutely tall.)

The earth says every summer have a ranch
that's minimum: one tree, one well, a landscape
that proclaims a universe—sermon
of the hills, hallelujah mountain,
highway guided by the way the world is tilted,
reduplication of mirage, flat evening:
a kind of ritual for the wavering.

The earth says where you live wear the kind
of color that your life is (gray shirt for me)
and by listening with the same bowed head that sings
draw all into one song, join
the sparrow on the lawn, and row that easy
way, the rage without met by the wings
within that guide you anywhere the wind blows.

Listening, I think that's what the earth says.

Further Reading

Allegiances. 1960.
Down in My Heart. 1947.
Kansas Poems of William Stafford. Ed. Denise Low. 1990.
Learning to Live in the World: Earth Poems. 1991.
The Rescued Year. 1966.
Sometime, Maybe. 1983.
Stories that Could Be True: New and Collected Poems. 1977.
Things that Happen Where There Aren't Any People. 1980.
West of Your Life. 1966.
Writing the Australian Crawl: Views on the Writer's Vocation. Ed. Donald Hall. 1978.

Reading about William Stafford

Andrews, Tom, ed. *On William Stafford: The Worth of Things.* Ann Arbor: University of Michigan Press, 1993.

Carpenter, David A. *William Stafford.* Western Writers Series. Boise ID: Boise State University, 1986.

Holden, Jonathan. *The Mark to Turn: A Reading of William Stafford's Poetry.* Lawrence: University Press of Kansas, 1976.

Roberts, J. Russell. "William Stafford." In *The Literary History of the American West.* Fort Worth: Texas Christian University Press, 1989. 458–67.

Greg Kuzma *(b. 1944)*

Greg Kuzma is a Nebraska poet, author of more than twenty books of poetry. He received his bachelor's and master's degrees from Syracuse University. Kuzma teaches at the University of Nebraska at Lincoln and edits the magazine *Pebble*. One critic has commented, "At his best, Kuzma is alert to landscape and rhythms of process, a land-bound creature alive with processes of living." "Songs," a catalog of birds by sound, is an illustration of Kuzma's awareness.

Songs (1984)

The mudlark sings its sad song.
So too the Spanish cormorant.
And I have heard the Garth flamingo
burleying at midnight, far from home.
Did you regard the lost last cry
of Thomas Arthur's Bulfinch mewing?
These are all sad singers, singers
of sad dark songs, beautiful in their way,
despite the mood, the overriding underscoring
heaviness, the negative aspects,
the lack, it may be argued,
of a sufficient balance. What rights
have they, I should like to ask myself,
these whose province is sunlight and
water (which is another light) (or
a light twice) to be acting so deprived?

Monday:
the curlews are twittering. Breakfast
at nine thirty. Awakened earlier, sevenish,
by the musketry of the hen hawkers,
an Audubon dishevelment. Trees
were flush in leaves, with wind.
Around ten, after forcing down some sopped toast,
blew out myself into the yard.

Called by the cardinal's entreaties,
attracted by the robin and her red cry.
A big mayhawk was perched like a piece of iron
or meteor, like a pinnacle on the garage,
its shadow drooping like wet raincoats
over the gravel.

Oh they are all lovely these singers.
They are all forgettably present, their
colors fading, their feathers fly about and
fall, fall out, go back to dust, and yet
these songs, their songs, deep as worry,
stay as a river through me.
Below the ear, down where the bones start.

Henry calls. A big trip into blue tip country.
Lots of provisions, set out on the back of
the crosscountry van. Emergency rations,
glasses, and recording books, reams, reels,
and the table of species. Jake will join us
at midpoint, a little high hill town,
poor on water and culture, thick with scenery.
"The Blue Tip ventures a wide radius from its
nest, deposits home three dark brown eggs,
blue tipped, from which derives the name.
The call, pure poetry."

In a clearing of stones we have made our fire.
In a thicket of thick trees we have placed our
stacks, sticks, jets and bricks, bats and racks.
The younger man is wild and green, he snorts
about decapitating ferns. And then from somewhere
overhead and to our right, knick knocking
through the trees, the Blue Tip sends her
luscious notes for free.

Back. The yellow newspapers.
Mail swollen in the mail slot. One piece—
a catalog from J and Edward's Sanctuary Press,
a big swollen picture of the Alder Hawk, feet
tucked sharply into a small rodent, looking
forlorn, the wash above them both an incipient
yellow. Sally writes. Bill. Charles
is up the peninsula, deep in. Last heard

from (like a Mirabelle Warbler really when he
gets excited) had reached the Far North Roosting
Place, intact, all the slides clear, the
tapes spinning. The lawn had come up
nearly to my boottops but I walked around.
Out by the tin shed, under the martin houses,
a shrivelled gray piece like a Brodkin's Tweeter
lay in the grass and sun. I examined the beak,
and little nasal grooves. And then, from the south,
and crossing, the shadow of the Grosshawk
past the fence, disintegrating at my feet.
A hunger welled up in me, and thirst.
The silence of being fully present,
an ache along the forearm, being fully home.
And let the fragment fall, flightless,
and went back in.

Further Reading

Selected Poems. 1996.

Dan O'Brien *(b. 1947)*

In western South Dakota Dan O'Brien ranches and chronicles the difficult lives of people on the northern plains. O'Brien is a biologist, naturalist, novelist, and falconer who has worked with the Peregrine Fund to restore these raptors to the Great Plains. His story collection, *Eminent Domain* (1987), won the 1986 Iowa School of Letters short fiction award. His novels explore the conflicts between those who value the land for its ineffable, intrinsic value and those who regard it as a source of profit. O'Brien's most recent work, *Buffalo for the Broken Heart: Restoring Life to a Black Hills Ranch* (2001), is an account of his foray into the buffalo business.

In *The Rites of Autumn* O'Brien chronicles his pilgrimage from Montana to the Gulf of Mexico with Dolly, a young captivity-raised falcon he is training to hunt as they migrate along the central flyway. Dolly is the only survivor of four peregrines whose release into the wild was thwarted by an alert and hungry golden eagle. Because the migrating season will come too soon to allow Dolly time to learn to hunt and kill before heading south, O'Brien is determined to accompany her (or perhaps it is the other way around) on her first journey south.

Seen from a falcon's point of view, certain features of the high plains stand out: the wetlands and prairie potholes, and the grasslands that are home to ducks and prairie grouse, both of which are among Dolly's favorite foods. In this passage O'Brien, with his ranch hand Erney and hunting dogs Spud and Jake, arrives for a brief stop at his ranch on their journey south. They have been delayed by a sudden snowstorm which forced them to stay in Sundance, Wyoming.

Excerpt from *The Rites of Autumn*

The sun came up brilliantly the next morning, and by nine o'clock I was digging in the back of the truck for a pair of sunglasses. The townspeople had been clearing the streets and driveways since before sunup, but we were in no hurry to leave. Interstate 90 was still closed. We ate caramel rolls at the local café, and I couldn't help thinking that the yuppies who lived around Kris in Denver would give two dollars for a roll like that. We'd paid fifty cents and another thirty-five for the coffee.

After our breakfast we let the dogs out, then walked downtown. Already the snow was beginning to melt, but we knew that even if the county roads had been cleared, the two-mile-long driveway to my ranch would likely be blocked. (We might not get home that day, but I knew that Dolly would need to be blocked out and flown that afternoon in any case.[1]) There was not much to do in Sundance, but we killed some time in the hardware store, then returned to the café for more coffee. We talked with ranchers and loggers who had not made it to work that morning. Just before noon, a trucker came in and said the Interstate was open.

By the time we got to the turnoff for my ranch, the county road had been plowed. I planned to spend only a week there, taking care of some business and flying Dolly nearby. Erney would stay to watch things for the winter.

Bear Butte, a sacred place, loomed four miles to the east when we turned into the driveway. The house was still two miles away, but the beginning of the driveway had been blown clear. We drove tentatively, until we came to the first drift. After looking it over, we decided we could get through it if we had enough speed. It was fifty yards long but not deep and not hard. We made it through and onto another spot the wind had cleared. The next drift was a little longer and deeper. Again, we decided that we would have a chance if we got our speed up. It would be a rough ride so we let the dogs out. Erney stood on the snowbank, holding Dolly on his fist while I drove. The pickup bucked and rolled through the worst of the drift, bogging down and finally stopping with only fifteen feet of drift to go. There were two shovels in the back, and it took only ten minutes to dig through the drift, but we were still a mile from the house.

Erney and I discussed our options. It would be impossible to turn around, but we could walk out to the county road and ask a neighbor to loan us a tractor. The other option was to keep going and take the chance of getting severely stuck. Because asking a neighbor for help did not appeal to either of us, we forged ahead. We bashed our way through two more drifts before we came to one that we could not see the end of. The sun shone powerfully, and the reflection from it was blinding. That country is stark and treeless, even when there is no snow. Now, with everything a uniform white except a few fence posts strung with dark barbed wire, the beautiful bleakness was even more striking. Erney walked ahead to find the end of the drift and came back shaking his head. He said it got shallower, but was a couple of hundred yards long. Even so, we were committed. He held Dolly, and I hit the drift as hard as I dared. I was only halfway through when the snow started coming over the hood, and we bogged down for good.

I had to crawl through the window. By the time I was out, Erney had blocked Dolly on the top of the snow and begun digging at the front tires. I was upset. "There's ten tons of snow between us and the house." I said. "We're stuck!"

Erney looked up from his work and then held the shovel for me to see. "We aren't stuck until the shovels break," he said.

We labored for two and a half hours with Bear Butte over our right shoulders, but finally we pulled the pickup onto a bare spot in front of the house. Drifts trailed off toward the southeast from all the buildings, bushes, posts, and trees. The old house, converted from a barn, stood defiantly in the landscape. When I stepped out of the truck, I looked around and remembered why I had chosen this particular place to live. You could look in any direction from the house, and not see another building. With the exception of a few fences and power lines in the distance, the time could have been a hundred years earlier. The landscape offered an unobstructed view. This rickety old house stood in the center of America's grasslands.

Seventeen years before, I had decided to call this area home. I had made the decision gravely, after spending an entire day in a university library. From climatic charts, demographic tables, old geological survey maps, and economic forecasts, I narrowed down the possibilities. I took this decision very seriously because, in a way, it was the first time I had had such a privilege. Prior to that day, I had had little to say about where I would live. For the first time since childhood, I was truly free. That decision was my first opportunity to take charge, and I wasn't going to bungle it. A week after I received a medical deferment from military service, I decided to live on the grasslands. Trees, pretty as they are, had always seemed a barrier to my vision. I had rewritten Joyce Kilmer's line in my mind. "I think that I shall never see, the other side of a tree." Here, a person could see as far as his vision would let him. It was a place too severe to be soon overpopulated, a land that the rest of the world might not consider worth fighting over. And when I stepped out of the pickup and looked at the house and landscape that most people would say was desolate, I knew that I was home.

Dolly was blocked out in the weathering yard and we unpacked those things needing cleaning or repair.[2] It was warm, and water ran off the roof, splattering into the shrubbery that was already beginning to reappear from the snow. By the next morning, the only hint that there had been a blizzard would be the mud. In a few days the only reminder would be the greenness of the grass.

By five o'clock, the clothesline and the fences separating the house from the pasture were draped with tarps, sleeping bags, and the tent. The burned-out stovepipe was repaired with a piece of flashing and a few rivets from the shop. The oil in the pickup was changed, and it was time to fly Dolly.

There are five ponds within walking distance of the house. Because the roads were impassable, we decided to walk a circle that would take us by three of them. With luck we would find ducks. Dolly had been flying stronger and stronger; we would want to graduate from ducks to more difficult quarry soon.

The small birds—lark buntings, blackbirds, and meadowlarks—had already left Montana. But here, two hundred miles south, they were plentiful. A group of meadowlarks huddled on the snowbank a hundred yards in front of the house. They looked out of place there with no green and brown grass to blend into. But they knew that this snow was freak, that it wasn't going to stay on the ground long.

Dolly did not even glance at the meadowlarks when I picked her up. She did not see them as food. She would have to learn that they were catchable. But that would come later. Now we would take a walk through the melting snow and hope we could find ducks. I hooded her and strapped the hawking bag around my waist as she stood on the scale. She weighed twenty-seven and three-quarter ounces; the cold weather had brought her weight down slightly. She should be ready to hunt.

As I waited for Erney to put Spud in the kennel, I enjoyed the smell of Dolly's feathers. The smell of falcon feathers is a secret fetish of people who keep them. The smell is spicy clean, a mixture of high mountain kinnikinnick, the ocean's salt spray, and the jungles of the Yucatan.[3] It is intoxicating. Erney and Jake caught me standing in the side yard with my eyes closed, my nose an inch from Dolly's back. Neither of them seemed to notice. Or perhaps they noticed and understood. When I looked up, Erney stood ten feet behind me staring at the ground. Jake sat beside him watching me intently and shaking slightly with excitement.

We hadn't walked twenty feet when Spud began to howl. We walked along the main draw that leads east from the buildings toward the first pond. Though the temperature had dropped again, the ground was not frozen, and the going was slower and more slippery than we had expected. We stayed on the high ground, keeping Jake at heel. At the rate we were going, it would be dark by the time we got to the third pond. There were no ducks on the first pond and I felt a little prick of fear that Dolly would not get flown that night.

The little ranch in South Dakota is not much, just a small piece of grassland with a couple of brushy draws running through it and a lot of rough land that most people would see as worthless. My banker, who is always trying to get me to plow part of it and plant crops or run more cattle, calls it a badland place. The man who used to own it, and whose defaulted loan I assumed, called it a cow-killing son of a bitch. But it suits me. Even though I have had to earn the money to make the payments by taking jobs that led me away, Erney and I were working for something we felt was important. Even if there weren't many cattle or crops, there were deer, rabbits, antelope, grouse, partridge, and ducks on this little patch of grassland, and we wanted to keep it that way. We had read every old account of this land that we could find and had determined that it was more fertile before the white man came with his plows and cattle. Our plan had always been to bring things back to what we considered full production. Recently, we had found people throughout the great plains who had the same idea.

As we moved, we looked around like two old painting conservators called to investigate an attic filled with long-forgotten oils. We commented on erosion, the deadly threat to birds and animals from barbed-wire fences set on the brink of hills, and the way the brush was coming back where we had excluded the cattle. We trudged through the wet snow to the second pond and found no ducks there either. The sun was sinking low, and the fear that Dolly would not get flown weighed me down, a responsibility not lived up to. We were hurrying toward the third pond, knowing that the light would be gone soon, when six sharp-tailed grouse purred over our heads and landed in a choke cherry thicket sixty yards away.

Jake's ears came up. Erney and I froze. Here was a dilemma. The plan had been to fly Dolly only at ducks until she was strong and confident. The sharp-tailed grouse in the brush ahead of us were as hard a quarry as there was. They would probably outfly her and perhaps discourage her. But we were running out of light and had not found any ducks. We retreated out of sight so we would not flush the grouse prematurely, and I removed Dolly's hood.[4]

The sun was nearly down and the temperature had dropped, which should have made Dolly keen to kill and eat. Even though the countryside was covered with snow and looked different from the way she had always seen it, she left my fist immediately. Erney had been peeking at the grouse through binoculars and said that they squatted down as soon as she appeared in the sky. Jake watched her fly, whining softly. Erney and I waited.

We had been leaving her in the air longer and longer each day. I checked my watch, resolving to not flush the grouse until she had been up five minutes. She flew south until she was almost out of sight, then turned back, gaining altitude as she came. By the time she was overhead, she was several hundred feet high. Now that the grouse could see her well and were likely to stay put, we moved closer. There was a shallow impression in the prairie fifty yards from the choke cherries, and we stopped there to wait for Dolly to make one more round. She made a tight circle and set her wings to glide for a moment. It was like a signal that she was ready, and I sent Jake ahead.

He knew this game too and streaked for the thicket. Erney and I ran along behind, watching Dolly as she flew ahead to see what had excited Jake. She was directly over the thicket when Jake flushed the grouse. Sharp-tailed grouse are very different from ducks. They reach full speed before they are ten feet in the air. Without good cover to land in, they usually try to outfly the falcon. And often they succeed. But this time Dolly was in perfect position and her vertical stoop was too much for the small hen who got up last.[5] I felt sure that the grouse would roll away from the stoop, evading a hit. But Dolly drove right through the grouse and hit it hard. It crashed into the snow with a plop, and Jake scared it back into the air just as Dolly reached the top of her pitch-up. The re-flush was not good falconry, but the timing was perfect. The grouse was rattled now and flew back toward the thicket. Dolly's second stoop knocked it down again, and this time she spun out of the air and snagged it on the ground.

I stared in disbelief. Although the style of the flight left much to be desired, Dolly had caught the first sharp-tailed grouse she had ever seen. It was disappointing that she hadn't killed it cleanly, over a point out in the open. But such aesthetics do not matter to falcons. Dolly reveled in her kill. She rolled the grouse on its back and plucked feathers proudly. Her eyes were very black and deep. She glared defiantly at Jake when he lay down in the snow hoping for a tidbit.

By then it was cold and nearly dark. I slipped in Dolly's jesses while she ate, securing her by snapping a leather bag filled with lead shot to her leash.[6] Erney and I talked while I held a flashlight for Dolly to eat by. This was the best training Dolly could get. She had learned that grouse were good to eat and that if she caught one she would not go hungry. After awhile I switched her to the lure and slid the grouse away without her knowing it. She continued to pull at the meat on the lure that I had gauged to keep her near her flying weight, while Erney and I examined the grouse. It was a small hen and though it was too dark to see the subtle mottling of the back feathers, the whiteness of the breast was clear. Here was one of the most beautiful and admirable birds in the world. Its adaptations for cold weather are marvelous. The feet are feathered, the nostrils designed to withstand winter nights buried in snowdrifts. Their flesh is dark red and delicious. Both the legs and half of the breast of this grouse were still good. We would eat grouse that night. I tossed what was left of the head to Jake and dug my fingers into the warm body cavity of the grouse to remove its heart. Before I picked Dolly up off the lure for the long walk home, I brushed the snow away from the roots of a choke cherry bush and forced the grouse heart into the soft dirt.

That was the first night I had the dream. In it, I was on the beach where I had seen my first peregrine, on Padre Island, off the Texas coast in the Gulf of Mexico. Many birds were there. Rails waded in the marshes, meadowlarks and vesper sparrows sang in the grass, sanderlings and avocets skimmed along the beach, and great blue herons stood motionless in the shallow waters. Somewhere ahead of me was the quarry, a drake pintail. And Dolly, her jesses cut away, was just leaving my fist. We had made the migration. I had come as far as I could and was sending her on alone; but not really alone because she was joining everything that surrounded us. She left my fist for the last time and flew with all the power of a completely wild peregrine. And as I walked, I thought of the country we had traveled together, but I did not look to find her in the sky. I knew that she was there and when the pintail flushed, I did not watch it go, did not look up, or anticipate the stoop. I turned and walked away, knowing that now it was up to Dolly. In my dream I walked back to the pickup and started home. In the dream I did not look back.

The morning sun did not find me in bed contemplating the dream, but on the trail to the top of Bear Butte. I had gotten up before light and driven to the parking lot of the state park where the trails begin. Below the parking lot, in the gray morning light, several Indians, Cheyennes I suppose, moved around a sweat lodge. This was their holy place, the center of their universe and, except during the most severe months, ceremonies were common in the natural amphitheater on the south side of the butte. It is not hard to understand why this place is important to the tribes of the Great Plains. It rises a thousand feet from the prairie in the shape of a sleeping bear. It is the Mount Sinai of the Plains Indian, where the seven sacred arrows that established their law were found, and it has been the object of pilgrimages for centuries.

Not far from the sweat lodge is a particularly sacred place where Crazy Horse addressed a gathering of tribes. Every time I make the hike to the top of the butte, along the trail that winds through pine trees laden with the personal prayer bundles of hundreds of Indians, and look down on that place, I wish I had been there. I imagine the 1870s on the Great Plains and try to understand what Crazy Horse was going through. It was a time of social turmoil, tribal politics, and general confusion. The world was falling apart for the Plains Indian, and the men in power tried to cut their losses. Great chiefs argued about how to react to the white men. Red Cloud would fight for a while, Sitting Bull would run to Canada. Many other chiefs would give in to the white man and try to convince other Indians to come to the reservation to live in frame houses and plow the fields. Finally all the chiefs would give in to one degree or another. All except Crazy Horse.

He was not really even a chief but became the symbol of resistance. Free Indians of all tribes flocked to his moving refuge camp. That huge, famous camp on the Little Big Horn was in part due to the magnetism of Crazy Horse. I have often wondered if he was one of the Indians who swam the day Custer made his strategic attack.

Mari Sandoz called him the strange man of the Oglala. He spent much of his life alone. When he was troubled he would disappear for weeks with only a horse, a blanket, and his weapons. He would return renewed, with meat for the poor of the village and perhaps an enemy scalp. Crazy Horse owned nearly nothing; he did not dress in the finery of other chiefs. He refused the flattery of the white men, scoffed at their invitations to come to Washington. He was religious, charismatic, and unswerving in his belief in his right to roam freely on the Great Plains. It has always amazed me that a man with these characteristics is not recognized as one of the truly great Americans. But he is not. Once, walking past the place where he addressed the tribes, I fantasized that the words of his speech were whispered into my ear and I was able to write them down. That, I imagined, would be all it would take. In no time those words would take their place in history. But sitting on the top of Bear Butte, I wondered what I would really do with the knowledge of Crazy Horse's words.

The temperature had continued to rise as I made my way to the top of the butte, and I could see the draws below running with melted snow. Except for the drifts, all the snow would be gone by evening. The sky was clear, and from my vantage point I could see into Montana and Wyoming. The Black Hills appeared very dark to the south. I stayed on top of the butte until noon as if I were waiting for something. Actually, I was charging my batteries for the next two months. The permits necessary to transport Dolly into Nebraska and Colorado had arrived, bringing the total permits I'd received so far to fourteen. Every unit of government required me to obtain a permit from them; permits to transport Dolly, hunting licenses, game restoration stamps, and falconry licenses. I had been required to supply proof of residency to obtain most of the permits and had been told several times that I could not be a nonresident unless I was a resident of another state, and that I had not been in South Dakota enough recently to establish residency there. I was told once that I was a resident of no state and therefore the permit was denied. It occurred to me that the twenty-odd permits required to travel from Montana to Texas were a conspiracy to keep me in one place. I thought of Crazy Horse again. But unlike Crazy Horse, I would probably get all the permits eventually. They would be sent to the ranch and Erney would forward them to me at Kris's place in Denver or Jim Weaver's camp in New Mexico.

I planned to leave South Dakota soon and head for Nebraska where the North American Falconers' Association would hold its national field meet. Later, I'd drive to Colorado, New Mexico, and finally Texas. There were a few things I needed to do before I left. I had to stop at the bank and try again to justify my loan on the ranch; and I needed to be sure the bills were paid at the feed store and the lumberyard. Still, I had the distinct feeling I was forgetting something. It was as if there was something I needed to do but was putting off. Just then a red-tailed hawk came off a rock below, set her wings and rode a thermal that had formed over the warming prairie. That is when I realized what it was I had to do.

I watched her ride the thermal, soaring effortlessly until she became a tiny spot in the blueness thousands of feet above my head. This reminded me: It was time Dolly learned to soar. The thought of it frightened me. Peregrine falcons are soaring masters. It is one of their favorite ways of hunting. They ride a thermal until they are so high that their prey cannot see them. A peregrine stoop from a soar is one of the most awesome events in nature. Dropping from perhaps a mile above the earth, they can dive at speeds approaching 238 miles per hour. The ancestors of the violet-green swallows flying around Bear Butte that day had no doubt witnessed such stoops before the peregrine became extinct in South Dakota. It was hard to believe that a peregrine could control such a stoop well enough to hit the shifty swallows. Soaring was something that Dolly had to learn to survive as a wild peregrine. It was also the best way I knew to lose a peregrine falcon.

Notes

1. A falcon is tied to a cylindrical piece of wood, called a block, that has a ring in it for attaching the falcon's leash. The blocked out falcon is placed out of doors.—Eds.

2. The weathering yard is the area where falcons are kept on blocks during the day.—Eds.

3. The kinnikinnik is a ground-hugging evergreen of the heath family having waxy leaves, tiny pink and red urn-shaped flowers, and bright red berries in the fall.—Eds.

4. To flush is to frighten a game bird from cover.—Eds.

5. Vertical stoop is the rapid descent of a falcon from a height, toward a quarry or a lure, with wings nearly closed.—Eds.

6. Jesses are the narrow strips of leather fastened around a falcon's legs so that the handler can hold her.—Eds.

Further Reading

Brendan Prairie. 1996.
The Contract Surgeon. 1999.
In the Center of the Nation. 1991.
Spirit of the Hills. 1988.

Paul A. Johnsgard *(b. 1931)*

In *Crane Music* Paul A. Johnsgard traces the sandhill cranes' existence from pre-historic fossil evidence to its present precarious place in the familiar tangle of tension between advocates of preservation and human population pressures. Any-one who has seen and heard the great flocks along Nebraska's Platte River or at other wetlands resting sites across the high plains will not soon forget the experi-ence. Those who have not yet made the trip to the rivers in spring can gain some appreciation of the birds in Johnsgard's prose.

Johnsgard, born in Fargo, North Dakota, is an authority on ornithology and bird behavior. He has written over thirty books, including volumes on waterfowl, hummingbirds, hawks, eagles, and snow geese. He received his bachelor of sci-ence degree from North Dakota State University, his master of science degree from Washington State University, and his Ph.D. from Cornell University. He joined the faculty at the University of Nebraska–Lincoln in 1961.

Seasons of the Sandhill Crane:
A Sandhills Spring (1991)

There is a river in the heart of North America that annually gathers together the watery largess of melting Rocky Mountain snowfields and glaciers and spills wildly down the eastern slopes of Colorado and Wyoming. Reaching the plains, it quickly loses its momentum and begins to spread out and flow slowly across Nebraska from west to east. As it does so, it cuts a sinuous tracery through the native prairies that has been followed for millennia by both men and animals. The river is the Platte.

There is a season in the heart of North America that is an unpredictable day-to-day battle between bitter winds carrying dense curtains of snow out of Canada and the high plains, turning the prairies into ice sculptures, and contrasting south-ern breezes that equally rapidly thaw out the native tall grasses and caress them gently. The season is sweetened each dawn by the compelling music of western meadowlarks, northern cardinals, and greater prairie-chickens, and the sky is neatly punctuated throughout the day with skeins of migrating waterfowl. The season is spring.

There is a bird in the heart of North America that is perhaps even older than the river, and far more wary than the waterfowl or prairie-chickens. It is as gray as the clouds of winter, as softly beautiful and graceful as the flower heads of Indian grass and big bluestem, and its penetrating bugle-like notes are as distinctive and memorable as the barking of a coyote or the song of a western meadowlark. The bird is the sandhill crane.

There is a magical time that occurs each year in the heart of North America, when the river and the season and the bird all come into brief conjunction. The cranes begin to arrive in Nebraska's Platte Valley about the end of February as the Platte begins to become ice-free. They funnel into the valley from wintering areas as far away as northern Mexico, but primarily from eastern New Mexico and adjoining Texas, where a variety of shallow, alkaline lakes have offered them safety through the coldest months. These areas are all at least 600 miles from the Platte, the equivalent of a 12-hour nonstop flight at 50 miles per hour. Some of the birds do stop en route, but probably the majority make the flight in a single day. They achieve their maximum air speed with the aid of south winds, and fly in uniformly spaced gooselike formations for optimum flight efficiency. As they reach the Platte near sunset, the formations begin to break up, and the birds start to circle above the river, looking for safe nighttime roosting sites. The occasional calls of the migrating birds gradually build into a deafening crescendo of crane music. Individual flock members try to maintain voice contact with parents, mates, and offspring as they begin to pour into roost sites on the river, and the darkening sky becomes a maelstrom of circling and descending birds.

Over 90 percent of the sandhill cranes using the Platte Valley in spring are lesser sandhill cranes, the smallest of all the races of sandhills and the one with the longest annual migration, from the American southwest to the arctic tundras of North America and eastern Siberia. At the time of their arrival in Nebraska the birds weigh about six and a half pounds, and they stand about four feet tall. Like all other sandhill crane races they are grayish in plumage, but the crown of birds at least a year old is bare and the skin is bright red.

A small percentage of the sandhill cranes on the Platte are larger-sized birds, averaging perhaps eight and a half pounds and with proportionately longer bills. These birds, Canadian sandhill cranes, are headed toward subarctic nesting areas in Ontario and the other interior provinces, to muskeg or boggy openings in the vast coniferous forest that covers the heart of Canada. A very few represent greater sandhill cranes, the largest of the migratory races of sandhills. These large and distinctively long-billed cranes often weigh ten pounds or more. Those using the Platte Valley are headed for nesting areas in northwestern Minnesota, but most of these very large sandhill cranes have quite different migratory routes that pass either well to the west or east of Nebraska.

Counting all races, the sandhill cranes in the Platte Valley build up to a total of perhaps 400,000–500,000 birds by late March. This number includes essentially all of the lesser sandhill cranes occurring east of the Rocky Mountains and is not only the largest concentration of sandhill cranes in North America, but easily the largest crane concentration in the world. (The other extremely widespread and next most common crane species, the Eurasian crane, has an overall world population of about 100,000 birds. Its largest reported migratory and wintering concentrations number only about 20,000 individuals.) The Platte Valley and the adjoining shallow marshes of the "Rainwater Basin" immediately to the south also host about a quarter-million greater white-fronted geese, or most of those that migrate through the interior of North America. Vast numbers of Canada geese, snow geese, and wild ducks, especially northern pintails and mallards, also migrate through the area. The overall migratory waterfowl numbers annually total about seven to nine million birds, one of the most spectacular concentrations of migratory birds to be found anywhere in the world.

Additionally, up to a hundred or more bald eagles often winter on the Platte. While the eagles normally feed mostly on dead or dying fish, they occasionally fly over and harass the flocks of ducks and geese, apparently to determine if any crippled or partially disabled birds might be present and perhaps provide fairly easy prey. They pay little attention to the sandhill cranes, whose sharp beaks are likely to pose a serious threat to an eagle, and rarely does the sight of an eagle put a crane flock to flight.

The origins of the long-term love affair between the sandhill cranes and the Platte River are lost in prehistory. The oldest known evidence suggesting its antiquity is a fossil humerus, or upper arm bone, found in Miocene deposits of western Nebraska that date from about nine million years ago. It has a structure virtually identical to that of modern sandhill cranes and, if accurately identified, represents not only the oldest sandhill crane fossil ever discovered, but also the oldest fossil attributable to any modern species of bird. At that time in Nebraska's preglacial history, the landscape was evidently a grassland somewhat similar to today's, but having an associated mammalian fauna more like that of present-day East Africa than of North America, with rhinos and horses instead of bison and domestic cattle.

More definite evidence of long-term sandhill crane use of the Platte comes from the writings of various early explorers such as John Thompson, who in the spring of 1834 reported seeing sandhill cranes gathered on the Platte. A somewhat later account was provided by a hunter-adventurer who described his attempts to stalk a large flock of sandhill cranes near Grand Island during the fall of 1841. These were among the earliest explorers and immigrants to use the Platte as a convenient overland route leading into the western wilderness. By the mid-1800s the Platte Valley of Nebraska Territory was to become the primary route leading to Utah and the Oregon Territory. During that time tens of thousands of people followed the Mormon and Oregon trails beside the Platte on their way to new lives and fresh frontiers. Doubtless the cranes and waterfowl of the Platte provided important sources of food along the way.

At this time, even though the Platte was generally placid, it was still a surprisingly treacherous river for much of its length, being both "too thick to drink and too thin to plough." Its generally shallow, muddy, and wide channels could easily hide quicksand-like bottoms, and its annual spring floods could easily carry away both men and their horses or livestock. Its innumerable channels were constantly adding to and subtracting from the land, producing new sandbars and islands as rapidly as other ones were erased. Its banks were kept almost wholly free of trees by the spring floods and ice floes, and especially by the lightning-set fires that periodically raged over the prairies.

It is hard to know just what the attraction of the Platte River was to sandhill and whooping cranes in presettlement days, but probably its wide channels and vegetation-free islands provided ideal protection from prairie wolves and coyotes, while the adjacent wet meadows certainly offered protein-rich foods in the form of seeds and invertebrates. In the century and a half since the first white explorers described these flocks, the river has changed greatly. Most obviously, about three-fourths of its volume has been lost as irrigation projects have diverted its flows. The once-raging spring floods that carried mountain meltwater down to the Missouri River have largely been replaced by dried or cut-off channels. Its once grassy or shrubby shorelines, now protected from uncontrolled prairie fires, have grown up to gallery forests lining the riverbanks. Finally, its innumerable islands have become shrub- and tree-covered as the annual ice scouring effects of early spring flooding have been progressively diminished.

With the loss of many of the Platte's historic channels, there has been an ever-increasing crowding of the birds into the few remaining acceptable roosting sites. These sites are now limited to a stretch of less than 100 miles of river distance between Kearney and Grand Island along the middle reaches of the Platte in east-central Nebraska. As a result, a population that was once distributed along at least 200 miles of river is now concentrated into fewer than 20 major roost sites, most of which are not on protected land and are subject to varying degrees of human disturbance.

Two major wildlife sanctuaries have recently been established on that part of the river that offers the best remaining crane habitat—the Audubon Society's Lillian Annette Rowe Sanctuary near Kearney, and the Mormon Island Crane Meadows sanctuary of the Whooping Crane Trust, near Grand Island. Both offer riverside blinds from which people can watch the daily drama in relative comfort and, more importantly, without unduly disturbing the cranes. The Rowe Sanctuary was funded by a single bequest, while the Crane Meadows sanctuary came about as the result of an environmental settlement in federal court. This settlement established a fund of more than seven million dollars, to be used for mitigating critical habitat losses for whooping cranes caused by the building of Grayrocks Dam on the Laramie River in Wyoming (a tributary of the North Platte, the single major source of water for the Platte). The other primary source, the South Platte, has already been seriously dewatered. Thus, in spite of the existence of these two important sanctuaries, the historic ties between the cranes and the Platte River are not guaranteed in perpetuity, and the conflicting needs of wildlife and the potential human exploitation of the Platte's water are likely to be brought into ever sharper focus in the future.

If the Platte has become so seriously degraded in recent decades, what then is it that draws the cranes back to it each year? The Platte still offers nighttime protection in the form of scattered sandbars and islands, though in ever fewer sites. Perhaps more importantly, the once vast wet meadows have largely been replaced by cornfields, in which the birds can feed daily for as long as five or six weeks, eating unharvested corn left over from the previous summer. In this way they can quickly build up their fat reserves to a maximum, adding about a pound of fat to their total body weight and putting them into ideal condition for their long remaining journey to the arctic. They must arrive on the nesting grounds in prime physiological readiness to breed, for there will be very little to eat during the first few weeks on the tundra.

Each day while the cranes are in the Platte Valley they leave their river roosts shortly after sunrise, as pairs, families, and small flocks spread out both north and south from the river to forage in nearby cornfields. They also feed in the few remaining wet meadows, where invertebrates still provide their best sources of high-protein foods. Each evening they return to traditional roost sites, each of which holds about 10,000–15,000 birds, located in the least disturbed portions of the river well away from bridges and easy human access. To these same roosts vast numbers of cranes return every night near sunset after they have finished their daytime foraging activities. The sunrise and sunset flights of tens of thousands of cranes provide a sight that overwhelms the senses, the din of the birds almost making one dizzy, and the sight of the wheeling flocks overhead seeming at times like a scene from fantasy or science fiction.

At almost any time while on their roosts or while foraging, "dancing" behavior may suddenly begin. This consists of bows, jumps, vegetation-tossing, and wing-flapping activities that are not limited by age or sex. Dancing may quickly spread through a small group of birds, and may just as suddenly end. Sometimes it is started by a sudden, possibly frightening stimulus, and under such circumstances the bounding movements of the birds may quickly change to actual flight, but at other times no apparent stimulus is evident. Although crane dancing vaguely resembles some primitive forms of human dancing and as such has been traditionally believed to represent courtship, in fact it probably has relatively little to do with pair bonding.

Cranes pair for life, and so true courtship is needed only infrequently. Instead, various pair-bonding activities by adults, such as "unison calling," serve periodically to reinforce existing pair bonds. In sandhill cranes, unison calling is done simultaneously by both members of a pair, the female usually uttering about two calls per male call and not throwing her head so far backward during the call as does the male. Perhaps these sex differences during unison calling help to reinforce sexual identity, and thus help to avoid same-sex pairings.

By early April, many of the sandhill cranes have begun to leave the Platte Valley, often beginning their migration by gaining great altitude, wheeling about in massive flocks that rise slowly, their broad wings riding the thermal updrafts produced by the warming April sun. Even before they leave, the birds often spend hours in such circling flocks above the Platte Valley, perhaps simply reveling in the sheer joy of such low-energy flying, or perhaps using these high-altitude maneuvers as reconnaissance flights to scan the river and commit its topographic features to the collective memories of the flock members. This procedure may be especially important for the younger and more inexperienced birds, which must eventually learn all of the species's most secure migratory stopping points along their several-thousand-mile journey.

Further Reading

Earth, Water, and Sky: A Naturalist's Stories and Sketches. 1999.
The Platte: Channels in Time. 1984.
This Fragile Land: A Natural History of the Nebraska Sandhills. 1995.
Those of the Gray Wind: The Sandhill Cranes. 1984.

Paul Gruchow *(b. 1947)*

Journal of a Prairie Year is Paul Gruchow's account of the seasonal cycle observed along the prairie's eastern edge, that is, southwest Minnesota and northwest Iowa. Like other prairie chroniclers Gruchow is aware of paradox: the wind created the prairie thousands of years ago and without its constant, malevolent presence the soil that holds the grasses that keep that soil in place would not have been deposited in deep, fertile drifts.

Gruchow's parents were organic farmers. He grew up in a rural area where his passion for the prairie landscape was first sparked. He graduated from the University of Minnesota and has written more than half a dozen books on Minnesota's environment. Gruchow frequently contributes to a variety of periodicals and lectures on environmental issues. He teaches at St. Olaf College and is a visiting writer in residence at Concordia College in Moorhead, Minnesota.

Spring 4 (1985)

In the fleeting days of April, in the first days of May:

The purple martins returned.

The butterflies emerged.

The frogs began to sing again in the dusk of evening at the waterholes.

The plums burst into fragrant blossom.

The nests of robins were filled with bright blue eggs.

The young cottontail rabbits made quivering forays from home and scampered back into hiding at the slightest sign of danger.

The bumblebees, the independent members of a gregarious family, settled their huge gilded bodies onto delicate flowers.

Violets and dandelions bloomed by the millions.

The prairie grasses began to awaken.

A visitor walking the edge of a prairie lake at dawn in these days was heralded along the way by the quacking of retreating ducks.

And these days brought the squalls and great winds of springtime. The winds seemed to follow the birds up from the south. They were like the furies in the ancient plays, like choruses of monsters come to hurl a final gale of insults at retreated winter before the shimmering and indolent days of summer. I set foot one late April afternoon in one of these torrents of wind. It was like a dream.

The sound of the wind overrode all other sounds. Birds disappeared. People disappeared. Automobile traffic disappeared. The wind wrapped around me like a skin.

The fine residue of topsoil in the air settled in my teeth and made a grinding grit at the nape of my neck. The dust settled in my eyes. They burned and watered. I narrowed them to slits and scowled.

I was carrying my mail. The wind whipped and tugged at it and tore it to shreds. The friction of the wind against my face began to burn the skin on my cheeks. I took on a blush.

The wind did not come at me in one steady blast. It was coquettish, but too rough to be really playful. It tossed me here and there, forward and back, rendered me as helpless as the treetops that also bowed and writhed before the wind.

On another day in early May, I went driving in a spring wind. My car bucked. The wind carried such a heavy load of earth that at times it was difficult to see through it to the center stripe on the highway. The earth filtered through the cracks of the car windows and settled in the furrows of my brow.

After such winds, I embraced the quiet of a house well-sheltered. In the peace of it, I tried to imagine how life must have been in the prairie days before sturdy houses and the shelter of full-grown trees, how desperately people must sometimes have yearned to be free of the winds, how reverently they came to worship and fear the winds that brought both feast and famine.

They are, I acknowledged, one of the requisite rigors of the prairie world. They both test and improve the character of its inhabitants. But I had just come in out of a spring wind. I was content for the moment to be neither tested nor improved.

There is a paradox in the havoc that the winds make upon the prairie: there would not be prairies without them. Actually, it is difficult to say what did make the prairies. They advanced and retreated in episodes stretching over millennia. When white people arrived to settle the country where I live, the prairies were in a period of retreat. I do not have to look very far back in history to find the time when the lands I have grown accustomed to thinking of as naturally prairie were, in fact, forests. Pollen samples from sediment cores taken in Lake Okoboji show my place was a spruce forest only 10,000 years ago. The deepest sediments in the core bear signs of musk oxen. The subarctic forest was wiped out by a glacier. Grasslands grew up in its place, but perhaps without the interruption of agriculture there would have been forest again. Whatever complex set of events made conditions favorable for prairie, the winds were prominent among them.

Before the ice, perhaps 65 million years ago at the end of the Cretaceous period, a geological riot, known as the Laramie Revolution, gave us the spectacular mountains of the West, the Rockies, the Sierra Madres, the Sierra Nevadas.

It was in the rain shadow of these mountains, perhaps 25 million years ago, that the grasslands of the central plains began to emerge. The air masses that reached the central plains still came from the Pacific, but by the time they got there, they had already been interrupted by three ranges of mountains, each extracting its own bit of the water vapor they were carrying. By the time the winds reached the plains they were nearly dry. Still they blew, speeding the transpiration of water from the plants, and drying out the highly permeable glacial soils that covered 70 percent of the land that would become the domain of the grasses. In the long shadow of the mountains, the climate became inhospitable to trees.

The great central grasslands took their present shape during the final ice age, which lasted 100,000 years during the Pleistocene era, and which made of the Upper Mississippi Valley a vast arctic waste. When the ice retreated, its water running away in great glacial rivers to the sea, a fine, mineral-rich till remained. It was exposed to the winds, which were even then prevailingly westerlies. These made of the powdered rock dust storms, which raged ceaselessly, eventually drifting what are now called loess soils across large stretches of the ice-flattened lands that were to become the prairies.

Four periods of glaciation occurred on the northern plains, the last of them still lingering in northern Minnesota scarcely 9,000 years ago. And there were fluctuations in climate. Now it was warmer; now it was colder; now there was drought; now the rainfall was heavier than usual. The forests advanced in warmer, wetter periods; they retreated in colder, drier times. But after the great mountain ranges of the West had risen, there was always a place on the plains where the critical ratio of precipitation to evaporation tilted in favor of the grasses. Grasses are wonderfully well suited to the capricious prairie winds.

For one thing, they grow from the roots up. A grass seedling shows only modest top growth for the first three or four years of its life. It spends much of its energy in building a dense underground support system. Its roots grow deep enough to take advantage of subsoil stores of water in times of drought, and they grow wide enough to catch the nutriment and moisture in the upper levels of the soil in times of normal rainfall. The grasses make a forest that grows underground instead of aboveground, and an incredible thicket it is. A square meter of prairie sod might contain twenty-five miles of roots.

The sod is a mighty armament against the vagaries of the weather. When the winds blow, it holds the movable soils firmly in place. When rains fall, it prevents the soils from washing away. The sod also sponges up the precious rainfall and releases it into the earth slowly so that as it percolates down, it becomes rich with the minerals the soil gives up. The sod acts as a cover to retard evaporation in the summer heat, and it insulates the life below its surface during the long winter freeze. It is a shield against the bruising hooves of the antelope and bison and elk. It is home to most of the creatures that have come to live upon the prairies; it made the raw material for the first homes of the white people.

When grass has rooted itself, it sends up its top growth, which might be a few inches high on the arid high plains or eight or nine feet high on the moistest prairies of the east. The stem of a grass is a hollow, silica-reinforced tube sturdied at regular intervals by thickened nodes. Its construction makes it incredibly strong—no stronger design exists in nature—but also quite flexible. It is made to take the steady beating of the winds.

Its leaves are long and narrow. It is possible to pack a great many of them into a small area. A stand of grass presents a far greater proportion of leaf surface to the sun than does an equivalent growth of trees. At the same time, these narrow leaves present a limited profile to the drying winds. When the sun is at its most brutal in mid-August, the grass leaves are made to curl in upon themselves, to hide their stoma from the devastating heat. The leaves are arranged in sheaves around the grass stems. When it rains, the arrangement breaks the fall of the water and channels it in streams down the stems to the central core of roots.

The dense sod and the happy arrangement of leaves have a dramatic effect on the climate at ground level, where the life of the prairie, given the limited reach of its canopy, is necessarily heavily concentrated. In a stand of native grasses, the temperature may be as much as 10 percent higher than at soil level in an adjacent field of corn.

The grasses, for the most part, have modest flowers. Although many of these are quite beautiful under the magnification of a hand lens, they are so unassuming in general that most people are never aware of them. The grasses do not need showy flowers to attract pollinating insects. They depend upon the winds for pollination, just as they depend upon the winds to scatter their seeds.

The grasses have several strategies for reproduction: they can extend their territory by seeds, which can remain viable for decades after they are produced; they regenerate themselves on shoots growing up from old roots; they send out runners on the surface of the soil to establish new plants.

Because it grows from its base rather than from its tip, a grass is made to withstand abuse. Break it off in the wind, cut it, trample it, mangle it to shreds in a hailstorm, pull it up—do what you might, in a week or two, a grass will be back as green and healthy as ever.

On the bare quartzite rocks atop the Blue Mounds, in the soggy alkaline seepages of the Silver Lake Fen, in the sand hills of western Nebraska, on the exposed knolls of gravel in the glacial moraines, wherever life is thin and stunted, there one can always find a species of grass, and not just one spear of it but a whole colony. Grass is by its nature a colonizer. It is the army that has always marched at the forefront of advanced life, even as it embraced, beginning 25 million years ago, the wide spaces of the American plains, where the winds blew, and tamed them into the wonder that now feeds the world.

Further Reading

Boundary Waters: The Grace of the Wild. 1997.

Grass Roots: The Universe of Home. 1995.

The Necessity of Empty Places. 1988.

Worlds within a World: Reflections on Visits to Minnesota Scientific and Natural Area Preserves. 1999.

Bruce Cutler *(1930–2001)*

In his carefully crafted poems Bruce Cutler sees below the surface and past the present. This poem evokes the elusive qualities of air and sky on the Great Plains. Anyone who has traveled across the high plains understands Cutler's idea of evolving drifts of smoke which slowly change the patterns in the great dome of sky.

Cutler, a native of Illinois, earned a bachelor's degree at the University of Iowa and a master's degree at Kansas State University. He was on the faculty at Wichita State University from 1960 until 1986. He traveled as a Fulbright Scholar to Italy, Paraguay, Argentina, Ecuador, and Spain, and he taught in Switzerland and several Central and South American countries for the U.S. Department of State. He also worked with migrants in a United Nations demonstration area in El Salvador.

All of these experiences clearly influenced Cutler's poetry, which is rich in allusions. His keen sense of history and theater found expression in his poetry, especially in his narrative poems and in a number of dramas.

From a Naturalist's Notebook: Smoke (1960)

Beyond the twirling keys of sycamores
and coil of anaconda hills,
smoke interrogates
a washed West Kansas sky.
As keen as cold
that tumbleweeds through trees,
white and icarian in a weight
of air, it soon convolves
and rises into space.

Not even a thrush
forgets itself to music
the way that silent smoke
involves itself in air.
Earth's own amplexity,
fat and fleshed and veined,
boned, limbed and skinned,
it grows somehow immune
to faltering or falling.

Evolving in a helicline
smoke commits itself
to constant reformation,
sometimes by drift of wind,
by sunlight and shade, humidity
and heat: existing
sometimes *no* and sometimes *yes,*
lost in a soul of sky,
inessential and complete.

Further Reading

Afterlife and Other Poems. 1997.
Dark Fire: A Narrative Poem. 1985.
Doctrine of Selective Depravity. 1985.
Maker's Name. 1980.
Massacre at Sand Creek: Narrative Voices. 1995.
Nectar in a Sieve. 1983.
Sun City: Sixteen Poems and a Translation. 1964.
A West Wind Rises. 1962.
The Year of the Green Wave. 1960.

Reading about Bruce Cutler

Kindrick, Robert. "Bruce Cutler and the Myth of the Land." *Late Harvest: Plains and Prairie Poets.* Ed. Robert Killoren. Kansas City: BkMkPress, 1977. 45–52.

Linda Hasselstrom *(b. 1943)*

Linda Hasselstrom views the Great Plains from ground level. A writer and western South Dakota rancher, she chronicles her struggles to operate her family's ranch in the face of real and potential economic and environmental catastrophes, mixing poetry and prose in her descriptions of the land, accounts of ranch routine, and observations about the ecological and economic pressures that make life on the arid high plains a precarious proposition. Everything she writes is solidly grounded: "Sense of place is the center of all good art," she has said. "Merely traveling through a region does not create intimacy, as Midwesterners have seen eastern writers prove often in our history. To write truly, to speak with authority of this place, one must put down roots, become involved, be battered and tested by the terrain, the weather, and the people." These two selections, found side by side in *Land Circle: Writings Collected from the Land*, reflect one of the plains' persistent themes: hard times are bearable in the company of others who face the same—or worse—difficulties.

Hasselstrom was born in Houston, Texas. When she was nine her mother remarried and they moved to John Hasselstrom's South Dakota ranch. Hasselstrom adopted Linda and gave her his name and a landscape where she feels deeply rooted. She received her bachelor's degree in English and journalism from the University of South Dakota and her master's in American literature from the University of Missouri. She has worked as a teacher, rancher, reporter, publisher, editor, and as director of Windbreak House Retreat, a women's writing workshop conducted on her South Dakota ranch. Numerous awards and honors recognize Hasselstrom's contribution to the arts in the Great Plains and the West.

Coffee Cup Cafe (1991)

Soon as the morning chores are done,
cows milked, pigs fed, kids packed
off to school, it's down to the cafe
for more coffee and some soothing
conversation.

"If it don't rain pretty soon, I'm
just gonna dry up and blow away."

"Dry? This ain't dry. You don't know
how bad it can get. Why, in the Thirties
it didn't rain any more than this for
(breathless pause) six years."

"I heard Johnson's lost ninety head of calves
in that spring snowstorm. They
were calving and heading for home
at the same time and they just walked
away from them."

"Yeah and when the cows
got home, half of them died
of pneumonia."

"I ain't had any hay on me since that hail
last summer; wiped out my hay crop, all
my winter pasture, and then the drouth
this spring. Don't know what I'll do."

"Yeah, but this is nothing yet.
Why in the Thirties the grasshoppers came
like hail and left nothing green on the ground.
They ate fenceposts, even. And the dust, why
it was deep as last winter's snow drifts,
piled against the houses. It ain't bad here yet,
and when it does come, there won't be so many of us
having coffee."

So for an hour they cheer each other, each story
worse than the last, each face longer. You'd think
they'd throw themselves under their tractors
when they leave, but they're bouncy as a new calf,
caps tilted fiercely into the sun.

They feel better, now they know
somebody's having a harder time
and that men like them
can take it.

Red Glow in the Western Sky (1991)

I worked hard in the garden that July afternoon, pulling weeds and moving hoses on the parched vegetables. Occasionally I'd straighten my aching back and look west, toward the sullen clouds hanging over the Black Hills, hoping for rain, but not expecting any.

After a hurried lunch with my husband and son, I drove the pickup down toward the garden, glancing west out of habit, then swung in a tight, dusty arc and roared back, honking. The column of smoke wasn't thick; it rose straight up and mingled with the clouds, but we hadn't had rain for months, and I knew the woods were flammable as gasoline.

The fire looked close. I called a foothills neighbor to ask if he's heard anything on his police scanner radio. He was casual, digesting lunch; no, he hadn't, and where did it look like it was? I told him to look behind his house, and hung up.

"Watch this," I said, leading my family to the porch, where we could see our neighbor's house and the black smoke exploding behind it. Aloud, I counted to five, and suddenly the red pickup by his back door roared backward, spun around, and raced down the ranch road toward the fire.

The column of smoke was building like a thunderhead, bubbling like a pot of water. It's always difficult to tell precisely where a fire is, but it was too close. The top of the column began to flow toward us as a west wind caught it.

A fire in trees is a dangerous place for inexperienced fire fighters, and our ranch was surrounded by acres of parched, crisp grass that could be ignited by a spark. We spent the afternoon filling the three-hundred-gallon water tank on the back of one truck, moving sprinklers in great circles around the house, and calling neighbors for news.

Breathing smoke as hot darkness came, we sat on the deck and joked about watching a live drama, better than television. Ash floated down, gentle as snowflakes. Often, summer nights are still, but when the wind began, it switched direction every few minutes, as if a thunderstorm was close. I knew I couldn't sleep, so I sent my family to bed and stayed on the deck.

About 10:30 P.M. I saw car lights on the driveway to my closest neighbors' house; they'd been gone all day, entertaining visitors from Germany. The car's brake lights flashed briefly as it topped the hill; I knew they were staring at the boiling red cloud.

Country neighbors never call each other after ten at night; too many of us get up early. I waited five minutes by the phone, and picked it up on the first ring.

"Where is the fire?" asked Margaret. I told her all I knew, and that I was staying up all night; she promised to call me when she got up at five.

All night I worked at my computer in the cool basement, and made trip every fifteen minutes to the deck. Sometimes the red glow seemed to cover the whole

western sky; at other times it flickered and dimmed. I listened with growing disbelief to the strange world of call-in talk shows, where people discussed with great
solemnity whether or not Elvis lived.

About midnight, a brief news flash reported Mount Rushmore threatened by a
forest fire. I could tell flames weren't close to the Shrine of Democracy, but for a
New York reporter, I suppose ten miles was close enough. Later, a talk-show caller
said, "I hope the forest fire blackens Lincoln's face on Mount Rushmore because
he'd be so shocked at what's happening in South Africa today." Trying to figure
out that logic kept me alert for an hour.

Several highways had been closed by fire fighters, and some residents were
desperate for news amid rumors ranch buildings had burned. I answered calls, but
could tell them little. Margaret sleepily called at five, and I went to bed.

By late afternoon, gray ash was falling on the deck, and we took our water truck
up to Margaret's yard. Her husband and brother were still on the fire line, and she
and her sister-in-law were discussing moving their cattle and buffalo out of the
pastures closest to the fire. But the job would be dangerous in the smoke, and the
animals might get out on the highway.

All day slurry bombers lumbered overhead; we could tell when they dropped
slurry—the engine sound changed.

The wind died during the night, the smoke moved east, and we woke to a
landscape that looked foggy. The sun was only a red glow, and we couldn't see
fences fifty feet away. It was impossible to tell if our own pastures were burning,
and the stead drone of the slurry bombers overhead was gone. No one could be
sure what the fire was doing; all flights were grounded.

On the fourth day, with the fire surrounded but not contained, I went into the
hills to teach a writer's conference. At midmorning, a sudden rain squall struck
so hard that we had to hold down the conference tents, and were laughingly
drenched. The squall paused directly over the fire, dropping so much rain that fire
fighters' truck were mired and sliding into trees. My neighbors, exhausted, having
spent four days away from their families and their work, came home.

They fought the fire, but they never controlled it; fire fighters say no equipment
exists to stop a fire of that intensity once it has begun. The conditions that brought
this one small fire in the West's summer of flame still exist. Even if we get snow and
rain, they will continue to exist. Our forests contain too much fuel; years of work
by environmentalists to stop logging in wilderness areas have resulted in a buildup
of brush and crowded trees that need only one spark to ignite. The danger is
particularly severe where disease or drought has left dead trees standing. We will
lose our wilderness forests to wildfire if we do not learn to manage them more
safely by removing some trees.

The joke among local fire fighters was that God looked down and said, "You
fellahs aren't managing your forest very well; you've got too much fuel buildup
down there," and sent a lightning storm to start a fire. Five days later he looked
down and said, "You guys don't fight fire very well, either," and sent a rainstorm.

Further Reading

Between Grass and Sky: Where I Live and Work. 2002.

Bittercreek Junction. 2000.

Caught By One Wing. 1993.

Dakota Bones: The Collected Poems of Linda Hasselstrom. 1993.

Feels Like Far: A Rancher's Life on the Great Plains. 1999.

Going Over East: Reflections of a Woman Rancher. 1987.

Leaning into the Wind: Women Write from the Heart of the West. Ed. Linda Hasselstrom, Gaydell Collier, and Nancy Curtis. 1997.

A Roadside History of South Dakota. 1994.

Windbreak: A Women Rancher on the Northern Plains. 1987.

Woven on the Wind: Women Write about Friendship in the Sagebrush West. Ed. Linda Hasselstrom, Gaydell Collier, and Nancy Curtis. 2001.

William Least Heat-Moon

In this passage from *PrairyErth* William Least Heat-Moon examines the Great Plains' most malevolent weather, the tornado: a very real threat to the region's inhabitants, and a metaphor for the power and capriciousness of Great Plains' nature.

For Heat-Moon's biography see page 44.

Under Old Nell's Skirt (1991)

I know a man, a Maya in the Yucatán, who can call up wind: he whistles a clear, haunting, thirteen-note melody set in the Native American pentatonic scale. He whistles, the wind moves, and for some moments the heat of the tropical forests eases. It's a talent there to appreciate. But does he summon the wind, or does he know just the right time to whistle before the wind moves? He says, in effect, that he is on speaking terms with the wind, and by that he means it is a phenomenon, yes, but also a presence, and it has a name, Ik, and it is Ik that brings the seasonal rain to Yucatán. You may call such a notion pantheism or primitivism or mere personification: he wouldn't care, because for him, for the Maya, for all of tribal America, the wind, the life bringer, is something to heed, to esteem: Ik.

In Kansas I've not heard any names for the nearly constant winds, the oldest of things here. When the Kansa Indians were pushed out of the state, they carried with them the last perception of wind as anything other than a faceless force, usually for destruction, the power behind terrible prairie wildfires, the clout in blizzards and droughts, and, most of all, in tornadoes that will take up everything, even fenceposts. But people here know wind well, they often speak of it, yet, despite the several names in other places for local American winds, in this state, whose very name may mean "wind-people," it has no identity but a direction, no epithet but a curse. A local preacher told me: *Giving names to nature is unchristian.* I said that it might help people connect with things and who knows where that might lead, and he said, *To idolatry.* Yet the fact remains: these countians are more activated by weather than religion.

Almost everything I see in this place sooner or later brings me back to the grasses; after all, this is the prairie, a topography that so surprised Anglo culture when it began arriving that it found for this grand-beyond no suitable word in its immense vocabulary, and it resorted to the French of illiterate trappers: prairie. Except in accounts of novice travelers, these grasslands have never been meadows, heaths, moors, downs, wolds. A woman in Boston once said to me, *Prairie is such a lovely word—and for so grim a place.*

More than all other things here, the grasses are the offspring of the wind, the power that helps evaporation equal precipitation to the detriment of trees, the power that breaks off leaves and branches, shakes crowns and rigid trunks to tear roots and disrupt transpiration, respiration, nutrient assimilation. But grasses before the wind bend and straighten and bend and keep their vital parts underground, and, come into season, they release their germ, spikelets, and seeds to the wind, the invisible sea that in this place must carry the code, the directions from the unfaced god, carry the imprint of rootlet and rhizome, blade and sheath, culm and rachis: the wind, the penisless god going and coming everywhere, the intercourse of the grasses, the sprayer of seed across the opened sex risen and waiting for the pattern set loose on the winds today of no name; and so the grasses pull the energy from the wind, the offspring of sunlight, to transmute soil into more grasses that ungulates eat into flesh that men turn into pot roasts and woolen socks.

Now: I am walking a ridge in the southern end of Saffordville quadrangle, and below me in the creek bottom are oaks of several kinds, cottonwood, hackberry, walnut, hickory, sycamore. Slippery elms, once providing a throat emulcent, try to climb the hills by finding rock crevices to shield their seed, and, if one sprouts, it will grow straight for a time, only to lose its inborn shape to the prevailing southerlies so that the windward sides of elms seem eaten off but the lee sides spread north like tresses unloosed in March. If a seedling succeeds on a ridge top, it will spread low as if to squat under the shears of windrush, and everywhere the elm trunks lean to the polestar and make the county appear as if its southern end had been lifted and tilted before the land could dry and set. A windmill must stand straight and turn into the wind to harvest water, but the slippery elm turns away to keep the wind from its wet pulp.

And there is another face to this thing from which life proceeds. Yesterday I walked down a ridge to get out of the November wind while I ate a sandwich, and I came upon a house foundation on a slope bereft of anything but grasses and knee-high plants. It was absolutely exposed, an oddity here, since most of the homes sit in the shelter of wooded vales. This one faced east—or it would have, had it still been there—and the only relief from the prevailing winds that the builder had sought was to set the back of the house to them. There was the foundation, some broken boards, a few rusting things, and, thirty feet away, a storm cellar, its door torn off, and that was all except for a rock road of two ruts. The cave, as people here call tornado cellars, was of rough-cut native stone with an arched roof, wooden shelves, and a packed-earth floor with Mason jar fragments glinting blue in the sunlight; one had been so broken that twin pieces at my feet said:

The shards seemed to be lost voices locked in silica and calling still.

These cellars once kept cool home-canned food (and rat snakes), and, when a tornado struck like a fang from some cloud-beast, they kept families that mocked their own timorousness by calling them *'fraidy holes,* and it did take nerve to go into the dim recesses with their spidered corners and dark, reptilian coils. I stepped down inside and sat on a stone fallen from the wall and ate safely in the doorway, but, even with the sun shafts, there was something dismal and haunted in the shadowed dust of dry rot here and dank of wet rot there. Things lay silent inside, the air quite stilled, and I felt something, I don't know what: something waiting.

Was there a connection between this cave and that house absent but for its foundation? The site, sloping southwest, seemed placed to catch a cyclone in a county in the heart of the notorious Tornado Alley of the Middle West, a belt that can average 250 tornadoes a year, more than anywhere else in the world. A hundred and sixty miles from here, Codell, Kansas, got thumped by a tornado every twentieth of May for three successive years, and five months ago a twister "touched down," mashed down really, a mile north of Saffordville at the small conglomeration of houses and trailers called Toledo, and the newspaper caption for a photograph of that crook'd finger of a funnel cloud was HOLY TOLEDO! Years earlier a cyclone wrecked a Friends meetinghouse there, but this time it skipped over the Methodist's church and went for their houses. In Chase County I've found a nonchalance about natural forces born of fatalism: *If it's gonna get me, it'll get me.* In Cottonwood Falls, on a block where a house once sat, the old cave remains, collapsing, yet around it are six house trailers. Riding out a tornado in a mobile home is like stepping into combine blades: trailers can become airborne chambers full of flying knives of aluminum and glass. No: if there is a dread in the county, it is not of dark skies but of the opposite, of clear skies, days and days of clear skies, of a drought nobody escapes, not even the shopkeepers. That any one person will suffer losses from a tornado, however deadly, goes much against the odds, and many residents reach high school before they first see a twister; yet, nobody who lives his full span in the county dies without a tornado story.

Tornado: a Spanish past participle meaning turned, from a verb meaning to turn, alter, transform, repeat, *and* to restore. Meteorologists speak of the reasons why the Midlands of the United States suffer so many tornadoes: a range of high mountains west of a great expanse of sun-heated plains at a much lower altitude, where dry and cold northern air can meet warm and moist southern air from a large body of water to combine with a circulation pattern mixing things up: that is to say, the jet stream from Arctic Canada crosses the Rockies to meet a front from the Gulf of Mexico over the Great Plains in the center of which sits Kansas, where, since 1950, people have sighted seventeen hundred tornadoes. It is a place of such potential celestial violence that the meteorologists at the National Severe Storms Forecast Center in Kansas City, Missouri, are sometimes called the Keepers of the Gates of Hell. Countians who have smelled the fulminous, cyclonic sky up close, who have felt the ground shake and heard the earth itself roar and have taken to a storm cellar that soon filled with a loathsome greenish air, find the image apt. The Keepers of the Gates of Hell have, in recent years, become adept at forecasting tornadoes, and they might even be able to suggest cures for them if only they could study them up close. Years ago a fellow proposed sending scientists into the eye of a tornado in an army tank until he considered the problem of transporting the machine to a funnel that usually lasts only minutes, and someone else suggested flying into a cyclone, whereupon a weather-research pilot said, yes, it was feasible if the aviator would first practice by flying into mountains.

Climatologists speak of thunderstorms pregnant with tornadoes, storm-breeding clouds more than twice the height of Mount Everest; they speak of funicular envelopes and anvil clouds with pendant mammati and of thermal instability of winds in cyclonic vorticity, of rotatory columns of air torquing at velocities up to three hundred miles an hour (although no anemometer in the direct path of a storm has survived), funnels that can move over the ground at the speed of a strolling man or at the rate of a barrel-assing semi on the turnpike; they say the width of the destruction can be the distance between home plate and deep center field and its length the hundred miles between New York City and Philadelphia. A tornado, although more violent than a much longer lasting hurricane, has a life measured in minutes, and weathercasters watch it snuff out as it was born: unnamed.

I know here a grandfather, a man as bald as if a cyclonic wind had taken his scalp—something witnesses claim has happened elsewhere—who calls twisters Old Nell, and he threatens to set crying children outside the back door for her to carry off. People who have seen Old Nell close, up under her skirt, talk about her colors: pastel-pink, black, blue, gray, and a survivor said this: *All at once a big hole opened in the sky with a mass of cherry-red, a yellow tinge in the center,* and another said: *a funnel with beautiful electric-blue light,* and a third person: *It was glowing like it was illuminated from the inside.* The witnesses speak of shapes: a formless black mass, a cone, cylinder, tube, ribbon, pendant, thrashing hose, dangling lariat, writhing snake, elephant trunk. They tell of ponds being vacuumed dry, eyes of geese sucked out, chickens clean-plucked from beak to bum, water pulled straight up out of toilet bowls, a woman's clothes torn off her, a wife killed after being jerked through a car window, a child carried two miles and set down with only scratches, a Cottonwood Falls mother (fearful of wind) cured of chronic headaches when a twister passed harmlessly within a few feet of her house, and, just south of Chase, a woman blown our of her living room window and dropped unhurt sixty feet away and falling unbroken beside her a phonograph record of "Stormy Weather."

London Harness, an eighty-five-year-old man who lives just six miles north of the county line, told me: *I knew a family years ago that was crossing open country here in a horse and wagon. A bad storm come on fast, and the man run to a dug well and said, "I'm going down in here—you do the best you can!" The wife hollered and screamed and run to a ditch and laid down with their two little kids. That funnel dropped right in on them. After the storm passed over, she and the kids went to the well to say, "Come on up, Pappy," but there weren't no water down there, and he weren't down there. If you're in that path, no need of running.*

Yesterday: in the sun the broken words on the Mason jar glinted and, against the foundation, the wind whacked dry grasses and seed pods, *tap-tap-tap, rasp-rasp,* and a yellow light lay over the November slope, and Ma and son: did they one afternoon come out of the cave to see what I see, an unhoused foundation, some twisted fence wire, and a sky turning golden in all innocence?

Denise Low *(b. 1949)*

Poet Denise Low was born in Emporia, Kansas. She received her bachelor's degree from the University of Kansas and her master of fine arts degree from Wichita State University. She has taught as Kansas State University, Washburn University in Topeka, and Haskell Indian College in Lawrence, Kansas.

Low grounds her poetry in her Kansas experiences. Like many plains dwellers, she defines the landscape in words that encompass the weather's legendary past and its very real present.

Another Tornado Dream (1988)

I am near Wakarusa River,
a rope of brown water centered
within wide terraces.
This valley marks
the ancient glacier's
southernmost margin.

This is the place a tornado
touched down in 'eighty-one.
The cloud moves away,
still formless,
but then it doubles back.
It explodes into a waterfall of wind.

In the dream I remember
a tornado will not touch
the fork of two rivers,
but I am miles from confluence.
I crouch by a forked tree
and wrap my arms around it

as though it were a father.
I can feel the tree
is a force, too,
like wind and water,

like the river of ice
that once bulged this valley open.

I pray to the tree so intently that I awaken.

Further Reading
Spring Geese and Other Poems. 1984.
Touching the Sky. 1994.
Tulip Elegies: An Alchemy of Writing. 1993.

Wallace Stegner (1909–1993)

Wallace Stegner has long been recognized as a preeminent chronicler of the American West. A novelist, historian, and environmentalist, Wallace Stegner was born in Lake Mills, Iowa, but spent much of his childhood moving around the West, a life chronicled in this autobiographical novel, *The Big Rock Candy Mountain* (1943). Author of more than thirty books, Stegener was awarded the National Book Award for *The Spectator Bird* in 1977 and the Pulitzer Prize for *Angle of Repose* in 1971. Stegner earned degrees at the University of Utah and Iowa State University. He taught writing at Stanford University from 1945 until his retirement in 1971. During the John F. Kennedy administration he served as assistant to the secretary of the interior. Throughout his life Stegner remained steadfastly committed to the environment, maintaining that the arid West could not withstand the levels of human population which the rest of the country supported.

Wolf Willow: A History, a Story, and a Memory of the Last Plains Frontier (1962) is Stegner's memoir of his boyhood on a wheat ranch near East End, Saskatchewan, on the Canada-Montana frontier border, where, as he imagined it, "the Plains, as an ecology, as native Indian culture, and as a process of white settlement, came to their climax and their end." The wheat farm that meant work, discouragement, and failure to his parents embodied mythic frontier freedom for the boy. As the full title suggests, *Wolf Willow* is part history, part affectionate memoir, and part fiction, all elements that represent the polar extremes of unrelenting reality and nostalgia that is the West in our collective American imagination.

The Question Mark in the Circle (1962)

An ordinary road map of the United States, one that for courtesy's sake includes the first hundred miles on the Canadian side of the Line, will show two roads, graded but not paved, reaching up into western Saskatchewan to link U.S. 2 with Canada 1, the Trans-Canada Highway. One of these little roads leads from Havre, on the Milk River, to Maple Creek; the other from Malta, also on the Milk, to Swift Current. The first, perhaps a hundred and twenty miles long, has no towns on it big enough to show on a map of this scale. The second, fifty miles longer, has two, neither of which would be worth comment except that one of them, Val Marie, is the site of one of the few remaining prairie-dog towns anywhere. The rest of that country is notable primarily for its weather, which is violent and prolonged; its emptiness, which is almost frighteningly total; and its wind, which blows all the time in a way to stiffen your hair and rattle the eyes in your head.

This is no safety valve for the population explosion, no prize in a latter-day land rush. It has had its land rush, and recovered. If you owned it, you might be able to sell certain parts of it at a few dollars an acre; many parts you couldn't give away. Not many cars raise dust along its lonely roads—it is country people do not much want to cross, much less visit. But that block of country between the Milk River and the main line of the Canadian Pacific, and between approximately the Saskatchewan-Alberta line and Wood Mountain, is what this book is about. It is the place where I spent my childhood. It is also the place where the Plains, as an ecology, as a native Indian culture, and as a process of white settlement, came to their climax and their end. Viewed personally and historically, that almost feature-less prairie glows with more color than it reveals to the appalled and misdirected tourist. As memory, as experience, those Plains are unforgettable; as history, they have the lurid explosiveness of a prairie fire, quickly dangerous, swiftly over.

I have sometimes been tempted to believe that I grew up on a gun-toting frontier. This temptation I trace to a stagecoach ride in the spring of 1914, and to a cowpuncher named Buck Murphy.

The stagecoach ran from Gull Lake, Saskatchewan, on the main line of the Canadian Pacific, to the town I shall call Whitemud, sixty miles southwest in the valley of the Whitemud or Frenchman River.[1] The grade from Moose Jaw already reached to Whitemud, and steel was being laid, but no trains were yet running when the stage brought in my mother, my brother, and myself, plus a red-faced cowpuncher with a painful deference to ladies and a great affection for little children. I rode the sixty miles on Buck Murphy's lap, half anesthetized by his whiskey breath, and during the ride I confounded both my mother and Murphy by fishing from under his coat a six-shooter half as big as I was.

A little later Murphy was shot and killed by a Mountie in the streets of Shauna-von, up the line. As I heard later, the Mountie was scared and trigger-happy, and would have been in real trouble for an un-Mountie-like killing if Murphy had not been carrying a gun. But instead of visualizing it as it probably was—Murphy coming down the street in a buckboard, the Mountie on the corner, bad blood between them, a suspicious move, a shot, a scared team, a crowd collecting—I have been led by a lifetime of horse opera to imagine that death in standard walk-down detail. For years, growing up in more civilized places, I got a comfortable sense of status out of recalling that in my youth I had been a friend of badmen and an eyewitness to gunfights in wide streets between false-fronted saloons. Not even the streets and saloons, now that I test them, were authentic, for I don't think I was ever in Shaunavon in my boyhood, and I could not have reconstructed an image from Whitemud's streets because at the time of Murphy's death Whitemud didn't have any. It hardly even had houses: we ourselves were living in a derailed dining car.

Actually Murphy was an amiable, drunken, sentimental, perhaps dishonest, and generally harmless Montana cowboy like dozens of others. He may have been in Canada for reasons that would have interested Montana sheriffs, but more likely not; and if he had been, so were plenty of others who never thought of themselves as badmen. The Cypress Hills had always made a comfortable retiring place just a good day's ride north of the Line. Murphy would have carried a six-shooter mainly for reasons of brag; he would have worn it inside his coat because Canadian law forbade the carrying of sidearms. When Montana cattle outfits worked across the Line they learned to leave their guns in their bedrolls. In the American West men came before law, but in Saskatchewan the law was there before settlers, before even cattlemen, and not merely law but law enforcement. It was not characteristic that Buck Murphy should die in a gunfight, but if he had to die by violence it was entirely characteristic that he should be shot by a policeman.

The first settlement in the Cypress Hills county was a village of *métis* win-terers,[2] the second was a short-lived Hudson's Bay Company post on Chimney Coulee, the third was the Mounted Police headquarters at Fort Walsh, the fourth was a Mountie outpost erected on the site of the burned Hudson's Bay Company buildings to keep an eye on Sitting Bull and other Indians who congregated in that country in alarming numbers after the big troubles of the 1870's. The Mountie post on Chimney Coulee, later moved down onto the river, was the predecessor of the town of Whitemud. The overgrown foundation stones of its cabins remind a historian why there were no Boot Hills along the Frenchman. The place was too well policed.

So as I have learned more I have had to give up the illusion of a romantic gun-toting past, and it is hardly glamour that brings me back, a middle-aged pilgrim, to the village I last saw in 1920. Neither do I come back with the expectation of returning to a childhood wonderland—or I don't think I do. By most estimates, including most of the estimates of memory, Saskatchewan can be a pretty depress-ing country.

The Frenchman, a river more American than Canadian since it flows into the Milk and thence into the Missouri, has changed its name since my time to con-form with American maps. We always called it the Whitemud, from the stratum of pure white kaolin exposed along its valley.[3] Whitemud or Frenchman, the river is important in my memory, for it conditioned and contained the town. But mem-ory, though vivid, is imprecise, without sure dimensions, and it is as much to test memory against adult observation as for any other reason that I return. What I remember are low bars overgrown with wild roses, cutbank bends, secret paths through the willows, fords across the shallows, swallows in the clay banks, days of indolence and adventure where space was as flexible as the mind's cunning and where time did not exist. That was at the heart of it, the sunken and sanctuary river valley. Out around, stretching in all directions from the benches to become coex-tensive with the disk of the world, went the uninterrupted prairie.

The geologist who surveyed southern Saskatchewan in the 1870's called it one of the most desolate and forbidding regions on earth. I can remember plenty of times when it seemed so to me and my family. Yet as I poke the car tentatively eastward into it from Medicine Hat, returning to my childhood through a green June, I took for desolation and can find none.

The plain spreads southward below the Trans-Canada Highway, an ocean of wind-troubled grass and grain. It has its remembered textures: winter wheat heavily headed, scoured and shadowed as if schools of fish move in it; spring wheat with its young seed-rows as precise as combings in a boy's wet hair; gray-brown summer fallow with the weeds disked under; and grass, the marvelous curly prairie wool tight to the earth's skin, straining the wind as the wheat does, but in its own way, secretly.

Prairie wool blue-green, spring wheat bright as new lawn, winter wheat gray-green at rest and slaty when the wind flaws it, roadside primroses as shy as prairie flowers are supposed to be, and as gentle to the eye as when in my boyhood we used to call them wild tulips, and by their coming date the beginning of summer.

On that monotonous surface with its occasional ship-like farm, its atolls of shelter-belt trees, its level ring of horizon, there is little to interrupt the eye. Roads run straight between parallel lines of fence until they intersect the circle of the horizon. It is a landscape of circles, radii, perspective exercises—a country of geometry.

Across its empty miles pours the pushing and shouldering wind, a thing you tighten into as a trout tightens into fast water. It is a grassy, clean, exciting wind, with the smell of distance in it, and in its search for whatever it is looking for it turns over every wheat blade and head, every pale primrose, even the ground-hugging grass. It blows yellow-headed blackbirds and hawks and prairie sparrows around the air and ruffles the short tails of meadowlarks on fence posts. In collaboration with the light, it makes lovely and changeful what might otherwise be characterless.

It is a long way from characterless; "overpowering" would be a better word. For over the segmented circle of earth is domed the biggest sky anywhere, which on days like this sheds down on range and wheat and summer fallow a light to set a painter wild, a light pure, glareless, and transparent. The horizon a dozen miles away is as clean a line as the nearest fence. There is no haze, neither the woolly gray of humid countries nor the blue atmosphere of the mountain West. Across the immense sky move navies of cumuli, fair-weather clouds, their bottoms as even as if they had scraped themselves flat against the flat earth.

The drama of this landscape is in the sky, pouring with light and always moving. The earth is passive. And yet the beauty I am struck by, both as present fact and as revived memory, is a fusion: this sky would not be so spectacular without this earth to change and glow and darken under it. And whatever the sky may do, however the earth is shaken or darkened, the Euclidean perfection abides. The very scale, the hugeness of simple forms, emphasizes stability. It is not hills and mountains which we should call eternal. Nature abhors an elevation as much as it abhors a vacuum; a hill is no sooner elevated than the forces of erosion begin tearing it down. These prairies are quiescent, close to static; looked at for any length of time, they begin to impose their awful perfection on the observer's mind. Eternity is a peneplain.

In a wet spring such as this, there is almost as much sky on the ground as in the air. The county is dotted with sloughs, every depression is full of water, the roadside ditches are canals. Grass and wheat grow to the water's edge and under it; they seem to grow right under the edges of the sky. In deep sloughs tules have rooted, and every such pond is dignified with mating mallards and the dark little automata that glide after them as if on strings.

The nesting mallards move in my memory, too, pulling after them shadowy, long-forgotten images. The picture of a drake standing on his head with his curly tailfeathers sticking up from a sheet of wind-flawed slough is tangled in my re-membering senses with the feel of the grassy edge under my bare feet, the smell of mud, the push of the traveler wind, the weight of the sun, the look of the sky with its level-floored clouds made for the penetration of miraculous Beanstalks.

Desolate? Forbidding? There was never a country that in its good moments was more beautiful. Even in drouth or dust storm or blizzard it is the reverse of monotonous, once you have submitted to it with all the senses. You don't get out of the wind, but learn to lean and squint against it. You don't escape sky and sun, but wear them in your eyeballs and on your back. You become acutely aware of yourself. The world is very large, the sky even larger, and you are very small. But also the world is flat, empty, nearly abstract, and in its flatness you are a challeng-ing upright thing, as sudden as an exclamation mark, as enigmatic as a question mark.

It is a country to breed mystical people, egocentric people, perhaps poetic people. But not humble ones. At noon the total sun pours on your single head; at sunrise or sunset you throw a shadow a hundred yards long. It was not prairie dwellers who invented the indifferent universe or impotent man. Puny you may feel there, and vulnerable, but not unnoticed. This is a land to mark the spar-row's fall.

Our homestead lay south of here, right on the Saskatchewan-Montana border—a place so ambiguous in its affiliations that we felt as uncertain as the drainage about which way to flow. It would be no more than thirty or forty miles out of my way, now, and yet I do not turn south to try to find it, and I know very well why. I am afraid to. In the Dust Bowl years all that country was returned to range by the Provincial Farm Rehabilitation Administration. I can imagine myself bumping across burnouts and cactus clumps, scanning the dehumanized waste for some mark—shack or wind-leaned chickencoop, wagon ruts or abandoned harrow with its teeth full of Russian thistle—to reassure me that people did once live there.

Worse, I can imagine actually finding the flat on which our house stood, the coulee that angled up the pasture, the dam behind which the spring thaw created our "rezavoy"—locating the place and standing in it ringed by emptiness and silence, while the wind fingered my face and whispered to itself like an old blind woman, and a burrowing owl, flustered by the unfamiliar visitor, bowed from the dirt mound of its doorstep, saying, "Who? Who?"

I do not want that. I don't want to find, as I know I will if I go down there, that we have vanished without trace like a boat sunk in mid-ocean. I don't want our shack to be gone, as I know it is; I would not enjoy hunting the ground around it for broken crockery and rusty nails and bits of glass. I don't want to know that our protective pasture fence has been pulled down to let the prairie in, or that our field, which stopped at the Line and so defined a sort of identity and difference, now flows southward into Montana without a break as restored grass and burnouts. Once, standing alone under the bell-jar sky gave me the strongest feeling of personal singularity I shall ever have. That was because it was all new, we were taking hold of it to make it ours. But to return hunting relics, to go down there armed only with memory and find every trace of our passage wiped away—that would be to reduce my family, myself, the hard effort of years, to solipsism, to make us as fictive as a dream.

If I say to the owl, "Your great-grandfather lived in my house, and could turn his head clear around and look out between his shoulder blades," I know he will bow, being polite, and then turn *his* head clear around and look out between his shoulder blades, and seeing only unbroken grass, will cough and say, "What house? Whose?" I know the very way the wind will ruffle his feathers as he turns; I can hear the dry silence that will resume as soon as he stops speaking. With the clarity of hallucination I can see my mother's weathered, rueful, half-laughing face, and hear the exact tone, between regretful and indomitable, in which she says the words with which she always met misfortune or failure: "Well," she will say, "better luck next time!"

I had much better let it alone. The town is safer. I turn south only far enough to come up onto the South Bench, and then I follow a dirt road eastward so as to enter Whitemud from the old familiar direction. That much I will risk.

It is a far more prosperous country than I remember, for I return at the crest of a wet cycle. The farms that used to jut bleakly from the prairie are bedded in cottonwoods and yellow-flowering caragana. Here and there the horizontal land is broken by a new verticality more portentous than windmills or elevators—the derricks of oil rigs. Farther north, prosperity rides on the uranium boom. Here it rides on wheat and oil. But though the country is no longer wild, this section within reach of town is even emptier, more thinly lived in, than in our time. Oil crews create no new towns and do not enlarge the old ones more than briefly. Even if they hit oil, they erect a Christmas tree on the well and go away. As for wheat, fewer and fewer farmers produce more and more of it.

To us, a half section was a farm. With modern machinery, a man by himself can plow, seed, and harvest a thousand or twelve hundred acres. The average Saskatchewan farm is at least a section; two sections, or even more, are not uncommon. And that is the good land, not the submarginal land such as ours which has been put back to grass. Even such a duchy of a farm is only a part-time job. A man can seed a hundred acres a day. Once the crop is in there is little to do until harvest. Then a week or two on the combine, a week or two of hauling, a week or two of working the summer fallow and planting winter wheat, and he is all done until May.

This is a strange sort of farming, with its dangers of soil exhaustion, drouth, and wind erosion, and with highly specialized conditions. Only about half of the farmhouses on the prairie are lived in any more, and some of those are lived in only part time, by farmers who spend all but the crop season in town, as we did. Many a farmer miles from town has no farmhouse at all, but commutes to work in a pickup. There is a growing class of trailer farmers, suitcase farmers, many of them from the United States, who camp for three or four months beside the field and return to Minneapolis or Bismarck when the crop is in.

Hence the look of extensive cultivation and at the same time the emptiness. We see few horses, few cattle. Saskatchewan farmers could go a long way toward supplying the world's bread, but they are less subsistence farmers than we were in 1915. They live in towns that have the essential form and function of medieval towns, or New England country towns, or Mormon villages in irrigated land: clusters of dwellings surrounded by the cultivated fields. But here the fields are a mile or two miles square and may be forty miles from the home of the man who works them.

So it is still quiet earth, big sky. Human intrusions seem as abrupt as the elevators that leap out of the plain to announce every little hamlet and keep it memorable for a few miles. The countryside and the smaller villages empty gradually into the larger centers; in the process of slow adaptation to the terms the land sets, the small towns get smaller, the larger ones larger. Whitemud, based strategically on railroad and river, is one of the ones that will last.

In the fall it was always a moment of pure excitement, after a whole day on the trail, to come to the rim of the South Bench. More likely than not I would be riding with my mother in the wagon while my father had my brother with him in the Ford. The horses would be plodding with their noses nearly to their knees, the colt would be dropping tiredly behind. We would be chocked with dust, cranky and headachy with heat, our joints loosened with fifty miles of jolting. Then miraculously the land fell away below us, I would lift my head from my mother's lap and push aside the straw hat that had been protecting my face from the glare, and there below, looped in its green coils of river, snug and protected in its sanctuary valley, lay town.

The land falls away below me now, the suddenness of my childhood town is the old familiar surprise. But I stop, looking, for adult perception has in ten seconds clarified a childhood error. I have always thought of the Whitemud as running its whole course in a deeply sunken valley. Instead, I see that the river has cut deeply only through the uplift of the hills; that off to the southeast, out on the prairie, it crawls disconsolately flat across the land. It is a lesson in how peculiarly limited a child's sight is: he sees only what he can see. Only later does he learn to link what he sees with what he already knows, or has imagined or heard or read, and so come to make perception serve inference. During my childhood I kept hearing about the Cypress Hills, and knew that they were somewhere nearby. Now I see that I grew up in them. Without destroying the intense familiarity, the flooding recognition of the moment, that grown-up understanding throws things a little out of line, and so it is with mixed feelings of intimacy and strangeness that I start down the dugway grade. Things look the same, surprisingly the same, and yet obscurely different. I tick them off, easing watchfully back into the past.

There is the Frenchman's stone barn, westward up the river valley a couple of miles. It looks exactly as it did when we used to go through the farmyard in wagon or buckboard and see the startled kids disappearing around every corner, and peeking out at us from hayloft door and cowshed after we passed. Probably they were *métis,* halfbreeds; to us, who had never heard the word *métis,* they were simply Frenchmen, part of the vague and unknown past that had given our river one of its names. I bless them for their permanence, and creep on past the cemetery, somewhat larger and somewhat better kept than I remember it, but without disconcerting changes. Down below me is the dam, with its wide lake behind it. It takes me a minute to recollect that by the time we left Whitemud Pop Martin's dam had long since washed out. This is a new one, therefore, but in approximately the old place. So far, so good.

The road I bump along is still a dirt road, and it runs where it used to run, but the wildcat oil derrick that used to be visible from the turn at the foot of the grade is not there any longer. I note, coming in toward the edge of town, that the river has changed its course somewhat, swinging closer to the southern hills and pinching the road space. I see a black iron bridge, new, that evidently leads some new road off into the willow bottoms westward, toward the old Carpenter ranch. I cannot see the river, masked in willows and alders, and anyway my attention is taken by the town ahead of me, which all at once reveals one element of the obscure strangeness that has been making me watchful. Trees.

My town used to be as bare as a picked bone, with no tree anywhere around it larger than a ten-foot willow or alder. Now it is a grove. My memory gropes uneasily, trying to establish itself among fifty-foot cottonwoods, lilac and honeysuckle hedges, and flower gardens. Searched for, plenty of familiarities are there: the Pastime Theater, identical with the one that sits across Main Street from the firehouse in my mind; the lumber yard where we used to get cloth caps advertising De Laval Cream Separators; two or three hardware stores (a prairie wheat town specializes in hardware stores), though each one now has a lot full of farm machinery next to it; the hotel, just as it was rebuilt after the fire; the bank, now remodeled into the post office; the Presbyterian church, now United, and the *Leader* office, and the square brick prison of the school, now with three smaller prisons added to it. These are old acquaintances that I can check against their replicas in my head and take satisfaction from. But among them are the evidences of Progress—hospital, Masonic Lodge, at least one new elevator, a big quonset-like skating rink—and all tree-shaded, altered and distorted and made vaguely disturbing by greenery. In the old days we all used to try to grow trees, transplanting them from the Hills or getting them free with any two-dollar purchase from one of the stores, but they always dried up and died. To me, who came expecting a dusty hamlet, the change is charming, but memory has been fixed by time as photographs fix the faces of the dead, and this reality is dreamlike. I cannot find myself or my family or my companions in it.

My progress up Main Street, as wide and empty and dusty as I remember it, has taken me to another iron bridge across the eastern loop of the river, where the flume of Martin's irrigation ditch used to cross, and from the bridge I get a good view of the river. It is disappointing, a quiet creek twenty yards wide, the color of strong tea, its banks a tangle of willow and wild rose. How could adventure ever have inhabited those willows, or wonder, or fear, or the other remembered emotions? Was it along here I shot at the lynx with my brother's .25–.20? And out of what log (there is no possibility of a log in these brakes, but I distinctly remember a log) did my bullet knock chips just under the lynx's bobtail?

A muddy little stream, a village grown unfamiliar with time and trees. I turn around and retrace my way up Main Street and park and have a Coke in the confectionery store. It is run by a Greek, as it used to be, but whether the same Greek or another I would not know. He does not recognize me, nor I him. Only the smell of his place is familiar, syrupy with old delights, as if the ghost of my first banana split had come close to breathe on me. Still in search of something or someone to make the town fully real to me, I get the telephone book off its nail by the wall telephone and run through it, sitting at the counter. There are no more than seventy or eighty names in the Whitemud section. I look for Huffman—none. Bickerton—none. Fetter—none. Orullian—none. Stenhouse—none. Young—one, but not by a first name I remember. There are a few names I do remember—Harold Jones and William Christenson and Nels Sieverud and Jules LaPlante. (That last one startles me. I always thought his name was Jewell.) But all of the names I recognize are those of old-timers, pioneers of the town. Not a name that I went to school with, not a single person who would have shared as a contemporary my own experience of this town in its earliest years, when the river still ran clear and beaver swam in it in the evenings. Who in town remembers Phil Lott, who used to run coyotes with wolfhounds out on the South Bench? Who remembers in the way I do the day he drove up before Leaf's store in his democrat wagon and unloaded from it two dead hounds and the lynx that had killed them when they caught him unwarily exposed out on the flats? Who remembers in *my* way that angry and disgusted scene, and shares my recollection of the stiff, half-disemboweled bodies of the hounds and the bloody grin of the lynx? Who feels it or felt it, as I did and do, as a parable, a moral lesson for the pursuer to respect the pursued?

Because it is not shared, the memory seems fictitious, and so do other memories: the blizzard of 1916 that marooned us in the schoolhouse for a night and a day, the time the ice went out and brought both Martin's dam and the CPR bridge in kindling to our doors, the games of fox-and-geese in the untracked snow of a field that is now a grove, the nights of skating with a great fire leaping from the river ice and reflecting red from the cutbanks. I have used those memories for years as if they really happened, have made stories and novels of them. Now they seem uncorroborated and delusive. Some of the pioneers still in the telephone book would remember, but pioneers' memories are not good to me. Pioneers would remember the making of the town; to me, it was made, complete, timeless. A pioneer's child is what I need now, and in this town the pioneer's children did not stay, but went on, generally to bigger places, farther west, where there was more opportunity.

Sitting in the sticky-smelling, nostalgic air of the Greek's confectionery store, I am afflicted with the sense of how many whom I have known are dead, and how little evidence I have that I myself have lived what I remember. It is not quite the same feeling I imagined when I contemplated driving out to the homestead. That would have been absolute denial. This, with its tantalizing glimpses, its hints and survivals, is not denial but only doubt. There is enough left to disturb me, but not to satisfy me. So I will go a little closer. I will walk on down into the west bend and take a look at our house.

In the strange forest of the school yard the boys are friendly, and their universal air of health, openness, and curiosity reassures me. This is still a good town to be a boy in. To see a couple of them on the prowl with air rifles (in my time we would have been carrying .22's or shotguns, but we would have been of the same tribe) forces me to readjust my disappointed estimate of the scrub growth. When one is four feet high, ten-foot willows are a sufficient cover, and ten acres are a wilderness.

By now, circling and more than half unwilling, I have come into the west end of town, have passed Corky Jones's house (put off till later that meeting) and the open field beside Downs's where we used to play run-sheep-run in the evenings, and I stand facing the four-gabled white frame house that my father built. It ought to be explosive with nostalgias and bright with recollections, for this is where we lived for five or six of my most impressionable years, where we all nearly died with the flu in 1918, where my grandmother "went crazy" and had to be taken away by a Mountie to the Provincial asylum because she took to standing silently in the door of the room where my brother and I slept—just hovered there for heaven knows how long before someone discovered her watching and listening in the dark. I try to remember my grandmother's face and cannot; only her stale old-woman's smell after she became incontinent. I can summon up other smells, too—it is the smells that seem to have stayed with me: baking paint and hot tin and lignite smoke behind the parlor heater; frying scrapple,[4] which we called head-cheese, on chilly fall mornings after the slaughtering was done; the rich thick odor of doughnuts frying in a kettle of boiling lard (I always got to eat the "holes"). With effort, I can bring back Christmases, birthdays, Sunday School parties in that house, and I have not forgotten the licking I got when, aged about six, I was caught playing with my father's loaded .30–.30 that hung above the mantel just under the Rosa Bonheur painting of three white horses in a storm. After that licking I lay out behind the chopping block all one afternoon watching my big dark heavy father as he worked at one thing and another, and all the time I lay there I kept aiming an empty cartridge case at him and dreaming murder.

Even the dreams of murder, which were bright enough at the time, have faded; he is long dead, and if not forgiven, at least propitiated. My mother too, who saved me from him so many times, and once missed saving me when he clouted me with a chunk of stove wood and knocked me over the woodbox and broke my collar-bone: she too has faded. Standing there looking at the house where our lives entangled themselves in one another, I am infuriated that of that episode I remember less her love and protection and anger than my father's inept contrition. And walking all around the house trying to pump up recollection, I notice principally that the old barn is gone. What I see, though less changed than the town in general, still has power to disturb me; it is all dreamlike, less real than memory, less convincing than the recollected odors.

Whoever lives in the house now is a tidy housekeeper; the yard is neat, the porch swept. The corner where I used to pasture my broken-legged colt is a bed of flowers, the yard where we hopefully watered our baby spruces is a lawn enclosed by a green hedge. The old well with the hand pump is still in the side yard. For an instant my teeth are on edge with the memory of the dry screech of that pump before a dipperful of priming water took hold, and an instant later I feel the old stitch in my side from an even earlier time, the time when we still carried water from the river, and I dipped a bucket down into the hole in the ice and toted it, staggering and with the other arm stuck stiffly out, up the dugway to the kitchen door.

Those instants of memory are persuasive. I wonder if I should knock on the door and ask the housewife to let me look around, go upstairs to our old room in the west gable, examine the ceiling to see if the stains from the fire department's chemicals are still there. My brother and I used to lie in bed and imagine scenes and faces among the blotches, giving ourselves inadvertent Rorschach tests. I have a vivid memory, too, of the night the stains were made, when we came out into the hard cold from the Pastime Theater and heard the firehouse bell going and saw the volunteer fire department already on the run, and followed them up the ditch toward the glow of the fire, wondering whose house, until we got close and it was ours.

It is there, and yet it does not flow as it should, it is all a pumping operation. I half suspect that I am remembering not what happened but something I have written. I find that I am as unwilling to go inside the house as I was to try to find the old homestead in its ocean of grass. All the people who once shared the house with me are dead; strangers would have effaced or made doubtful the things that might restore them in my mind.

Behind our house there used to be a footbridge across the river, used by the Carpenters and others who lived in the bottoms, and by summer swimmers from town. I pass by the opaque and troubling house to the cutbank. The twin shanties that through all the town's life have served as men's and women's bath houses are still there. In winter we used to hang our frozen beef in one of them. I remember iron evenings when I went out with a lantern and sawed and haggled steaks from a rocklike hind quarter. But it is still an academic exercise; I only remember it, I do not feel the numb fingers and the fear that used to move just beyond the lantern's glow.

Then I walk to the cutbank edge and look down, and in one step the past comes closer than it has yet been. There is the gray curving cutbank, not much lower than I remember it when we dug cave holes in it or tunneled down its drifted cliff on our sleds. The bar is there at the inner curve of the bend, and kids are wallowing in a quicksandy mudhole and shrieking on an otter slide. They chase each other into the river and change magically from black to white. The water has its old quiet, its whirlpools spin lazily into deep water. On the footbridge, nearly exactly where it used to be, two little girls lie staring down into the water a foot below their noses. Probably they are watching suckers that lie just as quietly against the bottom. In my time we used to snare them from the bridge with nooses of cooper wire.

It is with me all at once, what I came hoping to re-establish, an ancient, unbearable recognition, and it comes partly from the children and the footbridge and the river's quiet curve, but much more from the smell. For here, pungent and pervasive, is the smell that has always meant my childhood. I have never smelled it anywhere else, and it is as evocative as Proust's madeleine and tea.

But what is it? Somehow I have always associated it with the bath house, with wet bathing suits and damp board benches, heaps of clothing, perhaps even the seldom rinsed corners where desperate boys had made water. I go into the men's bath house, and the smell is there, but it does not seem to come from any single thing. The whole air smells of it, outside as well as in. Perhaps it is the river water, or the mud, or something about the float and footbridge. It is the way the old burlap-tipped diving board used to smell; it used to remain in the head after a sinus-flooding dive.

I pick up a handful of mud and sniff it. I step over the little girls and bend my nose to the wet rail of the bridge. I stand above the water and sniff. On the other side I strip leaves off wild rose and dogwood. Nothing doing. And yet all around me is that odor that I have not smelled since I was eleven, but have never forgotten—have *dreamed,* more than once. Then I pull myself up the bank by a gray-leafed bush, and I have it. The tantalizing and ambiguous and wholly native smell is no more than the shrub we called wolf willow, now blooming with small yellow flowers.

It is wolf willow, and not the town or anyone in it, that brings me home. For a few minutes, with a handful of leaves to my nose, I look across at the clay bank and the hills beyond where the river loops back on itself, enclosing the old sports and picnic ground, and the present and all the years between are shed like a boy's clothes dumped on the bath-house bench. The perspective is what it used to be, the dimensions are restored, the senses are as clear as if they had not been battered with sensation for forty alien years. And the queer adult compulsion to return to one's beginnings is assuaged. A contact has been made, a mystery touched. For the moment, reality is made exactly equivalent with memory, and a hunger is satisfied. The sensuous little savage that I once was is still intact inside me.

Later, looking from the North Bench hills across my restored town, I can see the river where it shallows and crawls southeastward across the prairie toward the Milk, the Missouri, and the Gulf, and I toy with the notion that a man is like the river or the clouds, that he can be constantly moving and yet steadily renewed. The sensuous little savage, at any rate, has not been rubbed away or dissolved; he is as solid a part of me as my skeleton.

And he has a fixed and suitably arrogant relationship with his universe, a relationship geometrical and symbolic. From his center of sensation and question and memory and challenge, the circle of the world is measured, and in that respect the years of experience I have loaded upon my savage have not altered him. Lying on the hillside where I once sprawled among the crocuses, watching the town herd and snaring May's emerging gophers, I feel how the world still reduces me to a point and then measures itself from me. Perhaps the meadowlark singing from a fence post—a meadowlark whose dialect I recognize—feels the same way. All points on the circumference are equidistant from him; in him all radii begin; all diameters run through him; if he moves, a new geometry creates itself around him.

No wonder he sings. It is a good country that can make anyone feel so.

And it is a fact that once I have, so to speak, recovered myself as I used to be, I can look at the town, whose childhood was exactly contemporary with my own, with more understanding. It turns out to have been a special sort of town—special not only to me, in that it provided the indispensable sanctuary to match the prairie's exposure, but special in its belated concentration of Plains history. The successive stages of the Plains frontier flowed like a pageant through these Hills, and there are men still alive who remember almost the whole of it. My own recollections cover only a fragment; and yet it strikes me that this is *my* history. My disjunct, uprooted, cellular family was more typical than otherwise on the frontier. But more than we knew, we had our place in a human movement. What this town and its surrounding prairie grew from, and what they grew into, is the record of my tribe. If I am native to anything, I am native to this.

Notes

1. Stegner calls the town of East End "Whitemud" in *Wolf Willow*. Today the town's website promotes itself as "Dino Country" in honor of the star of the local fossil beds, "Scotty," a Tyrannosaurus Rex.—Eds.

2. *Métis* refers to a person of French and Indian descent, a term that arose during the time of the fur trade in the prairie regions of Canada and the northern United States.—Eds.

3. Kaolin is white clay used in making porcelain and, when mixed with feldspar, paper.—Eds.

4. Scrapple: scraps of pork or other meat boiled with cornmeal or flour and made into cakes that are then sliced and fried. Head cheese: a jellied loaf made from the edible parts of the head and feet of hogs or other animals, cut up, cooked, and seasoned.—Eds.

Further Reading

All the Little Live Things. 1967.
Beyond the Hundredth Meridian: John Wesley Powell and the Second Opening of the West. 1954.
Collected Stories. 1990.
Crossing to Safety. 1987.
Recapitulation. 1979.
The Sound of Mountain Water. 1969.
The Spectator Bird. 1976.
Where the Bluebird Sings to the Lemonade Springs: Living and Writing in the West. 1992.

Reading about Wallace Stegner

Lewis, Merrill and Lorene. *Wallace Stegner*. Western Writers Series. Boise ID: Boise State University, 1972.

Rankin, Charles E., ed. *Wallace Stegner: Man and Writer*. Albuquerque: University of New Mexico Press, 1996.

Stegner, Wallace, and Richard Etulain. *Conversations with Wallace Stegner on Western History and Literature*. Salt Lake City: University of Utah Press, 1983.

2. Natives and Newcomers on the Great Plains

First Stories: *Native American Accounts*

Native inhabitants of the Great Plains developed complex cultures with rich religious and social traditions long before European and American explorers and travelers focused attention on the economic and political potential of the region. Indigenous histories, ritual practices, and material cultures are derived from coping with the plains environment. Among themselves, the Indians of the Great Plains were often in competition for resources, and this competition created intertribal rivalries. For example, the Sioux Nation, one of the largest tribes of the plains, refer to themselves as Lakota and Dakota; yet they are known as Sioux, a term derived from the word for snake in Ojibwe, the language of their enemy. Compounding the regional conflicts was the arrival in the early nineteenth century of the Eastern tribes who had been removed by the expanding white population to the Great Plains, an expanse still regarded as the "Great American Desert" and at that point designated "Indian Territory." The Five Civilized Nations from the southeastern United States—Cherokee, Chicasaw, Choctaw, Creek, and Seminole—found themselves being forced to live among various tribes that were already established on the Great Plains.

With the advent of residential boarding schools many American Indians acquired the literacy and English writing skills to record their oral literary traditions and their own life stories. Often their works were written for non-Native audiences in the hope of validating tribal beliefs and, through sentimental rhetoric, urging social justice. To the discerning observer these recorded cultural traditions and tales reveal the complex relationships between humans and animals and between the solid physical world and the metaphysical vision of a corresponding mythic world; however, it was many years before these stories were regarded by most American readers as anything more than quaint folk tales that were suitable only for children's entertainment.

The motto from the Carlisle Industrial Training School in Pennsylvania was "Kill the Indian, Save the Man." Yet, as former students recorded their boarding school experiences they maintained a sense of tribal identity and survival. Their accounts are attempts to explain to their white readers the full significance of their own removal and that of thousands of other children who were sent across the continent to be "civilized." Among these authors who recount both tribal stories and their own life experiences are Zitkala-Ša (Gertrude Simmons Bonnin), Charles Eastman, Luther Standing Bear, Black Elk, and Ella Deloria. All are from the Sioux Nation, and all but Black Elk were well versed in mainstream education. Zitkala-Ša is among the first American Indians to write without the assistance of a translator or editor. While Deloria is a later writer and an anthropologist by training, she, too, tried to tell the stories of historic Sioux life through her novel *Waterlily*.

After almost a century of American Indian writings, Great Plains literature includes a rich Native tradition of tales and legends, autobiographies, and stories that later writers have layered and transformed into their own retellings. From the beginning these indigenous tales of the Great Plains have been firmly rooted in place, acknowledging and enacting the deep past of the Great Plains.

Reading about Plains Indians

Alberts, Patricia, and Beatrice Medicine. *The Hidden Half: Studies of Plains Indian Women.* Washington DC: University Press of America, 1983.

Fixico, Donald. *Rethinking American Indian History.* Albuquerque: University of New Mexico Press, 1997.

Fowler, Loretta. *Shared Symbols, Contested Meanings.* Ithaca: Cornell University Press, 1987.

Hoxie, Frederick E., Peter C. Mancall, and James H. Merrell, eds. *American Nations: Encounters in Indian Country, 1850 to the Present.* New York: Routledge, 2001.

Iverson, Peter, ed. *The Plains Indians of the Twentieth Century.* Norman: University of Oklahoma Press, 1985.

Limerick, Patricia Nelson. *The Legacy of Conquest: The Unbroken Past of the American West.* New York: Norton, 1987.

Zitkala-Ša (Gertrude Simmons Bonnin) *(1876–1938)*

This story is only one account of the origin of the buffalo on the plains. As a fundamental source of both food and stories for Plains Indians, the buffalo was crucial; their decimation was catastrophic. An unnamed Indian woman appears to be the hero figure of the story, but once her ailing husband recovers they work together, expressing the gender complementarity of Plains Indians. The moral of the tale is that generosity is rewarded and greed is punished. The man's power comes from the sacred emblems of Buffalo Medicine—drum, flute, deer hoof, rattles—and the sounds they make. The screech of the owl only adds to the man's power. Like Ella Deloria's story "The Buffalo People," this tale has a sense of timelessness because of its setting in the mythological past and continuing influences on Sioux world view.* Zitkala-Ša (Yankton Sioux) concludes her rendering of the tale by introducing Iktomi, the Sioux trickster, and reiterating the central theme. The trickster is a complicated figure who, through humor, misbehavior, and negative example socializes moral behavior.

Gertrude Simmons Bonnin was born on the Yankton Reservation in South Dakota on 22 February 1876.† She recounted her early years and boarding school education in a series of articles published in *Atlantic Monthly* at the turn of the twentieth century. At the same time she also published a collection of traditional Sioux tales, *Old Indian Legends*. While she is most known in literary circles for these early writings, she also co-composed an opera and led a full life of political activism. She edited *American Indian Magazine,* gave numerous speeches for the General Federated Women's Clubs, and investigated fraud within the Indian Rights Association in her book "Oklahoma's Poor Rich Indians." With her husband, Raymond, she organized the National Council of American Indians. Bonnin died in Washington DC in 1938.

When the Buffalo Herd Went West (2001)

From a teepee among the trees, an Indian woman came forth to gather the seed-fruit of the wild rose. It was early springtime. Great white clouds drifted in the sky.

*For a discussion of Deloria's story see Julian Rice, *Ella Deloria's The Buffalo People* (Albuquerque: University of New Mexico Press, 1994), 94–126.

†As a young woman Bonnin gave herself the Lakota name Zitkala-Ša, Red Bird.

Her hunter husband, crippled by accident in a buffalo chase, lay within the teepee, slowly recovering. Every day his faithful wife gathered the rose berries and cooked them. It was all the food they had.

While picking the red berries from the thorny bush one day, she heard a distant noise of hurrying hoof beats upon the ground. Looking up quickly in the direction from which the sound came, she beheld a man mounted on a snow white pony, chasing a maddened buffalo. Her bewildered eyes, as they lit upon the roaring shaggy buffalo, seemed to draw his course straight toward her. On came the buffalo and the man on the white pony in hot pursuit. Instinctively she jumped behind a near tree for protection. Close at her feet the buffalo fell dead!

The man, dismounting, said in undisguised surprise, "Oh how came you here?" The Indian woman stood silent by the tree, her protector. She was loathe to speak to a stranger. The hunter did not wait for her reply. "You shall have choice meat, if you wait here and watch me cut up the buffalo," he said as he flourished a knife.

She watched him disrobe the dead buffalo and cut his bones asunder. He talked loud and fast all the while. He boasted of his prowess as a hunter and his unsurpassed skill with the knife. He claimed that he could carve a buffalo in the twinkling of an eye. He told of his wonderful generosity, how he always gave the choicest meats to the sick and hungry. Never a moment did he lose in his self praise. Having finished the carving of the buffalo he carried the meat, piece by piece, and packed it on his pony. The Indian woman who had waited, looking wistfully upon the tender steak, had said in her heart, "I will broil it upon the red hot coals for my sick husband." Now there was nothing left for her. The man of empty words, ready to go, tossed the tripe away, as if throwing it to a dog. He said, "Take that and make a good soup." Leading his pony laden with much meat, he went his way.

The woman hurried to her husband in the teepee and told him all that had happened. Carefully she washed the tripe and dashing boiling water upon it removed the outer skin until it was every whit clean and white. Over the center fire she cooked it quickly. It made a savory soup. Famished for long weary days, they ate the soup with a relish. The husband said he felt himself growing stronger. Both rejoiced that before long he would be able to go again in the hunt. Then they would have all the buffalo meat and venison that they could eat and some to share with their neighbors, somewhere in the big world.

It was after this occurrence, the soup having been eaten up, they were again very hungry. The woman went out to gather the rose berries. Her trained eye spied the same strange hunter, on his fleet white pony, chasing another buffalo! Again he killed it and began at once to cut it up. She was hungry but coveted the buffalo meat more for her sick husband than for herself. She stood close by, watching the strange man and his plunder. He chattered and chattered like a magpie. "I am the greatest hunter in the world. I am the most generous man in the world. I always give away the choicest pieces. I have great food bags stored in my teepee. I never hunger." Again, as he talked, he packed all the meat away, only the tripe, which he tossed aside, saying, "Take that and make soup with it."

This time, the woman became indignant and said, "Whoever you may be, you are the most unkind man in the world. You are a man of empty words. You boast of giving choice meat to the sick and poor, but instead you keep the best portion, only giving away the tripe. Now I am going to tell this to my husband, who is a medicine man. He will get his sacred drum, sing his mystery song, and no buffalo will come nigh you. He will scare the buffalo away from you."

The stranger shook with a sudden palsy—"Yun! Yun! Yun!" He groaned in pain. "Do not tell him! Do not let him bring his drum. I fear only four things in this world. These are the drum, flute, deer hoof rattles, and the screech owl. Do not let him bring any of these four wakan things and I will give you much meat. Every day I will come chasing the buffalo." He gave the woman all the meat she could carry. She went home and told her husband what had happened. He listened attentively. Being a man who understood many mysteries of the invisible power, he at once knew the stranger was misusing some sacred gift. "Let him fulfill his promises," he said.

But the man with the white pony failed to return. The Dakota and his wife again were without food. They made a drum and a deer hoof rattle. They traveled across a prairie in search of that man of empty words. With these four fears they would destroy him. They found his teepee. They approached it straight as an arrow flies and took their places on either side of the entrance way. The woman shook the deer hoof rattle and blew upon the flute; the man beat upon the sacred drum and hooted like an owl.

Out rushed the man of empty words, with his fingers stopping his ears. Like a mad man, he ran, shrieking, into the thick woods. The man and wife cautiously lifted the teepee door and peered into the cone shaped dwelling. The walls were lined with great food bags—bags that were decorated handsomely with beads and porcupine quills. They were filled to brim with dried meats and dried fruits and roots.

They entered in. From a tall pole hung a large bladder beautifully embroidered in the most wonderful designs with brightly colored quills. Ordinarily plain and undecorated bladders were filled with beef tallow and put away in the food bags. Very queer indeed that one should be decorated and hung upon a pole at the center of the teepee. This was certainly unusual. The man scrutinized it from a safe distance, reading some of the old symbols worked upon it. At last he whispered to his wife. "This appears to me like a powerful magic bag. It may be one of the ancient bags made at the beginning of the world." Nodding her head in assent, the wife gazed on the large bladder. It was very old; its skin was tough and wrinkled. It was tied at the neck with the sinews of the moose.

Many moons they lived in this teepee, where there was an abundance of dried meats and fruits. The man was now fully recovered, but one thing troubled them. It was the magic bag hanging overhead! Sometimes this bladder became agitated.

It swayed to and fro upon the string when there was no wind blowing without the teepee. At such times a tumultuous murmur as of many voices and noises issued from the bladder. There were sounds of hoof beats and the rumble of trampling herds, the bellowing of the buffalo mingled with the neighing of horses; far away shouts of men and women above the rattle of drum and clatter of gourds, dogs barking and coyotes howling. There seemed to be a faint trembling of the earth.

At such times the man and his wife sat in profound awe, eyeing the swaying old bladder. They burnt sweet herbs in smoke prayers to the Great Spirit.

At length their food bags were empty. They began to talk of going on a long hunt. One day as the sun hung low in the west, the woman went into the nearby woods to bring some sticks for the camp fire. She went about picking up fagots here and there. She came upon an old decayed log lying across her way. There, hiding under this log lay a frightened old man, the man of empty words.

He was terribly afraid at sight of her. He screeched out, "He! He! He! Do not harm me! Listen! In my teepee you have seen a bladder hanging. When you are out of meat you must untie the neck of the bladder and open it a little way. A buffalo will come out. Open it a little farther and a white pony will come out. Then close the bladder and let your husband mount the white pony and chase the buffalo. Thus you will always have plenty of meat."

Astounded by the man hiding like a culprit in the wildwood and who, begging for his life, told the sacred secret about the bladder, which no man dared to betray—she looked quickly around on all sides, like a deer, alert to see if any object moved in the quiet landscape. She turned to look again at the man. She saw nothing but an artichoke weed. She returned to the teepee and told her husband all she had seen and heard in the woods.

"Well then, let us open the magic bladder!" said he. They took it carefully down from the pole, carried it out of doors, and unloosed the neck of the bladder. Immediately a wild buffalo ran out, bellowing and pawing upon the earth, and a white pony followed closely behind.

They tied the bladder and the man caught the white pony, mounted it without saddle or bridle, and chased and killed the buffalo! Thus they had meat and skins in plenty. Never in their whole lives had they tasted such savory, tender meat. They talked together of sharing their game with their people. The man praised the fleetness of the pony's feet. He had never before mounted such a steed! He traveled like the wind! "At day break tomorrow I will ride him again. I shall go forth to invite the world to feast with us. For tonight I have tied the pony to our teepee pole that no prowling enemy may steal him away."

The next day the first streak of dawn awoke them. Their first thought was of the white pony. They went out together to water him at the river. He was gone! Only the rawhide rope remained tied to the tent at one end and a loop large enough for a horse's neck at the other. There was no track or sign of him save a white fleck in the sky. "I guess he is that white cloud in the sky! He is gone beyond our reach," sighed the man in deep regret.

Still, as the sun rose higher and higher, the man thought more and more about the white pony, saying, "I shall go on foot to invite the world and perhaps I may come upon the white pony on my way." He left his teepee.

During his absence, a tall, gaunt, man-like creature appeared at the oval teepee door. The Indian woman recognized old Iktomi, the mischief maker of camps. Unguardedly she told him of the white pony. She asked him if he had seen it on his way hither. "No, I have not seen any horse at all," Iktomi answered, twisting and twisting his neck, looking upward at the mystery pouch. He grew wild with curiosity. He startled her by suddenly declaring "I am going to open the mystery pouch! I want a buffalo to hunt and a white pony to ride." Oh hateful Iktomi, Mischief Maker! He always spoiled the happiness of others. In spite of her pleas not to touch the sacred bag, he strode roughly by her; he pushed her aside, saying, "You told me about its magic, now I am going to try it." He took down the magic pouch and carried out of doors. In his haste to untie the neck of the bladder, his clumsy fingers dropped the pouch to the ground! It fell wide open. Instantly a great herd of buffalo stampeded! A herd so great that it was impossible to number them. They rushed by, in a mad fury, bellowing shrilly and roaring with a voice of thunder. Under their hoofs the earth shook. They trampled upon Iktomi, the woman, and the tent. This, they say, is when the buffalo herd went west.

Further Reading

American Indian Stories. 1921; rpt. 1985.

Dreams and Thunder: Stories, Poems and the Sun Dance Opera by Zitkala-Ša. Ed. P. Jane Hafen. 2001.

Old Indian Legends. 1901; rpt. 1985.

Reading about Zitkala-Ša

Coleman, Michael. *American Indian Children at School: 1850–1930.* Jackson: University of Mississippi Press, 1993.

Deloria, Vine, Jr. *Singing for a Spirit: A Portrait of the Dakota Sioux.* Santa Fe: Clear Light Publishers, 1999.

Rappaport, Doreen. *The Flight of Red Bird: The Life of Zitkala-Ša.* New York: Dial, 1997.

Ruoff, A. LaVonne Brown. "Early Native American Women Authors: Jane Johnston Schoolcraft, Sarah Winnemucca, S. Alice Callahan, E. Pauline Johnson, and Zitkala-Ša." *Nineteenth-century American Women Writers: A Critical Reader.* Ed. Karen L. Kilcup. Malden MA: Blackwell, 1998.

Spack, Ruth. *America's Second Tongue: American Indian Education and the Ownership of English, 1860–1900.* Lincoln: University of Nebraska Press, 2002.

Willard, William. "Zitkala-Ša: A Woman Who Would Be Heard!" *Wicazo Sa Review* 1.1 (spring 1985): 11–16.

Charles Eastman (Ohiyesa) *(1888–1939)*

In "A Legend of Devil's Lake" Charles Eastman (Dakota) frames a narrative to accentuate the oral tradition of the story. Within that frame the narrator-listener sets forth proper and courteous behaviors. The tale is connected to specific geographic references. The story also invokes entities with great spiritual power among the Sioux: The Great Mystery (Wakan Tanka) and Lightning Beings.

During the 1862 Minnesota Sioux uprising when his father was imprisoned for taking part in it, four-year-old Eastman's Sioux relatives took him to Manitoba. Until he was fifteen he stayed with them and lived in a traditional setting. Then his father returned and he began Eastman's education in white schools. Eventually Eastman earned degrees from Dartmouth College and Boston University Medical School. He set up practice on South Dakota's Pine Ridge Reservation in 1890, an inauspicious time for the Sioux. The Ghost Dance religion stirred religious fervor among the tribes on the northern plains and then fear among whites that led, ultimately, to the massacre at Wounded Knee and to Eastman's resignation from his reservation post. Eastman found it difficult to establish a medical practice and spent most of his career working in Indian affairs.

In his many books Eastman, sometimes in collaboration with his wife, Elaine Goodale Eastman, presents and explains Sioux life and culture. *Indian Boyhood* (1902), an amalgam of autobiography and Sioux stories, focuses on his life among the Sioux. *From the Deep Woods to Civilization* (1916) recounts his frustrations and conflicts in blending his Sioux culture with a white world that is indifferent to his culture and to the suffering that persisted into the twentieth century. In all of his works Eastman attempts to bridge the divide between Sioux and white cultures, explaining the virtues of Sioux religion, the ideals of Sioux leaders, and the value of Sioux legends. His intended audience includes his own children and white adults and children. Many of his works remain in print, valuable as historical records and good reading.

A Legend of Devil's Lake (1902)

After the death of Smoky Day, old Weyuha was regarded as the greatest storyteller among the Wahpeton Sioux.

"Tell me, good Weyuha, a legend of your father's country," I said to him one evening, for I knew the country which is now known as North Dakota and South-ern Manitoba was their ancient hunting-ground. I was prompted by Uncheedah to make this request, after the old man had eaten in our lodge.

"Many years ago," he began, as he passed the pipe to uncle, "we traveled from the Otter-tail to Minnewakan (Devil's Lake). At that time the mound was very distinct where Chotanka lies buried. The people of his immediate band had taken care to preserve it.

"This mound under which lies the great medicine man is upon the summit of Minnewakan Chantay, the highest hill in all that region. It is shaped like an ani-mal's heart placed on its base, with the apex upward.

"The reason why this hill is called Minnewakan Chantay, or the Heart of the Mysterious Land, I will now tell you. It has been handed down from generation to generation, far beyond the memory of our great-grandparents. It was in Cho-tanka's line of descent that these legends were originally kept, but when he died the stories became everybody's, and then no one believed in them. It was told in this way."

I sat facing him, wholly wrapped in the words of the story-teller, and now I took a deep breath and settled myself so that I might not disturb him by the slightest movement while he was reciting his tale. We were taught this courtesy to our elders, but I was impulsive and sometimes forgot.

"A long time ago," resumed Weyuha, "the red people were many in number, and they inhabited all the land from the coldest place to the region of perpetual summer time. It seemed that they were all of one tongue, and all were friends.

"All the animals were considered people in those days. The buffalo, the elk, the antelope, were tribes of considerable importance. The bears were a smaller band, but they obeyed the mandates of the Great Mystery and were his favorites, and for this reason they have always known more about the secrets of medicine. So they were held in much honor. The wolves, too, were highly regarded at one time. But the buffalo, elk, moose, deer and antelope were the ruling people.

"These soon became conceited and considered themselves very important, and thought no one could withstand them. The buffalo made war upon the smaller tribes, and destroyed many. So one day the Great Mystery thought it best to change the people in form and in language.

"He made a great tent and kept it dark for ten days. Into this tent he invited the different bands, and when they came out they were greatly changed, and some could not talk at all after that. However, there is a sign language given to all the animals that no man knows except some medicine men, and they are under a heavy penalty if they should tell it.

"The buffalo came out of the darkened tent the clumsiest of all the animals. The elk and moose were burdened with their heavy and many-branched horns, while the antelope and deer were made the most defenseless of animals, only that they are fleet of foot. The bear and the wolf were made to prey upon all the others.

"Man was alone then. When the change came, the Great Mystery allowed him to keep his own shape and language. He was king over all the animals, but they did not obey him. From that day, man's spirit may live with the beasts before he is born a man. He will then know the animal language but he cannot tell it in human speech. He always retains his sympathy with them, and can converse with them in dreams.

"I must not forget to tell you that the Great Mystery pitched his tent in this very region. Some legends say that the Minnewakan Chantay was the tent itself, which afterward became earth and stones. Many of the animals were washed and changed in this lake, the Minnewakan, or Mysterious Water. It is the only inland water we know that is salt. No animal has ever swum in this lake and lived."

"Tell me," I eagerly asked, "is it dangerous to man also?"

"Yes," he replied, "we think so; and no Indian has ever ventured in that lake to my knowledge. That is why the lake is called Mysterious," he repeated.

"I shall now tell you of Chotanka. He was the greatest of medicine men. He declared that he was a grizzly bear before he was born in human form." Weyuha seemed to become very earnest when he reached this point in his story. "Listen to Chotanka's life as a grizzly bear."

" 'As a bear,' he used to say, 'my home was in sight of the Minnewakan Chantay. I lived with my mother only one winter, and I only saw my father when I was a baby. Then we lived a little way from the Chantay to the north, among scattered oak upon a hillside overlooking the Minnewakan.

" 'When I first remember anything, I was playing outside of our home with a buffalo skull that I had found near by. I saw something that looked strange. It walked upon two legs, and it carried a crooked stick, and some red willows with feathers tied to them. It threw one of the willows at me, and I showed my teeth and retreated within our den.

" 'Just then my father and mother came home with a buffalo calf. They threw down the dead calf, and ran after the queer thing. He had long hair upon a round head. His face was round, too. He ran and climbed up into a small oak tree.

" 'My father and mother shook him down, but not before he had shot some of his red willows into their sides. Mother was very sick, but she dug some roots and ate them and she was well again.' It was thus that Chotanka was first taught the use of certain roots for curing wounds and sickness," Weyuha added.

" 'One day' "—he resumed the grizzly's story—" 'when I was out hunting with my mother—my father had gone away and never came back—we found a buffalo cow with her calf in a ravine. She advised me to follow her closely, and we crawled along on our knees. All at once mother crouched down under the grass, and I did the same. We saw some of those queer beings that we called "two legs," riding upon big-tail deer (ponies). They yelled as they rode toward us. Mother growled terribly and rushed upon them. She caught one, but many more came with their dogs and drove us into a thicket. They sent the red willows singing after us, and two of them stuck in mother's side. When we got away at last she tried to pull them out, but they hurt her terribly. She pulled them both out at last, but soon after she lay down and died.

" 'I stayed in the woods alone for two days; then I went around the Minnewakan Chantay on the south side and there made my lonely den. There I found plenty of hazel nuts, acorns and wild plums. Upon the plains the teepsinna were abundant, and I saw nothing of my enemies.

" 'One day I found a footprint not unlike my own. I followed it to see who the stranger might be. Upon the bluffs among the oak groves I discovered a beautiful young female gathering acorns. She was of a different band from mine, for she wore a jet black dress.

" 'At first she was disposed to resent my intrusion; but when I told her of my lonely life she agreed to share it with me. We came back to my home on the south side of the hill. There we lived happy for a whole year. When the autumn came again Woshepee, for this was her name, said that she must make a warm nest for the winter, and I was left alone again.'

"Now," said Weyuha, "I have come to a part of my story that few people understand. All the long winter Chotanka slept in his den, and with the early spring there came a great thunder storm. He was aroused by a frightful crash that seemed to shake the hills; and lo! a handsome young man stood at his door. He looked, but was not afraid, for he saw that the stranger carried none of those red willows with feathered tips. He was unarmed and smiling.

" 'I come,' said he, 'with a challenge to run a race. Whoever wins will be the hero of his kind, and the defeated must do as the winner says thereafter. This is a rare honor that I have brought you. The whole world will see the race. The animal world will shout for you, and the spirits will cheer me on. You are not a coward, and therefore you will not refuse my challenge.'

" 'No,' replied Chotanka, after a short hesitation. The young man was fine-looking, but lightly built.

" 'We shall start from the Chantay, and that will be our goal. Come, let us go, for the universe is waiting!' impatiently exclaimed the stranger.

"He passed on in advance, and just then an old, old wrinkled man came to Chotanka's door. He leaned forward upon his staff.

" 'My son,' he said to him, 'I don't want to make you a coward, but this young man is the greatest gambler of the universe. He has powerful medicine. He gambles for life; be careful! My brothers and I are the only ones who have ever beaten him. But he is safe, for if he is killed he can resurrect himself—I tell you he is great medicine.

" 'However, I think that I can save you—listen! He will run behind you all the way until you are within a short distance of the goal. Then he will pass you by in a flash, for his name is Zig-Zag Fire! (lightning). Here is my medicine.' So speaking, he gave me a rabbit skin and the gum of a certain plant. 'When you come near the goal, rub yourself with the gum, and throw the rabbit skin between you. He cannot pass you.'

" 'And who are you, grandfather?' Chotanka inquired.

" 'I am the medicine turtle,' the old man replied. 'The gambler is a spirit from heaven, and those whom he outruns must shortly die. You have heard, no doubt, that all animals know beforehand when they are to be killed; and any man who understands these mysteries may also know when he is to die.'

"The race was announced to the world. The buffalo, elk, wolves and all the animals came to look on. All the spirits of the air came also to cheer for their comrade. In the sky the trumpet was sounded—the great medicine drum was struck. It was the signal for a start. The course was around the Minnewakan. (That means around the earth or the ocean.) Everywhere the multitude cheered as the two sped by.

"The young man kept behind Chotanka all the time until they came once more in sight of the Chantay. Then he felt a slight shock and he threw his rabbit skin back. The stranger tripped and fell. Chotanka rubbed himself with the gum, and ran on until he reached the goal. There was a great shout that echoed over the earth, but in the heavens there was muttering and grumbling. The referee declared that the winner would live to a good old age, and Zig-Zag Fire promised to come at his call. He was indeed great medicine," Weyuha concluded.

"But you have not told me how Chotanka became a man," I said.

"One night a beautiful woman came to him in his sleep. She enticed him into her white teepee to see what she had there. Then she shut the door of the teepee and Chotanka could not get out. But the woman was kind and petted him so that he loved to stay in the white teepee. Then it was that he became a human born. This is a long story, but I think, Ohiyesa, that you will remember it," said Weyuha, and so I did.

Further Reading

Old Indian Days. 1907.
The Soul of the Indian. 1911; rpt. 1980.

Reading about Charles Eastman

Copeland, Marion. *Charles Eastman.* Western Writers Series. Boise ID: Boise State University, 1978.

Eastman, Elaine Goodale. *Sister to the Sioux: The Memoir of Elaine Goodale Eastman 1885–1891.* Ed. Kay Graber. Lincoln: University of Nebraska Press, 1978.

McAllister, Mick. "American Indian Autobiographical Works." *Updating the Literary West.* Fort Worth: Texas Christian University Press, 1997. 141–49.

O'Brien, Lynn Woods. *Plains Indian Autobiography*. Western Writers Series. Boise: Boise State University. 1978.

Ruoff, A. LaVonne Brown. "Western American Indian Writers, 1854–1960." *Literary History of the American West*. Fort Worth: Texas Christian University Press, 1987. 1038–57.

Wilson, Raymond. *Ohiyesa: Charles Eastman, Santee Sioux*. Urbana: University of Illinois Press, 1983.

John G. Neihardt (1881–1973)

Black Elk (1863–1950), an Oglala holy man, lived through a period of incredible transition for the Sioux Nation. His narrative, told through the writing of John G. Neihardt, covers major events in the history of Plains Indians: the establishment of reservations, the Fetterman Battle, the Battle at the Little Big Horn (1876), and the massacre of Wounded Knee (1890). Black Elk even participated in Buffalo Bill's Wild West Show and traveled to Europe. All of these events pale alongside Black Elk's "Great Vision" in which as a young man he witnessed emblems and symbols that came to represent the spiritual foundations of the great Sioux Nation. Black Elk's description of the Sacred Hoop combined with the cardinal directions points to the wholeness of the earth itself. As Vine Deloria notes in the introduction to *Black Elk Speaks*, "To [a contemporary generation of young Indians] the book has become a North American bible of all tribes. They look to it for spiritual guidance, for sociological identity, for political insight, and for affirmation of the continuing substance of Indian tribal life."*

Literary and critical scholars have addressed Neihardt's role in telling Black Elk's narrative. Neihardt shaped the tragic ending, in which the flowering tree of hope and the future withers and Black Elk weeps in despair. *Black Elk Speaks* omits a description of more than half of Black Elk's life and his service to his tribal community. Providing a context and fuller view, Raymond J. DeMallie's *Sixth Grandfather* relies on stenographic notes of Neihardt's daughter, Enid. The most recent University of Nebraska Press edition of *Black Elk Speaks* includes ledger-style illustrations by Spotted Elk.

The Great Vision (1932)

What happened after that until the summer I was nine years old is not a story. There were winters and summers, and they were good; for the Wasichus had made their iron road[1] along the Platte and traveled there. This had cut the bison herd in two, but those that stayed in our country with us were more than could be counted, and we wandered without trouble in our land.

---

*Vine Deloria Jr., foreword in John G. Neihardt, *Black Elk Speaks* (1932; rpt. twenty-first-century edition, Lincoln: University of Nebraska Press, 2000), xiii.

Now and then the voices would come back when I was out alone, like someone calling me, but what they wanted me to do I did not know. This did not happen very often, and when it did not happen, I forgot about it; for I was growing taller and was riding horses now and could shoot prairie chickens and rabbits with my bow. The boys of my people began very young to learn the ways of men, and no one taught us; we just learned by doing what we saw, and we were warriors at a time when boys now are like girls.

It was the summer when I was nine years old, and our people were moving slowly towards the Rocky Mountains. We camped one evening in a valley beside a little creek just before it ran into the Greasy Grass,[2] and there was a man by the name of Man Hip who liked me and asked me to eat with him in his tepee.

While I was eating, a voice came and said: "It is time; now they are calling you." The voice was so loud and clear that I believed it, and I thought I would just go where it wanted me to go. So I got right up and started. As I came out of the tepee, both my thighs began to hurt me, and suddenly it was like waking from a dream, and there wasn't any voice. So I went back into the tepee, but I didn't want to eat. Man Hip looked at me in a strange way and asked me what was wrong. I told him that my legs were hurting me.

The next morning the camp moved again, and I was riding with some boys. We stopped to get a drink from a creek, and when I got off my horse, my legs crumpled under me and I could not walk. So the boys helped me up and put me on my horse; and when we camped again that evening, I was sick. The next day the camp moved on to where the different bands of our people were coming together, and I rode in a pony drag, for I was very sick. Both my legs and both my arms were swollen badly and my face was all puffed up.

When we had camped again, I was lying in our tepee and my mother and father were sitting beside me. I could see out through the opening, and there two men were coming from the clouds, head-first like arrows slanting down, and I knew they were the same that I had seen before. Each now carried a long spear, and from the points of these a jagged lightning flashed. They came clear down to the ground this time and stood a little way off and looked at me and said: "Hurry! Come! Your Grandfathers are calling you!"

Then they turned and left the ground like arrows slanting upward from the bow. When I got up to follow, my legs did not hurt me any more and I was very light. I went outside the tepee, and yonder where the men with flaming spears were going, a little cloud was coming very fast. It came and stooped and took me and turned back to where it came from, flying fast. And when I looked down I could see my mother and my father yonder, and I felt sorry to be leaving them.

Then there was nothing but the air and the swiftness of the little cloud that bore me and those two men still leading up to where white clouds were piled like mountains on a wide blue plain, and in them thunder beings lived and leaped and flashed.

Now suddenly there was nothing but a world of cloud, and we three were there alone in the middle of a great white plain with snowy hills and mountains staring at us; and it was very still; but there were whispers.

Then the two men spoke together and they said: "Behold him, the being with four legs!"

I looked and saw a bay horse standing there, and he began to speak: "Behold me!" he said, "My life-history you shall see." Then he wheeled about to where the sun goes down, and said: "Behold them! Their history you shall know."

I looked, and there were twelve black horses yonder all abreast with necklaces of bison hoofs, and they were beautiful, but I was frightened, because their manes were lightning and there was thunder in their nostrils.

Then the bay horse wheeled to where the great white giant lives (the north) and said: "Behold!" And yonder there were twelve white horses all abreast. Their manes were flowing like a blizzard wind and from their noses came a roaring, and all about them white geese soared and circled.

Then the bay wheeled round to where the sun shines continually (the east) and bade me look; and there twelve sorrel horses, with necklaces of elk's teeth, stood abreast with eyes that glimmered like the day-break star and manes of morning light.

Then the bay wheeled once again to look upon the place where you are always facing (the south), and yonder stood twelve buckskins all abreast with horns upon their heads and manes that lived and grew like trees and grasses.

And when I had seen all these, the bay horse said: "Your Grandfathers are having a council. These shall take you; so have courage."

Then all the horses went into formation, four abreast—the blacks, the whites, the sorrels, and the buckskins—and stood behind the bay, who turned now to the west and neighed; and yonder suddenly the sky was terrible with a storm of plunging horses in all colors that shook the world with thunder, neighing back.

Now turning to the north the bay horse whinnied, and yonder all the sky roared with a mighty wind of running horses in all colors, neighing back.

And when he whinnied to the east, there too the sky was filled with glowing clouds of manes and tails of horses in all colors singing back. Then to the south he called, and it was crowded with many colored, happy horses, nickering.

Then the bay horse spoke to me again and said: "See how your horses all come dancing!" I looked, and there were horses, horses everywhere—a whole skyful of horses dancing round me.

"Make haste!" the bay horse said; and we walked together side by side, while the blacks, the whites, the sorrels, and the buckskins followed, marching four by four.

I looked about me once again, and suddenly the dancing horses without number changed into animals of every kind and into all the fowls that are, and these fled back to the four quarters of the world from whence the horses came, and vanished.

Then as we walked, there was a heaped up cloud ahead that changed into a tepee, and a rainbow was the open door of it; and through the door I saw six old men sitting in a row.

The two men with the spears now stood beside me, one on either hand, and the horses took their places in their quarters, looking inward, four by four. And the oldest of the Grandfathers spoke with a kind voice and said: "Come right in and do not fear." And as he spoke, all the horses of the four quarters neighed to cheer me. So I went in and stood before the six, and they looked older than men can ever be—old like hills, like stars.

The oldest spoke again: "Your Grandfathers all over the world are having a council, and they have called you here to teach you." His voice was very kind, but I shook all over with fear now, for I knew that these were not old men, but the Powers of the World. And the first was the Power of the West; the second, of the North; the third, of the East; the fourth, of the South; the fifth, of the Sky; the sixth, of the Earth. I knew this, and was afraid, until the first Grandfather spoke again: "Behold them yonder where the sun goes down, the thunder beings! You shall see, and have from them my power; and they shall take you to the high and lonely center of the earth that you may see; even to the place where the sun continually shines, they shall take you there to understand."

And as he spoke of understanding, I looked up and saw the rainbow leap with flames of many colors over me.

Now there was a wooden cup in his hand and it was full of water and in the water was the sky.

"Take this," he said. "It is the power to make live, and it is yours."

Now he had a bow in his hands. "Take this," he said. "It is the power to destroy, and it is yours."

Then he pointed to himself and said: "Look close at him who is your spirit now, for you are his body and his name is Eagle Wing Stretches."

And saying this, he got up very tall and started running toward where the sun goes down; and suddenly he was a black horse that stopped and turned and looked at me, and the horse was very poor and sick; his ribs stood out.

Then the second Grandfather, he of the North, arose with a herb of power in his hand, and said: "Take this and hurry." I took and held it toward the black horse yonder. He fattened and was happy and came prancing to his place again and was the first Grandfather sitting there.

The second Grandfather, he of the North, spoke again: "Take courage, younger brother," he said; "on earth a nation you shall make live, for yours shall be the power of the white giant's wing, the cleansing wind." Then he got up very tall and started running toward the north; and when he turned toward me, it was a white goose wheeling. I looked about me now, and the horses in the west were thunders and the horses of the north were geese. And the second Grandfather sang two songs that were like this:

"They are appearing, may you behold!
They are appearing, may you behold!
The thunder nation is appearing, behold!

They are appearing, may you behold!
They are appearing, may you behold!
The white geese nation is appearing, behold!"

And now it was the third Grandfather who spoke, he of where the sun shines continually. "Take courage, younger brother," he said, "for across the earth they shall take you!" Then he pointed to where the daybreak star was shining, and beneath the star two men were flying. "From them you shall have power," he said, "from them who have awakened all the beings of the earth with roots and legs and wings." And as he said this, he held in his hand a peace pipe which had a spotted eagle outstretched upon the stem; and this eagle seemed alive, for it was poised there, fluttering, and its eyes were looking at me. "With this pipe," the Grandfather said, "you shall walk upon the earth, and whatever sickens there you shall make well." Then he pointed to a man who was bright red all over, the color of good and of plenty, and as he pointed, the red man lay down and rolled and changed into a bison that got up and galloped toward the sorrel horses of the east, and they too turned to bison, fat and many.

And now the fourth Grandfather spoke, he of the place where you are always facing (the south), whence comes the power to grow. "Younger brother," he said, "with the powers of the four quarters you shall walk, a relative. Behold, the living center of a nation I shall give you, and with it many you shall save." And I saw that he was holding in his hand a bright red stick that was alive, and as I looked it sprouted at the top and sent forth branches, and on the branches many leaves came out and murmured and in the leaves the birds began to sing. And then for just a little while I thought I saw beneath it in the shade the circled villages of people and every living thing with roots or legs or wings, and all were happy. "It shall stand in the center of the nation's circle," said the Grandfather, "a cane to walk with and a people's heart; and by your powers you shall make it blossom."

Then when he had been still a little while to hear the birds sing, he spoke again: "Behold the earth!" So I looked down and saw it lying yonder like a hoop of peoples, and in the center bloomed the holy stick that was a tree, and where it stood there crossed two roads, a red one and a black. "From where the giant lives (the north) to where you always face (the south) the red road goes, the road of good," the Grandfather said, "and on it shall your nation walk. The black road goes from where the thunder beings live (the west) to where the sun continually shines (the east), a fearful road, a road of troubles and of war. On this also you shall walk, and from it you shall have the power to destroy a people's foes. In four ascents you shall walk the earth with power."

I think he meant that I should see four generations, counting me, and now I am seeing the third.

Then he rose very tall and started running toward the south, and was an elk; and as he stood among the buckskins yonder, they too were elks.

Now the fifth Grandfather spoke, the oldest of them all, the Spirit of the Sky. "My boy," he said, "I have sent for you and you have come. My power you shall see!" He stretched his arms and turned into a spotted eagle hovering. "Behold," he said, "all the wings of the air shall come to you, and they and the winds and the stars shall be like relatives. You shall go across the earth with my power." Then the eagle soared above my head and fluttered there; and suddenly the sky was full of friendly wings all coming toward me.

Now I knew the sixth Grandfather was about to speak, he who was the Spirit of the Earth, and I saw that he was very old, but more as men are old. His hair was long and white, his face was all in wrinkles and his eyes were deep and dim. I stared at him, for it seemed I knew him somehow; and as I stared, he slowly changed, for he was growing backwards into youth, and when he had become a boy, I knew that he was myself with all the years that would be mine at last. When he was old again, he said: "My boy, have courage, for my power shall be yours, and you shall need it, for your nation on the earth will have great troubles. Come."

He rose and tottered out through the rainbow door, and as I followed I was riding on the bay horse who had talked to me at first and led me to that place.

Then the bay horse stopped and faced the black horses of the west, and a voice said: "They have given you the cup of water to make live the greening day, and also the bow and arrow to destroy." The bay neighed, and the twelve black horses came and stood behind me, four abreast.

The bay faced the sorrels of the east, and I saw that they had morning stars upon their foreheads and they were very bright. And the voice said: "They have given you the sacred pipe and the power that is peace, and the good red day." The bay neighed, and the twelve sorrels stood behind me, four abreast.

My horse now faced the buckskins of the south, and a voice said: "They have given you the sacred stick and your nation's hoop, and the yellow day; and in the center of the hoop you shall set the stick and make it grow into a shielding tree, and bloom." The bay neighed, and the twelve buckskins came and stood behind me, four abreast.

Then I knew that there were riders on all the horses there behind me, and a voice said: "Now you shall walk the black road with these; and as you walk, all the nations that have roots or legs or wings shall fear you."

So I started, riding toward the east down the fearful road, and behind me came the horsebacks four abreast—the blacks, the whites, the sorrels, and the buckskins—and far away above the fearful road the daybreak star was rising very dim.

I looked below me where the earth was silent in a sick green light, and saw the hills look up afraid and the grasses on the hills and all the animals; and everywhere about me were the cries of frightened birds and sounds of fleeing wings. I was the chief of all the heavens riding there, and when I looked behind me, all the twelve black horses reared and plunged and thundered and their manes and tails were whirling hail and their nostrils snorted lightning. And when I looked below again, I saw the slant hail falling and the long, sharp rain, and where we passed, the trees bowed low and all the hills were dim.

Now the earth was bright again as we rode. I could see the hills and valleys and the creeks and rivers passing under. We came above a place where three streams made a big one—a source of mighty waters[3]—and something terrible was there. Flames were rising from the waters and in the flames a blue man lived. The dust was floating all about him in the air, the grass was short and withered, the trees were wilting, two-legged and four-legged beings lay there thin and panting, and wings too weak to fly.

Then the black horse riders shouted "Hoka hey!" and charged down upon the blue man, but were driven back. And the white troop shouted, charging, and was beaten; then the red troop and the yellow.

And when each had failed, they all cried together: "Eagle Wing Stretches, hurry!" And all the world was filled with voices of all kinds that cheered me, so I charged. I had the cup of water in one hand and in the other was the bow that turned into a spear as the bay and I swooped down, and the spear's head was sharp lightning. It stabbed the blue man's heart, and as it struck I could hear the thunder rolling and many voices that cried "Un-hee!," meaning I had killed. The flames died. The trees and grasses were not withered any more and murmured happily together, and every living being cried in gladness with whatever voice it had. Then the four troops of horsemen charged down and struck the dead body of the blue man, counting coup; and suddenly it was only a harmless turtle.

You see, I had been riding with the storm clouds, and had come to earth as rain, and it was drouth that I had killed with the power that the Six Grandfathers gave me. So we were riding on the earth now down along the river flowing full from the source of waters, and soon I saw ahead the circled village of a people in the valley. And a Voice said: "Behold a nation; it is yours. Make haste, Eagle Wing Stretches!"

I entered the village, riding, with the four horse troops behind me—the blacks, the whites, the sorrels, and the buckskins; and the place was filled with moaning and with mourning for the dead. The wind was blowing from the south like fever, and when I looked around I saw that in nearly every tepee the women and the children and the men lay dying with the dead.

So I rode around the circle of the village, looking in upon the sick and dead, and I felt like crying as I rode. But when I looked behind me, all the women and the children and the men were getting up and coming forth with happy faces.

And a Voice said: "Behold, they have given you the center of the nation's hoop to make it live."

So I rode to the center of the village, with the horse troops in their quarters round about me, and there the people gathered. And the Voice said: "Give them now the flowering stick that they may flourish, and the sacred pipe that they may know the power that is peace, and the wing of the white giant that they may have endurance and face all winds with courage."

So I took the bright red stick and at the center of the nation's hoop I thrust it in the earth. As it touched the earth it leaped mightily in my hand and was a waga chun, the rustling tree,[4] very tall and fully of leafy branches and of all birds singing. And beneath it all the animals were mingling with the people like relatives and making happy cries. The women raised their tremolo of joy, and the men shouted all together: "Here we shall raise our children and be as little chickens under the mother sheo's wing."[5]

Then I heard the white wind blowing gently through the tree and singing there, and from the east the sacred pipe came flying on its eagle wings, and stopped before me there beneath the tree, spreading deep peace around it.

Then the daybreak star was rising, and a Voice said: "It shall be a relative to them; and who shall see it, shall see much more, for thence comes wisdom; and those who do not see it shall be dark." And all the people raised their faces to the east, and the star's light fell upon them, and all the dogs barked loudly and the horses whinnied.

Then when the many little voices ceased, the great Voice said: "Behold the circle of the nation's hoop, for it is holy, being endless, and thus all powers shall be one power in the people without end. Now they shall break camp and go forth upon the red road, and your Grandfathers shall walk with them." So the people broke camp and took the good road with the white wing on their faces, and the order of their going was like this:

First, the black horse riders with the cup of water; and the white horse riders with the white wing and the sacred herb; and the sorrel riders with the holy pipe; and the buckskins with the flowering stick. And after these the little children and the youths and maidens followed in a band.

Second, came the tribe's four chieftains, and their band was all young men and women.

Third, the nation's four advisers leading men and women neither young nor old.

Fourth, the old men hobbling with their canes and looking to the earth.

Fifth, old women hobbling with their canes and looking to the earth.

Sixth, myself all alone upon the bay with the bow and arrows that the First Grandfather gave me. But I was not the last; for when I looked behind me there were ghosts of people like a trailing fog as far as I could see—grandfathers of grandfathers and grandmothers of grandmothers without number. And over these a great Voice—the Voice that was the South—lived, and I could feel it silent.

And as we went the Voice behind me said: "Behold a good nation walking in a sacred manner in a good land!"

Then I looked up and saw that there were four ascents ahead, and these were generations I should know. Now we were on the first ascent, and all the land was green. And as the long line climbed, all the old men and women raised their hands, palms forward, to the far sky yonder and began to croon a song together, and the sky ahead was filled with clouds of baby faces.

When we came to the end of the first ascent we camped in the sacred circle as before, and in the center stood the holy tree, and still the land about us was all green.

Then we started on the second ascent, marching as before, and still the land was green, but it was getting steeper. And as I looked ahead, the people changed into elks and bison and all four-footed beings and even into fowls, all walking in a sacred manner on the good red road together. And I myself was a spotted eagle soaring over them. But just before we stopped to camp at the end of that ascent, all the marching animals grew restless and afraid that they were not what they had been, and began sending forth voices of trouble, calling to their chiefs. And when they camped at the end of the ascent, I looked down and saw that leaves were falling from the holy tree.

And the Voice said: "Behold your nation, and remember what your Six Grand-fathers gave you, for thenceforth your people walk in difficulties." Then the people broke camp again, and saw the black road before them towards where the sun goes down, and black clouds coming yonder; and they did not want to go but could not stay. And as they walked the third ascent, all the animals and fowls that were the people ran here and there, for each one seemed to have his own little vision that he followed and his own rules; and all over the universe I could hear the winds at war like wild beasts fighting.[6]

And when we reached the summit of the third ascent and camped, the nation's hoop was broken like a ring of smoke that spreads and scatters and the holy tree seemed dying and all its birds were gone. And when I looked ahead I saw that the fourth ascent would be terrible.

Then when the people were getting ready to begin the fourth ascent, the Voice spoke like someone weeping, and it said: "Look there upon your nation." And when I looked down, the people were all changed back to human, and they were thin, their faces sharp, for they were starving. Their ponies were only hide and bones, and the holy tree was gone.

And as I looked and wept, I saw that there stood on the north side of the starving camp a sacred man who was painted red all over his body, and he held a spear as he walked into the center of the people, and there he lay down and rolled. And when he got up, it was a fat bison standing there, and where the bison stood a sacred herb sprang up right where the tree had been in the center of the nation's hoop. The herb grew and bore four blossoms on a single stem while I was look-ing—a blue,[7] a white, a scarlet, and a yellow—and the bright rays of these flashed to the heavens.

I know now what this meant, that the bison were the gift of a good spirit and were our strength, but we should lose them, and from the same good spirit we must find another strength. For the people all seemed better when the herb had grown and bloomed, and the horses raised their tails and neighed and pranced around, and I could see a light breeze going from the north among the people like a ghost; and suddenly the flowering tree was there again at the center of the nation's hoop where the four-rayed herb had blossomed.

I was still the spotted eagle floating, and I could see that I was already in the fourth ascent and the people were camping yonder at the top of the third long rise. It was dark and terrible about me, for all the winds of the world were fighting. It was like rapid gun-fire and like whirling smoke, and like women and children wailing and like horses screaming all over the world.

I could see my people yonder running about, setting the smoke-flap poles and fastening down their tepees against the wind, for the storm cloud was coming on them very fast and black, and there were frightened swallows without number fleeing before the cloud.

Then a song of power came to me and I sang it there in the midst of that terrible place where I was. It went like this:

A good nation I will make live.
This the nation above has said.
They have given me the power to make over.

And when I had sung this, a Voice said: "To the four quarters you shall run for help, and nothing shall be strong before you. Behold him!"

Now I was on my bay horse again, because the horse is of the earth, and it was there my power would be used. And as I obeyed the Voice and looked, there was a horse all skin and bones yonder in the west, a faded brownish black. And a Voice there said: "Take this and make him over; and it was the four-rayed herb that I was holding in my hand. So I rode above the poor horse in a circle, and as I did this I could hear the people yonder calling for spirit power, "A-hey! a-hey! a-hey! a-hey!" Then the poor horse neighed and rolled and got up, and he was a big, shiny, black stallion with dapples all over him and his mane about him like a cloud. He was the chief of all the horses; and when he snorted, it was a flash of lightning and his eyes were like the sunset star. He dashed to the west and neighed, and the west was filled with a dust of hoofs, and horses without number, shiny black, came plunging from the dust. Then he dashed toward the north and neighed, and to the east and to the south, and the dust clouds answered, giving forth their plunging horses without number—whites and sorrels and buckskins, fat, shiny, rejoicing in their fleetness and their strength. It was beautiful, but it was also terrible.

Then they all stopped short, rearing, and were standing in a great hoop about their black chief at the center, and were still. And as they stood, four virgins, more beautiful than women of the earth can be, came through the circle, dressed in scarlet, one from each of the four quarters, and stood about the great black stallion in their places; and one held the wooden cup of water, and one the white wing, and one the pipe, and one the nation's hoop. All the universe was silent, listening; and then the great black stallion raised his voice and sang. The song he sang was this:

"My horses, prancing they are coming.
My horses, neighing they are coming;
Prancing, they are coming.
All over the universe they come.
They will dance; may you behold them.

(4 times)

A horse nation, they will dance. May you behold them."

(4 times)

His voice was not loud, but it went all over the universe and filled it. There was nothing that did not hear, and it was more beautiful than anything can be. It was so beautiful that nothing anywhere could keep from dancing. The virgins danced, and all the circled horses. The leaves on the trees, the grasses on the hills and in the valleys, the waters in the creeks and in the rivers and the lakes, the four-legged and the two-legged and the wings of the air—all danced together to the music of the stallion's song.

And when I looked down upon my people yonder, the cloud passed over, blessing them with friendly rain, and stood in the east with a flaming rainbow over it.

Then all the horses went singing back to their places beyond the summit of the fourth ascent, and all things sang along with them as they walked.

And a Voice said: "All over the universe they have finished a day of happiness." And looking down I saw that the whole wide circle of the day was beautiful and green, with all fruits growing and all things kind and happy.

Then a Voice said: "Behold this day, for it is yours to make. Now you shall stand upon the center of the earth to see, for there they are taking you."

I was still on my bay horse, and once more I felt the riders of the west, the north, the east, the south, behind me in formation, as before, and we were going east. I looked ahead and saw the mountains there with rocks and forests on them, and from the mountains flashed all colors upward to the heavens. Then I was standing on the highest mountain of them all, and round about beneath me was the whole hoops of the world.[8] And while I stood there I saw more than I can tell and I understood more than I saw; for I was seeing in a sacred manner the shapes of all things in the spirit, and the shape of all shapes as they must live together like one being. And I saw that the sacred hoop of my people was one of many hoops that made one circle, wide as daylight and as starlight, and in the center grew one mighty flowering tree to shelter all the children of one mother and one father. And I saw that it was holy.

Then as I stood there, two men were coming from the east, head first like arrows flying, and between them rose the day-break star. They came and gave a herb to me and said: "With this on earth you shall undertake anything and do it." It was the day-break-star herb, the herb of understanding, and they told me to drop it on the earth. I saw it falling far, and when it struck the earth it rooted and grew and flowered, four blossoms on one stem, a blue, a white, a scarlet, and a yellow; and the rays from these streamed upward to the heavens so that all creatures saw it and in no place was there darkness.

Then the Voice said: "Your Six Grandfathers—now you shall go back to them."

I had not noticed how I was dressed until now, and I saw that I was painted red all over, and my joints were painted black, with white stripes between the joints. My bay had lightning stripes all over him, and his mane was cloud. And when I breathed, my breath was lightning.

Now two men were leading me, head first like arrows slanting upward—the two that brought me from the earth. And as I followed on the bay, they turned into four flocks of geese that flew in circles, one above each quarter, sending forth a sacred voice as they flew: Br-r-r-p, br-r-r-p, br-r-r-p, br-r-r-p!

Then I saw ahead the rainbow flaming above the tepee of the Six Grandfathers, built and roofed with cloud and sewed with thongs of lightning; and underneath it were all the wings of the air and under them the animals and men. All these were rejoicing, and thunder was like happy laughter.

As I rode in through the rainbow door, there were cheering voices from all over the universe, and I saw the Six Grandfathers sitting in a row, with their arms held toward me and their hands, palms out; and behind them in the cloud were faces thronging, without number, of the people yet to be.

"He has triumphed!" cried the six together, making thunder. And as I passed before them there, each gave again the gift that he had given me before—the cup of water and the bow and arrows, the power to make live and to destroy; the white wing of cleansing and the healing herb; the sacred pipe; the flowering stick. And each one spoke in turn from west to south, explaining what he gave as he had done before, and as each one spoke he melted down into the earth and rose again; and as each did this, I felt nearer to the earth.

Then the oldest of them all said: "Grandson, all over the universe you have seen. Now you shall go back with power to the place from whence you came, and it shall happen yonder that hundreds shall be sacred, hundreds shall be flames! Behold!"

I looked below and saw my people there, and all were well and happy except one, and he was lying like the dead—and that one was myself. Then the oldest Grandfather sang, and his song was like this:

"There is someone lying on earth in a sacred manner.
There is someone—on earth he lies.
In a sacred manner I have made him to walk."

Now the tepee, built and roofed with cloud, began to sway back and forth as in a wind, and the flaming rainbow door was growing dimmer. I could hear voices of all kinds crying from outside: "Eagle Wing Stretches is coming forth! Behold him!"

When I went through the door, the face of the day of earth was appearing with the day-break star upon its forehead; and the sun leaped up and looked upon me, and I was going forth alone.

And as I walked alone, I heard the sun singing as it arose, and it sang like this:

"With visible face I am appearing.
In a sacred manner I appear.
For the greening earth a pleasantness I make.
The center of the nation's hoop I have made pleasant.
With visible face, behold me!
The four-leggeds and two-leggeds, I have made them to walk;
The wings of the air, I have made them to fly.
With visible face I appear.
My day, I have made it holy."

When the singing stopped, I was feeling lost and very lonely. Then a Voice above me said: "Look back!" It was a spotted eagle that was hovering over me and spoke. I looked, and where the flaming rainbow tepee, built and roofed with cloud, had been, I saw only the tall rock mountain at the center of the world.

I was all alone on a broad plain now with my feet upon the earth, alone but for the spotted eagle guarding me. I could see my people's village far ahead, and I walked very fast, for I was homesick now. Then I saw my own tepee, and inside I saw my mother and my father bending over a sick boy that was myself. And as I entered the tepee, some one was saying: "The boy is coming to; you had better give him some water."

Then I was sitting up; and I was sad because my mother and my father didn't seem to know I had been so far away.

Notes

1. The Union Pacific Railway.

2. The Little Big Horn River.

3. Black Elk thinks this was the Three Forks of the Missouri.

4. The cottonwood.

5. Prairie hen.

6. At this point Black Elk remarks: "I think we are near that place now, and I am afraid something very bad is going to happen all over the world." He cannot read and knows nothing of world affairs.

7. Blue as well as black may be used to represent the power of the West.

8. Black Elk said the mountain he stood upon in his vision was Harney Peak in the Black Hills. "But anywhere is the center of the world," he added.

Reading about Black Elk

Deloria, Vine, Jr., ed. *A Sender of Words: Essays in Memory of John G. Neihardt.* Salt Lake City: Howe, 1984.

DeMallie, Raymond J., ed. *Black Elk's Teachings Given to John G. Neihardt.* Lincoln: University of Nebraska Press, 2000.

Holler, Clyde. *Black Elk Reader.* Syracuse NY: Syracuse University Press, 2000.

Rice, Julian. *Black Elk's Story: Distinguishing Its Lakota Purpose.* Albuquerque: University of New Mexico Press, 1991.

Sayre, Robert. "Vision and Experience in Black Elk Speaks." *College English* 23 (1971): 509–35.

Steltenkamp, Michael F. *Black Elk: Holy Man of the Oglala.* Norman: University of Oklahoma Press, 1993.

Luther Standing Bear (1868–1939)

In "Crow Butte" Luther Standing Bear (Dakota) demonstrates the intertribal rivalry between the Crows and the Sioux. The physical demands of Great Plains geography play a role in the confidence the Sioux felt during the confrontation and in the ingenuity the Crows used in their escape.

The Sioux acquisition of the horse on the Great Plains is the subject of "The Holy Dog." The horse changed Sioux culture in many ways: it increased mobility, it could carry more material goods than dogs, and it increased the efficiency of the buffalo hunt. Here Standing Bear associates the arrival of the horse with a landmark of the plains.

Like many of his contemporaries, after writing his autobiographical work Standing Bear turned to political commentary. The generalizations that he makes about all American Indians are valid: "respect for life; enriching faith in a Supreme Power; and principles of truth, honesty, generosity, equity, and brotherhood as a guide to mundane relations." Standing Bear rightly suggests that the subjugation and dispossession of Indians and the labeling of them as savages rest at the hand of the white race.

Standing Bear grew up on the Rosebud Reservation in South Dakota. In 1879, when he was about ten years old he was one of the first children removed from the reservation and sent east to the Carlisle Indian School in Pennsylvania. There, instead of receiving the traditional training as a Sioux warrior that generations before him had experienced, Standing Bear learned a culture and trade that were useless to him when he returned to South Dakota after graduation. In 1902 Standing Bear became a member of Buffalo Bill's Wild West Show. Toward the end of his life Standing Bear moved to California where he lectured and acted in movies.

Standing Bear was a political advocate for Native Americans. Like other Indian activists in the early twentieth century, he spoke out on issues and policies that diminished the lives of Native Americans. In his published works Standing Bear recounts the tribe's deep knowledge of the plains' fecundity. Without plowing up or fencing off their territories, the Sioux knew how to live lightly and well on land that has proved hostile to white efforts at farming it. Ironically, when the settlers arrived it was gold they wanted, and so they ignored the air, the water, and the vast fertile grasslands, and instead set about carving their own version of America into the sacred Black Hills.

Crow Butte (1930)

In southeastern Dakota a long low line of hills runs out into the prairie as if it were going to level out and disappear into the plain, when suddenly it rises into a high rocky butte that can be seen for many miles around. So high and straight is this butte that it has long been a landmark for the Sioux. Later, when the white man came to the country, they used it for a landmark also. Standing straight and alone, one is reminded of a scout on the lookout for an enemy, or a soldier on guard.

The face of this butte is a sheer wall almost as smooth as a man's hand. Nothing grows on it. The smoothness of the stone wall is broken by a split from bottom to top, but that is all.

Though it stands in silence, this lone mountain speaks to the Indian, for it has watched the Sioux tribes pass back and forth before it for centuries.

At the opposite end from its stone face the bluff lowers slightly and joins the hills, but it is still steep and rocky, and there is only one path by which its top may be reached. This trail is rough and winding, and it takes a strong warrior to climb to the little plateau at the top. It is narrow, and only one man can travel it at a time. An army or a war-party would have to go up single-file. A pony could follow the trail only a short distance; it could never reach the top.

The level top of the bluff is covered with boulders, and a few pines grow here and there. White River runs not far from the foot of this bluff, and in summer the Sioux often camped in the timber which bordered the stream. Always this place, high in the air, had an attraction for the small boys of the camp, so one day we rode our ponies over and started up the steep path. Though the ponies were hardy and well trained, and the boys good riders, the animals were soon left by the path and the rest of the way was made on foot.

This is the story that the old folks told us younger ones in response to our questions.

One time a band of Crows came into the land of the Sioux, looking for a chance to steal some horses. As soon as the Crows were discovered, the Sioux gave chase. The Crows were unable to get away by running back the way they had come, and found themselves up against the bluff. With only one direction in which to run, they took to the steep path that led to the top of the butte. It was not a matter of choice with them, but their only means of escape. All along the way they abandoned their ponies, but managed to save themselves. At the end of the chase the Crows had all reached the top of the bluff, but the Sioux did not follow them, for it was late in the day. Guarding the path, the Sioux made camp, laughing and joking at the discomfort of the Crows up on top of the butte. The Sioux warriors gathered about their camp-fires enjoying their meal, and went to bed feeling that their enemy was securely imprisoned. High on top of the bluff, on its plateau, could be seen the glare of the Crow fires. All night they burned, lighting up the sky.

When morning came, no haste was made to attack the Crows. And not until some keen-eyed warrior saw footprints at the foot of the bluff were the Sioux aroused. Looking up, they saw, some fifty feet above, the end of a horse-hide rope, fresh and raw, swinging loose in the breeze. Sioux warriors climbed the path with all haste. When they reached the top of the bluff, the story was pictured there. One horse by some manner or means had reached the top with the Crows. It had been killed and skinned, and the hide used to lengthen the rawhide rope which some Crow warrior had. Around the stump of a pine tree the rope was secured, and down that, one by one, the Crow warriors had slid as far as they could go. Then they jumped and swam the river. It was a dangerous escape, and even the brave Sioux were amazed.

Since that time both Indians and white men have called this place Crow Butte. In the name is the story of the famous escape retained in the memory of the people.

The Holy Dog (1930)

In olden days the Sioux did not have horses. They had never even heard of one. Their travois were dragged along by large dogs, and when the camp was moved these big dogs served as pack-animals carrying tipis and household goods, and dragging the travois. Dogs were indispensable to the Sioux, and they had great numbers of them.

The Sioux dogs were big shaggy fellows, strong and intelligent. They had lived with the Sioux in this country and had been his companion, for a long, long time.

In those days the Indians lived peaceably with all animals. Even the buffalo would often wander into the camp of the Sioux and eat the grass that grew within the circle of the village. They would usually come during the night, and when the Sioux awoke in the morning there would be the buffalo feeding on the green grass. When the smoke began to rise from the tipis and the people began to stir about, the buffalo would move away. It was as if the Great Mystery sent the buffalo, so that if meat were needed it would be there at hand. In fact, many times if there was need for meat, a buffalo could be had for the morning meal. Those were the days of plenty for the Sioux.

One morning the Sioux came out of their tipis and there were the buffalo close by feeding as usual. Soon they moved away, but still feeding around was a strange-looking object such as had never before been seen. It seemed very gentle, not heeding the people, who stared at it curiously. No one ventured near at first, for the animal was too strange, and no one knew its habits. They did not know whether it would bite or kick or run. Everyone stared, but still the animal fed on, scarcely lifting its head to look at those who began to walk closer for a better view.

The head of this strange animal was not shaggy like that of the buffalo. Its eyes were large and soft-looking, like those of the deer, and its legs were slender and graceful. A mane flowed from its neck, and its tail reached nearly to the ground. The beauties of this strange animal were greatly praised by first one and then another.

Then some hunter got a rawhide rope. Maybe this animal would permit being tied, for it seemed so gentle. The rope was thrown, but the animal escaped, for it raised its head on its long slender neck and raced around a short distance, not in fright nor in anger, but as if annoyed. How handsome this animal was when it ran! It did not resemble the buffalo, nor deer, nor wolf, but was more beautiful than any of these.

The rope was thrown again and again, and at last it was on the neck of the animal. It seemed only more kind and gentle, and stood tamely while some dared to stroke it gently. Now and then it nibbled at the grass as if aware it was among friends. Admiration for the lovely animal grew. All wanted to stroke its neck and forehead, and the creature seemed at once to enjoy this extra attention. Finally a warrior grew brave enough to mount upon its back. Then all laughed and shouted with joy. What a wonderful creature! It must have come straight from the Great Mystery!

The people did not know that in later years this animal was to come to them in great numbers and was to become as great a friend to them as the dog. Both the hunter and the warrior came in time to think of it as an inseparable companion in peace and in war, for it faithfully shared the work of the long-time friend of the Sioux—the dog.

The Sioux loved their dogs—their daily companions in camp or on the trail. And liking the strange lovely animal so well, they could think of no better name to call it than the Holy Dog.

So to this day the horse to the Sioux is *Sunke Wakan*—'Holy Dog.'

Further Reading

Land of the Spotted Eagle. 1933; rpt. 1978.
My Indian Boyhood. 1959; rpt. 1988.
My People, the Sioux. 1928; rpt. 1975.

Ella Cara Deloria *(1889–1971)*

Waterlily is a novel about a young girl in the precontact Sioux society. In this selection, Ella Cara Deloria (Dakota) depicts life among the extended families who camped together in the fall on the plains. The description of daily life among the tipis includes storytellers and winter counts (a visual calendar method). Waterlily learns the proper way to listen to a story.

Deloria was born on the Yankton Reservation but reared at Standing Rock, South Dakota. She was educated at Oberlin College and Columbia University. She taught at All Saint's School in Sioux Falls, South Dakota, and at the Haskell Institute in Lawrence, Kansas. Deloria was among the first Native American bicultural, multilingual anthropologists. Under the training of Franz Boas at Columbia University she turned her analytical eye toward her Sioux heritage and produced a remarkable investigation in *Dakota Texts* (1932). Although she completed the novel *Waterlily* by 1944, she did not want it published during her lifetime fearing that it would be considered merely an ethnographic text rather than seen for its literary merit.

Excerpt from *Waterlily* (1988)

After traveling away from the region of Box Butte for many days, the people settled down into winter quarters in a deep valley with a high ridge on either side. There it was protected and cozy. Let the blizzard do its worst over the deserted uplands, it could not hit them broadside down there, even though they could not entirely escape it.

As usual in winter they dispensed with the regulation camp circle and broke up into small communities occupying the sheltering bends of the winding creek. The very large *tiyospayes* preempted entire bends while small groups that were congenial gathered together to occupy others. Thus, a series of villages were strung along the creek, on both sides. To go visiting one must follow the timberline instead of cutting across a common or following a curving line of tipis, as in summer.

It was a most sociable winter, for another camp circle had joined that of White Ghost by prearrangement, thus doubling the number of people. Such an encampment was always to everyone's liking. "That winter it was most agreeable—so many people!" the oral historians would be saying for years to come.

Each tipi was so placed that there was room to build a stockade of willows around it, with a runway between, where it was always somewhat milder than outside the stockade. The willows, set very close together, served as both a shelter for the tipi and a stable for the horses during severe storms. The people always went to great lengths to make their homes secure against winter. The tipi poles were all planted into deep holes, except for the hoisting pole by which the tent was raised. It was left resting on the ground, as always. And the entire framework of poles was anchored by guy ropes fastened to the top. These could be carried around and tied to heavy stakes in case of bad weather to brace the tipi against the prevailing wind. And finally, a single rope was dropped from the top into the tipi and left tied loosely to one of the rear poles where it was out of the way till needed. Then a stake was driven into the center of the tipi back of the fire, and to this the rope was tied very tautly to hold the tipi down solid.

Blue Bird took great pains to make her home both comfortable and ornamental inside, with an elaborately decorated dew-curtain that went completely around the room and was tied to the poles, to the height of her shoulder. It hung straight down and its lower edge was tucked beneath the fur rugs under the bed spaces. The space between the tipi itself and the dew-curtain provided a circular storage place where she kept surplus food and robes. It was always noticeably colder in this storage place than in the tipi. Thus further insulation was provided.

Backrests with fancy robes thrown over them, saddlebags, and other containers filled with the nicer gowns and other apparel, standing smartly around against the dew-curtain, and long, narrow Teton pillows, plain on one side for night and worked with porcupine quills of many colors on the other for daytime—all these touches helped to enhance the tipi. Such touches were a woman's pride, for they reflected her industry in preparing skins and her artistry in decorating them.

On the left side as one entered the tipi was where the men sat, ate, and slept, and the right side was where the women of the family belonged. The space across the back, behind the fireplace, was called the honor-place, for there all special guests were seated. As one entered, the first space to the right of the entrance was for fuel and drinking water, while the corresponding place on the left was for casual callers who dropped in for a little while and did not care to be settled too far in because they must leave shortly.

It was this callers' space where Little Chief sneaked in his pet dog during stormy nights and kept him hidden. Grownups frowned on the practice of letting dogs stay inside and the old grandfather was especially firm in the matter. "Grandson, do not harbor your dog inside," he would say. "It is not done. Dakota dogs should be as hardy as their owners. It weakens them to be kept in." And each time Little Chief would comply, only to repeat the practice when again his heart melted with pity for his shivering dog. Perhaps it was already unfit for storms.

Quite different were his grandmother's sturdy wood-gathering dogs. They were as important and useful as packhorses, eight noble and intelligent creatures that did all but speak. Gloku had provided a small travois for each one and made a set of harness of rawhide for pulling it. All day the dogs stayed on duty, for they knew their responsibility not to stray beyond call. When she announced her intention to go after wood they were ready. "Ah, my friends," she would talk to them, "you never fail me!"

The lead dog was especially fine, a huge wolflike animal by the name of Burnt Thigh, because Gloku got him from the Burnt Thigh, or Brulé, band of Tetons. In the morning she would call, "Burnt Thigh, where are you? Today you and I are going after fuel. Come!"

Soon Burnt Thigh would crawl into the tipi and sit up on his haunches in front of his mistress to be decorated. With her ceremonial vermilion paint she would first make a round circle on his forehead and then a thin line down his nose to its very tip. He would close his eyes and submit willingly, even proudly, to this little rite as though he knew what it meant. "There. Now we are relatives and won't be disloyal to each other," she would say half-solemnly. "Let's start!"

Outdoors the other dogs would be assembled and waiting, their tails wagging vigorously and their feet dancing, all eager to be off. She would harness each one in turn, talking to it all the while and calling it by name as she worked. Soon she would walk away toward the wood with her dogs in single file behind her, often to be gone the greater part of the day. Late in the afternoon she would return, the little procession following her, each dog dragging a disproportionate-looking load of fuel. Unhitching and feeding them was also a ceremony. She offered them food as generously as her store allowed and thanked them in formal speech.

It had been a late fall this year. The weather did not get noticeably colder for a long time even when all the natural indications, like the position of the stars and the behavior of birds and animals, said it should be winter. A great deal of life was still being lived in the open; women tanned hides pegged to the ground outside and men went out daily to hunt small game, while the children found themselves new playmates among the villages nearest their own and joined in games.

Black Eagle's group was an especially happy place. Everyone was delighted over the marriage of Rainbow. His mother was particularly pleased and said so on all occasions, feeling quite sure that it had been largely her doing. "Have you met my new daughter-in-law?" she asked her women friends. "She is a truly fine woman, so capable, and withal so kind, gentle, and respectful to her in-laws! One who knows her kinship obligations deserves nothing but respect in turn."

And then one night Gloku had a dream that for the time at least put an end to her preoccupation with her new daughter-in-law—a dream so vivid that she could not shake it off. She dreamed she stood on a great butte and looked eastward. Far off on another butte exactly like the one where she was, a huge man stood looking at her. She knew him at once though there was a distance of four days' journey between them. He was a certain Yankton Dakota medicine man and diviner who had once treated and healed her father. This man was famous throughout all the

Dakota bands because he used no herbs. He was so holy that he healed merely by the spoken word. Everyone revered and feared him.

Gloku and he stood looking at each other, and the thought came to her, "Can it be that the holy man has a message for me?" whereupon the man nodded slowly to indicate yes.

While she wondered what that message might be, four immense crows flew past her in a line, and she said, "Can it be that after four nights I shall be in danger?"

And again the man nodded yes. But now she could see him only dimly, for a sudden fog moved over the land between them. And she said, "Can it be that I shall be rendered invisible?" For the last time the holy man nodded yes.

After that she wakened with a heavy heart and was bothered all day. She went about her duties mechanically until her eldest daughter, First Woman, whom she described often as being direct and outspoken, remarked brusquely, "What ails you today, Mother? You are acting very strangely." But Gloku denied that anything ailed her. "If I tell my dream, it will surely come to pass, by other minds' dwelling on it to induce it," she told herself.

She lived through some wretched hours, and now it was the fourth day, *the* day. "If I can somehow get through this day safely, then I shall be free and I can laugh at that dream," she said to herself. But she was not laughing yet.

She stayed close to people, and though she ordinarily shunned idle gossip she actually sought it now; it was so normal and human. It looked as though she would get by—until a certain old woman who gadded about regularly came to see her and invited her to go and pick rose berries. "Cousin," she said, "I did not come merely to eat and pass the time but to have you go with me to the ravines yonder. You should see the rose berries now, so plentiful and so big and fleshy they are. Let's get in a good supply while we can."

Gloku wanted nothing so little as to venture from home. "Oh, who wants that common stuff?" she said. "Not while we are all well supplied with buffalo meat— the only real food."

Her caller pretended to scold her. "Don't spurn them so, cousin. There always comes a time when the meat is gone and we are glad enough for a pudding of rose berries. And who can ever say when a famine may overtake us?"

Gloku gave in and went with her. It was as her visitor had said: the berries covered all the rose thickets like one continuous red blanket. They were able to fill their containers rapidly and were soon safely back home. Gloku sighed. "Well, that's over and you've had your way. Now sit down and eat some of my best corn cakes before you go."

The old woman was ready enough to eat the delicacy but had no intention of going home yet. "I thought we might also go to the big river to get some real water," she said. "It is so much better than the salty creek water."

And somehow they were again on their way, past several clusters of tipis along the creek that flowed eastward to empty into the big river. After the last camp they still had to cross a lonely stretch of bottomland, where coarse slough grass grew tall and thick and useless all summer, to die each fall, only to send up new shoots each spring until an accumulation of the crops of countless years formed hard clumps that made walking very difficult.

Gloku complained as she went. "What a place to walk, today of all days. I wish I had never come. How headstrong you are!" but her companion feigned not to hear, quite satisfied to have had her way.

They found that the bank was high and steep and they had to make a path of sorts to reach the water. The nights had lately grown more than chilly and thin sheets of ice had formed along the edge. After drinking some water, Gloku hurriedly filled her container and climbed back to wait on the bank, but her companion took her time down at the water's edge. "Hurry up! Let's get home. The sun has already set," Gloku kept urging her in vain.

At last they were starting back when suddenly some terrifying war whoops filled the air as three men appeared on the bank upstream and made a dash for them, brandishing their tomahawks as they came. "This is it!" Gloku cried. "I was warned of this—run for your life! You wanted so badly to come!" And then, hardly knowing what she did, she grabbed up a handful of sand and tossed it behind her as she ran. Leaping over the huge clumps with miraculous ease she literally flew. Not until she had reached smoother ground did she dare look back. The men had her companion down and were beating and scalping her.

Gloku stopped at the first village and gave the alarm. The men who immediately went out brought the injured woman in and said the enemy had already left without a trace. The woman died that night. For days the members of the soldier societies formed scouting parties and went carefully over the surrounding country, but the first snowfall that night covered all tracks.

In afteryears this was Gloku's prize adventure story. Whenever she told it she began with the graphic dream, which she was sure was a prophecy. And in describing the way she threw sand behind her she would explain, "I was led to create a fog like the one in my dream and it rendered me invisible." She never failed to conclude with an extraordinary report that came out of a neighboring enemy tribe some years later, during a truce. "Some of our warriors claimed that a Dakota woman vanished before their eyes." That, she was morally certain to the day of her death, clinched her story.

That harrowing episode ushering in the winter might have been an evil omen for the days ahead, but it did not turn out that way. With many tribesmen living together and with plenty of food to last the winter, the people looked forward to a good season, and got it. There were always storms and blizzards, of course, but they were milder than on the flats and could be endured, as they always had been.

Winter was not the season for great gatherings; there were no big feasts, no ceremonials, little if any dancing. All of those activities were better suited to the milder seasons when the people lived in camp circle formation with the council tipi in the center. As always, there was still plenty to do. There were the usual winter sports, with target shooting and hurling the wooden snow-snake over the ice or snow as the men's principal games. Bowling on the ice with round stones was for women and especially for young girls. The moccasin game, a guessing game requiring skill in sleight-of-hand, was played by both men and women, though not in mixed groups. It was enjoyed in the tipi during winter though better outside in good weather, when great crowds could stand around and try to follow with the eye the lightning movements of the players' hands as they shuffled the hidden markers back and forth to confuse their opponents.

Indoors, women players in pairs engaged in toss-and-catch with deer hooves and sometimes in the plum-pit game, a favorite of old women particularly. It was something like dice. The tiny markings on the pits and the almost always limited vision of old women, especially in the dark tipis, made the accuracy of the points claimed a matter of doubt. But they enjoyed it anyway; enjoyed, too, occasionally wrangling over the score. In both the toss-and-catch and the plum-pit game, and for that matter the ice bowling and the rest, both players and spectators indulged in betting trinkets.

Boys spun cedar tops on the ice, whipping them to keep them spinning as long as possible. Smaller boys dramatized the old owl myths. Dressing up fantastically and wearing masks to resemble the owl spirit as they imagined him, they went around from tipi to tipi and from camp to camp, dancing. The audiences asked them to foretell the weather—assuming they had come from the north where winter weather was made—and then gave them sweetened corn cakes and pemmican mixed with wild fruits and similar treats. Little girls played their own dramatic games, some with singing, while small tots like Waterlily tried to understand the very simple games outgrown by their immediate predecessors and passed along to them.

Women visited around as they found time during the day and in the evenings congenial men gathered in the tipi of some person of prominence whose personal charm drew others to his company. There they sat sometimes long after midnight, smoking and talking and lunching occasionally amid much laughter and gaiety over funny stories and jokes. All kinds of talent came out. There were those who clowned cleverly on purpose, and those whose behavior, comical by nature, unintentionally sent the company into roars of laughter; those who could entertain by singing, and those who told stories professionally.

Of the last group the most famous was one called Woyaka (He Tells). Woyaka was a raconteur of exceptional skill and had a phenomenal memory. He was known everywhere, in every camp circle, for he sojourned in one or another as it pleased him. When he joined White Ghost's people for the winter everyone was delighted, looking forward to the time when he would come to tell stories, for he went the rounds as the heads of various groups of families invited him.

Meanwhile, in winter no less than in summer, the constants of life went on. Men and women worked, children played, old men sat dreaming of their youth and their past glories in war, and old women fussed over their grandchildren, for whom they would give their life if necessary, caring for them continuously and forgetting themselves in so doing. Always the young people went about subtly, with an eye for one another. And some people were marrying and some were dying and some were being born—all the natural and expectable things that happen wherever humans live together. It was a good winter all around.

The day came when there was great commotion in Black Eagle's group because Woyaka had finally got to them and sat in the tipi of Black Eagle on his special invitation. "It is important to me," that good leader said, "that the children of my relatives sit at the feet of a master and learn tribal lore from him. They must hear the myths and the legends; they must know our people's history, and to that end they must listen to the winter count," he said.

The winter count was a dramatic calendar of years that began with the previous winter and worked back in reverse chronological order. Woyaka was the man to give this, for, it was said, he alone could recite it farther back into the dim past than anyone else—three hundred winters and more. Each year was named after the most important event. Not only could Woyaka name off the years; he could, if asked, give the full story of the event referred to. "They hold a buffalo-calling ceremony," "Many expectant mothers die," "A man afflicted with sores kills himself," "A bear spends the winter with people" were some of the arresting titles that made the listeners wish they dared interrupt the flow of Woyaka's recitation to ask, "What killed the mothers with their unborn children?" or "How cold was it that a bear moved in?" or "Was it from shame or pain that the poor man killed himself?" or "How were the buffalo summoned? By whom? Did they answer?"

There was no denying Woyaka's gift as a storyteller and historian. How he became that, he told his youthful audiences. "Regard me, my grandchildren, and observe that I am very old. I have passed more than eighty winters. Many a man of lesser years finds his eyesight fading, his hearing gone, his memory faulty, while I retain all my powers and remember everything I hear. That is because my grandfather had a plan for me and he never rested in carrying it out. The day I was born he looked on me and vowed to make of me the best teller of stories that ever lived among the Tetons. And to that end he never gave up training me. I was, you might say, my grandfather's prisoner, for I did not have the liberty enjoyed by other boys; I did not go about at random; I did not run with my own kind or engage in idle play.

"Well might you think my childhood was austere, for at any instant and without warning my grandfather would grip me firmly by the shoulder until I winced, he being a powerful man. 'Now tell me,' he would say, 'what was that you heard last night?' And woe to me if I could not give it step by step without a flaw! Gravely he would then tell me, 'Grandson, speech is holy; it was not intended to be set free only to be wasted. It is for hearing and remembering.' Since I did not like to disappoint him I refused to trifle my time away on nothings. If I wakened during the night or too early to get up at dawn, I fixed my mind on rehearsing a new story or in going over what I already knew or in recalling some incident in all its details, just for practice.

"Did other boys find life easy? Could they daydream all they liked and fritter their time away? Then it was because their elders had no plan for them. My grandfather had a plan for me and that was why he had to be stern—to carry it out. In truth I was his very heart, and he was a kind man by nature. But he wanted me to be a storyteller and he spared no means to make me one. 'You owe it to our people,' he would say. 'If you fail them, there might be nobody else to remind them of their tribal history.'

"So determined was my grandfather that he even took me back to the very spot where I was born that there he might pray for me to have a clear mind. It was a long and hard journey and we walked all the way. Whenever I grew weary—being only eight years old—he carried me on his back. It rained every day, but we pressed on.

"The place was called Sandy Bend, on the north side of the beautiful Kampeska [Shell] River flowing eastward, far to the south [the Platte River in Nebraska]. I have visited it since. That lonely day my grandfather and I were the only humans in those parts. We came to the exact spot, on a little hill overlooking the river. It was smooth and hard-packed with white sand, a round spot like the inside of a tipi. The rain stopped and the morning sun came out, dazzling and blinding me.

" 'Come, stand here, grandson, in the very center,' my grandfather said. 'This is holy ground, for it was where you came into life.' And so I stood in the center of the round white spot while my grandfather moved a short distance away and there sent out his cry in my behalf: that I be enabled forever to hold captive everything I heard."

Some men were great warriors, some were seers and some hunters, some doctors of the sick, some workers of miracles and some diviners. It was believed that all such men were holy and that they succeeded in their undertaking in proportion as they enjoyed supernatural help. Of Woyaka the people said, "Surely he must enjoy more supernatural help than any other storyteller, for he is the greatest of them all."

Woyaka was a strange man in certain respects. He did not enter freely in the bantering and good-natured joking that went on about him. His eyes were fierce and searching and he went about with a great preoccupation that everlastingly set him apart and made ordinary men uneasy in his company unless he was telling a story. Then he came to life and both he and his hearers were lost in the things he so skillfully related. Otherwise he walked alone. Ordinary human camaraderie was not for him.

Nevertheless he held a universal respect that was close to veneration. He was showered with gifts and welcomed into any camp circle where he chose to stay for a time. He had no desire for things and promptly passed such gifts as moccasins and wearing apparel to others who needed them more. He seemed to prefer being unencumbered by things other than his mental possessions. People boasted, "Did you know that Woyaka is staying in our tipi at the present time?" Women from everywhere brought such dishes as were considered delicacies for him to feast on, though everyone knew that he ate only to live. Many went further: whenever they wished to act as handsomely as possible, they made a public feast and there announced to their guests that it was Woyaka who was feasting them, though he had had no hand in it. In such ways did the camp circles manifest their appreciation of so famous a man in their midst.

After the evening meal, which the children of Black Eagle's group could hardly eat, so great was their excitement, they hustled around getting ready for their first story hour. "What shall I take to the grandfather?" "What shall I?" "And I?" they asked, pulling on their mothers' skirts to gain their attention. Even Waterlily— copying the older ones as they insisted—wanted something to take along. A gift was no prerequisite. Though Black Eagle would certainly reward Woyaka at the end, however, it was customary to greet newcomers with a gift, and Woyaka was no ordinary newcomer, a fact that the children sensed.

Teton children loved to give. As far back as they could remember they had been made to give or their elders gave in their name, honoring them, until they learned to feel a responsibility to do so. Furthermore, they found it pleasant to be thanked graciously and have their ceremonial names spoken aloud. For giving was basic to Dakota life. The idea behind it was this: if everyone gives, then everyone gets; it is inevitable. And so old men and women preached continually, "Be hospitable; be generous. Nothing is too good for giving away." The children grew up hearing that, until it was a fixed notion.

The girls met in the grandmother's tipi for a final briefing. Always bent on making well-behaved women of them, she directed them thus: "Now, as you enter the tipi where the great man sits, move so quietly as not to attract attention; there are men sitting with him. Say nothing, and keep your eyes well down. At the same time, observe from under the eyelid just where to step. Do not be clumsy and trip over people's feet. It is rude even to step *over* any part of a human's body, even if your feet do not touch it. Go straight to the honor-place and there present your gift." She turned to the eldest granddaughter, Leaping Fawn, saying, "Grandchild, you know the proper side of the fire to walk in on—the left-hand side—and the proper side of the fire to walk out on—the right-hand side. So you lead the way, holding your little cousin by the hand.

"Sit like women. Never cross your legs like men. And be sure to keep your skirts pulled well down over your knees." To Leaping Fawn again, "See that your little cousin, young as she is, does the same. She must begin learning now. Above all, sit up straight; do not loll. Remember that no woman reclines in the presence of men, unless she is too ill to know."

All this had been told the girls many times but it was only by tireless repetition that proper habits could be fixed. Cautiously, as they had been instructed, the girls entered the tipi and approached the guest. One after the other they murmured, "Grandfather, for you," and made their gift. Then they took their places, barely aware of the man's quiet thanks or the exclamations of praise over the pretty gifts— moccasins and such things—from the adult guests present. They were far too busy in seating themselves correctly and tucking their skirts about their legs with only the tips of moccasins showing. And thus they sat all evening, composed and prim and quite different from the pile of irrepressible small boys in continuous motion on the other side.

Leaping Fawn was a well-bred girl with a sense of propriety. "How tractable she is," women said of her often. "Such a good girl!" She was called "good" because she fell into pattern easily, the exact opposite of a girl named Alila, from the neighboring settlement, who had been coming regularly of late to play with the girls of Black Eagle's camp. Though she was likable and friendly, Alila was at heart a young rebel who deliberately broke little rules of etiquette just for the fun of it. "There!" she seemed to be saying, "I've not conformed—and where is the dreadful result?"

Leaping Fawn had her troubles in trying to keep Waterlily still and in the proper posture. Her short legs would not stay flexed right and her skirts slipped up each time she moved, which was often, exposing chubby knees. Fortunately, she fell asleep almost at once, and Leaping Fawn was then free to fix her whole attention on the stories.

"I shall first tell you how our people caught the buffalo in the days before they had horses," Woyaka began. Then he smoked a while in silence, until his youthful hearers were wondering just how, and growing more eager by the minute to find out.

"When the people could not find any meat, when all the deer and other animals conspired to hide, until all food was nearly gone and a bad famine was certain, then they called upon a buffalo dreamer to help them.

"A buffalo dreamer was a man who, when he went fasting on some lonely butte, was visited by the spirit of the buffalo, who promised to be his brother for all time. 'Call me when you are hungry,' he said, 'and I will come. Sing this song I am about to teach you, and then I shall know you.' And he taught the buffalo dreamer a beautiful buffalo song, to be his alone. In afteryears, if another man wished to sing that song to entertain his friends, he must first say, 'This is the holy song of Such-an-one, a buffalo dreamer with greater power.' Then his listeners could not say he had stolen it.

"Now, when the buffalo dreamer had to call upon his brothers, he first made himself ready and worthy to receive power, by purifying himself in the sweatbath, by fasting and praying all night in a special tipi, and by abstaining from all physical appetites, so that he might keep his pending task sternly before him, for that was the only way to be sure of obtaining the gift he sought.

"Next day, all the people went out on open ground, away from their tipis, and there set up the small travois poles that their pack dogs dragged with loads bound to them. These poles were set up as tripods, close together, like the frames of tipis around a circle. Now every woman and child took a place behind this circle, each one armed with a stout club with which to strike the travois poles when the time was right. Meanwhile, all the hunters stood back of the women, with their arrows ready on their bows. And so they stood waiting, hoping, though as yet there was no sign of the buffalo anywhere.

"Then the holy man emerged from his tipi of preparation and made his way toward them. Outside the single opening to the circle he stopped and 'talked mystically.' That is to say, in sacred language he related his vision wherein he and the buffalo spirit became brothers. 'Do you remember? It is I, the man to whom you made that promise,' he said aloud. 'My children are hungry; they cry for food. I have no choice but to trouble you, my brothers. A vow is a vow. Keep it, then!' So he flung out a challenge.

"Then he sang his holy song from his vision; over and over he sang it, and paid attention to nothing but his song, a crying chant that had no ending. And as he sang he walked to and fro in front of the entrance, looking like a buffalo rampant himself, for he was wearing the head and skin of a buffalo and for the time he *was* a buffalo, talking to his own kind.

"And did they come? Most certainly they came. Looming large through the falling snow, they appeared over the hill and headed in a long, black line straight toward the circle. A magnificent buffalo bull led them; with eyes aglare he approached, frightening the people. But they knew they must stand their ground. Without their share of the responsibility the undertaking would fail; everyone must cooperate, for that was where the power finally lay.

"Hurrying past the holy man, who still sang and walked to and fro without seeing them, they entered the circle and began moving in a mass around inside, to the accompaniment of the continuous clatter, clatter, clatter of wood on wood, which the women and children made, striking their clubs in rhythm on the dog-travois poles. The singing of the holy man, the clatter, and the pace of the buffalo never slackened. Meantime each hunter picked out his animal and shot it from over the women's shoulders, aiming to kill by hitting the animal in the right spot. Arrowheads were priceless; let every one count!

"And soon the tribal leaders call a halt. 'Stop! It is enough. Our friends have kept their vow; once again they have given themselves to save us; once again they have extended hospitality to us. Let us kill no more than we need. It is enough.'

"And suddenly all was still, even the holy man's singing. And then, in the deafening stillness, the lead buffalo came to his senses; he had seemed to walk in his sleep before. The next time he came to the opening, which he had passed by time and again, leading the others after him, he turned and went out, and the rest went also. On and on in a single line, as deliberately and surely as they had come, they went until they disappeared over the hill. They knew they would not be shot at from behind, for they and the Dakotas were friends.

"And then came the ritual. The holy man cut off the tip of the tongue of the largest bull, the finest cow, and the prettiest calf, and reverently tied them into a bit of buckskin painted red. These, symbols of the buffalo's sacrifice, were buried while the people wailed ceremonially, as for dead relatives.

"Thus did our ancestors get food, when all else failed, with the help of the Great Mystery. Thus early they learned that man cannot manage alone. And, hungry as they were, nobody touched the animals until the ritual was decently finished. And then there was happy feasting again."

After this, Woyaka repeated some short myths, long familiar to the children, who never tired of them. And then he dismissed them, saying, "That will be enough for now, grandchildren. There will be many evenings that I shall sit here. Whenever you want to hear stories, come, for I have many to tell."

As they rose to go, and while Leaping Fawn was trying to rouse the sleeping Waterlily, Alila startled everyone by asking, "What will they be about, Grandfather?" for Alila never minded speaking out.

"They will be about many different things: of how the birds taught the Dakotas to play; of how West Wind and North Wind struggled for supremacy until West Wind emerged victorious. You shall hear also the story of Iron Hawk, the wonder-man of the east, and of Falling Star, the hero, and of the first man and woman to inhabit our world." He added, with one of his rare chuckles, "And such a time as their son had in managing his wives, Corn-woman and Buffalo-woman! For they were jealous of each other. It is from the son of the Buffalo-woman that we roving Tetons come. Is it any wonder that we love our buffalo brothers who sustain us so patiently? While they live we shall not die."

And the children went home singing, "While the buffalo live we shall not die!"

Further Reading

Speaking of Indians. 1998.

Reading about Ella Deloria

Medicine, Bea. "Ella C. Deloria: The Emic Voice." *MELUS* 7.4 (1980): 23–30.

Rice, Julian. *Deer Women and Elk Men: The Lakota Narratives of Ella Deloria*. Albuquerque: University of New Mexico Press, 1992.

Zitkala-Ša

This widely anthologized tale is Zitkala-Ša's account of her childhood among the Sioux when life is in transition on the Great Plains. She paints a portrait of the freedom she felt as she roamed unfettered, except for her mother's care. The missionaries who come to tempt her with "red, red apples" introduced her to a world and life beyond her childhood imagination. As a later selection shows, Zitkala-Ša uses her education to turn the critical eye back on those who removed her from her tribal home.

For the biography of and further reading about Zitkala-Ša see pages 125 and 129.

Impressions of an Indian Childhood (1921)

I. My Mother

A wigwam of weather-stained canvas stood at the base of some irregularly ascending hills. A footpath wound its way gently down the sloping land till it reached the broad river bottom; creeping through the long swamp grasses that bent over it on either side, it came out on the edge of the Missouri.

Here, morning, noon, and evening, my mother came to draw water from the muddy stream for our household use. Always, when my mother started for the river, I stopped my play to run along with her. She was only of medium height. Often she was sad and silent, at which times her full arched lips were compressed into hard and bitter lines, and shadows fell under her black eyes. Then I clung to her hand and begged to know what made the tears fall.

"Hush; my little daughter must never talk about my tears"; and smiling through them, she patted my head and said, "Now let me see how fast you can run today." Whereupon I tore away at my highest possible speed, with my long black hair blowing in the breeze.

I was a wild little girl of seven. Loosely clad in a slip of brown buckskin, and light-footed with a pair of soft moccasins on my feet, I was as free as the wind that blew my hair, and no less spirited than a bounding deer. These were my mother's pride,—my wild freedom and overflowing spirits. She taught me no fear save that of intruding myself upon others.

Having gone many paces ahead I stopped, panting for breath, and laughing with glee as my mother watched my every movement. I was not wholly conscious of myself, but was more keenly alive to the fire within. It was as if I were the activity, and my hands and feet were only experiments for my spirit to work upon.

Returning from the river, I tugged beside my mother, with my hand upon the bucket I believed I was carrying. One time, on such a return, I remember a bit of conversation we had. My grown-up cousin, Warca-Ziwin (Sunflower), who was then seventeen, always went to the river alone for water for her mother. Their wigwam was not far from ours; and I saw her daily going to and from the river. I admired my cousin greatly. So I said: "Mother, when I am tall as my cousin Warca-Ziwin, you shall not have to come for water. I will do it for you."

With a strange tremor in her voice which I could not understand, she answered, "If the paleface does not take away from us the river we drink."

"Mother, who is this bad paleface?" I asked.

"My little daughter, he is a sham,—a sickly sham! The bronzed Dakota is the only real man."

I looked up into my mother's face while she spoke; and seeing her bite her lips, I knew she was unhappy. This aroused revenge in my small soul. Stamping my foot on the earth, I cried aloud, "I hate the paleface that makes my mother cry!"

Setting the pail of water on the ground, my mother stooped, and stretching her left hand out on the level with my eyes, she placed her other arm about me; she pointed to the hill where my uncle and my only sister lay buried.

"There is what the paleface has done! Since then your father too has been buried in a hill nearer the rising sun. We were once very happy. But the paleface has stolen our lands and driven us hither. Having defrauded us of our land, the paleface forced us away.

"Well, it happened on the day we moved camp that your sister and uncle were both very sick. Many others were ailing, but there seemed to be no help. We traveled many days and nights; not in the grand, happy way that we moved camp when I was a little girl, but we were driven, my child, driven like a herd of buffalo. With every step, your sister, who was not as large as you are now, shrieked with the painful jar until she was hoarse with crying. She grew more and more feverish. Her little hands and cheeks were burning hot. Her little lips were parched and dry, but she would not drink the water I gave her. Then I discovered that her throat was swollen and red. My poor child, how I cried with her because the Great Spirit had forgotten us!

"At last, when we reached this western country, on the first weary night your sister died. And soon your uncle died also, leaving a widow and an orphan daughter, your cousin Warca-Ziwin. Both your sister and uncle might have been happy with us today, had it not been for the heartless paleface."

My mother was silent the rest of the way to our wigwam. Though I saw no tears in her eyes, I knew that was because I was with her. She seldom wept before me.

II. The Legends

During the summer days my mother built her fire in the shadow of our wigwam.

In the early morning our simple breakfast was spread upon the grass west of our tepee. At the farthest point of the shade my mother sat beside her fire, toasting a savory piece of dried meat. Near her, I sat upon my feet, eating my dried meat with unleavened bread, and drinking strong black coffee.

The morning meal was our quiet hour, when we two were entirely alone. At noon, several who chanced to be passing by stopped to rest, and to share our luncheon with us, for they were sure of our hospitality.

My uncle, whose death my mother ever lamented, was one of our nation's bravest warriors. His name was on the lips of old men when talking of the proud feats of valor; and it was mentioned by younger men, too, in connection with deeds of gallantry. Old women praised him for his kindness toward them; young women held him up as an ideal to their sweethearts. Every one loved him, and my mother worshiped his memory. Thus it happened that even strangers were sure of welcome in our lodge, if they but asked a favor in my uncle's name.

Though I heard many strange experiences related by these wayfarers, I loved best the evening meal, for that was the time old legends were told. I was always glad when the sun hung low in the west, for then my mother sent me to invite the neighboring old men and women to eat supper with us. Running all the way to the wigwams, I halted shyly at the entrances. Sometimes I stood long moments without saying a word. It was not any fear that made me so dumb when out upon such a happy errand; nor was it that I wished to withhold the invitation, for it was all I could do to observe this very proper silence. But it was a sensing of the atmosphere, to assure myself that I should not hinder other plans. My mother used to say to me, as I was almost bounding away for the old people: "Wait a moment before you invite any one. If other plans are being discussed, do not interfere, but go elsewhere."

The old folks knew the meaning of my pauses; and often they coaxed my confidence by asking, "What do you seek, little granddaughter?"

"My mother says you are to come to our tepee this evening," I instantly exploded, and breathed the freer afterwards.

"Yes, yes, gladly, gladly I shall come!" each replied. Rising at once and carrying their blankets across one shoulder, they flocked leisurely from their various wigwams toward our dwelling.

My mission done, I ran back, skipping and jumping with delight. All out of breath, I told my mother almost the exact words of the answers to my invitation. Frequently she asked, "What were they doing when you entered their tepee?" This taught me to remember all I saw at a single glance. Often I told my mother my impressions without being questioned.

While in the neighboring wigwams sometimes an old Indian woman asked me, "What is your mother doing?" Unless my mother had cautioned me not to tell, I generally answered her questions without reserve.

At the arrival of our guests I sat close to my mother, and did not leave her side without first asking her consent. I ate my supper in quiet, listening patiently to the talk of the old people, wishing all the time that they would begin the stories I loved best. At last, when I could not wait any longer, I whispered in my mother's ear, "Ask them to tell an Iktomi story, mother."

Soothing my impatience, my mother said aloud, "My little daughter is anxious to hear your legends." By this time all were through eating, and the evening was fast deepening into twilight.

As each in turn began to tell a legend, I pillowed my head in my mother's lap; and lying flat upon my back, I watched the stars as they peeped down upon me, one by one. The increasing interest of the tale aroused me, and I sat up eagerly listening to every word. The old women made funny remarks, and laughed so heartily that I could not help joining them.

The distant howling of a pack of wolves or the hooting of an owl in the river bottom frightened me, and I nestled into my mother's lap. She added some dry sticks to the open fire, and the bright flames leaped up into the faces of the old folks as they sat around in a great circle.

On such an evening, I remember the glare of the fire shown on a tattooed star upon the brow of the old warrior who was telling a story. I watched him curiously as he made his unconscious gestures. The blue star upon his bronzed forehead was a puzzle to me. Looking about, I saw two parallel lines on the chin of one of the old women. The rest had none. I examined my mother's face, but found no sign there.

After the warrior's story was finished, I asked the old woman the meaning of the blue lines on her chin, looking all the while out of the corners of my eyes at the warrior with the star on his forehead. I was a little afraid that he would rebuke me for my boldness.

Here the old woman began: "Why, my grandchild, they are signs,—secret signs I dare not tell you. I shall, however, tell you a wonderful story about a woman who had a cross tattooed upon each of her cheeks."

It was a long story of a woman whose magic power lay hidden behind the marks upon her face. I fell asleep before the story was completed.

Ever after that night I felt suspicious of tattooed people. Wherever I saw one I glanced furtively at the mark and round about it, wondering what terrible magic power was covered there.

It was rarely that such a fearful story as this one was told by the camp fire. Its impression was so acute that the picture still remains vividly clear and pronounced.

III. The Beadwork
Soon after breakfast mother sometimes began her beadwork. On a bright, clear day, she pulled out the wooden pegs that pinned the skirt of our wigwam to the ground, and rolled the canvas part way up on its frame of slender poles. Then

the cool morning breezes swept freely through our dwelling, now and then wafting the perfume of sweet grasses from newly burnt prairie.

Untying the long tasseled strings that bound a small brown buckskin bag, my mother spread upon a mat beside her bunches of colored beads, just as an artist arranges the paints upon his palette. On a lapboard she smoothed out a double sheet of soft white buckskin; and drawing from a beaded case that hung on the left of her wide belt a long, narrow blade, she trimmed the buckskin into shape. Often she worked upon small moccasins for her small daughter. Then I became intensely interested in her designing. With a proud, beaming face, I watched her work. In imagination, I saw myself walking in a new pair of snugly fitting moccasins. I felt the envious eyes of my playmates upon the pretty red beads decorating my feet.

Close beside my mother I sat on a rug, with a scrap of buckskin in one hand and an awl in the other. This was the beginning of my practical observation lessons in the art of beadwork. From a skein of finely twisted threads of silvery sinews my mother pulled out a single one. With an awl she pierced the buckskin, and skillfully threaded it with the white sinew. Picking up the tiny beads one by one, she strung them with the point of her thread, always twisting it carefully after every stitch.

It took many trials before I learned how to knot my sinew thread on the point of my finger, as I saw her do. Then the next difficulty was in keeping my thread stiffly twisted, so that I could easily string my beads upon it. My mother required of me original designs for my lessons in beading. At first I frequently ensnared many a sunny hour into working a long design. Soon I learned from self-inflicted punishment to refrain from drawing complex patterns, for I had to finish whatever I began.

After some experience I usually drew easy and simple crosses and squares. These were some of the set forms. My original designs were not always symmetrical nor sufficiently characteristic, two faults with which my mother had little patience. The quietness of her oversight made me feel strongly responsible and dependent upon my own judgment. She treated me as a dignified little individual as long as I was on my good behavior; and how humiliated I was when some boldness of mine drew forth a rebuke from her!

In the choice of colors she left me to my own taste. I was pleased with an outline of yellow upon a background of dark blue, or a combination of red and myrtle-green. There was another of red with a bluish-gray that was more conventionally used. When I became a little familiar with designing and the various pleasing combinations of color, a harder lesson was given me. It was the sewing on, instead of beads, some tinted porcupine quills, moistened and flattened between the nails of the thumb and forefinger. My mother cut off the prickly ends and burned them at once in the centre fire. These sharp points were poisonous, and worked into the flesh wherever they lodged. For this reason, my mother said, I should not do much alone in quills until I was as tall as my cousin Warca-Ziwin.

Always after these confining lessons I was wild with surplus spirits, and found joyous relief in running loose in the open again. Many a summer afternoon a party of four or five of my playmates roamed over the hills with me. We each carried a light sharpened rod about four feet long, with which we pried up certain sweet roots. When we had eaten all the choice roots we chanced upon, we shouldered our rods and strayed off into patches of a stalky plant under whose yellow blossoms we found little crystal drops of gum. Drop by drop we gathered this nature's rock-candy, until each of us could boast of a lump the size of a small bird's egg. Soon satiated with its woody flavor, we tossed away our gum, to return again to the sweet roots.

I remember well how we used to exchange our necklaces, beaded belts, and sometimes even our moccasins. We pretended to offer them as gifts to one another. We delighted in impersonating our own mothers. We talked of things we had heard them say in their conversations. We imitated their various manners, even to the inflection of their voices. In the lap of the prairie we seated ourselves upon our feet, and leaning our painted cheeks in the palms of our hands, we rested our elbows on our knees, and bent forward as old women were most accustomed to do.

While one was telling of some heroic deed recently done by a near relative, the rest of us listened attentively, and exclaimed in undertones, "Han! han!" (yes! yes!) whenever the speaker paused for breath, or sometimes for our sympathy. As the discourse became more thrilling, according to our ideas, we raised our voices in these interjections. In these impersonations our parents were led to say only those things that were in common favor.

No matter how exciting a tale we might be rehearsing, the mere shifting of a cloud shadow in the landscape near by was sufficient to change our impulses; and soon we were all chasing the great shadows that played among the hills. We shouted and whooped in the chase; laughing and calling to one another, we were like little sportive nymphs on that Dakota sea of rolling green.

On one occasion I forgot the cloud shadow in a strange notion to catch up with my own shadow. Standing straight and still, I began to glide after it, putting out one foot cautiously. When, with the greatest care, I set my foot in advance of myself, my shadow crept onward too. Then again I tried it; this time with the other foot. Still again my shadow escaped me. I began to run; and away flew my shadow, always just a step beyond me. Faster and faster I ran, setting my teeth and clenching my fists, determined to overtake my own fleet shadow. But ever swifter it glided before me, while I was growing breathless and hot. Slackening my speed, I was greatly vexed that my shadow should check its pace also. Daring it to the utmost, as I thought, I sat down upon a rock imbedded in the hillside.

So! my shadow had the impudence to sit down beside me!

Now my comrades caught up with me, and began to ask why I was running away so fast.

"Oh, I was chasing my shadow! Didn't you ever do that!" I inquired, surprised that they should not understand.

They planted their moccasined feet firmly upon my shadow to stay it, and I arose. Again my shadow slipped away, and moved as often as I did. Then we gave up trying to catch my shadow.

Before this peculiar experience I have no distinct memory of having recognized any vital bond between myself and my own shadow. I never gave it an after-thought.

Returning our borrowed belts and trinkets, we rambled homeward. That evening, as on other evenings, I went to sleep over my legends.

IV. The Coffee-Making

One summer afternoon my mother left me alone in our wigwam while she went across the way to my aunt's dwelling.

I did not much like to stay alone in our tepee for I feared a tall, broad-shouldered crazy man, some forty years old, who walked loose among the hills. Wiyaka-Napbina (Wearer of a Feather Necklace) was harmless, and whenever he came into a wigwam he was driven there by extreme hunger. He went nude except for the half of a red blanket he girdled around his waist. In one tawny arm he used to carry a heavy bunch of wild sunflowers that he gathered in his aimless ramblings. His black hair was matted by the winds, and scorched into a dry red by the constant summer sun. As he took great strides, placing one brown bare foot directly in front of the other, he swung his long lean arm to and fro.

Frequently he paused in his walk and gazed far backward, shading his eyes with his hand. He was under the belief that an evil spirit was haunting his steps. This was what my mother told me once, when I sneered at such a silly big man. I was brave when my mother was near by, and Wiyaka-Napbina walking farther and farther away.

"Pity the man, my child. I knew him when he was a brave and handsome youth. He was overtaken by a malicious spirit among the hills, one day, when he went hither and thither after his ponies. Since then he can not stay away from the hills," she said.

I felt so sorry for the man in his misfortune that I prayed to the Great Spirit to restore him. But though I pitied him at a distance, I was still afraid of him when he appeared near our wigwam.

Thus, when my mother left me by myself that afternoon I sat in a fearful mood within our tepee. I recalled all I had ever heard about Wiyaka-Napbina; and I tried to assure myself that though he might pass near by, he would not come to our wigwam because there was no little girl around our grounds.

Just then, from without a hand lifted the canvas covering of the entrance; the shadow of a man fell within the wigwam, and a large roughly moccasined foot was planted inside.

For a moment I did not dare to breathe or stir, for I thought that could be no other than Wiyaka-Napbina. The next instant I sighed aloud in relief. It was an old grandfather who had often told me Iktomi legends.

"Where is your mother, my little grandchild?" were his first words.

"My mother is soon coming back from my aunt's tepee," I replied.

"Then I shall wait awhile for her return," he said, crossing his feet and seating himself upon a mat.

At once I began to play the part of a generous hostess. I turned to my mother's coffeepot.

Lifting the lid, I found nothing but coffee grounds in the bottom. I set the pot on a heap of cold ashes in the centre, and filled it half full of warm Missouri River water. During this performance I felt conscious of being watched. Then breaking off a small piece of our unleavened bread, I placed it in a bowl. Turning soon to the coffeepot, which would never have boiled on a dead fire had I waited forever, I poured out a cup of worse than muddy warm water. Carrying the bowl in one hand and cup in the other, I handed the light luncheon to the old warrior. I offered them to him with the air of bestowing generous hospitality.

"How! how!" he said, and placed the dishes on the ground in front of his crossed feet. He nibbled at the bread and sipped from the cup. I sat back against a pole watching him. I was proud to have succeeded so well in serving refreshments to a guest all by myself. Before the old warrior had finished eating, my mother entered. Immediately she wondered where I had found coffee, for she knew I had never made any, and that she had left the coffeepot empty. Answering the question in my mother's eyes, the warrior remarked, "My granddaughter made coffee on a heap of dead ashes, and served me the moment I came."

They both laughed, and mother said, "Wait a little longer, and I shall build a fire." She meant to make some real coffee. But neither she nor the warrior, whom the law of our custom had compelled to partake of my insipid hospitality, said anything to embarrass me. They treated my best judgment, poor as it was, with the utmost respect. It was not till long years afterward that I learned how ridiculous a thing I had done.

V. The Dead Man's Plum Bush

One autumn afternoon many people came streaming toward the dwelling of our near neighbor. With painted faces, and wearing broad white bosoms of elk's teeth, they hurried down the narrow footpath to Haraka Wambdi's wigwam. Young mothers held their children by the hand, and half pulled them along in their haste. They overtook and passed by the bent old grandmothers who were trudging along with crooked canes toward the centre of excitement. Most of the young braves galloped hither on their ponies. Toothless warriors, like the old women, came more slowly, though mounted on lively ponies. They sat proudly erect on their horses. They wore their eagle plumes, and waved their various trophies of former wars.

In front of the wigwam a great fire was built, and several large black kettles of venison were suspended over it. The crowd were seated about it on the grass in a great circle. Behind them some of the braves stood leaning against the necks of their ponies, their tall figures draped in loose robes which were well drawn over their eyes.

Young girls, with their faces glowing like bright red autumn leaves, their glossy braids falling over each ear, sat coquettishly beside their chaperons. It was a custom for young Indian women to invite some older relative to escort them to the public feasts. Though it was not an iron law, it was generally observed.

Haraka Wambdi was a strong young brave, who had just returned from his first battle, a warrior. His near relatives, to celebrate his new rank, were spreading a feast to which the whole of the Indian village was invited.

Holding my pretty striped blanket in readiness to throw over my shoulders, I grew more and more restless as I watched the gay throng assembling. My mother was busily broiling a wild duck that my aunt had that morning brought over.

"Mother, mother, why do you stop to cook a small meal when we are invited to a feast?" I asked, with a snarl in my voice.

"My child, learn to wait. On our way to the celebration we are going to stop at Chanyu's wigwam. His aged mother-in-law is lying very ill, and I think she would like a taste of this small game."

Having once seen the suffering on the thin, pinched features of this dying woman, I felt a momentary shame that I had not remembered her before.

On our way I ran ahead of my mother and was reaching out my hand to pick some purple plums that grew on a small bush, when I was checked by a low "Sh!" from my mother.

"Why, mother, I want to taste the plums!" I exclaimed, as I dropped my hand to my side in disappointment.

"Never pluck a single plum from this brush, my child, for its roots are wrapped around an Indian's skeleton. A brave is buried here. While he lived he was so fond of playing the game of striped plum seeds that, at his death, his set of plum seeds were buried in his hands. From them sprang up this little bush."

Eyeing the forbidden fruit, I trod lightly on the sacred ground, and dared to speak only in whispers until we had gone many paces from it. After that time I halted in my ramblings whenever I came in sight of the plum bush. I grew sober with awe, and was alert to hear a long-drawn-out whistle rise from the roots of it. Though I had never heard with my own ears this strange whistle of departed spirits, yet I had listened so frequently to hear the old folks describe it that I knew I should recognize it at once.

The lasting impression of that day, as I recall it now, is what my mother told me about the dead man's plum bush.

VI. The Ground Squirrel

In the busy autumn days my cousin Warca-Ziwin's mother came to our wigwam to help my mother preserve foods for our winter use. I was very fond of my aunt, because she was not so quiet as my mother. Though she was older, she was more jovial and less reserved. She was slender and remarkably erect. While my mother's hair was heavy and black, my aunt had unusually thin locks.

Ever since I knew her she wore a string of large blue beads around her neck,— beads that were precious because my uncle had given them to her when she was a younger woman. She had a peculiar swing in her gait, caused by a long stride rarely natural to so slight a figure. It was during my aunt's visit with us that my mother forgot her accustomed quietness, often laughing heartily at some of my aunt's witty remarks.

I loved my aunt threefold: for her hearty laughter, for the cheerfulness she caused my mother, and most of all for the times she dried my tears and held me in her lap, when my mother had reproved me.

Early in the cool mornings, just as the yellow rim of the sun rose above the hills, we were up and eating our breakfast. We awoke so early that we saw the sacred hour when a misty smoke hung over a pit surrounded by an impassable sinking mire. This strange smoke appeared every morning, both winter and summer; but most visibly in midwinter it rose immediately above the marshy spot. By the time the full face of the sun appeared above the eastern horizon, the smoke vanished. Even very old men, who had known this country the longest, said that the smoke from this pit had never failed a single day to rise heavenward.

As I frolicked about our dwelling I used to stop suddenly, and with a fearful awe watch the smoking of the unknown fires. While the vapor was visible I was afraid to go very far from our wigwam unless I went with my mother.

From a field in the fertile river bottom my mother and aunt gathered an abundant supply of corn. Near our tepee they spread a large canvas upon the grass, and dried their sweet corn in it. I was left to watch the corn, that nothing should disturb it. I played around it with dolls made of ears of corn. I braided their soft fine silk for hair, and gave them blankets as various as the scraps I found in my mother's workbag.

There was a little stranger with a black-and-yellow-striped coat that used to come to the drying corn. It was a little ground squirrel, who was so fearless of me that he came to one corner of the canvas and carried away as much of the sweet corn as he could hold. I wanted very much to catch him and rub his pretty fur back, but my mother said he would be so frightened if I caught him that he would bite my fingers. So I was as content as he to keep the corn between us. Every morning he came for more corn. Some evenings I have seen him creeping about our grounds; and when I gave a sudden whoop of recognition he ran quickly out of sight.

When mother had dried all the corn she wished, then she sliced great pumpkins into thin rings; and these she doubled and linked together into long chains. She hung them on a pole that stretched between two forked posts. The wind and sun soon thoroughly dried the chains of pumpkin. Then she packed them away in a case of thick and stiff buckskin.

In the sun and wind she also dried many wild fruits,—cherries, berries, and plums. But chiefest among my early recollections of autumn is that one of the corn drying and the ground squirrel.

I have few memories of winter days at this period of my life, though many of the summer. There is one only which I can recall.

Some missionaries gave me a little bag of marbles. They were all sizes and colors. Among them were some of colored glass. Walking with my mother to the river, on a late winter day, we found great chunks of ice piled all along the bank. The ice on the river was floating in huge pieces. As I stood beside one large block, I noticed for the first time the colors of the rainbow in the crystal ice. Immediately I thought of my glass marbles at home. With my bare fingers I tried to pick out some of the colors, for they seemed so near the surface. But my fingers began to sting with the intense cold, and I had to bite them hard to keep from crying.

From that day on, for many a moon, I believed that glass marbles had river ice inside of them.

VII. The Big Red Apples

The first turning away from the easy, natural flow of my life occurred in an early spring. It was in my eighth year; in the month of March, I afterward learned. At this age I knew but one language, and that was my mother's native tongue.

From some of my playmates I heard that two paleface missionaries were in our village. They were from that class of white men who wore big hats and carried large hearts, they said. Running direct to my mother, I began to question her why these two strangers were among us. She told me, after I had teased much, that they had come to take away Indian boys and girls to the East. My mother did not seem to want me to talk about them. But in a day or two, I gleaned many wonderful stories from my playfellows concerning the strangers.

"Mother, my friend Judéwin is going home with the missionaries. She is going to a more beautiful country than ours; the palefaces told her so!" I said wistfully, wishing in my heart that I too might go.

Mother sat in a chair, and I was hanging on her knee. Within the last two seasons my big brother Dawée had returned from a three years' education in the East, and his coming back influenced my mother to take a farther step from her native way of living. First it was a change from the buffalo skin to the white man's canvas that covered our wigwam. Now she had given up her wigwam of slender poles, to live, a foreigner, in a home of clumsy logs.

"Yes, my child, several others besides Judéwin are going away with the palefaces. Your brother said the missionaries had inquired about his little sister," she said, watching my face very closely.

My heart thumped so hard against my breast, I wondered if she could hear it.

"Did he tell them to take me, mother?" I asked, fearing lest Dawée had forbidden the palefaces to see me, and that my hope of going to the Wonderland would be entirely blighted.

With a sad, slow smile, she answered: "There! I knew you were wishing to go, because Judéwin has filled your ears with the white man's lies. Don't believe a word they say! Their words are sweet, but, my child, their deeds are bitter. You will cry for me, but they will not even soothe you. Stay with me, my little one! Your brother Dawée says that going East, away from your mother, is too hard an experience for his baby sister."

Thus my mother discouraged my curiosity about the lands beyond our eastern horizon; for it was not yet an ambition for Letters that was stirring me. But on the following day the missionaries did come to our very house. I spied them coming up the footpath leading to our cottage. A third man was with them, but he was not my brother Dawée. It was another, a young interpreter, a paleface who had a smattering of the Indian language. I was ready to run out to meet them, but I did not dare to displease my mother. With great glee, I jumped up and down on our ground floor. I begged my mother to open the door, that they would be sure to come to us. Alas! They came, they saw, and they conquered!

Judéwin had told me of the great tree where grew red, red apples; and how we could reach out our hands and pick all the red apples we could eat. I had never seen apple trees. I had never tasted more than a dozen red apples in my life; and when I heard of the orchards of the East, I was eager to roam among them. The missionaries smiled into my eyes and patted my head. I wondered how mother could say such hard words against him.

"Mother, ask them if little girls may have all the red apples they want, when they go East," I whispered aloud, in my excitement.

The interpreter heard me, and answered: "Yes, little girl, the nice red apples are for those who pick them; and you will have a ride on the iron horse if you go with these good people."

I had never seen a train, and he knew it.

"Mother, I am going East! I like big red apples, and I want to ride on the iron horse! Mother, say yes!" I pleaded.

My mother said nothing. The missionaries waited in silence; and my eyes began to blur with tears, though I struggled to choke them back. The corners of my mouth twitched, and my mother saw me.

"I am not ready to give you any word," she said to them. "Tomorrow I shall send you my answer by my son."

With this they left us. Alone with my mother, I yielded to my tears, and cried aloud, shaking my head so as not to hear what she was saying to me. This was the first time I had ever been so unwilling to give up my own desire that I refused to hearken to my mother's voice.

There was a solemn silence in our home that night. Before I went to bed I begged the Great Spirit to make my mother willing I should go with the missionaries.

The next morning came, and my mother called me to her side. "My daughter, do you still persist in wishing to leave your mother?" she asked.

"Oh, mother, it is not that I wish to leave you, but I want to see the wonderful Eastern land," I answered.

My dear old aunt came to our house that morning, and I heard her say, "Let her try it."

I hoped that, as usual, my aunt was pleading on my side. My brother Dawée came for mother's decision. I dropped my play, and crept close to my aunt.

"Yes, Dawée, my daughter, though she does not understand what it all means, is anxious to go. She will need an education when she is grown, for then there will be fewer real Dakotas, and many more palefaces. This tearing her away, so young, from her mother is necessary, if I would have her an educated woman. The palefaces, who owe us a large debt for stolen lands, have begun to pay a tardy justice in offering some education to our children. But I know my daughter must suffer keenly in this experiment. For her sake, I dread to tell you my reply to the missionaries. Go, tell them that they may take my little daughter, and that the Great Spirit shall not fail to reward them according to their hearts."

Wrapped in my heavy blanket, I walked with my mother to the carriage that was soon to take us to the iron horse. I was happy. I met my playmates, who were also wearing their best thick blankets. We showed one another our new beaded moccasins, and the width of the belts that girdled our new dresses. Soon we were being drawn rapidly away by the white man's horses. When I saw the lonely figure of my mother vanish in the distance, a sense of regret settled heavily upon me. I felt suddenly weak, as if I might fall limp to the ground. I was in the hands of strangers whom my mother did not fully trust. I no longer felt free to be myself, or to voice my own feelings. The tears trickled down my cheeks, and I buried my face in the folds of my blanket. Now the first step, parting me from my mother, was taken, and all my belated tears availed nothing.

Having driven thirty miles to the ferryboat, we crossed the Missouri in the evening. Then riding again a few miles eastward, we stopped before a massive brick building. I looked at it in amazement, and with a vague misgiving, for in our village I had never seen so large a house. Trembling with fear and distrust of the palefaces, my teeth chattering from the chilly ride, I crept noiselessly in my soft moccasins along the narrow hall, keeping very close to the bare wall. I was as frightened and bewildered as the captured young of a wild creature.

Louise Erdrich *(b. 1954)*

The Antelope Wife brings together the indigenous peoples and the colonizers of the plains. This selection, the first chapter in the novel, sets the historical groundwork for families that will intersect throughout the twentieth century in the remainder of the novel. The lonely and guilty soldier Scranton Roy encounters the infant Chippewa survivor of a battle. Raising her on his own, he literally nurses her to flourish. A schoolteacher, Peace McKnight, relieves his loneliness. However, the bereft mother of the infant wanders the prairies to claim, with the antelope, her daughter.

Louise Erdrich (Ojibwe) was born in Little Falls, Minnesota, and raised in Wahpeton, North Dakota. She earned a bachelor's degree from Dartmouth College in 1976 and a master of fine arts degree from Johns Hopkins University in 1979. Erdrich returned to Dartmouth as poet in residence in 1981, and that same year married Michael Dorris (Modoc, 1945–1997), who was then director of Native American Studies at the college. With the collaborative support of Dorris she embarked on a prominent literary career, winning numerous awards. Her first novel, *Love Medicine* (1984), won the National Book Critics Circle Award, the first by an American Indian. Utilizing a style of multiple narrators in her novels, Erdrich creates a protagonist not of an individual character but of a tribal community based on an Ojibwe world view. Her novels epically intertwine an extended Ojibwe family and characters in a North Dakota setting.

Erdrich also has authored two volumes of poetry, a novel co-authored with Dorris, a personal memoir, children's books and several novels.

Father's Milk (1998)

Scranton Roy

Deep in the past during a spectacular cruel raid upon an isolated Ojibwa village mistaken for hostile during the scare over the starving Sioux, a dog bearing upon its back a frame-board tikinagun enclosing a child in moss, velvet, embroideries of beads, was frightened into the vast carcass of the world west of the Otter Tail River. A cavalry soldier, spurred to human response by the sight of the dog, the strapped-on child, vanishing into the distance, followed and did not return.

What happened to him lives on, though fading in the larger memory, and I relate it here in order that it not be lost.

Private Scranton Teodorus Roy was the youngest son of a Quaker father and a reclusive poet mother who established a small Pennsylvania community based on intelligent conversation. One day into his view a member of a traveling drama troupe appeared. Unmasked, the woman's stage glance broke across Roy's brow like fire. She was tall, stunningly slender, pale, and paler haired, resolute in her character, and simple in her amused scorn of Roy—so young, bright-faced, obedient. To prove himself, he made a rendezvous promise and then took his way west following her glare. An icicle, it drove into his heart and melted there, leaving a trail of ice and blood. The way was long. She glided like a snake beneath his footsteps in fevered dreams. When he finally got to the place they had agreed upon, she was not there, of course. Angry and at odds, he went against the radiant ways of his father and enlisted in the U.S. Cavalry at Fort Sibley on the banks of the Mississippi in St. Paul, Minnesota.

There, he was trained to the rifle, learned to darn his socks using a wooden egg, ate many an ill-cooked bean, and polished his officers' harness leather until one day, in a state of uneasy resignation, he put on the dark blue uniform, fixed his bayonet, set off marching due west.

The village his company encountered was peaceful, then not.

In chaos of groaning horses, dogs screaming, rifle and pistol reports, and the smoke of errant cooking fires, Scranton Roy was most disturbed not by the death yells of old men and the few warriors shocked naked from their robes, but by the feral quiet of the children. And the sudden contempt he felt for them all. Unexpected, the frigid hate. The pleasure in raising, aiming. They ran fleet as their mothers, heading for a brush-thick gully and a slough of grass beyond. Two fell. Roy whirled, not knowing whom to shoot next. Eager, he bayoneted an old woman who set upon him with no other weapon but a stone picked from the ground.

She was built like the broken sacks of hay he'd used for practice, but her body closed fast around the instrument. He braced himself against her to pull free, set his boot between her legs to tug the blade from her stomach, and as he did so tried to avoid her eyes but did not manage. His gaze was drawn into hers and he sank with it into the dark unaccompanied moment before his birth. There was a word she uttered in her language. Daashkikaa. Daashkikaa. A groan of heat and blood. He saw his mother, yanked the bayonet out with a huge cry, and began to run.

That was when he saw the dog, a loping dirt-brown cur, circle the camp twice with the child on its back and set off into open space. As much to escape the evil confusion of this village and his own dark act as out of any sympathy for the baby, though he glimpsed its face—mystified and calm—Scranton Roy started running after the two. Within moments, the ruckus of death was behind him. The farther away the village got, the farther behind he wanted it. He kept on, running, walking, managing to keep the dog in view only because it was spring and the new grass, after a burn of lightning, was just beginning its thrust, which would take it to well over a full-grown man's height.

From time to time, as the day went on, the dog paused to rest, stretched patient beneath its burden. Grinning and panting, she allowed Roy to approach, just so far. A necklace of blue beads hung from the brow guard of the cradle board. It swayed, clattered lightly. The child's hands were bound in the wrappings. She could not reach for the beads but stared at them as though mesmerized. The sun grew razor-hot. Tiny blackflies settled at the corners of her eyes. Sipped moisture from along her lids until, toward late afternoon, the heat died. A cold wind boomed against Scranton Roy in a steady rush. Still, into the emptiness, the three infinitesimally pushed.

The world darkened. Afraid of losing the trail, Roy gave his utmost. As night fixed upon them, man and dog were close enough to hear each other breathing and so, in that rhythm, both slept. Next morning, the dog stayed near, grinning for scraps. Afraid to frighten him with a rifle shot, Roy hadn't brought down game although he'd seen plenty. He managed to snare a rabbit. Then, with his tinderbox and steel, he started a fire and began to roast it, at which smell the dog dragged itself belly-down through the dirt, edging close. The baby made its first sound, a murmuring whimper. Accepting tidbits and bones, the dog was alert, suspicious. Roy could not touch it until the next day when he'd thought to wash himself all over and approach naked to diminish his whiteman's scent.

So he was able at last to remove the child from its wrappings and bathe it, a girl, and to hold her. He'd never done such a thing before. First he tried to feed her a tiny piece of the rabbit. She was too young to manage. He dripped water into her mouth, made sure it trickled down, but was perplexed at what to feed her, then alarmed when, after a night of deprivation, her tiny face crumpled in need. She peered at him in expectation and, at last, violently squalled. Her cries filled a vastness that nothing else could. They resounded, took over everything, and brought his heart clean to the surface. Scranton Roy cradled the baby, sang lewd camp tunes, then stalwart hymns, and at last remembered his own mother's lullabies. Nothing helped. It seemed, when he held her close upon his heart as women did, that the child grew angry with longing and desperately clung, rooted with its mouth, roared in frustration, until at last, moved to near insanity, Roy opened his shirt and put her to his nipple.

She seized him. Inhaled him. Her suck was fierce. His whole body was astonished, most of all the inoffensive nipple he'd never noticed or appreciated until, in spite of the pain, it served to gain him peace. As he sat there, the child holding part of him in its mouth, he looked around just in case there should be any witness to this act which seemed to him strange as anything that had happened in this sky-filled land. Of course, there was only the dog. Contented, freed, it lolled appreciatively near. So the evening passed and then the night. Scranton Roy was obliged to change nipples, the first one hurt so, and he fell asleep with the baby tucked beside him on his useless teat.

She was still there in the morning, stuck, though he pulled her off to slingshot a partridge, roasted that too, and smeared its grease on his two sore spots. That made her wild for him. He couldn't remove her then and commenced to walk, holding her, attached, toward a stand of cottonwood that wavered in the distance. A river. A place to camp. He'd settle there for a day or two, he thought, and try to teach the baby to eat something, for he feared she'd starve to death although she seemed, except for the times he removed her from his chest, surprisingly contented.

He slung the blue beads around the baby's neck. Tied the cradle board onto his own back. Then the man, child, and the dog struck farther into the wilderness. They reached hills of sand, oak covered, shelter. Nearby, sod he cut painstakingly with the length of his bayonet and piled into a square, lightless but secure, and warm. Hoarding his shots, he managed to bring down a buffalo bull fat-loaded with the summer grass. He fleshed the hide, dried the meat, seared the brains, stored the pounded fat and berries in the gut, made use of every bone and scrap of flesh even to the horns, carved into spoons, and the eyeballs, tossed to the dog. The tongue, cooked tender and mashed in his own mouth, he coaxed the baby to accept. She still much preferred him. As he was now past civilized judgment, her loyalty filled him with a foolish, tender joy.

He bathed each morning at the river. Once, he killed a beaver and greased himself all over against mosquitoes with its fat. The baby continued to nurse and he made a sling for her from his shirt. He lounged in the doorway of his sod hut, dreaming and exhausted, fearing that a fever was coming upon him. The situation was confusing. He did not know what course to take, how to start back, wondered if there'd be a party sent to search for him and then realized if they did find him he'd be court-martialed. The baby kept nursing and refused to stop. His nipples toughened. Pity scorched him, she sucked so blindly, so forcefully, and with such immense faith. It occurred to him one slow dusk as he looked down at her, upon his breast, that she was teaching him something.

This notion seemed absurd when he first considered it, and then, as insights do when we have the solitude to absorb them, he eventually grew used to the idea and paid attention to the lesson. The word *faith* hooked him. She had it in such pure supply. She nursed with utter simplicity and trust, as though the act itself would produce her wish. Half asleep one early morning, her beside him, he felt a slight warmth, then a rush in one side of his chest, a pleasurable burning. He thought it was an odd dream and fell asleep again only to wake to a huge burp from the baby, whose lips curled back from her dark gums in bliss, whose tiny fists were un-clenched in sleep for the first time, who looked, impossibly, well fed.

Ask and ye shall receive. Ask and ye shall receive. The words ran through him like a clear stream. He put his hand to his chest and then tasted a thin blue drop of his own watery, appalling, God-given milk.

Miss Peace McKnight

Family duty was deeply planted in Miss Peace McKnight, also the knowledge that if she did not nobody else would—do the duty, that is, of seeing to the future of the

McKnights. Her father's Aberdeen button-cart business failed after he ran out of dead sheep—his own, whose bones he cleverly thought to use after a spring disaster. He sawed buttons with an instrument devised of soldered steel, ground them to a luster with a polisher of fine sand glued to cloth, made holes with a bore and punch that he had self-invented. It was the absence, then, of sheep carcasses that forced his daughter to do battle with the spirit of ignorance.

Peace McKnight. She was sturdily made as a captain's chair, yet drew water with graceful wrists and ran dancing across the rutted road on curved white ankles. Hale, Scots, full-breasted as a pouter pigeon, and dusted all over like an egg with freckles, wavy brown-black hair secured with her father's gift—three pins of carved bone—she came to the Great Plains with enough education to apply for and win a teaching certificate.

Her class was piddling at first, all near grown, too. Three consumptive Swedish sisters not long for life, one boy abrupt and full of anger. A German. Even though she spoke plainly and slowly as humanly possible, her students fixed her with stares of tongueless suspicion and were incapable of following a single direction. She had to start from the beginning, teach the alphabet, the numbers, and had just reached the letter *v*, the word *cat*, subtraction, which they were naturally better at than addition, when she noticed someone standing at the back of her classroom. Quietly alert, observant, she had been there for some time. The girl stepped forward from the darkness.

She had roan coppery skin and wore a necklace of bright indigo beads. She was slender, with a pliable long waist, graceful neck, and she was about six years old.

Miss McKnight blushed pink-gold with interest. She was charmed, first by the confidence of the child's smile and next by her immediate assumption of a place to sit, study, organize herself, and at last by her listening intelligence. The girl, though silent, had a hungry, curious quality. Miss McKnight had a teaching gift to match it. Although they were fourteen years apart, they became, inevitably, friends.

Then sisters. Until fall, Miss McKnight slept in the school cloakroom and bathed in the river nearby. Once the river iced over at the edges, an argument developed among the few and far between homesteads as to which had enough room and who could afford her. No one. Matilda Roy stepped in and pestered her father, known as a strange and reclusive fellow, until he gave in and agreed that the new teacher could share the small trunk bed he had made for his daughter, so long as she helped with the poultry.

Mainly, they raised guinea fowl from keets that Scranton Roy had bought from a Polish widow. The speckled purple-black vulturine birds were half wild, clever. Matilda's task was to spy on, hunt down, and follow the hens to their hidden nests. The girls, for Peace McKnight was half girl around Matilda, laughed at the birds' tricks and hid to catch them. Fat, speckled, furious with shrill guinea pride, they acted as house watchdogs and scolded in the oak trees. Then from the pole shed where they wintered. In lard from a neighbor's pig, Scranton Roy fried strips of late squash, dried sand-dune morels, inky caps, field and oyster mushrooms, crushed acorns, the guinea eggs. He baked sweet bannock, dribbled on it wild aster honey aged in the bole of an oak, dark and pungent as mead.

The small sod and plank house was whitewashed inside and the deep sills of small bold windows held geraniums and started seeds. At night, the kerosene lamplight in trembling rings and halos, Miss Peace McKnight felt the eyes of Scranton Roy carve her in space. His gaze was a heat running up and down her throat, pausing elsewhere with the effect of a soft blow.

Scranton Roy

He is peculiar the way his mother was peculiar—writing poetry on the margins of bits of newspaper, tatters of cloth. His mother burned her life work and died soon after, comforted by the ashes of her words yet still in mourning for her son, who never did make his survival known but named his daughter for her. Matilda. One poem survived. A fragment. It goes like this. *Come to me, thou dark inviolate.* Scranton Roy prays to an unparticular god, communes with the spirit headlong each morning in a rush of ardor that carries him through each difficult day. He is lithe, nearly brown as his daughter, bearded, strong, and serene. He owns more than one dozen books and subscribes to periodicals that he lends to Miss McKnight.

He wants to be delivered of the burden of his solitude. A wife would help.

Peace tosses her sandy hair, feels the eyes of Scranton Roy upon her, appreciates their fire, and smiles into the eyes of his daughter. Technically, Miss McKnight soon becomes a stepmother. Whatever the term, the two women behave as though they've always known this closeness. Holding hands, they walk to school, kick dust, and tickle each other's necks with long stems of grama grass. They cook for Scranton Roy but also roll their eyes from time to time at him and break into fits of suppressed and impolite laughter.

Matilda Roy

Emotions unreel in her like spools of cotton.

When he rocks her, Matilda remembers the taste of his milk—hot and bitter as dandelion juice. Once, he holds her foot in the cradle of his palm and with the adept point of his hunting knife painlessly delivers a splinter, long and pale and bloody. Teaches her to round her *c*'s and put tiny teakettle handles on her *a*'s. Crooks stray hairs behind her ears. Washes her face with the rough palm of his hand, but gently, scrubbing at her smooth chin with his callus.

He is a man, though he nourished her. Sometimes across the room, at night, in his sleep, her father gasps as though stabbed, dies into himself. She is jolted awake, frightened, and thinks to check his breath with her hand, but then his ragged snore lulls her. In the fresh daylight, staring up at the patches of mildew on the ceiling,

Matilda watches him proudly from the corners of her eyes as he cracks the ice in the washing pail, feeds a spurt of hidden stove flame, talks to himself. She loves him like nothing else. He is her father, her human. Still, sometimes, afflicted by an anxious sorrow, she holds her breath to see what will happen, if he will save her. Heat flows up the sides of her face and she opens her lips but before her mouth can form a word she sees yellow, passes out, and is flooded by blueness, sheer blueness, intimate and strange, the color of her necklace of beads.

Kiss

Have you ever fallen from a severe height and had your wind knocked forth so that, in the strict jolt's sway, you did experience stopped time? Matilda Roy did when she saw her father kiss the teacher. The world halted. There sounded a great gong made of sky. A gasp. Silence. Then the leaves ticked again, the guineas scornfully gossiped, the burly black hound that had replaced the Indian dog pawed a cool ditch in the sand for itself. Sliding back from the casual window to the bench behind the house where she sat afternoons to shell peas, shuck corn, peel dinner's potatoes, pluck guinea hens, and dream, Matilda Roy looked at the gold-brown skin on her arms, turned her arms over, turned them back, flexed her pretty, agile hands.

The kiss had been long, slow, and of growing interest and intensity, more educational than any lesson yet given her by Miss Peace McKnight. Matilda shut her eyes. Within herself at all times a silent darkness sifted up and down. A pure emptiness fizzing and gliding. Now, along with the puzzling development between her friend and father, something else. It took a long concentration on her stillness to grasp the elusive new sensation of freedom, of relief.

Ozhawashkwamashkodeykway/Blue Prairie Woman

The child lost in the raid was still nameless, still a half spirit, yet her mother mourned her for a solid year's time and nearly died of the sorrow. A haunting uncertainty dragged the time out. Ozhawashkwamashkodekway might be picking blueberries and she feared she would come across her daughter's bones. In the wind at night, pakuks, she heard them wailing, black twig skeletons. Stirring the fire, a cleft of flame reminded her of the evil day itself, the massed piles of meat put to the torch, their robes and blankets smoldering, the stinking singe of hair, and the hot iron of the rifle barrels. At night, for the first month after that day, her breasts grew pale and hard and her milk impacted, spoiling in her, leaking out under her burnt clothes so that she smelled of sour milk and fire. An old midwife gave her a new puppy and she put it to her breasts. Holding to her nipple the tiny wet muzzle, cradling the needy bit of fur, she cried. All that night the tiny dog mercifully drew off the shooting pains in her breasts and at dawn, drowsy and comfortable, she finally cuddled the sweet-fleshed puppy to her, breathed its salty odor, and slept.

Wet ash when the puppy weaned itself. Blood. Her moons began and nothing she pressed between her legs could stop the rush of life. Her body wanting to get rid of itself. She ate white clay, scratched herself with bull thorns for relief, cut her hair, grew it long, cut it short again, scored her arms to the bone, tied the skull of a buffalo around her neck, and for six moons ate nothing but dirt and leaves. It must have been a rich dirt, said her grandmother, for although she slept little and looked tired, Blue Prairie Woman was healthy as a buffalo cow. When Shawano the younger returned from his family's wild rice beds, she gave her husband such a nigh of sexual pleasure that his eyes followed her constantly after that, narrow and hot. He grew molten when she passed near other men, and at night they made their own shaking tent. They got teased too much and moved farther off, into the brush, into the nesting ground of shy and holy loons. There, no one could hear them. In solitude they made love until they became gaunt and hungry, pale windi- gos with aching eyes, tongues of flame.

Twins are born of such immoderation.

By the time her husband left again with his sled of traps, she was pregnant and calm. During that winter, life turned more brutal. The tribe's stores had been burned by order, and many times in starving sleep Blue Prairie Woman dreamed the memory of buffalo fat running in rivulets across the ground, soaking into the earth, fat gold from piles of burning meat. She still dreamed, too, with wide-eyed clarity of the young, fleet brown dog, the cradle board bound to its body. Even carrying two, she dreamed of her first baby bewildered, then howling, then at last riding black as leather, mouth stretched wide underneath a waterless sky. She dreamed its bones rattled in the careful stitching of black velvet, clacked in the moss padding, grown thin. She heard their rhythm and saw the dog, the small pakuk flying. She howled and scratched herself half blind and at last so viciously took leave of her mind that the old ones got together and decided to change her name.

On a cool day in spring in the bud-popping moon the elders held a pitiful feast—only nothing seems pitiful to survivors. In weak sunlight they chewed spring-risen mud-turtle meat, roasted coot, gopher, the remaining sweet grains of manomin, acorns, puckoons from a squirrel's cache, and the fresh spears of dan- delion. Blue Prairie Woman's name was covered with blood, burned with fire. Her name was old and exquisite and had belonged to many powerful mothers. Yet the woman who had fit inside of it had walked off. She couldn't stop following the child and the dog. Someone else had taken her place. Who, as yet, was unclear. But the old ones did know, agreed between them, that the wrong name would kill what was in there and it had to go—like a husk dried off and scattered. Like a shell to a nut. Hair grown long and sacrificed to sorrow. They had to give her another name if they wanted her to return to the living.

The name they gave her had to be unused. New. Oshkay. They asked the strongest of the namers, the one who dreamed original names. This namer was nameless and was neither a man nor a woman, and so took power from the in-between. This namer had long, thick braids and a sweet shy smile, charming ways but arms tough with roped muscle. The namer walked like a woman, spoke in a man's deep voice. Hid coy behind a fan and yet agreed to dream a name to fit the new thing inside Blue Prairie Woman. But what name would help a woman who could only be calmed by gazing into the arrowing distance? The namer went away, starved and sang and dreamed, until it was clear that the only name that made any sense at all was the name of the place where the old Blue Prairie Woman had gone to fetch back her child.

Other Side of the Earth
Once she was named for the place toward which she traveled, the young mother was able to be in both places at once—she was following her child into the sun and also pounding the weyass between rocks to dried scruffs of pemmican. She was searching the thick underbrush of her own mind. She was punching holes to sew tough new soles on old moccasins and also sew new ones, tiny, the soles pierced before she beaded the tops. She starved and wandered, tracking the faint marks the dog left as he passed into the blue distance. At the same time, she knocked rice. She parched and stored the grains. Sugared. Killed birds. Tamed horses. Her mind was present because she was always gone. Her hands were filled because they grasped the meaning of empty. Life was simple. Her husband returned and she served him with indifferent patience this time. When he asked what had happened to her heat for him, she gestured to the west.

The sun was setting. The sky was a body of fire.

In the deep quiet of her blood the two babies were forming, creating themselves just as the first twin gods did at the beginning. As yet, no one had asked what might happen next. What would happen to the woman called Other Side of the Earth when Blue Prairie Woman found Matilda Roy?

A Dog Named Sorrow
The dog nursed on human milk grew up coyote gray and clever, a light-boned, loping bitch who followed Blue Prairie Woman everywhere. Became her second thought, lay outside the door when she slept, just within the outer flap when it rained, though not in. Not ever actually inside a human dwelling. Huge with pups or thin from feeding them, teats dragging, the dog still followed. Close and quiet as her shadow, it lived within touch of her, although they never did touch after the dog drew from Blue Prairie Woman's soaked and swollen nipples the heat, the night milk, the overpowering sorrow.

Always there, looking up alert at the approach of a stranger, guarding her in the dusk, waiting for a handout, living patiently on bits of hide, guts, offal, the dog waited. And was ready when Blue Prairie Woman set down her babies with their grandmother and started walking west, following at long last the endless invisible trail of her daughter's flight.

She walked for hours, she walked for years. She walked until she heard about them. The man. The young girl and the blue beads she wore. Where they were living. She heard the story. The twins, two girls, she left behind to the chances of baptism. They were named Mary, of course, for the good blue-robed woman, and Josephette, for the good husband. Only the Ojibwa tongue made Zosie of the latter name. Zosie. Mary. Their grandmother, Midass, who had survived the blue-coat massacre, would raise them as her own.

When she reached the place they lived, Blue Prairie Woman settled on a nearby rise, the dog near. From that distance, the two watched the house—small, immaculate, scent of a hearth fire made of crackling oak twigs. Illness. There was sickness in the house, she could sense it—the silence, then the flurries of motion. Rags hung out. Water to haul. One shrill cry. Silence again. All day in thin grass, the dog, the woman, sunlight brave on them, breathed each other's air, slept by turns, waited.

Matilda Roy

She heard the gentle approach that night, the scrawl of leaves, the sighing resonance of discovery. She sat up in her crazy quilt, knowing. Next to her, held in the hot vise of fever, Peace muttered endlessly of buttons and sheep bones. Sounds—a slight tap. The clatter of her beads. In the morning, there was no Matilda Roy in the trunk bed. There was only a note, folded twice, penned in the same exquisite, though feminized, handwriting of her father.

She came for me. I went with her.

Scranton Roy

Peace McKnight was never devout, so there was no intimacy of prayer between the newlyweds. Their physical passion suffered, as well, because of the shortness of his bed. There was, after all, very little space inside the sod house. Scranton Roy had slept in a tiny berth on one side of the room, his daughter on the other. Both slept curled like snails, like babies in the wombs of their mothers. More difficult with an extra person in the bedding. It wasn't long before, in order to get any rest at all, Peace slipped outside to sleep with the guineas, took up nightly residence apart from her husband.

Still, there were evenings when Scranton was inflicted with ardor and arranged them both, before she could leave, in the cramped and absurd postures of love. If only he had thought to use the armless rocking chair before the fire! Peace's mind flashed on the possibility, but she was too stubborn to mention it. Even the floor, packed dirt covered with skins, would have been preferable. Again, she didn't care to introduce that possibility into his mind. Anyway, as it happened she had every right to turn her back when the tiny knock of new life began in the cradle of her hipbones. And he retreated, missed the rasp of her breath, wondered about Matilda, and imagined the new life to come all at once. Prayed. Wrote poems in his head. *Come to me, thou dark inviolate.*

After her deliverance from the mottled skin sickness, the gasping and fever that made her bones ache, Peace was in her weakness even warier of her new husband. For the rest of her pregnancy, she made him sleep alone. Her labor began on a snowy morning. Scranton Roy set out for the Swedish housewife's in a swallowing blizzard that would have cost him his life but for his good sense in turning back. He reached the door. Smote, rattled, fell into the heat of a bloody scene in which Peace McKnight implored her neglected God in begging futility. For two days, then three, her labor shook her in its jaws. Her howls were louder than the wind. Hoarser. Then her voice was lost, a scrape of bone. A whisper. Her face bloated, dark red, then white, then gray. Her eyes rolled back to the whites, so she stared mystified with agony into her own thoughts when at last the child tore its way from her. A boy, plump and dead blue. Marked with cloudy spots like her earlier disease. There was no pulse in the birth cord but Scranton Roy thought to puff his own air into the baby's lungs. It answered with a startled bawl.

Augustus. She had already named her baby. Known that it would be a boy.

Scranton wrapped the baby in the skin of a dog and kissed the smoothed, ravaged temples of Peace with tender horror at the pains of his own mother, and of all mothers, and of the unfair limitations of our bodies, of the hopeless settlement of our life tasks, and finally, of the boundless iniquity of the God to whom she had so uselessly shrieked. *Look at her,* he called the unseen witness. And perhaps God did or Peace McKnight's mind, pitilessly wracked, finally came out of hiding and told her heart to beat twice more. A stab of fainting gold heeled through a scrap of window. Peace saw the wanton gleam, breathed out, gazed out. And then, as she stepped from her ripped body into the utter calm of her new soul, Peace McKnight saw her husband put his son to his breast.

Blue Prairie Woman

All that's in a name is a puff of sound, a lungful of wind, and yet it is an airy enclosure. How is it that the gist, the spirit, the complicated web of bone, hair, brain, gets stuffed into a syllable or two? How do you shrink the genie of human complexity? How the personality? Unless, that is, your mother gives you her name, Other Side of the Earth.

Who came from nowhere and from lucky chance. Whose mother bore her in shit and fire. She is huge as half the sky. In the milk from her rescuer's breasts she has tasted his disconcerting hatred of her kind and also protection, so that when she falls into the fever, she doesn't suffer of it the way Peace did. Although they stop, make camp, and Blue Prairie Woman speaks to her in worried susurrations, the child is in no real danger.

The two camp on the trail of a river cart. The sky opens brilliantly and the grass is hemmed, rife with berries. Blue Prairie Woman picks with swift grace and fills a new-made makuk. She dries the berries on sheaves of bark, in the sun, so they'll be easy to carry. Lying with her head on mother's lap, before the fire, Matilda asks what her name was as a little baby. The two talk on and on, mainly by signs.

Does the older woman understand the question? Her face burns. As she sinks dizzily onto the earth beside her daughter, she feels compelled to give her the name that brought her back. Other Side of the Earth, she says, teeth tapping. Hotter, hotter, first confused and then dreadfully clear when she sees, opening before her, the western door.

She must act at once if her daughter is to survive her.

The clouds are pure stratus. The sky is a raft of milk. The coyote gray dog sits patiently near.

Blue Prairie Woman, sick to death and knowing it, reaches swiftly to her left and sets her grip without looking on the nape of the dog's neck. First time she has touched the dog since it drank from her the milk of sorrow. She drags the dog to her. Soft bones, soft muzzle then. Tough old thing now. Blue Prairie Woman holds the dog close underneath one arm and then, knife in hand, draws her clever blade across the beating throat. Slices its stiff moan in half and collects in the berry-filled makuk its gurgle of dark blood. Blue Prairie Woman then stretches the dog out, skins and guts her, cuts off her head, and lowers the chopped carcass into a deep birch-bark container. Suspended over flames, just right, she knows how to heat water the old way in that makuk. Tending the fire carefully, weakening, she boils the dog.

When it is done, the meat softened, shredding off the bones, she tips the gray meat, brown meat, onto a birch tray. Steam rises, the fragrance of the meat is faintly sweet. Quietly, she gestures to her daughter. Prods the cracked oval pads off the cooked paws. Offers them to her.

It takes sixteen hours for Blue Prairie Woman to contract the fever and only eight more to die of it. All that time, as she is dying, she sings. Her song is wistful, peculiar, soft, questing. It doesn't sound like a death song; rather, is in it the tenderness and intimacy of seduction addressed to the blue distance.

Never exposed, healthy, defenseless, her body is an eager receptacle for the virus. She seizes, her skin goes purple, she vomits a brilliant flash of blood. Passionate, surprised, she dies when her chest fills, kicking and drumming her heels on the hollow earth. At last she is still, gazing west. That is the direction her daughter sits facing all the next day and the next. She sings her mother's song, holding her mother's hand in one hand and seriously, absently, eating the dog with the other hand—until in that spinning cloud light and across rich level earth, pale reddish curious creatures, slashed with white on the chest and face, deep-eyed, curious, pause in passing.

The antelope emerge from the band of the light at the world's edge.

A small herd of sixteen or twenty flickers into view. Fascinated, they poise to watch the girl's hand in its white sleeve dip. Feed herself. Dip. They step closer. Hooves of polished metal. Ears like tuning forks. Black prongs and velvet. They watch Matilda. Blue Prairie Woman's daughter. Other Side of the Earth. Nameless.

She is seven years old, tough from chasing poultry and lean from the fever. She doesn't know what they are, the beings, dreamlike, summoned by her mother's song, her dipping hand. They come closer, closer, grazing near, folding their legs under them to warily rest. The young nurse their mothers on the run or stare at the girl in fascinated hilarity, springing off if she catches their wheeling flirtation. In the morning when she wakens, still holding her mother's hand, they are standing all around. They bend to her, huff in excitement when she rises and stands among them quiet and wondering. Easy with their dainty precision, she wanders along in their company. Always on the move. At night she makes herself a nest of willow. Sleeps there. Moves on. Eats bird's eggs. A snared rabbit. Roots. She remembers fire and cooks a handful of grouse chicks. The herd flows in steps and spurting gallops deeper into the west. When they walk, she walks, following, dried berries in a sack made of her dress. When they run, she runs with them. Naked, graceful, the blue beads around her neck.

Further Reading

Baptism of Desire. 1989.
The Beet Queen. 1986.
The Bingo Palace. 1993.
The Birchbark House. 1999.
The Blue Jay's Dance: A Birth Year. 1995.
The Crown of Columbus. With Michael Dorris. 1991.
Grandmother's Pigeon. 1996.
Jacklight. 1984.
The Last Report on the Miracles at Little No Horse. 2001.
Love Medicine. 1984. Second ed., revised and expanded, 1993.
The Master Butchers Singing Club. 2003.
Tales of Burning Love. 1996.
Tracks. 1988.

Reading about Louise Erdrich

Beidler, Peter G., and Gay Barton. *A Reader's Guide to the Novels of Louise Erdrich*. Columbia: University of Missouri Press, 1999.

Catt, Catherine M. "Ancient Myth in Modern America: The Trickster in the Fiction of Louise Erdrich." *Platte Valley Review* 19 (winter 1991): 71–81.

Chavkin, Allan, and Nancy Feyl Chavkin. *Conversations with Louise Erdrich and Michael Dorris*. Jackson: University of Mississippi Press, 1994.

Hafen, P. Jane. "Louise Erdrich." *Concise Dictionary of Literary Biography, Supplement: Modern Writers, 1900–1998*. Ed. Tracy S. Bitonti. Detroit: Bruccoli, Clark Layman, 1998. 44–45.

Owens, Louis. "Erdrich and Dorris's Mixed Bloods and Multiple Narratives." *Other Destinies: Understanding the American Indian Novel.* American Indian Literature and Critical Studies Series. Ed. Gerald Vizenor. Norman: University of Oklahoma Press, 1992. 192–224.

Sarris, Greg. "Reading Louise Erdrich: Love Medicine as Home Medicine." *Keeping Slug Woman Alive: A Holistic Approach to American Indian Texts.* Berkeley: University of California Press, 1993. 115–45.

Wong, Hertha D. Sweet. *Louise Erdrich's Love Medicine: A Casebook.* New York: Oxford University Press, 2000.

Joy Harjo *(b. 1951)*

The poems by Joy Harjo (Muscogee Creek) represent her lyric voice and her social consciousness. Her invocations of the deer dances give tribute to her Native plains heritage. The poem "For Anna Mae Pictou Aquash . . . " is both a tribute and a protest to the 1970s conflict at Wounded Knee, South Dakota. Both of the deer poems refer to the natural relationship between animals and human beings.

Harjo was born in Tulsa, Oklahoma. She graduated from the University of New Mexico in 1976 and earned a master of fine arts degree from the University of Iowa in 1978. She has held various academic appointments at the Institute of American Indian Arts, Arizona State University, the University of Colorado, the University of Arizona, the University of New Mexico, and the University of California, Los Angeles. Harjo took a break from her academic career to play saxophone with the award-winning group, Poetic Justice, through which she also was able to perform her poetry.

Grace (1990)

I think of Wind and her wild ways the year we had nothing to lose
and lost it anyway in the cursed country of the fox. We still talk
about that winter, how the cold froze imaginary buffalo on the stuffed
horizon of snowbanks. The haunting voices of the starved and mutilated
broke fences, crashed our thermostat dreams, and we couldn't stand it
one more time. So once again we lost a winter in stubborn memory, walked
through cheap apartment walls, skated through fields of ghosts into
a town that never wanted us, in the epic search for grace.

Like Coyote, like Rabbit, we could not contain our terror and clowned
our way through a season of false midnights. We had to swallow
that town with laughter, so it would go down easy as honey. And one
morning as the sun struggled to break ice, and our dreams had found us
with coffee and pancakes in a truck stop along Highway 80,
we found grace.

I could say grace was a woman with time on her hands, or a white
buffalo escaped from memory. But in that dingy light it was a promise

of balance. We once again understood the talk of animals, and spring
was lean and hungry with the hope of children and corn.

I would like to say, with grace, we picked ourselves up and walked
into the spring thaw. We didn't; the next season was worse. You went
home to Leech Lake to work with the tribe and I went south. And, Wind,
I am still crazy. I know there is something larger than the memory
of a dispossessed people. We have seen it.

[For Wind and Jim Welch]

Deer Dancer (1990)

Nearly everyone had left that bar in the middle of winter except the
hardcore. It was the coldest night of the year, every place shut down, but
not us. Of course we noticed when she came in. We were Indian ruins. She
was the end of beauty. No one knew her, the stranger whose tribe we
recognized, her family related to deer, if that's who she was, a people
accustomed to hearing songs in pine trees, and making them hearts.

The woman inside the woman who was to dance naked in the bar of misfits
blew deer magic. Henry Jack, who could not survive a sober day, thought she
was Buffalo Calf Woman come back, passed out, his head by the toilet. All
night he dreamed a dream he could not say. The next day he borrowed
money, went home, and sent back the money I lent. Now that's a miracle.
Some people see vision in a burned tortilla, some in the face of a woman.

This is the bar of broken survivors, the club of shotgun, knife wound, of
poison by culture. We who were taught not to stare drank our beer. The
players gossiped down their cues. Someone put a quarter in the jukebox to
relive despair. Richard's wife dove to kill her. We had to hold her back,
empty her pockets of knives and diaper pins, buy her two beers to keep her
still, while Richard secretly bought the beauty a drink.

How do I say it? In this language there are no words for how the real world
collapses. I could say it in my own and the sacred mounds would come into
focus, but I couldn't take it in this dingy envelope. So I look at the stars in
this strange city, frozen to the back of the sky, the only promises that ever
make sense.

My brother-in-law hung out with white people, went to law school with a
perfect record, quit. Says you can keep your laws, your words. And

practiced law on the street with his hands. He jimmied to the proverbial
dream girl, the face of the moon, while the players racked a new game.
He bragged to us, he told her magic words and that's when she broke,
    became human.
But we all heard his bar voice crack:

What's a girl like you doing in a place like this?

That's what I'd like to know, what are we all doing in a place like this?

You would know she could hear only what she wanted to; don't we all? Left
the drink of betrayal Richard bought her, at the bar. What was she on? We all
wanted some. Put a quarter in the juke. We all take risks stepping into thin
air. Our ceremonies didn't predict this. Or we expected more.

I had to tell you this, for the baby inside the girl sealed up with a lick of
hope and swimming into praise of nations. This is not a rooming house, but
a dream of winter falls and the deer who portrayed the relatives of
strangers. The way back is deer breath on icy windows.

The next dance none of us predicted. She borrowed a chair for the stairway
to heaven and stood on a table of names. And danced in the room of children
without shoes.

You picked a fine time to leave me, Lucille.
With four hungry children and a crop in the field.

And then she took off her clothes. She shook loose memory, waltzed with the
empty lover we'd all become.

She was the myth slipped down through dreamtime. The promise of feast we
all knew was coming. The deer was crossed through knots of a curse to find
us. She was no slouch, and neither were we, watching.

The music ended. And so does the story. I wasn't there. But I imagined her
like this, not a stained red dress with tape on her heels but the deer who
entered our dream in white dawn, breathed mist into pine trees, her fawn a
blessing of meat, the ancestors who never left.

For Anna Mae Pictou Aquash, Whose Spirit Is Present Here and in the Dappled Stars (for we remember the story and must tell it again so we may all live) (1990)

Beneath a sky blurred with mist and wind,
                                        I am amazed as I watch the violet
heads of crocuses erupt from the stiff earth
                                after dying for a season,
as I have watched my own dark head
                                appear each morning after entering
the next world
                to come back to this one,
                                        amazed.
It is the way in the natural world to understand the place
                                        the ghost dancers named
after the heart/breaking destruction.
                                Anna Mae,
                                        everything and nothing changes.
You are the shimmering young woman
                                who found her voice,
when you were warned to be silent, or have your body cut away
from you like an elegant weed.
                        You are the one whose spirit is present in the dappled stars.
(They prance and lope like colored horses who stay with us
                through the streets of these steely cities. And I have seen them
                        nuzzling the frozen bodies of tattered drunks
                                        on the corner.)
This morning when the last star is dimming
                                and the buses grind toward
the middle of the city, I know it is ten years since they buried you
                        the second time in Lakota, a language that could
                                                free you.
I heard about it in Oklahoma, or New Mexico,
                how the wind howled and pulled everything down
        in a righteous anger.
                (It was the women who told me) and we understood wordlessly
the ripe meaning of your murder.
                As I understand ten years later after the slow changing
                                of the seasons

that we have just begun to touch
> the dazzling whirlwind of our anger,
we have just begun to perceive the amazed world the ghost dancers
> entered
> > crazily, beautifully.

In February 1976, an unidentified body of a young woman was found on the Pine Ridge Reservation in South Dakota. The official autopsy attributed death to exposure. The FBI agent present at the autopsy ordered her hands severed and sent to Washington for fingerprinting. John Trudell rightly called this mutilation an act of war. Her unnamed body was buried. When Anna Mae Aquash, a young Micmac woman who was an active American Indian Movement member, was discovered missing by her friends and relatives, a second autopsy was demanded. It was then discovered she had been killed by a bullet fired at close range to the back of her head. Her killer or killers have yet to be identified.

Deer Ghost (1990)

1.

I hear a deer outside; her glass voice of the invisible
calls my heart to stand up and weep in this fragile city.
The season changed once more, as if my childhood
was forced from me, stolen during the dream of the lion
fleeing the old-style houses my people used to make of mud
and straw to mother the source of burning. The skeleton
of stars encircling this misty world stares through the roof;
there is no hiding any more, and mystery is a skin that will never
quite fit. This is a night ghosts wander, and in this place
they are as nameless as the nightmare the muscles in my
left hand remember.

2.

I have failed once more and let the fire go out. I misunderstood
and left my world on your musk angel wings. Your fire scorched
my lips, but it was sweet, a bitter poetry. I can taste you
now as I squat on the earth floor of this home I abandoned
for you. On this street named for a warrior people, a street
named after bravery, I am lighting the fire that crawls from my spine
to the gods with a coal from my sister's flame. This is what names
me in the ways of my people, who have called me back.
The deer knows what it is doing wandering the streets of this
city; it has never forgotten the songs.

3.
I don't care what you say. The deer is no imaginary tale
I have created to fill this house because you left me.
There is more to this world than I have ever let on
to you, or anyone.

Further Reading

The Good Luck Cat. 2000.

The Last Song. 1975.

A Map to the Next World: Poetry and Tales. 2000.

Reinventing the Enemy's Language: Contemporary Native Women's Writings of North America.
    Ed. Joy Harjo and Gloria Bird. 1997.

Secrets from the Center of the World. Photographs by Stephen Strom. 1989.

She Had Some Horses. 1983.

The Spiral of Memory: Interviews/Joy Harjo. Ed. Laura Coltelli. 1996.

What Moon Drove Me to This. 1979.

The Woman Who Fell from the Sky: Poems. 1994.

Reading about Joy Harjo

Ancestral Voices. Videocassette. Public Affairs Television and David Grubin Productions.
    Princeton: Films for the Humanities and Sciences, 1994. (Joy Harjo, Mary Tallmoun-
    tain, and Garret Kaoru Hogo.)

Coltelli, Laura. "Joy Harjo." *Winged Words: American Indian Writing Speak.* Lincoln: Uni-
    versity of Nebraska Press, 1990.

Harjo, Joy, and Karen Strom. "Joy Harjo." Internet Public Library: Native Authors Project.
    23 October 2000. Online, AOL: *http://www.hanksville.org/storytellers/joy.*

Jaskoski, Helen. "A *MELUS* Interview: Joy Harjo." *MELUS* 16.1 (spring 1989–90): 5–13.

Wilson, Norma C. "Joy Harjo." *Dictionary of Native American Literature.* Ed. Andrew Wiget.
    New York: Garland, 1994. 437–44.

Stories of Exploration and Travel: *Newcomers' Accounts*

When President Thomas Jefferson finalized the Louisiana Purchase in 1803 the territory of the United States more than doubled, and neither the buyers nor the sellers knew the map of the interior. Extending from the Mississippi across the Rocky Mountains and from Louisiana to the Canadian border, the land purchased from France included the region we have labeled the Great Plains. Jefferson appointed his personal secretary, Meriwether Lewis, and William Clark, a seasoned army veteran of the Ohio and Kentucky frontier, to head a party of exploration and diplomatic introduction to the Native inhabitants. The trip, from 1804 to 1806, took them up the Missouri and across the northern Rocky Mountains to the Pacific Ocean—and back. The party returned with journals kept by Lewis, Clark, and other members of the party, maps of regions never before recorded, and written descriptions and specimens of 178 plants and 122 animal species never before scientifically identified.[1] The expedition's reports confirmed Jefferson's vision of new territories that promised nature's bounty and seemingly limitless space for the country's expansion.

Even before Lewis and Clark returned, other expeditions set out across other parts of the Great Plains, but for various reasons the accounts of these journeys do not appeal so much to our persistent romantic view of the region. The 1820 expedition led by Stephen Long explored parts of Kansas, Colorado, and Oklahoma. Concerned primarily with mapping the new territory, Long's report reflects a much more difficult journey over a much harsher landscape. Edwin James, a scientist and the chronicler of Long's 1820 expedition, wrote across the expedition's map "Great Desert," thereby declaring the prairies an effective barrier to the too-rapid growth of American settlement which might result in a scattered populace and a less-unified republic. Other accounts corroborated James's Great American Desert label that still remains firmly attached to the Great Plains in the popular imagination. Travelers and traders soon followed the mapmakers, spreading across the prairies and plains on the routes established by earlier explorers and trappers. William Becknell established the Santa Fe Trail and opened trade with Mexico's southwestern territories in 1821, and John Bidwell led the first settlers across the Great Plains on the trail to Oregon in 1841.

The West attracted Americans and Europeans eager for the opportunity to hunt buffalo and observe the "exotic" Indian. Their accounts became part of a popular nineteenth-century literary genre, the travel narrative. Artist-travelers such as the self-taught lawyer George Catlin and the Swiss artist Karl Bodmer, who both traveled up the Missouri with the German explorer and naturalist

Prince Maximilian, presented Indians in splendid ceremonial dress and also in everyday scenes. Their work contributed to the romantic myth of the noble savage but also to the growing interest among ethnographers and other scholars who were forming their own ideas about Native American culture. The grandiose landscapes of Albert Bierstadt and Thomas Moran helped Americans and Europeans visualize an exotic, outsized West of broad vistas and towering mountains. In most Bierstadt paintings the human, if visible, is a small presence barely visible off-center, dwarfed by the immense space of mountains, waterfalls, or the prairie's far horizon.

These early accounts appealed to the imagination of the pioneers set on heading west: the romantic and the realist both found enough variety within the reports of explorers and travelers to satisfy the visions they carried with them as they approached the Great Plains. These reports, written by traders, travelers, and settlers, combined with the promotions by railroad and land agents, fed the curiosity of Americans and Europeans alike during the years of expansion and migration, until the end of the nineteenth century.

Notes

1. For a full account of Lewis and Clark as naturalists, see Paul Russell Cutright, *Lewis and Clark: Pioneering Naturalists*. Lincoln: University of Nebraska Press, 1969, esp. appendix A, "Plants Discovered by Lewis and Clark," 399–423; appendix B, "Animals Discovered by Lewis and Clark," 424–47; and *The Herbarium of the Lewis and Clark Expedition*, in Gary Moulton, ed., *The Journals of Lewis and Clark*. vol. 12 (Lincoln: University of Nebraska Press, 1999).

Further Reading

Barclay, Donald A., James Maguire, and Peter Wild. *Into the Wilderness Dream: Exploration Narratives of the American West 1500–1805*. Salt Lake City: University of Utah Press, 1994.

deVoto, Bernard. *Across the Wide Missouri*. Boston: Houghton Mifflin, 1947.

Goetzmann, William E. *Exploration and Empire: The European and the Scientist in the Winning of the American West*. New York: Knopf, 1966.

Jones, Howard Mumford. *O Strange New World*. New York: Viking, 1952.

Ronda, James P. *Revealing America: Image and Imagination in the Exploration of North America*. Lexington MA: D. C. Heath, 1996.

Pedro de Castaneda *(c. 1510–1565)*

Spanish explorers provide the first European descriptions of the Great Plains. Traveling north from Mexico, they cared little for the soil's fertile potential or the value of a northwest passage to the rich Oriental trade because they imagined golden riches were to be found just ahead of their own expeditions. When those riches proved ephemeral they withdrew, leaving behind missionary priests intent on planting Roman Catholicism in the desert Southwest and the horses that would transform the prairie Indians' cultures.

One report of these Spanish explorations came from the pen of Pedro de Castaneda, who accompanied Coronado's ill-fated expedition from Mexico in 1540 across the southern Great Plains in search of the fabled Quivira, the seven cities of gold. Guided by an Indian they called the Turk, Coronado's forces crossed Arizona, New Mexico, and west Texas into Kansas, their guide's promised riches always a few days' march ahead. The Spaniards wandered across the featureless plains, while their scouts left crude markers for the army to follow. Some of the men who went out to hunt did not return, unable to find their way in a landscape with no directional landmarks. Finally, exhausted by months of marching, Coronado reached the ordinary village of Quivira located somewhere in central Kansas. Their guide, now home, admitted he had deliberately led them so far at the request of the Indians who had been mistreated by the Spaniards and wanted revenge on the weakened interlopers. The Turk was strangled for his role in the deception.

De Castaneda's account was written some twenty years after the expedition. Although his narrative undoubtedly contains inaccuracies that arise from faulty information and fading memories, it reflects de Castaneda's effort to report what he saw rather than repeating vague accounts of imagined, mythical cities of gold.

By 1600 Spanish settlers were traveling into present-day New Mexico attempting, with varying degrees of success, to establish permanent settlements, convert the natives, and establish routes to link their scattered outposts.

Excerpts from "The Narrative of the Expedition of Coronado" (1565)

Which treats of the plains that were crossed, of the cows, and of the people who inhabit them.

We have spoken of the settlements of high houses which are situated in what seems to be the most level and open part of the mountains, since it is 150 leagues across before entering the level country between the two mountain chains which I said were near the North Sea and the South Sea, which might better be called the Western Sea along this coast.[1] This mountain series is the one which is near the South Sea. In order to show that the settlements are in the middle of the mountains, I will state that it is eighty leagues from Chichilticalli, where we began to cross this country, to Cibola; from Cibola, which is the first village, to Cicuye, which is the last on the way across, is seventy leagues; it is thirty leagues from Cicuye to where the plains begin.[2] It may be we went across in an indirect or roundabout way, which would make it seem as if there was more country than if it had been crossed in a direct line, and it may be more difficult and rougher. This can not be known certainly, because the mountains change their direction above the bay at the mouth of the Firebrand (Tizon) River.

Now we will speak of the plains. The country is spacious and level, and is more than 400 leagues wide in the part between the two mountain ranges—one, that which Francisco Vazquez Coronado crossed, and the other that which the force under Don Fernando de Soto crossed, near the North Sea, entering the country from Florida. No settlements were seen anywhere on these plains.

In traversing 250 leagues, the other mountain range was not seen, nor a hill nor a hillock which was three times as high as a man. Several lakes were found at intervals; they were round as plates, a stone's throw or more across, some fresh and some salt. The grass grows tall near these lakes; away from them it is very short, a span or less.[3] The country is like a bowl, so that when a man sits down, the horizon surrounds him all around at the distance of a musket shot. There are no groves of trees except at the rivers, which flow at the bottom of some ravines where the trees grow so thick that they were not noticed until one was right on the edge of them. They are of dead earth. There are paths down into these, made by the cows when they go to the water, which is essential throughout these plains.[4] As I have related in the first part, people follow the cows, hunting them and tanning the skins to take to the settlements in the winter to sell, since they go there to pass the winter, each company going to those which are nearest, some to the settlements at Cicuye, others toward Quivira, and others to the settlements which are situated in the direction of Florida. These people are called Querechos and Teyas.[5] They described some large settlements, and judging from what was seen of these people and from the accounts they gave of other places, there are a good many more of these people than there are of those at the settlements. They have better figures, are better warriors, and are more feared. They travel like the Arabs, with their tents and troops of dogs loaded with poles and having Moorish pack-saddles with girths.[6] When the load gets disarranged, the dogs howl, calling some one to fix them right. These people eat raw flesh and drink blood. They do not eat human flesh. They are a kind people and not cruel. They are faithful friends. They are able to make themselves very well understood by means of signs. They dry the flesh in the sun, cutting it thin like a leaf, and when dry they grind it like meal to keep it and make a sort of sea soup of it to eat. A handful thrown into a pot swells up so as to increase very much. They season it with fat, which they always try to secure when they kill a cow. They empty a large gut and fill it with blood, and carry this around the neck to drink when they are thirsty. When they open the belly of a cow, they squeeze out the chewed grass and drink the juice that remains behind, because they say that this contains the essence of the stomach. They cut the hide open at the back and pull it off at the joints, using a flint as large as a finger, tied in a little stick, with as much ease as if working with a good iron tool. They give it an edge with their own teeth. The quickness with which they do this is something worth seeing and noting.

There are very great numbers of wolves on these plains, which go around with the cows. They have white skins. The deer are pied with white. Their skin is loose, so that when they are killed it can be pulled off with the hand while warm, coming off like pigskin. The rabbits, which are very numerous, are so foolish that those on horseback killed them with their lances. This is when they are mounted among the cows. They fly from a person on foot.

Of Quivira, of where it is and some information about it.

Quivira is to the west of those ravines, in the midst of the country, somewhat nearer the mountains toward the sea, for the country is level as far as Quivira, and there they began to see some mountain chains. The country is well settled. Judging from what was seen on the borders of it, this country is very similar to that of Spain in the varieties of vegetation and fruits. There are plums like those of Castile, grapes, nuts, mulberries, oats, pennyroyal, wild marjoram, and large quantities of flax, but this does not do them any good, because they do not know how to use it. The people are of almost the same sort and appearance as the Teyas. They have villages like those in New Spain. The houses are round, without a wall, and they have one story like a loft, under the roof, where they sleep and keep their belongings. The roofs are of straw. There are other thickly settled provinces around it containing large numbers of men. A friar named Juan de Padilla remained in this province, together with a Spanish-Portuguese and a negro and a half-blood and some Indians from the province of Capothan, in New Spain. They killed the friar because he wanted to go to the province of the Guas, who were their enemies. The Spaniard escaped by taking flight on a mare, and afterward reached New Spain, coming out by way of Panuco. The Indians from New Spain who accompanied the friar were allowed by the murderers to bury him, and then they followed the Spaniard and overtook him. This Spaniard was a Portuguese, named Campo.

The great river of the Holy Spirit (Espiritu Santo), which Don Fernando de Soto discovered in the country of Florida, flows through this country. It passes through a province called Arache, according to the reliable accounts which were obtained here. The sources were not visited, because, according to what they said, it comes from a very distant country in the mountains of the South Sea, from the part that sheds its waters onto the plains. It flows across all the level country and breaks through the mountains of the North Sea, and comes out where the people with Don Fernando de Soto navigated it. This is more than 300 leagues from where it enters the sea. On account of this, and also because it has large tributaries, it is so mighty when it enters the sea that they lost sight of the land before the water ceased to be fresh.

This country of Quivira was the last that was seen, of which I am able to give any description or information. Now it is proper for me to return and speak of the army, which I left in Tiguex, resting for the winter, so that it would be able to proceed or return in search of these settlements of Quivira, which was not accomplished after all, because it was God's pleasure that these discoveries should remain for other peoples and that we who had been there should content ourselves with saying that we were the first who discovered it and obtained any information concerning it, just as Hercules knew the site where Julius Cæsar was to found Seville or Hispales. May the all-powerful Lord grant that His will be done in everything. It is certain that if this had not been His will Francisco Vazquez [Coronado] would not have returned to New Spain without cause or reason, as he did, and that it would not have been left for those with Don Fernando de Soto to settle such a good country, as they have done, and besides settling it to increase its extent, after obtaining, as they did, information from our army.

Notes

1. A league is approximately 3 miles or 4.83 kilometers. In the years before the interior of North America was explored and mapped, scholars theorized that the region was drained by four great river systems that sprang from a single source, ran north, south, east, and west, and drained into the four great seas: the Atlantic, the Gulf of Mexico, the Arctic, and the Pacific. A number of expeditions searched along the coast of North America and made forays into the interior, looking for the theoretical Western River that would empty into the Pacific.—Eds.

2. Chichilticalli is north of Globe, Arizona; Cibola refers to the pueblos of Zuni and Acoma on the Arizona–New Mexico border; and Cicuye is Pecos, New Mexico.—Eds.

3. A span is approximately nine inches, the distance from the tip of the thumb to the tip of the little finger when the hand is fully extended.—Eds.

4. "Cows" is de Castaneda's word for bison.—Eds.

5. *Querechos* are Apaches.—Eds.

6. Before the Spanish introduced horses, some Plains Indians used dogs to haul supplies.
—Eds.

Reading about Early Explorations of the Great Plains

Barclay, Donald, and Peter Wild. "Pre-Lewis and Clark Narratives of Western North America." *Updating the Literary West.* Forth Worth: Texas Christian University Press, 1997. 150–61.

Flint, Richard, and Shirley Cushing Flint, eds. *The Coronado Expedition to Tierra Nueva: The 1540–1542 Route across the Southwest.* Niwot: University Press of Colorado, 1997.

Thacker, Robert. *The Great Prairie Fact and Literary Imagination.* Albuquerque: University of New Mexico Press, 1986.

Udall, Stewart. *To the Inland Empire: Coronado and Our Spanish Legacy.* Garden City NY: Doubleday, 1987.

Vigil, Ralph H., Frances Kaye, and John Wunder, eds. *Spain and the Plains: Myths and Realities of Spanish Exploration and Settlement on the Great Plains.* Niwot: University Press of Colorado, 1994.

Meriwether Lewis *(1774–1809) and*
William Clark *(1770–1838)*

The remarkable expedition led by Meriwether Lewis and William Clark has become so firmly embedded in our national mythology that the image of their Shoshone guide, Sacagawea, graces the one-dollar coin. A mere twenty-five years after the nation's formation it was obvious to many that the United States would, inevitably, spread westward, even though Spain, France, and Britain had already claimed large sections of the western parts of the North American continent where the Plains Indian tribes had lived for hundreds of years. Thomas Jefferson knew what he wanted Lewis and Clark to accomplish on their voyage across the continent, but he was careful to present the journey in different terms to different audiences. To Spain, which owned the region until they sold it to France, he presented it as a scientific undertaking. To Congress he presented it as a commercial venture to discover the illusive (that is, nonexistent) Northwest Passage that would open a water route to the lucrative trade with the Far East. To France it became a pragmatic necessity to sell the recently acquired region: war with England was brewing, thanks to Napoleon's ambitions. The expedition's goal was, of course, all of the above. In addition, Jefferson instructed Lewis and Clark to study the climate and the soil's fertility, to catalog the flowers and animals (especially those "not of the U.S."), to note the location of minerals such as salt and coal, and to assess possible trade routes as they mapped the region, known only from the fragmentary reports of trappers and British and Spanish explorers who had crossed various parts of the new Louisiana Territory.* The expedition was also meant to be a diplomatic mission to the Indian tribes they would encounter, informing them that the "Great White Father" now resided in Washington. And, while they were at it, Jefferson wanted Lewis and Clark to record their observations of the Indians' culture and to determine as much as they could about the regions stretching north and south from their route along the Missouri River. In the sections included here, for example, they note a report that Santa Fe is a twenty-five-day journey away.

The expedition set out from St. Louis on 14 May 1804. It took the party seven months to travel up the Missouri River, using sails if there was a favorable wind but more often rowing and sometimes, in shallow water, walking along the shore, pulling their heavily loaded boats against the current. They spent the winter in a Mandan village before embarking into the truly unknown territory across the

---

*Jefferson's instructions to the group are several pages long. See *The Journals of Lewis and Clark*, ed. Bernard deVoto (New York: Houghton Mifflin, 1953), 481–87.

Rocky Mountains. By the time they returned to St. Louis on 26 September 1805 the territory had become firmly attached to the United States.

These entries, from early in the expedition, reflect the multiple voices that make the record of this voyage unusually complete. During this month, July–August 1804, Lewis contributes some careful descriptions of animals they collect, but Clark is the principal journalist. In addition to entries from Lewis and Clark, there are reports by other Corps of Discovery members—Sgt. Patrick Gass, Sgt. Charles Floyd (who even reports on his illness that would prove fatal), Sgt. John Ordway, and Pvt. Joseph Whitehouse. The entries document the multiple tasks and duties the Corps had to attend to. Some search for wood or hunt game to feed fifty hard-working men. Others investigate Indian sites or perform routine tasks. Their entries reflect the aspects of the Corpsmen's daily life that Lewis and Clark would naturally overlook.

These journals were written under difficult circumstances. They are rough notes for the report that Lewis never managed to complete.* Sentence structure, capitalization, and spelling in the early nineteenth century were not so firmly fixed as they are today. Some words were created on the spot to name the thing or person or place being described. What one gets in return for the effort it takes to read the journals is the immediacy of discovery: the knowledge, in other words, that neither the reader nor the author knows what the next day or the next page may reveal.

The "Pani" are the Pawnee Indians, the "Mahar" the Omaha Tribe. "S.S." is the starboard or right side of the boat when facing forward; "L.S." is the larboard side of the boat when facing the front or bow. A perogue (or pirogue) is a large dugout canoe with oars.

Excerpt from *The Lewis and Clark Journals* (1815)

July 23, 1804

[Clark] at 11 oClock Sent off George Drewyer & *Peter Crousett* with Some tobacco to invite the Otteaus if at their town and Panies if they Saw them to Come and talk with us at our Camp &c. (at this Season the Indians on this river are in the Praries Hunting the Buffalow but from Some Signs of hunters near this place &

*Lewis was governor of Louisiana Territory and on his way to Washington when he died in 1809. Although some suspected murder, Jefferson, who knew of Lewis's periods of depression, believed his death was a suicide and most present-day scholars agree. If it was a suicide, one of the factors may have been the apparent difficulty Lewis was having with the journals. Stephen Ambrose has called it "the greatest writer's block of all time." From *The Journals of Lewis and Clark*, ed. Bernard deVoto (Boston: Houghton Mifflin, 1997), x.

the Plains being on fire near their towns induce a belief that they this nation have returned to get Some Green Corn or rosting Ears) raised a flag Staff Sund & Dryed our provisions &c. I commence Coppying a map of the river below to Send to the P[resident] U S . . . one man with a tumer on his breast. [Remained at Camp White Catfish.]

[Gass] Our people were all busily engaged in hunting, making oars, dressing skins, and airing our stores, provisions, and baggage. We killed two deer and caught two beaver. Beaver appear plenty in this part of the country.

July 24, 1804

[Clark] I am much engaged drawing off a map, Capt. Lewis also much engaged in prepareing Papers to Send back by a pirogue— Which we intended to Send back from the river Plate— observations at this place makes the Lattitude 41° 3′ 19″ North[1]

This evening Guthrege [Goodrich] Cought a *white Catfish*. [Remained at Camp White Catfish.]

[Floyd] Histed ouer Collars in the morning for the Reseptions of Indians who we expected Hear when the Rain and wind Came So that we wase forst to take it down.

July 25, 1804

[Clark] at 2 oClock *Drewyer & Peter* [Cruzatte] returned from the *Otteaus* Village; and informs that no Indians were at their towns, They Saw Some fresh Signs of a Small party but Could not find them. in their rout to the Towns (Which is about 18 miles West) they passed thro a open Prarie Crossed papillion or Butterfly Creek[2] and a Small butifull river which run into the Platt a little below the Town Called *Corne de charf*.[3] [Remained at Camp White Catfish.]

[Floyd] Continued Hear as the Capts is not Don there Riting.

July 26, 1804

[Clark] the wind blustering and hard from the South all day which blowed the Clouds of Sand in Such a manner that I could not complete my p[l]an in the tent, the Boat roled in Such a manner that I could do nothing in that, I was Compessed to go to the woods and Combat with the Musqutors, I opened the Tumer of a man on the left breast, which discharged half a point [pint?]. [Remained at Camp White Catfish.]

July 28, 1804

[Clark] G Drewyer brought in a *Missourie Indian* which he met with hunting in the Prarie This Indian is one of the fiew remaining of that nation, & lives with the Otteauz, his Camp about 4 miles from the river, he informs that the "great gangue" of the nation were hunting the Buffalow in the Plains. h[i]s party was Small Consisting only of about 20 Lodges. [Camped north of Council Bluffs, Pottawattamie County, Iowa.]

July 29, 1804

[Clark] Sent a french man *la Liberty* with the Indian to Otteaze Camp to invite the Indians to meet us on the river above. [Camped in Pottawattamie County,

Iowa, somewhat above the Washington-Douglas county line, Nebraska, on the opposite side.]

[Ordway] Willard Sent back to last nights Camp for his Tommahawk, which he left we Delayed about 2 hours. Willard lost his rifle in a large Creek Called Boyer.[4]

[Floyd] the Reasen this man Gives of His being with So Small a party is that He Has not Got Horses to Go in the Large praries after the Buflows but Stayes about the Town and River to Hunte the Elke to Seporte thare fameleys.

July 30, 1804

[Lewis] this day Joseph Fields killed a *Braro*[5] as it is called by the French *engáges*. this is a singular anamal not common to any part of the United States. it's weight is sixteen pounds. it is a carniverous anamal. on both sides of the upper jaw is fexed one long and sharp canine tooth. it's eye are small black and piercing. [Camped near Fort Calhoun, Washington County, Nebraska, the party's Council Bluff.]

[Clark] Capt. Lewis and my Self walked in the Prarie on the top of the Bluff and observed the most butifull prospects imagionable, this Prarie is Covered with grass about 10 or 12 Inch high, (Land rich) rises about 1/2 a mile back Something higher and is a Plain as fur as Can be Seen, under those high Lands next the river is butifull Bottom interspersed with Groves of timber, the River may be Seen for a great Distance both above & below meandering thro: the plains between two ranges of High land which appear to be from 4 to 20 ms. apart, each bend of the river forming a point which Contains tall timber, principally Willow Cotton wood some Mulberry elm Sycamore & ash. the groves Contain walnit coffeenut[6] & Oake in addition & Hickory & Lynn.

[Clark] everything in prime order. men in high Spirits.

July 31, 1804

[Floyd] I am verry Sick and Has ben for Somtime but have Recoverd my helth again. [Remained at the party's Council Bluff.]

August 1, 1804

[Clark] This being my birth day I order'd a Saddle of fat Vennison, an Elk fleece & a Bevertail to be cooked and a Desert of Cheries, Plumbs, Raspberries Currents and grapes of a Supr. quality. The Indians not yet arrived. a Cool fine eveninge Musquetors verry troublesom, the Praries Contain Cheres, Apple, Grapes, Currents, Rasp burry, Gooseberris Hastlenuts and a great Variety of Plants & flours not Common to the U S. What a field for a Botents [botanist] and a natirless [naturalist]. [Remained at the party's Council Bluff.]

August 2, 1804

[Clark] at Sunset Mr. *Fairfong* and a pt. of Otteau & Missourie Nation Came to Camp, among those Indians 6 were Chiefs, the principal Chiefs Capt. Lewis & myself met those Indians & informed them we were glad to See them, and would Speak to them tomorrow, Sent them Som rosted meat Pork flour & meal, in return they Sent us Water millions. [every?] man on his Guard & ready for any thing. [Remained at the party's Council Bluff.]

[Floyd] the Indianes Came whare we had expected thay fired meney Guns when thay Came in Site of us and we ansered them withe the Cannon.

[Whitehouse] They [Otoes] are a handsome stout well made set of Indians & have good open Countenances, and are of a light brown colour, and have long black hair, which they do wear without cutting; and they all use paint in order to compleat their dress.

August 3, 1804

[Clark] after Brackfast we Collected those Indians under an orning of our Main Sail, in presence of our Party paraded & Delivered a long Speech to them expressive of our journey the wirkes of our Government, Some advice to them and Directions how They were to Conduct themselves, the princapal Chief for the nation being absente we sent him the Speech *flag* Meadel & Some Cloathes. after hering what they had to say Delivered a medal of Second Grade to one for the Ottos & and one for the Missourie present and 4 medals of a third Grade to the inferior Chief two for each tribe. Those two parts of nations, Ottos & Missouries now residing together is about 250 men are the Ottoes Composeing 2/3 and Missourie 1/3 part . . . Those Chiefs all Delivered a Speech acknowledgeing Their approbation to the Speech and promissing to prosue the advice & Derictions given them that they wer happy to find that they had fathers which might be depended on &c. We gave them a Cannister of Powder and a Bottle of whiskey and delivered a few presents to the whole after giveing a *Br: Cth:* [breech cloth] Some Paint guartering[7] & a Meadele to those we *made* Cheifs after Capt Lewis's Shooting the air gun a feiw Shots (which astonished those nativs) we Set out and proceeded on five miles . . . The man *Liberty* whome we Sent for the Ottoes has not Come up. [Camped in either Harrison County, Iowa, or Washington County, Nebraska, some miles south of Blair, Nebraska.]

[Whitehouse] the Indians Beheavd. well while Incampd. Neer our party.

August 4, 1804

[Clark] proceeded on . . . the Banks washing away & trees falling in constantly for 1 mile, abov this place is the remains of an old Tradeing establishment L. S. where Petr. Crusett one of our hands Stayed two years & traded with the *Mahars* . . . *Reed* a man who went back to Camp for his knife has not joined us. [Camped in either Washington County, Nebraska, or Harrison County, Iowa, northeast of Blair, Nebraska.]

August 5, 1804

[Lewis] Killed a serpent[8] on the bank of the river adjoining a large prarie.

	F	Inch
Length from nose to tail	5	2
Circumpherence in largest part—		4½
Number of scuta on belly— 221		
Do. on Tale— 53		

No pison teeth therefore think him perfectly innocent— eyes, center black with a border of pale brown yellow Colour of skin on head yellowish green with black specks on the extremity of the scuta which are pointed or triangular colour of back, transverse stripes of black and dark brown of an inch in width, succeeded by a yellowish brown of half that width— the end of the tale hard and pointed like a cock's spur— the sides are speckled with yellowish brown and black. two roes of black spots on a lite yellow ground pass throughout his whole length on the upper points of the scuta of the belly and tale 1/2 Inch apart this snake is vulgarly called the cow or bull snake from a bellowing nois which it is said sometimes to make resembling that anamal, tho' as to this fact I am unable to attest it never having heard them make that or any other noise myself.

I have frequently observed an acquatic bird[9] in the cours of asscending this river but have never been able to procure one before today . . . they lay their eggs on the sand bars without shelter or nest, and produce their young from the 15th to the last of June, the young ones of which we caught several are covered with down of a yellowish white colour and on the back some small specks of a dark brown. they bear a great resemblance to the young quale of ten days oald, and apear like them to be able to runabout and peck their food as soon as they are hatched— this bird, lives on small fish, worms and bugs which it takes on the virge of the water it is seldom seen to light on trees an qu[i]te as seldom do they lite in the water and swim tho' the foot would indicate that they did it's being webbed . . . this bird is very noysey when flying which is dose exttreemly swift the motion of the wing is much like that of *kildee*[10] it has two notes one like the squaking of a small pig only on reather a high kee, and the other kit'-tee'-kit'-tee'- as near as letters can express the sound. [Camped in Harrison County, Iowa, across from the Burt-Washington county line, Nebraska.]

[Clark] In every bend the banks are falling in from the Current being thrown against those bends by the Sand points which inlarges and the Soil I believe from unquestionable appearns. of the entire bottom from one hill to the other being the mud or ooze of the River at Some former Period mixed with Sand and Clay easily melts and Slips into the River, and the mud mixes with the water & the Sand is washed down and lodges on the points— Great quantites of Grapes on the banks, I observe three different Kinds[11] at this time ripe, one Of the no. is large & has the flaver of the Purple grape.

August 6, 1804

[Clark] We have every reason to belive that one man has *Deserted Moses B: Reed* he has been absent three Days and one french man we Sent to the Indian Camps has not joined us, we have reasons to beleve he lost himself in attempting to join us at the *Council Bluff.* [Camped apparently in Harrison County, Iowa, about half-way between the Soldier and Little Sioux Rivers.]

August 7, 1804

[Clark] at 1 oClock dispatched George Drewyer, R. Fields, Wm. Bratten & Wm. Labieche back after the Deserter reid with order if he did not give up Peaceibly to put him to Death &c. to go to the Ottoes Village & enquire for La Liberty and bring him to the Mahars Village, also with a Speech on the occasion to the Ottoes & Missouries— and directing a few of their Chiefs to come to the Mahars, & we would make a peace between them & the Mahar and *Souex,* a String of wompom & a Carrot of Tobacco. [Camped a few miles below the mouth of the Little Sioux River, probably on the Iowa side in Harrison County.]

[Floyd] on the 4th of this month one of ouer men by the name of Moses B. Reed went Back to ouer Camp whare we had Left in the morning, to Git his Knife which he Had Left at the Camp . . . pon examining his nap-Sack we found that he had taken his Cloas and all His powder and Balles, and had hid them out that night and had made that an excuse to Desarte from us with out aney Jest Case.

August 8, 1804

[Gass] In a bag under the bill and neck of the pelican, which Captain Lewis killed, we put five gallons of water. [Camped probably on the Iowa side, in southwest Monona County, not far above the Harrison County line.]

August 9, 1804

[Clark] Musquetors worse this evening than ever I have Seen them. [Camped a mile or two south of Onawa, Harrison County, Iowa.]

August 11, 1804

[Clark] a hard wind accompanied with rain from the S. E. after the rain was over Capt. Lewis myself & 10 men assended the Hill on the L. S. under which there was Some fine Springs to the top of a high point where the *Mahars King Black* Bird[12] was burried 4 years ago. a mound of earth about 12 Diamuter at the base & 6 feet high is raised over him turfed, and a pole 8 feet high in the Center on this pole we fixed a white flage bound with red Blue & white. [Camped in the vicinity of Badger Lake, Monona County, Iowa.]

[Floyd] Capt Lewis and Clark . . . histed a flage on [Blackbird's] Grave as noner [honor] for him which will pleas the Indianes.

[Gass] His name was Blackbird, king of the Mahas; an absolute monarch while living, and the Indians suppose can exercise the power of one though dead.

August 12, 1804

[Clark] a *Prarie Wolf*[13] Come near the bank and Barked at us this evening, we made an attempt but could not git him, this Animale Barkes like a large *feste* [feist] Dog. Beever is verry Plenty on this part of the river. I prepare Some presents for to give the Indians of the *Mahars* nation. Wiser apt. Cook & Supentdt. of the Provisions of Sergt. Floyds Squad. [Camped in either Monona or Woodbury County, Iowa, near the county line.]

August 13, 1804

[Clark] [passed] the place Mr. Ja: McKey had a tradeing house in 95 & 96 & named it Fort Charles[14] . . . Detached Sergt. Ordeway Peter Crusatt, Geroge Shannon Werner & Carrn. to the Mahar Village[15] with a flag & Some Tobacco to invite the Nation to See & talke with us on tormorrow. [Camped a few miles south of Dakota City, Dakota County, Nebraska, or opposite in Woodbury County, Iowa, the party's Fish Camp.]

[Ordway] I and 3 more of the party went out to the [Omaha] Village or to the place where it formely Stood. we passed through high Grass in the low prarie & came to the Mahar Creek on our way . . . which was verry fatigueing for the high Grass Sunflowers & thistles &C all of which were above 10 feet high, a great quantity of wild peas among those weeds, we broke our way through them till we came to where their had been a village of about 300 Cabbins called the Mahar village. it was burned about 4 years ago immediately after near half the Nation died with the Small pox, which was as I was informed about 400, we found none of the natives about the place they were out hunting the Buffelow.

August 14, 1804

[Clark] Those people haveing no houses no Corn or any thing more than the graves of their ancesters to attach them to the old Village, Continue in pursuite of the Buffalow longer than others who had greater attachments to their native Village— the ravages of the Small Pox (which Swept off 400 men & women & Children in perpoposion) has reduced this Nation not exceeding 300 men and left them to the insults of their weaker neighbours which before was glad to be on friendly turms with them— I am told whin this fatal malady was among them they Carried ther franzey to verry extroadinary length, not only of burning their Village, but they put their *wives* & Children to *Dath* with a view of their all going together to Some better Countrey— They burry their Dead on the tops of high hills and rais mounds on the top of them, The cause or way those people took the Small Pox is uncertain, the most Probable from Some other Nation by means of a warparty. [Remained at Fish Camp.]

[Ordway] we Set out at light, & walked along down the hills past the Graves. we Saw also a number of large holes in the Ground where they used to hide their peltry &C. in, when they went out hunting and when they returned they would dig it out again, I put up a paper on a pole Stuck in a round hill, as a Signal for G. Drewyer &C . . . we walked along the ridge which is high prarie all back as far as my [eye?] could behold. we expected to have found Some corn or Something growing Some where in the bottom but we could not see any appearance of anythig being planted this year . . . Returned to the Boats about 10 oClock A. M.

August 15, 1804

[Clark] we mad a Drag and haulted up the Creek, and Cought 318 fish of different kind I'e' Peke,[16] Bass, Salmon,[17] perch, red horse, Small Cat,[18] and a kind of perch Called Silverfish,[19] on the Ohio. I cought a Srimp[20] prosisely of Shape Size & flavour of those about N. Orleans & the lower party of the Mississippi in this Creek which is only the pass or Streight from Beaver Pond to another, is Crouded with large Mustles[21] Verry fat, Ducks, Pliver of different Kinds are on those Ponds as well as on the river. [Remained at Fish Camp.]

[Gass] This day Sergeant Floyd became very sick and remained so all night. He was seized with a complaint somewhat like a violent colick.

August 17, 1804

[Clark] at 6 oClock this evening *Labieche* one of the Party Sent to the Ottoes joined, and informed that the Party was behind with one of the Deserters M B. Reed and the 3 principal Chiefs of the Nations— La Liberty they cought but he decived them and got away— the object of those Chiefs comeing forward is to make a peace with the Mahars thro: us. as the Mahars are not at home this great object cannot be accomplished at this time Set the Praries on fire to bring the Mahars & Soues if any were near, this being the usial Signal. [Remained at Fish Camp.]

August 18, 1804

[Clark] in the after part of the Day the Party with the Indians arrivd. we meet them under a Shade near the Boat and after a Short talk we gave them Provisions to eat & proceeded to the trial of Reed, he Confessed that he "Deserted & Stold a public Rifle[22] Shot-pouch Powder & Bals" and requested we would be as favourable with him as we Could consistantly with our Oathes—which we were and only Sentenced him to run the Gantlet four times through the Party & that each man with 9 Swichies Should punish him and for him not to be considered in future as one of the Party— The three principal Chiefs petitioned for Pardin for this man After we explained the injurey Such men could doe them by false representation, & explang. the Customs of our Countrey they were all Satisfied with the propriety of the Sentence & was witness to the punishment. after which we had Some talk with the Chiefs about the orrigan of the war between them & the Mahars &c. it commenced in this way I'e' in two of the Missouries Tribe resideing with the Ottoes went to the Mahars to Steel horses, they Killed them both which was a cause of revenge on the part of the Missouris & Ottoes, they also brought war on themselves Nearly in the Same way with the Panea Loups and they are greatly in fear of a just revenge from the Panies for takeing their Corn from the Pania Towns in their absence hunting this Summer. the evening was Closed with an extra Gill of Whiskey & a Dance untill 11 oClock. [Remained at Fish Camp.]

August 19, 1804

[Clark] at 10 oClock we assembled the Cheifs & Warriers under an Orning and delivered a Speech, explanitary of the One Sent to this Nation from the *Council Bluff,* &c.

Children When we Sent the 4 men to your towns, we expected to See & Speake with the Mahas by the time you would arrive and to lay the foundation of a peace between you and them

The Speech of Petieit Villeu Little Thief, If you think right and Can waite untill all our Warriers Come from the Buffalows hunt, we Can then tell you who is our men of Consequnce— My fathers always lived with the father of the B together & we always live with the Big hose— all the men here are the Suns of Chief and will be glad to get Something from the hands of their fathers. My father always directed me to be friendly with the white people, I have always done So and went often to the french, give my party pieces of Paper & we will be glad . . .

The Speach of the Big Horse I went to the hunt Buffalow I heard your word and I returned, I and all my men with me will attend to your words— you want to make peace with all, I want to make peace also, the young me[n] when they want to go to war where is the goods you give me to Keep them at home, if you give me Some Whisky to give a Drop to my men at home. I came here naked and must return home naked. if I have Something to give the young men I can prevent their going to war. You want to make peace with all, It is good we want Something to give my men at home. I am a pore man, and cant quiet without means, a Spoon ful of your milk will qui[e]t all . . .

Sergt. Floyd was taken violently bad with the Beliose Cholick [bilious colic] and is dangerously ill we attempt in Vain to releive him, I am much concerned for his Situation— we could get nothing to Stay on his Stomach a moment nature appear exosting fast in him every man is attentive to him. [Remained at Fish Camp.]

August 20, 1804

[Clark] Serjeant Floyd as bad as he can be no pulse & nothing will Stay a moment on his Stomach or bowels— Passed two Islands on the S. S. and at first Bluff on the S S. Serj.' Floyd Died with a great deel of Composure, before his death he Said to me, "I am going away" ["]I want you to write me a letter"— We buried him on the top of the bluff 1/2 Miles below a Small river to which we Gave his name, he was buried with the Honors of War much lamented; a Seeder post with the Name Sergt. C. Floyd died here 20th of August 1804 was fixed at the head of his grave— This Man at all times gave us proofs of his firmness and Detur-mined resolution to doe Service to his Countrey and honor to himself after paying all the honor to our Decesed brother we Camped in the mouth of *floyds* river about 30 yards wide, a butifull evening. [Camped just above the mouth of Floyd River, Sioux City, Woodbury County, Iowa.]

[Gass] Here Sergeant Floyd died, notwithstanding every possible effort was made by the commanding officers, and other persons, to save his life.

August 22, 1804

[Clark] this Bluff Contained alum, Copperas,[23] Cobalt, Pyrites; a alum rock Soft & Sand Stone. Capt. Lewis in proveing the quality of those minerals was near poisoning himself by the fumes & tast of the *Cabalt* which had the appearance of Soft Isonglass— Copperas & alum is verry pure . . . Seven miles above is a Clift of Allom Stone of a Dark Brown Colr. Containing also in crusted in the Crevises & Shelves of the rock great qts. of Cabalt, Semented Shels & a red earth . . . Capt Lewis took a Dost of Salts to work off the effects of the Arsenic[24] . . . ordered a vote for a Serjeant to chuse one of the three which may be the highest number the highest numbers are P. Gass had 19 Votes, Bratten & Gibson. [Camped south of Elk Point, Union County, South Dakota.]

August 23, 1804

[Ordway] Jo. Fields came to the Boat informed us that he had killed a Bull Buffelow.[25] [Camped in either Dixon County, Nebraska, or Clay County, South Dakota, a mile or so southeast of Vermillion, South Dakota.]

August 24, 1804

[Lewis] the Chronometer stoped again just after being wound up; I know not the cause, but fear it procedes from some defect which it is not in my power to remedy. [Camped near Vermillion, Clay County, South Dakota.]

[Clark] in an imence Plain a high Hill[26] is Situated, and appears of a Conic form and by the different nations of Indians in this quarter is Suppose to be the residence of Deavels. that they are in human form with remarkable large heads and about 18 Inches high, that they are Very watchfull, and are arm'd with Sharp arrows with which they Can Kill at a great distance; they are Said to Kill all persons who are So hardy as to attempt to approach the hill; they State that tradition informs them that many Indians have Suffered by those little people and among others three *Mahar* men fell a Sacrefise to their murceyless fury not many years Since— So much do the Maha, Souis, Ottoes and other neighbouring nations believe this fable that no Consideration is Suffecient to induce them to apporach the hill.

[Ordway] we found a great quantity of red berries[27] which grows on a handsome bush about as high as I could reach. these Berries are a little Sour (& are called Rabbit berries) (English) But pleasant to the taste.

Notes

1. The approximate latitude of Camp White Catfish is 41° 10′ 0″ N.

2. Papillion Creek, reaching the Missouri in Sarpy County, Nebraska.

3. Elkhorn River, entering the Platte in Sarpy County.

4. Boyer River, joining the Missouri in Pottawattamie County.

5. A badger.

6. Kentucky coffee tree.

7. Cloth used for making garters.

8. A bullsnake.

9. A least tern.

10. Killdeer.

11. The summer grape, river-bank grape, and winter grape.

12. Omaha chief Blackbird, who had a reputation for killing his adversaries through sorcery, or more likely, by the use of poison he obtained from traders.

13. Coyote.

14. Mackay's fort was southeast of Homer, Dakota County, Nebraska.

15. Tonwontonga, the main village of the Omaha tribe.

16. Pike.

17. Mooneye or goldeye.

18. Channel catfish.

19. Freshwater drum.

20. Crayfish.

21. Mussels.

22. Reed's "public Rifle" may have been one of the party's U.S. Model 1803 rifles that Lewis acquired at the federal arsenal at Harpers Ferry in present West Virginia.

23. Melanterite.

24. Lewis probably took Epsom or Glauber's salts as a purgative to work off the effects of an unknown substance.

25. Joseph Field killed the party's first buffalo.

26. Spirit Mound, about eight miles north of the town of Vermillion.

27. Buffaloberry.

Further Reading

Allen, John Logan. *Passage through the Garden: Lewis and Clark and the Image of the American Northwest*. Urbana: University of Illinois Press, 1975.

Ambrose, Stephen. *Undaunted Courage: Meriwether Lewis, Thomas Jefferson and the Opening of the American West*. New York: Simon and Schuster, 1996.

Cutright, Paul Russell. *Lewis and Clark: Pioneering Naturalists*. Urbana: University of Illinois Press, 1969.

deVoto, Bernard. *The Courage of Empire*. Boston: Houghton Mifflin, 1952.

——. *The Journals of Lewis and Clark*. Boston: Houghton Mifflin, 1953; rpt. 1997.

Duncan, Dayton. *Lewis and Clark: The Journey of the Corps of Discovery*. New York: Knopf, 1997.

Lavender, David S. *Way to the Western Sea: Lewis and Clark across the Continent*. 1988; rpt. Lincoln: University of Nebraska Press, 2001.

Ronda, James P. *Lewis and Clark among the Indians*. Lincoln: University of Nebraska Press, 1984; rpt. 2001.

Edwin James (*1797–1861*)

Maj. Stephen H. Long headed an expedition that crossed the Great Plains in the summer of 1820. The party followed the Platte River across Nebraska and then traveled south along the front range of the Rocky Mountains into New Mexico where the group turned southeast following the Canadian River across present-day Oklahoma to Fort Smith, Arkansas. The expedition crossed the driest, most difficult part of their route in August. In Long's party were the well-traveled naturalist Edwin James, who kept the record of the journey, and illustrators Samuel Seymour and Titian Peale. It was James who climbed and surveyed Pikes Peak (while Pike climbed Centennial Peak). They returned with scientific observations, to add to those collected by Lewis and Clark, and with the map that James prepared having the words "Great Desert" spread across the Great Plains topography.

James Fenimore Cooper assured Long's expedition at least a footnote in American literary history when he drew upon it as he wrote *The Prairie* (1827). Although Cooper referred to Long's report for his conception of the prairie, the novel's chronological timeframe coincides with the earlier Lewis and Clark exploration. Thus, the report of an expedition that crossed the plains in summer when temperatures read one hundred degrees became the empathetic setting for Cooper's story of intrigue, enmity, and abandonment against a bleak landscape.

The passages printed here were written for the most part by James (Long's notes were lost during the expedition's return trip). James judges the land's future value for settlement by applying his skills as a scientist, but he can report only what he sees that relates to what he already knows. Although the party relishes the berries they find and the bison meat they hunt, much of the land seems barren and useless to James. Nevertheless, there is, as we know, much about the country that none of them could imagine. James's frustration and confusion at the limitation of his knowledge are evident at times in this passage.

Excerpt from *From Pittsburgh to the Rocky Mountains* (1822)

Sand plains—Mississippi hawk—Small-leaved elm—Wild horses—Hail storm—Climate—Bisons—Grapes—Red-sand formation—Gypsum.
Extensive tracts of loose sand, so destitute of plants and so fine as to be driven by the winds, occur in every part of the saline sandstone formation southwest of

the Arkansa. They are, perhaps, invariably the detritus of the sandrock, deposited in vallies and depressions where the rapidity of the currents of water has been checked by permanent obstacles. This loose sand differs in colour from the sandstone, which is almost invariably red. The difference may have been produced simply by the operation of water suspending and removing the light colouring matter, no longer retained by the aggregation of the sandstone. These fields of sand have most frequently an undulated surface, occasioned, probably, not less by the operation of winds than by the currents of water. A few plum bushes, almost the only woody plants found on them, wherever they take root form points, about which the sand accumulates, and, in this manner, permanent elevations are produced. The yucca *angustifolia* and the shrubby cactus, the white argemone, and the night-flowering Bartonia, are the most conspicuous plants in these sandy wastes.

Our course, on the 15th, led us twice across the bed of the river, which we found one thousand and four hundred paces in width, and without water, except in a few small pools where it was stagnant. This wide and shallow bed is included between low banks, sometimes sloped gradually and sometimes, though rarely, perpendicular, and rising scarcely more than four feet from the common level of the bottom of the channel. Driftwood is occasionally seen without these banks, at an elevation of a few feet above them, affording evidence that they are, at times, not only full but overflowed. Whenever they are but partially filled it is easy to see that, what for a great part of the year is a naked sand-beach, then becomes a broad and majestic river. It must flow with a rapid current, and, in floods, its waters cannot be otherwise than of an intense red colour. The immediate valley of the river had now become little less than two miles in width, and had, in some places, a fertile soil. This happens wherever places occur having little elevation above the bed of the river, and which have not recently been covered with drifted sand.

Several species of locust were extremely frequent here, filling the air by day with their shrill and deafening cries, and feeding with their bodies great numbers of that beautiful species of hawk, the Falco *Mississippiensis* of Wilson. It afforded us a constant amusement to watch the motions of this greedy devourer, in the pursuit of the locust his favorite prey. The insect being large and not very active is easily taken; the hawk then poises on the wing, suspending himself in the air, while with his talons and beak he tears in pieces and devours his prey.

Prairie wolves, and vultures, occurred in unusual numbers, and the carcasses of several bisons, recently killed, had been seen. We could also distinguish the recent marks of a hunting party of Indians, the tracks of horses and men being still fresh in the sand. At four P.M. several bisons were discovered at a distance, and, as we were in the greatest want of provisions, we halted and sent the hunters in pursuit, and, being soon apprised of their success, the requisite preparations were made for jerking the meat. Near our camp was a scattering grove of small leaved elms. This tree (the Ulmus *alata, N.*) is not known in the Eastern States, but is common in many parts of Tennessee, Missouri, and Arkansa. When found in forests intermixed with other trees, it is usually of a smaller size than the Ulmus *Americana,* and is distinguished from it by the smallness of the leaves and the whiteness of the trunk. On the borders of the open country, where large trees often occur entirely isolated, the Ulmus *alata* has decidedly a more dense and flattened top than any other tree we have seen. When standing entirely alone, it rarely attains an elevation of more than thirty or thirty-five feet, but its top, lying close to the ground, is spread over an area of sixty or seventy feet in diameter, and is externally so close and smooth as to resemble, when seen from a distance, a small grassy hillock.

Near our camp was a circular breast-work, constructed like those already mentioned, and large enough to contain eighty or an hundred men. We were not particularly pleased at meeting these works so frequently, as they indicate a country subject to the incursions and ravages of Indian war parties.

16th. The greater part of the flesh of the bison, killed on the preceding evening, had been dried and smoked in the course of the night, so that we had now no fear of immediate suffering from hunger, having as much jerked meat as was sufficient to last several days.

The sky continued clear, but the wind was high, and the drifting of the sand occasioned much annoyance. The heat of the atmosphere became more intolerable, on account of the showers of burning sand driven against us, with such force as to penetrate every part of our dress, and proving so afflictive to our eyes, that it was with the greatest difficulty we could see to guide our horses. The sand is carried from the bed of the river, which is here a naked beach, of more than half a mile wide, and piled in immense drifts along the bank. Some of these heaps we have seen covering the trunk and a portion of the upper branches, of what appeared to be large trees. Notwithstanding we were now three hundred miles distant from the sources of the river, we found very little water, and that being stagnant and frequented by bisons and other animals, was so loathsome, both to sight and smell, that nothing but the most incontrollable thirst, could have induced us to taste it.

At a short distance below the place of our encampment, we passed the confluence of a large creek, entering from the southwest. Though like all the streams of this thirsty region its waters were entirely hid in the sand, yet it is evidently the bed of a large tributary; from its direction, we conclude it can be no other than the one on which the Kaskaias informed us they had encamped the night before we met them. Its name, if it have any among the Indians or Spaniards, we have not learned.

We had for some days observed a few wild horses, and they, as well as the bisons, were now becoming numerous. In the habits of the wild horse, we find little unlike what is seen in the domestic animal. He becomes the most timorous and watchful of the inhabitants of the wilderness. They show a similar attachment to each others' society, though the males are occasionally found at a distance from the herds. It would appear from the paths we have seen, that they sometimes perform long journies, and it may be worthy of remark, that along these paths are frequently found very large piles of horse-dung of different ages, affording sufficient evidence that this animal in a wild state, has, in common with some others, an inclination to drop his excrement where another has done so before him. This habit is sometimes faintly discovered in the domestic horse.

As we were about to halt for dinner, a male bison which had lingered near our path was killed, but the flesh was found in too ill a condition to be eaten, as is the case with all the bulls at this season.

Soon after we had mounted our horses in the afternoon, a violent thunder storm came on from the northwest. Hail fell in such abundance as to cover the surface of the ground, and some of the hailstones, which we examined, were near an inch in diameter. Falling with a strong wind, these heavy masses struck upon our bodies with considerable violence. Our horses, as they had done on a similar occasion before, refused to move, except before the wind. Some of the mules turned off from our course, and had run more than half a mile before they could be overtaken. For ourselves, we found some protection, by wrapping our blankets as loosely as possible around our bodies, and waited for the cessation of the storm, not without calling to mind some instances on record, of hailstones, which have destroyed the lives of men and animals. It is not improbable, that the climate of a portion of country, within the range of the immediate influence of the Rocky Mountains, may be more subject to hailstorms in summer, than other parts of the continent, lying in the same latitude. The radiation of heat from so extensive a surface of naked sand, lying along the base of this vast range of snowy mountains, must produce great local inequalities of temperature: the diminished pressure of the atmosphere, and the consequent rapidity of evaporation, may in these elevated regions also be supposed to have an important influence on the weather. We have not spent sufficient time in the country near the eastern border of the Rocky Mountains, to enable us to speak with confidence of the character of its climate. It is, however, sufficiently manifest that in summer it must be extremely variable, as we have found it; the thermometer often indicating an increase of near fifty degrees of temperature, between sunrise and the middle of the day. These rapid alternations of heat and cold must be supposed to mark a climate little favourable to health, though we may safely assert that this portion of the country is exempt from the operation of those causes, which produce so deleterious an atmosphere in the lower and more fertile portions of the Mississippi basin. If the wide plains of the Platte, the upper Arkansa, and the Red river of Louisiana, should ever become the seat of a permanent civilized population, the diseases most incident to such a population, will probably be fevers attended with pulmonary and pleuritic inflammations, rheumatism, scrofula, and consumption. It is true that few if any instances of pulmonary consumption, occur among the Indians of this region; the same remark is probably as true of the original native population of New York and New England.

Though much rain fell during this storm, it was so rapidly absorbed by the soil, that little running water was to be seen. The bed of the river was found smooth and unobstructed, and afforded us for several days the most convenient path for travelling. As we descended, we found it to expand in some places to a width of near two miles. Bisons became astonishingly numerous, and in the middle of the day countless thousands of them were seen, coming in from every quarter to the stagnant pools, which filled the most depressed places in the channel of the river. The water of these was of course too filthy to be used in cooking our meat, and though sometimes compelled to drink it, we found little alleviation to our thirst. At our encampments we were able to furnish ourselves with water of a better quality by digging in the sand, where we seldom failed to meet with a supply at a few feet from the surface.

On the 17th we halted in the middle of the day to hunt, as, although we had killed several bisons on our marches of the preceding days, none of them had been found in good condition. The flesh of the bulls in the months of August and September, is poor and ill-flavoured; but these are much more easily killed than the cows, being less vigilant, and sometimes suffering themselves to be overtaken by the hunter without attempting to escape. As the herds of cows were now seen in great numbers, we halted and the hunters went out and killed several. Our camp was on the southwest side of the river, under a low bluff, which separates the half wooded valley from the open and elevated plains. The small elms along this valley were bending under the weight of innumerable grape vines, now loaded with ripe fruit, the purple clusters crouded in such profusion as almost to give colouring to the landscape. On the opposite side of the river was a range of low sand hills, fringed with vines, rising not more than a foot or eighteen inches from the surface. On examination we found these hillocks had been produced, exclusively by the agency of the grape vines arresting the sand, as it was borne along by the wind, until such quantities had been accumulated as to bury every part of the plant except the ends of the branches. Many of these were so loaded with fruit, as to present nothing to the eye but a series of clusters so closely arranged as to conceal every part of the stem. The fruit of these vines is incomparably finer than that of any other, either native or exotic, which we have met with in the United States. The burying of the greater part of the trunk, with its larger branches, produces the effect of pruning, in as much as it prevents the unfolding of leaves and flowers on the parts below the surface, while the protruding ends of the branches enjoy an increased degree of light and heat from the reflection of the sand. It is owing undoubtedly to these causes that the grapes in question are so far superior to the fruit of the same vines in ordinary circumstances.

The treatment here employed by nature to bring to perfection the fruit of the vine may be imitated, but without the same peculiarities of soil and exposure, can with difficulty be carried to the same magnificent extent. Here are hundreds of acres covered with a surface of moveable sand, and abounding in vines, placed in more favorable circumstances, by the agency of the sun and the winds, than it is in the power of man, to afford to so great an extent. We indulged ourselves to excess, if excess could be committed in the use of such delicious and salutary fruit, and invited by the cleanness of the sand, and a refreshing shade, we threw ourselves down, and slept away with unusual zest, a few of the hours of a summer afternoon.

Our hunters had been as successful as could be wished, and at evening we assembled around a full feast of "marrow bones," a treat whose value must forever remain unknown to those who have not tried the adventurous life of the hunter. We were often surprised to witness in ourselves a proof of the facility, with which a part at least of the habits of the savage could be adopted. Having been in several instances compelled to practice a tedious abstinence, the return of plenty found us well disposed to make amends for these temporary privations, and we lingered almost involuntarily at every meal, as if determined not only to make amends for the deficiency of the past, but to secure so ample a supply as would enable us to defy the future.

The grapes and plums, so abundant in this portion of the country, are eaten by turkies and black bears, and the plums by wolves, as we conclude from observing plumstones in the excrement of these animals. It is difficult to conceive whence such numbers of predatory animals and birds, as exist in every part of the country where the bisons are present, can derive sufficient supplies for the sustenance of life; it is indeed sufficiently evident, their existence is but a protraction of the sufferings of famine.

The great flowering hibiscus is here a conspicuous and highly ornamental plant, among the scattering trees in the low ground. The occurrence of the black walnut for the first time, since we left the Missouri, indicated a soil somewhat adapted to the purposes of agriculture. Portions of the river valley, which are not covered with loose sand, have a red soil, resulting from the disintegration of the prevailing rocks, red sandstone and gypsum, intermixed with clay, and are covered with a dense growth of fine and nutritious grasses. Extensive tracts of the great woodless plain, at a distance from the river, appear to be based on a more compact variety of sandstone, usually of a dark gray colour, and less pervious to water than the red. For this reason some copious springs are found upon it, and a soil by no means destitute of fertility, yielding sustenance to inconceivable numbers of herbivorous animals, and through them to innumerable birds and beast's of prey. It must be supposed, however, that the herds of bisons, daily seen about the river, range over a much greater extent of the country than was comprised within our limited views; the want of water in many places, may compel them to resort frequently to the river in dry weather, though at other times they may be dispersed in the high plains.

18th. In speaking of a country, whose geography is so little known, as that of the region southwest of the Arkansa, we feel the want of ascertained and fixed points of reference.[1] Were we to designate the locality of a mineral or any other interesting object, as twenty or thirty days' journey from the Rocky Mountains, we should do nearly all in our power; yet this sort of information would probably be thought vague and useless. The smaller rivers of this region have as yet received no names from white hunters; if they have names among the Indians, these are unknown to us. There are no mountains, hills, or other remarkable objects, to serve as points of *reckoning*, nearer than the Rocky Mountains and the Arkansa. The river itself, which we supposed to be the Red river of Natchitoches, is a permanent land mark, but it is a line, and aids us only in one direction in our attempts to designate locality. The map accompanying this work was projected in conformity to the results of numerous astronomical observations for latitude and longitude, but many of these observations were made at places, not at present to be known by any names we might attempt to fix upon them. More extensive and minute examination, than we have been able to bestow, might establish something like a sectional division, founded on the distribution of certain remarkable plants. The great cylindric cactus, the American colycinth, (Cucumis *perennis*,) and the small-leaved elm, might be used in such an attempt, but it is easy to see that the advantages resulting from it, would be for the most part imaginary.

Discussions of this sort have been much insisted on, and may be important as aiding in the geography of climates and soils, but can afford little assistance to topography.

The geological features of the region under consideration, afford some foundation for a natural division, but this division must be so extremely general, as to afford little satisfaction. We could only distinguish the red sandstone, the argillaceous sandstone, and the trap districts, and though each of these have distinctive characters, not easy to be mistaken, they are so irregular in form and position, as to be in no degree adapted to aid in the description, and identifying of particular places. On the contrary it is to be regretted, there are no established points, to which we might refer, in communicating what we have observed of the position of these formations, and indicating the particular localities of some of the valuable minerals they contain.

The red sandstone, apparently the most extensive of the rocky formations of this region, shows, wherever it occurs, indications of the presence of muriate of soda, and almost as commonly discloses veins and beds of sulphate of lime. This substance had been growing more and more abundant, since we left the region of the trap rocks at the sources of the river. It was now so frequent as to be conspicuous in all the exposed portions of the sand-rock, and was often seen from a distance of several miles. It occurs under various forms; sometimes we met with the most beautiful selenite, disposed in broad reticulating veins, traversing the sandstone. The granular and fibrous varieties, whose snowy whiteness contrasts strongly with the deep red and brown of the sandstone, are sometimes seen in thin horizontal laminæ, or scattered about the surface, sometimes included in larger masses of the common amorphous plaister stone. This last is usually of a colour approaching to white, but the exposed surfaces are more or less tinged with the colouring matter of the sand-rock, and all the varieties are so soft as to disintegrate rapidly, when exposed to the air. Recent surfaces show no ferruginous tinge, in other words, this colour does not appear to have been contemporaneous to the formation of the sulphate of lime, but derived from the cement of the sandstone, and to have penetrated no farther than it has been carried by the infiltration of water.

We left our encampment at five o'clock; the morning fair; thermometer at 62°. Our courses, regulated entirely by the direction of the river, were north, fifty-five east, eleven miles, then north, ten east, seven miles, in all eighteen miles before dinner. The average direction of our course, for some days, had been rather to the north than south of east. This fact did not coincide with our previous ideas of the direction of Red River, and much less of the Faux Ouachitta or False Washita, which, being the largest of the upper branches of Red River from the north, we believed might be the stream we were descending. From observations taken at several points along the river we had ascertained that we must travel three or four days' journey to the south, in order to arrive at the parallel of the confluence of the Kiamesha with the Red river, and we were constantly expecting a change in the direction of our courses. The confident assurance of the Kaskaias, that we were on Red River, and but a few days' march above the village of the Pawnee Piquas, tended to quiet the suspicions we began to feel on this subject. We had now travelled, since meeting the Indians, a greater distance than we could suppose they had intended to indicate by the admeasurement of ten "lodge days," but we were conscious our communications with them had been made through inadequate interpreters, and it was not without reason we began to fear we might have received erroneous impressions. In the afternoon, however, the river inclined more to the direction we wished to travel; and we had several courses to the south of east. At sunset we pitched our tent on the north side of the river, and dug a well in the sand, which afforded a sufficient supply of wholesome, though brackish water. Throughout the night the roaring of immense herds of bisons, and the solemn notes of the hooting owl, were heard, intermixed with the desolate cries of the prairie wolf, and the screech owl. The mulberry and the guilandina growing near our camp, with many of the plants and birds we had been accustomed to see in the frontier settlements of the United States, reminded us of the comforts of home, and the cheering scenes of social life, giving us, at the same time, the assurance that we were about to arrive at the point where we should take leave of the desert.

19th. The mercury at sunrise stood at 71°. The morning was calm, and the sky tinged with that intense and beautiful blue which marks many of our summer skies, and is seen with greater pleasure, by those who know that home, or a good tavern, is near, than by such as have no prospect of shelter, save what a tent or a blanket can afford. We were now looking, with much impatience, for something to indicate an approach towards the village of the Pawnee Piquas; but instead of this the traces of Indians seemed to become less and less frequent. Notwithstanding the astonishing numbers of bison, deer, antelopes, and other animals, the country is less strewed with bones than almost any we have seen, affording an evidence that it is not a favourite hunting ground of any tribe of Indians. The animals also appeared wholly unaccustomed to the sight of men. The bisons and wolves moved slowly off to right and left, leaving a lane for the party to pass; but those on the windward side often lingered for a long time almost within the reach of our rifles, regarding us with little appearance of alarm. We had now nothing to suffer, either from the apprehension or the reality of hunger, and could have been content that the distance between ourselves and the settlements should have been much greater than we supposed it to be.

In the afternoon, finding the course of the river again bending towards the north, and becoming more and more serpentine, we turned off on the right side, and choosing an east course, travelled across the hills, not doubting but we would soon arrive again at the river. We found the country, at a distance from the bed of the river, somewhat elevated and broken; but, upon climbing some of the highest hills, we again saw the landscape of the unbounded and unvaried grassy plain spread out before us. All the inequalities of the surface have evidently been produced by the excavating operation of currents of water, and they are consequently most considerable near the channels of the large streams. This remark is applicable to the vallies of all the large rivers in the central portions of the great horizontal formation west of the Alleganies. We find, accordingly, that on the Ohio, the Missouri, the Platte, the Konzas, and many of the rivers tributary to the Mississippi, the surface becomes broken in proportion as we proceed from the interior towards the bed of the river; and all the hills bear convincing evidence that they have received their existence and their form from the action of the currents of water, which have removed the soil and other matters formerly occupying the vallies, and elevating the whole surface of the country nearly to a common level. Regarding in this view the extensive vallies of the Mississippi, and its tributaries, we naturally inquire how great a length of time must have been spent in the production of such an effect, the cause operating as it now does? It is scarce necessary to remark that where the vallies of the rivers in question are bounded on both sides, as they often are, by perpendicular cliffs of sandstone or limestone in horizontal strata, the seams and markings on one side correspond with those of the other, indicating the stratifications to have been originally continuous.

A ride of a few miles, in a direction passing obliquely from the river, brought us to a point which overlooked a large extent of the surrounding country. From this we could distinguish the winding course of a small stream uniting numerous tributaries from the ridge we occupied, and pursuing its way towards the southeast along a narrow and well wooded valley. The dense and verdant foliage of the poplars and elms contrasted faintly with the bright red of the sandstone cliffs, which rose on both sides, far surpassing the elevation of the tallest trees, and disclosing here and there masses of sulphate of lime of a snowy whiteness. Looking back upon the broad valley of the river we had left, the eye rested upon insulated portions of the sandy bed, disclosed by the inflections of its course, or the opening of ravines, and resembling pools of blood rather than wastes of sand. We had been so long accustomed to the red sands that the intensity of the colouring ceased to excite attention, until a distant view afforded us the opportunity of contrasting it with the general aspect of the country.

The elevated plains we found covered with a plenteous, but close fed crop of grasses, and occupied by extensive marmot villages. The red soil is usually fine, and little intermixed with gravel and pebbles, but too sandy to retain moisture enough for the purposes of agriculture. The luxuriance and fineness of the grasses, as well as the astonishing number and good condition of the herbivorous animals of this region clearly indicate its value for purposes of pasturage. There can be no doubt that more valuable and productive grasses than the native species can, with little trouble, be introduced. This may easily be effected by burning the prairies, at a proper season of the year, and sowing the seeds of any of the more hardy cultivated graminæ. Some of the perennial plants common in the prairies, will, undoubtedly, be found difficult to exterminate; their strong roots penetrating to a great depth, and enveloping the rudiments of new shoots placed beyond the reach of a fire on the surface. The soil of the more fertile plains is penetrated with such numbers of these as to present more resistance to the plough than the oldest cultivated pastures.

We had continued our march until near sunset, expecting constantly to come in view of the river, which we were persuaded must soon make a great bend to the south; but perceiving the night would overtake us in the plains, we began to search for a place to encamp. The bison paths in this country are as frequent, and almost as conspicuous, as the roads in the most populous parts of the United States. They converge from all directions to the places where water is to be found, and by following their guidance we were soon led to a spot where was a small spring, dripping from the side of a cliff of sandstone. The water collected in a little basin at the foot of the cliff, and flowing a few rods down a narrow ravine disappeared in the sand. Having established our camp, we travelled down this ravine, searching for plants, while any daylight remained. The rocks were beautifully exposed, but exhibited no appearance unlike what we had been accustomed to see along the river; the red indistinctly stratified sand-rock, spotted and veined with plaister stone and selenite. About the shelvings and crevices of the rocks the slender corrolla of the Oenothera macro *carpa* and the purple blossoms of the Pentstemon *bradburii* lay withering together, while the fading leaves and the ripening fruit reminded us that the summer was drawing to a close.

On the morning following we resumed our march, alternating our course from S.E. to N.E. The want of water in the hills compelled us again to seek the river. Falling in with a large bison path which we knew would conduct us by the easiest and most direct route, we travelled about fifteen miles, and encamped at noon on the bank of the river. In returning to the low grounds we pased some grassy pastures carpeted with the densest and finest verdure, and sprinkled with herds of deer, antelopes, and bisons. In some places the ground was covered with a purple mat of the prickly leaves and branches of a procumbent Eryngo intermixed with the tall and graceful Centaurea *speciosa,* with here and there a humble Dalea, or an ascending Petalostemon. As we approached the river we discovered a fine herd of bisons in the grove where we intended to place our camp, some lying down in the shade, others standing in the pool of water which extended along under the bank. Dismounting from our horses and approaching under cover of the bushes we shot two of the fattest, but before we had time to reload our pieces, after the second fire, we perceived a bull running towards us, evidently with the design to make battle; we, however, gave him the slip, by escaping into the thick bushes, and he turned off to follow the retiring herd.

It is only in the rutting season that any danger is to be apprehended from the strength and ferocity of the male bison. At all other times, whether wounded or not, their efforts are, to the last, directed solely towards an escape from their pursuers, and at this time it does not appear that their rage is provoked, particularly by an attack upon themselves, but their unusual intrepidity is directed indiscriminately against all suspicious intruders.

We had now, for some days, been excessively annoyed with large swarms of blowing flies, which had prevented our carrying fresh game along with us for more than a single day. It had been our custom at meals to place our boiled or roasted bison meat on the grass, or the broken boughs of a tree, in the middle of our circle; but this practice we now found it inexpedient to continue, as before we could finish our repast our table often became white with the eggs deposited by the flies. We were commonly induced to dispense with our roast meats, unless we chose to superintend the cooking ourselves; and afterwards it required the exertions of one hand to keep away the flies while with the other we helped ourselves to what we wished to eat. Our more common practice was to confine ourselves to the single dish of hunters' soup, suffering the meat to remain immersed in the kettle until we were ready to transfer it to our mouths.

Gnats had been rather frequent, and we began to feel once more the persecutions of the ticks, the most tormenting of the insects of this country.

The little pool near our tent afforded all the water that could be found within a very considerable distance. The bisons came in from every direction to drink, and we almost regretted that our presence frighted away the suffering animals with their thirst unslaked.

21st. The day was warm and somewhat rainy. Soon after leaving our camp we saw three black bears and killed one of them. This is the first animal of the kind we had eaten since we left the Missouri, and the flesh, though now not in the best condition, we found deserving the high encomiums commonly lavished upon it.

Experienced hunters prefer it to that of the bison, and indeed to almost every thing, except the tail of the beaver.

Black bears had been frequent in this country passed since the 15th. At this season they feed principally upon grapes, plums, the berries of the cornus *alba* and c. *cirunata* and the acorns of a small scrubby oak common about the sand hills.

They also eat the flesh of animals, and it is not uncommon to see them disputing with the wolves and buzzards for their share of the carcasses of bisons, and other animals, which have been left by the hunters, or have died of disease. Grapes had evidently been very abundant here, but had been devoured, and the vines torn in pieces by the bears and turkies.

In the middle of the day we found the heat more oppressive, with the mercury at 96°, than we had known it in many instances when the thermometer had indicated a higher temperature by six or eight degrees. This sultry calm was, however, soon succeeded by thunder showers, attended with their ordinary effects upon the atmosphere. In the afternoon, the country we passed was swarming with innumerable herds of bisons, wild horses, deer, elk, &c., while great numbers of minute sandpipers, yellow-shanked snipes, kill-deer plovers (charadrius *vociferus*) and tell-tale godwits, about the river, seemed to indicate the vicinity of larger bodies of water than we had been accustomed of late to see. During the afternoon and the night, there was a continual and rapid alternation of bright, calm, and cloudless skies, with sudden and violent thunder storms. Our horizon was a little obscured on both sides by the hills and the scattered trees which skirted along the sides of the valley. As we looked out of our tent, to observe the progress of the night, we found sometimes a pitchy darkness veiling every object; at others, by the clear light of the stars, and the constant flashing from some unseen cloud, we could distinguish all the features of the surrounding scene; our horses grazing quietly about our tent, and the famished prairie wolf prowling near, to seize the fragments of our plentiful supper. The thunder was almost incessant, but its low and distant mutterings were, at times, so blended with the roaring of the bisons, that more experienced ears than ours might have found a difficulty in distinguishing between them. At a late hour in the night some disturbance was perceived among the horses, occasioned by a herd of wild horses, which had come in and struck up a hasty acquaintance with their enslaved fellow-brutes. As it was near daylight we forbore to do any thing to frighten away the intruders, hoping, to have an opportunity to prove our skill in the operation of *creasing*, as soon as the light should be sufficient. A method sometimes adopted by hunters for taking the wild horse is to shoot the animal through the neck using the requisite care not to injure the spine. A horse may receive a rifle ball through a particular part of the neck without sustaining any permanent injury; the blow is, however, sufficient to occasion a temporary suspension of the powers of life, during which the animal is easily taken. This is called creasing; and requires for its successful performance a very considerable degree of skill and precision in the use of the rifle. A valuable but rather refractory mule, belonging to our party escaped from the cantonment near Council Bluff, a few days before we left that place. He was pursued by two men through the prairies of the Papillon, across the Elkhorn, and finally to the Platte, where, as they saw no prospect of taking him by other means, they resolved upon creasing. The ball however swerved an inch or two from its aim and broke the neck of the animal.

Notes

1. Despite James's frustration with the absence of easily mapped geographic features, he does recognize the changes in plants and accurately speculates about differences in climate and soil that coincide roughly with the area along the one-hundredth meridian, the customary dividing line between the tallgrass prairie and the high plains.—Eds.

Further Reading

Evans, Howard Ensign. *Natural History of the Long Expedition to the Rocky Mountains 1819–1820*. New York: Oxford University Press, 1997.

Goetzmann, William. *New Lands, New Men: America and the Second Great Age of Discovery*. New York: Viking, 1986.

Goodman, George J., Jr., and Cheryl A. Lawson. *Retracing Major Stephen H. Long's Expedition: The Itinerary and Botany*. Norman: University of Oklahoma Press, 1995.

Pike, Zebulon M. *Journals, with Letters and Related Documents*. Ed. Donald Jackson. Norman: University of Oklahoma Press, 1966.

Josiah Gregg *(1806–1850)*

In 1831 a sickly Josiah Gregg traveled west hoping, as many others did, to regain his health in the salubrious climate. As part of a caravan traveling from Independence, Missouri, to Santa Fe, New Mexico, he found renewed health and a new profession: until 1840 he was a Santa Fe merchant, traveling across Kansas and the corner of Oklahoma or Colorado (depending upon his choice of routes) into Santa Fe in Mexican territory. Gregg kept careful notes while on his journeys, and in 1844 he published them as *Commerce of the Prairies,* our most complete account of the earliest years of regular traffic by travelers and settlers across the Great Plains.

When he compiled his notes Gregg ordered them not by chronology but by subject. He evaluates the route not from a scientific point of view, as earlier explorers had, but as a businessman: he assesses the land's value as a trade route, especially along navigable rivers that were not only a means of transportation but also a source of goods such as salt or timber, and as land that would support settlers who would produce and purchase goods—a place conducive to steady trade. Gregg accepts the theory that cultivation, especially on the high plains, "might contribute to the multiplication of showers"—in other words, that rain will follow the plow, a widely accepted theory that led to settlement of the arid high plains and to concerted efforts to grow trees across the Great Plains. Unfortunately, the idea proved to be based not on fact but on wishful thinking.

This selection is an account of life on the trail that bisects Kansas from the eastern part of the state to its southwest corner.

On the Trail *(1844)*

Owing to the delays of organizing and other preparations, we did not leave the Council Grove camp till May 27th. Although the usual hour of starting with the prairie caravans is after an early breakfast, yet, on this occasion, we were hindered till in the afternoon. The familiar note of preparation, "Catch up! catch up!" was now sounded from the captain's camp, and re-echoed from every division and scattered group along the valley. On such occasions, a scene of confusion ensues, which must be seen to be appreciated. The woods and dales resound with the gleeful yells of the light-hearted wagoners, who, weary of inaction, and filled with joy at the prospect of getting under way, become clamorous in the extreme. Scarcely does the jockey on the race-course ply his whip more promptly at that magic word 'Go,' than do these emulous wagoners fly to harnessing their mules at the spirit-stirring sound of 'Catch up.' Each teamster vies with his fellows who shall be soonest ready; and it is a matter of boastful pride to be the first to cry out— "All's set!"

The uproarious bustle which follows—the hallooing of those in pursuit of animals—the exclamations which the unruly brutes call forth from their wrathful drivers; together with the clatter of bells—the rattle of yokes and harness—the jingle of chains—all conspire to produce a clamorous confusion, which would be altogether incomprehensible without the assistance of the eyes; while these alone would hardly suffice to unravel the labyrinthian manoeuvres and hurly-burly of this precipitate breaking up. It is sometimes amusing to observe the athletic wag- oner hurrying an animal to its post—to see him 'heave upon' the halter of a stubborn mule, while the brute as obstinately 'sets back,' determined not to 'move a peg' till his own pleasure thinks it proper to do so—his whole manner seeming to say, "Wait till your hurry's over!" I have more than once seen a driver hitch a harnessed animal to the halter, and by that process haul 'his mulishness' forward, while each of his four projected feet would leave a furrow behind; until at last the perplexed master would wrathfully exclaim, "A mule will be a mule any way you can fix it!"

"All's set!" is finally heard from some teamster—"All's set," is directly re- sponded from every quarter. "Stretch out!" immediately vociferates the captain. Then, the 'heps!' of drivers—the cracking of whips—the trampling of feet—the occasional creak of wheels—the rumbling of wagons—form a new scene of ex- quisite confusion, which I shall not attempt further to describe. "Fall in!" is heard from head-quarters, and the wagons are forthwith strung out upon the long in- clined plain, which stretches to the heights beyond Council Grove.

After fifteen miles' progress, we arrived at the 'Diamond Spring' (a crystal fountain discharging itself into a small brook), to which, in later years, caravans have sometimes advanced, before 'organizing.' Near twenty-five miles beyond we crossed the Cottonwood fork of the Neosho, a creek still smaller than that of Council Grove, and our camp was pitched immediately in its further valley.

When caravans are able to cross in the evening, they seldom stop on the near side of a stream—first, because if it happens to rain during the night, it may become flooded, and cause both detention and trouble: again, though the stream be not impassable after rain, the banks become slippery and difficult to ascend. A third and still more important reason is, that, even supposing the contingency of rain does not occur, teams will rarely pull as well in 'cold collars,' as wagoners term it—that is, when fresh geared—as in the progress of a day's travel. When a heavy pull is just at hand in the morning, wagoners sometimes resort to the expedient of driving a circuit upon the prairie, before venturing to 'take the bank.'

We experienced a temporary alarm during the evening, while we lay encamped at Cottonwood, which was rather more boisterous than serious in its consequences. The wagons had been 'formed' across the neck of a bend in the creek, into which the cattle were turned, mostly in their yokes; for though, when thoroughly trained, teamsters usually unyoke their oxen every night, yet at first they often leave them coupled, to save the trouble of re-yoking them in their unruly state. A little after dark, these animals started simultaneously, with a thundering noise and rattle of the yokes, towards the outlet protected by the wagons, but for which obstacle they might have escaped far into the prairie, and have been irrecoverably lost, or, at least, have occasioned much trouble and delay to recover them. The cause of the fright was not discovered; but oxen are exceedingly whimsical creatures when surrounded by unfamiliar objects. One will sometimes take a fright at the jingle of his own yoke-irons, or the cough of his mate, and, by a sudden flounce, set the whole herd in a flurry. This was probably the case in the present instance; although some of our easily excited companions immediately surmised that the oxen had scented a lurking Pawnee.

Our route lay through uninterrupted prairie for about forty miles—in fact I may say, for five hundred miles, except the very narrow fringes of timber along the borders of the streams. The antelope of the high prairies which we now occasionally saw, is sometimes found as far east as Council Grove; and as a few old buffaloes have sometimes been met with about Cottonwood, we now began to look out for this desirable game. Some scattering bulls are generally to be seen first, forming as it would appear the 'van' or 'piquet guards' of the main droves with their cows and calves. The buffalo are usually found much further east early in the spring, than during the rest of the year, on account of the long grass, which shoots up earlier in the season than the short pasturage of the plains.

Our hopes of game were destined soon to be realized; for early on the second day after leaving Cottonwood (a few miles beyond the principal Turkey creek), our eyes were greeted with the sight of a herd amounting to nearly a hundred head of buffalo, quietly grazing in the distance before us. Half of our company had probably never seen a buffalo before (at least in its wild state); and the excitement that the first sight of these 'prairie beeves' occasions among a party of novices, beggars all description. Every horseman was off in a scamper: and some of the wagoners, leaving their teams to take care of themselves, seized their guns and joined the race afoot. Here went one with his rifle or yager—there another with his double-barrelled shot-gun—a third with his holster-pistols—a Mexican perhaps with his lance—another with his bow and arrows—and numbers joined without any arms whatever, merely for the 'pleasures of the chase'—all helter-skelter—a regular John Gilpin race, truly 'neck or naught.' The fleetest of the pursuers were soon in the midst of the game, which scattered in all directions, like a flock of birds upon the descent of a hawk.

A few 'beeves' were killed during the chase; and as soon as our camp was pitched, the bustle of kindling fires and preparing for supper commenced. The new adventurers were curious to taste this prairie luxury; while we all had been so long upon salt provisions—now nearly a month—that our appetites were in exquisite condition to relish fresh meat. The fires had scarcely been kindled when the fumes of broiling meat pervaded the surrounding atmosphere; while all huddled about, anxiously watching their cookeries, and regaling their senses in anticipation upon the savory odors which issued from them.

For the edification of the reader, who had no doubt some curiosity on the subject, I will briefly mention, that the 'kitchen and tableware' of the traders usually consists of a skillet, a frying-pan, a sheet-iron campkettle, a coffee-pot, and each man with his tin cup and a butcher's knife. The culinary operations being finished, the pan and kettle are set upon the grassy turf, around which all take a 'lowly seat,' and crack their gleesome jokes, while from their greasy hands they swallow their savory viands—all with a relish rarely experienced at the well-spread tables of the most fashionable and wealthy.

The insatiable appetite acquired by travellers upon the Prairies is almost incredible, and the quantity of coffee drunk is still more so. It is an unfailing and apparently indispensable beverage, served at every meal—even under the broiling noon-day sun, the wagoner will rarely fail to replenish a second time, his huge tin cup.

Early the next day we reached the 'Little Arkansas,' which, although endowed with an imposing name, is only a small creek with a current but five or six yards wide. But, though small, its steep banks and miry bed annoyed us exceedingly in crossing. It is the practice upon the prairies on all such occasions, for several men to go in advance with axes, spades and mattocks, and by digging the banks and erecting temporary bridges, to have all in readiness by the time the wagons arrive. A bridge over a quagmire is made in a few minutes, by cross-laying it with brush (willows are best, but even long grass is often employed as a substitute), and covering it with earth, across which a hundred wagons will often pass in safety.

We had now arrived at the point nearest to the border, I believe, where any outrages have been perpetrated upon the traders to Santa Fé. One of the early packing companies lost their animals on this spot, and had to send back for a new supply.

Next day we reached Cow creek, where all the difficulties encountered at Little Arkansas had to be reconquered: but after digging, bridging, shouldering the wheels, with the usual accompaniment of whooping, swearing and cracking of whips, we soon got safely across and encamped in the valley beyond. Alarms now began to accumulate more rapidly upon us. A couple of persons had a few days before been chased to the wagons by a band of—buffalo; and this evening the encampment was barely formed when two hunters came bolting in with information that a hundred, perhaps of the same 'enemy,' were at hand—at least this was the current opinion afterwards. The hubbub occasioned by this fearful news had scarcely subsided, when another arrived on a panting horse, crying out "Indians, Indians! I've just escaped from a couple who pursued me to the very camp!" "To arms! to arms!" resounded from every quarter—and just then a wolf, attracted by the fumes of broiling buffalo bones, set up a most hideous howl across the creek. "Some one in distress!" was instantly shouted: "To his relief!" vociferated the crowd—and off they bolted, one and all, arms in hand, hurly-burly—leaving the camp entirely unprotected; so that had an enemy been at hand indeed, and approached us from the opposite direction, they might easily have taken possession of the wagons. Before they had all returned, however, a couple of hunters came in and laughed very heartily at the expense of the first alarmist, whom they had just chased into the camp.

Half a day's drive after leaving this camp of 'false alarms' brought us to the valley of Arkansas river. This point is about 270 miles from Independence. From the adjacent heights the landscape presents an imposing and picturesque appearance. Beneath a ledge of wave-like yellow sandy ridges and hillocks spreading far beyond, descends the majestic river (averaging at least a quarter of a mile in width), bespeckled with verdant islets, thickly set with cottonwood timber. The banks are very low and barren, with the exception of an occasional grove of stunted trees, hiding behind a swamp or sand-hill, placed there as it were to protect it from the fire of the prairies, which in most parts keeps down every perennial growth. In many places, indeed, where there are no islands, the river is so entirely bare of trees, that the unthinking traveller might approach almost to its very brink, without suspecting its presence.

Thus far, many of the prairies have a fine and productive appearance, though the Neosho river (or Council Grove) seems to form the western boundary of the truly rich and beautiful country of the border. Up to that point the prairies are similar to those of Missouri—the soil equally exuberant and fertile; while all the country that lies beyond, is of a far more barren character—vegetation of every kind is more stinted—the gay flowers more scarce, and the scanty timber of a very inferior quality: indeed, the streams, from Council Grove westward, are lined with very little else than cottonwood, barely interspersed here and there with an occasional elm or hackberry.

Following up the course of this stream for some twenty miles, now along the valley, and again traversing the points of projecting eminences, we reached Walnut creek. I have heard of a surgical operation performed at this point, in the summer of 1826, which, though not done exactly *secundum artem*, might suggest some novel reflections to the man of science. A few days before the caravan reached this place, a Mr. Broadus, in attempting to draw his rifle from a wagon muzzle foremost, discharged its contents into his arm. The bone being dreadfully shattered, the unfortunate man was advised to submit to an amputation at once; otherwise, it being in the month of August, and excessively warm, mortification would soon ensue. But Broadus obstinately refused to consent to this course, till death began to stare him in the face. By this time, however, the whole arm had become gangrened, some spots having already appeared above the place where the operation should have been performed. The invalid's case was therefore considered perfectly hopeless, and he was given up by all his comrades, who thought of little else than to consign him to the grave.

But being unwilling to resign himself to the fate which appeared frowning over him, without a last effort, he obtained the consent of two or three of the party, who undertook to amputate his arm merely to gratify the wishes of the dying man; for in such a light they viewed him. Their only 'case of instruments' consisted of a handsaw, a butcher's knife and a large iron bolt. The teeth of the saw being considered too coarse, they went to work, and soon had a set of fine teeth filed on the back. The knife having been whetted keen, and the iron bolt laid upon the fire, they commenced the operation: and in less time than it takes to tell it, the arm was opened round to the bone, which was almost in an instant sawed off; and with the whizzing hot iron the whole stump was so effectually seared as to close the arteries completely. Bandages were now applied, and the company proceeded on their journey as though nothing had occurred. The arm commenced healing rapidly, and in a few weeks the patient was sound and well, and is perhaps still living, to bear witness to the superiority of the 'hot iron' over ligatures, in 'taking up' arteries.

On the following day our route lay mostly over a level plain, which usually teems with buffalo, and is beautifully adapted to the chase. At the distance of about fifteen miles, the attention of the traveller is directed to the 'Pawnee Rock,' so called, it is said, on account of a battle's having once been fought hard by, between the Pawnees and some other tribe.[1] It is situated at the projecting point of a ridge, and upon its surface are furrowed, in uncouth but legible characters, numerous dates, and the names of various travellers who have chanced to pass that way.

We encamped at Ash creek, where we again experienced sundry alarms in consequence of 'Indian sign,' that was discovered in the creek valley, such as unextinguished fires, about which were found some old moccasins,—a sure indication of the recent retreat of savages from the vicinity. These constant alarms, however, although too frequently the result of groundless and unmanly fears, are not without their salutary effects upon the party. They serve to keep one constantly on the alert, and to sharpen those faculties of observation which would otherwise become blunted or inactive. Thus far also we had marched in two lines only; but, after crossing the Pawnee Fork, each of the four divisions drove on in a separate file, which became henceforth the order of march till we reached the border of the mountains. By moving in long lines as we did before, the march is continually interrupted; for every accident which delays a wagon ahead stops all those behind. By marching four abreast, this difficulty is partially obviated, and the wagons can also be thrown more readily into a condition of defence in case of attack.

Upon encamping the wagons are formed into a 'hollow square' (each division to a side), constituting at once an enclosure (or corral) for the animals when needed, and a fortification against the Indians. Not to embarrass this cattle-pen, the camp fires are all lighted outside of the wagons. Outside of the wagons, also, the travellers spread their beds, which consist, for the most part, of buffalo-rugs and blankets. Many content themselves with a single Mackinaw; but a pair constitutes the most regular pallet; and he that is provided with a buffalo-rug into the bargain, is deemed luxuriously supplied. It is most usual to sleep out in the open air, as well to be at hand in case of attack, as indeed for comfort; for the serene sky of the Prairies affords the most agreeable and wholesome canopy. That deleterious attribute of night air and dews, so dangerous in other climates, is but little experienced upon the high plains: on the contrary, the serene evening air seems to affect the health rather favorably than otherwise. Tents are so rare on these expeditions that, in a caravan of two hundred men, I have not seen a dozen. In time of rain the traveller resorts to his wagon, which affords a far more secure shelter than a tent; for if the latter is not beaten down by the storms which so often accompany rain upon the prairies, the ground underneath is at least apt to be flooded. During dry weather, however, even the invalid prefers the open air.

Prior to the date of our trip it had been customary to secure the horses by hoppling them. The 'fore-hopple' (a leathern strap or rope manacle upon the fore-legs) being most convenient, was more frequently used; though the 'side-line' (a hopple connecting a fore and a hind leg) is the most secure; for with this an animal can hardly increase his pace beyond a hobbling walk; whereas, with the fore-hopple, a frightened horse will scamper off with nearly as much velocity as though he were unshackled. But, better than either of these is the practice which the caravans have since adopted of tethering the mules at night around the wagons, at proper intervals, with ropes twenty-five or thirty feet in length, tied to stakes fifteen to twenty inches long, driven into the ground; a supply of which, as well as mallets, the wagoners always carry with them.

It is amusing to witness the disputes which often arise among wagoners about their 'staking ground.' Each teamster is allowed, by our 'common law,' a space of about a hundred yards immediately fronting his wagon, which he is ever ready to defend, if a neighbor shows a disposition to encroach upon his soil. If any animals are found 'staked' beyond the 'chartered limits,' it is the duty of the guard to 'knock them up,' and turn them into the *corral*. Of later years the tethering of oxen has also been resorted to with advantage. It was thought at first that animals thus confined by ropes could not procure a sufficient supply of food; but experience has allayed all apprehension on the subject. In fact, as the camp is always pitched in the most luxuriantly clothes patches of prairie that can be selected, a mule is seldom able to dispatch in the course of one night, all the grass within his reach. Again, when animals are permitted to range at liberty, they are apt to mince and nibble at the tenderest blades and spend their time in roaming from point to point, in search of what is most agreeable to their 'epicurean palates'; whereas if they are restricted by a rope, they will at once fall to with earnestness and clip the pasturage as it comes.

Although the buffalo had been scarce for a few days,—frightened off, no doubt, by the Indians whose 'sign' we saw about Ash creek, they soon became exceedingly abundant. The larger droves of these animals are sometimes a source of great annoyance to the caravans, as, by running near our loose stock, there is frequent danger of their causing *stampedes* (or general scamper), in which case mules, horses and oxen have been known to run away among the buffalo, as though they had been a gang of their own species. A company of traders, in 1824, lost twenty or thirty of their animals in this way. Hunters have also been deprived of their horses in the same way. Leaping from them in haste, in order to take a more determinate aim at a buffalo, the horse has been known to take fright, and, following the fleeing game, has disappeared with saddle, bridle, pistols and all—most probably never to be heard of again. In fact, to look for stock upon these prairies, would be emphatically to 'search for a needle in a haystack;' not only because they are virtually boundless, but that being everywhere alive with herds of buffalo, from which horses cannot be distinguished at a distance, one knows not whither to turn in search after the stray animals.

We had lately been visited by frequent showers of rain, and upon observing the Arkansas river, it was found to be rising, which seemed portentous of the troubles which the 'June freshet' might occasion us in crossing it; and, as it was already the 11th of this month, this annual occurrence was now hourly expected. On some occasions caravans have been obliged to construct what is called a 'buffalo-boat,' which is done by stretching the hides of these animals over a frame of poles, or, what is still more common, over an empty wagon-body. The 'June freshets,' however, are seldom of long duration; and, during the greatest portion of the year, the channel is very shallow. Still the bed of the river being in many places filled with quicksand, it is requisite to examine and mark out the best ford with stakes, before one undertakes to cross. The wagons are then driven over usually by double teams, which should never be permitted to stop, else animals and wagons are apt to founder, and the loading is liable to be damaged. I have witnessed a whole team down at once, rendering it necessary to unharness and drag each mule out separately: in fact, more than common exertion is sometimes required to prevent these dumpish animals from drowning in their fright and struggles through the water, though the current be but shallow at the place. Hence it is that oxen are much safer for fording streams than mules. As for ourselves, we forded the river without serious difficulty.

Rattlesnakes are proverbially abundant upon all these prairies, and as there is seldom to be found either stick or stone with which to kill them, one hears almost a constant popping of rifles or pistols among the vanguard, to clear the route of these disagreeable occupants, lest they should bite our animals. As we were toiling up through the sandy hillocks which border the southern banks of the Arkansas, the day being exceedingly warm, we came upon a perfect den of these reptiles. I will not say 'thousands,' though this perhaps were nearer the truth—but hundreds at least were coiled or crawling in every direction. They were no sooner discovered than we were upon them with guns and pistols, determined to let none of them escape.

In the midst of this amusing scramble among the snakes, a wild mustang colt, which had somehow or other, become separated from its dam, came bolting among our relay of loose stock to add to the confusion. One of our mules, evidently impressed with the impertinence of the intruder, sprang forward and attacked it, with the apparent intention of executing summary chastisement; while another mule, with more benignity of temper than its irascible compeer, engaged most lustily in defence of the unfortunate little mustang. As the contest was carried on among the wagons, the teamsters soon became very uproarious; so that the whole, with the snake fracas, made up a capital scene of confusion. When the mule skirmish would have ended, if no one had interfered, is a question which remained undetermined; for some of our company, in view of the consequences that might result from the contest, rather inhumanly took sides with the assailing mule; and soon after they entered the lists, a rifle ball relieved the poor colt from its earthly embarrassments, and the company from further domestic disturbance. Peace once more restored, we soon got under way, and that evening pitched our camp opposite the celebrated 'Caches,' a place where some of the earliest adventurers had been compelled to conceal their merchandise.

The history of the origin of these 'Caches' may be of sufficient interest to merit a brief recital. Beard, of the unfortunate party of 1812, alluded to in the first chapter, having returned to the United States in 1822, together with Chambers, who had descended the Canadian river the year before, induced some small capitalists of St. Louis to join in an enterprise, and then undertook to return to Santa Fé the same fall, with a small party and an assortment of merchandise. Reaching the Arkansas late in the season, they were overtaken by a heavy snow storm, and driven to take shelter on a large island. A rigorous winter ensued, which forced them to remain pent up in that place for three long months. During this time the greater portion of their animals perished; so that, when the spring began to open, they were unable to continue their journey with their goods. In this emergency they made a *cache* some distance above, on the north side of the river, where they stowed away most of their merchandise. From thence they proceeded to Taos, where they procured mules, and returned to get their hidden property.

Few travellers pass this way without visiting these mossy pits, some of which remain partly unfilled to the present day. In the vicinity, or a few miles to the eastward perhaps, passes the hundredth degree of longitude west from Greenwich, which, from the Arkansas to Red River, forms the boundary between the United States and the Mexican, or rather the Texan territory.

The term *cache,* meaning a *place of concealment,* was originally used by the Canadian French trappers and traders. It is made by digging a hole in the ground, somewhat in the shape of a jug, which is lined with dry sticks, grass, or anything else that will protect its contents from the dampness of the earth. In this place the goods to be concealed are carefully stowed away; and the aperture is then so effectually closed as to protect them from the rains. In *caching,* a great deal of skill is often required, to leave no signs whereby the cunning savage might discover the place of deposit. To this end, the excavated earth is carried to some distance and carefully concealed, or thrown into a stream, if one be at hand. The place selected for a cache is usually some rolling point, sufficiently elevated to be secure from inundations. If it be well set with grass, a solid piece of turf is cut out large enough for the entrance. The turf is afterward laid back, and taking root, in a short time no signs remains of its ever having been molested. However, as every locality does not afford a turfy site, the camp fire is sometimes built upon the place, or the animals are penned over it, which effectually destroys all traces of the cache.

This mode of concealing goods seems to have been in use from the time of the earliest French voyagers in America. Father Hennepin, during his passage down the Mississippi river, in 1680, describes an operation of this kind in the following terms: "We took up the green Sodd, and laid it by, and digg'd a hole in the Earth where we put our Goods, and cover'd them with pieces of Timber and Earth, and then put in again the Green Turf; so that 'twas impossible to suspect that any Hole had been digg'd under it, for we flung the Earth into the River." Returning a few weeks after, they found the cache all safe and sound.

Notes

1. Pawnee Rock is situated near the center of Kansas. It was a familiar landmark for travelers on the Santa Fe Trail. Names carved in the soft stone are still visible, though many are of a recent vintage. It is about half its original height: much of the rock has been carted off to be used as building material.—Eds.

Further Reading

Foster, Edward Halsey. *Josiah Gregg and Lewis H. Garrard.* Western Writers Series. Boise: Boise State University Press, 1977.

Horgan, Paul. *Josiah Gregg and His Vision of the Early West.* New York: Farrar, Straus & Giroux, 1979.

Diane Glancy *(b. 1941)*

In this prose poem Diane Glancy reminds us that, despite our attempts to explore and map the region, the Great Plains remain enigmatic and contradictory, a "flat space of prairie" where, ironically, the poet feels enclosed. Glancy, herself a child of immigrants and natives, senses the memory of early prairie trails—ruts in the land—with the imagination of someone who is still exploring the Great Plains.

Glancy was born in Kansas City, Missouri. She received a bachelor's degree from the University of Missouri and a master of fine arts degree from the University of Iowa. Her father is Cherokee and her mother is of English and German descent, a heritage evident in Glancy's poems, novels, plays, and essays. Glancy mixes oral and written traditions, poetry, and prose, and she experiments with various textual forms in ways that blur the lines between traditional literary forms.

October \ From the Back Screen of the Country
(1991)

I think I'm always trying to break thru the prairie into pockets of the world around me. It's because, even as I write, I still hear my mother's voice, don't leave the yard.

I search for diversity on the flat space of prairie where I feel enclosed. I make rigid blocks of imagery, which I try to transcend. Ordinary life & imagination are the tools.

But what of ordinary experience which is the frame? & where is this place from which I write? Not Midwest nor Southwest. The Great Plains. Possibly the Midlands. What else could it be called? & what am I doing here?

I was born in the middle of America. Some of my ancestors migrated by choice, some came during the forced march of the Cherokees to Indian Territory. Two generations later, my mother left the farm in Kansas, & my father left Arkansas. These two different people met, became my parents, & stuck it out. Later, I married & didn't. What could there be in our lives to provoke words? Especially the words of poetry: bearer of our cultures, mirror, road map, & releaser of emotions?

I raised two children, finished an education, divorced. I am burdened with
  rent & groceries, all the things my parents were burdened with. I groan
  as they groaned. But I will survive. It's the swale that runs through the
  land: depressions from wagon wheels moving west on the dining floor of
  the prairie. There's a memory of the trail & its hardships. Not a place
  for comfort, my mother said of the farm, long after the dust of those
  trails settled. My father never spoke of his upbringing, except to say that
  no one gave him anything, & it's true. Except maybe the Lord who
  blessed his path, & he never knew it.

This is a harsh land. Raw. A place everyone overlooks. Who'd want to
  come here? Isolated. Empty. 110° in the summer. Blizzardous out on the
  plains in winter. Narrow. Fundamental. Lonely as poetry itself.

In the early mornings, I sit on the back steps of my beige bungalow. I can
  tell by the chipped paint, the house used to be seagreen. Somewhere in
  memory, almost two thousand miles from either coast, boats float over
  the water like quilting needles on the farm.

It's much like the house where I grew up, which my parents owned. I rent.
  A backward step, a not-doing-as-well. A letting myself over the sea wall.

I hear rain on the leaves of the large old trees in the neighborhood, not yet
  soaked thru. I think of writing from the prairie as being in a colander. As
  I am aligned with the holes, I see the different views thru miniscule
  openings. Never the whole scene.

The death of both parents, the refining aspects of daily life. The empty
  bookcases in the house where I grew up. Impressions of experience.
  The feeling that far away something is happening. The hurt of lives that
  fall apart, love that doesn't hold. The voice of the Great Spirit. The fretwork of the mind on the rural concept of stay by the wagon & plow your
  own field. The ordinary life I write about from the harshness, the
  fullness of this land.

Further Reading

Boom Town. 1997.
The Cold-and-Hunger Dance. 1998.
Firesticks: A Novel. 1998.
Mask Maker. 2002.
The Only Piece of Furniture in the House. 1996.
Pushing the Bear. 1996.
Two Worlds Walking: Short Stories, Essays and Poetry by Writers with Mixed Heritages. 1994.
A Voice that Was in Travel: Stories. 1999.
The West Pole. 1997.

Susan Shelby Magoffin (1827–1855)

In 1846 Susan Shelby Magoffin, a girl of nineteen, set out for Santa Fe with her husband, Samuel, who was twenty-seven years older and a seasoned trader. She was, perhaps, the first white woman to make the journey along the Santa Fe Trail. The Magoffin brothers were well-established businessmen in New Mexico and Mexico and their influence extended beyond trade and commerce. The year that Susan set out for the Southwest coincided with the Mexican War that resulted in the annexation of New Mexico to the United States. Samuel's brother, James, was involved in annexation negotiations as a government agent for President James Polk.* As a result of the negotiations the Magoffins entered Santa Fe two weeks after U.S. troops took control of the town without using force.

Magoffin's journal provides a useful counterpoint to Josiah Gregg's more artfully organized account, with its emphasis on the region's economic viability. She was aware of Gregg's work and may have thought of publishing something herself, but her diary entries are intended primarily to be read by family and friends. The contrast in style and the details that each diarist selects underscore the differences in points of view of the seasoned trader going about his business and the young bride on an adventure. Notwithstanding the historical importance of the Magoffins, Susan's diary is more important as social rather than political commentary. She is a keen observer of life on the trail, with an eye for the telling details. In Santa Fe and Mexico she uses her knowledge of Spanish to learn about the lives around her, describing the social habits, customs, and daily routine of the region's Indian and Mexican inhabitants. As this sampling from the diary illustrates, everything interests her.

Despite her enthusiasm, life on the frontier was hard on Susan. The carriage rollover on the fourth of July, described in this selection, is followed on the twenty-first by a violent storm that collapses their tent. She is pregnant. These mishaps bring on an illness so alarming that her husband summons the doctor, who has traveled ahead with a faster party. On July twenty-seventh the party arrives at Bent's Fort, where the Magoffins have commodious private rooms. Nevertheless, Magoffin comments that "I am rather going down hill than up." July thirtieth is her nineteenth birthday, and on August sixth she has a miscarriage. Eight days later their party is again on the trail, covering the last leg of the long journey to

---

*For a full account of the historical background see the foreword by Howard R. Lamar in *Down the Santa Fe and into Mexico*, Stella Drumm, ed. (1926; rpt. Lincoln: University of Nebraska Press, 1982).

Santa Fe. They arrive there on August thirty-first, a journey of two months and twenty days.

Magoffin died in Missouri at the age of twenty-eight after suffering yellow fever, the loss of another child in Mexico, and the births of two daughters. Her diary provides one account of the precarious lives many women faced with varying degrees of fortitude during the years when thousands of men and women crossed the Great Plains on the overland trails.

Excerpts from *Down the Santa Fe Trail and into Mexico* (1926)

Noon. No. 20. Little Arkansas River. June 30th, 1846. Come my feeble pen, put on thy specks and assist this full head to unburthen itself! Thou hast a longer story than is usual to tell. How we left *Camp No. 19* yesterday (Monday) morning after a sleepless night, our tent was pitched in the musquito region and when will the God Somnus make his appearance in such quarters? It was slap, slap, all the time, from one party of the combatants, while the others came with a buz and a bite.

We traveled till 11 o'clock with the hope of finding water for the weary cattle. The sun was excessively oppressive. Col. Owens' mule teams left us entirely, but his oxen like ours were unable to stand the heat. They were before us and stoped—we followed their example, as much from necessity as any thing else. The oxen, some of them staggered under their yokes, and when we turned out for want of water—there was none within five miles of us that we knew of—some of the most fatigued absolutely crept under the wagons for shade, and did not move till they were driven up in the evening. One poor thing fell in the road and we almost gave him up for lost. His driver though, rather a tender hearted lad I presume, went with a bucket to a *mud hole* and brought the *wet mud* which was a little cool, and *plastered his body over with it.* He then got all the water from the water kegs after the men had drank, which was not more than two or three tin cups full; he took this and opening the ox's mouth poured it down his throat. He then made a covering over him with the ox yokes standing up and blankets spread over. In the course of an hour or two the poor thing could get up, and walk. But his great thirst for water led him to searching in the deep grass, and when the wagons started at 5 o'clock, he could not be found. Roman, the old Mexican who attended the loose stock, hunted some time for him, but to no purpose. Other sick ones needed his attention and it was probable this one had gone back to the last night's camp ground, and as it was too far to send on an uncertainty and pressing times, we gave up the search.

It blew up a little cooler towards sunset and we travelled pretty well, to make water was our object; both man and beast were craving it. The former could occasionally find a little to quench his parched thirst, by searching ravines that were grown up with tall weeds, this tho' muddy, and as warm as a scorching sun beaming into it all day could make it, was a luxurious draught. Now, about dark, we came into the musquito regions, and I found to my great *horror* that I have been complaining all this time for nothing, yes absolutely for *nothing;* for some two or hundred or even thousands are nothing compared with what we now encountered. The carriage mules became so restless that they passed all the wagons and switching their tails from side to side, as fast as they could, and slaping their ears, required some strength of our Mexican driver to hold them in. He would jerk the reins and exclaim "*hola los animal*[*es*] *cómo estande bravos!*" [Ho, animals! how wild you are!] The moon was not very bright and we could not see far before us. Suddenly one of the mules sprang to one side, reared, and pitched till I really believed we should turn over. Magoffin discouvered something lying in the road, and springing from the carriage pulled me out. It was a dead ox lying immediately in our way, and it is no wonder the mule was frightened.

In my own hurry to get out I had entirely forgotten the musquitoes, and on returning to the carriage I found my feet covered with stings, and my dress full, where they had gotten on me in the grass. About 10 o'clock we came upon a dark ravine, over which *las caras* [*los carros*—the wagons] would probably experience some difficulty in passing, so we stoped to see them over. The mules became perfectly frantic, and nothing could make them stand. They were turned out to shift for themselves, and Magoffin seeing no other alternative than to remain there all night, tied his head and neck up with pocket handkerchiefs and set about having the tent stretched. I drew my feet up under me, wraped my shawl over my head, till I almost smothered with heat, and listened to the din without. And such a noise as it was, I shall pray ever to be preserved. Millions upon millions were swarming around me, and their knocking against the carriage *reminded me of a hard rain.* It was equal to any of the plagues of Egypt. I lay almost in a perfect stupor, the heat and stings made me perfectly sick, till Magoffin came to the carriage and told me *to run if I could,* with my shawl, bonnet and shoes on (and without opening my mouth, Jane said, for they would *choke* me) straight to the bed.[1] When I got there they pushed me straight in under the musquito bar, which had been tied up in some kind of a fashion, and oh, dear, what a relief it was to breathe again. There I sat in my cage, like an imprisoned creature frightened half to death.

Magoffin now rolled himself up some how with all his cloths on, and lay down at my side, he dare not raise the bar to get in. I tried to sleep and towards daylight succeeded. On awaking this morning I found my forehead, arms and feet covered with knots. They were not little red places as musquitos generally make, but they were knots, some of them quite as large as a pea. We knocked up the tent as quick as possible and without thinking of breakfast came off to this place, passing on our way our own wagons and those of Col. Owens encamped at Mud Creek.

On our arrival here the buffalo and pillow were spread out and I layed down to sleep and I can say it took no rocking to accomplish the end. The tent was stretched with the intention of remaining here all night. The crossing is quite difficult, the sun extremely warm and it was supposed the oxen could not go on. About 11 o'clock *mi alma* came and raised me by my hand entirely up onto my feet without waking me. The whole scene had entirely changed. The sky was perfectly dark, wind blowing high, and atmosphere cool and pleasant and *no musquitoes,* with every appearance of a hard storm.

At 12 o'clock breakfast was ready, and after drinking a cup of tea I fell on the bed completely worn out. After two or three hours sound sleep I got up washed, combed my head, put on clean cloths—a luxury on the plains by the way—and sallied forth in the cool air somewhat refreshed. I brought out my writing implements and here I am.

Noon. 21. Little Cow Creek. July 1, 1846. According to the calculation of Mr. Gregg, a gentleman who made several expeditions across the Prairies and who wrote a history of the trade &c, we are 249 miles from Independence.

We camped last night at Arrow Rock creek—most of our travel yesterday was after 5 o'clock P.M. till 10—8 miles. I was quite sick and took medicine which has made me feel like a new being today. I am at least *50 per cent better.*

We had a fine dinner today and I enjoyed it exceedingly, for I had eaten nothing but a little tea and half a biscuit since yesterday dinner. It consisted of boiled chicken, soup, rice, and a dessert of *wine and gooseberry tart.* Such a thing on the plains would be looked upon by those at home as an utter impossibility. But nevertheless it is true. Jane and I went off as soon as we got here and found enough to make a fine pie. I wish the plumbs and grapes were ripe; there is any quantity of them along all the little streams we pass.

One of the wagoners chased a wolf today. We see them frequently lurking about, ready to come pick the scraps, if the dogs chance to leave any, where we have camped.

Camped tonight at big Cow Creek, three miles from the other which we left at seven o'clock. The crossing here is very bad and took us till moon down to cross. It is good water and wood, so we struck camp.

Camp No. 22. Bank of the Arkansas River. Prairie scenes are rather changing today. We are coming more into the buffalo regions. The grass is much shorter and finer. The plains are cut up by winding paths and every thing promises a *buffalo dinner* on the *4th.*

We left our last night's camp quite early this morning. About 9 o'clock we came upon "Dog City." This curiosity is well worth seeing. The Prairie dog, not much larger than a well grown rat, burrows in the ground. They generally make a regular town of it, each one making his house by digging a hole, and heaping the dirt around the mouth of this. Two are generally built together in a neighbourly way. They of course visit as regularly as man. When we got into this one, which lays on both sides of the road occupying at least a circle of some hundred yards, the little fellows like people ran to their doors to see the passing crowd. They could be seen all around with their heads poked out, and expressing their opinions I supposed from the loud barking I heard.

We nooned it on the Prairie without water for the cattle, within sight of the river, but some six miles from it. The banks are quite sandy and white, having the appearance, at a distance, of a large city. It is shaded by the trees in some places, having very much the appearance of white and coloured houses.

Came to camp tonight before sunset. Col. Owens' Company, which got before us this morning, were just starting after performing the last office to the dead body of a Mexican. He had consumption. Poor man, 'twas but yesterday that we sent him some soup from our camp, which he took with relish and today he is in his grave!

The manner of interring on the plains is necessarily very simple. The grave is dug very deep, to prevent the body from being found by the wolves. The corpse is rolled in a blanket—lowered and stones put on it. The earth is then thrown in, the sod replaced and it is well beat down. Often the corral is made over it, to make the earth still more firm, by the tromping of the stock. The Mexicans always place a cross at the grave.

Our camp is on the bank of the Arkansas tonight. Its dark waters remind me of the Mississippi.—It makes me sad to look upon it.—I am reminded of home. Though the Mississippi is a vast distance from there—it seems to me a near neighbour, compared with the distance I am from it—now three hundred miles from Independence. The time rolls on so fast I can scarcely realize its three weeks out.

Camp No. 23. This has indeed been a long day's travel. We left the Arkansas river, along which we have been traveling far and near since we first struck it, this morning by a little after 6 o'clock, and by 10 o'clock reached the Walnut Creek, a branch of the Arkansas, and eight miles from it. Crossed it with ease, the water quite deep though—and nooned it 4 miles father near the Arkansas. Today I have seen the first time wild buffalo. A herd of some ten or 12 were just across the river from our nooning place. The teamsters all afire to have a chase started off half a dozen of them—and much to our surprise, for we expected nothing of the kind, killed one—so after all we are to have a buffalo dinner tomorrow.

Started this P.M. about 4 o'clock traveled well till 6 o'clock, when a very hard thunder storm came up and detained us *in the road* till after eight. A thunder storm at sunset on the Prairie is a sublime and awing scene indeed. The vivid and forked lightning quickly succeeded by the hoarse growling thunder impresses one most deeply of his own weakness and the magnanimity of his God. With nothing before or near us in sight, save the wide expanse of Prairie resembling most fully in the pale light of the moon, as she occasionally appeared from under a murky cloud and between the vivid lightning, the wide sea. There was no object near higher than our own wagons, and how easy would it have been for one of them to be struck and consume the whole crowd, for with it was a high wind, sufficient to counteract the effects of the drenching rain.

We traveled on till 12 o'clock and stoped near the "Pawnee Rock"—a high mound with one side of sand stone. It derives its name from a battle once fought there between some company and a band of the Pawnee Indians. It has rather an awing name, since this tribe are the most treacherous and troublesome to the traders.

July 4th 1846. Pawnee Fork. Saturday. What a disasterous *celebration* I have today. It is certainly the greatest miracle that I have my head on my shoulders. I think I can never forget it if I live to be as old as my grandmother.

The wagons left Pawnee Rock some time before us.—For I was anxious to see this wonderful curiosity. We went up and while *mi alma* with his gun and pistols kept watch, for the wily Indian may always be apprehended here, it is a good lurking place and they are ever ready to fall upon any unfortunate trader behind his company—and it is necessary to be careful, so while *mi alma* watched on the rock above and Jane stood by to watch if any should come up on the front side of me, I cut my name, among the many hundreds inscribed on the rock and many of whom I knew. It was not done well, for fear of Indians made me tremble all over and I hurried it over in any way. This I remarked would be quite an adventure to celebrate the 4th! but woe betide I have yet another to relate.

The wagons being some distance ahead we rode on quite briskly to overtake them. In an hour's time we had driven some six miles, and at *Ash creek* we came up with them. No water in the creek and the crossing pretty good only a tolerably steep bank on the first side of it, all but two had passed over, and as these were not up we drove on ahead of them to cross first. The bank though a little steep was smooth and there could be no difficulty in riding down it.—However, we had made up our minds always to walk down such places in case of accident, and before we got to it *mi alma* hallowed "woe" as he always does when he wishes to stop, but as there was no motion made by the driver to that effect, he repeated it several times and with much vehemence. We had now reached the very verge of the cliff and seeing it a good way and apparently less dangerous than jumping out as we were, he said "go on." The word was scarcely from his lips, ere we were whirled completely over with a perfect crash. One to see the wreck of that carriage now with the top and sides entirely broken to pieces, could never believe that people had come out of it alive. But strange, wonderful to say, we are almost entirely unhurt! I was considerably stunned at first and could not stand on my feet. *Mi alma* forgetting himself and entirely enlisted for my safety carried me in his arms to a shade tree, almost entirely without my knowledge, and rubing my face and hands with whiskey soon brought me entire to myself.—My back and side are a little hurt, but is very small compared with what it might have been. *Mi alma* has his left hip and arm on which he fell both bruised and strained, but not seriously.

Dear creature 'twas for me he received this, for had he not caught me in his arms as we fell he could have saved himself entirely. And then I should perhaps have been killed or much crushed for the top fell over me, and it was only his hands that kept it off of me. It is better as it is, for we can sympathise more fully with each other.

It was a perfect mess that; of people, books, bottles—one of which broke, and on my head too I believe,—guns, pistols, baskets, bags, boxes and the dear knows what else. I was insensible to it all except when something gave me a hard knock and brought me to myself. We now sought refuge in Jane's carriage for our own could only acknowledge its incapability.

By 12 o'clock we reached this place six miles, when we found all the companies which have come on before us, having been stoped by an order of Government.

Sunday 5th. I am rather better of my bruises today. It is only for a little while though, I fear; such knocks seldom hurt so much for a day or two. I am yet to suffer for it.

We are still at "The Pawnee Fork." The traders are all stoped here by an order of Government, to wait the arrival of more troops than those already ahead of us, for our protection to Santa Fé.

We are quite a respectable crowd now with some seventy-five or eighty wagons of merchandise, beside those of the soldiers. When all that are behind us come up we shall number some hundred and fifty.

And it is quite probable we shall be detained here ten days or a week at the least. I shall go regularly to housekeeping. It is quite a nice place this, notwithstanding the number of wagons and cattle we have for our near neighbours. With the great Arkansas on the South of us, the Pawnee creek to the s.w. and extensive woods in the same direction. From the west the buffalo are constantly coming in, in bands of from three or four to more than fifty.

The sight of so many military coats is quite sufficient to frighten all the Indians entirely out of the country. So we have nothing to fear either on account of starvation, thirst or sudden murder.

Monday 6th. Camp No. 26. Ours is quite the picture of a hunter's home today.

The men, most of them, have been out since sun rise, and constantly mules loaded with the spoils of their several victories, are constantly returning to camp. It is a rich sight indeed to look at the fine fat meat stretched out on ropes to dry for our sustinence when we are no longer in the regions of the living animal. Such soup as we have made of the hump ribs, one of the most choice parts of the buffalo. I never eat its equal in the best hotels of N.Y. and Philad[a]. And the sweetest butter and most delicate oil I ever tasted tis not surpassed by the marrow taken from the thigh bones.

If one cannot live and grow fat here, he must be a strange creature. Oh, how much Papa would enjoy it! He would at once acknowledge that his venison camp never equaled it.

Mi alma was out this morning on a hunt, but I sincerely hope he will never go again. I am so uneasy from the time he starts till he returns. There is danger attached to it that the excited hunter seldom thinks of till it over take him. His horse may fall and kill him; the buffalo is apt too, to whirl suddenly on his persuer, and often serious if not fatal accidents occur. It is a painful situation to be placed in, to know that the being dearest to you on earth is in momentary danger of loosing his life, or receiving for the remainder of his days, whether long or short, a tormenting wound.

The servant who was with him today, was thrown from his horse by the latter stumbling in a hole, with which the Prairies are couvered, and had his head somewhat injured. And *mi alma's* horse was quite unruly.

Notes

1. Jane was Magoffin's "attendant."—Eds.

Reading about Women and Men on the Overland Trails

Chalfant, William Y. *Dangerous Passage: The Santa Fe Trail and the Mexican War*. Norman: University of Oklahoma Press, 1994.

Faragher, John Mack. *Women and Men on the Overland Trail*. New Haven: Yale University Press, 1979.

Meinig, D. W. *The Shaping of America: A Geographical Perspective on 500 Years of History*. vol. 2. *Contintental America 1800–1867*. New Haven: Yale University Press, 1993.

Meyer, Sandra. *Westering Women and the Frontier Experience 1800–1915*. Albuquerque: University of New Mexico Press, 1982.

Schlissel, Lillian. *Women's Diaries of the Westward Journey*. New York: Schocken, 1982.

Unruh, John, Jr. *The Plains Across: The Overland Emigrants and the TransMississippi West, 1840–1860*. Urbana: University of Illinois Press, 1979.

Washington Irving *(1783–1859)*

On his return from Europe where he had been living for seventeen years, Washington Irving accepted an invitation to accompany Henry L. Ellsworth, a newly appointed Indian commissioner, on a tour of the prairies in present-day Oklahoma. Irving joined an expedition that included his traveling companions Charles Latrobe, an English tutor, and Latrobe's nineteen-year-old charge, Count Albert-Alexander de Pourtales. It was 1832 and already Irving and others sensed that the central plains would soon be overrun by traders, trappers, and settlers. They mistakenly believed the wilderness would fade into memory and with it the great herds of bison and the American Indian peoples.

Irving was one of the first Americans to earn a living as a writer. When *A Tour on the Prairies* was published in 1835 his stories were already enjoying considerable popular and financial success. Irving's models were British and European authors and his audience was educated and well read. They expected polished prose and Irving did not disappoint them. He uses the elevated diction of an educated man addressing a sophisticated audience: only in Irving will a reader of Great Plains literature find ravines or draws referred to as "dells"; people "traversing" instead of crossing a valley; "beholding" not simply seeing a prairie landscape "diversified by hill and dale"; or a herd of buffalo transformed into "grazing cattle." Nevertheless, if Irving's narrative lacks the breathless enthusiasm of the young Susan Magoffin or the immediacy of the daily notes of Lewis and Clark, it does present, even for readers today, a rousing good story of imaginary Indians, adventures, and near catastrophes, all heightened by Irving's romantic embellishments of fancy words and elaborate similes.

The Grand Prairie—A Buffalo Hunt (1835)

After proceeding, about two hours, in a southerly direction, we emerged, towards mid-day, from the dreary belt of the Cross Timber, and, to our infinite delight, beheld "the Great Prairie" stretching to the right and left before us. We could distinctly trace the meandering course of the main Canadian and various smaller streams, by the strips of green forest that bordered them. The landscape was vast and beautiful. There is always an expansion of feeling in looking upon these boundless and fertile wastes; but I was doubly conscious of it after emerging from our "close dungeon of innumerable boughs."

From a rising ground Beatte pointed out to us the place where he and his comrades had killed the buffaloes; and we beheld several black objects moving in the distance, which he said were part of the herd. The Captain determined to shape his course to a woody bottom about a mile distant, and to encamp there, for a day or two, by way of having a regular buffalo hunt, and getting a supply of provisions. As the troops filed along the slope of the hill towards the camping-ground, Beatte proposed to my messmates and myself that we should put our-selves under his guidance, promising to take us where we should have plenty of sport. Leaving the line of march, therefore, we diverged towards the prairie, tra-versing a small valley, and ascending a gentle swell of land. As we reached the summit we beheld a gang of wild horses about a mile off. Beatte was immediately on the alert, and no longer thought of buffalo-hunting. He was mounted on his powerful half-wild horse, with a lariat coiled at the saddle-bow, and set off in pursuit: while we remained on a rising ground, watching his manœuvres with great solicitude. Taking advantage of a strip of woodland, he stole quietly along, so as to get close to them before he was perceived. The moment they caught sight of him, a grand scamper took place. We watched him skirting along the horizon, like a privateer in full chase of a merchantman:[1] at length he passed over the brow of a ridge, and down into a shallow valley; in a few moments he was on the opposite hill, and close upon one of the horses. He was soon head and head, and appeared to be trying to noose his prey; but they both disappeared again below the hill, and we saw no more of them. It turned out, afterwards, that he had noosed a powerful horse, but could not hold him, and had lost his lariat in the attempt.

While we were waiting for his return, we perceived two buffalo bulls descend-ing a slope towards a stream, which wound through a ravine fringed with trees. The young Count and myself endeavoured to get near them, under covert of the trees. They discovered us while we were yet three or four hundred yards off, and, turning about, retreated up the rising ground. We urged our horses across the ravine, and gave chase. The immense weight of head and shoulders causes the buffalo to labour heavily up hill, but it accelerates his descent. We had the advan-tage, therefore, and gained rapidly upon the fugitives, though it was difficult to get our horses to approach them, their very scent inspiring them with terror. The Count, who had a double-barrelled gun, loaded with ball, fired, but missed. The bulls now altered their course, and galloped down hill with headlong rapidity. As they ran in different directions, we each singled out one, and separated. I was provided with a brace of veteran brass-barrelled pistols, which I had borrowed at Fort Gibson, and which had evidently seen some service. Pistols are very effective in buffalo-hunting, as the hunter can ride up close to the animal, and fire at it while at full speed; whereas the long heavy rifles used on the frontier cannot be easily managed, nor discharged with accurate aim from horseback. My object, there-fore, was to get within pistol-shot of the buffalo. This was no very easy matter. I was well mounted, on a horse of excellent speed and bottom, that seemed eager for the chase, and soon overtook the game, but the moment he came nearly parallel he would keep sheering off, with ears forked and pricked forward, and every symptom of aversion and alarm. It was no wonder. Of all animals a buffalo, when close pressed by the hunter, has an aspect the most diabolical. His two short black horns curve out of a huge frontlet of shaggy hair; his eyes glow like coals; his mouth is open, his tongue parched and drawn up into a half-crescent; his tail is erect, and the tufted end whisking about in the air; he is a perfect picture of mingled rage and terror.

It was with difficulty I urged my horse sufficiently near, when, taking aim, to my chagrin, both pistols missed fire. Unfortunately, the locks of these veteran weapons were so much worn, that, in the gallop, the priming had been shaken out of the pans. At the snapping of the last pistol I was close upon the buffalo, when, in his despair, he turned round, with a sudden snort, and rushed upon me. My horse wheeled about, as if on a pivot, made a convulsive spring, and, as I had been leaning on one side with pistol extended, I came near being thrown at the feet of the buffalo.

Three or four bounds of the horse carried us out of reach of the enemy, who, having merely turned in desperate self-defence, quickly resumed his flight. As soon as I could gather in my panic-stricken horse, and prime the pistols afresh, I again spurred in pursuit of the buffalo, who had slackened his speed to take breath. On my approach, he again set off, full tilt, heaving himself forward with a heavy rolling gallop, dashing with headlong precipitation through brakes and ravines; while several deer and wolves, startled from their coverts by his thundering career, ran helter-skelter to right and left across the waste.

A gallop across the prairies in pursuit of game is by no means so smooth a career as those may imagine who have only the idea of an open level plain. It is true the prairies of the hunting-grounds are not so much entangled with flowering plants and long herbage as the lower prairies, and are principally covered with short buffalo grass; but they are diversified by hill and dale, and, where most level, are apt to be cut up by deep rifts and ravines, made by torrents after rains, and which, yawning from an even surface, are almost like pitfalls in the way of the hunter; checking him suddenly when in full career, or subjecting him to the risk of limb and life. The plains, too, are beset by burrowing holes of small animals, in which the horse is apt to sink to the fetlock and throw both himself and his rider. The late rain had covered some parts of the prairie, where the ground was hard, with a thin sheet of water through which the horse had to splash his way. In other parts there were innumerable shallow hollows, eight or ten feet in diameter, made by the buffaloes, who wallow in sand and mud like swine. These, being filled with water, shone like mirrors, so that the horse was continually leaping over them, or springing on one side. We had reached, too, a rough part of the prairie, very much broken and cut up: the buffalo, who was running for life, took no heed to his course, plunging down breakneck ravines, where it was necessary to skirt the borders in search of a safer descent. At length he came to where a winter stream had torn a deep chasm across the whole prairie, laying open jagged rocks, and forming a long glen bordered by steep crumbling cliffs of mingled stone and clay. Down one of these the buffalo flung himself, half tumbling, half leaping, and then scuttled off along the bottom; while I, seeing all farther pursuit useless, pulled up, and gazed quietly after him from the border of the cliff, until he disappeared amidst the windings of the ravine.

Nothing now remained but to turn my steed and rejoin my companions. Here, at first, was some little difficulty. The ardour of the chase had betrayed me into a long heedless gallop: I now found myself in the midst of a lonely waste, in which the prospect was bounded by undulating swells of land, naked and uniform, where, from the deficiency of landmarks and distinct features, an inexperienced man may become bewildered, and lose his way as readily as in the wastes of the ocean. The day, too, was overcast, so that I could not guide myself by the sun. My only mode was to retrace the track my horse had made in coming, though this I would often lose sight of, where the ground was covered with parched herbage. To one unaccustomed to it, there is something inexpressibly lonely in the solitude of a prairie: the loneliness of a forest seems nothing to it. There the view is shut in by trees, and the imagination is left free to picture some livelier scene beyond; but here we have an immense extent of landscape, without a sign of human existence. We have the consciousness of being far, far beyond the bounds of human habitation; we feel as if moving in the midst of a desert world. As my horse lagged slowly back over the scenes of our late scamper, and the delirium of the chase had passed away, I was peculiarly sensible to these circumstances. The silence of the waste was now and then broken by the cry of a distant flock of pelicans, stalking like spectres about a shallow pool, sometimes by the sinister croaking of a raven in the air, while occasionally a scoundrel wolf would scour off from before me, and, having attained a safe distance, would sit down and howl and whine, with tones that gave a dreariness to the surrounding solitude. After pursuing my way for some time, I descried a horseman on the edge of a distant hill, and soon recognised him to be the Count. He had been equally unsuccessful with myself. We were shortly afterwards rejoined by our worthy comrade, the virtuoso, who, with spectacles on nose, had made two or three ineffectual shots from horseback.

We determined not to seek the camp until we had made one more effort. Casting our eyes about the surrounding waste, we descried a herd of buffalo about two miles distant, scattered apart and quietly grazing near a small strip of trees and bushes. It required but little stretch of fancy to picture them so many cattle grazing on the edge of a common, and that the grove might shelter some lonely farm-house.

We now formed our plan to circumvent the herd, and, by getting on the other side of them, to hunt them in the direction where we knew our camp to be situated; otherwise the pursuit might take us to such a distance, as to render it impossible to find our way back before nightfall. Taking a wide circuit, therefore, we moved slowly and cautiously, pausing occasionally, when we saw any of the herd desist from grazing. The wind fortunately set from them, otherwise they might have scented us and have taken the alarm. In this way we succeeded in getting round the herd without disturbing it. It consisted of about forty head, bulls, cows, and calves. Separating to some distance from each other, we now approached slowly in a parallel line, hoping, by degrees, to steal near without exciting attention. They began, however, to move off quietly, stopping at every step or two to graze; when suddenly a bull that, unobserved by us, had been taking his siesta under a clump of trees to our left, roused himself from his lair, and hastened to join his companions. We were still at a considerable distance, but the game had taken the alarm. We quickened our pace, they broke into a gallop, and now commenced a full chase.

As the ground was level, they shouldered along with great speed, following each other in a line, two or three bulls bringing up the rear; the last of whom, from his enormous size and venerable frontlet and beard of sunburnt hair, looked like the patriarch of the herd, and as if he might long have reigned the monarch of the prairie.

There is a mixture of the awful and the comic in the look of these huge animals, as they heave their great bulk forwards, with an up and down motion of the unwieldy head and shoulders; their tail cocked up like the queue of Pantaloon in a pantomime,[2] the end whisking about in a fierce yet whimsical style; and their eyes glaring venomously with an expression of fright and fury.

For some time I kept parallel with the line, without being able to force my horse within pistol-shot, so much had he been alarmed by the assault of the buffalo in the preceding chase. At length I succeeded; but was again balked by my pistols missing fire. My companions, whose horses were less fleet and more wayworn, could not overtake the herd; at length, Mr. L., who was in the rear of the line, and losing ground, levelled his double-barrelled gun, and fired a long raking shot. It struck a buffalo just above the loins, broke its back bone, and brought it to the ground. He stopped, and alighted to despatch his prey, when, borrowing his gun, which had yet a charge remaining in it, I put my horse to his speed, again overtook the herd, which was thundering along pursued by the Count. With my present weapon there was no need of urging my horse to such close quarters; galloping along parallel, therefore, I singled out a buffalo, and by a fortunate shot brought it down on the spot. The ball had struck a vital part: it could not move from the place where it fell, but lay there struggling in mortal agony, while the rest of the herd kept on their headlong career across the prairie.

Dismounting, I now fettered my horse to prevent his straying, and advanced to contemplate my victim. I am nothing of a sportsman: I had been prompted to this unwonted exploit by the magnitude of the game and the excitement of an adventurous chase. Now that the excitement was over, I could not but look with commiseration upon the poor animal that lay struggling and bleeding at my feet. His very size and importance, which had before inspired me with eagerness, now increased my compunction. It seemed as if I had inflicted pain in proportion to the bulk of my victim, and as if there were a hundred-fold greater waste of life than there would have been in the destruction of an animal of inferior size.

To add to these after-qualms of conscience, the poor animal lingered in his agony. He had evidently received a mortal wound, but death might be long in coming. It would not do to leave him here to be torn piecemeal while yet alive, by the wolves that had already snuffed his blood, and were skulking and howling at a distance, and waiting for my departure, and by the ravens that were flapping about and croaking dismally in the air. It became now an act of mercy to give him his quietus,[3] and put him out of his misery. I primed one of the pistols, therefore, and advanced close up to the buffalo. To inflict a wound thus in cold blood, I found a totally different thing from firing in the heat of the chase. Taking aim, however, just behind the fore-shoulder, my pistol for once proved true: the ball must have passed through the heart, for the animal gave one convulsive throe, and expired.

While I stood meditating and moralising over the wreck I had so wantonly produced, with my horse grazing near me, I was rejoined by my fellow-sportsman, the virtuoso, who, being a man of universal adroitness, and, withal, more experience, and hardened in the gentle art of "venerie," soon managed to carve out the tongue of the buffalo, and delivered it to me to bear back to the camp as a trophy.

Notes

1. A privateer is a privately owned ship with a government's commission to attack and capture enemy ships in a time of war.—Eds.

2. Pantaloon is a stock figure in comedy; a lean, foolish old man, the butt of the clown's jokes.—Eds.

3. Quietus: release from life; death.—Eds.

Further Reading

The Complete Tales of Washington Irving. Ed. Charles Neider. 1975.
The Western Journals of Washington Irving. Ed. John Francis McDermott. 1944.

Reading about Washington Irving

Antelyes, Peter. *Tales of Adventurous Enterprise: Washington Irving and the Poetics of Western Expansion.* New York: Columbia University Press, 1990.

Cracroft, Richard. *Washington Irving.* Western Writers Series. Boise ID: Boise State University. 1974.

Hedges, William L. *Washington Irving: An American Study, 1802–1832.* Baltimore: Johns Hopkins University Press, 1965.

Leary, Lewis. *Washington Irving.* Minneapolis: University of Minnesota Press, 1963.

Francis Parkman (1823–1893)

The historian Francis Parkman began his career by writing an account of his travels across the Great Plains in 1846. With his cousin, Quincy Adams Shaw, expert guide Henry Chatillon, and muleteer Antoine De Laurier ("Delovier"), Parkman traveled along the Platte River immigrant trail through Nebraska to Fort Laramie in Wyoming, then turned south across what is now eastern Colorado to Bent's Fort in southeastern Colorado on the Santa Fe Trail (where Susan Shelby Magoffin stayed for some time the same year). Parkman and his party followed the Santa Fe Trail back to Missouri. The first installment of his account of the trip appeared in 1847.

Like Washington Irving, Parkman was an educated man who later went on to make his living as a writer. But, unlike Irving, Parkman's view of the Great Plains was not shaded by a romantic or European sensibility. The historian Parkman uses few similes or elaborate turns of phrases to detract the reader's attention from the narrative. His descriptions are relatively straightforward: a cup of water exhibits "an extraordinary variety and profusion of animal and vegetable life." Ironically, when Parkman first sees the Platte River he sees "no living thing" in a region now regarded as one of the most productive of the Great Plains. The prairie flowers only serve to remind him of the East and friends at home. Unlike Wright Morris, this traveler did not see what the prairie dwellers can see in their minds' eyes.

Parkman had the questionable opportunity to indulge in hindsight. In subsequent editions of *The Oregon Trail,* he added prefaces: two are included here. By 1892, the year before his death, Parkman acknowledges the radical changes in the "Wild West": his account is no longer a travel guide but rather the memory of a landscape and a way of life that disappeared in only forty-five years.

The Platte and the Desert (1847)

We were now at the end of our solitary journeyings along the St. Joseph trail. On the evening of the twenty-third of May we encamped near its junction with the old legitimate trail of the Oregon emigrants. We had ridden long that afternoon, trying in vain to find wood and water, until at length we saw the sunset sky reflected from a pool encircled by bushes and rocks. The water lay in the bottom of a hollow, the smooth prairie gracefully rising in ocean-like swells on every side. We pitched our tents by it; not however before the keen eye of Henry Chatillon had discerned some unusual object upon the faintly-defined outline of the distant swell. But in the moist, hazy atmosphere of the evening, nothing could be clearly distinguished. As we lay around the fire after supper, a low and distant sound, strange enough amid the loneliness of the prairie, reached our ears—peals of laughter, and the faint voices of men and women. For eight days we had not encountered a human being, and this singular warning of their vicinity had an effect extremely impressive.

About dark a sallow-faced fellow descended the hill on horseback, and splashing through the pool, rode up to the tents. He was enveloped in a huge cloak, and his broad felt hat was weeping about his ears with the drizzling moisture of the evening. Another followed, a stout, square-built, intelligent-looking man, who announced himself as leader of an emigrant party, encamped a mile in advance of us. About twenty wagons, he said, were with him; the rest of his party were on the other side of the Big Blue, waiting for a woman who was in the pains of childbirth, and quarrelling meanwhile among themselves.

These were the first emigrants that we had overtaken, although we had found abundant and melancholy traces of their progress throughout the course of the journey. Sometimes we passed the grave of one who had sickened and died on the way. The earth was usually torn up, and covered thickly with wolf-tracks. Some had escaped this violation. One morning, a piece of plank, standing upright on the summit of a grassy hill, attracted our notice, and riding up to it, we found the following words very roughly traced upon it, apparently with a red-hot piece of iron:—

MARY ELLIS.

DIED MAY 7TH, 1845.

AGED TWO MONTHS.

Such tokens were of common occurrence.

We were late in breaking up our camp on the following morning, and scarcely had we ridden a mile when we saw, far in advance of us, drawn against the horizon, a line of objects stretching at regular intervals along the level edge of the prairie. An intervening swell soon hid them from sight, until, ascending it a quarter of an hour after, we saw close before us the emigrant caravan, with its heavy white wagons creeping on in slow procession, and a large drove of cattle following behind. Half a dozen yellow-visaged Missourians, mounted on horseback, were cursing and shouting among them, their lank angular proportions enveloped in brown homespun, evidently cut and adjusted by the hands of a domestic female tailor. As we approached, they called out to us: "How are ye, boys? Are ye for Oregon or California?"

As we pushed rapidly by the wagons, children's faces were thrust out from the white coverings to look at us; while the care-worn, thin-featured matron, or the buxom girl, seated in front, suspended the knitting on which most of them were engaged to stare at us with wondering curiosity. By the side of each wagon stalked the proprietor, urging on his patient oxen, who shouldered heavily along, inch by inch, on their interminable journey. It was easy to see that fear and dissension prevailed among them; some of the men—but these, with one exception, were bachelors—looked wistfully upon us as we rode lightly and swiftly by, and then impatiently at their own lumbering wagons and heavy-gaited oxen. Others were unwilling to advance at all, until the party they had left behind should have rejoined them. Many were murmuring against the leader they had chosen, and wished to depose him; and this discontent was fomented by some ambitious spirits, who had hopes of succeeding in his place. The women were divided between regrets for the homes they had left and fear of the deserts and savages before them.

We soon left them far behind, and hoped that we had taken a final leave; but our companions' wagon stuck so long in a deep muddy ditch, that before it was extricated the van of the emigrant caravan appeared again, descending a ridge close at hand. Wagon after wagon plunged through the mud; and as it was nearly noon, and the place promised shade and water, we saw with satisfaction that they were resolved to encamp. Soon the wagons were wheeled into a circle: the cattle were grazing over the meadow, and the men, with sour, sullen faces, were looking about for wood and water. They seemed to meet but indifferent success. As we left the ground, I saw a tall, slouching fellow, with the nasal accent of "down east," contemplating the contents of his tin cup, which he had just filled with water.

"Look here, you," said he; "ir's chock-full of animals!"

The cup, as he held it out, exhibited in fact an extraordinary variety and profusion of animal and vegetable life.

Riding up the little hill, and looking back on the meadow, we could easily see that all was not right in the camp of the emigrants. The men were crowded together, and an angry discussion seemed to be going forward. R—— was missing from his wonted place in the line, and the Captain told us that he had remained behind to get his horse shod by a blacksmith attached to the emigrant party. Something whispered in our ears that mischief was on foot; we kept on, however, and coming soon to a stream of tolerable water, we stopped to rest and dine. Still the absentee lingered behind. At last, at the distance of a mile, he and his horse suddenly appeared, sharply defined against the sky on the summit of a hill; and close behind, a huge white object rose slowly into view.

"What is that blockhead bringing with him now?"

A moment dispelled the mystery. Slowly and solemnly, one behind the other, four long trains of oxen and four emigrant wagons rolled over the crest of the hill and gravely descended, while R—— rode in state in the van. It seems, that during the process of shoeing the horse, the smothered dissensions among the emigrants suddenly broke into open rupture. Some insisted on pushing forward, some on remaining where they were, and some on going back. Kearsley, their captain, threw up his command in disgust. "And now, boys," said he, "if any of you are for going ahead, just you come along with me."

Four wagons, with ten men, one woman, and one small child, made up the force of the "go-ahead" faction, and R———, with his usual proclivity toward mischief, invited them to join our party. Fear of the Indians—for I can conceive no other motive—must have induced him to court so burdensome an alliance. At all events, the proceeding was a cool one. The men who joined us, it is true, were all that could be desired; rude indeed in manners, but frank, manly, and intelligent. To tell them we could not travel with them was out of the question. I merely reminded Kearsley that if his oxen could not keep up with our mules he must expect to be left behind, as we could not consent to be farther delayed on the journey; but he immediately replied, that his oxen "*should* keep up; and if they couldn't, why, he allowed, he'd find out how to make 'em."

On the next day, as it chanced, our English companions broke the axle-tree of their wagon, and down came the whole cumbrous machine lumbering into the bed of a brook. Here was a day's work cut out for us. Meanwhile our emigrant associates kept on their way, and so vigorously did they urge forward their powerful oxen, that, what with the broken axle-tree and other mishaps, it was a full week before we overtook them; when at length we discovered them, one afternoon, crawling quietly along the sandy brink of the Platte. But meanwhile various incidents occurred to ourselves.

It was probable that at this stage of our journey the Pawnees would attempt to rob us. We began therefore to stand guard in turn, dividing the night into three watches, and appointing two men for each. Deslauriers and I held guard together. We did not march with military precision to and fro before the tents: our discipline was by no means so strict. We wrapped ourselves in our blankets, and sat down by the fire; and Deslauriers, combining his culinary functions with his duties as sentinel, employed himself in boiling the head of an antelope for our breakfast. Yet we were models of vigilance in comparison with some of the party; for the ordinary practice of the guard was to lay his rifle on the ground, and, enveloping his nose in his blanket, meditate on his mistress, or whatever subject best pleased him. This is all well enough when among Indians who do not habitually proceed further in their hostility than robbing travellers of their horses and mules, though, indeed, a Pawnee's forbearance is not always to be trusted; but in certain regions farther to the west, the guard must beware how he exposes his person to the light of the fire, lest some keen-eyed skulking marksman should let fly a bullet or an arrow from the darkness.

Among various tales that circulated around our campfire was one told by Boisverd, and not inappropriate here. He was trapping with several companions on the skirts of the Blackfoot country. The man on guard, knowing that it behooved him to put forth his utmost precaution, kept aloof from the fire-light, and sat watching intently on all sides. At length he was aware of a dark, crouching figure, stealing noiselessly into the circle of the light. He hastily cocked his rifle, but the sharp click of the lock caught the ear of the Blackfoot, whose senses were all on the alert. Raising his arrow, already fitted to the string, he shot it in the direction of the sound. So sure was his aim, that he drove it through the throat of the unfortunate guard, and then, with a loud yell, bounded from the camp.

As I looked at the partner of my watch, puffing and blowing over his fire, it occurred to me that he might not prove the most efficient auxiliary in time of trouble.

"Deslauriers," said I, "would you run away if the Pawnees should fire at us?"

"Ah! oui, oui, Monsieur!" he replied very decisively.

At this instant a whimsical variety of voices,—barks, howls, yelps, and whines,— all mingled together, sounded from the prairie, not far off, as if a conclave of wolves of every age and sex were assembled there. Deslauriers looked up from his work with a laugh, and began to imitate this medly of sounds with a ludicrous accuracy. At this they were repeated with redoubled emphasis, the musician being apparently indignant at the successful efforts of a rival. They all proceeded from the throat of one little wolf, not larger than a spaniel, seated by himself at some distance. He was of the species called the prairie-wolf: a grim-visaged, but harmless little brute, whose worst propensity is creeping among horses and gnawing the ropes of raw hide by which they are picketed around the camp. Other beasts roam the prairies, far more formidable in aspect and in character. These are the large white and gray wolves, whose deep howl we heard at intervals from far and near.

At last I fell into a doze, and awaking from it, found Deslauriers fast asleep. Scandalized by this breach of discipline, I was about to stimulate his vigilance by stirring him with the stock of my rifle; but, compassion prevailing, I determined to let him sleep a while, and then arouse him to administer a suitable reproof for such forgetfulness of duty. Now and then I walked the rounds among the silent horses, to see that all was right. The night was chill, damp, and dark, the dank grass bending under the icy dew-drops. At the distance of a rod or two the tents were invisible, and nothing could be seen but the obscure figures of the horses, deeply breathing, and restlessly starting as they slept, or still slowly champing the grass. Far off, beyond the black outline of the prairie there was a ruddy light, gradually increasing, like the glow of a conflagration; until at length the broad disk of the moon, blood-red, and vastly magnified by the vapors, rose slowly upon the darkness, flecked by one or two little clouds, and as the light poured over the gloomy plain, a fierce and stern howl, close at hand, seemed to greet it as an unwelcome intruder. There was something impressive and awful in the place and the hour; for I and the beasts were all that had consciousness for many a league around.

Some days elapsed, and brought us near the Platte. Two men on horseback approached us one morning, and we watched them with the curiosity and interest that, upon the solitude of the plains, such an encounter always excites. They were evidently whites, from their mode of riding, though, contrary to the usage of that region, neither of them carried a rifle.

"Fools!" remarked Henry Chatillon, "to ride that way on the prairie; Pawnee find them—then they catch it."

Pawnee *had* found them, and they had come very near "catching it;" indeed, nothing saved them but the approach of our party. Shaw and I knew one of them,—a man named Turner, whom we had seen at Westport. He and his companion belonged to an emigrant party encamped a few miles in advance, and had returned to look for some stray oxen, leaving their rifles, with characteristic rashness or ignorance, behind them. Their neglect had nearly cost them dear; for, just before we came up, half a dozen Indians approached, and, seeing them apparently defenceless, one of the rascals seized the bridle of Turner's horse and ordered him to dismount. Turner was wholly unarmed; but the other jerked a pistol out of his pocket, at which the Pawnee recoiled; and just then some of our men appearing in the distance, the whole party whipped their rugged little horses and made off. In no way daunted, Turner foolishly persisted in going forward.

Long after leaving him, and late that afternoon, in the midst of a gloomy and barren prairie, we came suddenly upon the great trail of the Pawnees, leading from their villages on the Platte to their war and hunting grounds to the southward. Here every summer passes the motley concourse: thousands of savages, men, women, and children, horses and mules, laden with their weapons and implements, and an innumerable multitude of unruly wolfish dogs, who have not acquired the civilized accomplishment of barking, but howl like their wild cousins of the prairie.

The permanent winter villages of the Pawnees stand on the lower Platte, but throughout the summer the greater part of the inhabitants are wandering over the plains,—a treacherous, cowardly banditti, who, by a thousand acts of pillage and murder, have deserved chastisement at the hands of government. Last year a Dahcotah warrior performed a notable exploit at one of these villages. He approached it alone, in the middle of a dark night, and clambering up the outside of one of the lodges, which are in the form of a half-sphere, looked in at the round hole made at the top for the escape of smoke. The dusky light from the embers showed him the forms of the sleeping inmates; and dropping lightly through the opening, he unsheathed his knife, and, stirring the fire, coolly selected his victims. One by one, he stabbed and scalped them; when a child suddenly awoke and screamed. He rushed from the lodge, yelled a Sioux war-cry, shouted his name in triumph and defiance, and darted out upon the dark prairie, leaving the whole village behind him in a tumult, with the howling and baying of dogs, the screams of women, and the yells of the enraged warriors.

Our friend Kearsley, as we learned on rejoining him, signalized himself by a less bloody achievement. He and his men were good woodsmen, well skilled in the use of the rifle, but found themselves wholly out of their element on the prairie. None of them had ever seen a buffalo; and they had very vague conceptions of his nature and appearance. On the day after they reached the Platte, looking towards a distant swell, they beheld a multitude of little black specks in motion upon its surface.

"Take your rifles, boys," said Kearsley, "and we'll have fresh meat for supper." This inducement was quite sufficient. The ten men left their wagons, and set out in hot haste, some on horseback and some on foot, in pursuit of the supposed buffalo. Meanwhile a high, grassy ridge shut the game from view; but mounting it after half an hour's running and riding, they found themselves suddenly confronted by about thirty mounted Pawnees. Amazement and consternation were mutual. Having nothing but their bows and arrows, the Indians thought their hour was come, and the fate that they were conscious of richly deserving about to overtake them. So they began, one and all, to shout forth the most cordial salutations, running up with extreme earnestness to shake hands with the Missourians, who were as much rejoiced as they were to escape the expected conflict.

A low, undulating line of sand-hills bounded the horizon before us. That day we rode ten hours, and it was dusk before we entered the hollows and gorges of these gloomy little hills. At length we gained the summit, and the long-expected valley of the Platte lay before us. We all drew rein, and sat joyfully looking down upon the prospect. It was right welcome; strange, too, and striking to the imagination, and yet it had not one picturesque or beautiful feature; nor had it any of the features of grandeur, other than its vast extent, its solitude, and its wildness. For league after league, a plain as level as a lake was outspread beneath us; here and there the Platte, divided into a dozen thread-like sluices, was traversing it, and an occasional clump of wood, rising in the midst like a shadowy island, relieved the monotony of the waste. No living thing was moving throughout the vast landscape, except the lizards that darted over the sand and through the rank grass and prickly pears at our feet.

We had passed the more tedious part of the journey; but four hundred miles still intervened between us and Fort Laramie; and to reach that point cost us the travel of three more weeks. During the whole of this time we were passing up the middle of a long, narrow, sandy plain, reaching like an outstretched belt nearly to the Rocky Mountains. Two lines of sand-hills, broken often into the wildest and most fantastic forms, flanked the valley at the distance of a mile or two on the right and left; while beyond them lay a barren, trackless waste, extending for hundreds of miles to the Arkansas on the one side, and the Missouri on the other. Before and behind us, the level monotony of the plain was unbroken as far as the eye could reach. Sometimes it glared in the sun, an expanse of hot, bare sand; sometimes it was veiled by long coarse grass. Skulls and whitening bones of buffalo were scattered everywhere; the ground was tracked by myriads of them, and often covered with the circular indentations where the bulls had wallowed in the hot weather.

From every gorge and ravine, opening from the hills, descended deep, well-worn paths, where the buffalo issue twice a day in regular procession to drink in the Platte. The river itself runs through the midst, a thin sheet of rapid, turbid water, half a mile wide, and scarcely two feet deep. Its low banks, for the most part without a bush or a tree, are of loose sand, with which the stream is so charged that it grates on the teeth in drinking. The naked landscape is, of itself, dreary and monotonous enough; and yet the wild beasts and wild men that frequent the valley of the Platte make it a scene of interest and excitement to the traveller. Of those who have journeyed there, scarcely one, perhaps, fails to look back with fond regret to his horse and his rifle.

Early in the morning after we reached the Platte, a long procession of squalid savages approached our camp. Each was on foot, leading his horse by a rope of bull-hide. His attire consisted merely of a scanty cincture, and an old buffalo robe, tattered and begrimed by use, which hung over his shoulders. His head was close shaven, except a ridge of hair reaching over the crown from the middle of the forehead, very much like the long bristles on the back of a hyena, and he carried his bow and arrows in his hand, while his meagre little horse was laden with dried buffalo meat, the produce of his hunting. Such were the first specimens that we met—and very indifferent ones they were—of the genuine savages of the prairie.

They were the Pawnees whom Kearsley had encountered the day before, and belonged to a large hunting party, known to be ranging the prairie in the vicinity. They strode rapidly by, within a furlong of our tents, not pausing or looking towards us, after the manner of Indians when meditating mischief, or conscious of ill desert. I went out to meet them, and had an amicable conference with the chief, presenting him with half a pound of tobacco, at which unmerited bounty he expressed much gratification. These fellows, or some of their companions, had committed a dastardly outrage upon an emigrant party in advance of us. Two men, at a distance from the rest, were seized by them, but, lashing their horses, they broke away and fled. At this the Pawnees raised the yell and shot at them, transfixing the hindmost through the back with several arrows, while his companion galloped away and brought in the news to his party. The panic-stricken emigrants remained for several days in camp, not daring even to send out in quest of the dead body.

Our New-England climate is mild and equable compared with that of the Platte. This very morning, for instance, was close and sultry, the sun rising with a faint oppressive heat; when suddenly darkness gathered in the west, and a furious blast of sleet and hail drove full in our faces, icy cold, and urged with such demoniac vehemence that it felt like a storm of needles. It was curious to see the horses; they faced about in extreme displeasure, holding their tails like whipped dogs, and shivering as the angry gusts, howling louder than a concert of wolves, swept over us. Wright's long train of mules came sweeping round before the storm, like a flight of snow-birds driven by a winter tempest. Thus we all remained stationary for some minutes, crouching close to our horses' necks, much too surly to speak, though once the Captain looked up from between the collars of his coat, his face blood-red, and the muscles of his mouth contracted by the cold into a most ludicrous grin of agony. He grumbled something that sounded like a curse, directed, as we believed, against the unhappy hour when he had first thought of leaving home. The thing was too good to last long; and the instant the puffs of wind subsided we pitched our tents, and remained in camp for the rest of a gloomy and lowering day. The emigrants also encamped near at hand. We being first on the ground, had appropriated all the wood within reach; so that our fire alone blazed cheerily. Around it soon gathered a group of uncouth figures, shivering in the drizzling rain. Conspicuous among them were two or three of the half-savage men who spend their reckless lives in trapping among the Rocky Mountains, or in trading for the Fur Company in the Indian villages. They were all of Canadian extraction; their hard, weather-beaten faces and bushy moustaches looked out from beneath the hoods of their white capotes with a bad and brutish expression, as if their owners might be the willing agents of any villany. And such in fact is the character of many of these men.

On the day following we overtook Kearsley's wagons, and thenceforward, for a week or two, we were fellow-travellers. One good effect, at least, resulted from the alliance; it materially diminished the fatigues of standing guard; for the party being now more numerous, there were longer intervals between each man's turns of duty.

Preface to *The Oregon Trail,* 4th ed. (1872)

The following sketches first appeared in 1847. A summer's adventures of two youths just out of college might well enough be allowed to fall into oblivion, were it not that a certain interest will always attach to the record of that which has passed away never to return. This book is the reflection of forms and conditions of life which have ceased, in great measure, to exist. It mirrors the image of an irrevocable past.

I remember that, as we rode by the foot of Pike's Peak, when for a fortnight we met no face of man, my companion remarked, in a tone any thing but complacent, that a time would come when those plains would be a grazing country, the buffalo give place to tame cattle, farm-houses be scattered along the water-courses, and wolves, bears, and Indians be numbered among the things that were. We condoled with each other on so melancholy a prospect, but we little thought what the future had in store. We knew that there was more or less gold in the seams of those untrodden mountains; but we did not foresee that it would build cities in the waste and plant hotels and gambling-houses among the haunts of the grizzly bear. We knew that a few fanatical outcasts were groping their way across the plains to seek an asylum from gentile persecution; but we did not imagine that the polygamous hordes of Mormon would rear a swarming Jerusalem in the bosom of solitude itself. We knew that, more and more, year after year, the trains of emigrant wagons would creep in slow procession towards barbarous Oregon or wild and distant California; but we did not dream how Commerce and Gold would breed nations along the Pacific, the disenchanting screech of the locomotive break the spell of weird mysterious mountains, woman's rights invade the fastnesses of the Arapahoes, and despairing savagery, assailed in front and rear, vail its scalp-locks and feathers before triumphant commonplace. We were no prophets to foresee all this; and, had we foreseen it, perhaps some perverse regrets might have tempered the ardor of our rejoicing.

The wild cavalcade that defiled with me down the gorges of the Black Hills, with its paint and war-plumes, fluttering trophies and savage embroidery, bows, arrows, lances, and shields, will never be seen again. Those who formed it have found bloody graves, or a ghastlier burial in the maws of wolves. The Indian of to-day, armed with a revolver and crowned with an old hat; cased, possibly, in trousers or muffled in a tawdry shirt, is an Indian still, but an Indian shorn of the picturesqueness which was his most conspicuous merit.

The mountain trapper is no more, and the grim romance of his wide, hard life is a memory of the past.

As regards the motives which sent us to the mountains, our liking for them would have sufficed; but in my case, another incentive was added. I went in great measure as a student, to prepare for a literary undertaking of which the plan was already formed, but which, from the force of inexorable circumstances, is still but half accomplished. It was this that prompted some proceedings on my part, which, without a fixed purpose in view, might be charged with youthful rashness. My business was observation, and I was willing to pay dearly for the opportunity of exercising it.

Two or three years ago, I made a visit to our guide, the brave and true-hearted Henry Chatillon, at the town of Carondelet, near St. Louis. It was more than twenty years since we had met. Time hung heavy on his hands, as usual with old mountain-men married and established; his hair was touched with gray, and his face and figure showed tokens of early hardship; but the manly simplicity of his character was unchanged. He told me that the Indians with whom I had been domesticated, a band of the hated Sioux, had nearly all been killed in fights with the white men.

The faithful Deslauriers is, I believe, still living on the frontier of Missouri. The hunter Raymond perished in the snow during Fremont's disastrous passage of the mountains in the winter of 1848.

Boston, March 30, 1872.

Preface to *The Oregon Trail,* illustrated ed. (1892)

In the preface to the fourth edition of this book, printed in 1872, I spoke of the changes that had already come over the Far West. Since that time change has grown to metamorphosis. For Indian teepees, with their trophies of bow, lance, shield, and dangling scalplocks, we have towns and cities, resorts of health and pleasure seekers, with an agreeable society, Paris fashions, the magazines, the latest poem, and the last new novel. The sons of civilization, drawn by the fascinations of a fresher and bolder life, thronged to the western wilds in multitudes which blighted the charm that had lured them.

The buffalo is gone, and of all his millions nothing is left but bones. Tame cattle and fences of barbed wire have supplanted his vast herds and boundless grazing grounds. Those discordant serenaders, the wolves that howled at evening about the traveller's camp-fire, have succumbed to arsenic and hushed their savage music. The wild Indian is turned into an ugly caricature of his conqueror; and that which made him romantic, terrible, and hateful, is in large measure scourged out of him. The slow cavalcade of horsemen armed to the teeth has disappeared before parlor cars and the effeminate comforts of modern travel.

The rattlesnakes have grown bashful and retiring. The mountain lion shrinks from the face of man, and even grim "Old Ephraim,"[1] the grizzly bear, seeks the seclusion of his dens and caverns. It is said that he is no longer his former self, having found by an intelligence not hitherto set to his credit, that his ferocious strength is no match for a repeating rifle; with which discovery he is reported to have grown diffident, and abated the truculence of his more prosperous days. One may be permitted to doubt if the blood-thirsty old savage has really experienced a change of heart; and before inviting him to single combat, the ambitious tenderfoot, though the proud possessor of a Winchester with sixteen cartridges in the magazine, would do well to consider not only the quality of his weapon, but also that of his own nerves.

He who feared neither bear, Indian, nor devil, the all-daring and all-enduring trapper, belongs to the past, or lives only in a few gray-bearded survivals. In his stead we have the cowboy, and even his star begins to wane.

The Wild West is tamed, and its savage charms have withered. If this book can help to keep their memory alive, it will have done its part. It has found a powerful helper in the pencil of Mr. Remington, whose pictures are as full of truth as of spirit, for they are the work of one who knew the prairies and the mountains before irresistible commonplace had subdued them.

Boston, 16 September, 1892.

Notes

1. Alias "Old Caleb" and "Old Enoch."

Reading about Francis Parkman

deVoto, Bernard. *The Year of Decision: 1846.* Boston: Little, Brown & Co., 1943.

Gale, Robert L. *Francis Parkman.* New York: Twayne, 1973.

Jacobs, Wilbur R. *Francis Parkman, Historian as Hero: The Formative Years.* Austin: University of Texas Press, 1991.

Kenneth Porter *(1905–1981)*

The poet, in a few short lines, encapsulates the character of the Great Plains, the region that Natives, explorers, and travelers describe in fragments. The long view in time and space provides the best summary.

Kenneth Wiggins Porter was born in central Kansas. He received a bachelor's degree from Sterling (Kansas) College, a master's degree from the University of Minnesota, and a doctoral degree from Harvard University. Porter taught history and political science at Southwestern College in Winfield, Kansas, and at Vassar, the University of Oregon, the University of Illinois, and Arizona State University. His scholarly work includes works on John Jacob Astor, the Humboldt Oil Company, and the Negro on the frontier. Poetry was his avocation.

Land of the Crippled Snake (1946)

The geographers have thrown a loop
north and south across the Great Plains,
a crippled snake—
tail at Lake Winnipeg,
crushed head near the mouth of the Rio Grande,
belly dragging
southwest across the Dakotas, Nebraska, Kansas,
south and southeast through Oklahoma, Texas,
by way of both Panhandles—
or maybe a length of discarded lariat,
dropped carelessly in the dust of a vast corral;
the geographers call it
"The Line of Semi-Aridity"—
which means that east there's usually enough rain for a crop
and west there usually isn't.
But you can't depend on either.
Let a thrill of awakening life
run through the snake's broken body,
let someone twitch idly at the frayed rope-end—
and farms west of the line are east;
again—

and farms that were east are west—
a game of skip-the-rope
in which a stumble is ruin. . . .

These are the High Plains,
the buffalo-lands
once matted with close curling grass
shaggy as the fell of the great beast
that grazed it and gave it a name—
shaggy beard mingling with the crisp grass,
drifting north or south with the grass in their thousands
till it seemed that the plain itself moved;
and on their flanks the naked hunters
feeding on the buffalo
as the buffalo
on the grass. . . .

From the east. . . .
the west. . . .
rapidly growing metal points
probing the continent's interior;
men in faded coats of blue or gray,
overalled Irish,
wide-straw-hatted Chinks—
their bodies going indistinguishably to iron
by chemistry of toil.
A grid of metal spanned the continent,
pushing apart the tribes,
the herds,
and along the bars
rushed hooting, puffing black monsters.
Buffalo, hunter,
alarmed by the smoke and the thunder,
stung by the Winchester-hail,
drifted north,
drifted south,
drifted west,
and across the horizon of time. . . .

But the grass did not long cure ungrazed.
Rattle of hooves,
snorting of thirst-reddened nostrils,
creak of leather,
yells and songs—

'Whoopee-ti-yi-yo! Get along little dogies! . . .'
'With my feet in the stirrups and my seat in the saddle
I go ridin' around these god-dam cattle—
Ti-yi-yippy-you-ya-ay! Ti-yi-yippy-you-yay!'—
the long horns,
the Texans,
surging north to Abilene, Ellsworth, Newton.
Wichita, Dodge City,
north and north to Ogallala and Cheyenne. . . .
and from the east the covered-wagons,
the immigrant-trains—
the 'nesters' with their plows,
following a rainbow—
the promise of rain.

Burrows in the hillside
beside the dens of coyote and badger;
oxen and horses moving
under the immense unbroken sky
slitting long thongs from the shaggy hide of the plain,
turning raw side up to cure under the sun.
A new green—
of sod-corn, of wheat;
grain heaped on the ground,
grain shoveled into stoves in blizzard-wrapped soddies,
covered wagons flaunting the slogan
"Kansas or Bust"
rolling—immense immigrating boulders,
schooners with canvas furled—
onto the plains
over which the belly of the crippled snake has twitched,
the lariat idly swung,
westward.

Further Reading
High Plains. 1938.

Mark Twain (Samuel Clemens) *(1835–1910)*

In 1861 Samuel Clemens, better known by his pen name, Mark Twain, accompanied his brother Orion to his new post as secretary to the governor of the territory of Nevada. He stayed until 1864, honing his writing skills as a newspaperman and humorist in the mining camp of Virginia City. Twain worked for the *Territorial Enterprise,* a newspaper with a remarkable staff of talented writers. The account of this period of his life, *Roughing It,* appeared in 1872 after his collection of Western tales and sketches, *The Celebrated Jumping Frog* (1867), and the chronicle of his romp through Europe, *Innocents Abroad* (1869), had brought him attention and some financial success.

Twain's companions were his brother Orion and another traveler, George Bemis. Although most of the book focuses on his adventures and misadventures in Nevada, with his typical humor Twain recounts his trip across the prairies twenty years after the first explorers and travelers visited the region and only a few years before the transcontinental railroad made the trip routine.

Twain knew his audience would be familiar with, perhaps even tired of, the travel narrative, a staple of popular reading in the nineteenth century. He could—and did—embellish his own account with the exaggeration and tall tales his readers were beginning to expect from him. As in this selection, Twain's humor often arises from his narrator's apparent innocence, gullibility, or discomfort.

Excerpts from *Roughing It* (1872)

About an hour and a half before daylight we were bowling along smoothly over the road—so smoothly that our cradle only rocked in a gentle, lulling way, that was gradually soothing us to sleep, and dulling our consciousness—when something gave away under us! We were dimly aware of it, but indifferent to it. The coach stopped. We heard the driver and conductor talking together outside, and rummaging for a lantern, and swearing because they could not find it—but we had no interest in whatever had happened, and it only added to our comfort to think of those people out there at work in the murky night, and we snug in our nest with the curtains down. But presently, by the sounds, there seemed to be an examination going on, and then the driver's voice said:

"By George, the thoroughbrace is broke!"

This startled me broad awake—as an undefined sense of calamity is always apt to do. I said to myself: "Now, a thoroughbrace is probably part of a horse; and doubtless a vital part, too, from the dismay in the driver's voice. Leg, maybe—and yet how could he break his leg waltzing along such a road as this? No, it can't be his leg. That is impossible, unless he was reaching for the driver. Now, what can be the thoroughbrace of a horse, I wonder? Well, whatever comes, I shall not air my ignorance in this crowd, anyway."

Just then the conductor's face appeared at a lifted curtain, and his lantern glared in on us and our wall of mail matter. He said:

"Gents, you'll have to turn out a spell. Thoroughbrace is broke."

We climbed out into a chill drizzle, and felt ever so homeless and dreary. When I found that the thing they called a "thoroughbrace" was the massive combination of belts and springs which the coach rocks itself in, I said to the driver:

"I never saw a thoroughbrace used up like that, before, that I can remember. How did it happen?"

"Why, it happened by trying to make one coach carry three days' mail—that's how it happened," said he. "And right here is the very direction which is wrote on all the newspaper-bags which was to be put out for the Injuns for to keep 'em quiet. It's most uncommon lucky, becuz it's so nation dark I should 'a' gone by unbeknowns if that air thoroughbrace hadn't broke."

I knew that he was in labor with another of those winks of his, though I could not see his face, because he was bent down at work; and wishing him a safe delivery, I turned to and helped the rest get out the mail-sacks. It made a great pyramid by the roadside when it was all out. When they had mended the thoroughbrace we filled the two boots again, but put no mail on top, and only half as much inside as there was before. The conductor bent all the seat-backs down, and then filled the coach just half full of mail-bags from end to end. We objected loudly to this, for it left us no seats. But the conductor was wiser than we, and said a bed was better than seats, and moreover, this plan would protect his thoroughbraces. We never wanted any seats after that. The lazy bed was infinitely preferable. I had many an exciting day, subsequently, lying on it reading the statutes and the dictionary, and wondering how the characters would turn out.

The conductor said he would send back a guard from the next station to take charge of the abandoned mail-bags, and we drove on.

It was now just dawn; and as we stretched our cramped legs full length on the mail-sacks, and gazed out through the windows across the wide wastes of greensward clad in cool, powdery mist, to where there was an expectant look in the eastern horizon, our perfect enjoyment took the form of a tranquil and contented ecstasy. The stage whirled along at a spanking gait, the breeze flapping curtains and suspended coats in a most exhilarating way; the cradle swayed and swung luxuriously, the pattering of the horses' hoofs, the cracking of the driver's whip, and his "Hi-yi! g'lang!" were music; the spinning ground and the waltzing trees appeared to give us a mute hurrah as we went by, and then slack up and look after us with interest, or envy, or something; and as we lay and smoked the pipe of peace and compared all this luxury with the years of tiresome city life that had gone before it, we felt that there was only one complete and satisfying happiness in the world, and we had found it.

After breakfast, at some station whose name I have forgotten, we three climbed up on the seat behind the driver, and let the conductor have our bed for a nap. And by and by, when the sun made me drowsy, I lay down on my face on top of the coach, grasping the slender iron railing, and slept for an hour or more. That will give one an appreciable idea of those matchless roads. Instinct will make a sleeping man grip a fast hold of the railing when the stage jolts, but when it only swings and sways, no grip is necessary. Overland drivers and conductors used to sit in their places and sleep thirty or forty minutes at a time, on good roads, while spinning along at the rate of eight or ten miles per hour. I saw them do it, often. There was no danger about it; a sleeping man *will* seize the irons in time when the coach jolts. These men were hard worked, and it was not possible for them to stay awake all the time.

By and by we passed through Marysville, and over the Big Blue and Little Sandy; thence about a mile, and entered Nebraska. About a mile further on, we came to the Big Sandy—one hundred and eighty miles from St. Joseph.

As the sun was going down, we saw the first specimen of an animal known familiarly over two thousand miles of mountain and desert—from Kansas clear to the Pacific Ocean—as the "jackass rabbit." He is well named. He is just like any other rabbit, except that he is from one third to twice as large, has longer legs in proportion to his size, and has the most preposterous ears that ever were mounted on any creature *but* a jackass. When he is sitting quiet, thinking about this sins, or is absent-minded or unapprehensive of danger, his majestic ears project above him conspicuously; but the breaking of a twig will scare him nearly to death, and then he tilts his ears back gently and starts for home. All you can see, then, for the next minute, is his long gray form stretched out straight and "streaking it" through the low sage-brush, head erect, eyes right, and ears just canted a little to the rear, but showing you where the animal is, all the time, the same as if he carried a jib. Now and then he makes a marvelous spring with his long legs, high over the stunted sage-brush, and scores a leap that would make a horse envious. Presently he comes down to a long, graceful "lope," and shortly he mysteriously disappears. He has crouched behind a sage-bush, and will sit there and listen and tremble until you get within six feet of him, when he will get under way again. But one must shoot at this creature once, if he wishes to see him throw his heart into his heels, and do the best he knows how. He is frightened clear through, now, and he lays his long ears down on his back, straightens himself out like a yard-stick every spring he makes, and scatters miles behind him with an easy indifference that is enchanting.

Our party made this specimen "hump himself," as the conductor said. The

Secretary started him with a shot from the Colt; I commenced spitting at him with my weapon; and all in the same instant the old "Allen's" whole broadside let go with a rattling crash, and it is not putting it too strong to say that the rabbit was frantic! He dropped his ears, set up his tail, and left for San Francisco at a speed which can only be described as a flash and a vanish! Long after he was out of sight we could hear him whiz.

I do not remember where we first came across "sage-brush," but as I have been speaking of it I may as well describe it. This is easily done, for if the reader can imagine a gnarled and venerable live-oak tree reduced to a little shrub two feet high, with its rough bark, its foliage, its twisted boughs, all complete, he can picture the "sage-brush" exactly. Often, on lazy afternoons in the mountains, I have lain on the ground with my face under a sage-bush, and entertained myself with fancying that the gnats among its foliage were liliputian birds, and that the ants marching and countermarching about its base were liliputian flocks and herds, and myself some vast loafer from Brobdignag waiting to catch a little citizen and eat him.

It is an imposing monarch of the forest in exquisite miniature, is the "sage-brush." Its foliage is a grayish green, and gives that tint to desert and mountain. It smells like our domestic sage, and "sage-tea" made from it tastes like the sage-tea which all boys are so well acquainted with. The sage-brush is a singularly hardy plant, and grows right in the midst of deep sand, and among barren rocks, where nothing else in the vegetable world would try to grow, except "bunch-grass." The sage-bushes grow from three to six or seven feet apart, all over the mountains and deserts of the Far West, clear to the borders of California. There is not a tree of any kind in the deserts, for hundreds of miles—there is no vegetation at all in a regular desert, except the sage-brush and its cousin the "greasewood," which is so much like the sage-brush that the difference amounts to little. Camp-fires and hot suppers in the deserts would be impossible but for the friendly sage-brush. Its trunk is as large as a boy's wrist (and from that up to a man's arm), and its crooked branches are half as large as its trunk—all good, sound, hard wood, very like oak.

When a party camps, the first thing to be done is to cut sage-brush; and in a few minutes there is an opulent pile of it ready for use. A hole a foot wide, two feet deep, and two feet long, is dug, and sage-brush chopped up and burned in it till it is full to the brim with glowing coals. Then the cooking begins, and there is no smoke, and consequently no swearing. Such a fire will keep all night, with very little replenishing; and it makes a very sociable camp-fire, and one around which the most impossible reminiscences sound plausible, instructive, and profoundly entertaining.

Sage-brush is very fair fuel, but as a vegetable it is a distinguished failure. Nothing can abide the taste of it but the jackass and his illegitimate child the mule. But their testimony to its nutritiousness is worth nothing, for they will eat pine knots, or anthracite coal, or brass filings, or lead pipe, or old bottles, or anything that comes handy, and then go off looking as grateful as if they had had oysters for dinner. Mules and donkeys and camels have appetites that anything will relieve temporarily, but nothing satisfy. In Syria, once, at the head-waters of the Jordan, a camel took charge of my overcoat while the tents were being pitched, and examined it with a critical eye, all over, with as much interest as if he had an idea of getting one made like it; and then, after he was done figuring on it as an article of apparel, he began to contemplate it as an article of diet. He put his foot on it, and lifted one of the sleeves out with his teeth, and chewed and chewed at it, gradually taking it in, and all the while opening and closing his eyes in a kind of religious ecstasy, as if he had never tasted anything as good as an overcoat before, in his life. Then he smacked his lips once or twice, and reached after the other sleeve. Next he tried the velvet collar, and smiled a smile of such contentment that it was plain to see that he regarded that as the daintiest thing about an overcoat. The tails went next, along with some percussion caps and cough candy, and some fig-paste from Constantinople. And then my newspaper correspondence dropped out, and he took a chance in that—manuscript letters written for the home papers. But he was treading on dangerous ground, now. He began to come across solid wisdom in those documents that was rather weighty on his stomach; and occasionally he would take a joke that would shake him up till it loosened his teeth; it was getting to be perilous times with him, but he held his grip with good courage and hopefully, till at last he began to stumble on statements that not even a camel could swallow with impunity. He began to gag and gasp, and his eyes to stand out, and his fore-legs to spread, and in about a quarter of a minute he fell over as stiff as a carpenter's work-bench, and died a death of indescribable agony. I went and pulled the manuscript out of his mouth, and found that the sensitive creature had choked to death on one of the mildest and gentlest statements of fact that I ever laid before a trusting public.

I was about to say, when diverted from my subject, that occasionally one finds sage-bushes five or six feet high, and with a spread of branch and foliage in proportion, but two or two and a half feet is the usual height.

When about five hundred and fifty miles from St. Joseph, our mud-wagon broke down. We were to be delayed five or six hours, and therefore we took horses, by invitation, and joined a party who were just starting on a buffalo hunt. It was noble sport galloping over the plain in the dewy freshness of the morning, but our part of the hunt ended in disaster and disgrace, for a wounded buffalo bull chased the passenger Bemis nearly two miles, and then he forsook his horse and took to a lone tree. He was very sullen about the matter for some twenty-four hours, but at last he began to soften little by little, and finally he said:

"Well, it was not funny, and there was no sense in those gawks making themselves so facetious over it. I tell you I was angry in earnest for a while. I should have shot that long gangly lubber they called Hank, if I could have done it without crippling six or seven other people—but of course I couldn't, the old 'Allen's' so confounded comprehensive I wish those loafers had been up in the tree;[1] they wouldn't have wanted to laugh so. If I had had a horse worth a cent—but no, the minute he saw that buffalo bull wheel on him and give a bellow, he raised straight up in the air and stood on his heels. The saddle began to slip, and I took him round the neck and laid close to him, and began to pray. Then he came down and stood up on the other end a while, and the bull actually stopped pawing sand and bellowing to contemplate the inhuman spectacle. Then the bull made a pass at him and uttered a bellow that sounded perfectly frightful, it was so close to me, and that seemed to literally prostrate my horse's reason, and make a raving distracted maniac of him, and I wish I may die if he didn't stand on his head for a quarter of a minute and shed tears. He was absolutely out of his mind—he was, as sure as truth itself, and he really didn't know what he was doing. Then the bull came charging at us, and my horse dropped down on all fours and took a fresh start—and then for the next ten minutes he would actually throw one hand-spring after another so fast that the bull began to get unsettled, too, and didn't know where to start in—and so he stood there sneezing, and shoveling dust over his back, and bellowing every now and then, and thinking he had got a fifteen-hundred-dollar circus horse for break-fast, certain. Well, I was first out on his neck—the horse's, not the bull's—and then underneath, and next on his rump, and sometimes head up, and sometimes heels—but I tell you it seemed solemn and awful to be ripping and tearing and carrying on so in the presence of death, as you might say. Pretty soon the bull made a snatch for us and brought away some of my horse's tail (I suppose, but do not know, being pretty busy at the time), but *something* made him hungry for solitude and suggested to him to get up and hunt for it. And then you ought to have seen that spider-legged old skeleton go! and you ought to have seen the bull cut out after him, too—head down, tongue out, tail up, bellowing like everything, and actually mowing down the weeds, and tearing up the earth, and boosting up the sand like a whirlwind! By George, it was a hot race! I and the saddle were back on the rump, and I had the bridle in my teeth and holding on to the pommel with both hands. First we left the dogs behind; then we passed a jackass rabbit; then we overtook a cayote, and were gaining on an antelope when the rotten girth let go and threw me about thirty yards off to the left, and as the saddle went down over the horse's rump he gave it a lift with his heels that sent it more than four hundred yards up in the air, I wish I may die in a minute if he didn't. I fell at the foot of the only solitary tree there was in nine counties adjacent (as any creature could see with the naked eye), and the next second I had hold of the bark with four sets of nails and my teeth, and the next second after that I was astraddle of the main limb and blaspheming my luck in a way that made my breath smell of brimstone. I *had* the bull, now, if he did not think of *one* thing. But that one thing I dreaded. I dreaded it very seriously. There was a possibility that the bull might not think of it, but there were greater chances that he would. I made up my mind what I would do in case he did. It was a little over forty feet to the ground from where I sat. I cautiously unwound the lariat from the pommel of my saddle—"

"Your *saddle?* Did you take your saddle up in the tree with you?"

"Take it up in the tree with me? Why, how you talk. Of course I didn't. No man could do that. It *fell* in the tree when it came down."

"Oh—exactly."

"Certainly. I unwound the lariat, and fastened one end of it to the limb. It was the very best green rawhide, and capable of sustaining tons. I made a slip-noose in the other end, and then hung it down to see the length. It reached down twenty-two feet—half way to the ground. I then loaded every barrel of the Allen with a double charge. I felt satisfied. I said to myself, if he never thinks of that one thing that I dread, all right—but if he does, all right anyhow—I am fixed for him. But don't you know that the very thing a man dreads is the thing that always happens? Indeed it is so. I watched the bull, now, with anxiety—anxiety which no one can conceive of who has not been in such a situation and felt that at any moment death might come. Presently a thought came into the bull's eye. I knew it! said I—if my nerve fails now, I am lost. Sure enough, it was just as I had dreaded, he started in to climb the tree—"

"What, the bull?"

"Of course—who else?"

"But a bull can't climb a tree."

"He can't, can't he? Since you know so much about it, did you ever see a bull try?"

"No! I never dreamt of such a thing."

"Well, then, what is the use of your talking that way, then? Because you never saw a thing done, is that any reason why it can't be done?"

"Well, all right—go on. What did you do?"

"The bull started up, and got along well for about ten feet, then slipped and slid back. I breathed easier. He tried it again—got up a littler higher—slipped again. But he came at it once more, and this time he was careful. He got gradually higher and higher, and my spirits went down more and more. Up he came—an inch at a time—with his eyes hot, and his tongue hanging out. Higher and higher—hitched his foot over the stump of a limb, and looked up, as much as to say, 'You are my meat, friend.' Up again—higher and higher, and getting more excited the closer he got. He was within ten feet of me! I took a long breath,—and then said I, 'It is now or never.' I had the coil of the lariat all ready; I paid it out slowly, till it hung right over his head; all of a sudden I let go of the slack, and the slip-noose fell fairly round his neck! Quicker than lightning I out with the Allen and let him have it in the face. It was an awful roar, and must have scared the bull out of his senses. When the smoke cleared away, there he was, dangling in the air, twenty foot from the ground, and going out of one convulsion into another faster than you could count! I didn't stop to count, anyhow—I shinned down the tree and shot for home."

"Bemis, is all that true, just as you have stated it?"

"I wish I may rot in my tracks and die the death of a dog if it isn't."

"Well, we can't refuse to believe it, and we don't. But if there were some proofs—"

"Proofs! Did I bring back my lariat?"

"No."

"Did I bring back my horse?"

"No."

"Did you ever see the bull again?"

"No."

"Well, then, what more do you want? I never saw anybody as particular as you are about a little thing like that."

I made up my mind that if this man was not a liar he only missed it by the skin of his teeth. This episode reminds me of an incident of my brief sojourn in Siam, years afterward. The European citizens of a town in the neighborhood of Bangkok had a prodigy among them by the name of Eckert, an Englishman—a person famous for the number, ingenuity and imposing magnitude of his lies. They were always repeating his most celebrated falsehoods, and always trying to "draw him out" before strangers; but they seldom succeeded. Twice he was invited to the house where I was visiting, but nothing could seduce him into a specimen lie. One day a planter named Bascom, an influential man, and a proud and sometimes irascible one, invited me to ride over with him and call on Eckert. As we jogged along, said he:

"Now, do you know where the fault lies? It lies in putting Eckert on his guard. The minute the boys go to pumping at Eckert he knows perfectly well what they are after, and of course he shuts up his shell. Anybody might know he would. But when we get there, we must play him finer than that. Let him shape the conversation to suit himself—let him drop it or change it whenever he wants to. Let him see that nobody is trying to draw him out. Just let him have his own way. He will soon forget himself and begin to grind out lies like a mill. Don't get impatient—just keep quiet, and let me play him. I will make him lie. It does seem to me that the boys must be blind to overlook such an obvious and simple trick as that."

Eckert received us heartily—a pleasant-spoken, gentle-mannered creature. We sat in the veranda an hour, sipping English ale, and talking about the king, and the sacred white elephant, the Sleeping Idol, and all manner of things; and I noticed that my comrade never led the conversation himself or shaped it, but simply followed Eckert's lead, and betrayed no solicitude and no anxiety about anything. The effect was shortly perceptible. Eckert began to grow communicative; he grew more and more at his ease, and more and more talkative and sociable. Another hour passed in the same way, and then all of a sudden Eckert said:

"Oh, by the way! I came near forgetting. I have got a thing here to astonish you. Such a thing as neither you nor any other man ever heard of—I've got a cat that will eat cocoanut! Common green cocoanut—and not only eat the meat, but drink the milk. It is so—I'll swear to it."

A quick glance from Bascom—a glance that I understood—then:

"Why, bless my soul, I never heard of such a thing. Man, it is impossible."

"I knew you would say it. I'll fetch the cat."

He went in the house. Bascom said:

"There—what did I tell you? Now, that is the way to handle Eckert. You see, I have petted him along patiently, and put his suspicions to sleep. I am glad we came. You tell the boys about it when you go back. Cat eat a cocoanut—oh, my! Now, that it just his way, exactly—he will tell the absurdest lie, and trust to luck to get out of it again. Cat eat a cocoanut—the innocent fool!"

Eckert approached with his cat, sure enough.

Bascom smiled. Said he:

"I'll hold the cat—you bring a cocoanut."

Eckert split one open, and chopped up some pieces. Bascom smuggled a wink to me, and proffered a slice of the fruit to puss. She snatched it, swallowed it ravenously, and asked for more!

We rode our two miles in silence, and wide apart. At least I was silent, though Bascom cuffed his horse and cursed him a good deal, notwithstanding the horse was behaving well enough. When I branched off homeward, Bascom said:

"Keep the horse till morning. And—you need not speak of this —— foolishness to the boys."

Notes

1. In a preceding chapter Twain describes Bemis's revolver, an "Allen": "Simply drawing the trigger back, cocked and fired the pistol. As the trigger came back the hammer would begin to rise and the barrel turn over, and presently down would drop the hammer and away would speed the ball. To aim along the turning barrel and hit the thing aimed at was a feat which was probably never done with an 'Allen' in the world. But George's was a reliable weapon, nevertheless, because, as one of the stage-drivers afterward said, 'If she didn't get what she went after, she would fetch something else.'"—Eds.

Reading about Mark Twain

Budd, Lewis J. *Our Mark Twain: The Making of His Public Personality.* Philadelphia: University of Pennsylvania Press, 1983.

deVoto, Bernard. *Mark Twain's America.* Boston: Little Brown, 1932.

Hoffman, Andrew. *Inventing Mark Twain: The Lives of Samuel Longhorne Clemens.* New York: W. Morrow, 1997.

Kaplan, Justin. *Mr. Clemens and Mark Twain.* New York: Simon and Schuster, 1966.

Lennon, Nigey. *Mark Twain in California.* San Francisco: Chronicle Books, 1982.

3. Arriving and Settling In

Pioneers

On the Great Plains the settlers' determination could keep the family tenaciously rooted to a place. The region has a deep map that determines what one sees with the mind's eye. On the deceptively empty space—the level plains, the sea of grass, the great bowl of sky—Great Plains writers impose their own variations. The images and stories they weave may be unraveled only to be caught up by another writer and rewoven into another story.

Almost as soon as the expeditions returned from mapping the "Great Desert," pioneers began stringing their wagons along the Oregon Trail. James Fenimore Cooper's quintessential frontiersman, Natty Bumppo, ends his life at the very edge of the frontier borderland. In 1827, when Cooper wrote his third "Leatherstocking Tale," that edge was the Great Plains, not his own New York. Although many of the earliest travelers were determined not to stop until they reached Oregon or Utah or California, others began settling along the trails. The fringes of white settlement spread westward, so that by the end of the Civil War much of the eastern Great Plains—the prairies—had been plowed and planted to corn and wheat. Diaries and journals of pioneers who settled, at least for a time, on the Great Plains in the first half of the nineteenth century record their struggles. Passed from generation to generation, these records, many of them written by women, were preserved by their descendants or deposited in some university or historical archive until, in recent years, an interest in the lives of ordinary people has drawn scholars and others to search them out.

During the Civil War the border wars between "free-staters" in Kansas and pro-slavery supporters from Missouri gained notoriety and some literary attention, but not until the Homestead Act of 1862, the legislative dispossession of Indian lands, encouraged men and women to settle on the remaining available government land did Americans consider the western regions of the central plains worth their interest. Thanks to persistent promotion, the grasslands, long regarded as a barren expanse, awoke, as Willa Cather once wrote, when attended to by those who recognized their fertile potential, "rich and strong and glorious."[1] Few of the pioneers who homesteaded the Great Plains, claiming by their hard work and residency neat squares of one hundred sixty acres, realized that their experiences were noteworthy enough to create stories or novels from those experiences. Most of the biographical accounts of pioneers and settlers have been written by their children. Ironically, the settlers' task, to break the sod and begin growing crops and communities, was not regarded as historically or scientifically important enough to record. Yet these pioneers' acts, multiplied by the thousands, profoundly changed the grasslands and the nation.

Notes

1. "For the first time, perhaps, since that land had emerged from the waters of geologic ages, a human face was set toward it with love and yearning. It seemed beautiful to her [Alexandra], rich and strong and glorious. Her eyes drank in the breadth of it, until her tears blinded her. Then the Genius of the Divide, the great, free spirit which breathes across it, must have bent lower than it had ever bent to a human will before. The history of every country begins in the heart of a man or a woman." Willa Cather, *O Pioneers!*

Reading about Women on the Great Plains

Fairbanks, Carol. *Prairie Women: Images in American and Canadian Fiction.* New Haven: Yale University Press, 1986.

Hampsten, Elizabeth. *Read This Only to Yourself: The Private Writings of Midwestern Women, 1880–1910.* Bloomington: Indiana University Press, 1982.

Kohl, Edith Eudora. *Land of the Burnt Thigh.* 1938; rpt. St. Paul: Minnesota Historical Society Press, 1986.

Riley, Glenda. *The Female Frontier: A Comparative View of Women on the Prairie and Plains.* Lawrence: University Press of Kansas, 1988.

James Fenimore Cooper (1789–1851)

James Fenimore Cooper's novel *The Prairie* (1827) recounts the last years and the death of the aged Natty Bumppo, who had moved on to the high plains to avoid encroaching settlements. The typically convoluted Cooper plot entwines the story of Bumppo's continuing attempt to live a peaceful life in harmony with the land and its romanticized Indian inhabitants with the story of Ishmael Bush and his family, who also seek to avoid civilization to escape the strictures of the law and conventions of society. Cooper structures the novel so that Bush's utter disregard for nature and for society's law is counterbalanced by Bumppo's preferences for untrammeled nature and idealized (yet demonized) Indian society, and his distrust of civilization's greed and dishonesty.

In the opening chapter Cooper draws on his reading of Stephen Long's expedition report to create a portrait of the Great Plains based on the scant knowledge that people had augmented with popular myth in the early nineteenth century. His description reflects the popular assumption that the Great Plains region was a "barrier of desert" that would prevent the too-rapid dispersal of the population; the "uninhabited" plains would be a safety valve, a place for "swarms of restless people" to go; this gradual expansion would assure a stable *United* States.* But Cooper also knew that soon the "multitude" would venture onto the Great Plains and that they would be more like Ishmael Bush than Natty Bumppo.

Before Cooper introduces Bumppo, he describes the approach of Bush's immigrant wagon train. They have ventured far beyond the settlements in search of their own El Dorado in a "bleak and solitary" landscape. The desert-like landscape reflects the character of Ishmael Bush, a "dull," "listless," and "inferior" man, the type of person the safety valve was meant to lure far from tidy eastern settlements. Clearly this party promises no good for the land: they are not people with the will or strength to make the prairie bloom. Though Bumppo regards the intruders as an unwelcome invasion, he is glad of the company and he helps them find a place to camp, thus acknowledging the inevitable invasion of land-seekers on the Great Plains. The conversation that passes between Bush and Bumppo explores a conundrum apparent in all of Cooper's Leatherstocking Tales: although Bumppo can live simply in nature's wilderness, outside the law, others cannot. He cautions Bush, who obviously has a limited understanding of law or society, that few can preserve their civilized ways beyond the limits of the law. The rest of the novel bears out Bumppo's observation.

*Some of Cooper's language in this chapter is lifted almost verbatim from James's report of the Long expedition.

The Prairie is the first fictional work set in the Great Plains. For many Americans in the nineteenth century, it no doubt provided the only description of the region they knew and thus formed the basis for the persistence of the Great Plains myths Cooper weaves into his narrative: the region is a desert—a safety valve for a restless, growing population, but no place for people without stamina, imagination, and a firmly fixed moral code.

Cooper was born into a wealthy family that had extensive landholdings in upstate New York, the setting for his first two historical Leatherstocking Tales, *The Pioneers* (1823) and *The Last of the Mohicans* (1826). *The Prairie* was intended to end the series with the death of Natty Bumppo on the farthest edge of America's western settlements. The public, however, demanded more tales, which led Cooper to write *The Pathfinder* (1840) and *The Deerslayer* (1841).

Ishmael Bush's Camp (1827)

> *"Up with my tent: here will I lie to night;*
> *But where, to-morrow?—Well, all's one for that."*

> Richard III, *V.iii. 7, 9.*

The travellers soon discovered the usual and unerring evidences, that the several articles necessary to their situation were not far distant. A clear and gurgling spring burst out of the side of the declivity, and joining its waters to those of other similar little fountains in its vicinity, their united contributions formed a run, which was easily to be traced, for miles along the Prairie, by the scattering foliage and verdure which occasionally grew within the influence of its moisture. Hither, then, the stranger held his way, eagerly followed by the willing teams, whose instinct gave them a prescience of refreshment and rest.

On reaching what he deemed a suitable spot, the old man halted, and with an enquiring look he seemed to demand if it possessed the needed conveniences. The leader of the emigrants cast his eyes understandingly about him, and examined the place with the keenness of one competent to judge of so nice a question, though in that dilatory and heavy manner which rarely permitted him to betray precipitation.

"Ay, this may do," he said, when satisfied with his scrutiny, "boys, you have seen the last of the sun; be stirring."

The young men manifested a characteristic obedience. The order, for such in tone and manner it was, in truth, was received with respect; but the utmost movement was the falling of an axe or two from the shoulder to the ground, while their owners continued to regard the place with listless and incurious eyes. In the mean time, the elder traveller, as if familiar with the nature of the impulses by which his children were governed, disencumbered himself of his pack and rifle, and, assisted by the man already mentioned as disposed to appeal so promptly to the rifle, he quietly proceeded to release the cattle from the gears.

At length the eldest of the sons stepped heavily forward, and, without any apparent effort, he buried his axe to the eye in the soft body of a cotton-wood tree. He stood, a moment, regarding the effect of the blow, with that sort of contempt with which a giant might be supposed to contemplate the puny resistance of a dwarf, and then flourishing the implement above his head, with the grace and dexterity with which a master of the art of offense would wield his nobler though less useful weapon, he quickly severed the trunk of the tree, bringing its tall top crashing to the earth, in submission to his prowess. His companions regarded the operation with indolent curiosity, until they saw the prostrate trunk stretch'd on the ground, when, as if a signal for a general attack had been given, they advanced in a body to the work, and in a space of time, and with a neatness of execution that would have astonished an ignorant spectator, they stripped a small but suitable spot of its burthen of forest, as effectually, and almost as promptly, as if a whirl-wind had passed along the place.

The stranger had been a silent, but attentive observer of their progress. As tree after tree came whistling down, he cast his eyes upward, at the vacancies they left in the heavens, with a melancholy gaze, and finally turned away, muttering to himself with a bitter smile, like one who disdained giving a more audible utter-ance to his discontent. Pressing through the groupe of active and busy children, who had already lighted a cheerful fire, the attention of the old man became next fixed on the movements of the leader of the emigrants and of his savage looking assistant.

These two had already liberated the cattle, which were eagerly browsing the grateful and nutritious extremities of the fallen trees, and were now employed about the wagon, which has been described, as having its contents concealed with so much apparent care. Notwithstanding this particular conveyance appeared to be as silent, and as tenantless as the rest of the vehicles, the men applied their strength to its wheels, and rolled it apart from the others, to a dry and elevated spot, near the edge of the thicket. Here they brought certain poles, which had seemingly been long employed in such a service, and fastening their larger ends firmly in the ground, the smaller were attached to the hoops that supported the covering of the wagon. Large folds of cloth were next drawn out of the vehicle, and after being spread around the whole, were pegged to the earth in such a manner as to form a tolerably capacious and an exceedingly convenient tent. After surveying their work with inquisitive, and perhaps jealous eyes, arranging a fold here and driving a peg more firmly there, the men once more applied their strength to the wagon, pulling it, by its projecting tongue, from the centre of the canopy, until it appeared in the open air, deprived of its covering, and destitute of any other freight than a few light articles of furniture. The latter were immediately removed, by the traveller into the tent with his own hands, as though to enter it were a privilege to which even his bosom companion was not entitled.

Curiosity is a passion that is rather quickened than destroyed by seclusion, and the old inhabitant of the Prairies did not view these precautionary and mysterious movements, without experiencing some of its impulses. He approached the tent, and was about to sever two of its folds, with the very obvious intention of examining, more closely, into the nature of its contents, when the man, who had once already placed his life in jeopardy, seized him by the arm, and with a rude exercise of his strength threw him from the spot he had selected as the one most convenient for his object.

"It's an honest regulation, friend," the fellow drily observed, though with an eye that threatened volumes, "and sometimes it is a safe one, which says, mind your own business."

"Men seldom bring any thing to be concealed into these deserts," retuned the old man, as if willing, and yet a little ignorant how to apologize for the liberty he had been about to take," and I had hop'd no offence, in examining your comforts."

"They seldom bring themselves, I reckon though this has the look of an old country, to my eye it seems not to be overly peopled."

"The land is as aged as the rest of the works of the Lord, I believe; but you say true, concerning its inhabitants. Many months have passed since I have laid eyes on a face of my own colour, before your own. I say again, friend, I meant no harm; I did not know, but there was something behind the cloth, that might bring former days to my mind."

As the stranger ended his simple explanation, he walked meekly away, like one who felt the deepest sense of the right which every man has to the quiet enjoyment of his own, without any troublesome interference on the part of his neighbour; a wholesome and just principle, that he had, also, most probably imbibed from the habits of his secluded life. As he passed towards the little encampment of the emigrants, for such the place had now become, he heard the voice of the leader calling aloud, in its hoarse tones, the name of—

"Ellen Wade."

The girl, who has been already introduced to the reader, and who was occupied with the others of her sex, around the fires, sprang willingly forward at this summons, and passing the stranger with the activity of a young antelope, she was instantly lost behind the forbidden folds of the tent. Neither her sudden disappearance, nor any of the arrangements we have mentioned, seemed, however, to excite smallest surprise among the remainder of the party. The young men, who had already completed their tasks with the axe, were all engaged after their lounging and listless manner; some in bestowing equitable portions of the fodder among the different animals; others in plying the heavy pestle of a moveable hommany-mortar,[1] and one or two, in wheeling the remainder of the wagons aside and arranging them in such a manner as to form a sort of outwork for their otherwise defenceless bivouac.

These several duties were soon performed, and, as darkness now began to conceal the objects on the surrounding Prairie, the shrill-toned termagant, whose voice since the halt had been diligently exercised among her idle and drowsy offspring, announced in tones that might have been heard at a dangerous distance, that the evening meal waited only for the approach of those who were to consume it. Whatever may be the other qualities of a border-man, he is seldom deficient in the virtue of hospitality. The emigrant no sooner heard the sharp call of his wife, than he cast his eyes about him in quest of the stranger, in order to offer him the place of distinction, in the rude entertainment to which they were so unceremoniously summoned.

"I thank you, friend," the old man replied to the rough invitation to take a seat nigh the smoking kettle; "you have my hearty thanks; but I have eaten for the day, and I am not one of them who dig their graves with their teeth. Well; as you wish it, I will take a place, for it is long sin' I have seen people of my colour eating their daily bread."

"You ar' an old settler, in these districts, then?" the emigrant rather remarked than inquired, with a mouth filled nearly to overflowing with the delicious hommany, prepared by his skillful, though repulsive spouse. "They told us below we should find settlers something thinnish, hereaway, and I must say, the report was mainly true; for, unless, we count the Canada traders on the big river, you ar' the first white face I have met, in a good five hundred miles; that is calculating according to your own reckoning."

"Though I have spent some years in this quarter, I can hardly be called a settler, seeing that I have no regular abode, and seldom pass more than a month, at a time, in the same range."

"A hunter, I reckon?" the other continued, glancing his eyes aside, as if to examine the equipments of his new acquaintance; "your fixen seem none of the best, for such a calling."

"They are old, and nearly ready to be laid aside, like their master," said the old man regarding his rifle, with a look in which affection and regret were singularly blended; "and I may say they are but little needed, too. You are mistaken, friend, in calling me a hunter; I am nothing better than a trapper."[2]

"If you ar' much of the one, I'm bold to say you ar' something of the other; for the two callings go mainly together, in these districts."

"To the shame of the man who is able to follow the first be it so said!" returned the trapper, whom in future we shall choose to designate by his pursuit; "for more than fifty years did I carry my rifle in the wilderness, without so much as setting a snare for even a bird that flies the heavens;—much less a beast, that has nothing but legs, for its gifts."

"I see but little difference whether a man gets his peltry by the rifle or by the trap," said the ill-looking companion of the emigrant, in his rough manner. "The 'arth was made for our comfort; and, for that matter, so ar' its creatur's."

"You seem to have but little plunder,[3] stranger, for one who is far abroad," bluntly interrupted the emigrant, as if he had a reason for wishing to change the conversation. "I hope you ar' better off for skins."

"I make but little use of either," the trapper quietly replied. "At my time of life, food and clothing be all that is needed, and I have little occasion for what you call plunder, unless it may be, now and then, to barter for a horn of powder or a bar of lead."

"You ar' not, then, of these parts, by natur', friend?" the emigrant continued, having in his mind the exception which the other had taken to the very equivocal word, which he himself, according to the custom of the country, had used for "baggage" or "effects."

"I was born on the sea-shore, though most of the my life has been passed in the woods."

The whole party now looked up at him, as men are apt to turn their eyes on some unexpected object of general interest. One or two of the young men, re-peated the words "sea-shore," and the woman tendered him one of those civilities with which, uncouth as they were, she was little accustomed to grace her hospi-tality, as if in deference to the travelled dignity of her guest. After a long, and seemingly a meditating silence, the emigrant, who had, however, seen no appar-ent necessity to suspend the functions of his masticating powers, resumed the discourse.

"It is a long road, as I have heard, from the waters of the west to the shores of the main sea?"

"It is a weary path, indeed, friend; and much have I seen, and something have I suffered in journeying over it."

"A man would see a good deal of hard travel in going its length?"

"Seventy and five years I have been upon the road, and there are not half that number of leagues in the whole distance, after you leave the Hudson, on which I have not tasted venison of my own killing. But this is vain boasting! of what use are former deeds, when time draws to an end!"

"I once met a man, that had boated on the river he names," observed the eldest son, speaking in a low tone of voice, like one who distrusted his knowledge, and deemed it prudent to assume a becoming diffidence in the presence of a man who had seen so much; "from his tell, it must be a considerable stream, and deep enough for a keelboat, from top to bottom."

"It is a wide and deep water-course, and many sightly towns are there growing on its banks," returned the trapper; "and yet it is but a brook, to the waters of the endless river!"

"I call nothing a stream, that a man can travel round," exclaimed the ill-looking associate of the emigrant; "a real river must be crossed; not headed, like a bear in a county hunt."[4]

"Have you been far towards the sun-down, friend?" interrupted the emigrant, as if he desired to keep his rough companion, as much as possible out of the discourse. "I find it is a wide tract of clearing, this, into which I have fallen."

"You may travel weeks, and you will see it the same. I often think the Lord has placed this barren belt of Prairie, behind the States, to warn men to what their folly may yet bring the land! Ay, weeks if not months, may you journey in these open fields, in which there is neither dwelling, nor habitation for man or beast. Even the savage animals travel miles on miles to seek their dens. And yet the wind seldom blows from the east, but I conceit the sounds of axes, and the crash of falling trees are in my ears."

As the old man spoke with the seriousness and dignity that age seldom fails to communicate even to less striking sentiments, his auditors were deeply attentive, and as silent as the grave. Indeed the trapper was left to renew the dialogue, himself, which he soon did by asking a question, in the indirect manner so much in use by the border inhabitants.

"You found it no easy matter to ford the water-courses, and to make your way so deep into the Prairies, friend, with teams of horses, and herds of horned beasts?"

"I kept the left bank of the main river," the emigrant replied, "until I found the stream leading too much to the north, when we rafted ourselves across, without any great suffering. The woman lost a fleece or two from the next year's sheering, and the girls have one cow less to their dairy. Since then, we have done bravely, by bridging a creek every day or two."

"It is likely you will continue west, until you come to land more suitable for a settlement?"

"Until I see reason to stop, or to turn ag'in," the emigrant bluntly answered, rising at the same time, and cutting short the dialogue, by the suddenness of the movement. His example was followed by the trapper, as well as the rest of the party, and then, without much deference to the presence of their guest, the travellers proceeded to make their dispositions to pass the night. Several little bowers, or rather huts, had already been formed of the tops of trees, blankets of coarse country manufacture, and the skins of buffaloes, united without much reference to any other object than temporary comfort. Into these covers the children with their mother soon drew themselves, and where, it is more than possible, they were all speedily lost in the oblivion of sleep. Before the men, however, could seek their rest, they had sundry little duties to perform; such as completing their works of defence; carefully concealing the fires; replenishing the fodder of their cattle, and setting the watch that was to protect the party, in the approaching hours of night.

The former was effected by dragging the trunks of a few trees into the intervals left by the wagons, and along the open space, between the vehicles and the thicket, on which, in military language, the encampment would be said to have rested; thus forming a sort of chevaux-de-frise on three sides of the position. Within these narrow limits (with the exception of what the tent contained), both man and beast were now collected; the latter being far too happy in resting their weary limbs, to give any undue annoyance to their scarcely more intelligent associates. Two of the young men took their rifles, and, first renewing the priming and examining the flints with the utmost care, they proceeded, the one to the extreme right and the other to the left of the encampment, where they posted themselves, within the shadows of the thicket, but in such positions, as enabled each to overlook a portion of the Prairie.

The trapper loitered about the place, declining to share the straw of the emigrant, until the whole arrangement was completed; and then, without the ceremony of an adieu, he slowly retired from the spot.

It was now in the first watch of the night, and the pale, quivering, and deceptive light, from a new moon, was playing over the endless waves of the Prairie, tipping the swells with gleams of brightness, and leaving the interval land in deep shadow. Accustomed to scenes of solitude like the present, the old man, as he left the encampment proceeded alone into the waste, like a bold vessel leaving its haven to enter on the trackless field of the ocean. He appeared to move for some time, without object, or indeed, without any apparent consciousness, whither his limbs were carrying him. At length, on reaching the rise of one of the undulations, he came to a stand, and for the first time, since leaving the band, who had caused such a flood of reflections and recollections to crowd upon his mind, the old man became aware of his present situation. Throwing one end of his rifle to the earth, he stood leaning on the other, again lost in deep contemplation for several minutes, during which time his hound came and crouched at his feet. A deep, menacing growl from the faithful animal, first aroused him from his musing.

"What now, dog?" he said, looking down at his companion, as if he addressed a being of an intelligence equal to his own, and speaking in a voice of great affection. "What is it, pup? ha! Hector; what is it noseing, now? It won't do, dog; it won't do; the very fa'ns play in open view of us, without minding so worn out curs, as you and I. Instinct is their gift, Hector; and they have found out how little we are to be fear'd, they have!"

The dog stretched his head upward, and responded to the words of his master by a long and plaintive whine, which he even continued after he had again buried his head in the grass, as if he held an intelligent communication with one who so well knew how to interpret his dumb discourse.

"This is a manifest warning, Hector!" The trapper continued, dropping his voice, to the tones of caution and looking warily about him. "What is it, pup; speak plainer, dog; what is it?"

The hound had, however, already laid his nose to the earth, and was silent; appearing to slumber. But the keen quick glances of his master, soon caught a glimpse of a distant figure, which seemed, through the deceptive light, floating along the very elevation on which he had placed himself. Presently its proportions became more distinct, and then an airy, female form appeared to hesitate, as if considering whether it would be prudent to advance. Though the eyes of the dog were now to be seen glancing in the rays of the moon, opening and shutting lazily, he gave no further signs of displeasure.

"Come nigher; we are friends," said the trapper, associating himself with his companion by long use, and, probably, through the strength of the secret tie that connected them together; "we are your friends; none will harm you."

Encouraged by the mild tones of his voice, and perhaps led on by the earnestness of her purpose, the female approached, until she stood at his side; when the old man perceived his visiter to be the young woman, with whom the reader, has already become acquainted by the name of Ellen Wade.

"I had thought you were gone," she said, looking timidly and anxiously around. "They said you were gone; and that we should never see you again. I did not think it was you!"

"Men are no common objects in these empty fields," returned the trapper, "and I humbly hope, though I have so long consorted with the beasts of the wilderness, that I have not yet lost the look of my kind."

"Oh! I knew you to be a man, and I thought I knew the whine of the hound, too," she answered hastily, as if willing to explain she knew not what, and then checking herself, like one fearful of having already said too much.

"I saw no dogs among the teams of your father," the trapper remarked.

"Father!" exclaimed the girl, feelingly, "I have no father! I had nearly said no friend."

The old man, turned towards her, with a look of kindness and interest, that was even more conciliating than the ordinary, upright, and benevolent expression of his weather-beaten countenance.

"Why then do you venture in a place where none but the strong should come?" he demanded. "Did you not know that, when you crossed the big river, you left a friend behind you that is always bound to look to the young and feeble, like yourself."

"Of whom do you speak?"

"The law—'Tis bad to have it, but, I sometimes think, it is worse to be entirely without it. Age and weakness have brought me to feel such weakness, at times. Yes—yes, the law is needed, when such as have not the gifts of strength and wisdom are to be taken care of. I hope, young woman, if you have no father, you have at least a brother."

The maiden felt the tacit reproach conveyed in this covert question, and for a moment she remained in an embarrassed silence. But catching a glimpse of the mild and serious features of her companion, as he continued to gaze on her with a look of interest, she replied, firmly, and in a manner that left no doubt she comprehended his meaning:

"Heaven forbid that any such as you have seen, should be a brother of mine, or any thing else near or dear to me! But, tell me, do you then actually live alone, in this desert district, old man; is there really none here besides yourself?"

"There are hundreds, nay, thousands of the rightful owners of the country, roving about the plains; but few of our own colour."

"And have you then met none who are white, but us?" interrupted the girl, like one too impatient to await the tardy explanation of age and deliberation.

"Not in many days—Hush, Hector, hush," he added in reply to a low, and nearly inaudible growl from his hound. "The dog scents mischief in the wind! The black bears from the mountains sometimes make their way, even lower than this. The pup is not apt to complain of the harmless game. I am not so ready and true with the piece as I used-to-could-be, yet I have struck even the fiercest animals of the Prairie, in my time; so, you have little reason for fear, young woman."

The girl raised her eyes, in that peculiar manner which is so often practised by her sex, when they commence their glances, by examining the earth at their feet, and terminate them by noting every thing within the power of human vision; but she rather manifested the quality of impatience, than any feeling of alarm.

A short bark from the dog, however, soon gave a new direction to the looks of both, then the real object of his second warning became dimly visible.

Notes

1. Hommany, is a dish composed chiefly of cracked corn, or maize. [1832]

2. It is scarcely necessary to say, that this American word means one who takes his game in a trap. It is of general use on the frontiers. The beaver, an animal too sagacious to be easily killed, is oftener taken in this way than in any other. [1832]

3. The cant word for luggage in the western States is "plunder." The term might easily mislead one as to the character of the people, who, notwithstanding their pleasant use of so expressive a word, are, like the inhabitants of all new settlements hospitable and honest. Knavery of the description conveyed by "plunder," is chiefly found in regions more civilized. [1832]

4. There is a practice, in the new countries, to assemble the men of a large district, sometimes of an entire county, to exterminate the beasts of prey. They form themselves into a circle of several miles in extent, and gradually draw nearer, killing all before them. The allusion is to this custom, in which the hunted beast is turned from one to another. [1832]

Reading about James Fenimore Cooper

Adams, Charles Hansford. *Guardians of the Law: Authority and Identity in James Fenimore Cooper.* University Park: Pennsylvania State University Press, 1990.

Clymer, William B. *James Fenimore Cooper.* New York: Haskell House, 1968.

Motley, Warren. *The American Abraham: James Fenimore Cooper and the Frontier Patriarch.* New York: Cambridge University Press, 1987.

Ringe, Donald A. *James Fenimore Cooper.* Boston: Twayne, 1965.

Spiller, Robert A. *James Fenimore Cooper.* Minneapolis: University of Minnesota Press, 1962.

Robert J. C. Stead *(1880–1959)*

Prairie writers have been an important part of Canadian literature through most of the twentieth century. Writers such as Margaret Laurence and Sinclair Ross, both closely identified with the prairie region, are among the country's major literary figures.

The reader should not be put off by the apparent frivolity of the women and Robert J. C. Stead's rather sentimental tone in this selection from his novel *The Homesteaders*. Not all stories of Canadian prairie settlements are as relentlessly grim as their southern counterparts, perhaps because settlement in much of Canada occurred a generation or two later than it did in the United States so that some "portable" conveniences made life less rigorous, or perhaps because there are often characters, in this case the Arthurses, who refuse to do without cultural amenities in the drive to possess land and economic wealth. The novel traces John Harris's obsession with wealth, the threat his actions bring to his family, and the Arthurs's equal determination to achieve a comfortable, if modest, life together.

When McCrae takes John Harris to search for a homesite he is following the standard practices of someone familiar with prairie soils, climate, and land use. Stead suggests that this very first act, the choice of a land claim, can determine the settler's success or failure.

Stead grew up on a Manitoba homestead. He had a career as a newspaperman and publicity director. In addition to those he used in his poetry and fiction, which gained him a wide audience, Stead adopted realistic techniques in his later novel *Grain* (1926). This novel has been generally regarded as his best work since its "rediscovery" in the 1960s. Much of *The Homesteaders* seems overwritten and the plot too dramatic to modern readers, but Stead balances these with his ability to re-create the time and place of the Canadian frontier.

Prairie Land (1916)

The afternoon that has just been described was typical of the days that were to follow as the immigrant party laboured its slow pilgrimage into the Farther West. True, they entered on the very next day a district having some pretence of settlement, where it was sometimes possible to secure shelter for the women and children under hospitable Mennonite roofs. The peculiar housekeeping principles of this class of settlers, however, which involved the lodging of cattle and horses in the same building with the human members of the family, discouraged too great intimacy with them, and for the most part the new-comers preferred the shelter of their own tent. They soon emerged from the Red River Valley, left the vast, level, treeless plain behind them, and plunged into the rolling and lightly wooded Pembina region.[1] Here clumps of small willows and, where repeated fires had not destroyed them, light bluffs of slender poplars afforded a measure of protection, and from the resources of the few scattered settlers already in the country they were able to replenish their supplies of fodder for the stock, and even to add to their own larder. Fortunately the wind continued to blow from the north, and, although the sun shone with astonishing fierceness in the middle of the day, the snow thawed but little and the trail remained passable. Other parties of settlers, wending their way westward to the region where homesteads were still available, or moving in to lands located the previous year, were overtaken; and again the party were themselves overtaken by more rapid-moving immigrants from behind, so that in the course of four or five days their cavalcade stretched far ahead and far to the rear. Acquaintanceships were made quickly—no one stood on ceremony; and as the journey wore on the Harrises began to feel that they already possessed many friends in the country, and that life on the prairie would not be altogether lonely.

After numerous consultations with McCrae, Harris had arranged that his immediate destination should be in a district where the scrub country melted into open prairie on the western side of the Pembina. The Arthurses, who were also of the party, had homesteaded there, and Fred Arthurs had built a little house on the land the year before. Arthurs was now bringing his young wife to share with him the privations and the privileges of their new home. A friendship had already sprung up between Mrs. Arthurs and Mrs. Harris, and nothing seemed more appropriate than that the two women should occupy the house together while Harris sought out new homestead land and Arthurs proceeded with the development of his farm. It was McCrae, whose interest in every member of the expedition was that of a father, that dropped the germ of this suggestion into Arthurs' receptive ear, and it was with paternal satisfaction he found the young couples speedily work out for themselves the arrangements which he had planned for them all along.

After the crossing of the Pembina the party began to scatter—some to homesteads already located; others to friends who would billet them until their arrangements were completed. As team after team swung out from the main road a certain sense of loss was experienced by those who were left, but it was cheery words and good wishes and mutual invitations that marked each separation. At length came the trail, almost lost in the disappearing snow, that led to Arthurs' homestead. A quick handshake with McCrae, Ned Beacon, and the doctor, and a few others who had grown upon them in the journey, and the two young couples turned out to break their way over the little-used route that now lay before them.

Darkness was settling down—darkness of the seventh night since their departure from Emerson—when, like a mole on the face of the plain, a little grey lump grew on the horizon. Arthurs rose in his sleigh and waved his fur cap in the air; Harris sent back an answering cheer; the women plied their husbands with questions; even the horses took on new energy, and plunged desperately through the frozen snow which one moment supported their weight and the next splintered in broken ice-cakes beneath them. Slowly the mole grew until in the gathering shadows it took on indistinctly the shape of a building, and just as the rising moon crested the ridge of the Pembina hills the travellers swung up at the door. Arthurs had carried the key of the padlock in his hand for the last mile; everybody was out of the sleighs in a moment, and the next they were stamping their cramped feet on the cold wooden floor of the little shack. Arthurs walked unerringly to a nail on the wall and took down a lantern; its dull flame drove the mist slowly down the glass, and presently the light was beating back from the glistening frost which sparkled on every log of the little room.

"Well, here we are in Hungry Hall," said Arthurs. "Everything just as I left it." Then, turning to his wife, "Come, Lil," he said. "Jack, perhaps you have an engagement of your own." He took his wife in a passionate embrace and planted a fervent kiss upon her lips, while Harris followed his example. Then they sat down on the boxes that served for chairs, amid a happiness too deep for words. . . . So the minutes passed until Mrs. Arthurs sprang to her feet. "Why, Mary," she exclaimed, "I do believe you're crying," while the moisture glistened on her own cheek. "Now, you men, clear out! I suppose you think the horses will stable themselves? Yes, I see you have the box full of wood, Fred. That's not so bad for a start. Leave some matches, and say, you might just get our boxes in here. Remember we've lived in these clothes for the best part of two weeks."

The young men sprang to their task, and as soon as they were out of the house the girls threw their arms about each other and wept like women together. It was only for a moment; a quick dash of the hand across the eyes, and both were busy removing coats and wraps. The door opened, and their "boxes," as well as other equipment from the sleighs, were carried in, and the men disappeared to the little stable at the back of the house. After several attempts the girls succeeded in starting a fire in the rusted stove, and soon its grateful heat was radiating to every corner of the room. As they busied themselves unpacking dishes and provisions they had opportunity to take observations of the new place that for one was to be a home and for the other a very welcome haven in a strange land.

The house was built of poplar logs, hewed and dovetailed at the corners with the skill of the Ontario woodsman. It was about twelve by sixteen feet in size, with collar-beams eight feet from the floor. The roof was of two thicknesses of elm boards, with tar-paper between. The floor was of poplar boards. The door was in the east side, near the south-east corner; the stove stood about the centre of the east wall. The only window was in the south; six panes of eight-by-ten glass sufficed for light. Through this window another lantern shone back from the darkness, and the flickering light from the stove danced in duplicate. A rough board table sat under the window; a box nailed in the south-west corner evidently served as cupboard. No tools or movables of any value had been left in the place, Arthurs having stored such effects with a neighbour, some dozen miles away, lest they be stolen from the cabin by some unscrupulous traveller during his absence.

"I like the plan of it very much," said Mrs. Arthurs, after a general survey of the room. "Don't you think Fred has shown good judgment in the design? This"— indicating the door—"will be my reception-room. And this, a little further in, is the parlour. The kitchen and pantry are right at hand—so convenient for the maid in serving, you know. And then our rooms. Fred and I will have the long room in the north-west wing, while you, of course, will occupy the guest-chamber in the north-east. Do not be alarmed, my dear; if the silence of the prairies weighs too heavily upon you we shall be within call. The bath may be reached from either room with equal convenience."

Both laughed, but Mary, more serious and sober-minded, was already slicing ham and greasing a frying-pan. "We need water, Lil—get some snow while I find the tea. The bread is hard, but there'll be coals presently, and we shall have toast. Lucky there were baked potatoes left over from last night's camp; they'll fry up fine along with this——" But already Lil was outside gathering snow.

She returned in breathless excitement. "Oh, Mary, I've just had a great thought. All my wedding china—presents, you know—is in that box, and I have my wedding clothes, too. Have you yours?"

"Of course. But why——"

"Why, dear, don't you see? The men are busy shovelling a path into the stable. It'll be an hour yet before they are in. Let's put on our wedding dresses, and set the table with our best dishes and best linen, just for a kind of post-nuptial. Let's!"

"But ham and friend potatoes!"

"And toast. Didn't you promise toast? And tea. And I'll wager there's some jam among these provisions. Oh, let's hurry."

An hour later, when the hungry men returned after making their horses and cattle comfortable, they stopped in amazement at the sight that confronted them. Snowy linen, delicate china, and sparkling glass returned the soft light from one of those great lamps such as are bought only for presentation; and beside the table, like fairies spirited from a strange land, stood two beautiful women, robed in the delicate draperies of their bridal hour. Exclamations of surprise were drowned in a flood of tender associations, and never in palace or banquet-hall did sweeter content and happiness reign than among these four young pioneers as they sat down to their first home-served meal in the new land.

The days that followed were days of intense activity for both men and women. There was much to do, inside and out. In the interior of the little house an extraordinary change was wrought; simple draperies and pictures relieved the bareness of the walls; shelves were built for the accommodation of many trinkets dear to the feminine heart; a rag carpet covered the centre of the floor; plain but appetising dishes peeked enticingly from behind the paper curtain that now clothed the bare ribs of the cupboard; and a sense of homeliness pervaded the atmosphere. The two men, in their own realm, had found much to occupy them, although for some days the range of their activities was limited owing to the necessity of giving the horses a much-needed rest before putting them back into the harness.

A week had passed, and no sign of life, other than that of the little party itself, had been seen about the Arthurses' homestead, when one day Harris's eyes already becoming keen to the prairie distances, espied a dark point on the horizon. It grew slowly from a point to a spot, from a spot to an object, and at length was defined as a man on horseback. Presently Aleck McCrae drew up at the door.

"Hello, farmers," he cried, "how goes the battle? An' the good wives? Building a little Eden in this wilderness, I'll warrant. Tell them to put another name in the pot, an' a hungry name at that. I haven't seen a white woman's meal I don't know when."

The friends gathered about the old-timer, plying him with questions, which he answered or discussed until the meal was over, holding his own business quietly in the background. But with supper ended, his pipe in his teeth and his feet resting comfortably in the oven, he broached his subject.

"Ready for the road in the morning, Jack? Don't want to break up your little honeymoon, y' know, but the month is wearing on. Nothing but horseback for it now, an' they do say the settlers are crowding up something wonderful. The best land's going fast. Most of them will hold up now, with the roads breaking, but by slipping out on our horses we can locate an' file before the real spring rush opens. You should get some kind of shelter up before the frost is out of the ground, so's to lose no time from ploughing once the spring opens."

Harris needed no urging, and in the early morning the two men, with blankets and provisions, started out on horseback for the still farther West. The snow was now going rapidly; water stood in a thousand pools and ponds on the face of the prairie, or ran with swift noiselessness in the creeks and ravines, although the real "break-up" of the streams would not occur until early in April. By avoiding the sleigh-trails and riding over the open prairie fairly sound footing was found for the horses and a good opportunity given to observe the land. Harris soon found that more judgment was required in the selection of a prairie farm than he had supposed, and he congratulated himself upon having fallen in with so experienced a plainsman as McCrae. On the first day they rode over mile after mile of beautiful country, following the survey stakes as closely as possible, and noting their location from time to time by the lettering on the posts.

"This is good enough for me," said Harris at length, as their horses crested a little elevation from which the prairie stretched away in all directions, smooth as a table. "Isn't it magnificent! And all free for the taking!"

"It's pretty to look at," said McCrae, "but I guess you didn't come West for scenery, did you?"

"Well, what's the matter with it? Look at that grass. If the soil wasn't all right it wouldn't grow native crops like that, would it?"

"The soil's all right," answered McCrae. "Nothing better anywhere, an' you can plough a hundred and sixty acres to every quarter-section. But this is in the frost belt. They get it every August—sometimes July. Shouldn't wonder but it'll be all right in time, when the country gets settled up, but most homesteaders can't afford to wait. We've got to get further West yet, into the higher land of the Turtle Mountain slopes. I know there's good stuff there that hasn't been taken."

And so they pressed on, until, in the bright sunshine, the blue line of the Turtle Mountain lay like a lake on the western horizon. Here McCrae began paying more minute attention to the soil, examining the diggings around badger holes, watching out for clumps of "wolf willow," with always a keen eye for stones and low-lying alkali patches and the general topography of the quarter.

"This is more rolling country, with more land broken up by sleughs an' creeks, but it's good stuff," he said.[2] "It's early to make predictions, but I'll risk one guess. There are two classes of people coming into this country—men who are looking for wheat land, nothing but wheat land, an' men who want some wheat land an' some stock land. I predict that in twenty-five years the wheat farmers will be working for the mortgage companies, an' the stock farmers will be building up bank accounts. Now stock must have water, an' if you can get natural shelter, so much the better. A creek may break your land a little, but it's worth more than it costs."

Many times in their explorations they passed over sections that Harris would have accepted, but McCrae objected, finding always some flaw not apparent to the untrained eye. Once, where a little river had worn its way across the plain, they came on a sod shack, where a settler was already located. "Nice spot," said Mc-Crae, "but too sandy. His farm'll blow away when he breaks the sod. There's an easy crossing there' though, an' perhaps he thinks the railway will hit him when it comes. That's all a gamble. It may go north of the lake; if it does we only bet on the wrong horse. We've got to take our chance on that."

But at length they rode over a quarter where McCrae turned his horse and rode back again. Forward and back, forward and back, they rode the whole hundred and sixty acres, until not a rood of it had escaped their scrutiny.[3] On the south-east corner a stream, in a ravine of some depth, cut off a triangle of a few acres' extent. Otherwise it was prairie sod, almost level, with yellow clay lying at the badger holes. Down in the ravine, where they had been sheltered from fire, were red willows, choke-cherry bushes, and a few little poplars and birches; a winding pond marked the course of the stream, which was running in considerable volume. Even as they stood on the bank a great cracking was heard, and huge blocks of ice rose to the surface of the pond. Some of these as they rose turned partly on their edge, showing two smooth sides.

"Good!" exclaimed McCrae. "There's some depth of water there. That pond hasn't frozen solid, or the ice wouldn't come up like that. That means water all winter for stock, independent of your well—a mighty important consideration, which a lot of these land-grabbers don't seem to reckon on. Now there's a good quarter, Jack. I don't say it's the best there is; they'll be opening up new land that'd make your teeth water twenty-five years from now. But we can't explore the whole North-West, an' you're far enough from the railroad here. This coulee will give shelter for your stock in raw weather, an' there's a bench looks at though it was put there for your little house. There's light timber to the north, fit for fuel an' building, within fifteen miles, an' there'll be neighbours here before the summer's over, or I'm no prophet. What do you say?"

"The quarter suits me," said Harris. "And the adjoining quarter is good stuff too. I can take pre-emption right on that. But there's just one thing I'm in doubt about."

"What's that?"

"How I'm going to square it with you for the service you have given. My cash is getting low, and——"

"Don't worry about that. I generally size up my customer an' bill him accordingly. If he has lots of money, an' seems likely to part with it foolishly, I put as much of it as I can in safe keeping. But there isn't any money fee as far as you're concerned. Fact is, I kinda figure on trading this bill out with you."

"Trading it out? How?"

"Well, I expect to be roving this country, east an' west, for some years to come, an' I've a little policy of establishing depots here an' there—places where I can drop in for a square meal an' a sleep an' a bit of Western hospitality. Places, too, if you like, where there are men to say a good word for Aleck McCrae. How's that suit you?"

Harris took his friend's hand in a warm grip. He rightly guessed that McCrae was not bartering his services for hospitality, but was making it easy for Harris to accept them by appearing to bargain for a service in return. So they shook hands together on the side of the bank overlooking the little coulee, and as they looked in each other's eyes Harris realized for the first time that McCrae was still a young man. A sense of comradeship came over him—a feeling that this man was more of a brother than a father. With admiring eyes he looked on McCrae's fine face, his broad shoulders, his wonderful physique, and the question he asked sprang from his lips before he could arrest it.

"Why don't you get married, Mac?"

"Who, me?" said McCrae, laughing; but Harris detected a tone in his voice that was not all happiness, and the thought came to him that McCrae's craving for hospitality might root deeper than he supposed.

"It's a long ride to the land office," continued McCrae, "an' you can't file a minute too soon. We'd better find a corner post an' make sure of the number of this section, an' put as much road behind us as we can tonight."

Notes

1. Red River Valley, Pembina: These and other places named are located along the border between Minnesota, North Dakota, and Manitoba.—Eds.

2. Sleugh (slough): a pond, march, or bog, usually stagnant and filled with mud.—Eds.

3. Rood: a British measure of length (5 1/2 to 8 yards) or area (as used here) of one-fourth of an acre.—Eds.

Further Reading: Canadian Prairie Fiction

PHILIP FREDERICK GROVE
Fruits of the Earth. 1933.
Over Prairie Trails. 1922.
Settlers of the Marsh. 1925.

MARGARET LAURENCE
A Bird in the House. 1970.
The Diviners. 1979.
The Fire Dwellers. 1969.
A Jest of God. 1966.
The Stone Angel. 1964.

W. O. MITCHELL
The Vanishing Point. 1973.
Who Has Seen the Wind. 1947.

MARTHA OSTENSO
Wild Geese. 1920.

RUDY WIEBE
Peace Shall Destroy Many. 1973.

Settlers

By the 1890s, when the U.S. census revealed that, mathematically, the frontier—defined as land with fewer than two people per square mile—was gone, much of the Great Plains region had been settled for a generation. Indian nations were resigned to being confined to reservations after the Massacre at Wounded Knee, 29 December 1890. The pioneers who created wheat fields out of prairie grass had moved on or settled in. Some of them became writers and began to tell their own stories and the stories of their parents. Linda Hogan celebrates her deep roots, grounded in countless generations, in her poetry. Hamlin Garland, in *Main-Travelled Roads* (1891) and other volumes, wrote stories about his family's experiences in Wisconsin, Iowa, and Dakota Territory. Garland's stories had an authenticity that appealed to readers, and his social agenda, grounded in the Populists' theories, made his stories popular, especially with disenfranchised groups such as farmers, who were concerned about the inequities becoming apparent in American society. William Allen White was a Kansas newspaper publisher who wrote novels and short stories set in and around his home town of Emporia. Garland and White were among the first to write stories and novels in the rising genre of Realism and the subgenre of Local Color, a term applied to stories by writers who are identified with a particular region and who depict the people and scenes peculiar to that place: mining camps, small towns, and rural areas.

Immigrants, blacks, and Indians met particular social and cultural challenges during the years of settlement on the Great Plains. Ole E. Rølvaag wrote what many regard as the classic Great Plains work, *Giants in the Earth*, published in 1927. His story of Norwegian immigrants is one of many novels that record the cultural barriers immigrants had to contend with in addition to the challenges of settling the land. Rølvaag himself immigrated from Norway and worked as a farmhand while he learned English and completed his education. Although the Exoduster Movement of former slaves from the South onto the Great Plains after the Civil War has been well documented, there are few literary works by African Americans about their early times on the Great Plains. Oscar Micheaux, who is best known as a pioneering black filmmaker, wrote two novels about his life as a farmer in South Dakota. Langston Hughes's autobiographical work, *Not Without Laughter* (1930), is set in a prairie town, and Gordon Park's *The Learning Tree* (1963) is based on his boyhood in Fort Scott, on the line between the prairies and the Ozarks in southeastern Kansas. Era Bell Thompson's *American Daughter* (1946) is an account of her family and other African Americans who tried to farm the northern Great Plains and fit into the rural society of white Americans and immigrants. James Welch documents the displacement and losses of his Blackfeet ancestors and, by extension, the losses of all the Plains Indian tribes forcibly removed from the land that the settlers claimed. In his search for the site of the Marias massacre Welch places the Indians' story within the context of Great Plains history.

Almost all of the stories here recount struggle and loss. Lands were taken from Indian owners, crops failed, and farmers lost their land by default. Settlers risked and sometimes lost their lives in the relentless storms on the plains. Children were denied school while Indian children were forced into schools as a tool of assimilation. Families were sometimes near starvation. At the end of the nineteenth century drought and depression sent thousands of settlers back-trailing, convinced as the eastern pundits had been that the Great Plains was not a place where people were meant to live. Nevertheless, many more stayed and even prospered.

Reading about Settling the Great Plains

Barns, Cass G. *The Sod House*. Lincoln: University of Nebraska Press, 1930.

Dick, Everett. *The Sod-House Frontier 1854–1890*. 1937; rpt. Lincoln: University of Nebraska Press, 1979.

Miner, Craig. *West of Wichita: Settling the High Plains of Kansas 1865–1890*. Lawrence: University Press of Kansas, 1986.

Sandoz, Mari. *Love Song to the Plains*. Lincoln: University of Nebraska Press, 1961.

Linda Hogan *(b. 1947)*

As a writer Linda Hogan first established herself as a poet. Her lyric voice stands out among writers whose roots stem from the plains. She has mastered a number of genres including poetry, drama, essay, fiction, and memoir. However, Hogan's roots are those of displacement and dispossession as a member of the Chickasaw nation that was removed to Oklahoma. She was born in Colorado and raised in different parts of the country while her father was in the military. After a series of menial jobs as a young woman she returned to her education, receiving a master of arts degree from the University of Colorado in 1978.

Hogan's writing has received numerous honors, and she has been awarded grants from the National Endowment for the Humanities and the Guggenheim Foundation. Committed to environmental issues, she writes with an awareness of human existence and responsibilities to the earth. Her awareness of place in the Great Plains, disenfranchisement, history, and hope are evident in these selections. From the 1991 collection *Red Clay* are three poems: "Calling Myself Home," "Red Clay," and "Heritage." From the more recent *Book of Medicines* (1993) are the poems "Return: Buffalo" and "Crossings."

Calling Myself Home (1991)

There were old women
who lived on amber.
Their dark hands
laced the shells of turtles
together, pebbles inside
and they danced
with rattles strong on their legs.

There is a dry river
between them and us.
Its banks divide up our land.
Its bed was the road
I walked to return.

We are plodding creatures
like the turtle

born of an old people.
We are nearly stone
turning slow as the earth.
Our mountains are underground
they are so old.

This land is the house
we have always lived in.
The women,
their bones are holding up the earth.
The red tail of a hawk
cuts open the sky
and the sun
brings their faces back
with the new grass.

Dust from yarrow
is in the air,
the yellow sun.
Insects are clicking again.

I came back to say good-bye
to the turtle
to those bones
to the shells locked together
on his back,
gold atoms dancing underground.

Red Clay (1991)

Turtle, old as earth
his slow neck has pushed aside
to bury him for winter.

His heart beats slow.
And the fish
are embedded in ice.

I photograph you
at the potter's wheel, the light
and the dark of you.

Tonight the turtle is growing
a larger shell, calcium
from inside sleep.

The moon grows
layer on layer
across iced black water.

On the clay your fingertips
are wearing away
the red soil.

We are here, the red earth
passed like light into us
and stays.

Heritage (1991)

From my mother, the antique mirror
where I watch my face take on her lines.
She left me the smell of baking bread
to warm fine hairs in my nostrils,
she left the large white breasts that weigh down
my body.

From my father I take his brown eyes,
the plague of locusts that leveled our crops,
they flew in formation like buzzards.

From my uncle the whittled wood
that rattles like bones
and is white
and smells like all our old houses
that are no longer there. He was the man
who sang old chants to me, the words
my father was told not to remember.

From my grandfather who never spoke
I learned to fear silence.
I learned to kill a snake
when begging for rain.

And grandmother, blue-eyed woman
whose skin was brown,
she used snuff.
When her coffee can full of black saliva
spilled on me
it was like the brown cloud of grasshoppers
that leveled her fields.
It was the brown stain
that covered my white shirt.
That sweet black liquid like the food
she chewed up and spit into my father's mouth
when he was an infant.

It was the brown earth of Oklahoma
stained with oil.
She said tobacco would purge your body of poisons.
It has more medicine than stones and knives
against your enemies.
That tobacco is the dark night that covers me.

She said it is wise to eat the flesh of deer
so you will be swift and travel over many miles.
She told me how our tribe has always followed a stick
that pointed west
that pointed east.
From my family I have learned the secrets
of never having a home.

Return: Buffalo (1993)

One man made a ladder
of stacked-up yellow bones
to climb the dead
toward his own salvation.
He wanted
light and fire, wanted
to reach and be close to his god.

But his god was the one
who opened his shirt
and revealed the scar of mortal climbing.

It is the scar
that lives in the house with me.
It goes to work with me.
It is the people I have loved
who fell
into the straight, unhealed
line of history.
It is a brother
who heard the bellowing cry of sacred hills
when nothing was there
but stories and rocks.

It was what ghost dancers heard
in their dream
of bringing buffalo down from the sky
as if song and prayer
were paths life would follow back
to land.

And the old women, they say,
would walk that land,
pick through bones for hide, marrow,
anything that could be used
or eaten.
Once they heard a terrible moan
and stood back,
and one was not dead
or it had come back from there,
walked out of the dark mountains
of rotted flesh and bony fur,
like a prophet
coming out from the hills
with a vision
too unholy to tell.

It must have traveled the endless journey
of fear,
returned from the far reaches
where men believed the world was flat
and they would fall over
its sharp edge
into pitiless fire,

and they must have thought
how life came together
was a casual matter,
war a righteous sin,
and betrayal
wasn't a round, naked thing
that would come back to them
one day.

Crossings (1993)

There is a place at the center of the earth
where one ocean dissolves inside the other
in a black and holy love;
It's why the whales of one sea
know songs of the other,
why one thing becomes something else
and sand falls down the hourglass
into another time.

Once I saw a fetal whale
on a block of shining ice.
Not yet whale, it still wore the shadow
of a human face, and fingers
that had grown before the taking
back and turning into fin.
It was a child from the curving world
of water turned square,
cold, small.

Sometimes the longing in me
comes from when I remember
the terrain of crossed beginnings
when whales lived on land
and we stepped out of water
to enter our lives in air.

Sometimes it's from the spilled cup of a child
who passed through all the elements
into the human fold,
but when I turned him over

I saw that he did not want to live
in air. He'd barely lost
the trace of gill slits
and already he was a member of the clan of crossings.
Like tides of water,
he wanted to turn back.

I spoke across elements
as he was leaving
and told him, Go.
It was like the wild horses
that night when fog lifted.
They were swimming across the river.
Dark was that water,
darker still the horses,
and then they were gone.

Further Reading

Dwellings: A Spiritual History of the Living World. 1995.
A Piece of Moon. 1981.
Power. 1998.
Savings. 1988.
Seeing Through the Sun. 1985.
Solar Storms: A Novel. 1995.
The Woman Who Watches Over the World: A Native Memoir. 2001.

Reading about Linda Hogan

Bonetti, Kay, ed. "Linda Hogan." *Conversations with American Novelists: The Best Interviews from The Missouri Review and the American Audio Prose Library.* Columbia: University of Missouri Press, 1997. 184–200.

Bruchac, Joseph. "To Take Care of Life: An Interview with Linda Hogan." *Survival This Way: Interviews with American Indian Poets.* Tucson: University of Arizona Press, 1987. 119–33.

Coltelli, Laura. "Linda Hogan." *Winged Words: American Indian Writers Speak.* Lincoln: University of Nebraska Press, 1990. 70–86.

Smith, Patricia Clark. "Linda Hogan." *This Is About Vision: Interviews with Southwestern Writers.* Ed. William Balassi, John F. Crawford, and Annie O. Eysturoy. Albuquerque: University of New Mexico Press, 1990. 141–55.

Hamlin Garland *(1860–1940)*

Hamlin Garland's collection of stories, *Main-Travelled Roads,* has been in print almost continuously since it was published in 1891. The first edition contained six stories. Garland added stories to subsequent editions until there were eleven in the 1922 edition. He was a successful writer and critic, and although he wrote novels, autobiographies, biographies, and literary commentary and criticism, his reputation today rests primarily on the stories found in *Main-Travelled Roads.*

Garland was both a practitioner and a theorist of what is usually termed Realism but what he called "Veritism" in his collection of critical essays, *Crumbling Idols* (1894). As he defined it, Veritism is "a passion for truth and individual expression" that originates in the artist's ability to convey a particular time and place. Garland's stories have also been identified with the Local Color movement that features stories about isolation, society's protocols, and the struggling economies of small towns in the early twentieth century.*

Garland focuses on a region he knows well: the hardscrabble farms of Wisconsin, Iowa, and Dakota Territory where his parents migrated in their search for economic security, if not success. In 1887, after a six-year absence, Garland traveled through Iowa to visit his parents. In the author's preface to the 1922 edition of *Main-Travelled Roads* Garland remembers his anger and bitterness at what he saw: "It was bad enough in our former home in Mitchell County [Iowa], but my pity grew more intense as I passed from northwest Iowa into southern Dakota. The houses, bare as boxes, dropped on the treeless plains, barbed-wire fences running at right angles, and the towns mere assemblages of flimsy wooden sheds with painted-pine battlement [*sic*], produced on me the effect of an almost helpless and sterile poverty."

"Among the Corn Rows" is one of Garland's cheerier stories. The Dakota prairie is a lush, productive green and yellow, not the dry prairie in "A Day's Pleasure," a story added to the 1893 edition of *Main-Travelled Roads.* Although the later story is especially grim, both stories are typical of Garland's early, most realistic work. Sentiment, apparent in Garland's later novels, is noticeably absent here: Rob's proposition to Julia is a purely practical one. In many of his stories

---

*The "local color" label has been used to describe works of Mary E. Wilkins Freeman and Sarah Orne Jewett in New England and Maine; of Mark Twain, Bret Harte, and others writing from the California gold fields; and of Glenway Wescott, Zona Gale, and Ruth Suckow in the Midwest. See Hamlin Hill, *The Revolt from the Village 1915–1930* (Chapel Hill: University of North Carolina Press, 1969).

Garland has a political agenda as well as a literary one. Like many farmers in the West who were dissatisfied with the policies of Eastern capitalists who controlled the railroads, the markets, and the distribution of goods, Garland advocated the single-tax theories of Henry George.* "Under the Lion's Paw" is Garland's best fictional use of the theories of George. Garland's crusading included Native Americans. In books, essays, and stories Garland argued for their rights long before such advocacy was popular.

Born in 1860, Garland, like his contemporary Mark Twain, spent much of his life moving between Wisconsin (where he was born), Iowa (where he grew up), and the East where he went to get away and where, in the fall and winter after his western trip, he began writing the stories that would establish his literary reputation. In Boston he pursued his education by reading in the public library and supported himself as an orator, often in support of Henry George's theories. Chicago was his home for several years, during a time when the city enjoyed an especially rich cultural life. Like William Allen White he knew important artists and public figures. Many of Garland's works remain in print, regarded as valuable resources for students of the Middle West, the Great Plains, and the cultural world of the late nineteenth century. Their authenticity still rings true. As Garland says in his 1922 preface, "I was there—a farmer."

Among the Corn Rows (1891)

I

"But the road sometimes passes a rich meadow, where the songs of larks and bobolinks and blackbirds are tangled."

Rob held up his hands, from which the dough depended in ragged strings.

"Biscuits," he said with an elaborate working of his jaws, intended to convey the idea that they were going to be specially delicious.

Seagraves laughed, but did not enter the shanty door. "How do you like baching it?"

"Oh, don't mention it!" entreated Rob, mauling the dough again. "Come in an' sit down. What in thunder y' standin' out there for?"

"Oh, I'd rather be where I can see the prairie. Great weather!"

"*Im*-mense!"

"How goes breaking?"

---

*Henry George advocated a single uniform tax on land, which he believed would prevent speculation and profit that left farmers at a disadvantage.

"Tip-top! A *leetle* dry now; but the bulls pull the plow through two acres a day. How's things in Boomtown?"

"Oh, same old grind."

"Judge still lyin'?"

"Still at it."

"Major Mullens still swearin' to it?"

"You hit it like a mallet. Railroad schemes are thicker'n prairie chickens. You've got grit, Rob. I don't have anything but crackers and sardines over to my shanty, and here you are making soda biscuit."

"I have t' do it. Couldn't break if I didn't. You editors c'n take things easy, lay around on the prairie, and watch the plovers and medderlarks; but we *settlers* have got to work."

Leaving Rob to sputter over his cooking, Seagraves took his slow way off down toward the oxen grazing in a little hollow. The scene was characteristically, wonderfully beautiful. It was about five o'clock in a day in late June, and the level plain was green and yellow, and infinite in reach as a sea; the lowering sun was casting over its distant swells a faint impalpable mist, through which the breaking teams on the neighboring claims plowed noiselessly, as figures in a dream. The whistle of gophers, the faint, wailing, fluttering cry of the falling plover, the whir of the swift-winged prairie pigeon, or the quack of a lonely duck, came through the shimmering air. The lark's infrequent whistle, piercingly sweet, broke from the longer grass in the swales nearby. No other climate, sky, plain, could produce the same unnamable weird charm. No tree to wave, no grass to rustle; scarcely a sound of domestic life; only the faint melancholy soughing of the wind in the short grass, and the voices of the wild things of the prairie.

Seagraves, an impressionable young man (junior editor of the *Boomtown Spike*), threw himself down on the sod, pulled his hat rim down over his eyes, and looked away over the plain. It was the second year of Boomtown's existence, and Seagraves had not yet grown restless under its monotony. Around him the gophers played saucily. Teams were moving here and there across the sod, with a peculiar noiseless, effortless motion that made them seem as calm, lazy, and unsubstantial as the mist through which they made their way; even the sound of passing wagons was a sort of low, well-fed, self-satisfied chuckle.

Seagraves, "holding down a claim" near Rob, had come to see his neighboring "bach" because of feeling the need of company; but now that he was near enough to hear him prancing about getting supper, he was content to lie alone on a slope of the green sod.

The silence of the prairie at night was well-nigh terrible. Many a night, as Seagraves lay in his bunk against the side of his cabin, he would strain his ear to hear the slightest sound, and be listening thus sometimes for minutes before the squeak of a mouse or the step of a passing fox came as a relief to the aching sense. In the daytime, however, and especially on a morning, the prairie was another thing. The pigeons, the larks, the cranes, the multitudinous voices of the ground birds and snipes and insects, made the air pulsate with sound—a chorus that died away into an infinite murmur of music.

"Hello, Seagraves!" yelled Rob from the door. "The biscuit are 'most done."

Seagraves did not speak, only nodded his head and slowly rose. The faint clouds in the west were getting a superb flame color above and a misty purple below, and the sun had shot them with lances of yellow light. As the air grew denser with moisture, the sounds of neighboring life began to reach the ear. Children screamed and laughed, and afar off a woman was singing a lullaby. The rattle of wagons and voices of men speaking to their teams multiplied. Ducks in a neighboring lowland were quacking. The whole scene took hold upon Seagraves with irresistible power.

"It is American," he exclaimed. "No other land or time can match this mellow air, this wealth of color, much less the strange social conditions of life on this sunlit Dakota prairie."

Rob, though visibly affected by the scene also, couldn't let his biscuit spoil or go without proper attention.

"Say, ain't y' comin' t' grub?" he asked impatiently.

"In a minute," replied his friend, taking a last wistful look at the scene. "I want one more look at the landscape."

"Landscape be blessed! If you'd been breakin' all day—Come, take that stool an' draw up."

"No; I'll take the candle box."

"Not much. I know what manners are, if I am a bull driver."

Seagraves took the three-legged and rather precarious-looking stool and drew up to the table, which was a flat broad box nailed up against the side of the wall, with two strips of board nailed at the outer corners for legs.

"How's that f'r a layout?" Rob inquired proudly.

"Well, you *have* spread yourself! Biscuit and canned peaches and sardines and cheese. Why, this is—is—prodigal."

"It ain't nothin' else."

Rob was from one of the finest counties of Wisconsin, over toward Milwaukee. He was of German parentage, a middle-sized, cheery, wide-awake, good-looking young fellow—a typical claimholder. He was always confident, jovial, and full of plans for the future. He had dug his own well, built his own shanty, washed and mended his own clothing. He could do anything, and do it well. He had a fine field of wheat, and was finishing the plowing of his entire quarter section.

"This is what I call settin' under a feller's own vine an' fig tree"—after Seagraves's compliments—"an' I like it. I'm my own boss. No man can say 'come here' 'n' 'go there' to me. I get up when I'm a min' to, an' go t' bed when I'm a min' t'."

"Some drawbacks, I s'pose?"

"Yes. Mice, f'r instance, give me a devilish lot o' trouble. They get into my flour barrel, eat up my cheese, an' fall into my well. But it ain't no use t' swear."

"The rats and the mice they made such a strife
He had to go to London to buy him a wife,"

quoted Seagraves. "Don't blush. I've probed your secret thought."

"Well, to tell the honest truth," said Rob a little sheepishly, leaning across the table, "I ain't satisfied with my style o' cookin'. It's good, but a little too plain, y' know. I'd like a change. It ain't much fun to break all day and then go to work an' cook y'r own supper."

"No, I should say not."

"This fall I'm going back to Wisconsin. Girls are thick as huckleberries back there, and I'm goin' t' bring one back, now you hear me."

"Good! That's the plan," laughed Seagraves, amused at a certain timid and apprehensive look in his companion's eye. "Just think what a woman 'd do to put this shanty in shape; and think how nice it would be to take her arm and saunter out after supper, and look at the farm, and plan and lay out gardens and paths, and tend the chickens!"

Rob's manly and self-reliant nature had the settler's typical buoyancy and hopefulness, as well as a certain power of analysis, which enabled him now to say: "The fact is, we fellers holdin' down claims out here ain't fools clear to the *rine*. We know a *couple* o' things. Now I didn't leave Waupac County f'r fun. Did y' ever see Waupac? Well, it's one o' the handsomest counties the sun ever shone on, full o' lakes and rivers and groves of timber. I miss 'em all out here, and I miss the boys an' girls; but they wa'n't no chance there f'r a feller. Land that was good was so blamed high you couldn't touch it with a ten-foot pole from a balloon. Rent was high, if you wanted t' rent, an' so a feller like me had t' get out, an' now I'm out here, I'm goin' t' make the most of it. Another thing," he went on, after a pause— "we fellers workin' out back there got more 'n' more like *hands*, an' less like human beings. Y'know, Waupac is a kind of summer resort, and the people that use' t' come in summers looked down on us cusses in the fields an' shops. I couldn't stand it. By God!" he said with a sudden impulse of rage quite unlike him, "I'd rather live on an iceberg and claw crabs f'r a livin' than have some feller passin' me on the road an' callin' me 'fellah!' "

Seagraves knew what he meant and listened in astonishment at this outburst.

"I consider myself a sight better 'n any man who lives on somebody else's hard work. I've never had a cent I didn't earn with them hands." He held them up and broke into a grin. "Beauties, ain't they? But they never wore gloves that some other poor cuss earned."

Seagraves thought them grand hands, worthy to grasp the hand of any man or woman living.

"Well, so I come West, just like a thousand other fellers, to get a start where the cussed European aristocracy hadn't got a holt on the people. I like it here—course I'd like the lakes an' meadows of Waupac better—but I'm my own boss, as I say, an' I'm goin' to *stay* my own boss if I haf to live on crackers an' wheat coffee to do it; that's the kind of a hairpin I am."

In the pause which followed, Seagraves, plunged deep into thought by Rob's words, leaned his head on his hand. This working farmer had voiced the modern idea. It was an absolute overturn of all the ideas of nobility and special privilege born of the feudal past. Rob had spoken upon impulse, but that impulse appeared to Seagraves to be right.

"I'd like to use your idea for an editorial, Rob," he said.

"*My* ideas!" exclaimed the astounded host, pausing in the act of filling his pipe. "My ideas! Why, I didn't know I had any."

'Well, you've given me some, anyhow."

Seagraves felt that it was a wild, grand upstirring of the modern democrat against the aristocratic against the idea of caste and the privilege of living on the labor of others. This atom of humanity (how infinitesimal this drop in the ocean of humanity!) was feeling the nameless longing of expanding personality, and had already pierced the conventions of society and declared as nil the laws of the land— laws that were survivals of hate and prejudice. He had exposed also the native spring of the emigrant by uttering the feeling that it is better to be an equal among peasants than a servant before nobles.

"So I have good reasons f'r liking the country," Rob resumed in a quiet way. "The soil is rich, the climate good so far, an' if I have a couple o' decent crops you'll see a neat upright goin' up here, with a porch and a bay winder."

"And you'll still be livin' here alone, frying leathery slapjacks an' choppin' taters and bacon."

"I think I see myself," drawled Rob, "goin' around all summer wearin' the same shirt without washin', an' wipin' on the same towel four straight weeks, an' wearin' holes in my socks, an' eatin' musty gingersnaps, moldy bacon, an' canned Boston beans f'r the rest o' my endurin' days! Oh, yes; I guess *not!* Well, see y' later. Must go water my bulls."

As he went off down the slope, Seagraves smiled to hear him sing:

"I wish that some kindhearted girl
Would pity on me take,
And extricate me from the mess I'm in.
The angel—how I'd bless her,
If this her home she'd make,
In my little old sod shanty on the plain!"

The boys nearly fell off their chairs in the Western House dining room, a few days later, at seeing Rob come into supper with a collar and necktie as the finishing touch of a remarkable outfit.

"Hit him, somebody!"

"It's a clean collar!"

"He's started f'r Congress!"

"He's going to get married," put in Seagraves in a tone that brought conviction.

"What!" screamed Jack Adams, O'Neill, and Wilson in one breath. "That man?"

"That man," replied Seagraves, amazed at Rob, who coolly took his seat, squared his elbows, pressed his collar down at the back, and called for the bacon and eggs.

The crowd stared at him in a dead silence.

"Where's he going to do it?" asked Jack Adams. "Where's he going to find a girl?"

"Ask him," said Seagraves.

"I ain't tellin'," put in Rob, with his mouth full of potato.

"You're afraid of our competition."

"That's right; *our* competition, Jack; not *your* competition. Come, now, Rob, tell us where you found her."

"I ain't found her."

"What! And yet you're goin' away t' get married!"

"I'm goin' t' bring a wife back with me ten days fr'm date."

"I see his scheme," put in Jim Rivers. "He's goin' back East somewhere, an' he's goin' to propose to every girl he meets."

"Hold on!" interrupted Rob, holding up his fork. "Ain't quite right. Every *good-lookin'* girl I meet."

"Well, I'll be blanked!" exclaimed Jack impatiently; "that simply lets me out. Any man with such a cheek ought to—"

"Succeed," interrupted Seagraves.

"That's what I say," bawled Hank Whiting, the proprietor of the house. "You fellers ain't got any enterprise to yeh. Why don't you go to work an' help settle the country like men? 'Cause y' ain't got no sand. Girls are thicker'n huckleberries back East. I say it's a dum shame!"

"Easy, Henry," said the elegant bank clerk, Wilson, looking gravely about through his spectacles. "I commend the courage and the resolution of Mr. Rodemaker. I pray the lady may not

"Mislike him for his complexion,
The shadowed livery of the burning sun."

"Shakespeare," said Adams at a venture.

"Brother in adversity, when do you embark? Another Jason on an untried sea."

"Hay!" said Rob, winking at Seagraves. "Oh, I go to-night—night train."

"And return?"

"Ten days from date."

"I'll wager a wedding supper he brings a blonde," said Wilson in his clean-cut, languid speech.

"Oh, come now, Wilson; that's too thin! We all know that rule about dark marryin' light."

"I'll wager she'll be tall," continued Wilson. "I'll wager *you*, friend Rodemaker, she'll be blonde and tall."

The rest roared at Rob's astonishment and confusion. The absurdity of it grew, and they went into spasms of laughter. But Wilson remained impassive, not the twitching of a muscle betraying that he saw anything to laugh at in the proposition.

Mrs. Whiting and the kitchen girls came in, wondering at the merriment. Rob began to get uneasy.

"What is it? What is it?" said Mrs. Whiting, a jolly little matron.

Rivers put the case. "Rob's on his way back to Wisconsin t' get married, and Wilson has offered to bet *him* that his wife will be a blonde and tall, and Rob dassent bet!" And they roared again.

"Why, the idea! The man's crazy!" said Mrs. Whiting.

The crowd looked at each other. This was hint enough; they sobered, nodding at each other.

"Aha! I see; I understand."

"It's the heat."

"And the Boston beans."

"Let up on him, Wilson. Don't badger a poor irresponsible fellow. I *thought* something was wrong when I saw the collar."

"Oh, keep it up!" said Rob, a little nettled by their evident intention to "have fun" with him.

"Soothe him—*soo-o-o-o-the* him!" said Wilson. "Don't be harsh."

Rob rose from the table. "Go to thunder! You make me tired."

"The fit is on him again!"

He rose disgustedly and went out. They followed him in single file. The rest of the town "caught on." Frank Graham heaved an apple at him and joined the procession. Rob went into the store to buy some tobacco. They followed and perched like crows on the counters till he went out; then they followed him, as before. They watched him check his trunk; they witnessed the purchase of the ticket. The town had turned out by this time.

"Waupac!" announced the one nearest the victim.

"Waupac!" said the next man, and the word was passed along the street up town.

"Make a note of it," said Wilson: "Waupac—a county where a man's proposal for marriage is honored upon presentation. Sight drafts."

Rivers struck up a song, while Rob stood around, patiently bearing the jokes of the crowd:

"We're lookin' rather seedy now,
While holdin' down our claims,
And our vittles are not always of the best,
And the mice play slyly round us
As we lay down to sleep
In our little old tarred shanties on the claim.

"Yet we rather like the novelty
Of livin' in this way,
Though the bill of fare is often rather tame;
An' we're happy as a clam
On the land of Uncle Sam
In our little old tarred shanty on the claim."

The train drew up at length, to the immense relief of Rob, whose stoical resignation was beginning to weaken.

"Don't y' wish y' had sand?" he yelled to the crowd as he plunged into the car, thinking he was rid of them.

But no; their last stroke was to follow him into the car, nodding, pointing to their heads, and whispering, managing in the half-minute the train stood at the platform to set every person in the car staring at the "crazy man." Rob groaned and pulled his hat down over his eyes—an action which confirmed his tormentors' words and made several ladies click their tongues in sympathy—"Tlck! tlck! poor fellow!"

"All *abo-o-o-a-rd!*" said the conductor, grinning his appreciation at the crowd, and the train was off.

"Oh, won't we make him groan when he gets back!" said Barney, the young lawyer who sang the shouting tenor.

"We'll meet him with the timbrel and the harp. Anybody want to wager? I've got two to one on a short brunette," said Wilson.

II

"Follow it far enough and it may pass the bend in the river where the water laughs eternally over its shallows."

A cornfield in July is a hot place. The soil is hot and dry; the wind comes across the lazily murmuring leaves laden with a warm sickening smell drawn from the rapidly growing, broad-flung banners of the corn. The sun, nearly vertical, drops a flood of dazzling light and heat upon the field over which the cool shadows run, only to make the heat seem the more intense.

Julia Peterson, faint with fatigue, was toiling back and forth between the corn rows, holding the handles of the double-shovel corn plow while her little brother

Otto rode the steaming horse. Her heart was full of bitterness, and her face flushed with heat, and her muscles aching with fatigue. The heat grew terrible. The corn came to her shoulders, and not a breath seemed to reach her, while the sun, nearing the noon mark, lay pitilessly upon her shoulders, protected only by a calico dress. The dust rose under her feet, and as she was wet with perspiration it soiled her till, with a woman's instinctive cleanliness, she shuddered. Her head throbbed dangerously. What matter to her that the king bird pitched jovially from the maples to catch a wandering bluebottle fly, that the robin was feeding its young, that the bobolink was singing? All these things, if she saw them, only threw her bondage to labor into greater relief.

Across the field, in another patch of corn, she could see her father—a big, gruff-voiced, wide-bearded Norwegian—at work also with a plow. The corn must be plowed, and so she toiled on, the tears dropping from the shadow of the ugly sunbonnet she wore. Her shoes, coarse and square-toed, chafed her feet; her hands, large and strong, were browned, or more properly *burned,* on the backs by the sun. The horse's harness "*creak*-cracked" as he swung steadily and patiently forward, the moisture pouring from his sides, his nostrils distended.

The field ran down to a road, and on the other side of the road ran a river—a broad, clear, shallow expanse at that point, and the eyes of the boy gazed longingly at the pond and the cool shadow each time that he turned at the fence.

"Say, Jule, I'm goin' in! Come, can't I? Come—say!" he pleaded as they stopped at the fence to let the horse breathe.

"I've let you go wade twice."

"But that don't do any good. My legs is all smarty, 'cause ol' Jack sweats so." The boy turned around on the horse's back and slid back to his rump. "I can't stand it!" he burst out, sliding off and darting under the fence. "Father can't see."

The girl put her elbows on the fence and watched her little brother as he sped away to the pool, throwing off his clothes as he ran, whooping with uncontrollable delight. Soon she could hear him splashing about in the water a short distance up the stream, and caught glimpses of his little shiny body and happy face. How cool that water looked! And the shadows there by the big basswood! How that water would cool her blistered feet! An impulse seized her, and she squeezed between the rails of the fence and stood in the road looking up and down to see that the way was clear. It was not a main-travelled road; no one was likely to come; why not?

She hurriedly took off her shoes and stockings—how delicious the cool, soft velvet of the grass!—and sitting down on the bank under the great basswood, whose roots formed an abrupt bank, she slid her poor blistered, chafed feet into the water, her bare head leaned against the huge tree trunk.

And now as she rested, the beauty of the scene came to her. Over her the wind moved the leaves. A jay screamed far off, as if answering the cries of the boy. A kingfisher crossed and recrossed the stream with dipping sweep of his wings. The river sang with its lips to the pebbles. The vast clouds went by majestically, far above the treetops, and the snap and buzzing and ringing whir of July insects made a ceaseless, slumberous undertone of song solvent of all else. The tired girl forgot her work. She began to dream. This would not last always. Some one would come to release her from such drudgery. This was her constant, tenderest, and most secret dream. *He* would be a Yankee, not a Norwegian; the Yankees didn't ask their wives to work in the field. He would have a home. Perhaps he'd live in town—perhaps a merchant! And then she thought of the drug clerk in Rock River who had looked at her—A voice broke in on her dream, a fresh, manly voice.

"Well, by jinks! if it ain't Julia! Just the one I wanted to see!"

The girl turned, saw a pleasant-faced young fellow in a derby hat and a fifteen-dollar suit of diagonals.

"Rob Rodemaker! How come—"

She remembered her situation, and flushed, looked down at the water, and remained perfectly still.

"Ain't ye goin' to shake hands? Y' don't seem very glad t' see me."

She began to grow angry. "If you had any eyes you'd see!"

Rob looked over the edge of the bank, whistled, turned away. "Oh, I see! Excuse *me!* Don't blame yeh a bit, though. Good weather f'r corn," he went on, looking up at the trees. "Corn seems to be pretty well forward," he continued in a louder voice as he walked away, still gazing into the air. "Crops is looking first-class in Boom-town. Hello! This Otto? H'yare y' little scamp! Get onto that horse agin. Quick, 'r I'll take y'r skin off an' hang it on the fence. What y' been doing?"

"Ben in swimmin'. Jimminy, ain't it fun! When 'd y' get back?" said the boy, grinning.

"Never you mind," replied Rob, leaping the fence by laying his left hand on the top rail. "Get onto that horse." He tossed the boy up on the horse, hung his coat on the fence. "I s'pose the ol' man makes her plow same as usual?"

"Yup," said Otto.

"Dod ding a man that'll do that! I don't mind if it's necessary, but it ain't necessary in his case." He continued to mutter in this way as he went across to the other side of the field. As they turned to come back, Rob went up and looked at the horse's mouth. "Gettin' purty near of age. Say, who's sparkin' Julia now—anybody?"

"Nobody 'cept some ol' Norwegians. She won't have them. Por wants her to, but she won't."

"Good f'r her. Nobody comes t' see her Sunday nights, eh?"

"Nope, only 'Tias Anderson an' Ole Hoover; but she goes off an' leaves 'em."

"Chk!" said Rob, starting old Jack across the field.

It was almost noon, and Jack moved reluctantly. He knew the time of day as well as the boy. He made this round after distinct protest.

In the meantime Julia, putting on her shoes and stockings, went to the fence and watched the man's shining white shirt as he moved across the cornfield. There had never been any special tenderness between them, but she had always liked him. They had been at school together. She wondered why he had come back at this time of the year, and wondered how long he would stay. How long had he stood looking at her? She flushed again at the thought of it. But he wasn't to blame; it was a public road. She might have known better.

She stood under a little popple tree, whose leaves shook musically at every zephyr, and her eyes through half-shut lids roved over the sea of deep-green glossy leaves, dappled here and there by cloud-shadows, stirred here and there like water by the wind, and out of it all a longing to be free from such toil rose like a breath, filling her throat, and quickening the motion of her heart. Must this go on forever, this life of heat and dust and labor? What did it all mean?

The girl laid her chin on her strong red wrists, and looked up into the blue spaces between the vast clouds—aerial mountains dissolving in a shoreless azure sea. How cool and sweet and restful they looked! If she might only lie out on the billowy, snow-white, sunlit edge! The voices of the driver and the plowman recalled her, and she fixed her eyes again upon the slowly nodding head of the patient horse, on the boy turned half about on the horse, talking to the white-sleeved man, whose derby hat bobbed up and down quite curiously, like the horse's head. Would she ask him to dinner? What would her people say?

"Phew! it's hot!" was the greeting the young fellow gave as he came up. He smiled in a frank, boyish way as he hung his hat on the top of a stake and looked up at her. "D' y' know, I kind o' enjoy getting at it again. Fact. It ain't no work for a girl, though," he added.

"When 'd you get back?" she asked, the flush not yet out of her face. Rob was looking at her thick, fine hair and full Scandinavian face, rich as a rose in color, and did not reply for a few seconds. She stood with her hideous sun bonnet pushed back on her shoulders. A kingbird was chattering overhead.

"Oh, a few days ago."

"How long y' goin' t' stay?"

"Oh, I d' know. A week, mebbe."

A far-off halloo came pulsing across the shimmering air. The boy screamed "Dinner!" and waved his hat with an answering whoop, then flopped off the horse like a turtle off a stone into water. He had the horse unhooked in an instant, and had flung his toes up over the horse's back, in act to climb on, when Rob said:

"H'yare, young feller! wait a minute. Tired?" he asked the girl with a tone that was more than kindly; it was almost tender.

"Yes," she replied in a low voice. "My shoes hurt me."

"Wel, here y' go," he replied, taking his stand by the horse and holding out his hand like a step. She colored and smiled a little as she lifted her foot into his huge, hard, sunburned hand.

"Oop-a-daisy!" he called. She gave a spring and sat the horse like one at home there.

Rob had a deliciously unconscious, abstracted, businesslike air. He really left her nothing to do but enjoy his company, while he went ahead and did precisely as he pleased.

"We don't raise much corn out there, an' so I kind o' like to see it once more."

"I wish I didn't have to see another hill of corn as long as I live!" replied the girl bitterly.

"Don't know as I blame yeh a bit. But, all the same, I'm glad you was working in it today," he thought to himself as he walked beside her horse toward the house.

"Will you stop to dinner?" she inquired bluntly, almost surlily. It was evident that there were reasons why she didn't mean to press him to do so.

"You bet I will," he replied; "that is, if you want I should."

"You know how we live," she replied evasively. "If you c'n stand it, why—" She broke off abruptly.

Yes, he remembered how they lived in that big, square, dirty, white frame house. It had been three or four years since he had been in it, but the smell of the cabbage and onions, the penetrating, peculiar mixture of odors, assailed his memory as something unforgettable.

"I guess I'll stop," he said as she hesitated. She said no more, but tried to act as if she were not in any way responsible for what came afterward.

"I guess I c'n stand f'r one meal what you stand all the while," he added.

As she left them at the well and went to the house, he saw her limp painfully, and the memory of her face so close to his lips as he helped her down from the horse gave him pleasure, at the same time that he was touched by its tired and gloomy look. Mrs. Peterson came to the door of the kitchen, looking just the same as ever. Broad-faced, unwieldly, flabby, apparently wearing the same dress he remembered to have seen her in years before—a dirty drab-colored thing—she looked as shapeless as a sack of wool. Her English was limited to "How de do, Rob?"

He washed at the pump, while the girl, in the attempt to be hospitable, held the clean towel for him.

"You're purty well used up, eh?" he said to her.

"Yes; it's awful hot out there."

"Can't you lay off this afternoon? It ain't right."

"No. *He* won't listen to that."

"Well, let me take your place."

"No; there ain't any use o' that."

Peterson, a brawny wide-bearded Norwegian, came up at this moment and spoke to Rob in a sullen, gruff way.

"He ain't *very* glad to see me," said Rob, winking at Julia. "He ain't b'ilin' over with enthusiasm; but I c'n stand it, for your sake," he added with amazing assurance; but the girl had turned away, and it was wasted.

At the table he ate heartily of the "bean swaagen," which filled a large wooden bowl in the center of the table, and which was ladled into smaller wooden bowls at each plate. Julia had tried hard to convert her mother to Yankee ways, and had at last given it up in despair. Rob kept on safe subjects, mainly asking questions about the crops of Peterson, and when addressing the girl, inquired of the school-mates. By skillful questioning, he kept the subject of marriage uppermost, and seemingly was getting an inventory of the girls not yet married or engaged.

It was embarrassing for the girl. She was all too well aware of the difference between her home and the home of her schoolmates and friends. She knew that it was not pleasant for her "Yankee" friends to come to visit her when they could not feel sure of a welcome from the tireless, silent, and grim-visaged old Norse, if, indeed, they could escape insult. Julia ate her food mechanically, and it could hardly be said that she enjoyed the brisk talk of the young man; his eyes were upon her so constantly and his smile so obviously addressed to her. She rose as soon as possible, and going outside, took a seat on a chair under the trees in the yard. She was not a coarse or dull girl. In fact, she had developed so rapidly by contact with the young people of the neighborhood that she no longer found pleasure in her own home. She didn't believe in keeping up the old-fashioned Norwegian customs, and her life with her mother was not one to breed love or confidence. She was more like a hired hand. The love of the mother for her "Yulyie" was sincere, though rough and inarticulate, and it was her jealousy of the young "Yankees" that widened the chasm between the girl and herself—an inevitable result.

Rob followed the girl out into the yard and threw himself on the grass at her feet, perfectly unconscious of the fact that this attitude was exceedingly romantic and becoming to them both. He did it because he wanted to talk to her and the grass was cool and easy: there wasn't any other chair, anyway.

"Do they keep up the ly-ceum and the sociables same as ever?"

"Yes. The others go a good 'eal, but I don't. We're gettin' such a stock round us, and Father thinks he needs me s' much, I don't git out much. I'm gettin' sick of it."

"I sh'd think y' would," he replied, his eyes on her face.

"I c'd stand the churnin' and housework, but when it comes t' working out-doors in the dirt an' hot sun, gettin' all sunburned and chapped up, it's another thing. An' then it seems as if he gets stingier 'n' stingier every year. I ain't had a new dress in—I d'—know—how—long. He says it's all nonsense, an' Mother's just about as bad. *She* don't want a new dress, an' so she thinks I don't." The girl was feeling the influence of a sympathetic listener and was making up for her long silence. "I've tried t' go out t' work, but they won't let me. They'd have t' pay a hand twenty dollars a month f'r the work I do, an' they like cheap help; but I'm not goin' t' stand it much longer, I can tell you that."

Rob thought she was very handsome as she sat there with her eyes fixed on the horizon, while these rebellious thoughts found utterance in her quivering, passionate voice.

"Yulie! Kom heat!" roared the old man from the well.

A frown of anger and pain came into her face. She looked at Rob. "That means more work."

"Say! let me go out in your place. Come, now; what's the use—"

"No; it wouldn't do no good. It ain't t'day s' much; it's every day, and—"

"Yu*lie!*" called Peterson again with a string of impatient Norwegian.

"Well, all right, only I'd like to—"

"Well, goodbye," she said, with a little touch of feeling. "When d'ye go back?"

"I don't know. I'll see y' again before I go. Goodbye."

He stood watching her slow, painful pace till she reached the well, where Otto was standing with the horse. He stood watching them as they moved out into the road and turned down toward the field. He felt that she had sent him away; but still there was a look in her eyes which was not altogether—

He gave it up in despair at last. He was not good at analyses of this nature; he was used to plain, blunt expressions. There was a woman's subtlety here quite beyond his reach.

He sauntered slowly off up the road after his talk with Julia. His head was low on his breast; he was thinking as one who is about to take a decided and important step.

He stopped at length, and turning, watched the girl moving along in the deeps of the corn. Hardly a leaf was stirring; the untempered sunlight fell in a burning flood upon the field; the grasshoppers rose, snapped, buzzed, and fell; the locust uttered its dry, heat-intensifying cry. The man lifted his head.

"It's a d—n shame!" he said, beginning rapidly to retrace his steps. He stood leaning on the fence, awaiting the girl's coming very much as she had waited his on the round he had made before dinner. He grew impatient at the slow gait of the horse and drummed on their rail while he whistled. Then he took off his hat and dusted it nervously. As the horse got a little nearer he wiped his face carefully, pushed his hat back on his head, and climbed over the fence, where he stood with elbows on the middle rail as the girl and boy and horse came to the end of the furrow.

"Hot, ain't it?" he said as she looked up.

"Jimminy Peters, it's awful!" puffed the boy. The girl did not reply till she swung the plow about after the horse, and set it upright into the next row. Her powerful body had a superb swaying motion at the waist as she did this—a motion which affected Rob vaguely but massively.

"I thought you'd gone," she said gravely, pushing back her bonnet till he could see her face dewed with sweat and pink as a rose. She had the high cheekbones of her race, but she had also their exquisite fairess of color.

"Say, Otto," asked Rob alluringly, "wan' to go swimming?"

"You bet!" replied Otto.

"Well, I'll go a round if—"

The boy dropped off the horse, not waiting to hear any more. Rob grinned; but the girl dropped her eyes, then looked away.

"Got rid o' him mighty quick. Say, Julyie, I hate like thunder t' see you out here; it ain't right. I wish you'd—I wish—"

She could not look at him now, and her bosom rose and fell with a motion that was not due to fatigue. Her moist hair matted around her forehead gave her a boyish look.

Rob nervously tried again, tearing splinters from the fence. "Say, now, I'll tell yeh what I came back here fer—t' git married; and if you're willin', I'll do it tonight. Come, now, whaddy y' say?"

"What 've *I* got t' do 'bout it?" she finally asked, the color flooding her face and a faint smile coming to her lips. "Go ahead. I ain't got anything—"

Rob put a splinter in his mouth and faced her. "Oh, looky here, now, Julyie! you know what I mean. I've got a good claim out near Boomtown—a *rattlin'* good claim; a shanty on it fourteen by sixteen—no tarred paper about it; and a suller to keep butter in; and a hundred acres o' wheat just about ready to turn now. I need a wife."

Here he straightened up, threw away the splinter, and took off his hat. He was a very pleasant figure as the girl stole a look at him. His black laughing eyes were especially earnest just now. His voice had a touch of pleading. The popple tree over their heads murmured applause at his eloquence, then hushed to listen. A cloud dropped a silent shadow down upon them, and it sent a little thrill of fear through Rob, as if it were an omen of failure. As the girl remained silent, looking away, he began, man-fashion, to desire her more and more as he feared to lose her. He put his hat on the post again and took out his jackknife. Her calico dress draped her supple and powerful figure simply but naturally. The stoop in her shoulders, given by labor, disappeared as she partly leaned upon the fence. The curves of her muscular arms showed through her sleeve.

"It's all-fired lonesome f'r me out there on that claim, and it ain't no picnic f'r you here. Now, if you'll come out there with me, you needn't do anything but cook f'r me, and after harvest we can git a good layout o' furniture, an' I'll lath and plaster the house, an' put a little hell [ell] in the rear." He smiled, and so did she. He felt encouraged to say: "An' there we be, as snug as y' please. We're close t' Boomtown, an' we can go down there to church sociables an' things, and they're a jolly lot there."

The girl was still silent, but the man's simple enthusiasm came to her charged with passion and a sort of romance such as her hard life had known little of. There was something enticing about this trip to the West.

"What 'll my folks say?" she said at last.

A virtual surrender, but Rob was not acute enough to see it. He pressed on eagerly:

"I don't care. Do you? They'll just keep y' plowin' corn and milkin' cows till the day of judgment. Come, Julyie, I ain't got no time to fool away. I've got t' get back t' that grain. It's a whoopin' old crop, sure's y'r born, an' that means som'pin' purty scrumptious in furniture this fall. Come, now." He approached her and laid his hand on her shoulder very much as he would have touched Albert Seagraves or any other comrade. "Whady y' say?"

She neither started, nor shrunk, nor looked at him. She simply moved a step away. "They'd never let me go," she replied bitterly. "I'm too cheap a hand. I do a man's work an' get no pay at all."

"You'll have half o' all I c'n make," he put in.

"How long c'n you wait?" she asked, looking down at her dress.

"Just two minutes," he said, pulling out his watch. "It ain't no use t' wait. The old man 'll be jest as mad a week from now as he is today. Why not go now?"

"I'm of age day after tomorrow," she mused, wavering, calculating.

"You c'n be of age tonight if you'll jest call on old Square Hatfield with me."

"All right, Rob," the girl said, turning and holding out her hand.

"That's the talk!" he exclaimed, seizing it. "An' now a kiss, to bind the bargain, as the fellah says."

"I guess we c'n get along without that."

"No, we can't. It won't seem like an engagement without it."

"It ain't goin' to seem much like one anyway," she answered with a sudden realization of how far from her dreams of courtship this reality was.

"Say, now, Julyie, that ain't fair; it ain't treatin' me right. You don't seem to understand that I *like* you, but I do."

Rob was carried quite out of himself by the time, the place, and the girl. He had said a very moving thing.

The tears sprang involuntarily to the girl's eyes. "Do you mean it? If y' do, you may."

She was trembling with emotion for the first time. The sincerity of the man's voice had gone deep.

He put his arm around her almost timidly and kissed her on the cheek, a great love for her springing up in his heart. "That settles it," he said. "Don't cry, Julyie. You'll never be sorry for it. Don't cry. It kind o' hurts me to see it."

He didn't understand her feelings. He was only aware that she was crying, and tried in a bungling way to soothe her. But now that she had given way, she sat down in the grass and wept bitterly.

"*Yulyie!*" yelled the old Norwegian, like a distant foghorn.

The girl sprang up; the habit of obedience was strong.

"No; you set right there, and I'll go round," he said. "*Otto!*"

The boy came scrambling out of the wood half dressed. Rob tossed him upon the horse, snatched Julia's sunbonnet, put his own hat on her head, and moved off down the corn rows, leaving the girl smiling through her tears as he whistled and chirped to the horse. Farmer Peterson, seeing the familiar sunbonnet above the corn rows, went back to his work, with a sentence of Norwegian trailing after him like the tail of a kite—something about lazy girls who didn't earn the crust of their bread, etc.

Rob was wild with delight. "Git up there Jack! Hay, you old corncrib! Say, Otto, can you keep your mouth shet if it puts money in your pocket?"

"Jest try me 'n' see," said the keen-eyed little scamp.

"Well, you keep quiet about my being here this afternoon, and I'll put a dollar on y'r tongue—hay?—what?—understand?"

"Show me y'r dollar," said the boy, turning about and showing his tongue.

"All right. Begin to practice now by not talkin' to me."

Rob went over the whole situation on his way back, and when he got in sight of the girl his plan was made. She stood waiting for him with a new look on her face. Her sullenness had given way to a peculiar eagerness and anxiety to believe in him. She was already living that free life in a far-off wonderful country. No more would her stern father and sullen mother force her to tasks which she hated. She'd be a member of a new firm. She'd work, of course, but it would be because she wanted to, and not because she was forced to. The independence and the love promised grew more and more attractive. She laughed back with a softer light in her eyes when she saw the smiling face of Rob looking at her from her sunbonnet.

"Now you mustn't do any more o' this," he said. "You go back to the house an' tell y'r mother you're too lame to plow any more today, and it's too late, anyhow. Tonight!" he whispered quickly. "Eleven! Here!"

The girl's heart leaped with fear. "I'm afraid."

"Not of *me*, are yeh?"

"No, I'm not afraid of you, Rob."

"I'm glad o' that. I—I want you to—to *like* me, Julyie; won't you?"

"I'll try," she answered with a smile.

"Tonight, then," he said as she moved away.

"Tonight. Goodbye."

"Goodbye."

He stood and watched her till her tall figure was lost among the drooping corn leaves. There was a singular choking feeling in his throat. The girl's voice and face had brought up so many memories of parties and picnics and excursions on far-off holidays, and at the same time such suggestions of the future. He already felt that it was going to be an unconscionably long time before eleven o'clock.

He saw her go to the house, and then he turned and walked slowly up the dusty road. Out of the May weed the grasshoppers sprang, buzzing and snapping their dull red wings. Butterflies, yellow and white, fluttered around moist places in the ditch, and slender striped water snakes glided across the stagnant pools at sound of footsteps.

But the mind of the man was far away on his claim, building a new house, with a woman's advice and presence.

It was a windless night. The katydids and an occasional cricket were the only sounds Rob could hear as he stood beside his team and strained his ear to listen. At long intervals a little breeze ran through the corn like a swift serpent, bringing to the nostrils the sappy smell of the growing corn. The horses stamped uneasily as the mosquitoes settled on their shining limbs. The sky was full of stars, but there was no moon.

"What if she don't come?" he thought. "Or *can't* come? I can't stand that. I'll go to the old man an' say, 'Looky here—' Sh!"

He listened again. There was a rustling in the corn. It was not like the fitful movement of the wind; it was steady, slower, and approaching. It ceased. He whistled the wailing, sweet cry of the prairie chicken. Then a figure came out into the road—a woman—Julia!

He took her in his arms as she came panting up to him.

"Rob!"

"Julyie!"

A few words, the dull tread of swift horses, the rising of a silent train of dust, and then the wind wandered in the growing corn. The dust fell, a dog barked down the road and the katydids sang to the liquid contralto of the river in its shallows.

Further Reading

Boy Life on the Prairie. 1899.
The Captain of the Gray-Horse Troop. 1902.
Daughter of the Middle Border. 1921.
Jason Edwards. 1892.
The Moccasin Ranch. 1909.
Other Main-Travelled Roads. 1892.
Rose of Dutcher's Coolly. 1895.
Selected Letters of Hamlin Garland. Ed. Keith Newlin and Joseph B. McCullough. 1998.
Son of the Middle Border. 1917.
Trail-Makers of the Middle Border. 1926.
Wayside Courtships. 1897.

Reading about Hamlin Garland

Gish, Robert. *Hamlin Garland: The Far West.* Western Writers Series. Boise ID: Boise State University, 1976.
McCullough, Joseph B. *Hamlin Garland.* Boston: Twayne, 1978.
Underhill, Joseph B., and Daniel E. Littlefield, Jr., eds. *Hamlin Garland's Observations on the American Indian, 1895–1905.* Tucson: University of Arizona Press, 1976.

William Allen White (1868–1944)

William Allen White, editor of the *Emporia (Kansas) Gazette*, was a popular figure in the first half of the twentieth century, known primarily for his editorials and his carefully nurtured persona as the wise, folksy, small-town editor. White chronicled the American scene in the heart of America, a kind of Norman Rockwell in print. Throughout much of the first half of the twentieth century he was an arbiter of popular taste and opinions, a role that he gained through the wide dissemination of his pithy editorials and his acquaintance with presidents, writers, and other public figures. As one of the founders of the Book-of-the-Month-Club, he even helped to form America's reading habits.

All of his adult life White was writing. One of his editorials won a Pulitzer Prize, and he earned another for his posthumous *Autobiography*. He wrote biographies of the politicians and other prominent people he knew (he seemed to know everyone), and in the early years even wrote the ads and obituaries for his paper.* His novels and short stories reflect the lives of ordinary citizens in a small town much like Emporia.

Although White was born in Emporia, he grew up in El Dorado, Kansas, on the edge of the frontier. His father was an ardent Democrat, his mother an equally committed Republican. White credited his fair-mindedness to this early exposure to radically different opinions. Over the years White defended free speech, labor unions, unwed mothers, and America's obligation to Europe in the years before the United States entered World War II. When he died in 1944, Americans knew and remembered him as the quintessential middle-class, small-town, hometown citizen. "A Story of the Highlands" was written in 1896 when, as he himself said, the western third of Kansas was still a questionable enterprise. White's story is unfortunately close to reality: depression and drought in the 1890s drove thousands of settlers from the high plains.† Towns that had sprung up during the unusually wet years of the 1880s—the boom years of settlement—disappeared entirely. The steady decline in population on the high plains continues into the twenty-first century.

*White purchased the *Emporia Gazette* in 1895. It is still owned and managed by the White family.

†Willa Cather, Hamlin Garland, and other Great Plains writers wrote their own versions of this story. Garland's story "A Day's Pleasure," Cather's story "El Dorado: A Kansas Recessional," and another of White's stories, "The Story of Aqua Pura," all recount the debilitating or tragic consequences of isolation and failure that drained the civilizing qualities out of men and women on the high plains.

A Story of the Highlands (1897)

Crossing the Missouri river into Kansas, the west-bound traveler begins a steady, upward climb, until he reaches the summit of the Rockies. The journey through Kansas covers in four hundred miles nearly five thousand feet of the long, upward slant. In that long hillside there are three or four distinct kinds of landscape, distinguished from one another by the trees that trim the horizon.

The hills and bluffs that roll away from the river are covered with scrub oaks, elms, walnuts, and sycamores. As the wayfarer pushes westward, the oak drops back, then the sycamore follows the walnut, and finally the elm disappears, until three hundred miles to the westward, the horizon of the "gently rolling" prairie is serrated by the scraggy cottonwood, that rises awkwardly by some sandbarred stream, oozing over the moundy land. Another fifty miles, and at Garden City, high up on the background of the panorama, even the cottonwood staggers; and here and there, around some sinkhole in the great flat floor of the prairie, droops a desolate willow—the last weary pilgrim from the lowlands.

When the traveler has mounted to this high table land, nearly four hundred miles from the Missouri, he may walk for days without seeing any green thing higher than his head. He may journey for hours on horseback, and not climb a hill, seeing before him only the level and often barren plain, scarred now and then by irrigation ditches.

The even line of the horizon is seldom marred. The silence of such a scene gnaws the glamour from the heart. Men become harsh and hard; women grow withered and sodden under its blighting power. The song of wood birds is not heard; even the mournful plaint of the meadow lark loses its sentiment, where the dreary clanking drone of the wind-mill is the one song which really brings good tidings with it. Long and fiercely sounds this unrhythmical monody in the night, when the traveler lies down to rest in the little sun-burned, pine-board town. The gaunt arms of the wheel hurl its imprecations at him as he rises to resume his journey into the silence, under the great gray dome, with its canopy pegged tightly down about him everywhere.

Crops are as bountiful in Kansas as elsewhere on the globe. It is the constant cry for aid, coming from this plateau—only a small part of the state—which reaches the world's ears, and the world blames Kansas. The fair springs on these highlands lure home-seekers to their ruin.

Hundreds of men and women have been tempted to death or worse, by this Lorelei of the prairies.

A young man named Burkholder came out to Fountain county in 1885. He had been a well-to-do young fellow in Illinois, was a graduate of an inland college, a man of good judgment, of sense, of a well-arranged mental perspective. In 1885 money was plentiful. He stocked his farm, put on a mortgage, and brought a wife back from the home of his boyhood. She was a young woman of culture, who put a bookshelf in the corner of the best of the three rooms in the yellow pine shanty, in which she and her husband lived. She brought her upright piano, and adorned her bed-room floor with bright rugs. She bought magazines at the "Post Office Book Store" of the prairie town. She was not despondent. The vast stretches of green cheered her through the hot summer. There was a novel fascination in the wide, treeless horizon which charmed her for a while. At first she never tired of glancing up from her work, through the south window of the kitchen, to see the level green stretches, and the road that merged into the distance. She sat in the shade of the house, and wrote home cheerful, rollicking letters. As for roughing it, she enjoyed it thoroughly.

The crops did not quite pay the expenses of the year; so "Thomas Burkholder and Lizzie his wife" put another mortgage on the farm. The books and magazines from home still adorned the best room. And all through the winter and spring, the prevailing spirits of the community buoyed up the young people. It was during the summer of 1887 that the first hot winds came. They blighted everything. The kaffir corn, the grass, the dust-laden weeds by the wayside curled up under their fiery breath from the southwestern desert. Mrs. Burkholder stayed indoors. The dust spread itself over everything. It came into the house like a flood, pouring through the loose window frames and weather-boarding. Mrs. Burkholder, looking out of her window on these days, could see only a great dust dragon, writhing up and down the brown road and over the prairie for miles and miles. The scene seemed weirdly dry. She found herself longing, one day, for a fleck of water in the land-scape. That longing grew upon her. She said nothing of it, but in her day dreams there was always a mental itching to put water into the lustreless picture framed by her kitchen window. It was a kind of soul thirst. In one of her letters she wrote:

"The hot winds have killed everything this year, but most of all I grieve for the little cottonwood saplings on the 'eighty' in front of the house. There is not a tree anywhere in sight, and as the government requires that we should plant trees on our place, as a partial payment for it, I was so in hopes that these would do well. They are burned up now. You do n't know how lonesome it seems without trees."

She did not tell the home folk that her piano and the books had gone to buy provisions for the winter. She did not tell the home folk that she had not bought a new dress since she left Illinois. She did not let her petty cares burden her letter. She wrote of generalities. "You do not know how I miss the hills. Tom and I rode twenty miles yesterday, to a place called the Taylor Bottom. It is a deep sink-hole, perhaps fifty feet deep, containing about ten square acres. By getting down into this we have the effect of hills. You cannot know how good and snug, and tucked in and 'comfy' it seemed. It is so naked at the house with the knife-edge on the horizon, and only the sky over you. Tom and I have been busy. I have n't had time to read the story in the magazine you sent me. Tom can't get corduroys out here. You should see him in overalls."

Mrs. Burkholder helped her husband look after the cattle. The hired man went away in the early fall. This she did not write home either. All through the winter days she heard the keen wind whistle around the house, and when she was alone a dread blanched her face. The great gray dome seemed to be holding her its prisoner. She felt chained under it. She shut her eyes and strove to get away from it in fancy, to think of green hills and woodland; but her eyes tore themselves open, and with a hypnotic terror she went to the window, where the prairie thrall bound her again in its chains.

The cemetery for the prairie town had been started during the spring before, and some one had planted therein a solitary cottonwood sapling. Its two dead, gaunt branches seemed to be beckoning her, and all day she thought she heard the winds shriek through the new iron fences around the graves and through the grass that grew wild about the dead. The scene haunted her. It was for this end that the gray dome held her, she thought, as she listened during the cold nights to the hard, dry snow as it beat against the board shanty wherein she lay awake.

In the spring the mover's caravan filed by the house, starting eastward before planting time. When the train of wagons had passed the year before, Mrs. Burkholder had been amused by the fantastic legends, which the wagon covers—white, clean, prosperous—had borne. "Kansas or bust," they used to read when headed westward. "Busted" was the laconic legend, written under the old motto on their first eastward trip. "Going back to wife's folks," had been a common jocose motto at first. Mrs. Burkholder and her husband had laughed over this the year before, but this year as she saw the long line file out of the west into the east, she missed the banners. She noticed, with a mental pang, that those who came out of the country this year seemed to be thankful to get out at all. There were times when she had to struggle to conceal her cowardice; for she wished to turn away from the fight, to flee from the gray dome, and from the beckoning of the dead cottonwood in the graveyard.

The spring slipped away, and another sultry summer came on, and then a long, dry fall. Mrs. Burkholder and her husband worked together.

There were whole weeks when she neglected her toilet; she tried to brighten up in the evening, and dutifully went at the magazines that were regularly sent to her by the home folks.

But she seemed to need sleep, and the cares of the day weighed upon her. The interests of the world of culture grew small in her vision. The work before her seemed to demand all her thought; so that serial after serial slipped through the magazines unread, and new literary men and fads rose and fell, all unknown to her. The pile of magazines at the foot of the bed grew dustier every day.

The Burkholders got their share of the seed-grain sent to Fountain county by the Kansas Legislature, and just after planting time in 1889, the land was gloriously green. But before July, the promises had been mocked by the hiss of the hot wind in the dead grass. That fall one of their horses died.

Saturday after Saturday, Burkholder went to the prairie town and brought home groceries and coal. It was a source of constant terror to him that some day his wife might ask how he got these supplies. She hid it from herself as long as she could. All winter they would not admit to each other that they were living on "aid." On many a gray, blustering afternoon, when Burkholder was in the village getting provisions, a straggler on the road might see his wife coming around the house, with two buckets of water in her hands, the water splashing against her feet, which were encased in a pair of her husband's old shoes, the wind pushing her thin calico skirts against her limbs, and her frail body bent stiffly in the man's coat that she wore. Her arms and shoulders seemed to shiver and crouch with the cold, and her blue features were so drawn that her friendly smile at the wayfarer was only a grimace.

In the spring many men in Fountain county went East looking for work. They left their wives with God and the county commissioners. Burkholder dumbly went with them. In March, the covered wagon train began to file past the Burkholder house. By April it was a continuous line—shabby, tattered, rickety, dying. Here came a wagon covered with bed quilts, there another topped with oil-cloth table covers; another followed, patched with everything. For two years, the mover's caravan trailing across the plains had taken the shape of a huge dust-colored serpent in the woman's fancy; now it seemed to Mrs. Burkholder that the terrible creature was withering away, that this was its skeleton. The treeless landscape worried her more and more; the steel dome seemed set tighter over her, and she sat thirsting for water in the landscape.

After a month's communion with her fancies, Mrs. Burkholder nailed a black rag over the kitchen window. But the arms of the dead sapling in the cemetery gyrated wildly in her sick imagination. It was a long summer, and when it was done, there was one more vacant house, one more among hundreds far out on the highlands. There is one more mound in the bleak country graveyard, where the wind, shrieking through the iron fences and the crackling, dead cottonwood branches, has never learned a slumber song to sob for a tired soul. But there are times when the wind seems to moan upon its sun-parched chords like the cry of some lone spirit groping its tangled way back to the lowlands, the green pastures, the still waters, and to the peace that passeth understanding.

Further Reading

The Autobiography of William Allen White. 1946.
A Certain Rich Man. 1909.
The Court of Boyville. 1899.
The Editor and His People. 1924.
Forty Years on Main Street. 1937.

In Our Town. 1906.
In the Heart of a Fool. 1918.
Masks in a Pageant. 1928.
Selected Letters of William Allen White. 1947.

Reading about William Allen White

Agran, Edward Gale. *"Too Good a Town": William Allen White, Community and the Emerging Rhetoric of Middle America.* Fayetteville: University of Arkansas Press, 1998.

Griffith, Sally Foreman. *Home Town News: William Allen White and the Emporia Gazette.* New York: Oxford, 1989.

——, ed. *The Autobiography of William Allen White.* 2d ed. Lawrence: University Press of Kansas, 1990.

Jernigan, Jay. *William Allen White.* Boston: Twayne, 1983.

McKee, John DeWitt. *William Allen White: Maverick on Main Street.* Westport CT: Greenwood Press, 1975.

Quantic, Diane D. *William Allen White.* Western Writers Series. Boise ID: Boise State University, 1993.

Diane Glancy

This poem echoes some of the sentiment expressed by William Allen White more than a century ago. Even though modern conveniences have made life possible on the high plains, the landscape can still be intimidating.

For Diane Glancy's biography see page 241.

September \ Peru, Kansas (1991)

The creek slutes north of town, a curve, a grocery, a few houses, fence slats, then the country blozomed to the land.

Warrior & squawl with towel hanging at the car window \ edges flapping like a bird trying to take off from the land.

Out here where water's scarce cows stand in ponds to hold them down. Language starts with their breath & the hurrrr of wind around grain elevators \ space ships in their towers.

Far away, turnpike tollgates are moons of Uranus. The dark sky \ transparent at night \ but for the black-eyed rudge of trees. In Peru \ salibales of words are hayrolled in fields. Look & you will find corridors of meaning in any direction, layers of it, anything you want \ a square box, root of fields, soy beanies & weet.

You can even feel the laps of the sky's tongue on your shoes. All directions, yet the openness doesn't take the hoe handle.

You still hold your loss as though it were something. The cutting into molars \ jaw \ the cold bone-white of the skull.

Driving thru Kansas is like being married to a man you didn't fit with \ not having money \ your days full of chores & boredom \ a towel in your window to keep out the sun. Robes of wheat whick by like crosses in a country cemetery.

You pass the unanimous bend of weeds. Just look where they are pointing \ the openness in fields. The opundance of language seeping to another.

Ee tabo cay moose \ Worriar & squaw \ their carwindow flapping over shed & galvanized tanks. Step anywhere & grasshoppers jump in the corn.

The wind flings you with dust from fields & gravel roads. Clouds in hopeless plight to wind patterns qpurting revolt from county line to line. Soon, the little sprats of rain on sunflars & gutturals of old stone houses \ sheds following like calves.

The space that sounds in brittle cornstalks is all yours \ the hinge of bugs opening Peru \ when you beat hollyhocks with your stick until the yard pinked with furzz & the grandmother yelled her tomahawk language.

All language defeats \ pulls out your tongue \ strips the loose string of bone from your back \ the bonds of ponds not giving in to earth, but kissing the sky.

All your life you want to feel ponded to the land \ enaporating upword. The sky thumbs through the cornrows as you pazz by head whacked off \ feet lifted from the floor in a car going fast to get thru.

O. E. Rølvaag *(1876–1931)*

O. E. Rølvaag's 1927 novel *Giants in the Earth* forms, with Willa Cather's *O Pioneers!* and *My Ántonia,* a kind of prairie trilogy. Cather's Alexandra Bergson and Antonia Shimerda, and Rølvaag's Per Hansa are models of the classic pioneer. Per Hansa is a man with a vision of heroic proportions and the strength to realize his dream kingdom in reality. He is so confident of his own powers that he cannot acknowledge his wife's fearful reaction to their new home. Pregnant and terrified by the apparently endless space around her, Beret fears, as so many others who sought new life on the plains, that in this "wilderness," despite the close community of Norwegians around her, they will become bestial, living in a sod house, the ground itself.

In *Giants in the Earth* and subsequent volumes, *Peder Victorious* (1929) and *Their Father's God* (1931), Rølvaag wrote an epic saga of immigrant pioneers battling malevolent forces *in* the earth, which is his metaphor for the Great Plains experience. *Giants in the Earth* relates Per Hansa's efforts to overcome these forces and his wife's resistance to them. After Per Hansa's death Beret proves to be a successful farmer, but because she insists on clinging to her Norwegian language and culture and because she suffers from periods of deep depression, she becomes more and more isolated from the community. Her own children, who embrace the English language and American customs, agree with the community that their mother is "odd."

Rølvaag was born on an island off the northwestern coast of Norway into a family of fisherman, a life he gave up after a violent storm during an early fishing trip. With help from an uncle in South Dakota, he emigrated in 1896. He learned English as he finished his high school education. After graduation from St. Olaf College in Minnesota and further study in Oslo, he joined the St. Olaf faculty as a professor of Norwegian. The opposing forces of cultural integrity and assimilation inform the plots and themes in many of Rølvaag's immigrant stories. Like his character Beret, he resisted surrender of his Norwegian culture in exchange for accepting America's cultural leveling. In fact, Rølvaag wrote his trilogy in Norwegian and then translated the novels into English. Rølvaag's notes, some of which are included in this selection, reflect his careful attention to Norwegian language and culture.

Home-founding (1927)

I

On the side of a hill, which sloped gently away toward the southeast and followed with many windings a creek that wormed its way across the prairie, stood Hans Olsa, laying turf. He was building a sod house. The walls had now risen breast-high; in its half-finished condition, the structure resembled more a bulwark against some enemy than anything intended to be a human habitation. And the great heaps of cut sod, piled up in each corner, might well have been the stores of ammunition for defence of the stronghold.

For a man of his strength and massive build, his motions were unusually quick and agile; but he worked by fits and starts to-day. At times he stopped altogether; in these pauses he would straighten himself up and draw his sleeve with a quick stroke across his troubled face; with each stroke the sleeve would come away damper; and standing so, he would fix his gaze intently on the prairie to the eastward. His eyes had wandered so often now over the stretch of land lying before them, that they were familiar with every tussock and hollow. . . . No—nothing in sight yet! . . . He would resume his task, as if to make up for lost time, and work hard for a spell; only to forget himself once more, pause involuntarily, and stand inert and abstracted, gazing off into the distance.

Beyond the house a tent had been pitched; a wagon was drawn up close beside it. On the ground outside of the tent stood a stove, a couple of chairs, and a few other rough articles of furniture. A stout, healthy-looking woman, whose face radiated an air of simple wisdom and kindliness, was busy preparing the midday meal. She sang to herself as she worked. A ten-year-old girl, addressed by the woman as Sofie, was helping her. Now and then the girl would take up the tune and join in the singing.

Less than a quarter of a mile away, in a southeasterly direction, a finished sod house rose on the slope of the hill. Smoke was winding up from it at this moment. This house, which had been built the previous fall, belonged to Syvert Tönseten.

Some distance north from the place where Hans Olsa had located, two other sod houses were under construction; but a hillock lay between, so that he could not see them from where he stood. There the two Solum boys had driven down their stakes and had begun building. Tönseten's completed house, and the other three half-finished ones, marked the beginning of the settlement on Spring Creek.

The woman who had been bustling about preparing the meal, now called to her husband that dinner was ready—he must come at once! He answered her, straightened up for the hundredth time, wiped his hands on his trousers, and stood for a moment gazing off eastward. . . . No use to look—not a soul in sight yet! . . . He sighed heavily, and walked with slow steps toward the tent, his eyes on the ground.

It was light and airy inside the tent, but stifling hot, because of the unobstructed sunlight beating down upon it. Two beds were ranged along the wall, both of them homemade; a big emigrant chest stood at the head of each. Nails had been driven into the centre pole of the tent, on which hung clothing; higher up a crosspiece, securely fastened, was likewise hung with clothes. Two of the walls were lined with furniture; on these pieces the dishes were displayed, all neatly arranged.

A large basin of water stood on a chair just inside the tent door. Hans Olsa washed his face and hands; then he came out and sat down on the ground, where his wife had spread the table. It was so much cooler outside. The meal was all ready; both mother and daughter had been waiting for him.

"I suppose you haven't seen any signs of them yet?" his wife asked at last.

"No—nothing at all!"

"Can you imagine what has become of them?"

"The Lord forgive us—if I only knew!"

Her husband looked so anxious that she asked no more questions. Out of her kind heart rose a hopeful, "Don't worry, they'll get here all right!" . . . But in spite of the cheerfulness of the words, she could not give them that ring of buoyant confidence which she would have liked to show. . . . "Of course!" said the girl with a laugh. "Store-Hans and Ola have two good pairs of eyes. Leave it to them—they'll find us!"

The father gave her a stern glance; he didn't tell her in words to stop her foolish chatter—but she said no more. Without speaking once, he ate his dinner. As soon as he had finished, he tossed his spoon on the blanket, thanked them for the food, got up gloomily, and went back to the half-completed wall. There he sat down awhile, as if lost in thought . . . gazing eastward. His large, rugged features were drawn and furrowed with anxiety. . . . "God Almighty!" he sighed, and folded his big hands. "What can have become of Per Hansa?"

His wife was watching his closely as he sat there on the wall. By and by she told her daughter to finish washing the dishes, and started to go over where he was. When he saw her coming, he tried to begin working as if there were nothing on his mind.

"Hans," she said, quickly, when she had reached his side, "I think you ought to go out and look for them!"

He waited until he had got a strip of sod in place before he answered: "Easier said than done . . . when we haven't the faintest idea where to look . . . on such stretches of prairie!"

"Yes, I know; but it would make us all feel better, anyway . . . as if we were doing something."

Hans Olsa laid another strip of turf; then he stopped, let his hands fall to his sides, and began thinking aloud as he gazed off into the distance. . . .

"I know this much—you don't often find a smarter fellow than Per Hansa. . . . That's what makes it so queer! I don't suppose he's able to get much speed out of his oxen; but one thing I'm certain of—he has been hurrying as fast as he could.

And we surely didn't come along very fast . . . but now it's the fifth day since we arrived here! If he made use of these bright moonlight nights, as he probably did, I begin to be afraid that he's gone on west of us somewhere, instead of being still to the eastward. . . . It's certainly no child's play to start looking for him!"

Hans Olsa slumped down on the wall, the picture of dejection. His wife quickly found a place beside him. Together they sat there in silence. The same fear that she felt him struggling with, a fear thrown into sharp relief by the things he had just been saying, had long since gripped her heart also.

"I feel so sorry for Beret, poor thing . . . and the children. You must remember, though, that he couldn't go very fast on account of her condition. . . . I think she is with child again!" She paused. "I dreamed about them last night . . . a bad dream. . . ."

Her husband glanced sidewise at her. "We mustn't pay attention to such things. A bad dream is a good sign, anyway—that's what my mother always said. . . . But I suppose I'll never forgive myself for not waiting for him." He got up heavily and laid another strip of turf. "He's always been like that, Per Hansa; he never would take help from any man. But this time he's carried it a little too far!"

His wife made no answer. She was watching a short stout man with a reddish beard who had started up the slope from the direction of the house to the south of them. He had cheeks like two rosy apples, a quick step, and eyes that flitted all about; he was noted among them for his glib tongue and the flood of his conversation. With hands stuck into the waistband of his trousers, and elbows out akimbo, the man looked half as broad again as he really was.

"Here comes Tönseten," said the woman. "Why don't you talk it over with him? I really think you ought to go out and look for them."

"Seen anything of them yet, Hans Olsa?" asked the man, without further greeting, as soon as he arrived. . . . "Well, well! this looks fine! Ha, ha! It's a warm house, you know, that's built by the aid of a woman's hand."

Hans Olsa wheeled on him. "You haven't caught sight of them yourself, Syvert, have you?"

"Caught sight of them? Why, man alive, that's just what I've come up here to tell you! I've had them in sight for over an hour now. Seems to me you ought to be able to see them easy enough—you who carry your eyes so high up in the air! . . . Good Lord! it won't be long before they arrive here, at the rate they're coming!"

"What's that you say?" the others burst out with one voice. . . . "Where are they?" . . .

"I reckon Per Hansa must have got off his course a little. Maybe the oxen didn't steer well, or maybe he didn't figure the current right. . . . Look to the westward, neighbours! Look over there about west-northwest, and you'll see him plain enough. . . . No need to worry. That fellow never would drown in such shallow water as this! . . . I wonder, now, how far west he's really been?"

Hans Olsa and his wife faced around in the direction that Tönseten had indicated. Sure enough, out of the west a little caravan was crawling up toward them on the prairie.

"Can that be them? . . . I really believe it is!" said Hans Olsa in a half whisper, as if hardly daring yet to give vent to his joy.

"*Of course* it is!" cried his wife, excitedly. . . . "Thank God!"

"Not the least doubt of it," Tönseten assured them. "You might as well go and put your coffeepot on the stove, Mother Sörrina![1] That Kjersti of mine is coming over pretty soon; she'll probably have something good tucked under her apron. . . . In half an hour we'll have the lost sheep back in the fold!"

"Yes! Heavens and earth, Sörrina!" cried Hans Olsa, "fetch out the best you've got! . . . Per, Per, is it really you, old boy? . . . But why are you coming from the west, I'd like to know?"

Tönseten coughed, and gave the woman a sly wink.

"Look here, Mother Sörrina," he said with a twinkle in his eyes, "won't you be good enough, please, to take a peek at Hans Olsa's Sunday bottle? . . . Not that *I* want anything to drink, you understand—I should say not. Good Lord, no! But think of that poor woman out there, who has been suffering all this time without a drop! And I'd be willing to bet that Per Hansa wouldn't object to having his stomach warmed up a little, too!"

At that they burst out laughing, from mingled joy and relief; but Tönseten's laughter at his own joke was the loudest of all. . . . Work was resumed at once; Syvert began to carry the sods for Hans Olsa to lay up, while Mother Sörrina went off in a happy frame of mind, to make her preparations for the reception of the wanderers.

II

Before the half hour allotted by Tönseten had passed, the caravan came slowly crawling up the slope. Per Hansa still strode in the van, with Store-Hans at his side; Ole walked abreast of the oxen, driving them with the goad. Beret and And-Ongen sat in the wagon. Rosie came jogging along behind at her own gait; she gave a loud, prolonged "moo-o-o-o" as she discovered the other animals across the prairie.

Both families stood ready to receive them; Hans Olsa and Sörine, Tönseten and his Kjersti, all watching intently the movements of the approaching company; but the girl couldn't possess her patience any longer, and ran down to meet the new arrivals. She took Store-Hans by the hand and fell in beside him; the first question she asked was whether he hadn't been terribly scared at night? . . .

As the slope of the hill grew steeper, the oxen had to bend to the yoke.

"Hey, there, folks!" shouted Per Hansa, boisterously. "Don't be standing around loafing, now! It's only the middle of the afternoon. Haven't you got anything to do around here?"

"Coffee time, coffee time, Per Hansa . . . ha, ha, ha!" Tönseten was bubbling over with good spirits. "We thought we might as well wait a little while for you, you know."

. . . "You've found us at last!" said Hans Olsa, with a deep, happy chuckle. . . . He didn't seem able to let go of Per Hansa's hand.

"Found you? Why, devil take it, it's no trick to follow a course out here! You just have to keep on steering straight ahead. And you had marked the trail pretty well, all the way along. I found plenty of traces of you. . . . I guess we stood a little too far to the westward, between Sioux Falls and here; that's how it happened. . . . So *this* is the place, is it? . . . The pastures of Goshen in the land of Egypt—eh?"

"Just so, just so!" cried Tönseten, nodding and laughing. "Pastures of Goshen—right you are! That's exactly what we are going to call the place—*Goshen*—if only you haven't sailed in to mix things up for us!" . . .

Beret and the child had now got down from the wagon; the other two women hovered around her, drawing her toward the tent. But she hung back for a moment; she wanted to stop and look around.

. . . Was this the place? . . . *Here!* . . . Could it be possible? . . . She stole a glance at the others, at the half-completed hut, then turned to look more closely at the group standing around her; and suddenly it struck her that *here something was about to go wrong*. . . . For several days she had sensed this same feeling; she could not seem to tear herself loose from the grip of it. . . . A great lump kept coming up in her throat; she swallowed hard to keep it back, and forced herself to look calm. Surely, surely, she mustn't give way to her tears now, in the midst of all this joy. . . .

Then she followed the other two women into the tent; seeing a chair, she sank down in it, as if her strength had gone!

Sörine was patting her on the shoulder. . . . "Come, get your things off, Beret. You ought to loosen up your clothes, you know. Just throw this dress of mine around you. . . . Here's the water to wash yourself in. Let down your hair, and take your time about it. . . . Don't mind Kjersti and me being around."

After they had bustled about for a little while the others left her. The moment they had gone she jumped up and crossed the tent, to look out of the door. . . . How will human beings be able to endure this place? she thought. Why, there isn't even a thing that one can *hide behind!* . . . Her sensitive, rather beautiful face was full of blank dismay; she turned away from the door and began to loosen her dress; then her eyes fell on the centre pole with its crosspiece, hung with clothes, and she stood a moment irresolute, gazing at it in startled fright. . . . It looked like the giants she had read about as a child; for a long while she was unable to banish the picture from her mind.

Outside the tent, Ole stood with his hand resting on one of the oxen. He was disgusted; the older people seemed to have clean forgotten his existence. They never would get done talking—when he, too, might have had a word to put in! . . .

"Hadn't we better unhitch the oxen, Dad?"

"Yes, yes—that's right, Ola. We might as well camp down here for the night, since we've run across some folks we used to know. . . . How about it, you fellows?" He turned to the other two. "I suppose there's a little more land left around here, isn't there, after you've got through?"

"*Land?* Good God! Per Hansa, what are you talking about? Take whatever you please, from here to the Pacific Ocean!" Tönseten's enthusiasm got so far away with him that he had to pull one of his hands out of his waistband and make a sweeping circle with it in the air.

"You must take a look around as soon as you can," Hans Olsa said, "and see if you find anything better that meets your fancy. In the meanwhile I've put down a stake for you on the quarter section that lies north of mine. We'll go over and have a look at it pretty soon. Sam Solum wanted it, but I told him he'd better leave it till you came. . . . You see, you would be next to the creek there; and then you and I would be the nearest neighbours, just as we've always planned. It makes no particular difference to Sam; he can take the quarter alongside his brother's."

Per Hansa drew a deep breath, as if filling himself with life's great goodness. . . . Here Hans Olsa had been worrying about him, and with kindly forethought had arranged everything to his advantage! . . . "Well, well, we'll have to settle all that later, Hans Olsa. For the present, I can only say that I'm deeply thankful to you! . . . Unhitch the beasts, there, Ola! . . . And now, if you folks have got anything handy, to either eat or drink, I'll accept it with pleasure."

. . . "Or *both*, Per Hansa!" put in Tönseten, excitedly.

"Yes, both, Syvert. I won't refuse!"

Soon they were all gathered around a white cloth which Mother Sörine had spread on the ground. On one side of it lay a whole leg of dried mutton; on the other a large heap of *flatbröd*, with cheese, bread, and butter; in the centre of the cloth stood a large bowl of sweet milk, and from the direction of the stove the breeze wafted to them a pleasant odour of fried bacon and strong coffee. Mother Sörine herself took charge of the ceremony, bringing the food and urging them all to sit down. The stocky figure of Per Hansa rocked back and forth in blissful delight as he squatted there with his legs crossed under him.

"Come, Sörrina, sit down!" he cried. "I guess we've fallen in with gentlefolks, by the looks of things around here. . . . I suppose you think you're old Pharaoh himself—eh, Hans Olsa?"

"Who do you call me, then?" inquired Tönseten.

"You, Syvert? Well, now, I really don't know what to say. Of course you'd like to be His Majesty's butler, but you mustn't be encouraged—remember what happened to that poor fellow! . . . I think we'd better make you the baker—it might be safer, all around. What's your idea, Hans Olsa?"

By this time they were all laughing together.

In the midst of the jollification came Sörine, carrying a plate with a large bottle and a dram glass[2] on it. . . . "Here, take this off my hands, Hans Olsa—you will know what to do with it!"

Tönseten fairly bubbled over in his admiration for her:

"Oh, you sweet Sörrina-girl!—you're dearer to my heart than a hundred women! . . . What a blessing it must be, to have a wife like that!"

"Stop your foolishness!" said Kjersti, but her voice didn't sound too severe.

For a long while they continued to sit around the cloth, chatting, eating, and drinking, and thoroughly enjoying themselves. Hans Olsa seemed like a different man from the one who had eaten here at noon. His loud voice led the cheerful talk; his ponderous bulk was always the centre of the merriment; it seemed as if he would never tire of gazing into that bearded, roguish face of Per Hansa's.

Once, as Per Hansa was slicing off a piece of mutton, he regarded the cut thoughtfully, and asked:

"I suppose you brought all your supplies through safe enough?"

"Oh, sure," answered Hans Olsa, innocently. "We had no trouble at all—didn't lose anything; that is, except for the leg that we left behind somewhere, east on the prairie. But that's hardly worth mentioning."

Per Hansa paused with the piece of meat halfway to his mouth, and looked at Sörine with an expression of deep concern:

"The devil you say! Did you lose one of your legs . . .?"

Mother Sörine laughed heartily at him. "Oh no—not quite so bad as that. . . . But a leg of mutton might come in handy later on, I'll tell you; there aren't too many of them to be had around here."

Per Hansa chewed away on the meat and looked very serious. At last he said:

"That's always the way with folks who have more of the world's goods than they can take care. . . . But I'll promise you one thing, Sörrina: if I can get my old blunderbuss to work, you're going to have your lost leg back again. . . . How about it, fellows? Have you seen any game that's fit to eat out here?"

III

They sat on until the first blue haze of evening began to spread eastward over the plain. The talk had now drifted to questions of a more serious nature, mostly concerned with how they should manage things out here; of their immediate prospects; of what the future might hold in store for them; of land and crops, and of the new kingdom which they were about to found. . . . No one put the thought into words, but they all felt it strongly; now they had gone back to the very beginning of things. . . .

As the evening shadows deepened the conversation gradually died away into silence. A peculiar mood came drifting in with the dusk. It seemed to float on the evening breeze, to issue forth out of the heart of the untamed nature round about them; it lurked in the very vastness and endlessness surrounding them on every hand; it even seemed to rise like an impalpable mist out of the ground on which they sat.

This mood brought vague premonitions to them, difficult to interpret. . . . No telling what might happen out here . . . for almost anything *could* happen!" . . .

They were so far from the world . . . cut off from the haunts of their fellow beings . . . so terribly far! . . .

The faces that gazed into one another were sober now, as silence claimed the little company; but lines of strength and determination on nearly every countenance told of an inward resolve to keep the mood of depression from gaining full control.

Per Hansa was the first to rouse himself and throw off the spell. He jumped up with nervous energy; a shiver passed over him, as if he were having a chill.

"What is it—are you cold?" asked his wife. She had instinctively sensed his mood as she looked at him—and loved him better for it. Until that moment, she had supposed that she herself was the only one who felt this peculiar influence.

"Such crazy talk!" he burst out. "I believe we've all lost our senses, every last one of us! Here we sit around celebrating in broad daylight, in the middle of summer, as if it was the Christmas holidays! . . . Come on, woman, let's go over to our new home!"

Everyone got up.

"You must do exactly as you please about it, Per Hansa," spoke up Hans Olsa with an apologetic air. "Don't feel that you must take this quarter if you don't like it. But as far as I can see, it's as good a piece of land as you could find anywhere around—every square foot of it plowland, except the hill over there. Plenty of water for both man and beast. . . . As for my part, if I can only sit here between you and Syvert, I certainly won't be kicking about my neighbours. . . . But I don't want you to feel that you have to take this quarter on my account, you understand. . . . If you do take it, though, we must get one of the Solum boys to go down to Sioux Falls with you the first thing to-morrow, so that you can file your claim. You'll have to do that in any case, you know, whichever quarter you take. . . . There's likely to be a lot of people moving into this region before the snow flies; we five oughtn't to part company or let anyone get in between us. . . . You've heard my best advice, anyway."

"Now, that's the talk!" Tönseten chimed in, briskly. "And considering the size of the head it comes from, it isn't half bad, either. You're damned well right, Hans Olsa. Before the snow flies you're going to see such a multitude swarming around these parts, that the thundering place won't be fit to live in! Remember what I say, boys, in times to come—bear it in mind that those were Syvert's very words! . . . You've got to go straight to Sioux Falls to-morrow morning, Per Hansa, and no two ways about it! If one of the Solum boys can't go along to do the talking for you, why, I shall have to buckle down to the job myself."

Once more Per Hansa's heart filled with a deep sense of peace and contentment as he realized how matters were being smoothed out for him. They seemed to move of their own accord, but he knew better. . . . Was he really to own it? Was it really to become his possession, this big stretch of fine land that spread here before him? Was he really to have his friends for neighbours, both to the north and to the south—folks who cared for him and wanted to help him out in every way? . . .

He was still chuckling with the rare pleasure of it as he asked, "You haven't discovered any signs of life since you came?"

"Devil, no!" Tönseten assured him. "Neither Israelites nor Canaanites! I was the first one to find this place, you know. . . . But there's no telling how soon the drift will loosen, the way folks were talking back East last winter. And now the land office for this whole section of country has been moved to Sioux Falls, too. That means business; the government, you may be certain, has good reason for doing such a thing." Tönseten spoke with all the importance of a man who has inside knowledge.

Per Hansa looked at him, and a bantering tone came into his voice:

"I see it clearly, Syvert—it would never do to keep you around here as a mere baker! We'll have to promote you to a higher office, right away. . . . Now, boys, I'm going over to see this empire that you two have set aside for me. Ola, you hitch up the oxen again and bring the wagons along."

With these commands he walked rapidly away; the others had almost to run in order to keep up with him. Strong emotions surged through him as he strode on. . . .

"It lies high," he observed after a while, when they had looked all the plowland over. . . . "There must be a fine view from the top of that hill."

They were bending their steps in this direction, and soon had reached the highest point. It seemed so spacious and beautiful to stand high above the prairie and look around, especially now, when the shades of evening were falling. . . . Suddenly Per Hansa began to step more cautiously; he sniffed the air like an animal; in a moment he stopped beside a small depression in the ground, and stood gazing at it intently for quite a while; then he said, quietly:

"There are people buried here. . . . That is a grave!"

"Oh no, Per Hansa! It can't be possible."

"No doubt about it," he said in the same subdued but positive tone.

Tönseten and Hans Olsa were so astonished that they could hardly credit the fact; they came over at once to where Per Hansa stood, and gazed down into the hollow.

Hans Olsa bent over and picked up a small stone that his eyes had lighted on; he turned it around in his hand several times. . . . "That's a queer-looking piece of stone! I almost believe people have shaped it for some use. . . . Here, see what you make of it, Syvert."

Tönseten's ruddy face grew sober and thoughtful as he examined the object.

"By thunder! It certainly looks as if the Indians had been here! . . . Now isn't that rotten luck?" . . .

"I'm afraid so," said Per Hansa, with a vigorous nod. Then he added, sharply, "But we needn't shout the fact from the house-tops, you know! . . . It takes so very little to scare some folks around here."

He waited no longer but walked hastily down the hill; at the foot he called to

Ole, telling him not to drive any farther; but first he turned to Hans Olsa to find out whether they were well across the line between the two quarters.

"No use in building farther away from you than is absolutely necessary," he said. "It's going to be lonesome for the women-folks at times." . . .

. . . Awhile later, Tönseten was dragging his way homeward. For reasons that he wouldn't admit even to himself, he walked a good deal heavier now than when he had climbed the slope that afternoon.

Per Hansa returned with his other neighbour to the wagons, where Beret and the children were waiting. Again he inquired about the line between the two quarters; then asked Beret and Hans Olsa to help pick the best building place; his words, though few and soberly spoken, had in them an unmistakable ring of determination. . . . This vast stretch of beautiful land was to be his—yes, *his*—and no ghost of a dead Indian would drive him away! . . . His heart began to expand with a mighty exaltation. An emotion he had never felt before filled him and made him walk erect. . . . "Good God" he panted. "This kingdom is going to be *mine!*"

IV

Early the next morning Per Hansa and one of the Solum boys set out on the fifty-two-mile journey to Sioux Falls, where Per Hansa filed an application for the quarter-section of land which lay to the north of Hans Olsa's. To confirm the application, he received a temporary deed to the land. The deed was made out in the name of *Peder Benjamin Hansen;* it contained a description of the land, the conditions which he agreed to fulfil in order to become the owner, and the date, *June 6, 1873.*

Sörine wanted Beret and the children to stay with her during the two days that her husband would be away; but she refused the offer with thanks. If they were to get ready a home for the summer, she said, she would have to take hold of matters right away.

. . . "For the summer?" exclaimed the other woman, showing her astonishment. "What about the winter, then?"

Beret saw that she had uttered a thought which she ought to have kept to herself; she evaded the question as best she could.

During the first day, both she and the boys found so much to do that they hardly took time to eat. They unloaded both the wagons, set up the stove, and carried out the table. Then Beret arranged their bedroom in the larger wagon. With all the things taken out it was quite roomy in there; it made a tidy bedroom when everything had been put in order. The boys thought this work great fun, and she herself found some relief in it for her troubled mind. But something vague and intangible hovering in the air would not allow her to be wholly at ease; she had to stop often and look about, or stand erect and listen. . . . Was that a sound she heard? . . . All the while, the thought that had struck her yesterday when she had first got down from the wagon, stood vividly before her mind: here there was nothing even to hide behind! . . . When the room was finished, and a blanket had been hung up to serve as a door, she seemed a little less conscious of this feeling. But back in the recesses of her mind it still was there. . . .

After they had milked the cow, eaten their evening porridge, and talked awhile to the oxen, she took the boys and And-Ongen and strolled away from camp. With a common impulse, they went toward the hill; when they had reached the summit, Beret sat down and let her gaze wander aimlessly around. . . . In a certain sense, she had to admit to herself, it was lovely up here. The broad expanse stretching away endlessly in every direction, seemed almost like the ocean—especially now, when darkness was falling. It reminded her strongly of the sea, and yet it was very different. . . . This formless prairie had no heart that beat, no waves that sang, no soul that could be touched . . . or cared. . . .

The infinitude surrounding her on every hand might not have been so oppressive, might even have brought her a measure of peace, if it had not been for the deep silence, which lay heavier here than in a church. Indeed, what was there to break it? She had passed beyond the outposts of civilization; the nearest dwelling places of men were far away. Here no warbling of birds rose on the air, no buzzing of insects sounded;[3] even the wind had died away; the waving blades of grass that trembled to the faintest breath now stood erect and quiet, as if listening, in the great hush of the evening. . . . All along the way, coming out, she had noticed this strange thing: the stillness had grown deeper, the silence more depressing, the farther west they journeyed; it must have been over two weeks now since she had heard a bird sing! Had they travelled into some nameless, abandoned region? Could no living thing exist out here, in the empty, desolate, endless wastes of green and blue? . . . How *could* existence go on, she thought, desperately? If life is to thrive and endure, it must at least have something to hide behind! . . .

The children were playing boisterously a little way off. What a terrible noise they made! But she had better let them keep on with their play, as long as they were happy. . . . She sat perfectly quiet, thinking of the long, oh, so interminably long march that they would have to make, back to the place where human beings dwelt. It would be small hardship for her, of course, sitting in the wagon; but she pitied Per Hansa and the boys—and then the poor oxen! . . . He certainly would soon find out for himself that a home for men and women and children could never be established in this wilderness. . . . And how could she bring new life into the world out here! . . .

Slowly her thoughts began to centre on her husband; they grew warm and tender as they dwelt on him. She trembled as they came. . . .

But only for a brief while. As her eyes darted nervously here and there, flitting from object to object and trying to pierce the purple dimness that was steadily closing in, a sense of desolation so profound settled upon her that she seemed unable to think at all. It would not do to gaze any longer at the terror out there, where everything was turning to grim and awful darkness. . . . She threw herself back in the grass and looked up into the heavens. But darkness and infinitude lay there, also—the sense of utter desolation still remained. . . . Suddenly, for the first time, she realized the full extent of her loneliness, the dreadful nature of the fate that had overtaken her. Lying there on her back, and staring up into the quiet sky across which the shadows of night were imperceptibly creeping, she went over in her mind every step of their wanderings, every mile of the distance they had travelled since they had left home. . . .

First they had boarded the boat at Sandnessjöen. . . . This boat had carried them southward along the coast. . . . In Namsos there had been a large ship with many white sails, that had taken her, with her dear ones, and sailed away—that had carried them off relentlessly, farther and farther from the land they knew. In this ship they had sailed for weeks; the weeks had even grown into months; they had seemed to be crossing an ocean which had no end. . . . There had been something almost laughable in this blind course, steadily fixed on the sunset! When head winds came, they beat up against them; before sweeping fair breezes they scudded along; but always they were westering! . . .

. . . At last they had landed in Quebec. There she had walked about the streets, confused and bewildered by a jargon of unintelligible sounds that did not seem like the speech of people. . . . Was this the Promised Land? Ah no—it was only the beginning of the real journey. . . . Then something within her had risen up in revolt: I will go no farther! . . .

. . . But they had kept on, just the same—had pushed steadily westward, over plains, through deserts, into towns, and out of them again. . . . One fine day they had stood in Detroit, Michigan. This wasn't the place, either, it seemed. . . . Move on! . . . Once more she had felt the spirit of revolt rising to shout aloud: I will go no farther! . . . But it had been as if a resistless flood had torn them loose from their foundations and was carrying them helplessly along on its current—flinging them here and there, hurling them madly onward, with no known destination ahead.

Farther and farther onward . . . always west. . . . For a brief while there had been a chance to relax once more; they had travelled on water again, and she could hear the familiar splash of waves against the ship's side. This language she knew of old, and did not fear; it had lessened the torture of that section of the journey for her, though they had been subjected to much ill-treatment and there had been a great deal of bullying and brawling on board.

At last the day had arrived when they had landed in Milwaukee. But here they were only to make a new start—to take another plunge into the unknown. . . . Farther, and always farther. . . . The relentless current kept whirling them along. . . . Was it bound nowhere, then? . . . Did it have no end? . . .

In the course of time they had come jogging into a place called Prairie du Chien. . . . Had that been in Wisconsin, or some other place named after savages? . . . It made no difference—they had gone on. They had floundered along to Lansing, in Iowa. . . . Onward again. Finally they had reached Fillmore County, in Minnesota. . . . But even that wasn't the place, it seemed! . . .

. . . Now she was lying here on a little green hillock, surrounded by the open, endless prairie, far off in a spot from which no road led back! . . . It seemed to her that she had lived many lives already, in each one of which she had done nothing but wander and wander, always straying farther away from the home that was dear to her.

She sat up at last, heaved a deep sigh, and glanced around as if waking from a dream. . . . The unusual blending of the gentle and forceful in her features seemed to be thrown into relief by the scene in which she sat and the twilight hovering about her, as a beautiful picture is enhanced by a well-chosen frame.

The two boys and their little sister were having great fun up here. So many queer things were concealed under the tufts of grass. Store-Hans came running, and brought a handful of little flat, reddish chips of stone that looked as though they had been carved out of the solid rock; they were pointed at one end and broadened out evenly on both sides, like the head of a spear. The edges were quite sharp; in the broad end a deep groove had been filed. Ole brought more of them, and gave a couple to his little sister to play with. . . . The mother sat for a while with the stones in her lap, where the children had placed them; at last she took them up, one by one, and examined them closely. . . . These must have been formed by human hands, she thought.

Suddenly Ole made another rare discovery. He brought her a larger stone, that looked like a sledge hammer; in this the groove was deep and broad.

The mother got up hastily.

"Where are you finding these things?"

The boys at once took her to the place; in a moment she, too, was standing beside the little hollow at the brow of the hill, which the men had discovered the night before; the queer stones that the children had been bringing her lay scattered all around.

"Ola says that the Indians made them!" cried Store-Hans, excitedly. "Is it true, mother? . . . Do you suppose they'll ever come back?"

"Yes, maybe—if we stay here long enough. . . ." She remained standing awhile beside the hollow; the same thought possessed her that had seized hold of her husband where he had first found the spot—here a human being lay buried. Strangely enough, it did not frighten her; it only showed her more plainly, in a stronger, harsher light, how unspeakably lonesome this place was.

The evening dusk had now almost deepened into night. It seemed to gather all its strength around her, to close in on every side, to have its centre in the spot where she stood. The wagons had become only a dim speck in the darkness, far, far away; the tent at Hans Olsa's looked like a tuft of grass that had whitened at the top; Tönseten's sod house she was unable to make out at all. . . . She could not bring herself to call aloud to the boys; instead, she walked around the hollow, spoke to them softly, and said that it was time to go home. . . . No, no, they mustn't take the stones with them to-night! But to-morrow they might come up here again to play.

. . . Beret could not go to sleep for a long time that night. At last she grew thoroughly angry with herself; her nerves were taut as bowstrings; her head kept rising up from the pillow to listen—but there was nothing to hear . . . nothing except the night wind, which now had begun to stir.

. . . It stirred with so many unknown things! . . .

V

Per Hansa came home late the following afternoon; he had so many words of praise for what she and the boys had accomplished while he had been gone, that he fairly bewildered her. Now it had taken possession of him again—that indomitable, conquering mood which seemed to give him the right of way wherever he went, whatever he did. Outwardly, at such times, he showed only a buoyant recklessness, as if wrapped in a cloak of gay, wanton levity; but down beneath all this lay a stern determination of purpose, a driving force, so strong that she shrank back from the least contact with it.

To-day he was talking in a steady stream.

"Here is the deed to our kingdom, Beret-girl! See to it that you take good care of the papers. . . . Isn't it stranger than a fairy tale, that a man can have such things here, just for the taking? . . . Yes—and years after he won the princess, too!" He cocked his head on one side. "I'll tell you what, it seems so impossible and unheard of, that I can't quite swallow it all yet. . . . What do you say, my Beret-girl?"

Beret stood smiling at him, with tears in her eyes, beside the improvised house that she had made; there was little for her to say. And what would be the use of speaking now? He was so completely wrapped up in his own plans that he would not listen nor understand. It would be wrong, too, to trouble him with her fears and misgivings. . . . When he felt like this he was so tender to her, so cheerful, so loving and kind. . . . How well she knew Per Hansa! . . .

"What are you thinking about it all, my Beret-girl?" He flung his arm around her, whirled her off her feet, and drew her toward him.

"Oh, Per, it's only this—I'm so afraid out here!" She snuggled up against him, as if trying to hide herself. "It's all so big and open . . . so empty. . . . Oh, Per! Not another human being from here to the end of the world!"

Per Hansa laughed loud and long, so that she winced under the force and meaning of it. "There'll soon be more people, girl . . . never you fear. . . . By God! there'll soon be more people here!"

But suddenly another idea took hold of him. He led her over to the large chest, made her sit down, and stood in front of her with a swaggering air:

"Now let me tell you what came into my mind yesterday, after I had got the papers. I went right out and bought ten sacks of potatoes! I felt so good, Beret—and you know how we men from Nordland like potatoes!" he added with a laugh. "This is the point of it: we're not going to start right in with building a house. The others are just foolish to do it." His voice grew low and eager. "They're beginning at the wrong end, you see. For my part, I'm going over to Hans Olsa's this very night and borrow his plow—and to-morrow morning I shall start breaking my ground! Yes, sir! I tell you those potatoes have got to go into the ground at once. Do you hear me, Beret-girl? If the soil out here is half as good as it's cracked up to be, we'll have a fine crop the very first fall! . . . Then I can build later in the summer, you know, when I am able to take my time about it. . . . Just wait, my girl, just wait. It's going to be wonderful; you'll see how wonderful I can make it for you, this kingdom of ours!" He laughed until his eyes were drawn out in two narrow slits. "And no old worn-out, thin-shanked, pot-bellied king is going to come around and tell me what I have to do about it, either!"

He explained to her at great length how he intended to arrange everything and how success would crown his efforts, she sitting there silently on the chest, he standing in front of her, waving his arms; while about them descended the grandeur of the evening. But with all his strength and enthusiasm, and with all her love, he didn't succeed in winning her heart over altogether—no, not altogether. She had heard with her own ears how no bird sang out here; she had seen with her own eyes how, day after day as they journeyed, they had left the abodes of men farther and farther behind. Wasn't she sitting here now, gazing off into an endless blue-green solitude that had neither heart nor soul? . . .

"Do you know," she said, quietly, as she got up once more and leaned close against him, "I believe there is a grave over there on the hill?"

"Why, Beret! Did you find it? Have you been going around brooding over that, too? . . . Don't worry, girl. He'll bring us nothing but good luck, the fellow who lies up there."

"Perhaps. . . . But it seems so strange that some one lies buried in unconsecrated ground right at our very door. How quiet it must be there! . . . The children found so many things to play with, while we were up on the hill last night, that I let them go again to-night. Come, we had better begin to look for them. . . . It is beautiful up there." She sighed, and moved away.

They climbed the hill together, holding each other's hands. There was something in that sad resignation of hers which he was powerless against. As he walked beside her and held her hand, he felt as if he could laugh and cry in the same breath. . . . She was so dear, so dear to him. Why could he never make her understand it fully? It was a strange, baffling thing! But perhaps the reason for it lay in this: she was not built to wrestle with fortune—she was too fine-grained. . . . Oh, well—he knew one person, at any rate, who stood ready to do the fighting for her!

Per Hansa had so much to think about that night that a long time passed before he could get to sleep. Now was a good chance to make his plans, while Beret lay at his side, sleeping safe and sound; he must utilize every moment now; he didn't feel very tired, either.

There seemed to be no end to the things he needed. But thirty dollars was all the money he had in the world; and when he thought of what would have to be bought in the near future, and of everything that waited to be done, the list grew as long as the distance they had travelled. . . . First of all, house and barn; that would need doors and windows. Then food and tobacco; shoes and clothing; and implements—yes, farming implements! If he only had horses and the necessary implements, the whole quarter-section would soon blossom like a garden. . . . The horses he would have to do without, to begin with. But he ought to get at least one more cow before fall came—no dodging that fact. . . . And pigs—he absolutely had to have some pigs for winter! . . . If the potatoes turned out well, there would be plenty to feed them on. . . . Then he would buy some chickens, as soon as he could run across any folks who had chickens to sell. Things like that would only be pleasant diversions for Beret. . . . There certainly seemed to be no end to all that he needed.

. . . But now came the main hitch in his calculations: Beret was going to have a baby again. . . . Only a blessing, of course—but what a lot of their time it would take up, just now! . . . Oh, well, she would have to bear the brunt of it herself, as the woman usually did. A remarkably brave and clever wife, that she was . . . a woman of tender kindness, of deep, fine fancies—one whom you could not treat like an ordinary clod.

. . . How hard he would strive to make life pleasant for her out here! Her image dominated all the visions which now seemed to come to him of their own accord. . . . The whole farm lay there before him, broken and under cultivation, yielding its fruitful harvests; there ran many horses and cows, both young and grown. And over on the location where to-day he was about to build the sod hut should stand a large dwelling . . . a *white* house, it would be! Then it would gleam so beautifully in the sun, white all over—but the cornices should be bright green! . . .

When, long ago, Per Hansa had had his first vision of the house, it had been painted white, with green cornices; and these colours had belonged to it in his mind ever since. But the stable, the barn, and all the rest of the outhouses should be painted red, with white cornices—for that gave such a fine effect! . . . Oh yes, that Beret-girl of his should certainly have a royal mansion for herself and her little princess! . . .

VI

As Per Hansa lay there dreaming of the future it seemed to him that hidden springs of energy, hitherto unsuspected even by himself, were welling up in his heart. He felt as if his strength were inexhaustible. And so he commenced his labours with a fourteen-hour day; but soon, as the plans grew clearer, he began to realize how little could be accomplished in that short span of time, with so much work always ahead of him; he accordingly lengthened the day to sixteen hours, and threw in another hour for good measure; at last he found himself wondering if a man couldn't get along with only five hours of rest, in this fine summer weather.

His waking dreams passed unconsciously into those of sleep; all that night a pleasant buoyancy seemed to be lifting him up and carrying him along; at dawn, when he opened his eyelids, morning was there to greet him—the morning of a glorious new day. . . . He saw that it was already broad daylight; with a guilty start, he came wide awake. Heavens! he might have overslept himself—on *this* morning! . . . He jumped into his clothes, and found some cold porridge to quiet his hunger for the time being; then he hurried out, put the yoke on the oxen, and went across to Hans Olsa's to fetch the plow. . . . Over there no life was stirring yet. Well, maybe they could afford to sleep late in the morning; but he had arrived five days behind the others, and had just been delayed for two days more; they had a big start over him already. His heart sang as he thought how he would have to hurry! . . . He led the oxen carefully, trying to make as little noise around the tent as possible.

Dragging the plow, he drove out for some distance toward the hillock, then stopped and looked around. This was as good a place as anywhere to start breaking. . . . He straightened up the plow, planted the share firmly in the ground, and spoke to the oxen: "Come now, move along, you lazy rascals!" He had meant to speak gruffly, but the thrill of joy that surged over him as he sank the plow in his own land for the first time, threw such an unexpected tone of gentleness into his voice that the oxen paid no attention to it; he found that he would have to resort to more powerful encouragement; but even with the goad it was hard to make them bend to the yoke so early in the morning. After a little, however, they began to stretch their muscles. Then they were off; the plow moved . . . sank deeper . . . the first furrow was breaking. . . .

It would have gone much easier now if Ole had only been there to drive the oxen, so that he could have given his whole attention to the plow. But never mind that! . . . The boy ought to sleep for at least another hour; the day would be plenty long enough for him, before it was through. . . . Young bulls have tender sinews— though for one of his age, Ole was an exceptionally able youngster.

That first furrow turned out very crooked for Per Hansa; he made a long one of it, too. When he thought he had gone far enough and halted the oxen, the furrow came winding up behind him like a snake. He turned around, drove the oxen back in the opposite direction, and laid another furrow up against the one he had already struck. . . . At the starting point again, he surveyed his work ruefully. Well, the second furrow wasn't any *crookeder* than the first, at all events! . . . When he had made another round he let the oxen stand awhile; taking the spade which he had brought out, he began to cut the sod on one side of the breaking into strips that could be handled. This was to be his building material. . . . Field for planting on the one hand, sods for a house on the other—that was the way to plow! . . . Leave it to Per Hansa—he was the fellow to have everything figured out beforehand!

By breakfast time he had made a fine start. No sooner had he swallowed the last morsel than he ordered both the boys to turn to, hitched the oxen to the old homemade wagon, and off they all went together toward the field, Per Hansa leading the way. . . . "You'd better cook the kettles full to-day!" he shouted back, as they were leaving. "We're going to punish a lot of food when we come in!"

Now Per Hansa began working in real earnest. He and Store-Hans, with plow and oxen, broke up the land; Ole used the hoe, but the poor fellow was having a hard time of it. The sod, which had been slumbering there undisturbed for countless ages, was tough of fibre and would not give up its hold on the earth without a struggle. It almost had to be turned by main strength, piece by piece; it was a dark brownish colour on the under side—a rich, black mould that gave promise of wonderful fertility; it actually gleamed and glistened under the rays of the morning sun, where the plow had carved and polished its upturned face. . . . Ole toiled on, settling and straightening the furrows as best he could, now and then cutting out the clods that fell unevenly. When Per Hansa had made a couple of rounds, he let the oxen stand awhile to catch their breath, and came over to Ole to instruct him. "This is the way to do it!" he said, seizing the hoe. "Watch me, now—*like this!*" He hewed away till the clods were flying around him. . . . When they quit work at noon a good many furrows lay stretched out on the slope, smiling up at the sun; they were also able to bring home with them a full wagonload of building material; at coffee time they brought another; at supper another. But when, arriving home at the end of the day, they found that supper was not quite ready, Per Hansa felt that he must go after still another load; they had better make use of every minute of time!

VII

He began building the house that same evening.

"You ought to rest, Per Hansa!" Beret pleaded. "Please use a little common sense!"

"Rest—of course! That's just what I propose to do! . . . Come along, now, all hands of you; you can't imagine what fun this is going to be. . . . Just think of it—a new house on our own estate! I don't mean that you've got to work, you know; but come along and watch the royal mansion rise!"

They all joined in, nevertheless . . . couldn't have kept their hands off. It gave them such keen enjoyment that they worked away until they could no longer see to place the strips of sod. Then Per Hansa called a halt—that was enough for one day. They had laboured hard and faithfully; well, they would get their wages in due time, every last one of them—but he couldn't bother with such trifles just now!

. . . That night sleep overpowered him at once; he was too tired even to dream.

From now on Per Hansa worked on the house every morning before breakfast, and every evening as soon as he had finished supper. The whole family joined in the task when they had nothing else to do; it seemed like a fascinating game.

To the eyes of Tönseten and Hans Olsa, it appeared as if nothing short of witchcraft must be at work on Per Hansa's quarter section; in spite of the fact that he and his entire family were breaking ground in the fields the whole day long, a great sod house shot up beside the wagon, like an enormous mushroom.

Per Hansa plowed and harrowed, delved and dug; he built away at the house, and he planted the potatoes; he had such a zest for everything and thought it all such fun that he could hardly bear to waste a moment in stupid sleep. It was Beret who finally put a check on him. One morning, as he threw off the blanket at dawn, on the point of jumping up in his wreckless way, she lay there awake, waiting for him. The moment he stirred, she put her arms lovingly around him and told him that he must stay in bed awhile longer. This would never do, she said; he ought to remember that he was only a human being. . . . She begged him so gently and soothingly that he gave in at last and stayed in bed with her. But he was ill at ease over the loss of time. It wouldn't take long to lay a round of sod, and every round helped. . . . This Beret-girl of his meant well enough, but she didn't realize the multitude of things that weighed on his mind—things that couldn't wait, that had to be attended to immediately!

. . . Yes, she was an exceptional woman, this Beret of his; he didn't believe that her like existed anywhere else under the sun. During the last two days she had hurried through her housework, and then, taking And-Ongen by the hand, had come out in the field with them; she had let the child roam around and play in the grass while she herself had joined in their labour; she had pitched in beside them and taken her full term like any man. It had all been done to make things easier for him . . . and now she was lying awake here, just to look after him!

. . . He thought of other things that she had done. When they had harrowed and hoed sufficient seed ground, Beret had looked over her bundles and produced all kinds of seed—he couldn't imagine how or where she had got them—turnips, and carrots, and onions, and tomatoes, and melons, even! . . . What a wife she was! . . . Well, he had better stay in bed and please her this time, when she had been so clever and thoughtful about everything.

However it was accomplished, on Per Hansa's estate they had a field all broken and harrowed and seeded down, and a large house ready for thatching, by the time that Hans Olsa and the Solum boys had barely finished thatching their houses and started the plowing. Tönseten, though, was ahead of him with the breaking—Per Hansa had to accept that—and was now busy planting his potatoes. But Syvert had every reason to be in the lead; his house had been all ready to move into when they had arrived. That little stable which he had built wasn't more than a decent day's work for an able man. And he had horses, too. . . . Of course, such things gave him a big advantage!

They finished planting the big field at Per Hansa's late one afternoon; all the potatoes that he had brought home from Sioux Falls had been cut in small pieces and tucked away in the ground. . . . "Only one eye to each piece!" he had warned

Beret as she sat beside him, cutting them up. "That's enough for such rich soil." . . . The other seed, which she had provided with such splendid fore-thought, had also been planted. The field looked larger than it really was. It stood out clearly against the fresh verdure of the hillside; from a little distance it appeared as if some one had sewn a dark brown patch on a huge green cloth. . . . That patch looked mighty good to Per Hansa as he stood surveying the scene, his whole being filled with the sense of completed effort. Here he had barely arrived in a new country; yet already he had got more seed into the ground than on any previous year since Beret and he had started out for themselves. . . . Just wait! What couldn't he do another year!

"Well, Beret-girl," he said, "we've cleaned up a busy spring season, all right! To-night we ought to have an extra-fine dish of porridge, to bless what has been put into the ground." He stood there with sparkling eyes, admiring his wonderful field.

Beret was tired out with the labour she had undergone; her back ached as if it would break. She, too, was looking at the field, but the joy he felt found no response in her.

. . . I'm glad that he is happy, she thought, sadly. Perhaps in time I will learn to like it, too. . . . But she did not utter the thought; she merely took the child by the hand, turned away, and went back to their wagon-home. There she measured out half of the milk that Rosie had given that morning, dipped some grits from the bag and prepared the porridge, adding water until it was thin enough. Before she served it up she put a small dab of butter in each dish, like a tiny eye that would hardly keep open; then she sprinkled over the porridge a small portion of sugar; this was all the luxury she could afford. Indeed, her heart began to reproach her even for this extravagance. But when she saw the joyful faces of the boys, and heard Per Hansa's exclamations over her merits as a housekeeper, she brightened up a little, cast her fears to the wind, and sprinkled on more sugar from the bag. . . . Then she sat down among them, smiling and happy; she was glad that she hadn't told them how her back was aching. . . .

. . . They all worked at the house building that night as long as they could see.

VIII

Per Hansa's house certainly looked as if it were intended for a royal mansion. When Tönseten saw it close at hand for the first time he exclaimed:

"Will you please inform me, Per Hansa, what the devil you think you're build-ing? Is it just a house, or is it a church and parsonage rolled in one? . . . Have you lost your senses altogether, man? You won't be able to get a roof over this crazy thing in a month of Sundays! . . . Why, damn it all, there aren't willows enough in this whole region to thatch a half of it! You might just as well tear it down again, for all the good it will do."

"The hell you say!" cried Per Hansa, genially. "But there it stands, as big as

Billy-be-damned, so what are you going to do about it? . . . The notion I had was this: I might as well build for my sons, too, while I was about it. Then when they got married and needed more room they could thatch a new section any time. . . . What ails you, Syvert? Isn't there plenty of sod for roofing, all the way from here to the Pacific coast?"

But Tönseten took a serious view of the affair:

"I tell you, Per Hansa, there's no sense in such a performance. It isn't the sod, it's the poles—you know it damned well! . . . You'd better go right ahead and tear it down as fast as ever you can!"

"Oh, well, I suppose I'll have to, then," said Per Hansa, dryly.

As a matter of fact, it was hardly to be wondered at that Tönseten grew excited when he saw this structure; it differed radically from the one he had built and from all the others that he had ever seen. He wondered if such a silly house as this could be found anywhere else in the whole country. . . . His own hut measured fourteen by sixteen feet; the one that the Solum boys were building was only fourteen feet each way; Hans Olsa had been reckless and had laid his out eighteen feet long and sixteen feet wide. . . . But look at this house of Per Hansa's—*twenty-eight* feet long and *eighteen* feet wide! Moreover, it had *two* rooms, one of them eighteen by eighteen, the other eighteen by ten. The rooms were separated by a wall; one had a door opening toward the south, the other a door opening toward the east. Two doors in a sod hut! My God! what folly! In the smaller room the sod even had been taken up, so that the floor level there was a foot below that of the larger room. What was the sense of that? . . . If we don't look out, thought Tönseten, this crazy man will start building a tower on it, too!

Things surely looked serious to Tönseten. In the first place, Per Hansa plainly was getting big-headed; heavens and earth, it was nothing but an ordinary sod hut that he was building! In the second place, it wasn't a practical scheme. If he were to search till doomsday, he wouldn't be able to find enough willows for the thatching. Why, he might just as well thatch the whole firmament, and be done with it! . . . As soon as he had looked his fill, Tönseten trotted right over to Hans Olsa's, told him all about it, and asked him to go and reason with the man. . . . But, no, Hans Olsa didn't care to meddle in that affair. Per Hansa had a considerable family already; it might grow in the next few years; at any rate, he needed a fairly large house. Above all, he wasn't the man to bite off more than he could chew.

"But that's just it—he doesn't know what he's bitten off! He doesn't know anything at all about building a house!" With these drastic words, Tönseten went directly to the Solum boys; they had been born and brought up in America, and knew what was what. Now they must go, right away, and talk to Per Hansa about this crazy building that he was putting up! The only way out of it that he could think of was for them and himself—and maybe Hans Olsa—to go in a body and show him what to do, and help him to build a house then and there. The thing that he had put up was frankly impossible; the poor man would ruin himself before he got a decent start! . . .

To his great disappointment, the Solum boys wouldn't go, either. It was Per Hansa's own business, they said, what sort of a house he wanted to build for himself. So Tönseten had to give it up as a bad job. He shook his head solemnly. . . . A damned shame, that a perfectly good man had to go to ruin through sheer folly!

Per Hansa had put a great deal of thought into this matter of building a house; ever since he had first seen a sod hut he had pondered the problem. On the day that he was coming home from Sioux Falls a brilliant idea had struck him—an idea which had seemed perhaps a little queer, but which had grown more attractive the longer he turned it over in his mind. How would it do to build house and barn under one roof? It was to be only a temporary shelter, anyway—just a sort of makeshift, until he could begin on his real mansion. This plan would save time and labour, and both the house and the barn would be warmer for being together. . . . He had a vague recollection of having heard how people in the olden days used to build their houses in that way—rich people, even! It might not be fashionable any longer; but it was far from foolish, just the same.

It will go hard with Beret, he thought; she won't like it. But after a while he picked up courage to mention his plan to her.

. . . House and barn under the same roof? . . . She said no more, but fell into deep and troubled thought. . . . Man and beast in one building? How could one live that way? . . . At first it seemed utterly impossible to her; but then she thought of how desolate and lonesome everything was here and of what a comfortable companion Rosie might be on dark evenings and during the long winter nights. She shuddered, and answered her husband that it made no difference to her whichever way he built, so long as it was snug and warm; but she said nothing about the real reason that had changed her mind.

This answer made Per Hansa very happy.

"Beret-girl, you are the most sensible woman that I know! . . . Of course it's better, all around, for us to build that way!"

He, too, had reasons that he kept to himself. . . . Now he would get ahead of both Hans Olsa and the Solum boys! None of them had even begun to think of building a barn yet; while according to his plan, his barn would be finished when his house was done.

IX

One evening Per Hansa came over with his oxen to Hans Olsa's to borrow his new wagon; the time had come to get his poles for the thatching. The others had been able to gather what they needed along the banks of a creek some ten miles to the southward, where a fringe of scattering willows grew; but it was small stock and a scanty supply at that; their roofs were certainly none too strong, and might not hold up through the next winter. . . . Per Hansa had a bigger and more original scheme in mind. If conditions were really as bad as Tönseten had made out, he'd have to find something besides willow poles for rafters on that house of his. The busy season of spring was over; now he proposed to rest on his oars awhile . . . take a little time to nose around the prairie at his leisure. He had been told that the Sioux River was only twenty-five or thirty miles away; big stands of timber were reported to lie in that direction, and several settlements of Trönders,[4] who had lived there for a number of years; many other interesting things would turn up, of course—things that he hadn't heard about; he wanted to see it all and get a running idea of the whole locality. He confided to Hans Olsa where he was going, but asked him not to mention it to anyone else. . . . "We might as well keep this matter to ourselves, you know. Besides, something has got to be done about getting fuel for the winter."

He brought the wagon home that evening, merely explaining that he and Store-Hans were going out to gather wood. Ole would have to look after the farm while they were away, and take the full responsibility on his shoulders. Store-Hans, who had been chosen to go on the trip, was overjoyed at the news; but his brother was reduced to the verge of tears at such an outrageous injustice. The idea of taking that *boy* along, and letting a grown man loaf around the house with nothing to do! For the first time his faith in his father's judgment was shattered. . . . And the situation grew worse and worse as Ole watched the extensive preparations for the trip; it looked for all the world as if they intended to move out West! The father was taking along a kettle, and was measuring out supplies of flour, and salt, and coffee, and milk, besides a big heap of *flatbröd* and plenty of other food. But, heaviest blow of all, the rifle—Old Maria—was brought out from the big chest! Ole wept at that in sheer anger. Ax, rope, and sacks, too—everything was going! . . . And on top of it all, this youngster who wasn't dry behind the ears yet had grown so conceited that he wouldn't deign to talk to his brother; he kept fussing and smirking around his father all the time, speaking to him in low, confidential tones, and pushing himself to the front on every occasion! He seemed to be bubbling over with foolish questions. Shouldn't they take this along, and *this,* and *this?* . . . But when at last he came dragging a piece of chain, even Per Hansa had to laugh outright. "That's the boy, now! I might have forgotten the chain. And how could we go to the woods without a chain, I'd like to know?"

Beret got the food ready for the journey. Her face wore a sad, sober expression. . . . Yes, of course, the house must have a roof; she knew that perfectly well. How could they live in a house without a roof? . . . But now he was going to be away for another two-day stretch—two whole days and a night! . . . It wasn't so bad in the daytime . . . but at night . . . !

"You'd better take the children with you and go over to Mother Sörrina's to-morrow evening," Per Hansa advised her, cheerfully. "You can spend the whole evening there, you know, visiting and talking. It'll make the time pass quicker, and you won't be so lonesome. . . . You do that, Beret!"

To this suggestion she answered neither yes nor no. In her heart she knew very well that she wouldn't follow his advice. She never could forget that evening of his trip to Sioux Falls, when she and the children had come down the hill toward the wagons; the air of the place had suddenly filled with terror and mystery. The wagons had floated like grey specks in the dusk; and all at once it had seemed as if the whole desolation of a vast continent were centring there and drawing a magic circle about their home. She had even seen the intangible barrier with her own eyes . . . had seen it clearly . . . had had to force herself to step across it. . . . Now she went on getting the food ready for them as well as she could; but from her sad lips there came not a word.

This was destined to be a memorable journey, both for those who went and for those who stayed at home. . . . Before it was over the latter were in a panic of apprehension and fear. The second day passed as the first had done; the second night, too; the third day came . . . noon, but no one in sight.

Beret had not really begun to expect them until sometime during the second day; Per Hansa had told her not to begin looking before they came in sight. Nevertheless, she had found herself unconsciously doing it shortly after dinner on the very first day. She knew that it was foolish—they hadn't even got there yet; but she couldn't refrain from scanning the sky line in the quarter where they had disappeared. . . . She went to bed with the children early that evening.

The following evening she took them up the hill; they sat there silently, gazing eastward over the plain. From this elevation her sight seemed to take flight and carry a long, long distance. . . . In the eastern sky the evening haze was gathering; it merged slowly into the purple dusk, out of which an intangible, mysterious presence seemed to be creeping closer and closer upon them. They sat trying to pierce it with their gaze; but neither wagon nor oxen crossed the line of their vision. . . . Ole took no interest in keeping watch; it was more fun for him to look for queer stones around the grave. . . . When the day was well-nigh dead and nothing had appeared, Beret suddenly felt that she must talk to some one to-night . . . hear some human voice other than those of the two children. Almost in spite of herself, she directed her steps toward Hans Olsa's.

—Hadn't Per Hansa returned yet?

—No. She couldn't imagine what had become of him! He surely ought to have been home by this time.

—Oh, well, she mustn't worry; he had probably travelled a long way on this trip; no doubt he had made use of the opportunity to look around for winter fuel.

—Winter fuel? . . . She had never given a thought to that before; but of course they would need wood if they were going to stay through the winter. It suddenly occurred to her how much there was for Per Hansa to plan about and worry over; but she also felt a twinge of jealousy because he had not confided in her. . . . Winter fuel? Of course; it was the thing they needed most of all!

Mother Sörine was well aware that her neighbour did not have any courage to spare. She realized, too, how lonesome it must be for Beret, to sleep over there in the wagon with only the children. As the visitors were leaving she got up, called her daughter, and insisted on accompanying them back to the wagon. They chatted gaily and freely all the way . . . and that night there was no magic circle to step across!

Some time after noon on the third day Per Hansa and Store-Hans came home with a load so big that the oxen were just barely able to sag up the slope with it. It was like an incident out of a fairy tale, that famous load. There was a stout timber for the ridgepole, there were crossbeams and scantlings, and rafters for the roof; but Ole only sneered at such prosaic things. Was *that* all they had gone for, he'd like to know? Farther down in the load, however, lay six bundles of young trees; their tops had been trimmed off, and the soil had been carefully wrapped around their roots with strips of bark. . . . "Those are to be planted around the house!" Store-Hans explained. "Would you believe it, Mother—in this bundle there are twelve plum trees! They grow great big plums! We met a man who told us all about them." Store-Hans caught his breath from sheer excitement. . . . There were still stranger things in that load. In the back of the wagon, as the father unloaded, an opening almost like a small room was gradually revealed. Here lay two great bags— two bags brimful of curious articles. One of them evidently contained fish; the other seemed to hold the flayed carcass of a calf; at least, Ole thought so, and wanted to know where it had come from.

"*Calf!*" exclaimed Store-Hans. "What makes you think it's a calf?" . . .

Per Hansa winked slyly at his travelling companion; the wink warned him that he'd better say no more—for a little while! . . . Store-Hans assumed a knowing silence; but it could be seen with half an eye that he was bursting with important secrets. At last he was no longer able to contain himself.

. . . "*Antelope!*" he burst out, ecstatically.

Beret watched with speechless admiration the unloading of all the wonderful things that they had brought; she was so overjoyed to have her dear ones with her again that she could have burst into hysterical tears; as she stood beside the oxen she stroked their necks fondly, murmuring in a low voice that they were nice fellows to have hauled home such a heavy load.

. . . "Well, there!" said Per Hansa at last, when he had cleared the wagon. "Now, this is the idea: Store-Hans and I have figured on having fresh fish to-day, cooked in regular Nordland fashion, with soup and everything. We nearly killed ourselves, and the beasts, too, to get here in time. . . . Beret, what the devil what we got to put all this meat and fish into?"

Store-Hans ate that day as if he could never get enough; there seemed to be no bottom to the boy. . . . When he had finished the father chased him off to bed at once; and strange to say, he wasn't at all unwilling though it was only the latter part of the afternoon. When evening came the mother tried to shake life into him again, but without success; once he roused enough to sit up in bed, but couldn't get so far as to take off his clothes; the next moment he had thrown himself flat once more and was sleeping like a log.

As time went on this first expedition of Per Hansa's came to be of great conse-quence to the new settlement on Spring Creek. . . . In the first place, there were all the trees that he had brought home and planted. This alone excited Tönseten's enthusiasm to such a pitch that he was for leaving at once to get a supply of his own; but Hans Olsa and the Solum boys advised him to wait until the coming fall, so Tönseten reluctantly had to give up still another plan.

. . . But there were other things to do when fall came, and several years went by before the others had followed Per Hansa's lead. This is the reason why, in the course of time, a stout grove of trees began to grow up around Per Hansa's house before anything larger than a bush was to be seen elsewhere in the whole neighbourhood.

But the most important result of all, perhaps, was the acquaintance with the Trönders eastward on the Sioux River, which sprang out of this journey. Amid these strange surroundings, confronted by new problems, the two tribes, Trönder and Helgelander, met in a quite different relationship than on the Lofoten fishing grounds. Here they were glad enough to join forces in their common fight against the unknown wilderness. . . .

. . . The Great Plain watched them breathlessly. . . .

Notes

1. The name properly is Sörine, with the accent on the second syllable; but in the dialect of Helgeland it is pronounced Sörrina, with the accent on the first. These people all came from the district of Helgeland, in Norway.

2. This bottle and glass would have been old family pieces from Norway, the bottle shaped something like an hourglass, with a contraction in the middle to be grasped by the hand.

3. Original settlers are agreed that there was neither bird nor insect life on the prairie, with the exception of mosquitoes, the first year that they came.

4. People from the district of Trondhjem, Norway.

Further Reading

The Boat of Longing. 1933.
Pure Gold. 1930.
When the Wind Is in the South and Other Stories. Selected and translated by Solveig T. Zempel. 1985.

Reading about O. E. Rølvaag

Haugen, Einer. *Ole Edvart Rølvaag.* Boston: Twayne, 1983.
Moseley, Ann. *Ole Edvart Rølvaag.* Western Writers Series. Boise ID: Boise State University, 1987.
Reigstad, Paul M. *Rølvaag: His Life and Art.* Lincoln: University of Nebraska Press, 1972.
Simonson, Harold P. *Prairies Within: The Tragic Trilogy of Ole Rølvaag.* Seattle: University of Washington Press, 1987.

John Ise *(1885–1969)*

In 1873 Henry Ise took his seventeen-year-old bride Rosie from her home in northeast Kansas to his homestead on the western Kansas plains. *Sod and Stubble* is a catalog of the failures and successes that thousands of average farm families like the Ises experienced in the first years of settlement. The author, John Ise, was uniquely qualified to write such a document. The seventh of the Ise children, he was a professor of economics at the University of Kansas. He began interviewing his mother, Rosie, about her life on the farm, planning to write a formal treatise on the economics of farming. Instead he found himself engrossed in his mother's stories, so he abandoned his scholarly manuscript to write instead a more personal memoir.* His attempts to find a publisher met with little success and he finally underwrote the publication himself.† When that publisher went out of business Ise found himself with the remaining unsold books. He gave them away to libraries and anyone else interested in his family's story.‡ Ironically, when the University of Nebraska Press published *Sod and Stubble* as a paperback in 1967, the story found an audience, and it has been in print ever since. Von Rothenberger's 1996 annotated edition includes chapters that Ise omitted in the 1939 edition and gives the reader much useful background information, including the identities of most of the characters in Ise's story.§

This selection recounts the arrival of the newlyweds on their homestead. They will live on their homestead for thirty-six years, lose one baby, have twelve children who grow to adulthood, and gradually build a successful farm. Rosie, who had only four days of formal schooling, with her husband's support encourages their children to get good educations. Nine of their children go on to college. At the end of the story, after Henry's death, Rosie moves to Lawrence to be near some of her children.

---

*John Ise, *Sod and Stubble: The Unabridged and Annotated Edition,* 2d ed., ed. Von Rothenberger (Lawrence: University Press of Kansas, 1996), 368.

†Ise, *Sod and Stubble,* 319.

‡Ise, *Sod and Stubble,* 370.

§The Ise farmhouse and the corner school are still (barely) standing, just east of Downs, Kansas. The home has been unoccupied for several years.

A New Homestead (1936)

At a spoken "Whoa!" the horses stopped. Rosie wrapped the lines around the bow of the wagon, stepped down onto the wheel, and gathering her skirts in her hand, leaped to the ground.

"Henry, come on now!" she called out, starting back to meet him. "I'll drive the cows a while again."

"You go on ahead," he replied, flourishing his switch at the laggards in his herd. "It's only a few miles yet."

She walked back to him and took the switch from his hand. "I'll drive'em," she said, smiling, but in a tone of finality.

A puzzled expression crossed Henry's face, then, apparently sensing the futility of argument, he climbed up into the wagon and untied the lines.

"Giddap Frank! Giddap Sam!" The horses started on, the tired cows and the young woman following.

With the new driver, the wagon moved more slowly, jogging sleepily along the ruts that served as a road; but the cows no longer lagged far behind, for Rosie indulged in no reveries. With resolute determination in every step, she not only kept the cows close behind the wagon, but found time to gather bouquets of the breadroot, prairie roses, larkspurs and daisies that grew along the roadside.

At the crest of a little knoll overlooking a level valley, Henry called out "Whoa!" and pointed out a little log cabin a half mile ahead.

"There it is!" That's my cabin—our cabin—and our claim. The corner is right there by the creek crossing; and it runs half a mile south, and half a mile west—not a creek on it, nor a hill, nor a rock! Doesn't it look like good land?" He turned to Rosie with unwonted enthusiasm, then looked down at the little cabin.

Rosie caught something of his enthusiasm, but said nothing. She sat gazing at the picture that lay before her, shimmering in the brightness of the noonday sun: the broad, green valley with its bordering grass-covered hills on the south and north, directly across the valley, a few miles distant, a high, flat-topped hill that rose above the rest, with a steep, conical mound on either side—three sentinels guarding the landscape; the river tracing its winding course with a fringe of cottonwoods—the only trees to be seen anywhere, except a few scattered willows and cottonwoods growing along the creek or draw that ran by the nearest corner of Henry's claim. A number of sod dugouts and log cabins were scattered here and there, most of them along the river and creek, the dugouts scarcely visible above the level of the ground, the cabins standing out stark and lonely, each dwelling with its sod stable, perhaps with a team of horses and one or two cows picketed out in the yard, and with a small patch of broken ground near, green with wheat that was already heading out, or newly planted to sod corn. The rain of the night before had brought fresh green life to the buffalo grass; and here and there, prairie flowers waved their faces in the wind. Over all was the sky, washed clean by the rain, wider and higher and bluer than any sky but that of the prairie, an intensely and vividly blue background for the scattered white clouds that drifted across the heavens, casting shadows that sped swiftly along the grass.

As Rosie looked at the happy scene, tears came to her eyes; but whether they were tears of happiness or of fear and foreboding, she never could have told. She only said, "I hope it will be a good home for us. It surely looks like good land."

"It *is* good land—all of it," he replied. "I plowed a furrow all around it, and never turned up anything but black soil. In two years I can get my patent—three years off, you know, for my war service. Then we can feel independent and can improve it better. I need a granary, and a corn crib—you see I haven't any granary or cribs at all—and a better stable, and some fences; and perhaps we can have a better house some day. It won't take long, if we have good luck."

"Oh yes, or maybe we can buy one of those claims next to us. It would be fine to have two quarters—bottom land like that."

"Maybe—if we want to. But let's not be too ambitious. We can live well enough on one good quarter." Looking at the cabin, they saw a man step out into the yard and gaze intently in their direction for a moment, then rush back, grab something from the door step—apparently the broom—and disappear in the door again.

"I know what's the matter," exclaimed Henry, laughing. "That's Frank Hagel. He's a bachelor—been taking care of my cabin; and I'll bet he hasn't swept out since I left—just thought of it when he saw us." He turned in his seat and leaped to the ground.

"Giddap there! Sam! Frank! Only half a mile yet!" He started back, and rounded up the cows while Rosie drove the horses on ahead.

The cavalcade soon reached the Dry Creek crossing, but here Rosie was brought face to face with that dark danger of all pioneer countries—high water. The creek was bank-full from the rain of the night before, apparently impassable to any wagon loaded with flour and cornmeal, or indeed to any wagon at all. They had travelled two hundred miles, and here, a quarter of a mile from their destination, they were for the first time stalled by flood waters. Dry Creek was not an imposing stream ordinarily, a mere gash across the face of the prairie, with a tiny stream trickling along its shallow bed; but today it was a raging torrent.

Rosie gazed longingly across at the cabin, then she looked at the muddy waters hurrying past with their burden of driftwood and broken sunflower stalks. Something in the dark, whirling eddies frightened her, and she would gladly have camped by the bank of the stream until the waters subsided; but she felt ashamed to express such fears. The horses stopped, obviously loth to enter the water.

Henry sat for a moment, looking in perplexity at the stream ahead, then at the contents of the wagon. Finally he jumped down from his seat, and began taking the cover off the bows. This he wrapped carefully around the wagon box and tied it firmly. He then drove the cows into the water. They waded and swam across safely.

"I believe we can make it!" he said, as he climbed to his seat again and drove rapidly into the whirling current. The water rose to the wagon box and boiled up along the sides. The wagon sank deeper—and then started to float—yes, it was floating down stream! The horses reared and plunged, but they were so nearly afloat themselves that they could get little traction on the load. Henry cracked the lines and shouted. For an instant he turned to Rosie with a look that made her grip the wagon bow tighter. He pulled out his knife and opened the blade.

"I'll cut the tugs." He stood up on the buckboard, ready to plunge into the water, when the wagon suddenly struck bottom, the horses got their footing, and with a mighty splashing pulled the wagon up the steep bank and out. It had all happened in less than a minute.

"Oh Henry, our flour!" cried Rosie, when they were safely on the bank.

"Yes, our flour, and our sorghum, and our wagon, and our horses, and our precious selves!" he replied. "I am glad enough to be out of there. I could have got you out, but I was afraid my horses were gone. It's washed since I was through there the last time."

He jumped down from his seat and pulled off the dripping wagon cover, while Rosie scratched the straw off the sacks of flour and cornmeal and examined their contents. She was vastly surprised and relieved to find that only a little water had seeped into the wagon box, and that their supplies were but slightly injured.

The team, still wet from their plunge in the water, soon stood before the little cabin. Henry vaulted over the wheel and helped Rosie down. "Home at last! Here Frank, this is my wife!"

"And Rosie, this is Frank Hagel . . . lives on the claim over west, and is keeping house for me. What have you got for dinner, Frank! We're hungry as coyotes . . . drove all the way from Glen Elder this morning."

While greetings were being spoken, Rosie's eye took in the premises: cabin of hewed logs, with sod roof, apparently twelve or fifteen by eighteen—almost spacious compared with the dugouts she had seen along the way that morning—with a home-made door and three small windows; a straw stable, made of wheat straw thrown over a frame of logs and saplings; a sod chicken house; a well, with a wheel and two buckets on a rope, and a small cow lot fenced in near the stable—about the only fence she had seen in the morning's drive. The well, only a few steps from the house, was a luxury that Rosie noted with joy, for at her old home she had always had to carry the water up from the creek, a distance of a quarter of a mile. There was a corn field of a few acres south of the cow lot; and a patch of wheat and one of oats lay west of it. The corn was up, and the wheat and oats, lush and green, were beginning to head. It must be good land, to grow such crops, was Rosie's silent observation; and that was the important thing. On good land one could surely build a good home. It would be her own home too, her very own, and Henry's, she thought to herself, with solid, possessive satisfaction, as she looked around at the smooth level land and the promising crops.

Entering the one-room cabin, she could hardly feel so cheerful. On the table was a pack of cards, which she promptly threw in the stove. Henry's cabin had been the rendezvous of several bachelors living near, and they had been playing cards to pass the time—not a Christian form of amusement, Rosie thought. Frank Hagel was obviously no housekeeper; but dirt and disorder were only a challenge to Rosie, a challenge that she accepted as a confident trooper accepts the gage of battle. The cabin had a floor, as Henry had promised—she did not yet realize what a luxury this was—and was chinked between the logs with a kind of clay mortar. There was no ceiling, but there were wide cottonwood boards underneath the sod roof.

Of furniture there was little enough, and that of the most primitive construction; but Rosie appraised it all without consternation: a bedstead made of cottonwood boards, without springs, with a bed tick filled with straw, a table made also of warped cottonwood boards, and a tiny cook stove. Two empty nail kegs and two boxes served as chairs, and on another nail keg by the door there was a washpan, half full of soapy water. A hammer and a saw hung from nails driven in one of the logs, a coffee grinder was screwed onto the log just below, and a few other household utensils were scattered about the room: a broom leaning against the wall, a boiler and washboard behind the stove, and on the shelf near the stove, a kettle, two bread pans, a few iron knives and forks and tin spoons. There was no bureau, no cupboard, no clock, no rug, no tablecloth; there were no curtains nor blinds on the windows, no sheets on the bed, no pictures on the walls. Rather bare and primitive, the little cabin seemed.

"It's better though, than we had at Holton, at first," thought Rosie, as she looked around; "and I'll soon have it looking different." A dozen plans were soon shaping in her mind for building shelves for the cooking utensils and flower pots that she hoped to get.

While Frank Hagel took charge of the horses and cows, Henry brought in a bucket of cold water from the well for Rosie to wash and comb her long, black hair. Henry then proceeded to carry in the flour and cornmeal, the churn-ful of molasses, and the varied contents of the scuttle box and wagon.

After dinner, Rosie set to work, and before nightfall a new home was there: table scoured and floor scrubbed—not with a mop, for there was no mop in the cabin, or in the country, but with a scrap of grain sack found in the stable; a shelf was up, and on it were several tin cans of flowers, transplanted from the feed box. The sacks of flour and cornmeal were set in a neat row behind the bed, and the kitchen utensils were washed and scoured and deftly arranged on one end of the shelf. The churn, with its delectable saccharine contents, and the lard and butter were stored away in the small cellar under the house. Outside, two precious sheets and pillow slips, and a few articles of clothing, were spread out on the grass to dry. When Henry came in from the field that evening, he marveled at the transformation; and when he sat down to supper at the clean little table, he had no doubt that it was going to be a good home. After supper, he made a potato masher and a rolling pin out of two sticks of wood, while Rosie set out the rose bushes and asparagus they had brought along.

The next morning Henry took Rosie with him on a ride around the claim, to show her the boundaries and let her see for herself how fine and black the soil was. When they got back, he helped her plant a garden of peas, turnips, lettuce, and cucumbers in the sod at the end of the little cornfield. Henry had a few chickens, and several hens were given settings of eggs in the chicken coop.

Further Reading

Ruede, Howard. *Sod-House Days: Letters from a Kansas Homesteader, 1877–78*. Ed. John Ise. New York: Columbia University Press, 1937.

William Stafford

Jonathan Holden points out the distances in space and time in this poem that separate the poet from his childhood place, a farm in the Great Plains.★ Holden reads this separation as negative, "a grimmer sense of 'home' he has learned to accept as an adult." But in his own brief comment on this poem, William Stafford expresses a more benign view. He acknowledges his regrets but links them with the "emergences of consciousness" in the poem. The solid things in the poem, "plains, farm, home, winter," he suggests "might . . . signal something like austere hope."†

At any rate, this is a poem about the memory of place. For the biography and bibliography of William Stafford see pages 68–69.

The Farm on the Great Plains (1998)

A telephone lines goes cold;
birds tread it wherever it goes.
A farm back of a great plain
tugs an end of the line.

I call that farm every year,
ringing it, listening, still;
no one is home at the farm,
the line gives only a hum.

Some year I will ring the line
on a night at last the right one,
and with an eye tapered for braille
from the phone on the wall

I will see the tenant who waits—
the last one left at the place;
through the dark my braille eye
will lovingly touch his face.

★*The Mark to Turn: A Reading of William Stafford's Poetry* (Lawrence: University Press of Kansas, 1976), 53.

†"William Stafford," in *The Poet's Choice*, ed. Paul Engle and Joseph Langland (New York: Dial, 1962), 143.

"Hello, is Mother at home?"
No one is home today.
"But Father—he should be there."
No one—no one is here.

"But you—are you the one . . . ?"
Then the line will be gone
because both ends will be home:
no space, no birds, no farm.

My self will be the plain,
wise as winter is gray,
pure as cold posts go
pacing toward what I know.

Era Bell Thompson *(1905–1986)*

With some exceptions, most of the Exodusters—the former slaves who migrated into Kansas and Nebraska and other plains states after the Civil War—did not stay long on their homesteads or rented farms. Like the family in Langston Hughes's autobiographical novel *Not Without Laughter,* they settled into prairie towns. Others back-trailed to eastern cities or pursued jobs off of the farm. Nevertheless, the black migration wave that swept across the Great Plains in the late nineteenth century is an important part of the region's history.

Era Bell Thompson tells the story of her introduction to the Great Plains landscape and community in this selection from *American Daughter.* At age thirty-eight, "not taking any chances," Thompson wrote this autobiography before she began a successful career as a journalist and editor at *Negro Digest, Ebony Magazine,* and Johnson Publishing. Thompson's father followed his brother, John, to North Dakota in 1899, but he retreated to Iowa where Era Bell was born, and where Era Bell reports, "we Thompsons were a constant surprise to the good people of Des Moines." The family was modestly prosperous, but Uncle John wrote glowingly of North Dakota where "a farm could be had even without money." In 1914 the Thompsons returned to North Dakota where John Thompson hoped to prosper as a farmer and where his teenaged sons could stay out of trouble.

The author's account of her family's life in North Dakota presents a balanced kind of ambivalence. They have to overcome ethnic and racial antipathy in the community and even within their own extended family—from Thompson's Aunt Ann, who is white. Unlike many other settlers, the family has not farmed before, but Thompson's father makes up for inexperience with sheer determination. Thompson's story is one of adaptation and compromise, prejudice and friendship, among people isolated from the sterner social division as well as the more cosmopolitan tolerance of other regions and the society of other blacks. Life in North Dakota is a tradeoff of sorts for families like the Thompsons.

God's Country *(1946)*

It was a strange and beautiful country my father had come to, so big and boundless he could look for miles and miles out over the golden prairies and follow the unbroken horizon where the midday blue met the bare peaks of the distant hills. No tree or bush to break the view, miles and miles of grass, acre after acre of waving grain, and, up above, God and that fiery chariot which beat remorsely down upon a parching earth.

The evenings, bringing relief, brought also a greater, lonelier beauty. A crimson blur in the west marked the waning of the sun, the purple haze of the hills crept down to pursue the retreating glow, and the whole new world was hushed in peace.

Now and then the silence was broken by the clear notes of a meadowlark on a nearby fence or the weird honk of wild geese far, far above, winging their way south.

This was God's country. There was something in the vast stillness that spoke to Pop's soul, and he loved it.

But not the first day.

John Evans, taking precious time out from his threshing to meet Father and Tom, drove them to the farm and whisked them out to the field as soon as they had changed their clothes.

Father was disappointed in his brother's house—a low, colorless shanty squatting down among the lesser sheds in awe of the big hood-shaped barn, whose silver lightning rods and bright red paint could be seen for miles. He was soon to learn that, in this country, livestock came first, man second.

He hardly recognized Ann. She was very fat now—fat and white. Bossy white. He was shocked all over again by the sight of her, again resented her whiteness. Ann was effusive in her greeting. She kissed him twice, and he was ashamed of his thoughts of her, hoped they could learn to get along.

Clad in straw hats and faded overalls, Pop and Tom clung hard to the sides of the big grain wagon as it lumbered out across the rough stubble fields towards a funnel of smoke and the chug of an engine.

"All this yours?" Father was impressed.

"All this as far as eye can see," said the wiry little man, with a munificent sweep of his hand, "is my land, Tony." He drew up in front of the busy threshing machine. "All this machinery is mine, an' all these men work for me." John was on his favorite topic; he swelled visibly as he hooked his rough, brown fingers in his suspenders and waited for his brother's gasp.

"My Lord, John! You own all this? You must be rich, rich, man!" There was pride and awe in Father's voice, and the last sentence was mingled with a new personal hope.

"Sue! O Sue!" John shouted.

A pretty, buxom girl of fifteen tumbled down from the top of the separator and ran towards them. Her sloppy overalls ill concealed the fast developing curves of her healthy body.

"So this is Uncle Tony." She wrung his hand until he winced.

"Tom," called Pop. "Where's that boy? Tom, come meet your cousin!"

But Tom had vanished among the bundle-wagons. Drawn by the magic of machinery, he found himself staring up into the cabin of the big, hot engine, staring at a boy his own age, a boy with white skin and sandy hair. When Sue guided Pop to the noisy engine, Tom was in the cab with his cousin, Ben, and they were already fast friends.

The tour ended, John assigned father and son to a bundle rack, and they were on their own. The prairie sun hung suspended in the white-hot sky, its lambent flame playing upon their tender necks and arms. The slick, round handle of the pitchfork galled their city hands as they staggered under the burden of the golden bundles; prickly beards of wheat worked down their shirts and into their bodies to torture them; dry stubble cut through thin city soles. Other threshers passed them going to the machine with full loads, passed them returning in empty racks, while Pop and Tom struggled in sweat and silence.

"Hey there, Tony!" yelled John from the top of the separator. "What's the matter with you city fellas? You've missed three turns." John laughed loudly as he sauntered towards them.

"John," said Pop, hot and aggravated, "you know I ain't used to no hard work like this."

"You'll git used to it out here. Do you good, eh, Tom?" John winked broadly. He was enjoying himself; he wanted to see his brother sweat, wanted to see if he could take it. This was his country, his land. He was sure of himself with the soil, scornful of those who had never slaved for the bare essentials of life. While light-skinned Tony cooked in fine hotels and served the rich, he, dark-skinned John, had swung the anvils, shoveled the coal, hoed the corn. Two broken ribs from a mining mule, a broken leg from a Washington mountain slide, a missing finger from the sharp blade of a metal shear were his souvenirs. And all this—the acres of land, the stock, the expensive machinery, and the crew of thirty hands—had come gradually, slowly, after years of struggle with the stubborn earth, after long, frozen winters, self-denial, and personal deprivations for himself and his family. Tony, too, should learn. There was little mercy left in John Evans. He laughed with his men and goaded his brother on.

The next morning when the big, bad Dakota sun sent its golden feelers up over the rim of the earth, Pop's urban bones creaked and rattled, and when Old Sol emerged from his lair, red and ready, every part of Pop rebelled. John relented and made him handyman around the machine, responsible for the stray bundles that missed or overflowed the jaws of the separator—a job reserved for old men, cripples, or the mentally disturbed. That morning Pop was all three.

Tom took the bundle-wagon out alone. He was already a man.

Late that fall Father sent for us. Harry and I were excited, for at last we were going to fight the Indians, and ride the range in search of buffalo—we hoped. Sadly Mother sold the house and turned back the shiny veneer piano. All through the last day, white and colored neighbors came with gifts of parting and words of sympathy; for them our destiny was an untimely death in the frozen wilds of Dakota. Smiling through her tears, Mother packed our things, and at last we were on our way.

As the train sped along through amber fields of corn dotted with yellow pumpkins and bright orange squash, through the mellow haze of an Iowa autumn, Harry and I sat glued to the windows, entranced by the passing panorama, enthralled by the miracle of locomotion. Leaving Minneapolis and the wide Mississippi River the next morning, the scenery gradually grew gray and hushed; trees, baring their limbs, looked sad and forlorn; the last flowers were withering and dying, and with them went some of the glamor of the journey. Past Fargo and the Red River Valley came the barren prairies of North Dakota—vast, level, gray-brown country, treeless and desolate.

Suddenly there was snow—miles and miles of dull, white snow, stretching out to meet the heavy, gray sky; deep banks of snow drifted against wooden snow fences along the railroad right-of-way. And with the snow went our dreams of Indians, for somehow they did not fit into this strange white world. We could sense the cold wind without feeling it, without hearing it. Here and there was a tiny cluster of buildings, a windmill or silo towering above the snow-covered roofs; strawstacks sheltering thick-coated horses and cows that had eaten their way deep into the sides of the stacks away from the wind and the snow. Occasionally we passed through tiny country towns with their inevitable grain elevators, one-room, dull red depots, and companion section houses.

All day long we rode through the silent fields of snow, a cold depression spreading over us. I looked at Mother. She tried to smile, but there were new tears in her eyes. She was thinking of the green hills of Virginia, thinking, too, of the lush valleys of Iowa. All these things, these friendly things that she knew and loved, were far behind her now. I think she knew then that she would never come that way again.

Weary and hungry, we arrived at last at Driscoll. I tumbled down the steps of the train into the outstretched arms of my father, hidden in the collar of a huge sheepskin coat, his face buried in the folds of a wool muffler, only the merry eyes visible. Pop was beside himself with joy. He and Uncle John loaded us into the straw-covered bed of a big sled and covered us with horse blankets. I was so thoroughly bundled and so firmly lodged between my mother and father that I could see very little, but I could smell the clean, fresh odor of straw and feel the sideways jolt of the runners as they bumped into rocks underneath the snow. The steady, rhythmic beat of horses' hoofs sounded pleasantly beneath my uncle's constant chatter.

"But aren't there any colored people here?" asked Mother incredulously.

"Lord, no!" said Father.

"What'd you want with colored folks, Mary? Didn't you come up here to get away from 'em? Me, I could do without 'em for the rest of my days." Uncle John laughed. "There's a couple of colored families over north of Steele, about thirty miles from here—Williams brothers, Ted and Mack. Both of 'em got kids; got right nice farms, too. A little gal there about your age, too, Dick." Uncle John looked at my brother and winked.

All too soon we arrived at the house. Ann's "Hello there!" boomed out above the barking of the dogs and the general din of welcome. It was good to see Tom again. He didn't take on like the others—just patted my head as I leaned against his sturdy legs. Soon the Thompson and Evans clans were gathered around a bountiful feast, as Ann prided herself on setting a good table.

"We ain't got nothin' fancy, but we always got enough fer everybody. If you folks can put up with what we got, you're welcome. We've took many a one in in our time, divided everything we had with 'em, and didn't even git thanks." She was talking on and on in a singsong fashion. "John's too easy; he's always doin' fer others, but you don't see nobody doin' nothin' fer him. There's them Murdocks. John took 'em food and grain and even give 'em the clothes off his back."

"Oh, for Christ's sake, Ma! Ya gonna go over that again?"

"Ben, you shut your face!" Ann's martyrlike voice vanished as she lashed out at her son.

"This is for your benefit, folks." Ben grinned maliciously. "Anything you get out of the Evanses you earn."

"The clothes we give away can't nobody wear," chimed in Sue.

"They're better'n they had." Ann was on the defensive now.

"Go on, Ma, tell 'em what they did for us, tell 'em." Ben's eyes sparkled as he egged her on.

"What'd they ever do? Tell me that. What'd they ever do fer us?"

"Remember all that grain Murdock hauled? Remember that calf he saved?" Ben's eyes became crafty, his speech slow and deliberate. "Remember those three stacks of hay we stole?"

"Ben!" shouted John. "You shut your damned mouth!"

Ann's placid, white face turned fiery red, and a big blood vessel in the center of her forehead throbbed with her mounting anger. "We never stole a dern thing! That hay was rightfully our'n!"

"Benjamin, you're a liar," Sue announced happily.

"Sue's right," barked John.

"Sue's always right, everything she says is right; but every time Ben opens his mouth you're ready to cuss him out."

"Oh, for Christ's sake!" Ben threw down his fork and left the table.

"Now see what you've done," said Ann triumphantly.

"His feelings ain't hurt. He's just getting out of cleaning up all that food on his plate," said Sue knowingly.

The Murdocks and the hay were forgotten, as father and daughter lined up against mother and son. It was a familiar pattern, as old as family life itelf; but this alliance was accentuated, maybe motivated by another division: Ben was as white as Ann, his sandy hair straight, his eyes gray; only his features gave slight indication of mixed heritage. Sue was sallow, with big brown eyes and brown freckles, her reddish-brown hair a mass of heavy curls. She was a far cry from John's copper color, but not so far as Ben.

"I'm sorry you folks had to listen in on a family row the first meal," Ann apologized, still bristling.

"They might as well get used to our wrangling, gonna hear it from now on." John's good nature was already restored. He looked at my mother and laughed. "What's the matter, Mary? Scared?"

Mother smiled uneasily; Pop grunted. We Thompsons sat that one out.

Mother, Father, and I took Sue's tiny room with its magazine pictures pasted on the walls and embroidered shams over the pillows, a cozy, little-girl room, not large enough for a big girl, let alone the three of us. My aunt and uncle slept on the wooden folding bed that let out in the living room beside Sue's cot, and the boys were billeted on pallets on the floor, a sheet separating them from the beds. Ten of us in a three-room house was crowded, but not stuffy. The heater in the center of the room offered little competition to the cold north wind that whipped around the corners of the building and in through its many cracks and crevices. Manure banked around the outside of the house kept out some of the drafts, and each night Ann put old rugs against the threshold and chinked up the windows with rags, before she blew out the lamp.

Mother and Father talked far into the night. "Tony, I don't like it here. All this fussing and crowding."

"I know, I know, but we've got to put up with it somehow, until spring anyway, when we can get a place of our own. You'll like the country in the spring, Mary, when the snow is gone."

"Let's go back to Iowa."

"Can't go back. Cost money to go back, and besides, our home's gone. What'd we do when we got back?"

"You've got some money, haven't you? Where's the money you and Tom made working this fall?"

"Time we paid John back for train fare and clothes and things, we didn't have nothin' comin'. It's like Ben said tonight, John always gets his. Time he got through figuring, we owed *him* money.

"But Ann, is she always like that?"

"Old Brother Satan hisself couldn't get along with that old white woman. Lord, honey, she's. . . . " Pop's Christianity was making it difficult to find a word. He searched, failed, put his religion aside. "She's a bitch."

"Tony!" screamed Mother, sitting bolt upright in bed. "What's that? Wolves?" A long, weird howl pierced the night. It was followed by short, sharp yelps.

Father pulled Mother back down on the pillow. "Them's coyotes; them ain't wolves. Them rascals howl like that all night."

"They—they sound so close."

"They just up the hill there a piece. The dogs keep 'em away. Jepp, the big dog, he's part coyote hisself. Lord! Lord! Dogs and coyotes chasin' each other up and down the hills all night long."

Suddenly Mother remembered all the stories she had heard about timber wolves and early pioneers, how a young couple overtaken by wolves, threw their only baby to the animals to save themselves. "Tony, what'd you bring me and my children out to this place for? We'll all be froze to death or eaten up alive!"

"Now, now," soothed Father. "They can't get in here, and ain't nobody been set up by them things recently. You'll get used to 'em by and by. Yes, Lord." Father continued without much conviction. "You'll get used to 'em, maybe, but God knows I won't!"

The Monday after our arrival, Harry and I were bundled off to our first day of rural schooling. Ben, like many farm youths, had quit school early, so my parents, remembering what they went through in Iowa, most eagerly excused Tom and Dick. In the gray-white cold of early morning, with the temperature hovering around thirty-five below, Harry, Sue, and I climbed into the big sled, John whipped up the horses, and we bounded off in a flurry of snow.

Driscoll was a typical small North Dakota town, population about one hundred. Main Street, a broad, snow-packed road, was lined on both sides with frame store buildings, and its few homes were scattered out to the west of Main and south towards the Lutheran and Protestant cemeteries. A four-room consolidated school sat up on a hill, midway between the cemeteries and town.

A canvas-covered school rig was pulling away as we drew up to the gate. Sue herded us into the tiny entrance hall and up the three shallow steps to the first floor, where a short, red-haired woman gasped in disbelief.

"Good morning, Miss Breen," said Sue perfunctorily. "These are my cousins; they're both in your room."

Miss Breen had spent most of her three years at Driscoll trying to classify the Evans' offspring. They weren't white and they weren't black. Some of the children, drawing their own reckless conclusions, had called them "skunks" and fought it out. Miss Breen didn't know what it was the mulattoes objected to: the skunk's predominance of black fur over white or its more distinctive qualities. Now, suddenly, without warning, here were two studies in brown, not quite like the pictures in the geography or funny papers, but near enough to be identified. They were the first bona fide Negro children she or the pupils had ever seen.

We left our wraps and overshoes in the cloakroom and, still stiff with cold, joined the other children by the big tin drum which surrounded the stove. Every eye was upon us. One or two little girls snickered; a boy pushed another against me and grinned. Miss Breen rang a little handbell, and the eighteen children marched reluctantly to their seats. Summoning Harry and me to her desk, she plied us with questions—questions far from educational lines, questions about our parents, what they did in Des Moines, where they were born, about the South. She questioned us until my mouth began to quiver, and I had to blink hard to keep back the tears. Finally she led me to an empty seat in the fourth grade section and took Harry to the sixth grade on the opposite side of the room. The two middle rows were filled with disappointed fifth graders who felt left out of this new thing that was happening to them and the community.

A girl seated across the aisle from me, delicately featured, and with long, flaxen curls, smiled. The girl directly in front of me turned around. "Hello," she whispered. "My name's Ollie Koch." She laid her open reader on my desk. "You can use my book." There was method in her kindness. Without a book she was free to sit in the next aisle with her cousin, Tillie. Tillie made a face at me and buried her head in her arms laughing silently. I didn't like her; I wanted to go home.

At recess the blonde girl came to my seat. "I'm Jewel Nordland," she said. Her name was like a poem, and her voice was like music. I liked her.

At noon the children gathered around the stove to eat lunch from their round syrup cans and their tin tobacco baskets. It was like a picnic back in Iowa when it rained. I choked a little when I thought of Iowa, and ate my half-frozen sandwiches in silence. One of Sue's friends put her arm around me and felt of my hair; Tillie stared at the white palms of my hands, and I closed my fists tight until they hurt. For the first time I began to wonder about that and about the soles of my feet and my pink toes, and I was glad she couldn't see my feet where the color ran out. Long before four o'clock I had had enough school.

Mother, standing in the yard that night waiting for us, clasped me in her arms, hugging me as though she had never expected to see me again, and I soon forgot about the soles of my feet and the palms of my hands.

On those frigid winter evenings after our homework was done, we joined the others in games of checkers and dominoes or listened to the hard-to-believe tales of Uncle John's pioneers and Pop's ghosts. Then Ben would bring out his harmonica and play far into the night. As he played the songs of the prairies the tempo became slower and the music saddened. I liked the sad cowboy laments best, for they were a part of the whistling winds and the lone prairies.

Sunday afternoons, curious but friendly neighbors stopped by to visit the Evanses and welcome the Thompsons. They wanted to see for themselves if the family was white or black, and the brownness of us was a surprise.

The monotony of the long winter days and the increased bickering and quarreling between the two families made Father's short temper shorter. The friction with Ann increased in the narrow confines of the little house, and he and Mother spent more and more time in their room, talking in low, bitter tones.

"It won't last always," Mother would say. It was she, now, who mollified him. "Try not to say things to aggravate Ann. You know how she is."

"I tell you, Mary, I'm goin' to forget myself one of these days and hit that woman, so help me!"

The first open break came one morning at breakfast when Aunt Ann set before me a warmed-over plate of codfish balls and a half-eaten biscuit—my supper from the night before. "You eat that up before you git any more, young lady. We ain't got food to waste around here."

I looked at Mother. There was a hurt look in her soft brown eyes, her lips tightly closed. I looked at Pop, and got the green light. His thin, yellow nostrils were quivering, his blue-black eyes like slits of steel. I drew a deep breath and began to howl. Aunt Ann hovered by the table, alert and waiting, like a big polar bear. Ann was fast tiring of her husband's relatives.

Pop pushed my plate roughly aside. "She don't have to eat leftovers!"

"It's her own plate. I make my kids clean up their plates; she ain't no better'n them."

"Ann, I've seen you give better'n that to the dogs. I've seen you give 'em buttered biscuits right off the stove. My children's as good as your dogs!"

"Sure I feed our dogs. Dogs got to eat same as you, but they don't waste it. Nobody's gonna waste food around here, as hard as John has to work fer it!"

Pop jumped to his feet. He was cold with fury, his words measured, brittle. "You white, Irish devil, you!" I stopped crying to listen. "You can take your food and . . . "

"Tony!" Mother was beside him. "Tony," she pleaded, taking him by the arm. "Don't say anything more. You're angry now. Come." She led him from the table into the bedroom and shut the door.

Ann was pallid, and her hands trembled. Suddenly she threw a coat over her head and rushed from the house in search of Uncle John. Left alone at the table, I helped myself to fried mush and, for the first time, got enough Karo syrup.

Before the week was up, John gave Sue a whipping—a noisy, farcical affair with a lot of unhelpful coaching from the sidelines. I was so greatly impressed that I told the kids at school.

"You're going to get it!" Sue hissed in my ear at recess time. "You told on me!"

The rest of the day I suffered as only a guilty nine-year-old can suffer. By four I was terrified. All the way home I waited for her to tell Uncle John, but she said nothing. When both families gathered at the supper table, I was sick with apprehension; still Sue was silent, biding her time. In that satisfied and satiated lull that precedes dessert, she spoke.

"Papa," she said dramatically, "do you know what happened today?"

"No. What?"

"Sissy told. She told everybody in school that you beat me. I was never so mortified!"

All eyes turned towards me. John carefully laid down his knife and fork. "Did you repeat at school what happened in the sanctity of this house?"

I nodded my head, not trusting myself to speak.

"What made you do it?"

"Yes, dear, you knew it was wrong." Mother took the play away from John.

Ben grinned. "She didn't have to tell 'em. They could hear her, all the hollerin' and screamin' she was doin'. Lord, you coulda . . ."

"You shut your face, Ben Evans," snapped Sue, forgetting her look of martyrdom. "I didn't holler any more than you do."

"Did you hear that, Dick?"

"Did I! Man, oh, man! I was down at the other end of the lane . . ."

"You stop that lie," Pop silenced him. Tom and Harry were convulsed with laughter.

"What'd you think it was, boy—a train whistle or that old sow with the little pigs?"

"Papa!" wailed Sue.

"Shut up now, all of you!" bellowed Uncle John. "And I don't want to ever hear of anyone telling tales outside of this house again. Not anyone."

It would have come anyway—the end, I mean. The old axiom about the one roof was never more true. Things were nearing a climax. Ann and Pop weren't speaking, the Thompsons were eating alone—after the Evanses—and even Ben's harmonica couldn't fill in the long silences.

So I broke the emery wheel. I was forbidden to touch anything in my uncle's toolshed, but the foot-propelled emery wheel was irresistible. I sneaked out to the shed, mounted the machine, and began to pedal. The chain snapped, and the pedals went limp. Sue walked in.

Uncle John said he was going to whip me. Pop didn't say anything; he just hitched up a team and drove into Driscoll. When he returned, we piled all our belongings into the big sled and moved to the empty hotel on the edge of town.

The hotel was an old, eighteen-room barn of a building, bare and cold, but we set up living quarters in the spacious kitchen, and that night Pop made southern hoecake on top of the gigantic range and fried thick steaks in butter. The tightness was gone from the corners of his eyes as he threw his head back and sang:

"I'm so glad, trouble don't last alway,
Oh, I'm so glad, trouble don't last alway!"

Chef's cap tilted, eyes shining, Pop shouted above the roaring stove and the sizzling steak, "Sing it, Mary; sing it, chillun! 'Oh, I'm so glad!' "

We all joined in, loud, off-key maybe, but united, together again, a whole hotel in which to sing and play and fight.

The food we ate that night was purchased on credit from Old Lady Anderson's store across the street. "Yah, yah," she had said, "I give you credit, you farm soon. Little ones must eat." And Pop borrowed twenty-five dollars from the bank on our furniture to buy coal and the little things we needed. Debt was no disgrace in North Dakota; everybody was in debt, everything was mortgaged—that's why they didn't need money out there.

At night the family sat around the big range and played checkers or got out the old Baptist hymnal that somehow followed us and sang the old songs in a setting the old folks never knew. For the first time, the folks didn't have to worry about the whereabouts of the boys.

One night I came in from school to find a Norwegian couple and a colored missionary woman visiting us. I stared rudely, not at the couple, but at the colored woman. Aside from my mother, I hadn't seen one since we left Des Moines. They stayed for dinner, a meal freely interspersed with "Amens," "Hallelujahs," and "Word-of-Gods." Hallelujah, coming between bites of boiled pig's feet, was too much for Dick. He choked and left the table, Tom and Harry following.

After supper Mother, Father, and I accompanied these new and voluble friends home. For twenty miles we drove over the silvery, moon-swept snow, the runners of the sled singing out in the harsh cold. The unabated conversation of five newly met people who had just found a common ground—religion—went eagerly on, unmindful of the distance and the cold.

The man, Oscar Olson, spoke fervently in broken English. Twenty-five years before, he had left his native land and come to America to get rich. His first wife was dead ten years before he married the loquacious Scotch widow and mail-order bride, who, one soon gathered, was not very popular with her half-grown stepchildren.

The missionary woman was a little off the heathen trail, but still preaching the Gospel to all who would listen—and contribute to the price of a railroad ticket towards a warmer land. Just how the lump little woman got that far out into the sparsely settled country was a mistake she never explained. "All I wants to do, praise God, is to get back to Kansas, hallelujah, and preach the Word, yes, Jesus!" That was her problem.

When I awoke, Father was carrying me into a big warm kitchen. Fresh coffee was boiling on the stove, and the whole Olson household was waiting up to greet us. A big girl, with wide blue eyes and the smell of clean milk about her, took me gently from my father's arms and deftly removed the many layers of wraps around me. A younger girl, a thin, pale child, with white pigtails bouncing about her sharp shoulders, hurried back and forth from pantry to table with butter and cheese and fresh coffee cake. The task completed, she stood before me, gazing solemnly and silently. The older boy was defiant and sullen, openly hating his stepmother; but the other one teased everybody, laughed at everything. The "Hallelujahs" had a hard time maintaining their sacred intonations in his presence. Pop, a little out of practice, a long time out of church, caught himself grinning with the boy, cast a furtive glance at Mother, and dropped his head.

Those three pleasant days with the Olsons were the first of many such weekends and the beginning of a strong and lasting friendship, one wrought with prayer and much drinking of coffee.

Several weeks passed before Uncle John came to see us. "Blood's thicker than marriage," he said. "If Ann could learn to keep her darned mouth shut, you folks would still be with us."

"No," Pop demurred, "it's better this way. We'll get along somehow."

"Anything I can do for you? Have you got enough to eat?"

"No, John; no, thanks. We're doin' all right. The Lord will provide."

"He won't provide no horses." John winked at Mother. "That colt, Major, that I promised the boys, he's still theirs."

"Yes, John. Thanks. If you can just keep him till spring, till I can find a farm, I'll be mighty grateful." Pop didn't believe Major would live until spring. He was about to die when John became philanthropic, but somehow he survived and grew into a scrawny, hump-backed horse.

After that visit Sue occasionally came home with me at noon, and Ben came often, but Ann never lightened our door.

Diligently Father searched for a suitable farm to rent, one on which we could gain experience and make enough money for a down payment on a farm of our own. Just before the spring thaws, he heard about the Old Hansmeyer place, two and a half miles west of Driscoll.

Hank Hansmeyer, owner of the local blacksmith shop, was tight and shrewd. The rock-ridden quarter section had never made a living for anyone, but a man with three sturdy sons, a man who didn't know wheat from barley, Hank reasoned, would make a good tenant, wouldn't be too choosey or too demanding. He drove my parents out to the farm one Sunday and with pleasant generalities and heavy emphasis upon the hidden possibilities of the soil (hidden two feet under the snow) explained his terms. He, Hank, party of the first part, would furnish the land, the buildings, and the horses, if we, parties of the second part, would furnish the seed, do the work, and give him half the profits. The sod-covered barn leaned heavily to the south, and the corral fence was broken down in many places, but the house looked pleasant and bright in its once-white paint. The small frustrated grove of stunted willows gave faint hope of living things. My parents were impressed.

"Now, where are the horses?" Pop asked.

"Oh, yes," said Hank and drove out towards the open range. Half an hour later he sighted them, eight or ten broncos far to the north, galloping across the snow like streaks of flame, their long manes and tails shining in the cold sun. "There they are. Now you just get them in the barn and feed them up a little, and you've got fine horses, good working horses."

"Umm umph!" Pop squinted. "How you tell them wild things your horses—ten miles away?"

"Oh, they're mine, all right. I know all of my horses. Let 'em run the range every winter—saves feed, makes 'em self-reliant."

"You say, put 'em in the barn. Who's gonna git them rascals in a barn when you can't even git close enough to read the brand—if they got a brand? Tell me that."

Hank Hansmeyer laughed tolerantly. "When the snow begins to thaw, they'll come closer in. They're not wild horses; they've been broke, had harness on."

Pop liked horses, thought he knew horseflesh, all the time he'd spent with racehorse men. "Them's the wildest tame horses I ever see. But ain't no horse livin' I can't handle. No, siree. Ain't no horse livin'." Hank looked straight ahead; Mother looked at Pop and crossed her fingers. Pop looked back at the fleeing horses. "Ummm umph!" There was admiration and excitement in his grunt. "It's a deal."

Hank Hansmeyer stopped the team and pulled out a prepared contract. "Sign right here," he said, trying to appear casual.

Right there in the middle of the prairie, Pop pulled off his glove and, with fingers numb with cold, shaking with emotion, signed his name. "Lord, today!" he said with a start. "I'm a farmer, Mary, I'm a farmer."

Further Reading

Micheaux, Oscar. *The Conquest: The Story of A Negro Pioneer.* 1913; rpt. Lincoln: University of Nebraska Press.

——. *The Homesteader: A Novel.* 1917; rpt. Lincoln: University of Nebraska Press, 1994.

Reading about African Americans on the Great Plains

Athearn, Robert G. *In Search of Canaan: Black Migration to Kansas, 1879–80.* Lawrence: University Press of Kansas, 1978.

Leckie, William H. *The Buffalo Soldier: A Narrative of the Negro Cavalry in the West.* Norman: University of Oklahoma Press, 1967.

Painter, Nell Irvin. *Exodusters: Black Migration to Kansas after Reconstruction.* New York: Norton, 1976.

Ravage, John W. *Black Pioneers: Images of the Black Experience on the North American Frontier.* Salt Lake City: University of Utah Press, 1997.

Taylor, Quintard. *In Search of the Racial Frontier: African-Americans in the American West, 1528–1990.* New York: Norton, 1998.

James Welch (b. 1940)

While working on a documentary for the Public Broadcasting Service's American Experience series, James Welch traversed the Montana plains. *Killing Custer* is an account of Welch's experience while writing the script for the film. The first chapter places the Battle of the Little Bighorn in retrospect with Welch's own Blackfeet–Gros Ventre histroy in a recounting of the 1870 Massacre on the Marias River. Welch also places the massacre within the context of Plains Indian history.

Welch was born in Browning, Montana. He graduated with a bachelor's degree from the University of Montana and began a master of fine arts degree program there under the direction of poet Richard Hugo. Welch has taught at the University of Washington, Cornell University, and most recently, at Colorado College. He began his literary career auspiciously, with his novel of a modernist, alienated, unnamed Blackfeet hero, *Winter in the Blood* (1974). In many ways the coming-of-age novel is the same story set historically with transliterated Blackfeet signifiers in the award-winning *Fools Crow* (1986). Welch continues to examine the historical experience of Plains Indians with his most recent novel, *The Heartsong of Charging Elk* (2000), the story of a Sioux performer in Buffalo Bill's Wild West show who gets left behind in Europe.

Excerpt from *Killing Custer* (1994)

On August 17, 1869, a young Pikuni warrior, Owl Child, led his small gang of dissidents under cover of darkness to the ranch of Malcolm Clarke, a man who had accumulated much wealth by trading with the Blackfeet for over thirty years. Clarke, known as Four Bears, was a respected man among the whites of Montana for having opened up trade with a tribe that possessed the reputation of being the most fearsome on the northern Great Plains. Unlike the Sioux, the Cheyennes, the Arapahos, the Crow, the Assiniboins, the Crees, and the Gros Ventres, the Pikunis, the southernmost tribe of the Blackfeet Nation, did not tolerate the earlier Americans who came west to trap, to trade, to settle among them.

Their territory in Montana had been invaded for the first time by Americans in the summer of 1806. Captain Meriwether Lewis, in an attempt to locate the headwaters of the Marias River (named by him for his fair cousin Maria Wood), ran into a small party of Pikuni warriors. He believed them to be Gros Ventres, and through his sign-talker, George Drouillard, beseeched them to live in peace with their neighbors and to trade with him in the future, an obvious ruse to save his hide, since he had no intention of returning to that barren, often hostile country. He gave a flag to one and a medal to another, men he perceived to be chiefs. That night the two parties camped together. Toward dawn a great commotion developed when a brave attempted to steal one of the white men's firesticks. Other attempts were made for guns; then the Indians tried to drive off Lewis's horses. By the time the dust settled, one of the Pikunis, the man to whom Lewis gave the medal, was killed, and another wounded. Lewis took back the flag but left the medal around the dead man's neck so the Pikunis would know who they were. Lewis then beat a hasty retreat down the river to join the other half of the expedition led by William Clark.

Much has been made of this incident by the whites, the only truly hostile encounter of the Lewis and Clark expedition, but more was made of it by the Blackfeet. From that time forward, they considered the Americans their enemies, although they still traded with the French, and then with the English across the Medicine Line in Canada. They considered the French the Real Old Man People, because they were the first to come from that place where Sun Chief rises to begin his journey across the sky.

But the Americans were not to be outdone by the Canadian traders. They returned to Blackfeet territory and in 1831 built a trading post, Fort Piegan, at the confluence of the Marias and the Missouri. The American Fur Company, a John Jacob Astor enterprise, wanted a special item from the Indians, and not only did the company have the goods to trade for that item, it had the means to transport it back to civilization—the keelboat. So began the trade in buffalo hides. Hides for goods—copper kettles, foodstuffs, beads, blankets, knives, mirrors, guns, ammunition, and eventually the white man's water, a potent brew of tobacco, capsicum, molasses, peppers, and alcohol mixed with river water and whatever else could produce a fire in the belly.

Although that first trading season went well, the Blackfeet burned the fort when the white men left. Subsequent trading posts were built. Fort McKenzie was built on very nearly the same site in time for the next trading season. Later, a few miles upriver at a very natural landing, Fort Benton, known as Many Houses to the Blackfeet, became the ultimate trading center on that part of the Missouri. The keelboats carried goods and people upriver, hides and pelts downriver. Eventually they were replaced by large steamboats, which could carry even greater quantities of trade items, as well as people and their supplies bound for the gold fields of Montana and to points west along the Mullan Trail, which culminated at Fort Walla Walla on the Columbia River. Here they could go down the river all the way to the Pacific Ocean.

In 1847, one of the traders for the American Fur Company, Malcolm Clarke, married a Pikuni, Cutting-off-head Woman, a member of the Many Chiefs band like her cousin, Owl Child. The Many Chiefs were led by Mountain Chief, a great leader who resisted the invasion of the white settlers and their soldiers, the seizers. Clarke, by marrying into Mountain Chief's band, secured his position as principal trader among the Blackfeet. He also gained the respect of the elders of all the bands by marrying one of their women. They brought their buffalo hides to Many Houses and returned to their camps with goods that were meant to make their lives easier, but in fact made them more complicated.

Owl Child, several years before, had ridden with a war party against the Assiniboins (Cutthroats) and had claimed a kill, although most in the party insisted that the kill belonged to Bear Head. During a heated argument, Owl Child leveled his rifle and killed Bear Head. Since that incident, Owl Child had become an outcast among the Blackfeet, although he did live off and on with Mountain Chief's band. But mostly Owl Child roamed, and his bitterness toward his own people increased. He considered the Pikunis weak for signing treaties with the *napikwans*— the whites—and allowing them to steal the land, to settle on the buffalo ranges. He did his part to make the *napikwans* suffer—stealing animals, destroying houses and property, occasionally killing a settler or miner. But in 1867, an incident occurred that would focus Owl Child's anger.

Malcolm Clarke had retired from his position as principal trader among the Blackfeet and began to ranch on a small tributary of the Missouri River called Prickly Pear Creek, north of Helena. He moved his family into a comfortable home, complete with attached smokehouse and several outbuildings for tack, grain, and equipment. It was a prosperous ranch by any standards, and those Blackfeet who saw it were impressed. In the spring of 1867, several of Cutting-off-head Woman's relatives came to visit and look over the large spread. Owl Child was among them. As fate would have it, Owl Child's horses were stolen during the visit. Naturally, he blamed Malcolm Clarke, and shortly afterward he stole some of Clarke's horses, driving them back to Mountain Chief's camp.

Clarke and his son, Horace, followed the trail and found both Owl Child and the horses in the encampment. Horace struck Owl Child with a whip and called him a dog. Clarke called him an old woman, and the men left with their horses. Now, it is not good to insult and beat a young Pikuni in front of his people. Such an action requires revenge, and although many of the chiefs were trying desperately to avoid trouble with the *napikwans,* they understood what Owl Child had to do.

So it came as no surprise that on the night of August 17, 1869, Owl Child and twenty-five young Pikuni warriors paid a visit to the ranch on Prickly Pear Creek. When they left, Clarke was dead and his son, Horace, was seriously wounded by gunfire.

More than any other of the many depredations against the white invaders, this single incident triggered the retaliation that would lead to the swift punishment of the Blackfeet, from which they would never recover. It was simply the last straw. Powerful men in the press and in the territorial capital of Helena roared loud and clear. They wanted nothing less than the total annihilation of these savages. They wanted the army to settle the Indian problem once and for all. United States Marshal William F. Wheeler produced a document listing fifty-six whites who had been murdered and more than a thousand horses stolen by the Blackfeet in 1869 alone. The *Helena Weekly Herald* stated that "the pleasant and innocent amusement of butchering and scalping the palefaces is believed by some likely soon to begin in good earnest."

Ironically, it was the United States Army that tried to mollify the outraged Montanans. General Philip H. Sheridan, originator of the famous maxim "The only good Indian is a dead Indian," Civil War hero and now commander of the Department of the Missouri, informed the citizens that he did not have enough men at present to attack "these Indian marauders." But he promised that as soon as recruits could be sent west he would propose a plan to punish the malfeasants. Actually, he already had a plan, a plan that he had used successfully against the Southern Cheyennes of the southern plains. He spelled out his plan in that earlier incident: "Let me find out exactly where these Indians are going to spend the winter, and about the time of a good heavy snow I will send out a party and try and strike them." That party, in 1868, had been led by General George Armstrong Custer, and that place of heavy snow was the Washita River in the Indian Territory of Oklahoma. Although Sheridan's superior, General of the Army William T. Sherman, approved an identical plan against the Pikunis, a few of Sheridan's experienced officers had misgivings. General Philippe de Trobriand, in command of Fort Shaw, reported, "I do not see so far an opportunity for striking a successful blow. The only Indians within reach are friendly, and nothing could be worse, I think, than to chastise them for offenses of which they are not guilty."

On New Year's Day, 1870, General Alfred H. Sully met with four peace chiefs of the Blackfeet Nation—Heavy Runner, Little Wolf, and Big Lake of the Pikunis, and Gray Eyes of the Bloods, or Kainahs. The one chief he wanted to speak with, Mountain Chief, head chief of the Pikunis, leader of the opposition to white encroachment, did not show up. Nevertheless, Sully outlined the conditions imposed by the United States Army to avoid war: capture, kill, and bring back the bodies of Owl Child and the others in his war party named in an indictment, and return all, or as many as possible, of the horses and other livestock stolen from the citizens of Montana Territory—and from the army itself. All to be done within two weeks.

Heavy Runner and the other peace chiefs agreed to these conditions, but they knew they were powerless to find, much less kill, the young warriors. They were rumored to be with Mountain Chief's band north of the Medicine Line in Canada. As for the livestock, many of the animals had been sold to traders and the others were hopelessly scattered among the bands.

Sully knew that the meeting had been futile, and when the two weeks were up, Sheridan's plan was put into effect. De Trobriand's scouts reported that Mountain Chief and his band had crossed back into Montana and were wintering on the Marias River, a good day's ride south of the Medicine Line. Colonel E. M. Baker was in charge of four companies of cavalry stationed at Fort Shaw on the Sun River. The army had finally mustered up enough troops to carry out Sheridan's command, which put simply in a telegraph on January 15 read: "If the lives and property of the citizens of Montana can best be protected by striking Mountain Chief's band, I want them struck. Tell Baker to strike them hard."

On January 19, Colonel Baker led his four cavalry companies, along with fifty-five mounted infantrymen and a company of foot soldiers, northward from Fort Shaw. The weather was almost as bad as it gets in that part of the country. Temperatures never rose above twenty below zero, and the winds swept off the Rocky Mountain slope in a constant fury. But Baker was determined to carry out Sheridan's command. He knew that the Pikuni band would be bundled up in their lodges, waiting out the storm. But one can only imagine what some of the green recruits, many of them from the east and south, thought as they hunkered down in their buffalo coats, riding across the godforsaken plains in treacherous weather toward an encounter with savages they had only read about in comic books and dime novels.

One of the men knew what he was getting into. Joe Kipp, a half-white, half-Pikuni scout also known as Raven Quiver, knew these people; he had married a Pikuni woman and had lived and traded with them for several years. And now he led the United States Army toward the Big Bend of the Marias River, where his own people were camped. He had to have known the likely results of such an expedition.

It has been stated by scouts and troops alike (and also by civilian Horace Clarke, who accompanied the expedition) that Colonel Baker was drunk when the attack began, that he had been drinking during the whole of the journey north. If he was drunk, it would not be an uncommon occurrence. Several of the officers out west had a similar problem. The same charge would be leveled against Major Marcus A. Reno six years later when he attacked, under Custer's orders, the large Indian encampment on the Little Bighorn River. The fact that Baker was drunk might not have mattered much in the overall scheme of things—life was hard and dreary and monotonous on the western plains—had it not been for a small but significant incident just prior to the attack.

In the dark hour just before dawn on January 23, 1870, the men were in position on a ridge above the Indian camp, waiting for light and the order from Baker to commence the attack. As the darkness turned to steel gray, Joe Kipp recognized some of the quiet lodges, recognized the painted designs on the buffalo-skin covers. It was the wrong camp. And he understood immediately what must have happened—Mountain Chief had gotten wind of the army's plan of attack and had moved his winter camp, and Heavy Runner, one of the peace chiefs, had moved his people to the site. Because the Big Bend of the Marias was well protected from the winter winds and because the game was fairly plentiful most winters, it was a popular camping area among the Pikunis. Kipp at once reported to Baker, "Colonel, that is not Mountain Chief's camp. It is the camp of Black Eagle and Heavy Runner. I know it by its differently painted lodges." To which Baker replied, "That makes no difference, one band or another of them; they are all Piegans [Pikunis] and we will attack them." Then he said to one of his men, "Sergeant, stand behind this scout, and if he yells or makes a move, shoot him."

Some in the camp said that the first volley of firing brought Heavy Runner from his lodge. He waved a piece of paper in his hand, an order of safe conduct signed by General Sully during that futile meeting on New Year's Day. Although Heavy Runner was at peace with the *napikwans,* he was among the first to fall. After thousands of rounds of ammunition had turned the air blue and thick with gunsmoke, 173 people lay dead, most still in their lodges. The soldiers approached the camp to quell what little resistance was left. They then cut the bindings of the lodges, collapsing them, and burned them with the people still inside. They gathered up all the food, weapons, and supplies they could carry and rode off toward Fort Shaw, driving the band's horse herds before them.

Although the numbers became a matter of controversy, it is clear that most of the dead were women and children and old people. Baker, in his report of the incident, claimed that all but fifty-three were able-bodied warriors, which even by army standards is an absurd body count. Most reports state that a great many of the able-bodied men were out hunting. The winter had already been cruel, many were hungry, and the hunters were out to get meat. Perhaps a more realistic breakdown of the dead was in a report submitted to his superiors by W. A. Pease, the Indian agent: Only fifteen of the dead Indians had been fighting men between the ages of twelve and thirty-seven, while ninety were women and fifty were children. One suspects that the rest of the dead were old people.

As if the massacre weren't bad enough, it came during a smallpox winter. The white scabs disease, as it was known to the Pikunis, was probably the most effective weapon the white people brought to the new world. More deadly than rifles, swords, artillery pieces, Gatling guns, and battle-tested horses, this disease killed many thousands of Indians, reducing tribal populations by a third, by a half, by three-quarters, often by even more. And it was deliberately used as a weapon on occasions.

As far back as 1763, Jeffrey Amherst, the English commander in chief during the latter part of the French and Indian War, called the Indians "more nearly allied to the Brute than to the Human Creation" and saw no reason to get along with this "execrable race." He further stated, "I am fully resolved whenever they give me an occasion to extirpate them root and branch." Amherst, after whom the college town in Massachusetts is named, made a suggestion to one of his subordinates: "Could it not be contrived to send the small pox among the disaffected tribes of Indians? . . . You will do well to try to inoculate the Indians by means of blankets. . . ." Smallpox became a routine weapon of war against the powerless immune systems of the savages.

Throughout the contact period with the whites, smallpox epidemics raged periodically, almost systematically. In 1837, three years after Prince Maximilian, the German naturalist and explorer, and the Swiss artist Karl Bodmer visited a Mandan village on the upper Missouri and remarked on the Indians' fine appearance, the tribe had been reduced from sixteen hundred to only one hundred. Villages along the Missouri were decimated, mothers, brothers, daughters, and fathers turned away from each other in desperation. Frozen bodies were stacked like firewood on the edge of camps.

So it was that the latest epidemic of the white scabs in 1869 and 1870 had laid low the camps of the Pikunis. The soldiers had massacred a village of helpless people. Ironically, the target of the United States Army, the "bad head" who had precipitated the action against the Pikunis, Owl Child, lay dying of the disease in Mountain Chief's camp, seventeen miles down the Marias River from the massacre site.

Baker's report of the incident, issues two months later, claimed that he did not know that the camp was that of the friendly chief Heavy Runner. Another report claimed that the Indians put up heavy resistance, firing from inside the tipis, which justified the heavy return fire that killed all within those lodges, women and children included. But word got out back east that the attack had involved friendly Indians and had been a cruel and indefensible act of savagery. It was especially the great numbers of women and children killed that outraged citizens and legislators alike. Vincent Collyer, secretary to the Board of Indian Commissioners, wrote: "At last the sickening details of Colonel Baker's attack have been received." His revelation of the casualty figures opened up a public debate that fiercely questioned the army's policy toward Indians.

Congressman Daniel Vorhees of Indiana stated: "I wash my hands of all responsibility for this system of warfare. It cannot be justified here or before the country; it cannot be justified before the civilization of the age, or in the sight of God or man." Another congressman also invoked the white man's God: "I say there is no warrant in the laws of God or of man for destroying women and children merely because their husbands and fathers may be marauders. I say that civilization shudders at horrors like this."

But there were military apologists in the halls of Congress. Job Stevenson of Ohio stood to "enter my protest against these sweeping condemnations of the Government and its officers. I for one, if I stand alone, avow my approval of the sentiment expressed in the orders of General Sheridan. They express the sentiments of war, and I have always believed . . . that in war the most vigorous policy is not only the best policy, but is the most merciful policy. General Sheridan says we must strike a blow with telling effect, and that is the only way to make war." He went on to state, "These savages who themselves never care for age or sex, these savages whose women and children make war on white women and children, these savages who dance for joy around the burning stake, these savages whose women and children are instruments and demons of torture to white women and children, are only to be warred upon, when you war at all, by a war of extermination."

Stevenson's speech was received by the majority of the membership as belli-cose, even bloodthirsty. Many expressed amazement that one of their own could enter a plea supporting the army's "monstrous transaction," as Congressman Vorhees put it.

Much of the press around the country appeared to be equally incensed by the actions of Sheridan and Baker. The *Chicago Tribune* editorialized, "The account given by Vincent Collyer did not by any means present the worst features of the affair. There is nothing in the records of the Indian Office which surpasses the atrocities detailed in this paper. Several members of the House have been in-formed of its character, and steps are pretty sure to be taken in Congress looking to dismissing from the service those officers directly responsible for the atrocities committed." A couple of days later, the same paper wrote, "The affair is looked on at the Interior Department as the most disgraceful butchery in the annals of our dealings with the Indians." The *New York Tribune* was a little more circumspect: "This matter must be investigated and the facts obtained. It is shameful to have such statements [accounts of the atrocities] published by authority, if they are false; it is terrible to think of what happened, if they are true."

Closer to the frontier, the actions of Sheridan and Baker were received much differently. The *Helena Herald* of March 30, 1870, commented: "There is every reason to believe that the raid of Colonel Baker, in addition to ridding the Territory of the most murderous band of Indians in the country, has also had a very salutary effect on the other tribes of the Blackfeet Nation. There is a good prospect of future peace and security." The *Platte Journal* asked, "Shall we Williampennize or Sheridanize the Indians?" And the *New North-west of Montana* celebrated the victory but warned that "all the namby-pamby, sniffling old maid sentimentalists of both sexes who leave most of their brains on their handkerchiefs when under excitement, will join the jargon of discontent." In Congress, Montana's James T. Cavanaugh led a group of army supporters by pointing out that it is necessary to chastise those responsible for "atrocities that shock humanity—atrocities that are nameless . . . nameless mutilations of both men and women . . . witnessed by my own eyes. . . . I endorse the order of General Phil Sheridan. I endorse the act of General Hancock. I endorse the conduct of Colonel Baker." In answer to a ques-tion involving his support of killing of defenseless women and children, he said, ". . . in the words of General Harney after the battle of Ash Hollow [in Nebraska], years ago . . . they are nits, and will become lice."

The national debate raged. Wendell Philips, a Boston abolitionist, stated in a speech to a Reform League meeting, "I only know the names of three savages upon the Plains—Colonel Baker, General Custer [for his part in leading the massacre on the sleeping village on the Washita in December 1868, little more than a year before the Massacre on the Marias], and at the head of all, general Sheridan. . . ." Other reformers condemned the action in equally vigorous terms.

But the military authorities, from Sherman and Sheridan on down the chain of command, supported Baker's attack, calling it justified and necessary. Sheridan wrote to Sherman, "Since 1862, at least eight hundred men, women and children have been murdered within the limits of my present command, in most fiendish manner, the men usually scalped and mutilated, their privates cut off and placed in their mouths; women ravished sometimes fifty and sixty times in succession, then killed and scalped, sticks stuck up their persons before and after death. I have myself conversed with one woman, who, while some months gone in pregnancy, was ravished over thirty times successively by different Indians, becoming insensible two or three times during this fearful ordeal; and each time on recovering consciousness, mutely appealing for mercy, if not for herself, for her unborn child. Also another woman ravished with more fearful brutality, over forty times, and the last sticking the point of his saber up the person of the woman. I could give the names of these women were it not for delicacy." Sheridan may have been obsessed with numbers, but his point that the Indians were savages was not lost on Sherman.

Sherman, a man of ingenuity, presented this line of defense in a letter to Sheridan: "The Piegans [Pikunis] were attacked on the application of General Sully and the Interior Department, and that these should now be shocked at the result of their requisitions and endeavor to cast blame on you and Colonel Baker is unfair."

Finally, the United States Army's internal investigation found Sheridan and Baker innocent of any wrongdoing and considered the matter closed. The debate died down, then ended. Congress got on to other pressing matters, the newspapers had other news to report, and the reformers had other reforms to press. But two important decisions that would affect Indian policy forever came out of the Baker Massacre. One, although there had been a very strong movement in Congress to transfer control of Indian affairs from the Department of the Interior to the War Department, Congress now had no stomach for it. Most felt that it would be the old story of appointing the fox to guard the henhouse. And two, the military would henceforth have nothing to do with supervising the reservation Indians. Until the massacre, the Indian agents had been military men. Now, President Grant proposed to the Quakers, as part of his Quaker policy, that they select from among themselves capable individuals who could run the reservations in a more humane way. Although only a few Quakers answered the call, other church groups became involved. The bottom line of this new policy was that civilians, acting as agents of the government, would administer to the Indians. The military was out—at least, officially. As we shall see, the army maintained a strong presence in Indian country.

And so the matter ended on a national level. Despite the support of Sherman and Sheridan, "Piegan" Baker, as he came to be known, did not get promoted for his action at the Big Bend of the Marias River; in fact, he never got promoted at all. In August 1872, while escorting Northern Pacific Railroad surveyors, his command was attacked by a Sioux war party. Baker was so drunk that he refused to admit that a fight was going on around him. That was about the last anyone heard of the man whose actions prompted such sweeping change in Indian policy.

As for the Blackfeet, they never raised arms against the United States again.

The Big Bend of the Marias River was a favorite wintering spot among the Blackfeet. The black clay walls rise almost vertically from the river bottom to the top of the prairies. The river itself makes a large horseshoe bend, the apex of the bend striking the cliffs to the south. On the west side of the cliffs a series of ridges cut by deep ravines look down on the brushy flats which flank the river. It was onto these flats that Heavy Runner's people moved when Mountain Chief's band moved out. The dark, almost black ridges provided protection from the cold winds which blew above them. It was from these ridges that the soldiers waited for dawn to begin their killing.

One has to imagine what the camp looked like on that January day in 1870. The river has changed course several times in the ensuing years; the vegetation has changed from cottonwoods and willows to mostly greasewood and brush, in large part because of the presence of the backup from Tiber Dam, a few miles downstream. The trees have been cut down and the willows have disappeared from the yearly floods.

The massacre, as well as the site, has disappeared from public consciousness. It is dutifully noted in historical texts as a small paragraph or a footnote, then forgotten, while the writers get on to bigger and better things, such as the Battle of the Little Bighorn. Even the Blackfeet, while aware of the event, have not given it the attention it deserves in their tribal history. (Recently, educators George Heavy Runner and Darryl Kipp, descendants of the chief and the scout, have begun a series of field trips to the site, during which they tell Blackfeet children the history of the event and how it affects their people today). When I was writing my historical novel *Fools Crow,* I felt that I needed to visit the site in order to describe it truly, the way it must have been over a hundred years ago. Of course, I should have known that the spring runoff from the Rocky Mountains had altered the course of the river somewhat, but I didn't expect that the backup from Tiber Dam would reach this far upriver; nor that the woodcutters had cleared out the trees to accommodate a full reservoir in the spring.

It was in the late fall of 1985 that I decided to find the massacre site. I had talked it over with my wife, Lois, and a couple of friends—Bill Bevis, who teaches in the English Department with my wife at the University of Montana in Missoula, and Ripley Hugo, a poet and the widow of Richard Hugo, the celebrated poet and teacher, who died in 1982.

Ripley's family has always owned a cabin on the south fork of the Teton River, a river which, like the tributaries of the Marias (Badger Creek, Birch Creek, Cut-bank Creek, and the Two Medicine River), runs directly east out of the Rocky Mountains onto the plains to eventually empty into the Missouri River.

I should note here that Montana is loosely but definitively divided into two parts—western Montana, which is the mountainous part; and eastern Montana, which is the plains part. They are separated by the Continental Divide. All the rivers on the west side flow into the Pacific Ocean; all the rivers on the east side flow into the Atlantic (via the Missouri, the Mississippi, the Gulf of Mexico). Very simple and neat. Eastern Montana comprises two-thirds of the state and is by far the more interesting part from a historical standpoint. It was here on the eastern plains that the great conflicts between the settlers from the east and the native peoples took place. It was here that the Massacre on the Marias in 1870 and the Battle of the Little Bighorn in 1876 took place. Since Montana is so enormous, the two conflicts took place many hundreds of miles apart and involved different Indian tribes' territories.

I live in western Montana but I come from eastern Montana. I was born on the Blackfeet Reservation, a figurative stone's throw from the Rocky Mountains. If I had been born with my eyes open I might have looked out the Indian Health Service hospital window and my first vision would have been the snow-capped Chief Mountain, the sacred mountain in the Rockies where many a youth went to have his vision. Nevertheless, the reservation was just off the foothills onto the plains, and that makes it eastern Montana.

But it was in Missoula, across the Continental Divide, official western Montana, that I decided with the help of my wife and friends to find the place where Heavy Runner, possibly an ancestor of mine, met his fate on that cold January dawn. I did have another motive, apart from the fact that I wanted to describe the site truly: My great-grandmother Red Paint Woman had been a member of Heavy Runner's band and, although shot in the leg by the soldiers, had managed to escape upriver, to the west, with a few other survivors. Red Paint Woman had told my father many stories of that time when he was a boy. Although an old woman, who refused to learn even grocery-store English, she remembered everything that had happened to her and her people. It was her stories, related to me by my father, that informed the many stories I told in *Fools Crow*, an account of the Blackfeet (Pikuni) people of that era that culminates in the Massacre on the Marias.

Bill Bevis had done some research in the Montana Historical Society library in Helena and in the University of Montana library, but nowhere could he find a reference to the exact site of the massacre. He asked several historians if they knew where it had taken place. I asked some Blackfeet friends if they could locate the site for me. Nobody knew where it was. Finally Bevis found a slim book written by a man named Ege and published by the Old Army Press in 1970. It is a discussion of the tactics used by the military in that campaign. It does not concern itself with the morality of the act of such wholesale slaughter. Fair enough. It was a place to start.

Ege makes a point of the fact that the exact site had been lost for several years prior to his own looking. There can be no doubt that after much sleuthing he found it. With a metal detector he found thousands of cartridge cases of the type used by the military during that period. On a black ridge just above the Big Bend of the Marias River.

In the center of the book, on two pages, is a grainy, poorly reproduced photograph of the site. It is taken from a ridge almost due west of the site. One can see the cliffs and the ridges, the bend of the river, the dark bottomlands, prominent features, but because it was taken from such a distance, the site looks like many other large river bends cut through the plains of eastern Montana. Try as I might, I could see nothing—not a pattern of trees or willows, not a flat that would look like a natural camping area, not a sign of man-made material—that would distinguish this particular landscape as a site of one of the most horrific massacres in western history.

We drove from Missoula to Ripley's cabin on the Teton River, a distance of four hours, late one cool, sunny September day. The drive was lovely, and we remarked on the first frosting of snow on the higher peaks, the gold of the turning aspen trees, the deer standing in thickets beside the road, and the ducks and geese in the marshes and potholes of the high valleys. We were happy to be on such a mission of high purpose, and when we crossed the Continental Divide at Rogers Pass, we were giddy with anticipation.

But it is when you break out of the mountains and suddenly you see the foothills, and beyond them the rolling golden plains that stretch east as far as the earth's curve will allow the eye to see, that you realize you live in a country uncommon in its sweep. This is the Big Sky, so named from the great novel by A. B. Guthrie, Jr. The sky is so big here that clouds, even the thunderheads that appeared south of us, seem as insignificant as the thousands of cars and motor homes each summer, filled with visitors who suddenly feel vulnerable and threatened by such vastness. Their predecessors, the settlers and homesteaders, felt this same vulnerability, modified somewhat by their faint hopes of "taming the land."

That night in Ripley's cabin we studied the photograph of the massacre site and several topographical maps that Bevis had gotten from the Bureau of Land Management. We read every word of Ege's description until we felt confident we could find the site in our sleep. I think we all may have been secretly wondering what we were going to do with the knowledge we would acquire the next day. After all, the site had been lost both before and after Ege's discovery. Would we tell the world? Would the world come and erect a visitor center, a blacktop parking lot for tour buses? Would it become another Little Bighorn Battlefield Monument, a shrine visited by thousands and thousands of curiosity seekers each year?

We made the two-hour drive the next morning across numberless county roads bordering sagebrush plains, wheat fields, abandoned homesteads and rusty machinery, new homesteads of house trailers and metal buildings, always heading north and east, until we stopped on a bridge that spanned the Marias River not far from present-day Shelby. By our calculations the site should have been about a quarter mile downriver from where we stood. We could see that far, and what we saw was a field of alfalfa and a line of cottonwoods along the river. That land was neatly farmed, and the alfalfa, ready for a third cutting, was bright green beneath a threatening gray sky. In fact, the weather had changed drastically from the day before. A biting north wind had driven the clouds down from Canada. As I stood on that bridge, my mood changed as surely as the weather. I knew that nothing significant had happened in that particular bend of the river. It just didn't have the look of the Big Bend of the Marias.

Back in the car we studied the maps again. We looked up and down the river, but there were no roads, not even any cow trails that we could see. Furthermore, both sides were fenced off, the fence posts spray-painted orange. An ominous warning in the west even without the NO TRESPASSING signs.

We had passed a farmstead at the top of the grade on the east side of the road. Now as we looked up and down the gray slow-moving river, we began to realize that the farm was our best, perhaps our only, prospect. But again, like the bright green alfalfa field, the trim buildings settled on an old landscape didn't offer much hope.

But we did try it. We pulled into the yard in front of a small but nicely kept double-wide trailer with several outbuildings behind it. But there was no one at home. After ringing the doorbell and waiting, Bevis and Ripley went around back to a large metal barn. They had a copy of Ege's book in hand. Lois and I waited in the car. After almost half an hour they came back, looking somber. Then with a sudden rush of wind they were in the car, laughing and yelling.

They had asked the farmer, an early-middle-aged man who was in his coveralls preparing his machinery for a long winter of idleness, if he had heard of the Massacre on the Marias. No, he hadn't. They said it had to have happened near there. Nope, doesn't ring a bell. Are you sure? Lived here all my life, never heard of it. Maybe your wife . . . ? Nope. Then they showed him the double-page photograph in Ege's book. Look familiar? Can't say that it does. Nothing around here looks like this? Everything around here looks like that. Well, thanks for your help. . . . Wait a minute, let me look at that picture again. After some studying he pointed to a slender object in the left forefront of the grainy photograph. I recognize that fencepost. The fencepost was on the promontory of a high bluff from which the photograph was taken looking down into the big bend. Yeah, I've been there. I know exactly where it is. He gave directions. You take the county road south about three miles, you come to a little dirt road on your left, it's easy to miss, it almost doubles back in this direction, but you stay on it, you go past the missile silo, you come to a gate, go through, and maybe a mile or so you're right here. He pounded the book for emphasis.

We did as we were told and we did pass a Cyclone-fenced missile site. It looked like nothing above ground—the only signs were the electronic presence detectors and a large slab of concrete—but deep beneath the earth a silo housed a Minuteman missile as tall as a six-story building. There are maybe a thousand such missiles in Montana. Montanans like to say they are the fourth-largest nuclear power in the world. (But this is no longer true. At the time of this writing, the Cold War has ended and the missiles are being deactivated.)

We passed through the barbed-wire gate and drove another half mile until the road ended. I turned off the motor and we stared straight ahead at the wooden fence post. Beyond it lay a vast space of sky, as gray as the day looked in the Ege photograph of 1970. I've often wondered if it was a clear day that January of 1870 when all hell broke loose and the spirits of 173 Blackfeet traveled to the Sand Hills, the resting place of departed souls. Nothing I have read indicates whether the sky was clear or cloudy, only that it was dawn and the temperature was around thirty below.

We got out of the car and walked up the rise to the promontory, and suddenly we could see a long way, all the way down the valley of the Marias to the backup of the Tiber Dam reservoir. We could see even farther than that, but we didn't need to. What we had come to see lay just below the promontory—the Big Bend of the Marias. And the landscape was black. The valley floor, the cliffs and ridges above it, the scrub brush upon it, even the river—all black beneath the gray sky. The only flashes of light were the windward sides of silvery sagebrush bending beneath the relentless north wind. We stood in silence for a few minutes, trying to take in that formidable landscape. Even without looking at the Ege photograph, we knew what we were seeing.

Lois found a game trail on the side of the promontory, a steep descent on the diagonal, tricky going. We slipped and skidded the hundred yards down until we were standing on the flat at the base of the promontory. The wind was not as strong as it had been on the top, but it still burned the cheeks and ears.

I remember wondering, as I wandered across the wasted flat, what the village must have looked like on January 22, 1870, the day before the massacre. It would have been a winter camp, bundled up against the cold, of less than forty lodges. Perhaps a few women would have been walking back to their homes with water or a sheaf of sticks or buffalo chips to heat the lodge and cook what little winter stores they had. Normally, there would have been a few children outside playing with buffalo-rib sleds or small bows and spears. The men would have been visiting or perhaps gambling or making arrows. But it was a camp of death already. Small-pox, the white scabs disease, the white man's gift, had visited the Pikuni camps that winter. Medicine men, the many-faces men, the heavy-singers-for-the-sick, would have been singing, praying, administering their useless medicines to the dying. By the time that winter was over, a third to a half of all the people in all the bands would be dead. So it would have been a quiet camp on the surface, but within the lodges there would be much sickness, agony, terror, hunger, and exhaustion. And the Pikunis, the Blackfeet, would never fully recover from that winter. Even to this day.

I also remember noticing that as we walked across the flat we began to drift apart. By the time I got to where the heart of the camp must have been, beneath a low black ridge from which the soldiers fired their rounds into the lodges, I was standing by myself. As I looked up the gentle slope to the top of the ridge, I thought, This would be where the children played on their sleds. Perhaps Heavy Runner, or my great-grandmother Red Paint Woman, had stood on this very spot and watched them, heard their cries of delight. Perhaps Red Paint, who was not yet a teenager, was one of them. Some years later, as I stood on the bank of the Little Bighorn River, on the southern end of the immense camp of Lakotas, Cheyennes, and Arapahos, where Reno made his charge, I thought of the children playing in the river, riding their ponies, the girls picking flowers with which to make crowns or bracelets. In both instances I thought of children, perhaps because they are truly the innocents.

We stayed for two to three hours, climbing the ridge, looking at the slow dark river, leaving our always circling footprints in the crumbling dark gumbo, and then we left.

How does one compare this incident in western history with the one at the Little Bighorn, Custer's Last Stand? The difference could not be in the numbers alone. Here, 173 Indians were killed. There, 263 white men, 210 under Custer's command, not to mention sixty to one hundred Indians, died. Both were large numbers of fatalities by western standards of that time. Why, then, is Custer's Last Stand such an important part of this nation's history, and why is the Massacre on the Marias known to so few people? In both cases, the United States Army and Plains Indians were involved. The Indians would say they were defending their territory, or exercising their right to be free upon it, to follow the buffalo as they had for centuries; the white authorities would say that they were punishing the Indians for depredations against the white settlers, traders, rivermen, wood gatherers, and miners, or for leaving the reservations without permission. In any case, contrary to some opinion, these actions resulted from a clash of cultures. What caused this clash is evident. The Indians lived on territories that the whites wanted. Most such collisions occur when one culture wants something from the other. It is always astonishing when the invading culture feels it has the divine right (call it Manifest Destiny or whatever) to take that something in this case, land— from the other.

It is important to point out, with the quincentennial year of Columbus's "discovery" of America just past, that initially the Indian tribes of the North American continent, for the most part, welcomed the pale-skinned men who came to these shores and eventually began to move west. They were not the bloodthirsty savages that later yellow journalists and dime novelists made them out to be. In the beginning the Indians wanted something from the whites—commerce. They wanted coffee, and sugar to put into that coffee; they wanted pans to cook their meat in; they wanted guns to kill that meat; and they wanted horses to give them the mobility to find that meat more readily. They were willing to give up some of their territories to get these commodities. To be sure, there were incidents begun by Indians that resulted in localized hostilities; but there were more incidents begun by the whites' desire to dispossess these "savages," who did not know how to use the land "properly." By the time the whites invaded the northern plains in force in the 1850s and 1860s, the general consensus of opinion in America was that the Indians should be driven off these lands permanently. Some in the Congress, in the government, and in the army echoed the cries of those on the frontier that if the Indians did not relinquish their land peacefully and move to ever-shrinking reservations, then genocide should be considered a reasonable option. So when Sheridan's order came down that "if the lives and property of the citizens of Montana can best be protected by striking Mountain Chief's band, I want them struck," it didn't matter a whit to the army and to the citizens of Montana that the wrong band, a band led by a peace chief, had been struck. "Annihilation" was a word used frequently by the whites of that period. "Nits make lice" was a common phrase. For those who think "annihilation" is too strong a word, consider that it has been estimated that there were 75 million Indians in the Americas, perhaps six million in the contiguous United States area, when Columbus arrived. By 1900, only 237,000 Indians in the United States remained.

Perhaps the largest difference (and the most ignored) between the Massacre on the Marias and the Battle of the Little Bighorn six years later was that Baker was successful in carrying out the army's orders and Custer wasn't. In one incident a large number of Indians were killed; in the other, a popular western hero's entire command was wiped out. Was Custer a fool who rode to his death, as Sitting Bull, the great Sioux leader, stated, or was he a martyr who died in the cause of righteousness, as both the frontier and eastern press contended? Did it matter that some perceived Custer as a fool, others as a hero? Not much. The fact that Custer *died* mattered. His death was proof that the Indians were savages and should be dealt with just as the whites dealt with all the savages they encountered around the world. Ironically, Baker, who was successful in killing a lot of Indians, never became a hero and died an obscure drunk. Custer, in being killed, was elevated to mythical status by the press and the poets. The Custer Myth was born.

And that myth of the martyr making a heroic Last Stand against a red horde versus the mundane fact of an unruly drunk successfully killing the wrong Indians was probably the big difference between the two events. In spite of the outcry from Quakers, abolitionists, preachers, civil rights groups, and a few prominent congressmen and government officials, not many Americans lost sleep over the Massacre on the Marias. Most felt the Indians deserved it for standing in the way of progress. Tough. But the Custer "massacre" (in spite of the fact that he attacked a peaceful camp) touched a wellspring of hysteria. It became the rallying cry for the final push westward ("Get the first scalp for Custer!") and the subjugation or annihilation of the "red fiends," as they became known in the press. And thus began the long determined effort by the whites to destroy Indian cultures, which goes on today in a more subtle form in government, schools, and churches.

One more thing—whites wrote the history of these and all the other conflicts that resulted from the coming together of the two races. Needless to say, this history has been carefully distorted throughout the years to justify the invasion and subjugation of the indigenous people. While there is some "lo, the poor Indian" rhetoric in these historical accounts, the writers were as much a part of the invading culture's establishment as the politicians and military men. In 1859, Horace Greeley wrote, "To the prosaic observer, the average Indian of the woods and prairies is a being who does little credit to human nature—a slave of appetite and sloth, never emancipated from the tyranny of one animal passion save by the more ravenous demands of another. . . . I could not help saying, 'These people must die out—there is no help for them. God has given this earth to those who will subdue and cultivate it, and it is vain to struggle against His righteous decree.' " Custer himself wrote a similar description of the Native Americans in his *My Life on the Plains.*

It has been only recently that historians have begun to incorporate Indian accounts of events like the Battle of the Little Bighorn into "official" accounts. Perhaps the first book to do this in a popular way was *Bury My Heart at Wounded Knee,* by Dee Brown. Because it was deemed subjective and too slanted in favor of the Indians by the Custer Battlefield Historical and Museum Association, it is not, as of this writing, sold in the bookshop at the visitor center.

The Indian wars on the plains are a tragic part of this country's history. The Battle of the Little Bighorn is but one of many battles fought as the hostile forces sought to sweep away the Indians and the Indians fought to stay alive. The Massacre on the Marias is far more emblematic of the Indians' fate, as they were defeated tribe by tribe by the whites who pushed into their territories in violation of treaty after treaty. The outcome of the Indian wars was never in doubt. It is a tribute to the Indians' spirit that they resisted as long as they did. Custer's Last Stand has gone down in history as an example of what savagery the Indians were capable of; the Massacre on the Marias is a better example of what man is capable of doing to man.

Further Reading

The Death of Jim Loney. 1979.
Indian Lawyer. 1990.
Riding the Earthboy 40. 1976.

Reading about James Welch

Bevis, William. "James Welch." *Updating the Literary West*. Fort Worth: Texas Christian University Press, 1997. 808–26.

McFarland, Ron, ed. *James Welch*. Lewiston ID: Confluence Press, 1986.

——. *Understanding James Welch*. Columbia: University of South Carolina Press, 2000.

Owens, Louis, "Earthboy's Return: James Welch's Acts of Recovery." *Other Destinies: Understanding the American Indian Novel*. Norman: University of Oklahoma Press, 1992. 128–66.

Wild, Peter. *James Welch*. Western Writers Series. Boise ID: Boise State University, 1983.

Louise Erdrich

This short poem is Louise Erdrich's view of the dilemma James Welch considers in his book *Killing Custer*, a deep if invisible disjuncture between American Indians' view of themselves and the white hero stereotype embodied in the movie star John Wayne. In addition to presenting an indigenous perspective, Erdrich shows how Natives must mediate popular representations of themselves.

For the biography of and further reading about Erdrich see pages 179 and 191.

Dear John Wayne (1984)

August and the drive-in picture is packed.
We lounge on the hood of the Pontiac
surrounded by the slow-burning spirals they sell
at the window, to vanquish the hordes of mosquitoes.
Nothing works. They break through the smoke screen for blood.

Always the lookout spots the Indians first,
spread north to south, barring progress.
The Sioux or some other Plains bunch
in spectacular columns, ICBM missiles,
feathers bristling in the meaningful sunset.

The drum breaks. There will be no parlance.
Only the arrows whining, a death-cloud of nerves
swarming down on the settlers
who die beautifully, tumbling like dust weeds
into the history that brought us all here
together: this wide screen beneath the sign of the bear.

The sky fills, acres of blue squint and eye
that the crowd cheers. His face moves over us,
a thick cloud of vengeance, pitted
like the land that was once flesh. Each rut,
each scar makes a promise: *It is
not over, this fight, not as long as you resist.*

Everything we see belongs to us.

A few laughing Indians fall over the hood
slipping in the hot spilled butter.
The eye sees a lot, John, but the heart is so blind.
Death makes us owners of nothing.
He smiles, a horizon of teeth
the credits reel over, and then the white fields
again blowing in the true-to-life dark.
The dark films over everything.
We get into the car
scratching our mosquito bites, speechless and small
as people are when the movie is done.
We are back in our skins.

How can we help but keep hearing his voice,
the flip side of the sound track, still playing:
Come on, boys, we got them
where we want them, drunk, running.
They'll give us what we want, what we need.
Even his disease was the idea of taking everything.
Those cells, burning, doubling, splitting out of their skins.

4. Adapting to a New Country

Surviving Nature's Storms

When the first good crops brought settlers some cash, they turned their sod houses into corn cribs or storage sheds and built wood frame houses that looked oddly inappropriate until the trees the farm wives insisted upon planting began to provide some protecting shade that connected the buildings to the landscape. The frame houses, exposed to the wind, dust, and cold of the Great Plains, sometimes made the occupants long for the thick sod walls of their first homes. Most of the farmers were too busy trying to grow another good crop, to save cattle from thirst or blizzard or wheat from hail or locusts, to care much about the house. It was up to the women to make the houses into homes and the homes into integral parts of the communities. The women added the details: porches, flowers, fly-discouraging screens.

"Surviving" is a fact of life for plains dwellers and has been a miraculous imperative for Native peoples. Even town and city residents must pay attention to what grows—or doesn't grow—in the fields just beyond the latest suburban development. The farmers' crops stored in the city's grain elevators and the cattle in the town's feedlots provide a large portion of the plains states' exports. The blizzard that means a day off at home for the urban dweller means more hard work for the farmer. Roads closed by snow, dust, or the occasional flood are more than an inconvenience to people who must drive long distances to do almost everything— shop, work, or get away. Economic disaster is a real possibility if cattle prices drop below the price of feed or if the farmer's crop is worth less in the elevator than it cost to put it in the ground. When a farmer gives up, sells out, and moves on, the region is diminished. The writers in this section know that the most basic part of this interlocking pattern, the house, is more than a warm kitchen or a porch and the clutter under it. If there is no one in the porch swing, no child to claim the clutter, the neighbors and casual passers-by know that something is missing in the landscape.

The stories and poems in this section are hard stories of the struggle to survive the worst that nature can present to those who assume that they will survive by sheer force of will on the Great Plains. Any hesitation will turn into a loss. Physical and economic forces wear down many a family's resolve. They give up the effort to make the Great Plains the Garden of the World and head to the cities back east or west for sunny California.

Reading about the Great Plains in Literature

Hafen, P. Jane. "Native American Writers of the Midwest." In *Updating the Literary West.*
Ed. Diane D. Quantic. Fort Worth: Texas Christian University Press, 1997. 711–20.

Harrison, Dick. *Unnamed Country: The Struggle for a Canadian Prairie Fiction.* Edmonton:
University of Alberta Press, 1977.

Meyer, Roy. *The Middle Western Farm Novel in the Twentieth Century.* Lincoln: University of
Nebraska Press, 1965.

Quantic, Diane D., ed. "The Midwest and the Great Plains." In *Updating the Literary West.*
Fort Worth: Texas Christian University Press, 1997. 641–727.

———. *The Nature of the Place: A Study of Great Plains Fiction.* Lincoln: University of Nebraska Press, 1995.

Ricou, Laurence. *Vertical Man–Horizontal World: Man and Landscape in Canadian Prairie
Fiction.* Vancouver: University of British Columbia Press, 1973.

Smith, Henry Nash. *Virgin Land: The American West as Symbol and Myth.* 1950; rpt. Cambridge: Harvard University Press, 1970.

Thacker, Robert. *The Great Prairie Fact and Literary Imagination.* Albuquerque: University
of New Mexico Press, 1984.

Ron Hansen *(b. 1947)*

A unifying theme in Ron Hansen's writing is the individual's struggle with essential moral questions of integrity and survival in a complex, secular, and apparently indifferent world. Hansen explores these issues in his collection of stories about Nebraska, some based on actual events and some originating in his vivid imagination. 'Wickedness" is a collection of vignettes about a blizzard's physical threat. Hansen acknowledges the storm's apparent conscious malevolence: "Everything about the blizzard seems to have personality and hateful intentions." Hansen joins other Great Plains writers who write about the hard winters, especially in the late 1880s, that are a frequent motif in Great Plains literature.*

Hansen was born in Omaha, Nebraska. He received an undergraduate degree from Omaha's Creighton University and an MFA from the University of Iowa. He has taught at Stanford University, Cornell University, the State University of New York at Binghamton, and at the University of California at Santa Cruz, where he is the Gerard Manley Hopkins Professor of Writing. His settings and genres are as varied as his teaching venues, ranging from juvenile fiction to murder mystery and the Western, from the past to the present.

Wickedness (1989)

At the end of the nineteenth century a girl from Delaware got on a milk train in Omaha and took a green wool seat in the second-class car. August was outside the window, and sunlight was a yellow glare on the trees. Up front, a railway conductor in a navy-blue uniform was gingerly backing down the aisle with a heavy package in a gunnysack that a boy was helping him with. They were talking about an agreeable seat away from the hot Nebraska day that was persistent outside, and then they were setting their cargo across the runnered aisle from the girl and tilting it against the shellacked wooden wall of the railway car before walking back up the aisle and elsewhere into August.

She was sixteen years old and an Easterner just recently hired as a county schoolteacher, but she knew enough about prairie farming to think the heavy

*Fierce blizzards are an important part of Rølvaag's *Giants in the Earth,* Laura Ingalls Wilder's *The Long Winter,* and several of the stories in Sinclair Ross's *The Lamp at Noon and Other Stories.*

package was a crank-and-piston washing machine or a boxed plowshare and coulter, something no higher than the bloody stump where the poultry were chopped with a hatchet and then wildly high-stepped around the yard. Soon, however, there was a juggling movement and the gunnysack slipped aside, and she saw an old man sitting there, his limbs hacked away, and dark holes where his ears ought to have been, the skin pursed at his jaw hinge like pink lips in a kiss. The milk train jerked into a roll through the railway yard, and the old man was jounced so that his gray cheek pressed against the hot window glass. Although he didn't complain, it seemed an uneasy position, and the girl wished she had the courage to get up from her seat and tug the jolting body upright. She instead got to her page in *Quo Vadis* and pretended to be so rapt by the book that she didn't look up again until Columbus, where a doctor with liquorice on his breath sat heavily beside her and openly stared over his newspaper before whispering that the poor man was a carpenter in Genoa who'd been caught out in the great blizzard of 1888. Had she heard of that one?

The girl shook her head.

She ought to look out for their winters, the doctor said. Weather in Nebraska could be the wickedest thing she ever saw.

She didn't know what to say, so she said nothing. And at Genoa a young teamster got on in order to carry out the old man, whose half body was heavy enough that the boy had to yank the gunnysack up the aisle like sixty pounds of mail.

In the year 1888, on the twelfth day of January, a pink sun was up just after seven and southeastern zephyrs of such soft temperature were sailing over the Great Plains that squatters walked their properties in high rubber boots and April jackets and some farmhands took off their Civil War greatcoats to rake silage into the cattle troughs. However, sheep that ate whatever they could the night before raised their heads away from food and sniffed the salt tang in the air. And all that morning streetcar mules were reported to be acting up, nipping each other, jingling the hitch rings, foolishly waggling their dark manes and necks as though beset by gnats and horseflies.

A Danish cattleman named Axel Hansen later said he was near the Snake River and tipping a teaspoon of saleratus into a yearling's mouth when he heard a faint groaning in the north that was like the noise of a high waterfall at a fair distance. Axel looked toward Dakota, and there half the sky was suddenly gray and black and indigo blue with great storm clouds that were seething up as high as the sun and wrangling toward him at horse speed. Weeds were being uprooted, sapling trees were bullwhipping, and the top inches of snow and prairie soil were being sucked up and stirred like the dirty flour that was called red dog. And then the onslaught hit him hard as furniture, flying him onto his back so that when Axel looked up, he seemed to be deep undersea and in icehouse cold. Eddying snow made it hard to breathe any way but sideways, and getting up to just his knees and hands seemed a great attainment. Although his sod house was but a quarter-mile away, it took Axel four hours to get there. Half his face was frozen gray and hard as weatherboarding so the cattleman was speechless until nightfall, and then Axel Hansen simply told his wife, That was not pleasant.

Cow tails stuck out sideways when the wind caught them. Sparrows and crows whumped hard against the windowpanes, their jerking eyes seeking out an escape, their wings fanned out and flattened as though pinned up in an ornithologist's display. Cats died, dogs died, pigeons died. Entire farms of cattle and pigs and geese and chickens were wiped out in a single night. Horizontal snow that was hard and dry as salt dashed and seethed over everything, sloped up like rooftops, tricked its way across creek beds and ditches, milkily purled down city streets, stole shanties and coops and pens from a bleak landscape that was even then called the Great American Desert. Everything about the blizzard seemed to have personality and hateful intention. Especially the cold. At six A.M., the temperature at Valentine, Nebraska, was thirty degrees above zero. Half a day later the temperature was fourteen below, a drop of forty-four degrees and the difference between having toes and not, between staying alive overnight and not, between ordinary concerns and one overriding idea.

Ainslie Classen was hopelessly lost in the whiteness and tilting low under the jamming gale when his right elbow jarred against a joist of his pigsty. He walked around the sty by skating his sore red hands along the upright shiplap and then squeezed inside through the slops trough. The pigs scampered over to him, seeking his protection, and Ainslie put himself among them, getting down in their stink and their body heat, socking them away only when they ganged up or when two or three presumed he was food. Hurt was nailing into his finger joints until he thought to work his hands into the pigs' hot wastes, then smeared some onto his skin. The pigs grunted around him and intelligently snuffled at his body with their pink and tender noses, and Ainslie thought, *You are not me but I am you,* and Ainslie Classen got through the night without shame or injury.

Whereas a Hartington woman took two steps out her door and disappeared until the snow sank away in April and raised her body up from her garden patch.

An Omaha cigar maker got off the Leavenworth Street trolley that night, fifty yards from his own home and five yards from another's. The completeness of the blizzard so puzzled him that the cigar maker tramped up and down the block more than twenty times and then slept against a lamppost and died.

A cattle inspector froze to death getting up on his quarter horse. The next morning he was still tilting the saddle with his upright weight, one cowboy boot just inside the iced stirrup, one bear-paw mitten over the horn and reins. His quarter horse apparently kept waiting for him to complete his mount, and then the quarter horse died too.

A Chicago boy visiting his brother for the holidays was going to a neighbor's farm to borrow a scoop shovel when the night train of blizzard raged in and overwhelmed him. His tracks showed the boy mistakenly slanted past the sod house he'd just come from, and then tilted forward with perhaps the vain hope of running into some shop or shed or railway depot. His body was found four days later and twenty-seven miles from home.

A forty-year-old wife sought out her husband in the open range land near O'Neill and days later was found standing up in her muskrat coat and black bandanna, her scarf-wrapped hands tightly clenching the top strand of rabbit wire that was keeping her upright, her blue eyes still open but cloudily bottled by a half inch of ice, her jaw unhinged as though she'd died yelling out a name.

The one A.M. report from the Chief Signal Officer in Washington, DC, had said Kansas and Nebraska could expect "fair weather, followed by snow, brisk to high southerly winds gradually diminishing in force, becoming westerly and warmer, followed by colder."

Sin Thomas undertook the job of taking Emily Flint home from their Holt County schoolhouse just before noon. Sin's age was sixteen, and Emily was not only six years younger but also practically kin to him, since her stepfather was Sin's older brother. Sin took the girl's hand and they haltingly tilted against the uprighting gale on their walk to a dark horse, gray-maned and gray-tailed with ice. Sin cracked the reins loose of the crowbar tie-up and helped Emily up onto his horse, jumping up onto the croup from a soapbox and clinging the girl to him as though she were groceries he couldn't let spill.

Everything she knew was no longer there. She was in a book without descriptions. She could put her hand out and her hand would disappear. Although Sin knew the general direction to Emily's house, the geography was so duned and drunk with snow that Sin gave up trying to nudge his horse one way or another and permitted its slight adjustments away from the wind. Hours passed and the horse strayed southeast into Wheeler County, and then in misery and pneumonia it stopped, planing its overworked legs like four parts of an argument and slinging its head away from Sin's yanks and then hanging its nose in anguish. Emily hopped down into the snow and held on to the boy's coat pocket as Sin uncinched the saddle and jerked off a green horse blanket and slapped it against his iron leggings in order to crack the ice from it. And then Sin scooped out a deep nook in a snow slope that was high and steep as the roof of a New Hampshire house. Emily tightly wrapped herself in the green horse blanket and slumped inside the nook in the snow, and the boy crept on top of her and stayed like that, trying not to press into her.

Emily would never say what was said or was cautiously not said that night. She may have been hysterical. In spite of the fact that Emily was out of the wind, she later said that the January night's temperature was like wire-cutting pliers that snipped at her ears and toes and fingertips until the horrible pain became only a nettling and then a kind of sleep and her feet seemed as dead as her shoes. Emily wept, but her tears froze cold as penny nails and her upper lip seemed candlewaxed by her nose and she couldn't stop herself from feeling the difference in the body on top of her. She thought Sin Thomas was responsible, that the night suited his secret purpose, and she so complained of the bitter cold that Sin finally took off his Newmarket overcoat and tailored it around the girl; but sixty years later, when Emily wrote her own account of the ordeal, she forgot to say anything about him giving her his overcoat and only said in an ordinary way that they spent the night inside a snowdrift and that "by morning the storm had subsided."

With daybreak Sin told Emily to stay there and, with or without his Newmarket overcoat, the boy walked away with the forlorn hope of chancing upon his horse. Winds were still high, the temperature was thirty-five degrees below zero, and the snow was deep enough that Sin pulled lopsidedly with every step and then toppled over just a few yards away. And then it was impossible for him to get to his knees, and Sin only sank deeper when he attempted to swim up into the high wave of snow hanging over him. Sin told himself that he would try again to get out, but first he'd build up his strength by napping for just a little while. He arranged his body in the snow gully so that the sunlight angled onto it, and then Sin Thomas gave in to sleep and within twenty minutes died.

His body was discovered at noon by a Wheeler County search party, and shortly after that they came upon Emily. She was carried to a nearby house where she slumped in a kitchen chair while girls her own age dipped Emily's hands and feet into pans of ice water. She could look up over a windowsill and see Sin Thomas's body standing upright on the porch, his hands woodenly crossed at his chest, so Emily kept her brown eyes on the pinewood floor and slept that night with jars of hot water against her skin. She could not walk for two months. Even scissoring tired her hands. She took a cashier's job with the Nebraska Farm Implements Company and kept it for forty-five years, staying all her life in Holt County. She died in a wheelchair on a hospital porch in the month of April. She was wearing a glamorous sable coat. She never married.

The T. E. D. Schusters' only child was a seven-year-old boy named Cleo who rode his Shetland pony to the Westpoint school that day and had not shown up on the doorstep by two P.M., when Mr. Schuster went down into the root cellar, dumped purple sugar beets onto the earthen floor, and upended the bushel basket over his head as he slung himself against the onslaught in his second try for Westpoint. Hours later Mrs. Schuster was tapping powdered salt onto the night candles in order to preserve the wax when the door abruptly blew open and Mr. Schuster stood there without Cleo and utterly white and petrified with cold. She warmed him up with okra soup and tenderly wrapped his frozen feet and hands in strips of gauze that she'd dipped in kerosene, and they were sitting on milking stools by a red-hot stove, their ankles just touching, only the usual sentiments being expressed, when they heard a clopping on the wooden stoop and looked out to see the dark Shetland pony turned gray and shaggy-bearded with ice, his legs as wobbly as if he'd just been born. Jammed under the saddle skirt was a damp, rolled-up note from the Scottish schoolteacher that said, Cleo is safe. The Schusters invited the pony into the house and bewildered him with praises as Cleo's mother scraped ice from the pony's shag with her own ivory comb, and Cleo's father gave him sugar from the Dresden bowl as steam rose up from the pony's back.

Even at six o'clock that evening, there was no heat in Mathias Aachen's house, and the seven Aachen children were in whatever stockings and clothing they owned as they put their hands on a Hay-burner stove that was no warmer than soap. When a jar of apricots burst open that night and the iced orange syrup did not ooze out, Aachen's wife told the children, You ought now to get under your covers. While the seven were crying and crowding onto their dirty floor mattresses, she rang the green tent cloth along the iron wire dividing the house and slid underneath horse blankets in Mathias Aachen's gray wool trousers and her own gray dress and a ghastly muskrat coat that in hot weather gave birth to insects.

Aachen said, Every one of us will be dying of cold before morning. Freezing here. In Nebraska.

His wife just lay there, saying nothing.

Aachen later said he sat up bodingly until shortly after one P.M., when the house temperature was so exceedingly cold that a gray suede of ice was on the teapot and his pretty girls were whimpering in their sleep. You are not meant to stay here, Aachen thought, and tilted hot candle wax into his right ear and then his left, until he could only hear his body drumming blood. And then Aachen got his Navy Colt and kissed his wife and killed her. And then walked under the green tent cloth and killed his seven children, stopping twice to capture a scuttling boy and stopping once more to reload.

Hattie Benedict was in her Antelope County schoolyard overseeing the noon recess in a black cardigan sweater and gray wool dress when the January blizzard caught her unaware. She had been impatiently watching four girls in flying coats playing Ante I Over by tossing a spindle of chartreuse yarn over the one-room schoolhouse, and then a sharp cold petted her neck and Hattie turned toward the open fields of hoarfrosted scraggle and yellow grass. Just a half mile away was a gray blur of snow underneath a dark sky that was all hurry and calamity, like a nighttime city of sin-black buildings and havoc in the streets. Wind tortured a creekside cottonwood until it cracked apart. A tin water pail rang in a skipping roll to the horse path. One quarter of the tar-paper roof was torn from the schoolhouse and sailed southeast forty feet. And only then did Hattie yell for the older boys with their cigarettes and clay pipes to hurry in from the prairie twenty rods away, and she was hustling a dallying girl inside just as the snowstorm socked into her Antelope County schoolhouse, shipping the building awry off its timber skids so that the southwest side heavily dropped six inches and the oak-plank floor became a slope that Hattie ascended unsteadily while ordering the children to open their *Webster Franklin Fourth Reader* to the Lord's Prayer in verse and to say it aloud. And then Hattie stood by her desk with her pink hands held theatrically to her cheeks as she looked up at the walking noise of bricks being jarred from the chimney and down the roof. Every window view was as white as if butchers' paper had been tacked up. Winds pounded into the windowpanes and dry window putty trickled onto the unpainted sills. Even the slough grass fire in the Hay-burner stove was sucked high into the tin stack pipe so that the soot on it reddened and snapped. Hattie could only stare. Four of the boys were just about Hattie's age, so she didn't say anything when they ignored the reading assignment and earnestly got up from the wooden benches in order to argue *oughts* and *ought nots* in the cloakroom. She heard the girls saying Amen and then she saw Janusz Vasko, who was fifteen years old and had grown up in Nebraska weather, gravely exiting the cloakroom with a cigarette behind one ear and his right hand raised high overhead. Hattie called on him, and Janusz said the older boys agreed that they could get the little ones home, but only if they went out right away. And before she could even give it thought, Janusz tied his red handkerchief over his nose and mouth and jabbed his orange corduroy trousers inside his antelope boots with a pencil.

Yes, Hattie said, please go, and Janusz got the boys and girls to link themselves together with jump ropes and twine and piano wire, and twelve of Hattie Benedict's pupils walked out into a nothingness that the boys knew from their shoes up and dully worked their way across as though each crooked stump and tilted fence post was a word they could spell in a plain-spoken sentence in a book of practical knowledge. Hours later the children showed up at their homes, aching and crying in raw pain. Each was given cocoa or the green tea of the elder flower and hot bricks were put next to their feet while they napped and newspapers printed their names incorrectly. And then, one by one, the children disappeared from history.

Except for Johan and Alma Lindquist, aged nine and six, who stayed behind in the schoolhouse, owing to the greater distance to their ranch. Hattie opened a week-old Omaha newspaper on her desktop and with caution peeled a spotted yellow apple on it, eating tan slices from her scissor blade as she peered out at children who seemed irritatingly sad and pathetic. She said, You wish you were home.

The Lindquists stared.

Me too, she said. She dropped the apple core onto the newspaper page and watched it ripple with the juice stain. Have you any idea where Pennsylvania is?

East, the boy said. Johan was eating pepper cheese and day-old rye bread from a tin lunch box that sparked with electricity whenever he touched it. And his sister nudged him to show how her yellow hair was beguiled toward her green rubber comb whenever she brought it near.

Hattie was talking in such quick English that she could tell the Lindquists couldn't quite understand it. She kept hearing the snow pinging and pattering against the windowpanes, and the storm howling like clarinets down the stack pipe, but she perceived the increasing cold in the room only when she looked to the Lindquists and saw their Danish sentences grayly blossoming as they spoke. Hattie went into the cloakroom and skidded out the poorhouse box, rummaging from it a Scotch plaid scarf that she wrapped twice around her skull and ears just as a squaw would, and snipping off the fingertips of some red knitted gloves that were only slightly too small. She put them on and then she got into her secondhand coat and Alma whispered to her brother but Hattie said she'd have no whispering, she hated that, she couldn't wait for their kin to show up for them, she had too many responsibilities, and nothing interesting ever happened in the country. Everything was stupid. Everything was work. She didn't even have a girlfriend. She said she'd once been sick for four days, and two by two practically every woman in Neligh mistrustfully visited her rooming house to squint at Hattie and palm her forehead and talk about her symptoms. And then they'd snail out into the hallway and prattle and whisper in the hawk and spit of the German language.

Alma looked at Johan with misunderstanding and terror, and Hattie told them to get out paper and pencils; she was going to say some necessary things and the children were going to write them down. She slowly paced as she constructed a paragraph, one knuckle darkly striping the blackboard, but she couldn't properly express herself. She had forgotten herself so absolutely that she thought forgetting was a yeast in the air; or that the onslaught's only point was to say over and over again that she was next to nothing. Easily bewildered. Easily dismayed. The Lindquists were shying from the crazy woman and concentrating their shame on a nickel pad of Wisconsin paper. And Hattie thought, *You'll give me an ugly name and there will be cartoons and snickering and the older girls will idly slay me with jokes and imitations.*

She explained she was taking them to her rooming house, and she strode purposefully out into the great blizzard as if she were going out to a garden to fetch some strawberries, and Johan dutifully followed, but Alma stayed inside the schoolhouse with her purple scarf up over her mouth and nose and her own dark sandwich of pepper cheese and rye bread clutched to her breast like a prayer book. And then Johan stepped out of the utter whiteness to say Alma had to hurry up, that Miss Benedict was angrily asking him if his sister had forgotten how to use her legs. So Alma stepped out of the one-room schoolhouse, sinking deep in the snow and sloshing ahead in it as she would in a pond until she caught up with Hattie Benedict, who took the Lindquists' hands in her own and walked them into the utter whiteness and night of the afternoon. Seeking to blindly go north to her rooming house, Hattie put her high button shoes in the deep tracks that Janusz and the schoolchildren had made, but she misstepped twice, and that was enough to get her on a screw-tape path over snow humps and hillocks that took her south and west and very nearly into a great wilderness that was like a sea in high gale.

Hattie imagined herself reaching the Elkhorn River and discovering her rooming house standing high and honorable under the sky's insanity. And then she and the Lindquist children would duck over their teaspoons of tomato soup and soda crackers as the town's brooms and scarecrows teetered over them, hooking their green hands on the boy and girl and saying, Tell us about it. She therefore created a heroine's part for herself and tried to keep to it as she floundered through drifts as high as a four-poster bed in a white room of piety and weeping. Hattie pretended gaiety by saying once, See how it swirls! but she saw that the Lindquists were tucking deep inside themselves as they trudged forward and fell and got up again, the wind drawing tears from their squinting eyes, the hard, dry snow hitting their skin like wildly flying pencils. Hours passed as Hattie tipped away from the press of the wind into country that was a puzzle to her, but she kept saying, Just a little farther, until she saw Alma playing Gretel by secretly trailing her right hand along a high wave of snow in order to secretly let go yet another crumb of her rye bread. And then, just ahead of her, she saw some pepper cheese that the girl dropped some time ago. Hissing spindrifts tore away from the snow swells and spiked her face like sharp pins, but then a door seemed to inch ajar and Hattie saw the slight, dark change of a haystack and she cut toward it, announcing that they'd stay there for the night.

She slashed away an access into the haystack and ordered Alma to crawl inside, but the girl hesitated as if she were still thinking of the gingerbread house and the witch's oven, and Hattie acidly whispered, You'll be a dainty mouthful. She meant it as a joke but her green eyes must have seemed crazy, because the little girl was crying when Hattie got inside the haystack next to her, and then Johan was crying, too, and Hattie hugged the Lindquists to her body and tried to shush them with a hymn by Dr. Watts, gently singing, Hush, my dears, lie still and slumber. She couldn't get her feet inside the haystack, but she couldn't feel them anyway just then, and the haystack was making everything else seem right and possible. She talked to the children about hot pastries and taffy and Christmas presents, and that night she made up a story about the horrible storm being a wicked old man whose only thought was to eat them up, but he couldn't find them in the haystack even though he looked and looked. The old man was howling, she said, because he was so hungry.

At daybreak a party of farmers from Neligh rode out on their high plowhorses to the Antelope County schoolhouse in order to get Hattie and the Lindquist children, but the room was empty and the bluetick hound that was with them kept scratching up rye bread until the party walked along behind it on footpaths that wreathed around the schoolyard and into a haystack twenty rods away where the older boys smoked and spit tobacco juice at recess. The Lindquist girl and the boy were killed by the cold, but Hattie Benedict had stayed alive inside the hay, and she wouldn't come out again until the party of men yanked her by the ankles. Even then she kept the girl's body hugged against one side and the boy's body hugged to the other, and when she was put up on one horse, she stared down at them with green eyes that were empty of thought or understanding and inquired if they'd be okay. Yes, one man said. You took good care of them.

Bent Lindquist ripped down his kitchen cupboards and carpentered his own triangular caskets, blacking them with shoe polish, and then swaddled Alma and Johan in black alpaca that was kindly provided by an elder in the Church of Jesus Christ of Latter-Day Saints. And all that night Danish women sat up with the bodies, sopping the Lindquists' skin with vinegar so as to impede putrefaction.

Hattie Benedict woke up in a Lincoln hospital with sweet oil of spermaceti on her hands and lips, and weeks later a Kansas City surgeon amputated her feet with a polished silver hacksaw in the presence of his anatomy class. She was walking again by June, but she was attached to cork-and-iron shoes and she sighed and grunted with every step. Within a year she grew so overweight that she gave up her crutches for a wicker-backed wheelchair and stayed in Antelope County on a pension of forty dollars per month, letting her dark hair grow dirty and leafy, reading one popular romance per day. And yet she complained so much about her helplessness, especially in winter, that the Protestant churches took up a collection and Hattie Benedict was shipped by train to Oakland, California, whence she sent postcards saying she'd married a trolley repairman and she hated Nebraska, hated their horrible weather, hated their petty lives.

On Friday the thirteenth some pioneers went to the upper stories of their houses to jack up the windows and crawl out onto snow that was like a jeweled ceiling over their properties. Everything was sloped and planed and caped and whitely fur-belowed. One man couldn't get over his boyish delight in tramping about on deer-hide snowshoes at the height of his roof gutters, or that his dogwood tree was forgotten but for twigs sticking out of the snow like a skeleton's fingers. His name was Eldad Alderman, and he jabbed a bamboo fishing pole in four likely spots a couple of feet below his snowshoes before the bamboo finally thumped against the plank roof of his chicken coop. He spent two hours spading down to the coop and then squeezed in through the one window in order to walk among the fowl and count up. Half his sixty hens were alive; the other half were still nesting, their orange beaks lying against their white hackles, sitting there like a dress shop's hats, their pure white eggs not yet cold underneath them. In gratitude to those thirty chickens that withstood the ordeal, Eldad gave them Dutch whey and curds and eventually wrote a letter praising their constitutions in the *American Poultry Yard*.

Anna Shevschenko managed to get oxen inside a shelter sturdily constructed of oak scantling and a high stack of barley straw, but the snow powder was so fine and fiercely penetrating that it sifted through and slowly accumulated on the floor. The oxen tamped it down and inchingly rose toward the oak scantling rafters, where they were stopped as the snow flooded up, and by daybreak were overcome and finally asphyxiated. Widow Shevschenko decided then that an old woman could not keep a Nebraska farm alone, and she left for the East in February.

One man lost three hundred Rhode Island Red chickens; another lost two hundred sixty Hereford cattle and sold their hides for two dollars apiece. Hours after the Hubenka boy permitted twenty-one hogs to get out of the snowstorm and join their forty Holsteins in the upper barn, the planked floor in the cattle linter collapsed under the extra weight and the livestock perished. Since even coal picks could no more than chip the earth, the iron-hard bodies were hauled aside until they could be put underground in April, and just about then some Pawnee Indians showed up outside David City. Knowing their manner of living, Mr. Hubenka told them where the carcasses were rotting in the sea wrack of weed tangles and thaw-water jetsam, and the Pawnee rode their ponies onto the property one night and hauled the carrion away.

And there were stories about a Union Pacific train being arrested by snow on a railway siding near Lincoln, and the merchandisers in the smoking car playing euchre, high five, and flinch until sunup; about cowboys staying inside a Hazard bunkhouse for three days and getting bellyaches from eating so many tins of anchovies and saltine crackers; about the Omaha YMCA where shop clerks paged through inspirational pamphlets or played checkers and cribbage or napped in green leather Chesterfield chairs until the great blizzard petered out.

Half a century later, in Atkinson, there was a cranky talker named Bates, who maintained he was the fellow who first thought of attaching the word *blizzard* to the onslaught of high winds and slashing dry snow and ought to be given credit for it. And later, too, a Lincoln woman remembered herself as a little girl peering out through yellowed window paper at a yard and countryside that were as white as the first day of God's creation. And then a great white Brahma bull with street-wide horns trotted up to the house, the night's snow puffing up from his heavy footsteps like soap flakes, gray funnels of air flaring from his nostrils and wisping away in the horrible cold. With a tilt of his head the great bull sought out the hiding girl under a Chesterfield table and, having seen her, sighed and trotted back toward Oklahoma.

Wild turkey were sighted over the new few weeks, their wattled heads and necks just above the snow like dark sticks, some of them petrified that way but others simply waiting for happier times to come. The onslaught also killed prairie dogs, jackrabbits, and crows, and the coyotes that relied upon them for food got so hungry that skulks of them would loiter like juveniles in the yards at night and yearn for scraps and castaways in old songs of agony that were always misunderstood.

Addie Dillingham was seventeen and irresistible that January day of the great blizzard, a beautiful English girl in an hourglass dress and an ankle-length otter-skin coat that was sculpted brazenly to display a womanly bosom and bustle. She had gently agreed to join an upperclassman at the Nebraska School of Medicine on a journey across the green ice of the Missouri River to Iowa, where there was a party at the Masonic Temple in order to celebrate the final linking of Omaha and Council Bluffs. The medical student was Repler Hitchcock of Council Bluffs—a good companion, a Republican, and an Episcopalian—who yearned to practice electro-therapeutics in Cuernavaca, Mexico. He paid for their three-course luncheon at the Paxton Hotel and then the couple strolled down Douglas Street with four hundred other partygoers, who got into cutters and one-horse open sleighs just underneath the iron legs and girders of what would eventually be called the Ak-Sar-Ben Bridge. At a cap-pistol shot the party jerked away from Nebraska and there were champagne toasts and cheers and yahooing, but gradually the party scattered and Addie could only hear the iron shoes of the plowhorse and the racing sleigh hushing across the shaded window glass of river, like those tropical flowers shaped like saucers and cups that slide across the green silk of a pond of their own accord.

At the Masonic Temple there were coconut macaroons and hot syllabub made with cider and brandy, and quadrille dancing on a puncheon floor to songs like the "Butterfly Whirl" and "Cheater Swing" and "The Girl I Left Behind Me." Although the day was getting dark and there was talk about a great snowstorm roistering outside, Addie insisted on staying out on the dance floor until only twenty people remained and the quadrille caller had put away his violin and his sister's cello. Addie smiled and said, Oh what fun! as Repler tidily helped her into her mother's otter-skin coat and then escorted her out into a grand empire of snow that Addie thought was thrilling. And then, although the world by then was wrathfully meaning everything it said, she walked alone to the railroad depot at Ninth and Broadway so she could take the one-stop train called The Dummy across to Omaha.

Addie sipped hot cocoa as she passed sixty minutes up close to the railroad depot's coal stoker oven and some other partygoers sang of Good King Wenceslaus over a parlor organ. And then an old yardman who was sheeped in snow trudged through the high drifts by the door and announced that no more trains would be going out until morning.

Half the couples stranded there had family in Council Bluffs and decided to stay overnight, but the idea of traipsing back to Repler's house and sleeping in his sister's trundle bed seemed squalid to Addie, and she decided to walk the iron railway trestle across to Omaha.

Addie was a half hour away from the Iowa railway yard and up on the tracks over the great Missouri before she had second thoughts. White hatchings and tracings of snow flew at her horizontally. Wind had rippled snow up against the southern girders so that the high white skin was pleated and patterned like oyster shell. Every creosote tie was tended with snow that angled down into dark troughs that Addie could fit a leg through. Everything else was night sky and mystery, and the world she knew had disappeared. And yet she walked out onto the trestle, teetering over to a catwalk and sidestepping along it in high-button shoes, forty feet above the ice, her left hand taking the yield from one guy wire as her right hand sought out another. Yelling winds were yanking at her, and the iron trestle was swaying enough to tilt her over into nothingness, as though Addie Dillingham were a playground game it was just inventing. Halfway across, her gray tam-o'-shanter was snagged out just far enough into space that she could follow its spider-drop into the night, but she only stared at the great river that was lying there moon-white with snow and intractable. Wishing for her jump.

Years later Addie thought that she got to Nebraska and did not give up and was not overfrightened because she was seventeen and could do no wrong, and accidents and dying seemed a government you could vote against, a mother you could ignore. She said she panicked at one jolt of wind and sank down to her knees up there and briefly touched her forehead to iron that hurt her skin like teeth, but when she got up again, she could see the ink-black stitching of the woods just east of Omaha and the shanties on timber piers just above the Missouri River's jagged stacks of ice. And she grinned as she thought how she would look to a vagrant down there plying his way along a rope in order to assay his trotlines for gar and catfish and then, perhaps, appraising the night as if he'd heard a crazy woman screaming in a faraway hospital room. And she'd be jauntily up there on the iron trestle like a new star you could wish on, and as joyous as the last high notes of "The Girl I Left Behind Me."

Further Reading

The Assassination of Jesse James by the Coward Robert Ford. 1983.
Atticus: A Novel. 1996.
Desperadoes. 1979.
Hitler's Niece. 1999.
Isn't It Romantic? An Entertainment. 2003.
Mariette in Ecstasy. 1991.
The Shadowmaker. 1987.
Stay against Confusion: Essays on Faith and Fiction. 2001.

Sinclair Ross *(1908–1996)*

Writers, including many of those who write about the Great Plains, often focus on physical survival in order to explore the ways men and women respond to each other in crises. Life on the Great Plains provides a writer many choices: blizzards, floods, drought, tornadoes, dust, isolation, space. In this story Sinclair Ross focuses on the irony of a hailstorm that hits just as the crops are ripening for harvest: hailstones can pummel and destroy a field in a matter of minutes. At its most sinister the storm can kill animals and people as well.

Ross's stories often use some elemental natural phenomenon as the central motif—dust, hail, blizzard—but Ross is primarily interested in human relations. The characters in his stories and novels are usually married couples who cannot be honest with each other. The destructive ferocity of the storm exposes the unspoken tensions two people endure.

Born on a Saskatchewan homestead, Ross lived most of his life in small prairie towns where he was an employee of the Royal Bank of Canada. These places color his fiction. Although writing was an avocation for Ross, he is regarded by many readers and scholars as a major Canadian author.

A Field of Wheat (1968)

It was the best crop of wheat that John had ever grown; sturdy, higher than the knee, the heads long and filling well; a still, heat-hushed mile of it, undulating into a shimmer of summer-colts and crushed horizon blue. Martha finished pulling the little patch of mustard that John had told her about at noon, stood a minute with her shoulders strained back to ease the muscles that were sore from bending, then bunched up her apron filled with the yellow-blossomed weeds and started towards the road. She walked carefully, placing her feet edgeways between the rows of wheat to avoid trampling and crushing the stalks. The road was only a few rods distant, but several times she stopped before reaching it, holding her apron with one hand and with the other stroking the blades of grain that pressed close against her skirts, luxuriant and tall. Once she looked back, her eyes shaded, across the wheat to the dark fallow land beside it. John was there; she could see the long, slow-settling plume of dust thrown up by the horses and the harrow-cart. He was a fool for work, John. This year he was farming the whole section of land without help, managing with two outfits of horses, one for the morning and one for the afternoon; six, and sometimes even seven hours a shift.

It was John who gave such allure to the wheat. She thought of him hunched black and sweaty on the harrow-cart, twelve hours a day, smothering in dust, shoulders sagged wearily beneath the glare of sun. Her fingers touched the stalks of grain again and tightened on a supple blade until they made it squeak like a mouse. A crop like this was coming to him. He had had his share of failures and set-backs, if ever a man had, twenty times over.

Martha was thirty-seven. She had clinched with the body and substance of life; had loved, borne children—a boy had died—and yet the quickest aches of life, travail, heartbrokenness, they had never wrung as the wheat wrung. For the wheat allowed no respite. Wasting and unending it was struggle, struggle against wind and insects, drought and weeds. Not an heroic struggle to give a man courage and resolve, but a frantic, unavailing one. They were only poor, taunted, driven things; it was the wheat that was invincible. They only dreaded, built bright futures; waited for the first glint of green, watched timorous and eager while it thickened, merged, and at last leaned bravely to a ripple in the wind; then followed every slip of cloud into the horizon, turned to the wheat and away again. And it died tantalizingly sometimes, slowly: there would be a cool day, a pittance of rain.

Or perhaps it lived, perhaps the rain came, June, July, even into August, hope climbing, wish-patterns painted on the future. And then one day a clench and tremble to John's hand; his voice faltering, dull. Grasshoppers perhaps, sawflies or rust; no matter, they would grovel for a while, stand back helpless, then go on again. Go on in bitterness and cowardice, because there was nothing else but going-on.

She had loved John, for these sixteen years had stood close watching while he died—slowly, tantalizingly, as the parched wheat died. He had grown unkempt, ugly, morose. His voice was gruff, contentious, never broke into the deep, strong laughter that used to make her feel she was living at the heart of things. John was gone, love was gone; there was only wheat.

She plucked a blade; her eyes travelled hungrily up and down the field. Serene now, all its sting and torment sheathed. Beautiful, more beautiful than Annabelle's poppies, than her sunsets. Theirs—all of it. Three hundred acres ready to give perhaps a little of what it had taken from her—John, his love, his lips unclenched.

Three hundred acres. Bushels, thousands of bushels, she wouldn't even try to think how many. And prices up this year. It would make him young again, lift his head, give him spirit. Maybe he would shave twice a week as he used to when they were first married, buy new clothes, believe in himself again.

She walked down the road towards the house, her steps quickening to the pace of her thoughts until the sweat clung to her face like little beads of oil. It was the children now, Joe and Annabelle: this winter perhaps they could send them to school in town and let them take music lessons. Annabelle, anyway. At a pinch Joe could wait a while; he was only eight. It wouldn't take Annabelle long to pick up her notes; already she played hymn tunes by ear on the organ. She was bright, a real little lady for manners; among town people she would learn a lot. The farm was no place to bring her up. Running wild and barefoot, what would she be like in a few years? Who would ever want to marry her but some stupid country lout?

John had never been to school himself; he knew what it meant to go through life with nothing but his muscles to depend upon; and that was it, dread that Annabelle and Joe would be handicapped as he was, that was what had darkened him, made him harsh and dour. That was why he breasted the sun and dust a frantic, dogged fool, to spare them, to help them to a life that offered more than sweat and debts. Martha knew. He was a slow, inarticulate man, but she knew. Sometimes it even vexed her, brought a wrinkle of jealousy, his anxiety about the children, his sense of responsibility where they were concerned. He never seemed to feel that he owed her anything, never worried about her future. She could sweat, grow flat-footed and shapeless, but that never bothered him.

Her thoughts were on their old, trudging way, the way they always went; but then she halted suddenly, and with her eyes across the wheat again found freshening promise in its quiet expanse. The children must come first, but she and John— mightn't there be a little of life left for them too? A man was young at thirty-nine. And if she didn't have to work so hard, if she could get some new clothes, maybe some of the creams and things that other women had. . . .

As she passed through the gate, Annabelle raced across the yard to meet her. "Do you know what Joe's done? He's taken off all his clothes and he's in the trough with Nipper!" She was a lanky girl, sunburned, barefoot, her face oval and regular, but spoiled by an expression that strained her mouth and brows into a reproachful primness. It was Martha who had taught her the expression, dinning manners and politeness into her, trying to make her better than the other little girls who went to the country school. She went on, her eyes wide and aghast, "And when I told him to come out he stood right up, all bare, and I had to come away."

"Well, you tell him he'd better be out before I get there."

"But how can I tell him? He's all bare."

Then Joe ran up, nothing on but little cotton knee-pants, strings of green scum from the water-trough still sticking to his face and arms. "She's been peekin'." He pointed at Annabelle. "Nipper and me just got into the trough to get cooled off, and she wouldn't mind her own business."

"Don't you tell lies about me." Annabelle pounced on him and slapped his bare back. "You're just a dirty little pig anyway, and the horses don't want to drink after you've been in the trough."

Joe squealed, and excited by the scuffle Nipper yelped and spattered Martha with a spray of water from his coat and tail. She reached out to cuff him, missed, and then to satisfy the itch in her fingers seized Joe and boxed his ears. "You put your shirt on and then go and pick peas for supper. Hurry now, both of you, and only the fat ones, mind. No, not you, Annabelle." There was something about Annabelle's face, burned and countrified, that changed Martha's mind. "You shell the peas when he gets them. You're in the sun too much as it is."

"But I've got a poppy out and if he goes to the garden by himself he'll pick it—just for spite." Annabelle spun round, and leaving the perplexity in her voice behind her, bolted for the garden. The next minute, before Martha had even reached the house, she was back again triumphant, a big fringed pink and purple poppy in her hand. Sitting down on the doorstep to admire the gaudy petals, she complained to herself, "They go so fast—the first little winds blows them all away." On her face, lengthening it, was bitten deeply the enigma of the flowers and the naked seed-pods. Why did the beauty flash and the bony stalks remain?

Martha had clothes to iron, and biscuits to bake for supper; Annabelle and Joe quarelled about the peas until she shelled them herself. It was hot—heat so intense and breathless that it weighed like a solid. An ominous darkness came with it, gradual and unnoticed. All at once she turned away from the stove and stood strained, inert. The silence seemed to gather itself, hold its breath. She tried to speak to Nipper and the children, all three sprawled in a heap alongside the house, but the hush over everything was like a raised finger, forbidding her.

A long immobile minute; suddenly a bewildering awareness that the light was choked; and then, muffled, still distant, but charged with resolution, climaxing the stillness, a slow, long brooding heave of thunder.

Martha darted to the door, stumbled down the step and around the corner of the house. To the west there was no sky, only a gulf of blackness, so black that the landscape seemed slipping down the neck of a funnel. Above, almost overhead, a heavy, hard-lined bank of cloud swept its way across the sun-white blue in august, impassive fury.

"Annabelle!" She wanted to scream a warning, but it was a bare whisper. In front of her the blackness split—an abrupt, unforked gash of light as if angry hands had snatched to seal the rent.

"Annabelle! Quick—inside!" Deep in the funnel shaggy thunder rolled, emerged and shook itself, then with hurtling strides leaped up to drum and burst itself on the advancing peak of cloud.

"Joe, come back here!" He was off in pursuit of Nipper, who had broken away from Annabelle when she tried to pull him into the house. "Before I warm you!"

Her voice broke. She stared into the blackness. There it was—the hail again—the same white twisting little cloud against the black one—just as she had seen it four years ago.

She craned her neck, looking to see whether John was coming. The wheat, the acres and acres of it, green and tall, if only he had put some insurance on it. Damned mule—just work and work. No head himself and too stubborn to listen to anyone else.

There was a swift gust of wind, thunder in a splintering avalanche, the ragged hail-cloud low and close. She wheeled, with a push sent Annabelle toppling into the house, and then ran to the stable to throw open the big doors. John would turn the horses loose—surely he would. She put a brace against one of the doors, and bashed the end into the ground with her foot. Surely—but he was a fool—such a fool at times. It would be just like him to risk a runaway for the sake of getting to the end of the field.

The first big drops of rain were spitting at her before she reached the house. Quietly, breathing hard, she closed the door, numb for a minute, afraid to think or move. At the other side of the kitchen Annabelle was tussling with Joe, trying to make him go down cellar with her. Frightened a little by her mother's excitement, but not really able to grasp the imminence of danger, she was set on exploiting the event; and to be compelled to seize her little brother and carry him down cellar struck her imagination as a superb way of crystallizing for all time the dreadfulness of the storm and her own dramatic part in it. But Martha shouted at her hoarsely, "Go and get pillows. Here, Joe, quick, up on the table." She snatched him off his feet and set him on the table beside the window. "Be ready now when the hail starts, to hold the pillow tight against the glass. You, Annabelle, stay upstairs at the west window in my room."

The horses were coming, all six at a break-neck gallop, terrified by the thunder and the whip stripes John had given them when he turned them loose. They swept past the house, shaking the earth, their harness jangling tinny against the brattle of thunder, and collided headlong at the stable door.

John, too; through Joe's legs Martha caught sight of his long, scarecrow shape stooped low before the rain. Distractedly, without purpose, she ran upstairs two steps at a time to Annabelle. "Don't be scared, here comes your father!" Her own voice shook, craven. "Why don't you rest your arms? It hasn't started yet."

"As she spoke there was a sharp, crunching blow on the roof, its sound abruptly dead, sickening, like a weapon that has sunk deep into flesh. Wildly she shook her hands, motioning Annabella back to the window, and started for the stairs. Again the blow came; then swiftly a stuttered dozen of them.

She reached the kitchen just as John burst in. With their eyes screwed up against the pommelling roar of the hail they stared at each other. They were deafened, pinioned, crushed. His face was a livid blank, one cheek smeared with blood where a jagged stone had struck him. Taut with fear, her throat aching, she turned away and looked through Joe's legs again. It was like a furious fountain, the stones bouncing high and clashing with those behind them. They had buried the earth, blotted out the horizon; there was nothing but their crazy spew of whiteness. She cowered away, put her hands to her ears.

Then the window broke, and Joe and the pillow tumbled off the table before the howling inrush of the storm. The stones clattered on the floor and bounded up to the ceiling, lit on the stove and threw out sizzling steam. The wind whisked pots and kettles off their hooks, tugged at and whirled the sodden curtains, crashed down a shelf of lamps and crockery. John pushed Martha and Joe into the next room and shut the door. There they found Annabelle huddled at the foot of the stairs, round-eyed, biting her nails in terror. The window she had been holding was broken too; and she had run away without closing the bedroom door, leaving a wild tide of wind upstairs to rage unchecked. It was rocking the whole house, straining at the walls. Martha ran up to close the door, and came down whimpering.

There was hail heaped on the bed, the pictures were blown off the walls and broken, the floor was swimming; the water would soak through and spoil all the ceilings.

John's face quietened her. They all crowded together, silent, averting their eyes from one another. Martha wanted to cry again, but dared not. Joe, awed to calmness, kept looking furtively at the trickle of blood on his father's face. Annabelle's eyes went wide and glassy as suddenly she began to wonder about Nipper. In the excitement and terror of the storm they had all forgotten him.

When at last they could go outside they stumbled over his body on the step. He had run away from Joe before the storm started, crawled back to the house when he saw John go in, and crouching down against the door had been beaten lifeless. Martha held back the children, while John picked up the mangled heap and hurried away with it to the stable.

Neither Joe nor Annabelle cried. It was too annihilating, too much like a blow. They clung tightly to Martha's skirts, staring across the flayed yard and garden. The sun came out, sharp and brilliant on the drifts of hail. There was an icy wind that made them shiver in their thin cotton clothes. "No, it's too cold on your feet." Martha motioned them back to the step as she started towards the gate to join John. "I want to go with your father to look at the wheat. There's nothing anyway to see."

Nothing but the glitter of sun on hailstones. Nothing but their wheat crushed into little rags of muddy slime. Here and there an isolated straw standing bolt upright in headless defiance. Martha and John walked to the far end of the field. There was no sound but their shoes slipping and rattling on the pebbles of ice. Both of them wanted to speak, to break the atmosphere of calamity that hung over them, but the words they could find were too small for the sparkling serenity of wasted field. Even as waste it was indomitable. It tethered them to itself, so that they could not feel or comprehend. It had come and gone, that was all; before its tremendousness and havoc they were prostrate. They had not yet risen to cry out or protest.

It was when they were nearly back to the house that Martha started to whimper. "I can't go on any longer; I can't, John. There's no use, we've tried." With one hand she clutched him and with the other held her apron to her mouth. "It's driving me out of my mind. I'm so tired—heart-sick of it all. Can't you see?"

He laid his big hands on her shoulders. They looked at each other for a few seconds, then she dropped her head weakly against his greasy smock. Presently he roused her. "Here come Joe and Annabelle!" The pressure of his hands tightened. His bristly cheek touched her hair and forehead. "Straighten up, quick, before they see you!"

It was more of him than she had had for years. "Yes, John, I know—I'm all right now." There was a wistful little pull in her voice as if she would have had him hold her there, but hurriedly instead she began to dry her eyes with her apron. "And tell Joe you'll get him another dog."

Then he left her and she went back to the house. Mounting within her was a resolve, a bravery. It was the warming sunlight, the strength and nearness of John, a feeling of mattering, belonging. Swung far upwards by the rush and swell of recaptured life, she was suddenly as far above the desolation of the storm as a little while ago she had been abject before it. But in the house she was alone; there was no sunlight, only a cold wind through the broken window; and she crumpled again.

She tried to face the kitchen, to get the floor dried and the broken lamps swept up. But it was not the kitchen; it was tomorrow, next week, next year. The going on, the waste of life, the hopelessness.

Her hands fought the broom a moment, twisting the handle as if trying to unscrew the rusted cap of a jar; then abruptly she let it fall and strode outside. All very fine for John: he'd talk about education for Joe and Annabelle, and she could worry where the clothes were to come from so that they could go clean and decent even to the country school. It made no difference that she had wanted to take out hail insurance. He was the one that looked after things. She was just his wife; it wasn't for her to open her mouth. He'd pat her shoulder and let her come back to this. They'd be brave, go on again, forget about the crop. Go on, go on—next year and the next—go on till they were both ready for the scrap-heap. But she'd had enough. This time he'd go on alone.

Not that she meant it. Not that she failed to understand what John was going through. It was just rebellion. Rebelling because their wheat was beaten to the ground, because there was this brutal, callous finish to everything she had planned, because she had will and needs and flesh, because she was alive. Rebellion, not John at all—but how rebel against a summer storm, how find the throat of a cloud?

So at a jerky little run she set off for the stable, for John. Just that she might release and spend herself, no matter against whom or what, unloose the fury that clawed within her, strike back a blow for the one that had flattened her.

The stable was quiet, only the push of hay as the horses nosed through the mangers, the lazy rub of their flanks and hips against the stall partitions; and before its quietness her anger subsided, took time for breath. She advanced slowly, almost on tiptoe, peering past the horses' rumps for a glimpse of John. To the last stall, back again. And then there was a sound different from the stable sounds. She paused.

She had not seen him the first time she passed because he was pressed against one of the horses, his head pushed into the big deep hollow of its neck and shoulder, one hand hooked by the fingers in the mane, his own shoulders drawn up and shaking. She stared, thrust out her head incredulously, moved her lips, but stood silent. John sobbing there, against the horse. It was the strangest, most frightening moment of her life. He had always been so strong and grim; had just kept on as if he couldn't feel, as if there were a bull's hide over him, and now he was beaten.

She crept away. It would be unbearable to watch his humiliation if he looked up and saw her. Joe was wandering about the yard, thinking about Nipper and disconsolately sucking hailstones, but she fled past him, head down, stricken with guilty shame as if it were she who had been caught broken and afraid. He had always been so strong, a brute at times in his strength, and now—

Now—why now that it had come to this, he might never be able to get a grip of himself again. He might not want to keep on working, not if he were really beaten. If he lost heart, if he didn't care about Joe and Annabelle any more. Weeds and pests, drought and hail—it took so much fight for a man to hold his own against them all, just to hold his own, let alone make headway.

"Look at the sky!" It was Annabelle again, breathless and ecstatic. "The far one—look how it's opened like a fan!"

Withdrawn now in the eastern sky the storm clouds towered, gold-capped and flushed in the late sunlight, high still pyramids of snowiness and shadow. And one that Annabelle pointed to, apart, the farthest away of them all, this one in bronzed slow splendour spread up mountains high to a vast, plateau-like summit.

Martha hurried inside. She started the fire again, then nailed a blanket over the broken window and lit the big brass parlour lamp—the only one the storm had spared. Her hands were quick and tense. John would need a good supper tonight. The biscuits were water-soaked, but she still had the peas. He liked peas. Lucky that they had picked them when they did. This winter they wouldn't have so much as an onion or potato.

Further Reading

As For Me and My House. 1941.
Sawbones Memorial. 1974.

Reading about Sinclair Ross

Stouck, David. *Major Canadian Authors: A Critical Introduction to Canadian Literature in English.* Lincoln: University of Nebraska Press, 1984.

May Williams Ward *(1882–1975)*

A dust storm can darken the sky and creep through every crevice of a house, coating everything with a fine mist that clogs the nose and fills the lungs. Each of us has probably tasted the grit of dust or tried to get it out of our eyes at least once. Multiply that unpleasantness a thousand times to understand the frustration of those who lived through storms that turned the sky dark for days at time. As May Williams Ward says, "all our values are shaken when earth and air reverse their function."

In 1933 Ward and her husband moved to Wellington, Kansas, to operate the Ward Hotel. Before this move the Wards lived for twenty-eight years in various eastern Colorado and western Kansas towns, where Ward's husband was a bookkeeper and later co-owner of grain elevator companies. Ward knew about dust.

In the 1920s Ward's poetry began to appear in national magazines such as *Life* and *The New York Times*. In 1925 she was one of thirty writers in residence at the MacDowell Colony in New Hampshire, a group that included luminaries such as Edward Arlington Robinson and Sara Teasdale. In her long career Ward was a publishing poet, editor and writing coach, a writer of song lyrics, and an artist, working mostly in block prints. She was an active member of various state and national authors' associations as well.

Ward's life is typical of many writers, especially women, who were not professional writers but enjoyed wide readership during their lifetimes. Their contributions to our literature have been largely forgotten.

Dust Bowl (A Sequence)

I—Reversal

> Dust again. All our values are shaken
> When earth and air reverse their functions,
> When earth flies upward and air presses downward,
>   when earth is taken
> And swirled in the sky, earth that should be massive
>   and hard
> Beneath our feet; and when air

Symbol of lightness, is choke and curse and heaviness
Pushing despair
Under the sill and into the hard-pressed lung—
Bright air flung
Down in the dust.
We could not bear it except we must
For all our values are shaken. What is earth?
Is there anything solid and sure? And what is air?
Is there sun anywhere?

II—Long after Spring
The spring seems no spring when the pall
Of dust is over all
A winterish death to the green of the land,
When the hand
Opens and gathers nothing;
After no harvest in fall after such a spring, if the rain
Comes, however late, unfruitful, out of season,
    illogical hope springs again
Now too late, too long after spring. The mind
    cannot cope
With the strangeness of this untimely swing
Upward, but even with hopeless hope
The heart can cope.
Itself is a strange thing.

III—Rain
We had known we should not really starve
Though the cows and the grass had died,
But we moved like sleepwalkers half alive
Our hearts were dry inside.
Today when it rained we ran out doors
And stood and cried.

Further Reading
From Christmas Time to April. 1938.
In Double Rhythm. 1929.
In That Day: Poems. 1969.
No Two Years Alike. 1960.

Seesaw. 1929.
Wheatlands. 1954..

Reading about May Williams Ward

"The Papers of May Williams Ward." Wichita State University. *www.wichita.edu/library/special collections.*

Lois Phillips Hudson *(b. 1927)*

The special characteristic of drought is its devastating longevity. In the 1920s and 1930s drought persisted for a decade across the Great Plains. Families that weathered floods or blizzards could not wait for the rains to return. Topsoil was scoured off of fields, orchards disappeared under dust dunes, and mortgages inevitably came due.

As Lois Phillips Hudson notes in this story about a "water witch"—a man who uses divination or intuition to find water below the dried-out surface—the cloudburst that ends the drought and renews the farmer's wells is merely a clumsy irony. Hudson comments, "I was not clear . . . as to whether the drought made the depression or the depression made the drought. . . . I do know that a lone man trying to wrest consistency out of the prairies can be tragically out of scale."

Hudson was born in North Dakota. She taught in secondary schools and at the University of Washington in Seattle. For many of her stories she draws on her own experiences. Throughout her career Hudson remained committed to her responsibility as an artist, not to solve problems but to examine them. As she explained, "artists must be responsible for articulating the things our species must know to remain civilized."*

The Water Witch (1957)

Benjamin the water witch lived in a dark little shed attached to the rear wall of his grandnephew's blacksmith shop, with a layer of clotted sawdust for a rug between him and the boards that served as a floor. For his purposes the sawdust was better than a rug, because he shook too much to be very accurate with his coffee-can spittoons.

Besides the day-long din that would have maddened almost anybody but the person making it, Benjamin had to bear the bitter cold of the shed in winter and a heat like that of Leroy's forge in the summer. But if he hadn't been Leroy's great-uncle he might not have had any place at all to live, and anyway the temperature of the air around him obtruded only vaguely on the world he lived in. All year round, the cuffs of his one union suit flapped about his wrists and flared over the tops of

---

Contemporary Authors vol. 64 (Detroit), 191.

his ankle-high shoes. Sometimes, during those drought years in our little North Dakota town, when the thermometer under the awning of the barbershop was hovering around a hundred degrees, old Benjamin would take off his blue work shirt and reveal the scalloped lines of sweat creeping like a lava flow down the chest of his underwear.

In a time of general affliction, a creature who is even more afflicted than the rest is either shunned and feared as the most disfavored subject of the gods, or else esteemed as the possessor, through his unimaginable misfortune, of a special purpose in life. When that creature is a water witch in the midst of an unprecedented drought, it is not hard to see why he should be sought after, if not accepted or understood. Thus it was that after a lifetime of being supported by the parched but unpatronizing charity of the community, the old man was elevated, in his last years, to a status of full self-support.

Even the Russian immigrants who scarcely spoke English knew that staring, palsied Benjamin was their last hope. In a universe so populated with inimical forces, it seemed reasonable that a few creatures of malign aspect were in fact good spirits in disguise, waiting only for a demonstration of belief in the goodness under their bestial exteriors to unleash that beneficence upon the believers. Mythology is full of tales of such creatures. Hardship and ignorance made the myths, and they are still revived and leaned upon whenever people cannot get along without them.

Like most other people, I have gotten my water out of a faucet for a long time now—a faucet that presumably is connected to a limitless supply of water—but I still experience a vestigial terror of being waterless if for some peculiar reason no water comes out of the faucet. It is like a racial memory of desperate hunts for water. Such desperate hunts went on over millions of square miles of the breadbasket that was becoming the Dust Bowl in the fourteen summers of desolation.

There are poems, sometimes written by people riding a train from one ocean to the other across that stricken expanse of the continent, which celebrate the pathos of a house abandoned in the blowing fields, but I have never seen a poem which deals with the day on which a child of that house is sent out for a half a bucket of water and comes running back through the dust to report that the well is dry.

The hunt for wells was so intense that in 1931, when the drought was only seven years old, the government of British Columbia employed a Cornishwoman named Evelyn Penrose as its official Government Water-Diviner, and sent her into the homesteads in the Okanagan Valley, where she often found herself as far as ninety miles from a place where there was enough water for a bath. There were many other instances, in those days, of the hiring of dowsers by official agencies. It is not surprising that Benjamin, who offered the added persuasion of an affliction, should have been catapulted to eminence in our little dying town.

Even so, I don't think my father believed in water-witching, and I don't think he asked old Benjamin to come out to our half-section. I was six years old then, three

years younger than the drought, which had dominated my life like a cruel unnatural stepsister out of a fairy tale. We had been living with my grandparents after
a depression business failure, and were continuing to live with them until we got
the new place in shape and found water. However, my father and I happened to be
on the farm for a special reason the day Benjamin came shambling down the
rutted lane that connected our farm to the county road. He must have heard at the
blacksmith shop that we were planning to dig a well, and simply assumed that we
would be waiting for him. A passing neighbor had given him a ride from town,
but, in an inarticulate graciousness, did not offer to go out of his way for him,
pretending that a quarter-mile walk for a spastic was no more than for anyone else.
Benjamin came just as were slamming the door of our new home against the
raging fumes of the sulphur we had set in cans on a stoked-up stove—the way we
fumigated for vermin in those pre-DDT days. We planned to stay the day to make
sure the house didn't catch fire, so my father had a little spare time in which to
indulge the water witch (if that was indeed the way he looked at it). I tagged after
them all morning, partly because I was afraid of the deadly house with the awful
gases swirling around its insides, and partly because I did not want to lose sight of
my father while a creature like Benjamin was around. His twitching lips drooled
tobacco juice, his lower eyelids sagged away from the red-lined globes of his
eyeballs, and his hands fluttered from his buttonless shirt sleeves in a terrible
anarchy. A high, stumbling voice came out of his massive chest, and his clothes
and shoes were heavy with the deep fine dust of the land in which he proposed to
find water.

He mumbled repetitiously about veins and depths, which his missing teeth
rendered into "depfs," shuffling over the fields, with us at a patient pace behind
him. He held his Y-shaped branch high, straight out from his chest like the drummer in the American Legion band. Suddenly the branch in his hand flipped over
and the tail of the Y pointed rigidly at his feet. He had had such an odd grip on the
branch that when it flipped over it appeared to have thrown both his wrists out of
joint. He began to shake much more violently.

"It's right below me here!" he cried. "There's a lot of it—a whole lot—I can tell
by the way it's pullin' at me—it's just like it was taking the stomach right out of me.
It's close or it couldn't do like that—depf of eighteen feet, not more. Set a stake here
quick, I tell ye—it's rilin' my stomach to stand here."

My father obediently drove a stake down through the billowing dust into the
hard earth beneath the palsied branch. Then he said coaxingly to the old man,
"Do you feel up to following this vein along for a ways, Ben?"

"Well, I dunno what you want that fer," he said in pleased complaint, "but if
you think I can find something even better than what we've got right here I reckon
I can try—but I tell ye this is hard on a man. It's mighty hard on a man."

The old man "followed the vein" down the hill to a spot under a huge elm tree
where his dowsing rod, green as it was, cracked loudly in its wrenching somer-

sault. He stood there transfixed, while the leaves of the great tree above him quivered in the wind and flickered darts of light over the wavering lines of his body.

Crowded as my world was with invisible beings and magical forces, I had never expected to be an actual witness of supernatural energies at work.

Even my father jumped a little, but he recovered himself quickly enough to say a little too loudly and nonchalantly, "Well, now, Ben, I think you did it! I reckon I ought to dig right here, don't you?"

I thought that was about as superfluous a question as he could have asked. The kind of power that had just been demonstrated to us could have called all the water in the world to that spot under our elm.

My father did dig there. He found no water until he had gone three times as deep as old Benjamin's rod had said, but finally the sand began to whisper and slide in around him as he spaded it into the bucket my grandfather cranked up and dumped aside, and then the water began to seep up around his legs and to fill faster than he could bail and dig. After we got the pump installed and the water had a chance to clear, we realized that we had a well bordering on the miraculous. The water was wonderful. Most wells in that area yielded water so strong with minerals that it was often almost as unpotable as it was good for the teeth. When old Benjamin tasted the water from our well he trembled in pride, and my father gave him five dollars out of gratitude to the earth.

As the drought became worse that summer, we came to see what a remarkable well we had. I, of course, accepted both the unusual taste and abundance of the water as the natural result of Benjamin's water-witching. I was sure that he had not just found that water, but had an absolute control over keeping it there. As soon as we had transplanted the vegetables that we had started indoors while we were staying with my grandparents, we began hauling water from the well up the long hill to the garden. My father would hitch the team to the stoneboat, load an oil drum on it, empty a dozen buckets into the drum, then flick the reins with a specious optimism at the sweating horses. Their mosquito-covered thighs vibrated with effort as they yanked and dug for footing to move the first inch that would jolt the loaded sledge out of its inertia. When they had finally dragged and scraped it to the top of the miserable incline, my father would pour the water, bucket by bucket, into the trenches along the garden rows, and then drive the weary animals back down the hill to get another load.

For weeks the well supplied us and our stock and our flourishing garden, while all around us the wells of neighbors began to go dry. The water table receded from one sputtering pump shaft after another, and men went shamefaced and frantic to their friends, who became suddenly aloof and cautious. There was, after all, nothing anybody could barter for water—not seed wheat or labor or even money. People who had lived for three generations under the homesteaders' law of unconditional hospitality to those in need now began to live under another law—the law of the desert—the law that had caused the wells of Isaac to be called such names as "Hatred" and "Contention." None dared to ask for more than enough to water their animals and themselves. Their winter's vegetables, begun in the hopeful boxes of earth propped against kitchen windows looking out on March snow, faded into dead yellow strings lying in the dust of their gardens. If Benjamin could not find new wells for them, there was nothing left for them to do but slaughter their bony milch cows, take the proceeds from their lugubrious auctions, and go West.

The heat wilted even the wind, and the normally restless windmills stood mute against the silent sky, while the water in the great tanks below them evaporated through a covering of green scum. I was so hungry for water that I could bring myself to play in one of those round wooden tanks, and I still remember climbing into it and scraping my heels and calves down against the hairy growths on its sides. The tank was in our neighbor's horse pasture, and my mother would take us there in our old Ford, driving across the hard useless fields, and would then sit in the shade of the car reading the Jamestown *Sun* while my three-year-old sister and I jumped and paddled about in the lukewarm mixture for an hour or so. Then we would come home and sponge off the green that coated our bodies and matted our hair.

At night, ten minutes in bed was a long time—long enough for a person no bigger than I to have searched out every un-slept-on cooler piece of sheet, and to have made the whole bed as hot as I with my searching. Every night was like the worst two days of the measles.

But despite my miserable nights I had no way of knowing that things were worse than usual. I was making a bird-nest collection and I spent my days visiting various bird homes, admiring the eggs, then the baby birds, and finally taking the nests for my own when the birds were done with them. My favorites were the twin doves who hatched in a nest built every year in the same place—on top of a low stump in the center of a mound so charmingly furnished with hundreds of tiny toadstools that there was no doubt it was the dancing ring for the fairies who belonged on our farm. Since my sister was too little to be of any real interest, the birds and the shy beings that only the birds ever saw were the sole companions of my long summer days and the only recipients of my wistful affections. They absorbed me utterly, and they could make me forget the worrisome conversations between my mother and father that I could hear every night after I had been put to bed.

But then came the three days of heat. The thermometer in the shade of our porch registered one hundred and twelve degrees at one o'clock in the afternoon of the first day. So unobtrusively that we never knew exactly when it happened, eleven of our fattest hens drew their last breaths through beaks straining away from their hard dry tongues and slumped into the hollows they had made while dusting themselves, as though they had dug their own graves.

That was also the day that our well finally betrayed us. We used up all the priming water in the can by the watering trough and then we brought down the last of the water we had in the house, but all we heard was the rasp of sand in the shaft. My father put four barrels on the wagon and drove the team to town, three miles away. There they would allow him only three barrels at a time, afraid the supply would not hold out. The stock required all the water he could get, and the garden, after only one day of such punishment, contracted a mortal thirst.

The next morning there was still no water, but I visited the first nest on my route as usual. I could barely see the three-day-old babies under their undulating blanket of gluttonous red ants, their frail necks drooped comfortingly across each other's backs and their little heads swollen with the blue bruises of their eyes under the lids that would never open. During those first two days the whole generation of nestlings in our north and south windbreaks perished and their parents disappeared. Only the twin doves on the enchanted stump survived, for their mother's throat made milk as well as lullabies, and they drank and were spared the crawling red feast.

There was still one more day of heat and then we had the cloudburst. The irony was clumsy, but the meteorological principles behind it were perfectly sound. We crouched in the earth-floored cellar while the wind tore at the splintered wooden door over us and the tornado ripped apart a barn and a house a few miles to the south of us. Then the sky that had been so hot and dry and far away lowered itself to our roof and spilled out the flood that removed the last skeletal traces of our garden. It seemed to me that all the water in the world, after disobeying the water witch for three days, had come back to us through the sky. There was more water than anybody could have imagined without believing in magic.

Still, the damage was local enough not to be mentioned in the newspapers of places any farther away then Fargo. It just happened that nine years of drought, three years of depression wheat prices, and the treason of a well had exhausted our capacity to exist any longer in an environment which offered no semblance of cosmic hospitality. Even our meek-hearted doves decided to leave.

Thus it was that we joined the caravan of destitute nomads who sought the western ocean, where the people had no experience of the perfidy of wells and therefore concluded that our difficulties must be the result of a lazy shiftlessness. They called us Okies if we had come from north of Texas, and Arkies otherwise, and generally treated us the way people with such names would expect to be treated.

Perhaps it was only the depression that made so much depend on so little. I know I was not clear, at the time, as to whether the drought made the depression or the depression made the drought. Even now I don't know whether it is nomads who make the desert or the desert that makes nomads. I do know that a lone man trying to wrest consistency out of the prairies can be tragically out of scale. Only nomads can live in the wastelands of the sea, sand, ice, or dust, where the figures of men are forever out of scale.

If we had all been birds, we could simply have forgotten a lost generation and migrated to the next nesting site. If we had been Indians, we would be there still, having followed the buffalo, which would have followed the grass that was sure to be green enough somewhere, for there is usually a greener valley for people to find, if only they are not encumbered by the idea of human permanence.

Since we were not nomads by nature, we were obliged to shrink on the outskirts of the small group of farmers at our auction, who made humiliating bids on the sad trappings of our permanence and bought them at sums that made my mother's eyes seek my father's in frightened dismay. We had counted on getting much more to help us move to another place where there would not be so many enemies of roots.

Inexplicably the veins of several wells old Benjamin had dowsed were renewed after the cloudburst, and the desperate people, renewed in their faith, came ever more frequently to the blacksmith shop. They would bring in a singletree that was about ready to be welded or a horse that was about to lose a nail, and then they would drift back to the corner where Benjamin sat propped against the wall on a cracked anvil draped with gunny sacks. The drought had promoted him from his shed into the shop. A man would start to speak of how the east forty was a little dry, and he was thinking of spying out a vein to open there. Softly and casually they spoke, as people will to a being who might be easily offended because of his terrible affliction and the pride it takes to bear it. They spoke as people do to a being who may be cajoled into bestowing on suppliants who hit upon the proper ritual a stay of execution, a drink of real water out of a mirage.

My father and I saw Benjamin the water witch for the last time—sitting on his anvil, trembling and rolling his eyes, whittling aimlessly on the tail of a dowsing rod—on the day we went down to Leroy's shop to get a little welding job done on the wagon box we were converting into a trailer. We didn't mention anything to him about the well, or even tell him why we were there in Leroy's shop, because we too bore our affliction with pride.

Further Reading
Bones of Plenty. 1962.

Further Reading: Stories of Survival on the Great Plains
Haldeman-Julius, Emmanuel, and Anna Marcet Haldeman-Julius. *Dust.* 1921; rpt. Charlottesville: University of Virginia Library, 1997.

Low, Ann Marie. *Dust Bowl Diary.* Lincoln: University of Nebraska Press, 1984.

Scarborough, Dorothy. *The Wind.* 1925; rpt. Austin: University of Texas Press, 1979.

Svobida, Lawrence. *An Empire of Dust.* Reprinted as *Farming the Dust Bowl: A First-Hand Account from Kansas.* Lawrence: University Press of Kansas, 1986.

Creating Communities in America

Creating communities among the scattered farms on the Great Plains presents particular challenges for settlers, and those who immigrated to America face even more difficulties. Not only must they learn to survive on the open plains, they must also learn to live as Americans. What can—or should—one give up in a new country? Language? Cultural tradition? Religion? For older immigrants change is not always possible. How can newcomers convey to Americans their own values that may stand in stark contrast to the mainstream's? If public policy denies basic human rights to both immigrants and Native Indians, how can they interact with the larger American society while maintaining their identity?

For immigrants, language differences make it hard to explain their own practices that are apparently at odds with the community's expectations, and they cannot comprehend the town's traditions. The Russian peasant may wear odd clothing and go barefoot because she or he has no other clothes. As their children blend into the American culture, parents, especially mothers, become more isolated from their own families and from the surrounding community. Yet many are willing, even eager, for their children to attend American schools and learn to be American: it is why they came to America.

Indians had fewer choices in adapting to encroaching white culture and systematic programs of assimilation. There are fewer shared values and even more misunderstandings, often deliberate on the part of settlers and official U.S. policymakers. Even during the early part of the twentieth century, when some sympathetic men and women directed Indian affairs for the United States, tribal peoples had little say in conducting their own affairs. The gap persists between what mainstream American culture wants to believe about Indians and how indigenous peoples view themselves.

Further Reading: Immigrants' Stories on the Great Plains

JOHAN BOJER
The Emigrants. Trans. A. G. Joyne. 1925; rpt. Lincoln: University of Nebraska Press, 1978.
Rachel Calof's Story: Jewish Homesteader on the Northern Plains. Trans. Jacob Calof. Bloomington: Indiana University Press, 1995.

WILLA CATHER
My Ántonia. 1918; rpt. Lincoln: University of Nebraska Press, 1995.
O Pioneers! 1913; rpt. Lincoln: University of Nebraska Press, 1992.

MELA MEISNER LINDSAY
Shukar Balan: The White Lamb. Lincoln: The American Historical Society of Germans
    from Russia, 1976.

WILHELM MOBERG
The Emigrants. Trans. Gustaf Lannestock. 1951; rpt. St. Paul: Minnesota Historical Society
    Press, 1995.
Last Letter Home. Trans. Gustaf Lannestock. 1957; rpt. St. Paul: Minnesota Historical
    Society Press, 1995.
The Settlers. Trans. Gustaf Lannestock. 1956; rpt. St. Paul: Minnesota Historical Society
    Press, 1995.
Unto a Good Land. Trans. Gustaf Lannestock. 1954; rpt. St. Paul: Minnesota Historical
    Society Press, 1995.

AAGOT RANEN
Grass of the Earth: Immigrant Life in the Dakota Country. 1950; rpt. St. Paul: Minnesota
    Historical Society Press, 1994.

LINDA MACK SCHLOFF
"And Prairie Dogs Weren't Kosher": Jewish Women in the Upper Midwest since 1855. St. Paul:
    Minnesota Historical Society Press, 1996.

HOPE WILLIAMS SYKES
Second Hoeing. 1935; rpt. Lincoln: University of Nebraska Press, 1982.

SOPHIE TRUPIN
Dakota Diaspora: Memoirs of a Jewish Homesteader. 1984; rpt. Lincoln: University of Ne-
    braska Press, 1988.

SOPHUS KEITH WINTHER
Mortgage Your Heart. 1937; rpt. New York: Arno Press, 1979.
Take All to Nebraska. 1936; rpt. Lincoln: University of Nebraska Press, 1976.
This Passion Never Dies. New York: Macmillan, 1938.

Willa Cather *(1873–1947)*

Willa Cather wrote "Neighbour Rosicky" in 1932 when she was taking stock of her own life after the death of her father in 1928 and of her mother in 1931.* First published in *Obscure Destinies* with the stories "Old Mrs. Harris" and "Two Friends," the three stories together form a nostalgic portrait of the lives of people who grow old in the small prairie towns that are always Cather's Red Cloud, Nebraska, no matter what she calls them in the stories. In a sense this is the story of John Pavelka, the husband of her friend Annie Pavelka, whose story forms the basis for her earlier novel, *My Ántonia.*

The following narrative, like many other Cather works, reflects her interest in the immigrants who farmed in Webster County, Nebraska. She uses this story's frame to explore the ways that one family found their own place on the edges of a community on the Great Plains. Much has been written about this work. It is often read as an elegy or as a way of approaching life that Cather valued after she had enough years away from Red Cloud to appreciate men like Rosicky and her own father.

Cather was born in Virginia. Her family followed her grandparents to Webster County, Nebraska, in 1883. Used to the woods and mountains of western Virginia, the young Cather experienced a profound emotional shock when she found herself on the flat and treeless plains. Over the years her appreciation of Nebraska grew, especially when she realized that it would be her literary material. Upon graduating from the University of Nebraska, Cather left Nebraska for the East. She was a teacher and an editor for *McClure's Magazine,* one of the leading magazines at the turn of the twentieth century. She published her first successful novel, *O Pioneers!* in 1913, and from then on she supported herself as a writer. She won the Pulitzer Prize for her 1922 novel *One of Ours.*

Neighbour Rosicky (1932)

I

When Doctor Burleigh told neighbour Rosicky he had a bad heart, Rosicky protested.

*See Kari Ronning, "Historical Essay," in *Obscure Destinies,* scholarly ed. (Lincoln: University of Nebraska Press, 1998), 200.

"So? No, I guess my heart was always pretty good. I got a little asthma, maybe. Just a awful short breath when I was pitchin' hay last summer, dat's all."

"Well now, Rosicky, if you know more about it than I do, what did you come to me for? It's your heart that makes you short of breath, I tell you. You're sixty-five years old, and you've always worked hard, and your heart's tired. You've got to be careful from now on, and you can't do heavy work any more. You've got five boys at home to do it for you."

The old farmer looked up at the Doctor with a gleam of amusement in his queer triangular-shaped eyes. His eyes were large and lively, but the lids were caught up in the middle in a curious way, so that they formed a triangle. He did not look like a sick man. His brown face was creased but not wrinkled, he had a ruddy colour in his smooth-shaven cheeks and in his lips, under his long brown moustache. His hair was thin and ragged around his ears, but very little grey. His forehead, naturally high and crossed by deep parallel lines, now ran all the way up to his pointed crown. Rosicky's face had the habit of looking interested,— suggested a contented disposition and a reflective quality that was gay rather than grave. This gave him a certain detachment, the easy manner of an onlooker and observer.

"Well, I guess you ain't got no pills fur a bad heart, Doctor Ed. I guess the only thing is fur me to git me a new one."

Doctor Burleigh swung round in his desk-chair and frowned at the old farmer. "I think if I were you I'd take a little care of the old one, Rosicky."

Rosicky shrugged. "Maybe I don't know how. I expect you mean fur me not to drink my coffee no more."

"I wouldn't, in your place. But you'll do as you choose about that. I've never yet been able to separate a Bohemian from his coffee or his pipe. I've quit trying. But the sure thing is you've got to cut out farm work. You can feed the stock and do chores about the barn, but you can't do anything in the fields that makes you short of breath."

"How about shelling corn?"

"Of course not!"

Rosicky considered with puckered brows.

"I can't make my heart go no longer'n it wants to, can I, Doctor Ed?"

"I think it's good for five or six years yet, maybe more, if you'll take the strain off it. Sit around the house and help Mary. If I had a good wife like yours, I'd want to stay around the house."

His patient chuckled. "It ain't no place fur a man. I don't like no old man hanging round the kitchen too much. An' my wife, she's a awful hard worker her own self."

"That's it; you can help her a little. My Lord, Rosicky, you are one of the few men I know who has a family he can get some comfort out of; happy dispositions, never quarrel among themselves, and they treat you right. I want to see you live a few years and enjoy them."

"Oh, they're good kids, all right," Rosicky assented.

The Doctor wrote him a prescription and asked him how his oldest son, Rudolph, who had married in the spring, was getting on. Rudolph had struck out for himself, on rented land. "And how's Polly? I was afraid Mary mightn't like an American daughter-in-law, but it seems to be working out all right."

"Yes, she's a fine girl. Dat widder woman bring her daughters up very nice. Polly got lots of spunk, an' she got some style, too. Da's nice, for young folks to have some style." Rosicky inclined his head gallantly. His voice and his twinkly smile were an affectionate compliment to his daughter-in-law.

"It looked like a storm, and you'd better be getting home before it comes. In town in the car?" Doctor Burleigh rose.

"No, I'm in de wagon. When you got five boys, you ain't got much chance to ride round in de Ford. I ain't much for cars, noway."

"Well, it's a good road out to your place; but I don't want you bumping around in a wagon much. And never again on a hay-rake, remember!"

Rosicky placed the Doctor's fee delicately behind the desk-telephone, looking the other way, as if this were an absent-minded gesture. He put on his plush cap and his corduroy jacket with a sheepskin collar, and went out.

The Doctor picked up his stethoscope and frowned at it as if he were seriously annoyed with the instrument. He wished it had been telling tales about some other man's heart, some old man who didn't look the Doctor in the eye so knowingly, or hold out such a warm brown hand when he said good-bye. Doctor Burleigh had been a poor boy in the country before he went away to medical school; he had known Rosicky almost ever since he could remember, and he had a deep affection for Mrs. Rosicky.

Only last winter he had had such a good breakfast at Rosicky's, and that when he needed it. He had been out all night on a long, hard confinement case at Tom Marshall's,—a big rich farm where there was plenty of stock and plenty of feed and a great deal of expensive farm machinery of the newest model, and no comfort whatever. The woman had too many children and too much work, and she was no manager. When the baby was born at last, and handed over to the assisting neighbour woman, and the mother was properly attended to, Burleigh refused any breakfast in that slovenly house, and drove his buggy—the snow was too deep for a car—eight miles to Anton Rosicky's place. He didn't know another farm-house where a man could get such a warm welcome, and such good strong coffee with rich cream. No wonder the old chap didn't want to give up his coffee!

He had driven in just when the boys had come back from the barn and were washing up for breakfast. The long table, covered with a bright oilcloth, was set out with dishes waiting for them, and the warm kitchen was full of the smell of coffee and hot biscuit and sausage. Five big handsome boys, running from twenty to twelve, all with what Burleigh called natural good manners,—they hadn't a bit of the painful self-consciousness he himself had to struggle with when he was a lad. One ran to put his horse away, another helped him off with his fur coat and hung it up, and Josephine, the youngest child and the only daughter, quickly set another place under her mother's direction.

With Mary, to feed creatures was the natural expression of affection,—her chickens, the calves, her big hungry boys. It was a rare pleasure to feed a young man whom she seldom saw and of whom she was as proud as if he belonged to her. Some country housekeepers would have stopped to spread a white cloth over the oilcloth, to change the thick cups and plates for their best china, and the wooden-handled knives for plated ones. But not Mary.

"You must take us as you find us, Doctor Ed. I'd be glad to put out my good things for you if you was expected, but I'm glad to get you any way at all."

He knew she was glad,—she threw back her head and spoke out as if she were announcing him to the whole prairie. Rosicky hadn't said anything at all; he merely smiled his twinkling smile, put some more coal on the fire, and went into his own room to pour the Doctor a little drink in a medicine glass. When they were all seated, he watched his wife's face from his end of the table and spoke to her in Czech. Then, with the instinct of politeness which seldom failed him, he turned to the Doctor and said slyly: "I was just tellin' her not to ask you no questions about Mrs. Marshall till you eat some breakfast. My wife, she's terrible fur to ask questions."

The boys laughed, and so did Mary. She watched the Doctor devour her biscuit and sausage, too much excited to eat anything herself. She drank her coffee and sat taking in everything about her visitor. She had known him when he was a poor country boy, and was boastfully proud of his success, always saying: "What do people go to Omaha for, to see a doctor, when we got the best one in the State right here?" If Mary liked people at all, she felt physical pleasure in the sight of them, personal exultation in any good fortune that came to them. Burleigh didn't know many women like that, but he knew she was like that.

When his hunger was satisfied, he did, of course, have to tell them about Mrs. Marshall, and he noticed what a friendly interest the boys took in the matter.

Rudolph, the oldest one (he was still living at home then), said: "The last time I was over there, she was lifting them big heavy milk-cans, and I knew she oughtn't to be doing it."

"Yes, Rudolph told me about that when he come home, and I said it wasn't right," Mary put in warmly. "It was all right for me to do them things up to the last, for I was terrible strong, but that woman's weakly. And do you think she'll be able to nurse it, Ed?" She sometimes forgot to give him the title she was so proud of. "And to think of your being up all night and then not able to get a decent breakfast! I don't know what's the matter with such people."

"Why, Mother," said one of the boys, "if Doctor Ed had got breakfast there, we wouldn't have him here. So you ought to be glad."

"He knows I'm glad to have him, John, any time. But I'm sorry for that poor woman, how bad she'll feel the Doctor had to go away in the cold without his breakfast."

"I wish I'd been in practice when these were getting born." The Doctor looked down the row of close-clipped heads. "I missed some good breakfasts by not being."

The boys began to laugh at their mother because she flushed so red, but she stood her ground and threw up her head. "I don't care, you wouldn't have got away from this house without breakfast. No doctor ever did. I'd have had something ready fixed that Anton could warm up for you."

The boys laughed harder than ever, and exclaimed at her: "I'll bet you would!" "She would, that!"

"Father, did you get breakfast for the doctor when we were born?"

"Yes, and he used to bring me my breakfast, too, mighty nice. I was always awful hungry!" Mary admitted with a guilty laugh.

While the boys were getting the Doctor's horse, he went to the window to examine the house plants. "What do you do to your geraniums to keep them blooming all winter, Mary? I never pass this house that from the road I don't see your windows full of flowers."

She snapped off a dark red one, and a ruffled new green leaf, and put them in his buttonhole. "There, that looks better. You look too solemn for a young man, Ed. Why don't you git married? I'm worried about you. Settin' at breakfast, I looked at you real hard, and I seen you've got some grey hairs already."

"Oh, yes! They're coming. Maybe they'd come faster if I married."

"Don't talk so. You'll ruin your health eating at the hotel. I could send your wife a nice loaf of nut bread, if you only had one. I don't like to see a young man getting grey. I'll tell you something, Ed; you make some strong black tea and keep it handy in a bowl, and every morning just brush it into your hair, an' it'll keep the grey from showin' much. That's the way I do!"

Sometimes the Doctor heard the gossipers in the drug-store wondering why Rosicky didn't get on faster. He was industrious, and so were his boys, but they were rather free and easy, weren't pushers, and they didn't always show good judgment. They were comfortable, they were out of debt, but they didn't get much ahead. Maybe, Doctor Burleigh reflected, people as generous and warm-hearted and affectionate as the Rosickys never got ahead much; maybe you couldn't enjoy your life and put it into the bank, too.

II

When Rosicky left Doctor Burleigh's office he went into the farm-implement store to light his pipe and put on his glasses and read over the list Mary had given him. Then he went into the general merchandise place next door and stood about until the pretty girl with the plucked eyebrows, who always waited on him, was free. Those eyebrows, two thin India-ink strokes, amused him, because he remembered how they used to be. Rosicky always prolonged his shopping by a little joking; the girl knew the old fellow admired her, and she liked to chaff with him.

"Seems to me about every other week you buy ticking, Mr. Rosicky, and always the best quality," she remarked as she measured off the heavy bolt with red stripes.

"You see, my wife is always makin' goose-fedder pillows, an' de thin stuff don't hold in dem little down-fedders."

"You must have lots of pillows at your house."

"Sure. She makes quilts of dem, too. We sleeps easy. Now she's makin' a fedder quilt for my son's wife. You know Polly, that married my Rudolph. How much my bill, Miss Pearl?"

"Eight eighty-five."

"Chust make it nine, and put in some candy fur de women."

"As usual. I never did see a man buy so much candy for his wife. First thing you know, she'll be getting too fat."

"I'd like dat. I ain't much for all dem slim women like what de style is now."

"That's one for me, I suppose, Mr. Bohunk!" Pearl sniffed and elevated her India-ink strokes.

When Rosicky went out to his wagon, it was beginning to snow,—the first snow of the season, and he was glad to see it. He rattled out of town and along the highway through a wonderfully rich stretch of country, the finest farms in the county. He admired this High Prairie, as it was called, and always liked to drive through it. His own place lay in a rougher territory, where there was some clay in the soil and it was not so productive. When he bought his land, he hadn't the money to buy on High Prairie; so he told his boys, when they grumbled, that if their land hadn't some clay in it, they wouldn't own it at all. All the same, he enjoyed looking at these fine farms, as he enjoyed looking at a prize bull.

After he had gone eight miles, he came to the graveyard, which lay just at the edge of his own hay-land. There he stopped his horses and sat still on his wagon seat, looking about at the snowfall. Over yonder on the hill he could see his own house, crouching low, with the clump of orchard behind and the windmill before, and all down the gentle hill-slope the rows of pale gold cornstalks stood out against the white field. The snow was falling over the cornfield and the pasture and the hay-land, steadily, with very little wind,—a nice dry snow. The graveyard had only a light wire fence about it and was all overgrown with long red grass. The fine snow, settling into this red grass and upon the few little evergreens and the head-stones, looked very pretty.

It was a nice graveyard, Rosicky reflected, sort of snug and homelike, not cramped or mournful,—a big sweep all round it. A man could lie down in the long grass and see the complete arch of the sky over him, hear the wagons go by; in summer the mowing-machine rattled right up to the wire fence. And it was so near home. Over there across cornstalks his own roof and windmill looked so good to him that he promised himself to mind the Doctor and take care of himself. He was awful fond of his place, he admitted. He wasn't anxious to leave it. And it was a comfort to think that he would never have to go farther than the edge of his own hayfield. The snow, falling over his barnyard and the graveyard, seemed to draw things together like. And they were all old neighbours in the graveyard, most of them friends; there was nothing to feel awkward or embarrassed about. Embarrassment was the most disagreeable feeling Rosicky knew. He didn't often have it,—only with certain people whom he didn't understand at all.

Well, it was a nice snowstorm; a fine sight to see the snow falling so quietly and graciously over so much open country. On his cap and shoulders, on the horses' backs and manes, light, delicate, mysterious it fell; and with it a dry cool fragrance was released into the air. It meant rest for vegetation and men and beasts, for the ground itself; a season of long nights for sleep, leisurely breakfasts, peace by the fire. This and much more went through Rosicky's mind, but he merely told himself that winter was coming, clucked to his horses, and drove on.

When he reached home, John, the youngest boy, ran out to put away his team for him, and he met Mary coming up from the outside cellar with her apron full of carrots. They went into the house together. On the table, covered with oilcloth figured with clusters of blue grapes, a place was set, and he smelled hot coffee-cake of some kind. Anton never lunched in town; he thought that extravagant, and anyhow he didn't like the food. So Mary always had something ready for him when he got home.

After he was settled in his chair, stirring his coffee in a big cup, Mary took out of the oven a pan of *kolache* stuffed with apricots, examined them anxiously to see whether they had got too dry, put them beside his plate, and then sat down opposite him.

Rosicky asked her in Czech if she wasn't going to have any coffee.

She replied in English, as being somehow the right language for transacting business: "Now what did Doctor Ed say, Anton? You tell me just what."

"He said I was to tell you some compliments, but I forgot 'em." Rosicky's eyes twinkled.

"About you, I mean. What did he say about your asthma?"

"He says I ain't got no asthma." Rosicky took one of the little rolls in his broad brown fingers. The thickened nail of his right thumb told the story of his past.

"Well, what is the matter? And don't try to put me off."

"He don't say nothing much, only I'm a little older, and my heart ain't so good like it used to be."

Mary started and brushed her hair back from her temples with both hands as if she were a little out of her mind. From the way she glared, she might have been in a rage with him.

"He says there's something the matter with your heart? Doctor Ed says so?"

"Now don't yell at me like I was a hog in de garden, Mary. You know I always did like to hear a woman talk soft. He didn't say anything de matter wid my heart, only it ain't so young like it used to be, an' he tell me not to pitch hay or run de corn-sheller."

Mary wanted to jump up, but she sat still. She admired the way he never under any circumstances raised his voice or spoke roughly. He was city-bred, and she was country-bred; she often said she wanted her boys to have their papa's nice ways.

"You never have no pain there, do you? It's your breathing and your stomach that's been wrong. I wouldn't believe nobody but Doctor Ed about it. I guess I'll go see him myself. Didn't he give you no advice?"

"Chust to take it easy like, an' stay round de house dis winter. I guess you got some carpenter work for me to do. I kin make some new shelves for you, and I want dis long time to build a closet in de boys' room and make dem two little fellers keep dere clo'es hung up."

Rosicky drank his coffee from time to time, while he considered. His moustache was of the soft long variety and came down over his mouth like the teeth of a buggy-rake over a bundle of hay. Each time he put down his cup, he ran his blue handkerchief over his lips. When he took a drink of water, he managed very neatly with the back of his hand.

Mary sat watching him intently, trying to find any change in his face. It is hard to see anyone who has become like your own body to you. Yes, his hair had got thin, and his high forehead had deep lines running from left to right. But his neck, always clean shaved except in the busiest seasons, was not loose or baggy. It was burned a dark reddish brown, and there were deep creases in it, but it looked firm and full of blood. His cheeks had a good colour. On either side of his mouth there was a half-moon down the length of his cheek, not wrinkles, but two lines that had come there from his habitual expression. He was shorter and broader than when she married him; his back had grown broad and curved, a good deal like the shell of an old turtle, and his arms and legs were short.

He was fifteen years older than Mary, but she had hardly ever thought about it before. He was her man, and the kind of man she liked. She was rough, and he was gentle,—city-bred, as she always said. They had been shipmates on a rough voyage and had stood by each other in trying times. Life had gone well with them because, at bottom, they had the same ideas about life. They agreed, without discussion, as to what was most important and what was secondary. They didn't often exchange opinions, even in Czech,—it was as if they had thought the same thought together. A good deal had to be sacrificed and thrown overboard in a hard life like theirs, and they had never disagreed as to the things that could go. It had been a hard life, and a soft life, too. There wasn't anything brutal in the short, broad-backed man with the three-cornered eyes and the forehead that went on to the top of his skull. He was a city man, a gentle man, and though he had married a rough farm girl, he had never touched her without gentleness.

They had been at one accord not to hurry through life, not to be always skimping and saving. They saw their neighbours buy more land and feed more stock than they did, without discontent. Once when the creamery agent came to the Rosickys to persuade them to sell him their cream, he told them how much money the Fasslers, their nearest neighbours, had made on their cream last year.

"Yes," said Mary, "and look at them Fassler children! Pale, pinched little things, they look like skimmed milk. I'd rather put some colour into my children's faces than put money into the bank."

The agent shrugged and turned to Anton.

"I guess we'll do like she says," said Rosicky.

III

Mary very soon got into town to see Doctor Ed, and then she had a talk with her boys and set a guard over Rosicky. Even John, the youngest, had his father on his mind. If Rosicky went to throw hay down from the loft, one of the boys ran up the ladder and took the fork from him. He sometimes complained that though he was getting to be an old man, he wasn't an old woman yet.

That winter he stayed in the house in the afternoons and carpentered, or sat in the chair between the window full of plants and the wooden bench where the two pails of drinking-water stood. This spot was called "Father's corner," though it was not a corner at all. He had a shelf there, where he kept his Bohemian papers and his pipes and tobacco, and his shears and needles and thread and tailor's thimble. Having been a tailor in his youth, he couldn't bear to see a woman patching at his clothes, or at the boys'. He liked tailoring, and always patched all the overalls and jackets and work shirts. Occasionally he made over a pair of pants one of the older boys had outgrown, for the little fellow.

While he sewed, he let his mind run back over his life. He had a good deal to remember, really; life in three countries. The only part of his youth he didn't like to remember was the two years he had spent in London, in Cheapside, working for a German tailor who was wretchedly poor. Those days, when he was nearly always hungry, when his clothes were dropping off him for dirt, and the sound of a strange language kept him in continual bewilderment, had left a sore spot in his mind that wouldn't bear touching.

He was twenty when he landed at Castle Garden in New York, and he had a protector who got him work in a tailor shop in Vesey Street, down near the Washington Market. He looked upon that part of his life as very happy. He became a good workman, he was industrious, and his wages were increased from time to time. He minded his own business and envied nobody's good fortune. He went to night school and learned to read English. He often did overtime work and was well paid for it, but somehow he never saved anything. He couldn't refuse a loan to a friend, and he was self-indulgent. He liked a good dinner, and a little went for beer, a little for tobacco; a good deal went to the girls. He often stood through an opera on Saturday nights; he could get standing-room for a dollar. Those were the great days of opera in New York, and it gave a fellow something to think about for the rest of the week. Rosicky had a quick ear, and a childish love of all the stage splendour; the scenery, the costumes, the ballet. He usually went with a chum, and after the performance they had beer and maybe some oysters somewhere. It was a fine life; for the first five years or so it satisfied him completely. He was never hungry or cold or dirty, and everything amused him: a fire, a dog fight, a parade, a storm, a ferry ride. He thought New York the finest, richest, friendliest city in the world.

Moreover, he had what he called a happy home life. Very near the tailor shop was a small furniture-factory, where an old Austrian, Loeffler, employed a few skilled men and made unusual furniture, most of it to order, for the rich German housewives up-town. The top floor of Loeffler's five-storey factory was a loft, where he kept his choice lumber and stored the odd pieces of furniture left on his hands. One of the young workmen he employed was a Czech, and he and Rosicky became fast friends. They persuaded Loeffler to let them have a sleeping-room in one corner of the loft. They bought good beds and bedding and had their pick of the furniture kept up there. The loft was low-pitched, but light and airy, full of windows, and good-smelling by reason of the fine lumber put up there to season. Old Loeffler used to go down to the docks and buy wood from South America and the East from the sea captains. The young men were as foolish about their house as a bridal pair. Zichec, the young cabinet-maker, devised every sort of convenience, and Rosicky kept their clothes in order. At night and on Sundays, when the quiver of machinery underneath was still, it was the quietest place in the world, and on summer nights all the sea winds blew in. Zichec often practised on his flute in the evening. They were both fond of music and went to the opera together. Rosicky thought he wanted to live like that for ever.

But as the years passed, all alike, he began to get a little restless. When spring came round, he would begin to feel fretted, and he got to drinking. He was likely to drink too much of a Saturday night. On Sunday he was languid and heavy, getting over his spree. On Monday he plunged into work again. So he never had time to figure out what ailed him, though he knew something did. When the grass turned green in Park Place, and the lilac hedge at the back of Trinity churchyard put out its blossoms, he was tormented by a longing to run away. That was why he drank too much; to get a temporary illusion of freedom and wide horizons.

Rosicky, the old Rosicky, could remember as if it were yesterday the day when the young Rosicky found out what was the matter with him. It was on a Fourth of July afternoon, and he was sitting in Park Place in the sun. The lower part of New York was empty. Wall Street, Liberty Street, Broadway, all empty. So much stone and asphalt with nothing going on, so many empty windows. The emptiness was intense, like the stillness in a great factory when the machinery stops and the belts and bands cease running. It was too great a change, it took all the strength out of one. Those blank buildings, without the stream of life pouring through them, were like empty jails. It struck young Rosicky that this was the trouble with big cities; they built you in from the earth itself, cemented you away from any contact with the ground. You lived in an unnatural world, like the fish in an aquarium, who were probably much more comfortable than they ever were in the sea.

On that very day he began to think seriously about the articles he had read in the Bohemian papers, describing prosperous Czech farming communities in the West. He believed he would like to go out there as a farm hand; it was hardly possible that he could ever have land of his own. His people had always been workmen; his father and grandfather had worked in shops. His mother's parents had lived in the country, but they rented their farm and had a hard time to get along. Nobody in his family had ever owned any land,—that belonged to a different station of life altogether. Anton's mother died when he was little, and he was sent into the country to her parents. He stayed with them until he was twelve, and formed those ties with the earth and the farm animals and growing things which are never made at all unless they are made early. After his grandfather died, he went back to live with his father and stepmother, but she was very hard on him, and his father helped him to get passage to London.

After that Fourth of July day in Park Place, the desire to return to the country never left him. To work on another man's farm would be all he asked; to see the sun rise and set and to plant things and watch them grow. He was a very simple man. He was like a tree that has not many roots, but one tap-root that goes down deep. He subscribed for a Bohemian paper printed in Chicago, then for one printed in Omaha. His mind got farther and farther west. He began to save a little money to buy his liberty. When he was thirty-five, there was a great meeting in New York of Bohemian athletic societies, and Rosicky left the tailor shop and went home with the Omaha delegates to try his fortune in another part of the world.

IV

Perhaps the fact that his own youth was well over before he began to have a family was one reason why Rosicky was so fond of his boys. He had almost a grandfather's indulgence for them. He had never had to worry about any of them—except, just now, a little about Rudolph.

On Saturday night the boys always piled into the Ford, took little Josephine, and went to town to the moving-picture show. One Saturday morning they were talking at the breakfast table about starting early that evening, so that they would have an hour or so to see the Christmas things in the stores before the show began. Rosicky looked down the table.

"I hope you boys ain't disappointed, but I want you to let me have de car tonight. Maybe some of you can go in with de neighbours."

Their faces fell. They worked hard all week, and they were still like children. A new jack-knife or a box of candy pleased the older one as much as the little fellow.

"If you and Mother are going to town," Frank said, "maybe you could take a couple of us along with you, anyway."

"No, I want to take de car down to Rudolph's, and let him an' Polly go in to de show. She don't git into town enough, an' I'm afraid she's gettin' lonesome, an' he can't afford no car yet."

That settled it. The boys were a good deal dashed. Their father took another piece of apple-cake and went on: "Maybe next Saturday night de two little fellers can go along wid dem."

"Oh, is Rudolph going to have the car every Saturday night?"

Rosicky did not reply at once; then he began to speak seriously: "Listen, boys; Polly ain't lookin' so good. I don't like to see nobody lookin' sad. It comes hard fur a town girl to be a farmer's wife. I don't want no trouble to start in Rudolph's family. When it starts, it ain't so easy to stop. An American girl don't git used to our ways all at once. I like to tell Polly she and Rudolph can have the car every Saturday night till after New Year's, if it's all right with you boys."

"Sure it's all right, Papa," Mary cut in. "And it's good you thought about that. Town girls is used to more than country girls. I lay awake nights, scared she'll make Rudolph discontented with the farm."

The boys put as good a face on it as they could. They surely looked forward to their Saturday nights in town. That evening Rosicky drove the car the half-mile down to Rudolph's new, bare little house.

Polly was in a short-sleeved gingham dress, clearing away the supper dishes. She was a trim, slim little thing, with blue eyes and shingled yellow hair, and her eyebrows were reduced to a mere brush-stroke, like Miss Pearl's.

"Good evening, Mr. Rosicky. Rudolph's at the barn, I guess." She never called him father, or Mary mother. She was sensitive about having married a foreigner. She never in the world would have done it if Rudolph hadn't been such a handsome, persuasive fellow and such a gallant lover. He had graduated in her class in the high school in town, and their friendship began in the ninth grade.

Rosicky went in, though he wasn't exactly asked. "My boys ain't goin' to town tonight, an' I brought de car over fur you two to go in to de picture show."

Polly, carrying dishes to the sink, looked over her shoulder at him. "Thank you. But I'm late with my work tonight, and pretty tired. Maybe Rudolph would like to go in with you."

"Oh, I don't go to de shows! I'm too old-fashioned. You won't feel so tired after you ride in de air a ways. It's a nice clear night, an' it ain't cold. You go an' fix yourself up, Polly, an' I'll wash de dishes an' leave everything nice fur you."

Polly blushed and tossed her bob. "I couldn't let you do that, Mr. Rosicky. I wouldn't think of it."

Rosicky said nothing. He found a bib apron on a nail behind the kitchen door. He slipped it over his head and then took Polly by her two elbows and pushed her gently toward the door of her own room. "I washed up de kitchen many times for my wife, when de babies was sick or somethin'. You go an' make yourself look nice. I like you to look prettier'n any of dem town girls when you go in. De young folks must have some fun, an' I'm goin' to look out fur you, Polly."

That kind, reassuring grip on her elbows, the old man's funny bright eyes, made Polly want to drop her head on his shoulder for a second. She restrained herself, but she lingered in his grasp at the door of her room, murmuring tearfully: "You always lived in the city when you were young, didn't you? Don't you ever get lonesome out here?"

As she turned round to him, her hand fell naturally into his, and he stood holding it and smiling into her face with his peculiar, knowing, indulgent smile without a shadow of reproach in it. "Dem big cities is all right fur de rich, but dey is terrible hard fur de poor."

"I don't know. Sometimes I think I'd like to take a chance. You lived in New York, didn't you?"

"An' London. Da's bigger still. I learned my trade dere. Here's Rudolph comin', you better hurry."

"Will you tell me about London some time?"

"Maybe. Only I ain't no talker, Polly. Run an' dress yourself up."

The bedroom door closed behind her, and Rudolph came in from the outside, looking anxious. He had seen the car and was sorry any of his family should come just then. Supper hadn't been a very pleasant occasion. Halting in the doorway, he saw his father in a kitchen apron, carrying dishes to the sink. He flushed crimson and something flashed in his eye. Rosicky held up a warning finger.

"I brought de car over fur you an' Polly to go to de picture show, an' I made her let me finish here so you won't be late. You go put on a clean shirt, quick!"

"But don't the boys want the car, Father?"

"Not tonight dey don't." Rosicky fumbled under his apron and found his pants pocket. He took out a silver dollar and said in a hurried whisper: "You go an' buy dat girl some ice cream an' candy tonight, like you was courtin'. She's awful good friends wid me."

Rudolph was very short of cash, but he took the money as if it hurt him. There had been a crop failure all over the county. He had more than once been sorry he'd married this year.

In a few minutes the young people came out, looking clean and a little stiff. Rosicky hurried them off, and then he took his own time with the dishes. He scoured the pots and pans and put away the milk and swept the kitchen. He put some coal in the stove and shut off the draughts, so the place would be warm for them when they got home late at night. Then he sat down and had a pipe and listened to the clock tick.

Generally speaking, marrying an American girl was certainly a risk. A Czech should marry a Czech. It was lucky that Polly was the daughter of a poor widow woman; Rudolph was proud, and if she had a prosperous family to throw up at him, they could never make it go. Polly was one of four sisters, and they all worked; one was book-keeper in the bank, one taught music, and Polly and her younger sister had been clerks, like Miss Pearl. All four of them were musical, had pretty voices, and sang in the Methodist choir, which the eldest sister directed.

Polly missed the sociability of a store position. She missed the choir, and the company of her sisters. She didn't dislike housework, but she disliked so much of it. Rosicky was a little anxious about this pair. He was afraid Polly would grow so discontented that Rudy would quit the farm and take a factory job in Omaha. He had worked for a winter up there, two years ago, to get money to marry on. He had done very well, and they would always take him back at the stockyards. But to Rosicky that meant the end of everything for his son. To be a landless man was to be a wage-earner, a slave, all your life; to have nothing, to be nothing.

Rosicky thought he would come over and do a little carpentering for Polly after the New Year. He guessed she needed jollying. Rudolph was a serious sort of chap, serious in love and serious about his work.

Rosicky shook out his pipe and walked home across the fields. Ahead of him the lamplight shone from his kitchen windows. Suppose he were still in a tailor shop on Vesey Street, with a bunch of pale, narrow-chested sons working on machines, all coming home tired and sullen to eat supper in a kitchen that was a parlour also; with another crowded, angry family quarrelling just across the dumb-waiter shaft, and squeaking pulleys at the windows where dirty washings hung on dirty lines above a court full of old brooms and mops and ash-cans. . . .

He stopped by the windmill to look up at the frosty winter stars and draw a long breath before he went inside. That kitchen with the shining windows was dear to him; but the sleeping fields and bright stars and the noble darkness were dearer still.

V

On the day before Christmas the weather set in very cold; no snow, but a bitter, biting wind that whistled and sang over the flat land and lashed one's face like fine wires. There was baking going on in the Rosicky kitchen all day, and Rosicky sat inside, making over a coat that Albert had outgrown into an overcoat for John. Mary had a big red geranium in bloom for Christmas, and a row of Jerusalem cherry trees, full of berries. It was the first year she had every grown these; Doctor Ed brought her the seeds from Omaha when he went to some medical convention. They reminded Rosicky of plants he had seen in England; and all afternoon, as he stitched, he sat thinking about those two years in London, which his mind usually shrank from even after all this while.

He was a lad of eighteen when he dropped down into London, with no money and no connexions except the address of a cousin who was supposed to be working at a confectioner's. When he went to the pastry shop, however, he found that the cousin had gone to America. Anton tramped the streets for several days, sleeping in doorways and on the Embankment, until he was in utter despair. He knew no English, and the sound of the strange language all about him confused him. By chance he met a poor German tailor who had learned his trade in Vienna, and could speak a little Czech. This tailor, Lifschnitz, kept a repair shop in a Cheapside basement, underneath a cobbler. He didn't much need an apprentice, but he was sorry for the boy and took him in for no wages but his keep and what he could pick up. The pickings were supposed to be coppers given you when you took work home to a customer. But most of the customers called for their clothes themselves, and the coppers that came Anton's way were very few. He had, however, a place to sleep. The tailor's family lived upstairs in three rooms; a kitchen, a bedroom, where Lifschnitz and his wife and five children slept, and a living-room. Two corners of this living-room were curtained off for lodgers; in one Rosicky slept on an old horsehair sofa, with a feather quilt to wrap himself in. The other corner was rented to a wretched, dirty boy, who was studying the violin. He actually practised there. Rosicky was dirty, too. There was no way to be anything else. Mrs. Lifschnitz got the water she cooked and washed with from a pump in a brick court, four flights down. There were bugs in the place, and multitudes of fleas, though the poor woman did the best she could. Rosicky knew she often went empty to give another potato or a spoonful of dripping to the two hungry, sad-eyed boys who lodged with her. He used to think he would never get out of there, never get a clean shirt to his back again. What would he do, he wondered, when his clothes actually dropped to pieces and the worn cloth wouldn't hold patches any longer?

It was still early when the old farmer put aside his sewing and his recollections. The sky had been a dark grey all day, with not a gleam of sun, and the light failed at four o'clock. He went to shave and change his shirt while the turkey was roasting. Rudolph and Polly were coming over for supper.

After supper they sat round in the kitchen, and the younger boys were saying how sorry they were it hadn't snowed. Everybody was sorry. They wanted a deep snow that would lie long and keep the wheat warm, and leave the ground soaked when it melted.

"Yes, sir!" Rudolph broke out fiercely; "if we have another dry year like last year, there's going to be hard times in this country."

Rosicky filled his pipe. "You boys don't know what hard times is. You don't owe nobody, you got plenty to eat an' keep warm, an' plenty water to keep clean. When you got them, you can't have it very hard."

Rudolph frowned, opened and shut his big right hand, and dropped it clenched upon his knee. "I've got to have a good deal more than that, Father, or I'll quit this farming gamble. I can always make good wages railroading, or at the packing house, and be sure of my money."

"Maybe so," his father answered dryly.

Mary, who had just come in from the pantry and was wiping her hands on the roller towel, thought Rudy and his father were getting too serious. She brought her darning-basket and sat down in the middle of the group.

"I ain't much afraid of hard times, Rudy," she said heartily. "We've had a plenty, but we've always come through. Your father wouldn't never take nothing very hard, not even hard times. I got a mind to tell you a story on him. Maybe you boys can't hardly remember the year we had that terrible hot wind, that burned everything up on the Fourth of July? All the corn an' the gardens. An' that was in the days when we didn't have alfalfa yet,—I guess it wasn't invented.

"Well, that very day your father was out cultivatin' corn, and I was here in the kitchen makin' plum preserves. We had bushels of plums that year. I noticed it was terrible hot, but it's always hot in the kitchen when you're preservin', an' I was too busy with my plums to mind. Anton come in from the field about three o'clock, an' I asked him what was the matter.

" 'Nothin',' he says, 'but it's pretty hot, an' I think I won't work no more today.' He stood round for a few minutes, an' then he says: 'Ain't you near through? I want you should git up a nice supper for us tonight. It's Fourth of July.'

"I told him to git along, that I was right in the middle of preservin', but the plums would taste good on hot biscuit. 'I'm goin' to have fried chicken, too,' he says, and he went off an' killed a couple. You three oldest boys was little fellers, playin' round outside, real hot an' sweaty, an' your father took you to the horse tank down by the windmill an' took off your clothes an' put you in. Them two box-elder trees was little then, but they made shade over the tank. Then he took off all his own clothes, an' got in with you. While he was playin' in the water with you, the Methodist preacher drove into our place to say how all the neighbours was goin' to meet at the schoolhouse that night, to pray for rain. He drove right to the windmill, of course, and there was your father and you three with no clothes on. I was in the kitchen door, an' I had to laugh, for the preacher acted like he ain't never seen a naked man before. He surely was embarrassed, an' your father couldn't git to his clothes; they was all hangin' up on the windmill to let the sweat dry out of 'em. So he laid in the tank where he was, an' put one of you boys on top of him to cover him up a little, an' talked to the preacher.

"When you got through playin' in the water, he put clean clothes on you and a clean shirt on himself, an' by that time I'd begun to get supper. He says: 'It's too hot in here to eat comfortable. Let's have a picnic in the orchard. We'll eat our supper behind the mulberry hedge, under them linden trees.'

"So, he carried our supper down, an' a bottle of my wild-grape wine, an' everything tasted good, I can tell you. The wind got cooler as the sun was goin' down, and it turned out pleasant, only I noticed how the leaves was curled up on the linden trees. That made me think, an' I asked your father if that hot wind all day hadn't been terrible hard on the gardens an' the corn.

" 'Corn,' he says, 'there ain't no corn.'

" 'What you talkin' about?' I said. 'Ain't we got forty acres?'

" 'We ain't got an ear,' he says, 'nor nobody else ain't got none. All the corn in this country was cooked by three o'clock today, like you'd roasted it in an oven.'

" 'You mean you won't get no crop at all?' I asked him. I couldn't believe it, after he'd worked so hard.

" 'No crop this year,' he says. 'That's why we're havin' a picnic. We might as well enjoy what we got.'

"An' that's how your father behaved, when all the neighbours was so discouraged they couldn't look you in the face. An' we enjoyed ourselves that year, poor as we was, an' our neighbours wasn't a bit better off for bein' miserable. Some of 'em grieved till they got poor digestions and couldn't relish what they did have."

The younger boys said they thought their father had the best of it. But Rudolph was thinking that, all the same, the neighbours had managed to get ahead more, in the fifteen years since that time. There must be something wrong about his father's way of doing things. He wished he knew what was going on in the back of Polly's mind. He knew she liked his father, but he knew, too, that she was afraid of something. When his mother sent over coffee-cake or prune tarts or a loaf of fresh bread, Polly seemed to regard them with a certain suspicion. When she observed to him that his brothers had nice manners, her tone implied that it was remarkable they should have. With his mother she was stiff and on her guard. Mary's hearty frankness and gusts of good humour irritated her. Polly was afraid of being unusual or conspicuous in any way, of being "ordinary," as she said!

When Mary had finished her story, Rosicky laid aside his pipe.

"You boys like me to tell you about some of dem hard times I been through in London?" Warmly encouraged, he sat rubbing his forehead along the deep creases. It was bothersome to tell a long story in English (he nearly always talked to the boys in Czech), but he wanted Polly to hear this one.

"Well, you know about dat tailor shop I worked in in London? I had one Christmas dere I ain't never forgot. Times was awful bad before Christmas; de boss ain't got much work, an' have it awful hard to pay his rent. It ain't so much fun, bein' poor in a big city like London, I'll say! All de windows is full of good t'ings to eat, an' all de pushcarts in de streets is full, an' you smell 'em all de time, an' you ain't got no money,—not a damn bit. I didn't mind de cold so much, though I didn't have no overcoat, chust a short jacket I'd outgrowed so it wouldn't meet on me, an' my hands was chapped raw. But I always had a good appetite, like you all know, an' de sight of dem pork pies in de windows was awful fur me!

"Day before Christmas was terrible foggy dat year, an' dat fog gits into your bones and makes you all damp like. Mrs. Lifschnitz didn't give us nothin' but a little bread an' drippin' for supper, because she was savin' to try for to give us a good dinner on Christmas Day. After supper de boss say I can go an' enjoy myself, so I went into de streets to listen to de Christmas singers. Dey sing old songs an' make very nice music, an' I run round after dem a good ways, till I got awful hungry. I t'ink maybe if I go home, I can sleep till morning an' forget my belly.

"I went into my corner real quiet, and roll up in my fedder quilt. But I ain't got my head down, till I smell somet'ing good. Seem like it git stronger an' stronger, an' I can't git to sleep noway. I can't understand dat smell. Dere was a gas light in a hall across de court, dat always shine in at my window a little. I got up an' look round. I got a little wooden box in my corner fur a stool, 'cause I ain't got no chair. I picks up dat box, and under it dere is a roast goose on a platter! I can't believe my eyes. I carry it to de window where de light comes in, an' touch it and smell it to find out, an' den I taste it to be sure. I say, I will eat chust one little bite of dat goose, so I can go to sleep, and tomorrow I won't eat none at all. But I tell you, boys, when I stop, one half of dat goose was gone!"

The narrator bowed his head, and the boys shouted. But little Josephine slipped behind his chair and kissed him on the neck beneath his ear.

"Poor little Papa, I don't want him to be hungry!"

"Da's long ago, child. I ain't never been hungry since I had your mudder to cook fur me."

"Go on and tell us the rest, please," said Polly.

"Well, when I come to realize what I done, of course, I felt terrible. I felt better in de stomach, but very bad in de heart. I set on my bed wid dat platter on my knees, an' it all come to me; how hard dat poor woman save to buy dat goose, and how she get some neighbour to cook it dat got more fire, an' how she put it in my corner to keep away from dem hungry children. Dere was a old carpet hung up to shut my corner off, an' de children wasn't allowed to go in dere. An' I know she put it in my corner because she trust me more'n she did de violin boy. I can't stand it to face her after I spoil de Christmas. So I put on my shoes and go out into de city. I tell myself I better throw myself in de river; but I guess I ain't dat kind of a boy.

"It was after twelve o'clock, an' terrible cold, an' I start out to walk about London all night. I walk along de river awhile, but dere was lots of drunks all along; men, and women too. I chust move along to keep away from de police. I git onto de Strand, an' den over to New Oxford Street, where dere was a big German restaurant on de ground floor, wid big windows all fixed up fine, an' I could see de people havin' parties inside. While I was lookin' in, two men and two ladies come out, laughin' and talkin' and feelin' happy about all dey been eatin' an' drinkin', and dey was speakin' Czech,—not like de Austrians, but like de home folks talk it.

"I guess I went crazy, an' I done what I ain't never done before nor since. I went right up to dem gay people an' begun to beg dem: 'Fellow-countrymen, for God's sake give me money enough to buy a goose!'

"Dey laugh, of course, but de ladies speak awful kind to me, an' dey take me back into de restaurant and give me hot coffee and cakes, an' make me tell all about how I happened to come to London, an' what I was doin' dere. Dey take my name and where I work down on paper, an' both of dem ladies give me ten shillings.

"De big market at Covent Garden ain't very far away, an' by dat time it was open. I go dere an' buy a big goose an' some pork pies, an' potatoes and onions, an' cakes an' oranges fur de children,—all I could carry! When I git home, everybody is still asleep. I pile all I bought on de kitchen table, an' go in an' lay down on my bed, an' I ain't waken up till I hear dat woman scream when she come out into her kitchen. My goodness, but she was surprise! She laugh an' cry at de same time, an' hug me and waken all de children. She ain't stop fur no breakfast; she git de Christmas dinner ready dat morning, and we all sit down an' eat all we can hold. I ain't never seen dat violin boy have all he can hold before.

"Two three days after dat, de two men come to hunt me up, an' dey ask my boss, and he give me a good report an' tell dem I was a steady boy all right. One of dem Bohemians was very smart an' run a Bohemian newspaper in New York, an' de odder was a rich man, in de importing business, an' dey been travelling togedder. Dey told me how t'ings was easier in New York, an' offered to pay my passage when dey was goin' home soon on a boat. My boss say to me: 'You go. You ain't got no chance here, an' I like to see you git ahead, fur you always been a good boy to my woman, and fur dat fine Christmas dinner you give us all.' An' da's how I got to New York."

That night when Rudolph and Polly, arm in arm, were running home across the fields with the bitter wind at their backs, his heart leaped for joy when she said she thought they might have his family come over for supper on New Year's Eve. "Let's get up a nice supper, and not let your mother help at all; make her be company for once."

"That would be lovely of you, Polly," he said humbly. He was a very simple, modest boy, and he, too, felt vaguely that Polly and her sisters were more experienced and worldly than his people.

VI

The winter turned out badly for farmers. It was bitterly cold, and after the first light snows before Christmas there was no snow at all,—and no rain. March was as bitter as February. On those days when the wind fairly punished the country, Rosicky sat by his window. In the fall he and the boys had put in a big wheat planting, and now the seed had frozen in the ground. All that land would have to be ploughed up and planted over again, planted in corn. It had happened before, but he was younger then, and he never worried about what had to be. He was sure of himself and of Mary; he knew they could bear what they had to bear, that they would always pull through somehow. But he was not so sure about the young ones, and he felt troubled because Rudolph and Polly were having such a hard start.

Sitting beside his flowering window while the panes rattled and the wind blew in under the door, Rosicky gave himself to reflection as he had not done since those Sundays in the loft of the furniture-factory in New York, long ago. Then he was trying to find what he wanted in life for himself; now he was trying to find what he wanted for his boys, and why it was he so hungered to feel sure they would be here, working this very land, after he was gone.

They would have to work hard on the farm, and probably they would never do much more than make a living. But if he could think of them as staying here on the land, he wouldn't have to fear any great unkindness for them. Hardships, certainly; it was a hardship to have the wheat freeze in the ground when seed was so high; and to have to sell your stock because you had no feed. But there would be other years when everything came along right, and you caught up. And what you had was your own. You didn't have to choose between bosses and strikers, and go wrong either way. You didn't have to do with dishonest and cruel people. They were the only things in his experience he had found terrifying and horrible; the look in the eyes of a dishonest and crafty man, of a scheming and rapacious woman.

In the country, if you had a mean neighbour, you could keep off his land and make him keep off yours. But in the city, all the foulness and misery and brutality of your neighbours was part of your life. The worst things he had come upon in his journey through the world were human,—depraved and poisonous specimens of man. To this day he could recall certain terrible faces in the London streets. There were mean people everywhere, to be sure, even in their own country town here. But they weren't tempered, hardened, sharpened, like the treacherous people in cities who live by grinding or cheating or poisoning their fellow-men. He had helped to bury two of his fellow-workmen in the tailoring trade, and he was distrustful of the organized industries that see one out of the world in big cities. Here, if you were sick, you had Doctor Ed to look after you; and if you died, fat Mr. Haycock, the kindest man in the world, buried you.

It seemed to Rosicky that for good, honest boys like his, the worst they could do on the farm was better than the best they would be likely to do in the city. If he'd had a mean boy, now, one who was crooked and sharp and tried to put anything over on his brothers, then town would be the place for him. But he had no such boy. As for Rudolph, the discontented one, he would give the shirt off his back to anyone who touched his heart. What Rosicky really hoped for his boys was that they could get through the world without ever knowing much about the cruelty of human beings. "Their mother and me ain't prepared them for that," he sometimes said to himself.

These thoughts brought him back to a grateful consideration of his own case. What an escape he had had, to be sure! He, too, in his time, had had to take money for repair work from the hand of a hungry child who let it go so wistfully; because it was money due his boss. And now, in all these years, he had never had to take a cent from anyone in bitter need,—never had to look at the face of a woman become like a wolf's from struggle and famine. When he thought of these things, Rosicky would put on his cap and jacket and slip down to the barn and give his work-horses a little extra oats, letting them eat it out of his hand in their slobbery fashion. It was his way of expressing what he felt, and made him chuckle with pleasure.

The spring came warm, with blue skies,—but dry, dry as a bone. The boys began ploughing up the wheat-fields to plant them over in corn. Rosicky would stand at the fence corner and watch them, and the earth was so dry it blew up in clouds of brown dust that hid the horses and the sulky plough and the driver. It was a bad outlook.

The big alfalfa-field that lay between the home place and Rudolph's came up green, but Rosicky was worried because during that open windy winter a great many Russian thistle plants had blown in there and lodged. He kept asking the boys to rake them out; he was afraid their seed would root and "take the alfalfa." Rudolph said that was nonsense. The boys were working so hard planting corn, their father felt he couldn't insist about the thistles, but he set great store by that big alfalfa-field. It was a feed you could depend on,—and there was some deeper reason, vague, but strong. The peculiar green of that clover woke early memories in old Rosicky, went back to something in his childhood in the old world. When he was a little boy, he had played in fields of that strong blue-green colour.

One morning, when Rudolph had gone to town in the car, leaving a work-team idle in his barn, Rosicky went over to his son's place, put the horses to the buggy-rake, and set about quietly raking up those thistles. He behaved with guilty caution, and rather enjoyed stealing a march on Doctor Ed, who was just then taking his first vacation in seven years of practice and was attending a clinic in Chicago. Rosicky got the thistles raked up, but did not stop to burn them. That would take some time, and his breath was pretty short, so he thought he had better get the horses back to the barn.

He got them into the barn and to their stalls, but the pain had come on so sharp in his chest that he didn't try to take the harness off. He started for the house, bending lower with every step. The cramp in his chest was shutting him up like a jack-knife. When he reached the windmill, he swayed and caught at the ladder. He saw Polly coming down the hill, running with the swiftness of a slim greyhound. In a flash she had her shoulder under his armpit.

"Lean on me, Father, hard! Don't be afraid. We can get to the house all right."

Somehow they did, though Rosicky became blind with pain; he could keep on his legs, but he couldn't steer his course. The next thing he was conscious of was lying on Polly's bed, and Polly bending over him wringing out bath towels in hot water and putting them on his chest. She stopped only to throw coal into the stove, and she kept the tea-kettle and the black pot going. She put these hot applications on him for nearly an hour, she told him afterwards, and all that time he was drawn up stiff and blue, with the sweat pouring off him.

As the pain gradually loosed its grip, the stiffness went out of his jaws, the black circles round his eyes disappeared, and a little of his natural colour came back. When his daughter-in-law buttoned his shirt over his chest at last, he sighed.

"Da's fine, de way I feel now, Polly. It was a awful bad spell, an' I was so sorry it all come on you like it did."

Polly was flushed and excited. "Is the pain really gone? Can I leave you long enough to telephone over to your place?"

Rosicky's eyelids fluttered. "Don't telephone, Polly. It ain't no use to scare my wife. It's nice and quiet here, an' if I ain't too much trouble to you, just let me lay still till I feel like myself. I ain't got no pain now. It's nice here."

Polly bent over him and wiped the moisture from his face. "Oh, I'm so glad it's over!" she broke out impulsively. "It just broke my heart to see you suffer so, Father."

Rosicky motioned her to sit down on the chair where the tea-kettle had been, and looked up at her with that lively affectionate gleam in his eyes. "You was awful good to me, I won't never forgit dat. I hate it to be sick on you like dis. Down at de barn I say to myself, dat young girl ain't had much experience in sickness, I don't want to scare her, an' maybe she's got a baby comin' or somet'ing."

Polly took his hand. He was looking at her so intently and affectionately and confidingly; his eyes seemed to caress her face, to regard it with pleasure. She frowned with her funny streaks of eyebrows, and then smiled back at him.

"I guess maybe there is something of that kind going to happen. But I haven't told anyone yet, not my mother or Rudolph. You'll be the first to know."

His hand pressed hers. She noticed that it was warm again. The twinkle in his yellow-brown eyes seemed to come nearer.

"I like mighty well to see dat little child, Polly," was all he said. Then he closed his eyes and lay half-smiling. But Polly sat still, thinking hard. She had a sudden feeling that nobody in the world, not her mother, not Rudolph, or anyone, really loved her as much as old Rosicky did. It perplexed her. She sat frowning and trying to puzzle it out. It was as if Rosicky had a special gift for loving people, something that was like an ear for music or an eye for colour. It was quiet, unobtrusive; it was merely there. You saw it in his eyes,—perhaps that was why they were merry. You felt it in his hands, too. After he dropped off to sleep, she sat holding his warm, broad, flexible brown hand. She had never seen another in the least like it. She wondered if it wasn't a kind of gypsy hand, it was so alive and quick and light in its communications,—very strange in a farmer. Nearly all the farmers she knew had huge lumps of fists, like mauls, or they were knotty and bony and uncomfortable-looking, with stiff fingers. But Rosicky's was like quicksilver, flexible, muscular, about the colour of a pale cigar, with deep, deep creases across the palm. It wasn't nervous, it wasn't a stupid lump; it was a warm brown human hand, with some cleverness in it, a great deal of generosity, and something else which Polly could only call "gypsy-like,"—something nimble and lively and sure, in the way that animals are.

Polly remembered that hour long afterwards; it had been like an awakening to her. It seemed to her that she had never learned so much about life from anything as from old Rosicky's hand. It brought her to herself; it communicated some direct and untranslatable message.

When she heard Rudolph coming in the car, she ran out to meet him.

"Oh, Rudy, your father's been awful sick! He raked up those thistles he's been worrying about, and afterwards he could hardly get to the house. He suffered so I was afraid he was going to die."

Rudolph jumped to the ground. "Where is he now?"

"On the bed. He's asleep. I was terribly scared, because, you know, I'm so fond of your father." She slipped her arm through his and they went into the house. That afternoon they took Rosicky home and put him to bed, though he protested that he was quite well again.

The next morning he got up and dressed and sat down to breakfast with his family. He told Mary that his coffee tasted better than usual to him, and he warned the boys not to bear any tales to Doctor Ed when he got home. After breakfast he sat down by his window to do some patching and asked Mary to thread several needles for him before she went to feed her chickens,—her eyes were better than his, and her hands steadier. He lit his pipe and took up John's overalls. Mary had been watching him anxiously all morning, and as she went out of the door with her bucket of scraps, she saw that he was smiling. He was thinking, indeed, about Polly, and how he might never have known what a tender heart she had if he hadn't got sick over there. Girls nowadays didn't wear their heart on their sleeve. But now he knew Polly would make a fine woman after the foolishness wore off. Either a woman had that sweetness at her heart or she hadn't. You couldn't always tell by the look of them; but if they had that, everything came out right in the end.

After he had taken a few stiches, the cramp began in his chest, like yesterday. He put his pipe cautiously down on the window-sill and bent over to ease the pull. No use,—he had better try to get to his bed if he could. He rose and groped his way across the familiar floor, which was rising and falling like the deck of a ship. At the door he fell. When Mary came in, she found him lying there, and the moment she touched him she knew that he was gone.

Doctor Ed was away when Rosicky died, and for the first few weeks after he got home he was hard driven. Every day he said to himself that he must get out to see that family that had lost their father. One soft, warm moonlight night in early summer he started for the farm. His mind was on other things, and not until his road ran by the graveyard did he realize that Rosicky wasn't over there on the hill where the red lamplight shone, but here, in the moonlight. He stopped his car, shut off the engine, and sat there for a while.

A sudden hush had fallen on his soul. Everything here seemed strangely moving and significant, though signifying what, he did not know. Close by the wire fence stood Rosicky's mowing-machine, where one of the boys had been cutting hay that afternoon; his own work-horses had been going up and down there. The new-cut hay perfumed all the night air. The moonlight silvered the long, billowy grass that grew over the graves and hid the fence; the few little evergreens stood out black in it, like shadows in a pool. The sky was very blue and soft, the stars rather faint because the moon was full.

For the first time it struck Doctor Ed that this was really a beautiful graveyard. He thought of city cemeteries; acres of shrubbery and heavy stone, so arranged and lonely and unlike anything in the living world. Cities of the dead, indeed; cities of the forgotten, of the "put away." But this was open and free, this little square of long grass which the wind for ever stirred. Nothing but the sky overhead, and the many-coloured fields running on until they met that sky. The horses worked here in summer; the neighbours passed on their way to town; and over yonder, in the corn-field, Rosicky's own cattle would be eating fodder as winter came on. Nothing could be more undeathlike than this place; nothing could be more right for a man who had helped to do the work of great cities and had always longed for the open country and had got to it at last. Rosicky's life seemed to him complete and beautiful.

Further Reading

"The Bohemian Girl." 1912; rpt. 1965 in *Willa Cather's Collected Short Fiction, 1892–1912*.
"Eric Hermannsson's Soul." 1900; rpt. 1965 in *Willa Cather's Collected Short Fiction, 1892–1912*.
My Ántonia. 1918.
"On the Divide." 1896; rpt. 1965 in *Willa Cather's Collected Short Fiction, 1892–1912*.

Reading about Willa Cather

Arnold, Marilyn. *Willa Cather's Short Fiction*. Athens: Ohio University Press, 1984.
Bennet, Mildred. *The World of Willa Cather*. 1951; rpt. Lincoln: University of Nebraska Press, 1995.
Bohlke, Brent. *Willa Cather in Person: Interviews, Speeches, and Letters*. Lincoln: University of Nebraska Press, 1986.
Bohlke, Brent, and Sharon Hoover, eds. *Willa Cather Remembered*. Lincoln: University of Nebraska Press, 2002.
Murphy, John. "The Cather Enterprise." *Udpating the Literary West*. Fort Worth: Texas Christian University Press, 1997. 658–69.
Rosowski, Susan. *Approaches to Teaching "My Ántonia"*. New York: MLA, 1989.
Wasserman, Loretta. *Willa Cather: A Study of the Short Fiction*. Boston: Twayne, 1991.
Woodress, James. *Willa Cather: A Literary Life*. Lincoln: University of Nebraska Press, 1987.

O. E. Rølvaag

Peder Victorious, the sequel to Rølvaag's novel *Giants in the Earth,* follows Per Hansa's wife, Beret, in the years after her husband's death in a blizzard, the event that ends the first novel. A central theme in this work is the increasing distance between Beret, who stubbornly refuses to accept English and American customs, and her children, who eagerly embrace English and their Norwegian, Irish, Lutheran, and Catholic neighbors and classmates. The idea that the children would mix with, much less marry, people who are not Norwegian Lutherans is unimaginable to their mother.

In her dreams Beret imagines her children being transformed into evil spirits that represent American behaviors and attitudes. For Beret, to cease being Norwegian is to cease to *be* at all. In this selection from the novel the conflict is between Beret and her youngest son, Peder, who was born on Christmas day in their first hard year in the Dakota Territory. Beret's fear and resentment reach a climax when Peder refuses to read to her in Norwegian. For Rølvaag the issue is not simply a matter of semantics but a deeply psychological matter: to lose language is to lose one's soul, to be cut off from any firm anchor in either language or culture.*

For the biography and bibliography of Rølvaag see pages 341 and 367.

Excerpt from *Peder Victorious* (1929)

II

All that summer thoughts of Norway bore more strongly in upon the mind of Beret than at any time since her coming to America. Not that she longed greatly for her fatherland, but Norway was beautiful and now she was her own master. Nothing could compare with summer in Nordland, for that was enchantment itself—she had heard many people say so. On warm nights, when she found it difficult to sleep, she would sometimes get up and go out to sit on the porch in order to let the night air soothe her mind and body. Then old scenes would come back to her, the mood of the prairie night round about her being strangely reminiscent of them. It might happen that she would sit here on her own porch and watch

---

*Like Beret, Rølvaag believed in staying close to his Norwegian cultural roots. He wrote his novels in Norwegian and then translated them into English.

a lazy sea billowing listlessly into a quiet cove, washing up against kelp-covered rocks. . . . Clear, quiescent night. Drowsy, sated light upon heathery hills. Purple inland mountains dozing in a hazy sun. She could hear the call of the gull in the meadows. Down on the bay floated flocks of eider ducks, dreaming, their bills tucked under their wings. . . . A boat paddled its way toward shore. Put in at the landing. A man in heavy sea boots ascended the rocky path. That was Father. Tonight he had been out coal fishing.

Her memory became trance-like; she would see all as clearly as if she were standing by the corner of the cottage at home. . . . Yes, there came Father! Who took care of the house for him after Mother had gone? He never wrote to her, and it seemed she never could make herself write to him. How could she write to people who didn't understand how things were over here? . . . She could sell, to be sure, and go back to Norway. . . . Wondered if that might not be wise? For then the children would regain race and fatherland and their mother tongue. . . . Was it possible to atone for sin that way? In old times people made long pilgrimages to distant lands, she had heard. . . . It would not be easy for her. . . . No. . . . Over in the churchyard yonder lay Per Hansa watching every move she made. Ought she leave him to lie here alone in this alien land? . . . Whenever these thoughts came she would feel like a traitor. He had had such great dreams about how things were to be in the New Kingdom, had talked about a royal mansion and many other wonders. Were she to get up and leave it all, how would she account to him if they ever met again? He would surely want to know how she had carried on the work. . . . No, the move would not be easy for her. And the children—what would they say? . . .

But the thought of Norway would not give her peace. One Sunday, when on a visit to Sörine, she mentioned the idea to her. What did she think? Ought they sell and move back to Norway?

Sörine sat playing with the child. "If it weren't for the children," she answered as though she had thought a great deal about the matter, "I'd be on my way now. With the money you and I would get if we sold, we could live very comfortably there."

"What makes you think it wouldn't be all right for the children?"

"Oh, you know that as well as I. You surely don't wish that they should be strangers in Norway, the way we've been here? . . . That would be terrible!"

"But that could never happen," Beret objected . . . "they'd be coming back to their own people!"

"Well, I wonder now? Sofie doesn't remember much of Norway, and the baby was born here, you know. Besides, you wouldn't want your boys to slave on the sea for a living, would you? . . . Here we have plenty both to eat and to drink."

To which Beret made no reply. After that the subject was never discussed between them.

That summer Beret tried several times to write to her father, each effort to end only by her burning the letter. She never could say what she wished to, it seemed; either she would tell altogether too little, and thereby make the whole picture untrue, or she would have to include so much that she could never finish.

Moreover, she scarcely had time to think of more than what each day demanded. The moment dawn crimsoned her bedroom window she was up; and she never went to bed until long after dark. In her work outside she wore men's clothing, a habit she continued until she discovered that the children didn't like it.

Duties multiplied and made increasing demands on her time. The days were always too short. The weariness at night gave pleasant relief. More than anything else she enjoyed taking care of the cattle; every creature on the farm responded to her voice. How good to feel that all life was fond of her! The first spring and summer she let every creature born on the farm live. Not until late in the fall did she sell any cattle, and then only because the boys compelled her to. Just suppose now, they argued, that they had another winter like the last one; what would she do with all the stock? They certainly didn't intend to slave the way they did last year!

On warm evenings that summer, as soon as the children had gone to bed, Beret would heat water, and undressing in her bedroom and putting out the light, she would go back of the house and bathe her whole body. Then, with only her night clothes on, she would often sit on the porch to rest awhile before going to bed. On such nights it frequently happened that an intense longing for her husband came upon her; she actually ached to feel masculine strength embrace her. All the endearing terms Per Hansa had used, the many kinds of caresses he could think of when he was in the mood, now came back to her with all the poignancy of actuality. . . . One thing she realized more and more clearly as time went on: She and her husband had not lived together as they ought during the last years, and it was, she thought, mostly her fault. And never could it be done over again! . . . Gnawing remorse filled her mind—it might have been heaven between her and Per Hansa, and instead it had become hell. Now she lived in bereavement, a strong, healthy woman in her best years!

That these balmy moon-nights, burning a verdigris green, were dangerous to her, she did not realize! It often happened that Tambur-Ola's face, springing out of nowhere, would stand gazing at her, the expression of his face changing from ironic mockery to a quiet peacefulness—the whole man a poor wounded creature begging for kindness from hearts that could understand. She didn't wonder that he begged! Strange feelings stole over her. She let herself be carried away by them . . . liked them. But the next day she would go about feeling so ashamed of herself that she did not dare look at the children. Nevertheless, she couldn't banish the man from her thoughts; and truth to tell, she didn't want to either. And so she must go about dreading that sin too.

. . . Could she only have known how many of her troubles had been ordained by God! . . . Assuredly, His ways were unsearchable. Never had truer words been spoken by human tongue. Here He had worked the greatest of miracles with her,

had restored full understanding and reason to her. Had it been done only that she
might do yet greater wrongs? . . . Why had He let Tambur-Ola come into her life?
. . . "You must learn to find the good in your fellow man."

The words would keep ringing in Beret's ears. Perhaps the minister was right?
There was more goodness in the world than she had seen. Could it be that she was
still stricken with blindness? . . . Folks had been remarkably kind to her since Per
Hansa died. The neighbours had banded together and helped her with the work
during both the spring and the harvest season that first year. Even the hardest
labour had been nothing but fun. Those who had helped had enjoyed it like
children playing a game. Not that she had needed help, for she could afford to hire,
and they were three grown persons themselves. Nevertheless, the neighbours'
kindness had been of great comfort to her. It felt pleasant, as though someone, after
a hard day's toil, had pushed an armchair up to her and invited her to sit down.

It might be that the minister was right. There were the children, for example. At
times she didn't know what to do with them because they had the notion that they
must carry her on their hands. Their eagerness often become embarrassing. Did
they actually think she was helpless? Surely they weren't guarding her? Beret
laughed outright at the thought. The idea—couldn't they understand that she
must be both first and last herself? . . . And Ole, so impulsive by nature—never
before had she known what a heart there was in the boy. He would look out for her
continually. Had she permitted it, he would have worked nights too in order to
spare her. He and his brother literally competed to see who could be the more
diligent and the more manly. . . . And here toddled Permand, that dear ridiculous
little youngster, always asking questions and always wanting to help. Tears would
come into her eyes when she thought of the child. Well, him at least she would take
good care of! . . . A more difficult matter with the older ones. Not so easy to know
just what they might be up to the moment she wasn't around; children were, after
all, only children. . . . Once while the boys were busy patching up the barn for the
winter, Store-Hans had run a rusty nail through his foot. But they had kept the
accident a secret until several days later. Ole had simply ordered his brother to pull
off his shoe and sock, and had lain down to suck the blood out. After supper they
had had an errand to Tönseten's and had driven over. That night they had gone to
Crazy-Brita's west on the prairie to get ointment for the foot. . . . Always thus with
anything which might cause her to worry. Merciful heaven, could it be that they
feared there was something wrong with her?

. . . Queer this—about the good in people. There it was, and then again it would
be gone, like an object bobbing up and down in the sea over on the horizon. If one
looked hard it would disappear altogether. . . . No one saw things as she saw them.
People talked politics until they got drunk with excitement; the discussion only
made her still more aloof and silent. She saw how, by it, good will and neighbourli-
ness were being blighted, like beautiful wheat by rust. Abominableness and hatred, and a futile chasing after wind were all the fruits they harvested! What

difference would it make whether they had two states or one? What for all this hate? Did quarreling and bitter wrangling make for sweeter temper? . . . Supposing they spent all that energy in trying to live peaceably together and in helping one another? . . . It really was possible to make life pleasant out here.

Was she so different from all others? . . . She craved to be understood but found no response. If she spoke her thoughts, she was sure to be greeted with laughter, just as if she had been a child trying to talk grown-up. . . . She had tried to talk but had learned to keep silent.

This summer the minister had died of a stroke. Beret, mourning his death as though he had been her own father, felt the need of being alone, that in solitude she might thank God for what He, through this man, had done for her. No one seemed to share her feeling. The whole congregation was soon in a stew as to whom they should call to succeed him. And so they had gone to work and called that dolt of a man! Then Beret had had to protest because she must prevent a calamity, and had said more than was proper for an ignorant farmer woman. . . . That Simple Simon to explain the mysterious workings of God with man! . . . No one had listened to her; people had seemed stricken with blindness. He looked so nice in the pulpit; he had the best of recommendations; he was very well educated; he was so tactful in his associations; he came of good family; and he didn't use tobacco, they had argued. Sörine, in her amiable way, had laughed at her and said they surely weren't going to marry the man! . . . Now they were lying in the bed they had made for themselves. But where a people are being stunted by spiritual starvation, the knowledge that they are themselves to blame gives small comfort. That, too, was in Beret's mind.

III

How could it be that she always seemed to see things that others scarcely noticed? Was she really more stupid than anyone else?

One evening the first winter after Per Hansa died, Kjersti was sitting in the kitchen at Beret's knitting a sock, and bubbling over with gossip.

A terrible rumpus in the settlement now! Hadn't Beret heard about it? Really? Could it be possible? Why, people weren't talking about anything else! Ole Tallaksen had gone off and got married to Rose Mary. Awful commotion on account of it. Reverend Isaksen had refused to marry them unless Rose Mary turned Lutheran and joined the church. Tallaksen himself was on a terrible rampage; fierce the way he was cussing and carrying on; he declared that before he'd let any of his marry a Catholic he'd see him buried alive! Foolish of Tallaksen to talk that way. Two young people loving each other in that manner didn't stop to consider their faith—she certainly could remember what happened summers in Nordland when the herring fishers came! . . . Kjersti had dropped a stitch, necessitating that she unravel to pick it up. . . . Let's see now, what was she saying? Oh, yes, well—the boy wasn't so slow; nor the girl either, you bet! They had run away and got themselves squared; things had probably gone a bit too far with them, 'cording to what people said! Young folks will be thoughtless, you know. And now the Catholic priest was maintaining that they weren't married at all, but that they were living in sin and adultery! She wondered about that though. *Her* husband said that 'cording to law it was right enough, no doubt about that, just so it was done properly and in a Christian way; but of course it depended on how the Lord would look at it! Well, that's what *he* said, and he ought to know, for it was Syvert who had married Johannes Mörstad and Josie, and with them it had turned out just fine! . . . A lot going on these days. Much jollier now than the first years when they saw nothing but gophers and Indians. . . .

A far away look came over Beret's face as she listened to the story. Back in her mind a Scripture passage strove to come out into the light, something about the sons of God going in to the daughters of men, and wickedness increasing fearfully on account of it. . . . The second marriage of the kind in less than two years. Out here people seemed no longer to care with whom they mixed and whored. Had the like of it ever been known before among either humans or beasts? It was terrible! . . . But He who reigns in heaven laughs.

During the winter of the terrible snow the school had fared badly; for weeks it had been closed altogether, the pupils attending irregularly the time it was in session; none of Beret's had been there after the memorable February blizzards.

But the following winter she sent the three youngest. Permand had teased and fussed so long that she had finally let him go also. Store-Hans was still attending and could look after him; it probably wasn't so easy for a little tot the first year. Later she came to regret having let the child start so early.

The school seemed to exert an influence that Beret could not understand. The children, once started, would think of nothing else. Evenings as soon as they had swallowed the last bite, they would clear the kitchen table and sit down to their books. In a moment they were off in a world where she could not follow. And they would act as if possessed; they neither heard nor saw. Never had she seen the like of it, for it was school, school, school all the time; as far as they were concerned nothing else seemed to exist.

At first, she had not realized what was taking place, feeling contented because she had the children at home, right here by the kitchen table; Ole, too, having subscribed for an English farm paper, sat here with the others. At times she would think of questions to ask just to make them come out of their world. What were they doing now? What was the lesson about? Yes, but couldn't they say it in Norwegian? . . . Well, was that anything for grown folks to learn? Either she would be ignored altogether, or she would get an answer so nonsensical that it vexed her. They could at least listen to what she asked, could they not? If the two younger were called upon to explain, they would stammer or stumble over the words, and immediately switch into English; then they weren't stuck for words!

Peder had not attended many weeks before he would talk nothing but English. He had started school knowing only a few English words, such as were used daily in the Norwegian speech at home. Returning one day he had left behind him the language he had spoken all his life. The mother talked to him in Norwegian; Peder answered her in English; his voice loud and boisterous, the boy seemed almost beside himself. The others had to join in the laugh, which only emboldened him so that he went on with still greater swagger, talking nothing but English. Finally his mother stopped talking to him altogether. That same evening, taking the Norwegian primer, she sat down to teach him from it; then all ambition and joy vanished. But he didn't escape for all that, either that night or later.

Henceforth a peculiar uneasiness hovered about Beret. At times she wasn't particularly aware of it; but it never quite disappeared; it merely lay there, existing, enjoying itself until an opportunity should come. Suddenly, stirring, it would rise up and breathe apprehension, making her sensibilities painfully acute.

For a long time she couldn't quite comprehend the nature of her uneasiness. Nor did she want to think about it either. Nevertheless, it was there, would come stealing upon her at intervals, throwing shadows, uncertain, fleeting—yet shadows which persisted; they approached and passed on, might move so far that she thought they were gone; before she was aware, they were upon her again, threatening like black clouds, and now nearer than ever.

As time passed the dread of impending evil grew. Turn where she might she saw no escape. And though realizing more and more clearly the inevitableness of what she was facing, she could not make herself believe it—no, not altogether. Merciful God! was it possible that a people could disappear utterly and yet continue to exist? Was this retributive justice for having torn themselves loose from kindred and fatherland? If so, then there would be many in America that would be brought low! . . . There had been many in Noah's day too—God hadn't hesitated on that account! . . . No, she could not fathom it. Perhaps it was with the Norwegians in this country as with the fertilizer she scattered on the fields in spring? She spread it there that it might give strength and virility to the growth which was to come. . . .

The dread would paint pictures for her, especially on sleepless nights when she wasn't able to get up and read it away. One picture often returned. She saw herself sitting on a lone rock far out at sea. The surf sucked and boomed. There must be a terrible storm brewing. The tide had begun to rise. Never had it risen more circumstantially. She watched it come. Little by little the surf began sucking her feet. A skua kept circling about the rock.[1] That bird hacked rapaciously at dead bodies floating on the surface—always the eyes first. She remembered her father telling her that once. . . . She might lie and look at the picture so long that she would involuntarily draw her feet up under her and in suspense raise herself from the pillow. . . . Oh, no, America would not be satisfied with getting their bodies only!

Hidden forces were taking the children away from her—Beret saw it clearly. And strangely enough, they were enticing the youngest first. Permand and Anna Marie would watch every opportunity to talk English to each other, surreptitiously; the two older boys, she felt sure, did the same the moment she was out of their sight. Nor would they talk anything but English when youngsters of their own age came to the farm. And never did she hear them so much as mention what pertained to them as Norwegians. . . . Here was a people going away from itself, and not realizing it!

Fairytales she had heard in childhood and now only vaguely remembered came back to her, stories about sorcerers—Lapps skilled in the black art, her mother had said—who, slipping out of their human integument, would roam about in the guise of animals; if anyone in the meantime chanced upon their forms and touched them, their owners could never again become human; for ever and ever they must wander about as evil spirits. Was that what was happening to the children now? . . . At times, as she listened to their talk she would fall to wondering whether she actually was their mother—their language was not hers. Here, so it seemed, each did not bring forth after its own kind as the Lord had ordained. Wheat did not yield wheat; nor cattle beget cattle. . . . Had nature's laws been annulled altogether in this land?

One evening while she was sitting by the kitchen table reading the *Skandinaven,*[2] the two youngest, opposite her, were poring over their books. Peder, now in the third year of school, had already reached the fourth grade. Coming upon an awfully good story, he straightway wanted to read it to Anna Marie. His sister, remembering the selection from the year before, showed no interest. But Peder, undismayed, launched into the reading at once, loudly throwing himself into it with all the enthusiasm and vim he possessed—he'd make them listen all right!

Beret looked up and waited till he had finished the story; then she asked him to come and sit down beside her—here she had found an interesting story.

At first he pretended not to have heard her. But after a little, slowly and unwillingly, he came shuffling around the table and plumped himself down next to her.

"What is it then?" he asked apathetically.

"You read this to me, my eyes bother me so."

"Huh!" he grunted and was silent.

"You can do that much for your mother, can't you?"

Peder bethought himself long, his whole figure indifferent and miserably bored. When at length he began to read, his voice sounded resentful and was husky with tears. Every other word he hacked to pieces or carelessly mispronounced. The boy acted as though he were being tortured, slowly.

Beret listened to him awhile. Unable to endure his behaviour any longer she grabbed him by the arm and shook him.

"Now you read decently!"

Silence.

"Don't you hear me?"

Peder put his fists to his eyes and rubbed.

"Ain't I reading?" he whined.

His obstinacy infuriated her. Springing up, she boxed his ear, then seized him by the shoulders and shook him violently; letting go of his shoulders, she grabbed hold of one ear, and held while she beat the other unmercifully.

"Now will you read?" she panted hoarsely.

It was deathly quiet in the room. Store-Hans, repairing a harness, looked up and coughed lightly. Ole jumped up, seized his cap, and went out. The sister, realizing how this would end, had retreated to the living room. After a little, sounds of the organ began coming from there—subdued, hesitating. Suddenly Store-Hans, too, got up, put the harness on his arm and walked toward the door. Before he reached it, he stopped.

"If you two are going to keep this up, the rest of us better move to the barn."

"Might as well. Soon we'll be like the beasts anyway!"

Store-Hans fingered a strap, cast a look at his mother, and left, slamming the door hard.

That wasn't the only set-to between the mother and Peder. But the winter he read the Bible through Beret experienced serene peace. Perhaps the Lord had listened to her supplications and was ordaining all for the best? Her own Bible, a family heirloom, was difficult to read because it was written in the Danish language of two hundred years ago. And so she sent after a new one for the boy, a beautiful book with clear type, bound in leather, and gilt-edged. Elated over the gift, Peder went at his reading with still greater diligence.

Until the fall she had him transferred to the Tallaksen School, things seemed to go tolerably well. But she soon realized that that move had been a mistake; from now on she found it increasingly difficult to keep him to his Norwegian lessons; and because the farm constantly demanded more of her attention she had little time to help him.

Notes

1. *Skua:* an artic sea bird that is an aggressive predator.—Eds.

2. A Norwegian newspaper, published in Chicago.

Mari Sandoz (1896–1966)

Mari Sandoz is best known for the biography of her father, *Old Jules* (1935). Jules Sandoz, a Swiss immigrant, settled along the Niobrara River in the Sandhills of northwest Nebraska. Despite the harsh climate he built a successful farm. He was especially proud of his orchards, which brought statewide recognition. But Jules was a hard man to live with. His first three wives fled. Mary, who stayed and bore six children with him, worked harder than Jules did on the farm itself. Jules focused much of his energy on building a community in this remote region. He was a locator, helping newcomers find available land. He fought a continual battle to keep the post office in his house, a common practice in the rural areas. For Jules the post office was a kind of symbol: his house as the center of the community.

Even today some readers are appalled at Sandoz's frank descriptions of cruelty and violence in her works, but Sandoz was, above all else, an honest and accurate writer. The violence is based on her own experience growing up during a period of open conflict between ranchers and settlers and on her extensive research into Sandhills history. The years of settlement were violent times.

Mari was the eldest child of Jules and Mary Sandoz. She grew up in poverty, often the object of her father's temper, but Jules also depended on her. Over the years, as they worked together, he told her his stories. Mari began teaching school when she was fourteen, married briefly, and then moved to Lincoln. Although she visited her family often, she never lived in the Sandhills again, the only child of Jules and Mary to leave the region. She worked various jobs in Lincoln and was admitted to the University of Nebraska despite her lack of a high school education. When *Old Jules* won the *Atlantic Monthly* prize for nonfiction in 1935, the prize money enabled her to turn to writing full-time. She moved to New York and lived there until her death. She is buried on a hillside overlooking the Sandoz family homestead in the Sandhills south of Gordon, Nebraska.

Like Willa Cather's "Neighbour Rosicky," this story was written late in Sandoz's life.* It focuses not on the violence but on the power of music to create a community out of enemies as well as friends. Instead of buying needed supplies or paying his creditors, Jules spends most of an inheritance he received from his father's estate—$2,100—on a phonograph and eight hundred wax cylinder records.† This story has been one of Sandoz's most popular, perhaps because of its

---

*The story was published posthumously.

†Helen Stauffer, "Battles Won and Lost," in *Mari Sandoz, Story Catcher of the Plains* (Lincoln: University of Nebraska Press, 1982), 251.

seasonal appeal, but also because the story itself is a welcome relief for the reader from the violence and disappointment in so many Great Plains stories.

The Christmas of the Phonograph Records (1966)

It seems to me that I remember it all quite clearly. The night was very cold, footsteps squeaking in the frozen snow that had lain on for over two weeks, the roads in our region practically unbroken. But now the holidays were coming and wagons had pushed out on the long miles to the railroad, with men enough to scoop a trail for each other through the deeper drifts.

My small brother and I had been asleep in our attic bed long enough to frost the cover of the feather tick at our faces when there was a shouting in the road before the house, running steps, and then the sound of the broom handle thumping against the ceiling below us, and Father booming out, "Get up! The phonograph is here!"

The phonograph! I stepped out on the coyote skin at our bed, jerked on my woolen stockings and my shoes, buttoning my dress as I slipped down the outside stairs in the fading moon. Lamplight was pouring from the open door in a cloud of freezing mist over the back end of a loaded wagon, with three neighbors easing great boxes off, Father limping back and forth shouting, "Don't break me my records!" his breath white around his dark beard.

Inside the house Mother was poking sticks of wood into the firebox of the cookstove, her eyes meeting mine for a moment, shining, her concern about the extravagance of a talking machine when we needed overshoes for our chilblains apparently forgotten. The three largest boxes were edged through the doorway and filled much of the kitchen–living room floor. The neighbors stomped their felt boots at the stove and held their hands over the hot lids while Father ripped at the boxes with his crowbar, the frozen nails squealing as they let go. First there was the machine, varnished oak, with a shining cylinder for the records, and then the horn, a great black, gilt-ribbed morning glory, and the crazy angled rod arm and chain to hold it in place.

By now a wagon full of young people from the Dutch community on Mirage Flats turned into our yard. At a school program they had heard about the Edison phonograph going out to Old Jules Sandoz. They trooped in at our door, piled their wraps in the leanto and settled along the benches to wait.

Young Jule and James, the brothers next to me in age, were up too, and watching Father throw excelsior aside,[1] exposing a tight packing of round paper containers a little smaller than a middle-sized baking powder can, with more layers under these, and still more below. Father opened one and while I read out the instructions in my German-accented fifth-grade country school English, he slipped the brown wax cylinder on the machine, cranked the handle carefully, and set the needle down. Everybody waited, leaning forward. There was a rhythmic frying in the silence, and then a whispering of sound, soft and very, very far away.

It brought a murmur of disappointment and an escaping laugh, but gradually the whispers loudened into the sextet from *Lucia,* into what still seems to me the most beautiful singing in the world. We all clustered around, the visitors, fourteen, fifteen by now, and Mother too, caught while pouring hot chocolate into cups, her long-handled pan still tilted in the air. Looking back I realize something of the meaning of the light in her face: the hunger for music she must have felt, coming from Switzerland, the country of music, to a western Nebraska government claim. True, we sang old country songs in the evenings, she leading, teaching us all she knew, but plainly it had not been enough, really nothing.

By now almost everybody pushed up to the boxes to see what there was to play, or called out some title hopefully. My place in this was established from the start. I was to run the machine, play the two-minute records set before me. There were violin pieces for Father, among them *Alpine Violets* and *Mocking Bird* from the first box opened; *Any Rags, Red Wing,* and *I'm Trying so Hard to Forget You* for the young people; *Rabbit Hash* for my brothers, their own selection from the catalog; and Schubert's *Serenade* and *Die Kapelle* for Mother, with almost everyone laughing over *Casey at the Telephone,* all except Father. He claimed he could not understand such broken English, he who gave even the rankest westernism a French pronunciation.

With the trail broken to the main bridge of the region, just below our house, and this Christmas Eve, there was considerable travel on the road, people passing most of the night. The lighted windows, the music, the gathering of teams and saddlehorses in the yard, and the sub-zero weather tolled them in to the weathered little frame house with its leanto.

"You better set more yeast. We will have to bake again tomorrow," Mother told me as she cut into a *zopf,* one of the braids of coffee cake baked in tins as large as the circle of both her arms. This was the last of five planned to carry us into the middle of holiday week.

By now the phonograph had been moved to the top of the washstand in our parents' kalsomined bedroom,[2] people sitting on the two double beds, on the round-topped trunk and on benches carried in, some squatting on their heels along the wall. The little round boxes stood everywhere, on the dresser and on the board laid from there to the washstand and on the window sills, with more brought in to be played and Father still shouting over the music, "Don't break me my records!" Some were broken, the boxes slipping out of unaccustomed or cold-stiffened hands, the brown wax perhaps already cracked by the railroad.

When the Edison Military Band started a gay, blaring galop, Mother looked in at the bedroom door, pleased. Then she noticed all the records spread out there, and in the kitchen–living room behind her, and began to realize their number.

"Three hundred!" she exclaimed in German, speaking angrily in Father's direction, "Looks to me like more than three thousand!"

Father scratched under his bearded chin, laughing slyly. "I added to the order," he admitted. He didn't say how many, nor that there were other brands besides the Edison here, including several hundred foreign recordings obtained through a Swiss friend in New York, at a stiff price.

Mother looked at him, her blue eyes tragic, as she could make them. "You paid nothing on the mortgage! All the twenty-one-hundred-dollar inheritance wasted on a talking machine!"

No, Father denied, puffing at his corncob pipe. Not all. But Mother knew him well. "You did not buy the overshoes for the children. You forgot everything except your stamp collection, your guns, and the phonograph!"

"The overshoes are coming. I got them cheaper on time, with the guns."

"More debts!" she accused bitterly, but before she could add to this one of the young Swiss, Maier perhaps, or Paul Freye, grabbed her and, against the stubbornness of her feet, whirled her back into the kitchen in the galop from the Edison band. He raced Mother from door to stove and back again and around and around, so her blue calico skirts flew out and the anger died from her face. Her eyes began to shine in an excitement I had never seen in them, and I realize now, looking back, all the fun our mother missed in her working life, even in her childhood in the old country, and during the much harder years later.

That galop started the dancing. Hastily the table was pushed against the wall, boxes piled on top of it, the big ones dragged into the leanto. Waltzes, two-steps, quadrilles, and schottisches were sorted out and set in a row ready for me to play while one of the men shaved a candle over the kitchen floor. There was room for only one set of square dancers but our bachelor neighbor, Charley Sears, called the turns with enthusiasm. The Peters girls, two school teachers, and several other young women whom I've forgotten were well outnumbered by the men, as is common in new communities. They waltzed, two-stepped, formed a double line for a Bohemian polka, or schottisched around the room, one couple close behind the other to, perhaps, *It Blew, Blew, Blew.* Once Charley Sears grabbed my hand and drew me out to try a quadrille, towering over me as he swung me on the corner and guided me through the allemande left. My heart pounded in shyness and my home-made shoes compounded my awkwardness. Later someone else dragged me out into a step-step, saying, "Like this: 'one, two; one, two.' Just let yourself go."

Ah, so that was how it was done. Here started a sort of craze that was to hold me for over twenty years, through the bear dance, the turkey trot, the Charleston, and into the Lindy hop. But that first night with the records even Old Jules had to try a round polka, even with his foot crippled in a long-ago well accident. When he took his pipe out of his mouth, dropped it lighted into his pocket, and whirled Mother around several times we knew that this was a special occasion. Before this we had never seen him even put an arm around her.

After the boys had heard their selection again, and *The Preacher and the Bear,* they fell asleep on the floor and were carried to their bed in the leanto. Suddenly I remembered little Fritzlie alone in the attic, perhaps half-frozen. I hurried up the slippery, frosted steps. He was crying, huddled together under the feather tick, cold and afraid, deserted by the cat too, sleeping against the warm chimney. I brought the boy down, heavy hulk that he was, and laid him in with his brothers. By then the last people started to talk of leaving, but the moon had clouded over, the night-dark roads winding and treacherous through the drifts. Still, those who had been to town must get home with the Christmas supplies and such presents as they could manage for their children when they awoke in the morning.

Toward dawn Father dug out *Sempach,* a song of a heroic Swiss battle, in which one of Mother's ancestors fell, and *Andreas Hofer,* of another national hero. Hiding her pleasure at these records, Mother hurried away to the cellar under the house for two big hams, one to boil while the Canada goose roasted for the Christmas dinner. From the second ham she sliced great red rounds for the frying pan and I mixed up a triple batch of baking powder biscuits and set on the two-gallon coffee pot. When the sun glistened on the frosted snow, the last of the horses huddled together in our yard were on the road. By then some freighters forced to camp out by an upset wagon came whipping their teams up the icy pitch from the Niobrara River and stopped in. Father was slumped in his chair, letting his pipe fall into his beard, but he looked up and recognized the men as from a ranch accused of driving out bona fide settlers. Instead of rising to order them off the place he merely said "How!" in the Plains greeting, and dropped back into his doze. Whenever the music stopped noticeably, he lifted his shaggy head, complaining, "Can't you keep the machine going?" even if I had my hands in the biscuits. "Play the *Mocking Bird* again," he might order, or a couple of the expensive French records of pieces he had learned to play indifferently in the violin lessons of his boyhood in Neuchatel. He liked *Spring Song* too, and *La Paloma,* an excellent mandolin rendition of *Come ye Disconsolate,* and several German love songs he had learned from his sweetheart, in Zurich, who had not followed him to America.

Soon my three brothers were up again and calling for their favorites as they settled to plates of ham with red gravy and biscuits, Fritzlie from the top of two catalogs piled on a chair shouting too, just to be heard. None of them missed the presents that we never expected on Christmas; besides, what could be finer than the phonograph?

While Mother fed our few cattle and the hogs I worked at the big stack of dishes with one of the freighters to wipe them. Afterward I got away to the attic and slept a little, the music from below faint through my floating of dreams. Suddenly I awoke, remembering what day this was and that young Jule and I had hoped Father might go cottontail hunting in the canyons up the river and help us drag home a little pine tree. Christmas had become a time for a tree, even without presents, a tree and singing, with at least one new song learned.

I dressed and hurried down. Father was asleep and there were new people in the bedroom and in the kitchen too, talking about the wonder of the music rolling steadily from the big horn. In our Swiss way we had prepared for the usual visitors during the holidays, with family friends on Christmas and surely some of the European homeseekers Father had settled on free land, as well as passers by just dropping in to get warm and perhaps be offered a cup of coffee or chocolate or a glass of Father's homemade wine if particularly privileged. Early in the forenoon the Syrian peddler we called Solomon drew up in the yard with his high four-horse wagon. I remember him every time I see a picture of Krishna Menon—the tufted hair, the same lean yellowish face and long white teeth.[3] Solomon liked to strike our place for Christmas because there might be customers around and besides there was no display of religion to make him uncomfortable in his Mohammedanism, Father said, although one might run into a stamp-collecting priest or a hungry preacher at our house almost any other time.

So far as I know, Solomon was the first to express what others must have thought. "Excuse it please, Mrs. Sandoz," he said, in the polite way of peddlers, "but it seem to uneducated man like me the new music is for fine palace—"

Father heard him. "Nothing's too good for my family and my neighbors," he roared out.

"The children have the frozen feet—" the man said quietly.

"Frozen feet heal! What you put in the mind lasts!"

The peddler looked down into his coffee cup, half full of sugar, and said no more.

It was true that we had always been money poor and plainly would go on so, but there was plenty of meat and game, plenty of everything that the garden, the young orchard, the field, and the open country could provide, and for all of which there was no available market. Our bread, dark and heavy, was from our hard macaroni wheat ground at a local water mill. The hams, sausage, and bacon were from our own smokehouse, the cellar full of our own potatoes, barrels of pickles and sauerkraut, and hundreds of jars of canned fruit and vegetables, crocks of jams and jellies, wild and tame, including buffalo berry, that wonderful, tart, golden-red jelly from the silvery bush that seems to retreat before close settlement much like the buffalo and the whooping crane. Most of the root crops were in a long pit outside, and the attic was strung with little sacks of herbs and poppy seed, bigger ones of dried green beans, sweetcorn, chokecherries, sandcherries, and wild plums. Piled along the low sides of the attic were bushel bags of popcorn, peas, beans, and lentils, the flour stacked in rows with room between for the mousing cat.

Sugar, coffee, and chocolate were practically all we bought for the table, with perhaps a barrel of blackstrap molasses for cookies and brown cake, all laid in while the fall roads were still open.

When the new batch of coffee cake was done and the fresh bread and buns, the goose in the oven, we took turns getting scrubbed at the heater in the leanto, and put on our best clothes, mostly made-over from some adult's but well-sewn. Finally we spread Mother's two old country linen clothes over the table lengthened out by boards laid on salt barrels for twenty-two places. While Mother passed the platters, I fed the phonograph with records that Mrs. Surber and her three musical daughters had selected, soothing music: Bach, Mozart, Brahms, and the *Moonlight Sonata* on two foreign records that Father had hidden away so they would not be broken, along with an a capella *Stille Nacht* and some other foreign ones Mother wanted saved. For lightness, Mrs. Surber had added *The Last Rose of Summer,* to please Elsa, the young soprano soon to be a professional singer in Cleveland, and a little Strauss and Puccini, while the young people wanted Ada Jones and *Monkey Land* by Collins and Harlan.

There was stuffed Canada goose with the buffalo berry jelly; ham boiled in a big kettle in the leanto; watercress salad; chow-chow and pickles, sweet and sour; dried green beans cooked with bacon and a hint of garlic; carrots, turnips, mashed potatoes and gravy, with coffee from the start to the pie, pumpkin and gooseberry. At the dishpan set on the high water bench, where I had to stand on a little box for comfort, the dishes were washed as fast as they came off the table, with a relay of wipers. There were also waiting young men and boys to draw water from the bucket well, to chop stove wood and carry it in.

As I recall now, there were people at the table for hours. A letter of Mother's says that the later uninvited guests got sausage and sauerkraut, squash, potatoes, and fresh bread, with canned plums and cookies for dessert. Still later there was a big roaster full of beans and sidemeat brought in by a lady homesteader, and some mince pies made with wild plums to lend tartness instead of apples, which cost money.

All this time there was the steady stream of music and talk from the bedroom. I managed to slip in the *Lucia* a couple of times until a tart-tongued woman from over east said she believed I was getting addled from all that hollering. We were not allowed to talk back to adults, so I put on the next record set before me, this one *Don't Get Married Any More, Ma,* selected for a visiting Chicago widow looking for her fourth husband, or perhaps her fifth. Mother rolled her eyes up at this bad taste, but Father and the other old timers laughed over their pipes.

We finally got Mother off to bed in the attic for her first nap since the records came. Downstairs the floor was cleared and the Surber girls showed their dancing-school elegance in the waltzes. There was a stream of young people later in the afternoon, many from the skating party at the bridge. Father, red-eyed like the rest of us, limped among them, soaking up their praise, their new respect. By this time my brothers and I had given up having a tree. Then a big boy from up the river rode into the yard dragging a pine behind his horse. It was a shapely tree, and small enough to fit on a box in the window, out of the way. The youth was the son of Father's worst enemy, the man who had sworn in court that Jules Sandoz shot at him, and got our father thirty days in jail, although everybody, including the judge, knew that Jules Sandoz was a crack shot and what he fired at made no further appearances.

As the son came in with the tree, someone announced loudly who he was. I saw Father look toward his Winchester on the wall, but he was not the man to quarrel with an enemy's children. Then he was told that the boy's father himself was in the yard. Now Jules Sandoz paled above his bearding, paled so the dancers stopped, the room silent under the suddenly foolish noise of the big-horned machine. Helpless, I watched Father jump toward the rifle. Then he turned, looked to the man's gaunt-faced young son.

"Tell your old man to come in. We got some good Austrian music."

So the man came in, and sat hunched over near the door. Father had left the room, gone to the leanto, but after a while he came out, said his "How!" to the man, and paid no attention when Mrs. Surber pushed me forward to make the proper thanks for the tree that we were starting to trim as usual. We played *The Blue Danube* and some other pieces long forgotten now for the man, and passed him the coffee and *küchli* with the others. He tasted the thin flaky frycakes. "Your mother is a good cook," he told me. "A fine woman."

When he left with the skaters all of Father's friends began to talk at once, fast, relieved. "You could have shot him down, on your own place, and not got a day in the pen for it," one said.

Old Jules nodded. "I got no use for his whole outfit, but the music is for everybody."

As I recall now, perhaps half a dozen of us, all children, worked at the tree, looping my strings of red rose hips and popcorn around it, hanging the people and animal cookies with chokecherry eyes, distributing the few Christmas tree balls and the tinsel and candleholders that the Surbers had given us several years before. I brought out the boxes of candles I had made by dipping string in melted tallow, and then we lit the candles and with my schoolmates I ran out into the cold of the road to look. The three showed fine through the glass.

Now I had to go to bed, although the room below me was alive with dancing and I remembered that Jule and I had not sung our new song, *Amerika ist ein schönes Land* at the tree.

Holiday week was much like Christmas, the house full of visitors as the news of the fine music and the funny records spread. People appeared from fifty, sixty miles away and farther so long as the new snow held off, for there was no other such collection of records in all of western Nebraska, and none with such an open door. There was something for everybody, Irishmen, Scots, Swedes, Danes, Poles, Czechs as well as the Germans and the rest, something pleasant and nostalgic. The greatest variety in tastes was among the Americans, from *Everybody Works but Father, Arkansas Traveler,* and *Finkelstein at the Seashore* to love songs and the sentimental *Always in the Way;* from home and native region pieces to the patriotic and religious. They had strong dislikes too, even in war songs. One settler, a GAR veteran, burst into tears and fled from the house at the first notes of *Tenting Tonight.* Perhaps it was the memories it awakened. Many Americans were as interested in classical music as any European, and it wasn't always a matter of cultivated taste. One illiterate little woman from down the river cried with joy at Rubinstein's *Melody in F.*

"I has heard me talkin' and singin' before," she said apologetically as she wiped her eyes, "but I wasn't knowin' there could be something sweet as that come from a horn."

Afternoons and evenings, however, were still the time for the dancers. Finally it was New Year, the day when the Sandoz relatives, siblings, uncles and cousins, gathered, perhaps twenty of them immigrants brought in by the land locator, Jules. This year they were only a sort of eddy in the regular stream of outsiders. Instead of nostalgic jokes and talk of the family and the old country, there were the records to hear, particularly the foreign ones, and the melodies of the old violin lessons that the brothers had taken, and the guitar and mandolin of their one sister. Jules had to endure a certain amount of joking over the way he spent most of his inheritance. One brother was building a cement block home in place of his soddy with his, and a greenhouse. The sister was to have a fine large barn instead of a new home because her husband believed that next year Halley's comet would bring the end of the world. Ferdinand, the youngest of the brothers, had put his money into wild-cat oil stock and planned to become very wealthy.

Although most of their talk was in French, which Mother did not speak, they tried to make up for this by complimenting her on the excellence of her chocolate and her golden fruit cake. Then they were gone, hot bricks at their feet, and calling back their adieus from the freezing night. It was a good thing they left early, Mother told me. She had used up the last of the chocolate, the last cake of the twenty-five pound caddies. We had baked up two sacks of flour, forty-nine pounds each, in addition to all that went into the Christmas preparations before the phonograph came. Three-quarters of a hundred pound bag of coffee had been roasted, ground, and used during the week, and all the winter's sausage and ham. The floor of the kitchen–living room, old and worn anyway, was much thinner for the week of dancing. New Year's night a man who had been there every day, all week, tilted back on one of the kitchen chairs and went clear through the floor.

"Oh, the fools!" Father shouted at us all. "Had to wear out my floor dancing!"

But plainly he was pleased. It was a fine story to tell for years, all the story of the phonograph records. He was particularly gratified by the praise of those who knew something about music, people like the Surbers and a visitor from a Czech community, a relative of Dvorak, the great composer. The man wrote an item for the papers, saying, "This Jules Sandoz has not only settled a good community of homeseekers, but is enriching their cultural life with the greatest music of the world."

"Probably wants to borrow money from you," Mother said. "He has come to the wrong door."

Gradually the records for special occasions and people were stored in the leanto. For those used regularly, Father and a neighbor made a lot of flat boxes to fit under the beds, always handy, and a cabinet for the corner at the bedroom door. The best, the finest from both the Edison and the foreign recordings, were put into this cabinet, with a door that didn't stay closed. One warmish day when I was left alone with the smaller children, the water pail needed refilling. I ran out to draw a bucket from the well. It was a hard and heavy pull for a growing girl and I hated it, always afraid that I wouldn't last, and would have to let the rope slip and break the windlass.

Somehow, in my uneasy hurry, I left the door ajar. The wind blew it back and when I had the bucket started up the sixty-five foot well, our big old sow, loose in the yard, pushed her way into the house. Horrified, I shouted to Fritzlie to get out of her way, but I had to keep pulling and puffing until the bucket was at the top. Then I ran in. Fritzlie was up on a chair, safe, but the sow had knocked down the record cabinet and scattered the cylinders over the floor. Standing among them as in corn, she was chomping down the wax records that had rolled out of the boxes, eating some, box and all. Furiously I thrashed her out with the broom, amidst squealings and shouts. Then I tried to save what I could. The sow had broken at least thirty or thirty-five of the best records and eaten all or part of twenty more. *La Paloma* was gone, and *Traumerei* and *Spring Song; Evening Star* too, and half of the *Moonlight Sonata* and many others, foreign and domestic, including all of Brahms.

I got the worst whipping of my life for my carelessness, but the loss of the records hurt more, and much, much, longer.

Notes

1. Excelsior: short, fine, curled soft wood shavings used to pack fragile items.—Eds.
2. Kalsomined: Alternative spelling for calcimine, used as a noun and a verb. A mixture of lime and glue that could be tinted any color and applied to walls. A cheap substitute for paint.—Eds.
3. Krishna Menon: India's minister of defense from 1957 to 1962, blamed by Indian people for the defeat of India by China in 1962.—Eds.

Further Reading

The Beaver Men. 1964.
The Buffalo Hunters. 1954.

The Cattlemen. 1958.

Cheyenne Autumn. 1953.

Crazy Horse, Strange Man of the Oglalas. 1942.

The Horsecatcher. 1957.

Hostiles and Friendlies: Selected Short Works of Mari Sandoz. Ed. Virginia Faulkner. 1957, 1976.

Love Song to the Plains. 1961.

Miss Morissa, Doctor of the Gold Trail. 1955.

Sandhill Sundays and Other Recollections. Ed. Virginia Faulkner. 1970.

Slogum House. 1937.

The Story Teller. 1963.

There Were the Sioux. 1961.

Reading about Mari Sandoz

Stauffer, Helen, ed. *Letters of Mari Sandoz.* Lincoln: University of Nebraska Press, 1992.

——. *Mari Sandoz: Story Catcher of the Plains.* Lincoln: University of Nebraska Press, 1982.

Will Weaver *(b. 1950)*

In Will Weaver's story the clash between immigrants' culture and American regulations is reduced to a simple issue: the burial of Inge, wife of Olaf, mother and grandmother of the children. This contemporary story suggests that the prejudicial political barriers Americans established to keep out unwelcome foreigners in the early years of the twentieth century eventually translated into irrelevant rules and regulations that became deeply embedded in American society.

Weaver was born in Minnesota. His father was a farmer. He received degrees from the University of Minnesota and Stanford University. In his professional life he has been a farmer and an English professor at Bemidji State University in Minnesota. When his sons reached the oxymoronic "young adult" stage Weaver began writing his Billy Baggs novels about baseball. His early novel *Red Earth, White Earth* explores the progressive exploitation of Indians by settlers, farmers, and profit-seeking creditors in northern Minnesota.

A Gravestone Made of Wheat (1989)

"You can't bury your wife here on the farm," the sheriff said. "That's the law."

Olaf Torvik looked up from his chair by the coffin; he did not understand what the sheriff was saying. And why was the sheriff still here, anyway? The funeral was over. They were ready for the burial—a family burial. There should be only Torviks in the living room.

"Do you understand what he's saying, Dad?" Einar said.

Olaf frowned. He looked to his son, to the rest of the family.

"He's saying we can't bury Mom here on the farm," Einar said slowly and deliberately. "He's saying she'll have to be buried in town at Greenacre Cemetery."

Olaf shook his head to clear the gray fuzz of loss, of grief, and Einar's words began to settle into sense. But suddenly a fly buzzed like a chainsaw—near the coffin—inside—there, walking the fine white hair on Inge's right temple. Olaf lurched forward, snatching at the fly in the air but missing. Then he bent over her and licked his thumb and smoothed the hair along her temple. Looking down at Inge, Olaf's mind drew itself together, cleared; he remembered the sheriff.

"Dad?" Einar said.

Olaf nodded. "I'm okay." He turned to the sheriff, John Carlsen, whom he had known for years and who had been at the funeral.

"A law?" Olaf said. "What do you mean, John?"

"It's a public health ordinance, Olaf," the sheriff said. "The state legislature passed it two years ago. It's statewide. I don't have it with me 'cause I had no idea . . . The law prohibits home burials."

"The boys and me got her grave already dug," Olaf said.

"I know," the sheriff said. "I saw it at the funeral. That's why I had to stay behind like this. I mean I hate like hell to be standing here. You should have told me that's the way you wanted to bury her, me or the county commissioners or the judge. Somebody, anyway. Maybe we could have gotten you a permit or something."

"Nothing to tell," Olaf said, looking across to Einar and Sarah, to their son Harald and his wife, to Harald's children. "This is a family affair."

The sheriff took off his wide-brimmed hat and mopped his forehead with the back of his sleeve. "The times are changing, Olaf. There's more and more people now, so there's more and more laws, laws like this one."

Olaf was silent.

"I mean," the sheriff continued, "I suppose I'd like to be buried in town right in my own backyard under that red maple we got. But what if everybody did that? First thing you know, people would move away, the graves would go untended and forgotten, and in a few years you wouldn't dare dig a basement or set a post for fear of turning up somebody's coffin."

"There's eighteen hundred acres to this farm," Olaf said softly. "That's plenty of room for Inge—and me, too. And nobody in this room is likely to forget where she's buried. None of us Torviks, anyway."

The sheriff shook his head side to side. "We're talking about a law here, Olaf. And I'm responsible for the law in this county. I don't make the laws, you understand, but still I got to enforce them. That's my job."

Olaf turned and slowly walked across the living room; he stood at the window with his back to the sheriff and the others. He looked out across his farm—the white granaries, the yellow wheat stubble rolling west, and far away, the grove of Norway pine where Inge liked to pick wildflowers in the spring.

"She belongs here on the farm," Olaf said softly.

"I know what you mean," the sheriff said, and began again to say how sorry . . .

Olaf listened but the room came loose, began to drift, compressing itself into one side of his mind, as memories, pictures of Inge pushed in from the past. Olaf remembered one summer evening when the boys were still small and the creek was high and they all went there at sundown after chores and sat on the warm rocks and dangled their white legs in the cold water.

"Dad?" Einar said.

The sheriff was standing close now, as if to get Olaf's attention.

"You been farming here in Hubbard County how long, fifty years?"

Olaf blinked. "Fifty-three years."

"And I've been sheriff over half that time. I know you, I know the boys. None of you has ever broken a law that I can think of, not even the boys. The town folk respect that. . . ."

Olaf's vision cleared and something in him hardened at the mention of town folk. He had never spent much time in town, did not like it there very much. And he believed that, though farmers and townspeople did a lot of business together, it was business of necessity; that in the end they had very little in common. He also had never forgotten how the town folk treated Inge when she first came to Hubbard County.

"What I mean is," the sheriff continued, "you don't want to start breaking the law now when you're seventy-five years old."

"Seventy-eight," Olaf said.

"Seventy-eight," the sheriff repeated.

They were all silent. The sheriff mopped his forehead again. The silence went on for a long time.

Einar spoke. "Say we went ahead with the burial. Here, like we planned."

The sheriff answered to Olaf. "Be just like any other law that was broken. I'd have to arrest you, take you to town. You'd appear before Judge Kruft and plead guilty or not guilty. If you pled guilty, there would be a small fine and you could go home, most likely. Then your wife would be disinterred and brought into town to Greenacre."

"What if he was to plead not guilty?" Einar said.

The sheriff spoke again to Olaf. "The judge would hold a hearing and review the evidence and pass sentence. Or, you could have a trial by jury."

"What do you mean by evidence?" Olaf asked, looking up. That word again after all these years.

The sheriff nodded toward the coffin. "Your wife," he said. "She'd be the evidence."

Evidence . . . evidence; Olaf's mind began to loop back through time, to when Inge first came from Germany and that word meant everything to them. But by force of will Olaf halted his slide into memory, forced his attention to the present. He turned away from the window.

"She told me at the end she should be buried here on the farm," Olaf said softly.

They were all silent. The sheriff removed his hat and ran his fingers through his hair. "Olaf," he said. "I've been here long enough today. You do what you think is best. That's all I'll say today."

The sheriff's car receded south down the gravel road. His dust hung over the road like a tunnel and Olaf squinted after the car until the sharp July sunlight forced his gaze back into the living room, to his family.

"What are we going to do, Dad?" Einar said.

Olaf was silent. "I . . . need some more time to think," he said. He managed part of a smile. "Maybe alone here with Inge?"

The others quietly filed through the doorway, but Einar paused, his hand on the doorknob.

"We can't wait too long, Dad," he said quietly.

Olaf nodded. He knew what Einar meant. Inge had died on Wednesday. It was now Friday afternoon, and the scent of the wilting chrysanthemums had been joined by a heavier, sweeter smell.

"I've sent Harald down to Penske's for some ice," Einar said.

Olaf nodded gratefully. He managed part of a smile, and then Einar closed the door to the living room.

Olaf sat alone by Inge. He tried to order his thoughts, to think through the burial, to make a decision; instead, his mind turned back to the first time he set eyes upon Inge, the day she arrived in Fargo on the Northern Pacific. His mind lingered there and then traveled further back, to his parents in Norway, who had arranged the marriage of Olaf and Inge.

His parents, who had remained and died in Norway, wrote at the end of a letter in June of 1918 about a young German girl who worked for the family on the next farm. They wrote how she wished to come to America; that her family in Germany had been lost in the bombings; that she was dependable and could get up in the morning; that she would make someone a good wife. They did not say what she looked like.

Olaf carried his parents' letter with him for days, stopping now and again in the fields, in the barn, to unfold the damp and wrinkled pages and read the last part again—about the young German girl. He wondered what she looked like. But then again, he was not in a position to be too picky about that sort of thing. It was hard to meet young, unmarried women on the prairie because the farms were so far apart, several miles usually, and at day's end Olaf was too tired to go anywhere, least of all courting. He had heard there were lots of young women in Detroit Lakes and Fargo, but he was not sure how to go about finding one in such large cities. Olaf wrote back to his parents and asked more about the German girl. His parents replied that she would be glad to marry Olaf, if he would have her. He wrote back that he would. His parents never did say what she looked like.

Because of the war, it was nearly two years later, April of 1920, before Olaf hitched up the big gray Belgian to his best wheat wagon, which he had swept as clean as his bedroom floor, and set off to Fargo to meet Inge's train.

It was a long day's ride and there was lots to see—long strings of geese rode the warm winds north, and beyond Detroit Lakes the swells of wheat fields rose up from the snow into black crowns of bare earth. But Olaf kept his eyes to the west, waiting for the first glimpse of Fargo. There were more wagons and cars on the road now, and Olaf stopped nodding to every one as there were far too many. Soon his wagon clattered on paved streets past houses built no more than a fork's handle apart. The Belgian grew skittish and Olaf stopped and put on his blinders before asking the way to the Northern Pacific Railroad station.

Inge's train was to arrive at 3:55 P.M. at the main platform. Olaf checked his watch against the station clock—2:28 P.M.—and then reached under the wagon seat. He brought out the smooth cedar shingle with his name, Olaf Leif Torvik, printed on it in large black letters. He placed it back under the seat, then on second thought, after glancing around the station, slipped the shingle inside his wool shirt. Then he grained and watered the Belgian and sat down to wait.

At 3:58 her train rumbled into the station and slowly drew to a stop, its iron wheels crackling as they cooled. People streamed off the train. Olaf held up his shingle, exchanging a shy grin with another man—John William Olsen—who also held a name-sign.

But there seemed to be few young women on the train, none alone.

A short Dutch-looking woman, small-eyed and thick, came toward Olaf—but at the last second passed him by. Olaf did not know whether to give thanks or be disappointed. But if the Dutch-looking woman passed him by, so did all the others. Soon Olaf was nearly alone on the platform. No one else descended from the Pullman cars. Sadly, Olaf lowered his shingle. She had not come. He looked at his shingle again, then let it drop to the platform.

He turned back to his wagon. If he was honest with himself, he thought, it all seemed so unlikely anyway; after all, there were lots of men looking for wives, men with more land and money, men certainly better-looking than Olaf.

"Maybe my folks made the mistake of showing her my picture," Olaf said to the Belgian, managing a smile as the horse shook his head and showed his big yellow teeth. Olaf wondered if he would ever take a wife. It seemed unlikely.

Before he unhitched the Belgian, he turned back to the platform for one last look. There, beside the train, staring straight at him, stood a tall, slim girl of about twenty. Her red hair lit the sky. In one hand she clutched a canvas suitcase, and in the other, Olaf's cedar shingle.

Inge Altenberg sat straight in Olaf's wagon seat, her eyes scared and straight ahead; she nodded as Olaf explained, in Norwegian, that there was still time today to see about the marriage. She spoke Norwegian with a heavy German accent, said yes, that is what she had come for.

They tried to get married in Fargo, in the courthouse, but a clerk there said that since Olaf was from Minnesota, they should cross the river and try at the courthouse in Moorhead. Olaf explained this to Inge, who nodded. Olaf opened his watch.

"What time do they close in Minnesota?" he asked the clerk.

"Same as here, five o'clock."

It was 4:36; they could still make it today. Olaf kept the Belgian trotting all the way across the Red River Bridge to the Moorhead Courthouse.

Inside, with eight minutes to spare, Olaf found the office of the Justice of the Peace; he explained to the secretary their wish to be married, today, if possible.

The secretary, a white-haired woman with gold-rimmed glasses, frowned.

"It's a bit late today," she said, "but I'll see what I can do. You do have all your papers in order?" she asked of Inge.

"Papers?" Olaf said.

"Her birth certificate and citizenship papers."

Olaf's heart fell. He had not thought of all this. He turned to Inge, who already was reaching under her sweater for the papers. Olaf's hopes soared as quickly as they had fallen.

"All right," the secretary said, examining the birth certificate, "now the citizenship papers."

Inge frowned and looked questioningly at Olaf. Olaf explained the term. Inge held up her hands in despair.

"She just arrived here," Olaf said, "she doesn't have them yet."

"I'm so sorry," the secretary said, and began tidying up her desk.

Olaf and Inge walked out. Inge's eyes began to fill with tears.

"We'll go home to Park Rapids," Olaf told her, "where they know me. There won't be any problem, any waiting, when we get home."

Inge nodded, looking down as she wiped her eyes. Olaf reached out and brushed away a teardrop, the first time he had toucher her. She flinched, then burst into real tears.

Olaf drew back his hand, halfway, but then held her at her shoulders with both his hands.

"*Ich verstehe,*" he said softly, "I understand."

They stayed that night in a hotel in Detroit Lakes. Olaf paid cash for two single rooms, and they got an early start in the morning. Their first stop was not Olaf's farm, but the Hubbard County Courthouse in Park Rapids.

At the same counter Olaf and Inge applied for both her citizenship and their marriage license. When Inge listed her nationality as German, however, the clerk raised an eyebrow in question. He took her papers back to another, larger office; the office had a cloudy waved-glass door and Olaf could see inside, as if underwater, several dark-suited men passing Inge's papers among themselves and murmuring. After a long time—thirty-eight minutes—the clerk returned to the counter.

"I'm afraid we have some problems with this citizenship application," he said to Inge.

When Inge did not reply, the clerk turned to Olaf. "She speak English?"

"I don't believe so, not much anyway."

"Well, as I said, there are some problems here."

"I can't think of any," Olaf said, "we just want to get married."

"But your wife—er, companion—lists that she's a German national."

"That's right," Olaf answered, "but she's in America now and she wants to become an American."

The clerk frowned. "That's the problem—it might not be so easy. We've got orders to be careful about this sort of thing."

"What sort of thing?"

"German nationals."

"Germans? Like Inge? But why?"

"You do realize we've been at war with Germany recently?" the clerk said, pursing his lips. "You read the papers?"

Olaf did not bother to answer.

"I mean the war's over, of course," the clerk said, "but we haven't received any change orders regarding German nationals."

Olaf laughed. "You think she's a spy or something? This girl?"

The clerk folded his arms across his chest. Olaf saw that he should not have laughed, that there was nothing at all to laugh about.

"We've got our rules," the clerk said.

"What shall we do?" Olaf asked. "What would you recommend?"

The clerk consulted some papers. "For a successful citizenship application she'll need references in the form of letters, letters from people who knew her in Germany and Norway, people who can verify where she was born, where she has worked. We especially need to prove that she was never involved in any capacity in German military or German government work."

"But that might take weeks," Olaf said.

The clerk shrugged. Behind him one of the county commissioners, Sig Hansen, had stopped to listen.

"There's nothing else we can do?" Olaf asked, directing his question beyond the clerk to the commissioner. But Sig Hansen shook his head negatively.

"Sorry, Olaf, that's out of my control. That's one area I can't help you in." The commissioner continued down the hall.

"Sorry," the clerk said, turning to some other papers.

With drawn lips Olaf said, "Thanks for your time."

They waited for Inge's letters to arrive from Europe. They waited one week, two weeks, five weeks. During this time Olaf slept in the hayloft and Inge took Olaf's bed in the house. She was always up and dressed and had breakfast ready by the time Olaf came in from the barn. Olaf always stopped at the pumphouse, took off his shirt and washed up before breakfast. He usually stepped outside and toweled off his bare chest in the sunlight; once he noticed Inge watching him from the kitchen window.

At breakfast Olaf used his best table manners, making sure to sit straight and hold his spoon correctly. And though they usually ate in silence, the silence was not uncomfortable. He liked to watch her cooking. He liked it when she stood at the wood range with her back to him, flipping pancakes or shaking the skillet of potatoes; he liked the way her body moved, the way strands of hair came loose and curled down her neck. Once she caught him staring. They both looked quickly away, but not before Olaf saw the beginnings of a smile on Inge's face. And it was not long after that, in the evening when it was time for Olaf to retire to the hayloft, that they began to grin foolishly at each other and stay up later and later. Though Olaf was not a religious man, he began to pray for the letters' speedy return.

Then it was July. Olaf was in the field hilling up his corn plants when Inge came running, calling out to him as she came, holding up her skirts for speed, waving a package in her free hand. It was from Norway. They knelt in the hot dirt and tore open the wrapping. The letters! Three of them. They had hoped for more, just to make sure, but certainly three would be enough.

Olaf and Inge did not even take time to hitch up the wagon, but rode together bareback on the Belgian to Park Rapids. They ran laughing up the courthouse steps, Olaf catching Inge's hand on the way. Once inside, however, they made themselves serious and formal, and carefully presented the letters to the clerk. The clerk examined them without comment.

"I'll have to have the Judge look at these," he said, "he's the last word on something like this." The clerk then retreated with their letters down the hall and out of sight.

The Judge took a long time with the letters. Twenty minutes. Thirty-nine minutes. Olaf and Inge waited at the clerk's window, holding hands below the cool granite counter. As they waited, Inge began to squeeze Olaf's hand with increasing strength until her fingers dug into his palm and hurt him; he did not tell her, however. Finally the clerk returned. He handed back the letters.

"I'm sorry," he said, "but the Judge feels these letters are not sufficient."

Olaf caught the clerk's wrist. The clerk's eyes jumped wide and round and scared; he tried to pull back his arm but Olaf had him.

"We want to get married, that's all," he said hoarsely.

"Wait—" the clerk stammered, his voice higher now, "maybe you should see the Judge yourselves."

"That's a damned good idea," Olaf said. He let go of the clerk's arm. The clerk rubbed his wrist and pointed down the hall.

Olaf and Inge entered the Judge's chambers, and Olaf's hopes plummeted. All the old books, the seals under glass on the walls, the papers; the white hair and expressionless face of the Judge himself: they all added up to power, to right-of-way. The Judge would have it his way.

Olaf explained their predicament. The Judge nodded impatiently and flipped through the letters again.

"Perhaps what we should do for you," the Judge said, "is to have you wait on this application for a period of say, one calendar year. If, during that time, it is determined that Inge Altenburg is loyal and patriotic, then we can consider her for citizenship. And, of course, marriage."

"One year!" Olaf exclaimed.

The Judge drew back and raised his eyebrows. Sig Hansen, the commissioner, had paused in the doorway. He shook his head at the Judge.

"Christ, Herb," he said, "you ought to run it through, let 'em get married. They're harmless. They're just farmers."

Inge rose up from her chair. There was iron in her face. "Come—" she commanded Olaf, in English, "it is time we go to home."

They rode home slowly, silently. The Belgian sensed their sorrow and kept turning his wide brown eyes back to Olaf. But Olaf had no words for the big animal. Inge held Olaf around his waist. As they came in sight of their buildings she leaned her head on his shoulder and he could feel her crying.

They ate their dinner in silence, and then Olaf returned to his cornfield. At supper they were silent again.

Come sundown, Olaf climbed the ladder to the hayloft and unrolled his bedroll in the hay. He wished he could have found some good thing to say at supper, but it was not in him. Not tonight. Olaf felt old, tired beyond his thirty-three years. He lay back on the loose prairie hay and watched the sun set in the knotholes of the west barn wall, red, then violet, then purple, then blue shrinking to gray. He hardly remembered going to sleep. But then he knew he must be dreaming. For standing above him, framed in the faint moonlight of the loft, stood Inge. She lay down beside him in the hay and when her hair fell across his face and neck he knew he could not be dreaming. He also knew that few dreams could ever be better than this. And in his long life with Inge, none were.

Olaf rose from his chair by her casket. That night when she came to him in the loft was forty-five years past. That night was Olaf's last in the hayloft, for they considered themselves married, come morning—married by body, by heart, and by common law.

And Inge never forgot her treatment at the Hubbard County Courthouse in Park Rapids; she rarely shopped in the town, preferring instead Detroit Lakes, which was twelve miles farther but contained no unpleasant memories.

Nor did she become a citizen; she remained instead without file or number, nonexistent to federal, state, or local records. She was real, Olaf thought, only to those who knew her, who loved her. And that, Olaf suddenly understood, was the way she should remain. As in her life, her death.

Before Olaf called the family back into the room, he thought he should try to pray. He got down on his knees on the wood floor by the coffin and folded his hands. He waited, but no words came. he wondered if he had forgotten how to pray. Olaf knew that he believed in a great God of some kind. He had trouble with

Jesus, but with God there was no question. He ran into God many times during the year: felt of him in the warm field-dirt of May; saw his face in the shiny harvest grain; heard his voice among the tops of the Norway pines. But he was not used to searching him out, to calling for him.

Nor could he now. Olaf found he could only cry. Long, heaving sobs and salty tears that dripped down his wrists to the floor. He realized, with surprise, that this was the first time he had cried since Inge's death; that his tears in their free flowing were a kind of prayer. He realized, too, that God was with him these moments. Right here in this living room.

When the family reassembled, Olaf told them his decision. He spoke clearly, resolutely.

"We will bury Inge here on the farm as we planned," he said, "but in a little different fashion."

He outlined what they would do, asked if anyone disagreed, if there were any worries. There were none. "All right then, that's settled," Olaf said. He looked around the room at his family—Einar, Sarah, the children, the others.

"And do you know what else we should do?" Olaf said.

No one said anything.

"Eat!" Olaf said. "I'm mighty hungry."

The others laughed, and the women turned to the kitchen. Soon they all sat down to roast beef, boiled potatoes with butter, dill pickles, wheat bread, strong black coffee, and pie. During lunch Harald returned with the ice. Einar excused himself from the table and went to help Harald.

Once he returned and took from a cupboard some large black plastic garbage bags. Olaf could hear them working in the living room, and once Einar said, "Don't let it get down along her side, there."

Olaf did not go into the living room while they worked. He poured himself another cup of coffee, which, strangely, made him very tired. He tried to remember when he had slept last.

Sarah said to him, "Perhaps you should rest a little bit before we . . ."

Olaf nodded. "You're right," he said, "I'll go upstairs and lie down a few minutes. Just a few minutes."

Olaf started awake at the pumping thuds of the John Deere starting. He sat up quickly—too quickly, nearly pitching over, and pushed aside the curtain. It was late—nearly dark. How could he have slept so long? It was time.

He hurriedly laced his boots and pulled on a heavy wool jacket over his black suit-coat. Downstairs, the women and children were sitting in the kitchen, dressed and waiting for him.

"We would have wakened you," Sarah said.

Olaf grinned. "I thought for a minute there . . ." Then he buttoned his coat and put on a woolen cap. He paused at the door. "One of the boys will come for you when everything is ready," he said to Sarah.

"We know," she said.

Outside, the sky was bluish purple and Harald was running the little John Deere tractor in the cow lot. The tractor carried a front-end loader and Harald was filling the scoop with fresh manure. Beyond the tractor some of the Black Angus stretched stiffly and snorted at the disturbance. Harald drove out of the lot when the scoop was rounded up and dripping. He stopped by the machine shed, went inside, and returned with two bags of commercial nitrogen fertilizer.

"Just to make sure, Grandpa," he said. His smile glinted white in the growing dark.

"Won't hurt," Olaf said. Then he tried to think of other things they would need.

"Rope," Olaf said. "And a shovel." Then he saw both on the tractor.

"Everything's ready," Harald said, pointing to the little John Deere. "She's all yours. We'll follow."

Olaf climbed up to the tractor's seat and then backed away from the big machine-shed doors. Einar and Harald rolled open the mouth of the shed and went inside.

The noise of their two big tractors still startled Olaf, even in daylight, and he backed up farther as the huge, dual-tandem John Deeres rumbled out of their barn. A single tire on them, he realized, was far bigger than the old Belgian he used to have. And maybe that's why he never drove the big tractors. Actually, he'd never learned, hadn't wished to. He left them to the boys, who drove them as easily as Olaf drove the little tractor. Though they always frightened him a little, Olaf's long wheat fields called for them—especially tonight. Behind each of the big tractors, like an iron spine with twelve shining ribs, rode a plow.

Olaf led the caravan of tractors. They drove without lights into the eighty-acre field directly west from the yellow-lit living-room window of the house. At what he sensed was the middle of the field, Olaf halted. He lowered the manure and fertilizer onto the ground. Then, with the front-end digger, he began to unearth Inge's grave.

Einar and Harald finished the sides of the grave with shovels. Standing out of sight in the hole, their showers of dirt pumped rhythmically up and over the side. Finished, they climbed up and brushed themselves off, and then walked back to the house for the others.

Olaf waited alone by the black hole. He stared down into its darkness and realized that he probably would not live long after Inge, and yet felt no worry or fear. For he realized there was, after all, a certain order to the events and times of his life: all the things he had worked for and loved were now nearly present.

Behind, he heard the faint rattle of the pickup. He turned to watch it come across the field toward the grave. Its bumper glinted in the moonlight, and behind, slowly walking, came the dark shapes of his family. In the bed of the pickup was Inge's coffin.

The truck stopped alongside the grave. Einar turned off the engine and then he and Harald lifted the coffin out and onto the ground. The family gathered around. Sarah softly sang "Rock of Ages," and then they said together the Twenty-third Psalm. Olaf could not speak past "The Lord is my . . ."

Then it was over. Einar climbed onto the tractor and raised the loader over the coffin. Harald tied ropes to the loader's arms and looped them underneath and around the coffin. Einar raised the loader until the ropes tightened and lifted the long dark box off the ground. Harald steadied the coffin, kept it from swinging, as Einar drove forward until the coffin was over the dark hole. Olaf stepped forward toward it as if to—to what?

Einar turned questioningly toward Olaf. "Now, Dad?" he said.

Olaf nodded.

Swaying slightly in the moonlight, the coffin slowly sank into the grave. There was a scraping sound as it touched bottom. Harald untied the ropes and then Einar began to push forward the mound of earth; the sound of dirt thumping on the coffin seemed to fill the field. When the grave was half filled, Einar backed the tractor to the pile of manure and pushed it forward into the hole. Harald carried the two bags of nitrogen fertilizer to the grave, slit their tops, and poured them in after the manure. Then Einar filled in the earth and scattered what was left over until the grave was level with the surrounding field.

Olaf tried to turn away, but could not walk. For with each step he felt the earth rising up to meet his boots as if he were moving into some strange room, an enormous room, one that went on endlessly. He thought of his horses, his old team. He heard himself murmur some word that only they would understand.

"Come Dad," Sarah said, taking Olaf by the arm. "It's over."

Olaf let himself be led into the pickup. Sarah drove him and the children to the field's edge by the house where Einar had parked the little John Deere.

"You coming inside now?" Sarah asked as she started the children toward the house.

"No, I'll wait here until the boys are finished," Olaf said, "you go on ahead."

Even as he spoke the big tractors rumbled alive. Their running lights flared on and swung around as Einar and Harald drove to the field's end near Olaf. They paused there a moment, side by side, as their plows settled onto the ground. Then their engine RPMs came up and the tractors, as one, leaned into their work and headed straight downfield toward Inge's grave.

The furrows rolled up shining in the night light. Olaf knew this earth. It was heavy soil, had never failed him. He knew also that next year, and nearly forever after, there would be one spot in the middle of the field where the wheat grew greener, taller, and more golden than all the rest. It would be the gravestone made of wheat.

Olaf sat on the little tractor in the darkness until the boys had plowed the field black from side to side. Then they put away the tractors and fed the Angus. After that they ate breakfast, and went to bed at dawn.

Further Reading

Farm Team: A Billy Baggs Novel. 1995.
Hard Ball: A Billy Baggs Novel. 1998.
Memory Boy. 2000.
Red Earth, White Earth. 1986.
Striking Out: A Billy Baggs Novel. 1993.

Luther Standing Bear

Luther Standing Bear tallies the things that all Americans have lost in their efforts to "Americanize" the Indians. In contrast to the stories of Americans' survival and defeat on the plains, Standing Bear points out that the American Indian fits into the landscape "both physically and spiritually."

Standing Bear is writing to a white audience. He wants his readers to realize that if they would pause and consider his philosophy, they might learn valuable lessons to live by on the Great Plains and in America.

For the biography and bibliography of Standing Bear see pages 150 and 153.

What the Indian Means to America (1933)

The feathered and blanketed figure of the American Indian has come to symbolize the American continent. He is the man who through centuries has been moulded and sculpted by the same hand that shaped its mountains, forests, and plains, and marked the course of its rivers.

The American Indian is of the soil, whether it be the region of forests, plains, pueblos, or mesas. He fits into the landscape, for the hand that fashioned the continent also fashioned the man for his surroundings. He once grew as naturally as the wild sunflowers; he belongs just as the buffalo belonged.

With a physique that fitted, the man developed fitting skills—crafts which today are called American. And the body had a soul, also formed and moulded by the same master hand of harmony. Out of the Indian approach to existence there came a great freedom—an intense and absorbing love for nature; a respect for life; enriching faith in a Supreme Power; and principles of truth, honesty, generosity, equity, and brotherhood as a guide to mundane relations.

Becoming possessed of a fitting philosophy and art, it was by them that native man perpetuated his identity; stamped it into the history and soul of this country—made land and man one.

By living—struggling, losing, meditating, imbibing, aspiring, achieving—he wrote himself into ineraceable evidence—an evidence that can be and often has been ignored, but never totally destroyed. Living—and all the intangible forces that constitute that phenomenon—are brought into being by Spirit, that which no man can alter. Only the hand of the Supreme Power can transform man; only

Wakan Tanka can transform the Indian. But of such deep and infinite graces finite man has little comprehension. He has, therefore, no weapons with which to slay the unassailable. He can only foolishly trample.

The white man does not understand the Indian for the reason that he does not understand America. He is too far removed from its formative processes. The roots of the tree of his life have not yet grasped the rock and soil. The white man is still troubled with primitive fears; he still has in his consciousness the perils of this frontier continent, some of its fastnesses not yet having yielded to his questing footsteps and inquiring eyes. He shudders still with the memory of the loss of his forefathers upon its scorching deserts and forbidding mountain-tops. The man from Europe is still a foreigner and an alien. And he still hates the man who questioned his path across the continent.

But in the Indian the spirit of the land is still vested; it will be until other men are able to divine and meet its rhythm. Men must be born and reborn to belong. Their bodies must be formed of the dust of their forefathers' bones.

The attempted transformation of the Indian by the white man and the chaos that has resulted are but the fruits of the white man's disobedience of a fundamental and spiritual law. The pressure that has been brought to bear upon the native people, since the cessation of armed conflict, in the attempt to force conformity of custom and habit has caused a reaction more destructive than war, and the injury has not only affected the Indian, but has extended to the white population as well. Tyranny, stupidity, and lack of vision have brought about the situation now alluded to as the 'Indian Problem.'

There is, I insist, no Indian problem as created by the Indian himself. Every problem that exists today in regard to the native population is due to the white man's cast of mind, which is unable, at least reluctant, to seek understanding and achieve adjustment in a new and a significant environment into which it has so recently come.

The white man excused his presence here by saying that he had been guided by the will of his God; and in so saying absolved himself of all responsibility for his appearance in a land occupied by other men.

Then, too, his law was a written law; his divine decalogue reposed in a book. And what better proof that his advent into this country and his subsequent acts were the result of divine will! He brought the Word! There ensued a blind worship of written history, of books, of the written word, that has denuded the spoken word of its power and sacredness. The written word became established as a criterion of the superior man—a symbol of emotional fineness. The man who could write his name on a piece of paper, whether or not he possessed the spiritual fineness to honor those words in speech, was by some miraculous formula a more highly developed and sensitized person than the one who had never had a pen in hand, but whose spoken word was inviolable and whose sense of honor and truth was paramount. With false reasoning was the quality of human character mea-

sured by man's ability to make with an implement a mark upon paper. But grant-
ing this mode of reasoning be correct and just, then where are to be placed the
thousands of illiterate whites who are unable to read and write? Are they, too,
'savages'? Is not humanness a matter of heart and mind, and is it not evident in the
form of relationship with men? Is not kindness more powerful than arrogance; and
truth more powerful than the sword?

True, the white man brought great change. But the varied fruits of his civilization, though highly colored and inviting, are sickening and deadening. And if it be
the part of civilization to maim, rob, and thwart, then what is progress?

I am going to venture that the man who sat on the ground in his tipi meditating
on life and its meaning, accepting the kinship of all creatures, and acknowledging
unity with the universe of things was infusing into his being the true essence of
civilization. And when native man left off this form of development, his humaniza-
tion was retarded in growth.

Another most powerful agent that gave native man promise of developing into
a true human was the responsibility accepted by parenthood. Mating among
Lakotas was motivated, of course, by the same laws of attraction that motivate all
beings; however, considerable thought was given by parents of both boy and girl to
the choosing of mates. And a still greater advantage accrued to the race by the law
of self-mastery which the young couple voluntarily placed upon themselves as
soon as they discovered they were to become parents. Immediately, and for some
time after, the sole thought of the parents was in preparing the child for life. And
true civilization lies in the dominance of self and not in the dominance of other
men.

How far this idea would have gone in carrying my people upward and toward a
better plane of existence, or how much of an influence it was in the development of
their spiritual being, it is not possible to say. But it had its promises. And it cannot
be gainsaid that the man who is rising to a higher estate is the man who is putting
into his being the essence of humanism. It is self-effort that develops, and by this
token the greatest factor today in dehumanizing races is the manner in which the
machine is used—the product of one man's brain doing the work for another. The
hand is the tool that has built man's mind; it, too, can refine it.

Zitkala-Ša

Known primarily for her early stories and autobiographical writings, Zitkala-Ša was intense in her political activism and writings. Although this piece is not dated, it seems consistent with her writings of the early 1920s and her association with the General Federated Women's Clubs, and probably written prior to the congressional act that granted American Indians U.S. citizenship in 1924. While today some might disagree with her political agenda, her aim was clear: to establish equal rights and treatment for American Indians. She draws on her heritage from the Great Plains to create images of contrasting freedom and discrimination. Her political incarnation of the Sioux image of the sacred hoop is harmonious with Black Elk's sacred vision.

For the biography and bibliography of Zitkala-Ša see pages 125 and 129.

Americanize the First American

During two summer moons I followed Indian trails over an undulating prairie. The blue canopy of sky came down and touched the earth with a circular horizon. Within such an enclosure of infinite space, virgin soil appeared like a heaving brown sea, slight tinged with green—a profoundly silent sea. Far out upon its eternal waves now and then came into sight a lone houseboat of crude logs. A captain on one of these strange crafts wirelessed to me an "S.O.S." My inquiry brought the answer: "many of these houseboats are set adrift with a funeral pyre for a burial at sea."

In low log huts, adrift upon their reservation containing approximately 5,000 square miles, are the souls of 7,500 Sioux. So widely scattered are they that time and perseverance were required to make even a limited round of visits in the burning sun and parching wind of midsummer.

Listening one day to a sad story of the influenza epidemic among these Indians two years ago, I closed my eyes and tried to imagine this great wild area held in the frigid embrace of winter. I tried to visualize two Government physicians going forth in a Dakota blizzard to visit the sick and dying Sioux. Had they divided the territory evenly between them, each would have had to traverse 2,500 square miles to attend to 3,750 Indian people. Could they have traveled like whirlwinds to respond to the cries for help, their scant supply of medicines would have been exhausted far too soon. It would have been a physical impossibility for these two wise men to vie with the wind, so they did not. They received their salary as quickly for treating one Indian as if they had cared for a thousand. Therefore, the small medical supply was saved and the Indians died unattended.

How bitter is the cold of this frozen landscape where the fire of human compassion is unkindled! It is a tragedy to the American Indian and the fair name of American that the good intentions of a benevolent Government are turned into channels of inefficiency and criminal neglect. Nevertheless, the American Indian is our fellow-man. The time is here when for our own soul's good we must acknowledge him. In the defense of democracy his utter self-sacrifice was unequaled by any other class of Americans. What now does democracy mean to him and his children?

Many Indian children are orphans through the inevitable havoc of war and influenza epidemic. Poor little Indian orphans! Who in this world will love them as did their own fathers and mothers? Indians love their children dearly. Never in all history was there an Indian mother who left her darling in a basket upon a doorstep. Indians do not believe in corporal punishment. They are keenly aware that children are spirits from another realm, come for a brief sojourn on earth. When and where they found this great truth is wrapped in as much mystery as the origin of their race which ever puzzles thinking men and women of today. If a correction is necessary, they speak quietly and tenderly to the intelligent soul of the child. Appreciation of the spiritual reality of the child places the Indian abreast with the most advanced thought of the age—our age, in which one of the notable signs of progress is the co-ordination of humanitarian and education organizations for child welfare. It is a wonderful work to inculcate in the world's children today the truths accrued from the ages, that in the near future, when they are grown-up men and women, the world shall reap an ideal harvest. Children are to play, on the world stage, their role in solving the riddle of human redemption.

Speaking of the constructive and widespread activities of the Junior Red Cross, Arthur William Dunn, specialist in civic education, said: "The aim is to cultivate not only a broad human sympathy but also an Americanism with a world perspective." Among other things, a school of correspondence is started between the children of America, Europe and Asia. Loving the wee folks as I do, and concerned for the salvation of my race, I am watching eagerly for the appearance of the Indian child in the world drama.

Where are those bright-eyes, black-haired urchins of the out-of-doors? Where are those children whose fathers won so much acclaim for bravery in the World War now closed?

They are on Indian reservations—small remnants of land not shown on our maps. They are in America, but their environment is radically different from that surrounding other American children. A prolonged wardship, never intended to be permanent, but assumed by our Government as an emergency measure, has had its blighting effect upon the Indian race. Painful discrepancies in the meaning of American freedom to the Indian are revealed in the following comparisons:

1920

Town of White Americans	Pine Ridge Indian Reservation
Population 7,500.	Population 7,500.
All American citizens.	Citizenship withheld from large majority.
City government by vote of inhabitants.	Arbitrary rule by Government official.
Commercial Club.	None. No voice in their business affairs.
Banks, where depositors check on their accounts at will.	None. Not allowed to handle their moneys.
Public accounts audited and reported.	No itemized account of expenditure of Indian funds or audited statements furnished to Indians.
Amusements—Theaters, movies, dances, education programs.	None. No recreation halls. Dances forbidden [except] only at long intervals.
Public libraries.	None.
Open forums.	None. Open forums forbidden.
Many competing physicians.	None. Only two Government physicians.
Dentists.	None. Teeth neglected.
Hospitals.	None.
Common school.	Government school to sixth grade, inclusive. Holy Rosary Mission teaches eighth grade, inclusive, fortunately for the Sioux.
Fraternities.	None. Get-together meetings forbidden.

These differences prevail not only on one, but on every Indian reservation.[1] Suffice it to say that by a system of solitary isolation from the world the Indians are virtually prisoners of war in America. Treaties with our government made in good faith by our ancestors are still unfulfilled, while the Indians have never broken a single promise they pledged to the American people. American citizenship is withheld from some three-fourths of the Indians of the United States. On their reservations they are held subservient to political appointees upon whom our American Congress confers discretionary powers. These are unlovely facts, but they are history. Living conditions on the reservations are growing worse. In the fast approach of winter I dread to think of the want and misery the Sioux will suffer on the Pine Ridge Reservation.

Womanhood of America, to you I appeal in behalf of the Red Man and his children. Heed the lonely mariner's signal of distress. Give him those educational advantages pressed with so much enthusiasm upon the foreigner. Revoke the tyrannical powers of Government superintendents over a voiceless people and extend American opportunities to the first American—the Red man.

Beaureaucracy [*sic*] Versus Democracy

We have a bureaucracy wheel with a $14,000,000 hub and a rim of autocratic discretionary power. Between the two are the segments suppressing the energies of the Indian people. About 90 years ago the American Congress created the

Bureau of Indian Affairs as a temporary measure, and it was not intended for a permanent institution. Steadily, through 90 years, the bureau has enlarged itself regardless of the diminishing Indian population, "educated and civilized" all this time.

Official power, official business and official numbers have been augmented, impinging upon the liberty loving Indians of America a wardship growing more deadly year by year.

Whenever a plea for our human rights is made this despotic-grown bureaucracy issues contrary arguments through its huge machinery for reasons best known to itself. It silences our inquiring friends by picturing to them the Indians' utter lack of business training and how easily they would fall victims to the wiles of unscrupulous white men were bureau supervision removed from all Indians.

I would suggest that Congress enact more stringent laws to restrain the unscrupulous white men. It is a fallacy in a democratic government to de-franchise a law-abiding race that the lawless may enjoy the privileges of citizenship. Further would I suggest that this bureau be relieved of its supervising an orderly people and assigned to the task of restraining the unscrupulous citizens of whatsoever color who are menacing the liberty and property of the Indians. It is true the Indians lack business training and experience. Therefore, I would suggest business schools for the Indians, together with a voice in the administration of their own affairs, that they may have the opportunity to overcome their ignorance and strengthen their weakness.

We insist upon our recognition by America as really normal and quite worth-while human beings.

We want American citizenship for every Indian born within the territorial limits of the United States.

We want a democracy wheel whose hub shall be an organization of progressive Indian citizens and whose rim shall be the Constitution of your American Government—a wheel whose segments shall become alive with growing community interests and thrift activities of the Indians themselves.[2] Indians require first-hand experience as others do to develop their latent powers. They proved their loyalty to country by their unequaled volunteer service in your army in the World War now closed.

You have enfranchised the black race, and are now actively waging a campaign of Americanization among the foreign-born. Why discriminate against the noble aborigines of America—they who have no other father-motherland? The gospel of humanitarianism, like charity, must begin at home, among home people, and from thence, spread out into all the world.

Americanize the first Americans. Give them freedom to do their own thinking; to exercise their judgment; to hold open forums for the expression for their thought, and finally permit them to manage their own personal business. Let no one deprive the American Indians of life, liberty or property without due process of law.

Notes

Originally written for *The Pen Woman Magazine,* later published independently as a pamphlet with Zitkala-Ša's picture (in costume) on the cover.—Eds.

1. For a discussion of the abrogation of American Indian rights on reservations see John R. Wunder, *"Retained by the People," A History of American Indians and the Bill of Rights* (New York: Oxford University Press, 1994).—Eds.

2. The circular model has broad historical and political implications by referring to the sacred hoop of the Plains cultures and the decentering of power. The original document contains two large circular organizational charts.—Eds.

Elizabeth Cook-Lynn *(b. 1930)*

This essay is consistent with Elizabeth Cook-Lynn's style of seeing the political impact of personal experience and individual reading. As she reflects on her life experiences by returning as an acclaimed scholar to South Dakota, she unveils the bigotry and imperialism behind the disguised language of admiration. As is often the case with her writing, Cook-Lynn knows that the consequences of writing are much larger than mere intellectual or sentimental play in metaphor; they directly impact indigenous peoples and their rights.

Cook-Lynn (Crow Creek Dakota) was born in Fort Thomson, South Dakota, and she pursued higher education in South Dakota and Nebraska. She is a professor emerita from Eastern Washington University. In addition to her writing, she helped pioneer American Indian Studies as a discipline. Along with William Willard and Beatrice Medicine (Lakota), she founded *Wicazo Sa Review,* a journal of American Indian studies devoted to tribal and intellectual sovereignty.

End of the Failed Metaphor (1996)

It is hard to say what will survive and why as the world moves forward. Only in retrospect can that be known. As I think about the writing we are doing currently as Native Americans, I am disappointed in the congeniality of most of it, because in the face of astonishing racism of one people toward another, there continues to be great risk. My thoughts turn with some trepidation to survival and place, the New World, and the old—this place once known only by the tribes but a place at once named, described, misnamed, and renamed by those who followed the colonist's prince.

My thoughts are about the nature of our lives as indigenous peoples in the modern world, and the nature of our survival, and because I am a writer, the function of literary voice. In the twentieth century, the survival of indigenous peoples everywhere, not just here in my homelands, but everywhere in the world, has been nothing if not miraculous. In the face of efficient colonial land theft, which has made up poor, the environmental wastelands caused by virulent economic interests, the attempted ethnocide, deicide, and genocide brought about by the failure of one federal policy after another toward our peoples, we continue to say, *anpetu wi,* the sun, lives on forever. And we continue to say that we will forever call him *tunkashina,* "Grandfather." *Tunkashinayapi*—"All of our grandfathers surround us." This continuation is, truly, a miracle. *Anpetu wi,* the day light, to whom we speak in our prayers, is symbolic of the cultural spirit of the Sioux in traditional terms. Every day, every glimpse of the sun reminds us of who we are and to whom we are related.

What I want to focus on in this last essay of this collection has to do with the emblematic use of our histories and cultures outside of those traditions to tell our stories. I want to focus on the literary creations, that is, the symbols and metaphors which are developed in contemporary literary terms and in foreign places outside of our traditional languages and lifeways to describe who we are and where we have been. This seems appropriate in this last decade of the century, during which we have paid much attention to the quincentennial of "discovery."

Indigenous peoples are no longer in charge of what is imagined about them, and this means that they can no longer freely imagine themselves as they once were and as they might become. Perhaps a separation of culture and place and voice has never been more contextualized in modernity than it is for Indians today. This means that the literary metaphors devised for the purposes of illumination belong more often than not to those outside of the traditional spheres. What comes immediately to mind is the metaphor of Mother Earth, and others such as the characterization of the literary figure, the Trickster.

Mother Earth, some have argued, was really an example of the evolution of female earth imagery in Europe rather than in North America; therefore, she rightly becomes available to every writer in all of Christendom. She is used to express a wide variety of ideals and has accounted for a number of arguments between scholars. In this essay I review some personal issues concerning the use of metaphor and pose some questions which may be useful in analyzing the consequences of literary acts.

As spring came upon us a few years ago, I was asked to participate in the Great Plains Writers' Conference at South Dakota State University, my alma mater. This was to be the first time I had returned to that place since the late 1950s, and I was overcome by nostalgia. It was there, in the college town of Brookings in central South Dakota, miles away from my home reservation, that I first met a tall, young Minneconjou Sioux from Cheyenne River, just back from Korea. My father, a Santee, had known of this young man's French and Indian family for generations, so our meeting seemed somehow fortuitous; we married and had children together. And then we left one another—and that was the end of that story. Such a return to what might be called a place of origin, however, as this recent visit to my old alma mater reminded me of what Sartre was supposed to have said, that the greatest happiness is always a little sad, and so I walked about the streets alone during the first few hours, recalling the events of a past life.

At the conference table the next morning, we were asked to move out of our own individual spheres and speculate about broader historical matters. The year was 1990, one hundred years after the Wounded Knee massacre, and our conference title was "Wounded Knee: The Literary Legacy." We were there to speculate specifically about "Wounded Knee as Metaphor for Tragedy." I read a poem about Wounded Knee which I had written years earlier. The first line was, "All things considered, Crow Dog should be removed." The second line was, "With Sitting Bull dead, it was easier said." I thought about Shelley, the great English poet who told the literati of his day that poetry was supposed to be a mirror which makes beautiful that which is distorted. That kind of theory seemed indefensible at that conference. The bleak truth is that even my subversive sensibility concerning poetry was invaded that day, and I left as soon as the conference ended.

From there I went to the University of South Dakota, another college campus a couple of hours' drive away at Vermillion, South Dakota, where I participated in a discussion entitled "Land, Law, and Ethics," with many white and Indian scholars, politicians, and tribal leaders who are locked into a pathology of racial hatred and good intentions as complex as any in the world, in a state where the largest daily newspaper refused to call the killing of innocent women and children at Wounded Knee, all of them under a white flag of truce, a "massacre." In South Dakota it is publicly called, one hundred years after the fact, an "event," "an incident," or an "affair." And now, poets were invited to speak on the idea of Wounded Knee as a metaphor for tragedy.

These two incidents are responsible, more than any others in recent times, for my renewed interest in and present discussion of the function of literary device. Out of these experiences, I have formed questions to which I have no answers. What are the consequences of such metaphors? What is the effect of taking one of the most vicious criminal acts in history and imagining it as literary device? What happens to history? What happens morally and ethically to the people in such a process? Will our children know who their relatives are? Will they be able to know themselves in the context of a new history, a literary history rather than an actual one? Is it possible that poetry flattens value systems, so that what was once not talked about becomes useful only for sensation?

When I returned to my office at Eastern Washington University after these public events, I read quite by accident "The New World Man," an essay by the gifted, Spanish-speaking novelist Rudolfo Anaya. It is an essay in which he analyzes the important metaphor with which this essay began, the metaphor of Mother Earth.

Anaya says that the people in the Southwest are the "fruit of the Spanish Father and the Indian Mother." He alternately labels them Hispanic and Chicano. He glorifies Malinche, who was the first Indian woman of Mexico to bear children fathered by a Spaniard. Without talking much about the fact that she was a captive of men and had little free choice in the matter of who was to father her children, Anaya says "in our mothers is embodied the archetype of the indigenous Indian Mother of the Americas," and he urges that "it is her nature we must know." As I read this essay I wondered how I could understand this glorification within the context of Wounded Knee.

I recognized Anaya's glorification as similar to the argument for the glorification of Sacajawea, the Plains Indian girl (barely in her teens, we are told) who led Lewis and Clark, the precursors of those who stole the land and forced millions into Christianity against their wills, the Shoshone youngster who eventually lived with the Frenchman Charbonneau and died bearing his children. Pocohantas and Tekakwitha also came to mind. And I began to understand that, as American Indian literatures are often used to serve the white man's needs, so the Indian woman archetype is used for the colonist's pleasure and profit.

We have all become collaborators without intention, and we all bear responsibility for our common histories. It is not just those people (the colonists) who came and invaded the lives and lands of our ancestors, implanted their seed and began from that moment on to contend their ownership. It is what we have done to ourselves. Thinking of collaborators, I flipped the pages of an unpublished manuscript lying on my desk and read a poem I had written years before, in 1980, that expressed the troubling fracture in which I saw us living our lives:

Collaborator
Ensuring Domestic Tranquility

I remember the fallen trees, thin and pale as frost smoke;
and how the wounded river's rippling presence,
witness to the outrage, intentionally or not,
consoled the venal among us. Poor, wind-swept,
the miles and miles of prairie dog towns
kept our secret. We swam and knew this could become the place
of the unburied, here where the peace treaty
was signed and it was said crimes on both sides
would be forgotten. Buzzards and Old Spotted Eagle
kept watch.

In this mythological Hades descendants
of cowpokes, stirring the tainted water with glimmerous
wands meant to disrupt the questions we would ask
about the sweet creation of life, and death,
and meaning, take up residence in Buffalo Gap,
the farthest fields. Jedediah Smith was said to tear the hide
from grizzlies, his life inimical to the lives of all living things.
Thin, pale children run
on Cedar street.

Persistent jets, unseen and ominous
as the shrill of the imagined Red Telephone

whisper in the river's gorge, lapping at the water's edge.
And I walk, intentional or not, amongst
the tourists who are here again
to see the Indians dance.

Forgive me, my children.
I barely hear the soft raindrops on shrouded drums
of my father and his father. And yours.

Periodic, unpredictable,
their songs sway in the gloom
of my forfeiture.

This poem suggests that we all bear the weight of history. It suggests that poets must ask, what is our responsibility, and what of the future? Anaya poses the question in his essay very specifically, I think, but we may generalize it for the purposes of this discussion. Anaya says, "As I think of the quincentennial of Columbus's crossing, I ask myself how I relate to that Hispanic legacy which left the peninsula in 1492 to implant itself in the New World. How do I relate to the peninsular consciousness of the people who crossed the Atlantic five hundred years ago to deposit their seed on the earth of the New World?"

This is the essential question for all of us who are now called Native American writers, or Third World writers, to answer. It is especially important for those of us who are native women writers. For myself, I am reluctant to forget about *anpetu wi* (just as I am reluctant to talk of Wounded Knee in terms of metaphor), for I know that without *anpetu wi*, the *indigenous* male presence, Mother Earth is a silent, barren place of death.

I shudder at Anaya's answer, which rings with confidence and finality: "I am the son of Spanish and Mexican colonists who settled the fertile Rio Grand Valley of New Mexico. I am the New World Man I have sought: I am an indigenous man taking his essence and perspective from the earth and people of the New World, from the Earth which is my Mother. By naming ourselves Chicanos we reaffirmed our humanity by exploring and understanding the nature of our mothers, the indigenous American woman."

He describes his duality in this way: "The Spanish character is the aggressive, conquest-oriented part of our identity; the Native American nature is the more harmonious, earth-oriented side." He calls for the assimilation of those two natures.

The fragility of this resolution lies in Anaya's willful dismissal of indigenous myth. Yet he must know that there are no versions of origin, no discussions of wisdom, goodness, kindness, hospitality, nor any of the other virtues of indigenous, tribal society without the seed, and spirit, and power of the indigenous fathers. There is no mythic cycle from the spiritual journey into the real world that is not associated with both indigenous maleness and femaleness. What about the lands the people say they possess, lands which are possessed legitimately both in the recent treaty process and in the ancient imagination?

I want to ask about the utter disregard of this maleness as it is dismissed by the colonists of the past and the present in favor of the mother goddess as lone repositor of history. For those who have prayed to *tunkashinayapi*, there is the certain knowledge that the earth's survival is not possible without those indigenous male figures, those rights of possession, that occupancy, that vision.

To accept the indigenous woman's role as the willing and cooperating recipient of the colonist's seed and as the long repositor of culture is to legitimize the destruction of ancient religions, the murder of entire peoples, the rape of the land, not to mention the out-and-out theft of vast native homelands. To do so dismisses the centuries of our modern American Indian histories when our fathers fought and died and made treaties in order to save us from total annihilation.

Metaphor has sometimes been used, if not to legitimize colonization, then to tolerate it in the modern world. "Wounded Knee as Metaphor for Tragedy" implies the absence of human control in the killing of hundreds of Indians. Nothing could be more wrong, and conferring medals of heroism on the killer troops exposes the lie of it. Because America refuses to reject its colonial past, it continues its acts of destruction, murder, rape, and theft. We will read, therefore, in our morning newspapers that a waste dump is to be put on top of the traditional burial mounds of the Yakima Indian people of Washington State; that the U.S. courts have ruled, again, against the indigenous religious leaders of the peyote religion, as old as any in the world, and harassment of its communicants will continue. We will hear that some members of the Senate Select Committee on Indian Affairs have vowed secretly that they will never allow hearings on the legislative proposal for the return of stolen land in the sacred Black Hills to its rightful owners. We will watch while white affluent Americans tie green paper ribbons on trees on Earth Day (more metaphors) and drive away from the scene in the latest, gas-guzzling automobiles, the most potent producers of the toxic gases which cause global warming.

In order for these crimes to be stopped, they must be recognized as emblematic of the dismissal of our native fathers in favor of our colonial ones. In the final analysis, you see, what kind of seed is implanted matters to Mother Earth. To continue to use her as a receptacle for the seeds of exploitation and extermination against her will holds no promise for the future.

The function of metaphor is to clarify, to illuminate, not to add to the confusion. Many other writers of America have taken up the issues of a ruined world. Many have contemplated the meaning of the mother goddesses of all times, though they seldom spend much time asking why or how we reached Gilead, only saying that we are there. America's colonial past, its dismissal of indigenous maleness, its glorification of the fecund native woman as bearer of alien children, the continuing aggressiveness of the colonist's exploitation of the earth for profit may be the essential causes of the horrors of Gilead. Margaret Atwood does not tell us that in her horrific *Handmaid's Tale*. But, she certainly illustrates what happens when we fail to know the function of history and metaphor.

And so, as I raise more questions than I can answer, I want to say that we must resist the argument that the American Mother Earth, the native earth, should be legitimized as receptacle for the male colonist's seed, for it leads to a new and disastrous religion in which *anpetu wi* and *tunkashina* cannot collaborate. I would like to suggest, also, that there are at least two unexamined moral axioms in this argument that have kept the audience we have clamoring to hear more of the theory of the female-indigenous receptacle of the colonist's seed. The first is that there is no male seed which is indigenous; it has, as expected, vanished. The second is that even if there were such a survivor, he is not deserving, and he must not, therefore, be allowed to compete for his own life either historically or imaginatively.

To what extent our recent Native American literatures have expressed, denied, or trivialized our reality depends, one supposes, on the ways of thinking which have captured the public's attention. For now, we contend with the idea that Crazy Horse is either an alcoholic drink or a steak house in California, that Dakota is a pick-up with four-wheel drive, and the Braves are alive and well in Atlanta doing the tomahawk chop.

Metaphors are complex and disturbing things. We must claim them when they are useful to our literary legacies and disclaim them when they are failed. If we do not, we will have become the hired intellectuals of the disciplines of academia that we have so often feared. For the Sioux Oyate, the male creator figures are inseparable from the female. They are inseparable from specific geography. They have been with us in life and death and at Wounded Knee. How dare we suggest that Mahpiyato, Inyan, Tunkashina, Anpetu Wi and all the other fathers of the people are nonexistent, irrelevant, undeserving, and thus appropriately displaced by the colonist's seed in our Mother. How dare we say that crimes of history are mere tragedy for which no one but God is responsible?

We must make hard choices if we expect the plot to keep moving.

Further Reading

Anti-Indianism in Modern America: A Voice from Tatekeya's Earth. 2001.

Aurelia: A Crow Creek Trilogy. 1999.

I Remember the Fallen Trees: New and Selected Poems. 1998.

The Politics of Hallowed Ground: Wounded Knee and the Struggle for Indian Sovereignty. Coauthored with Mario Gonzalez. 1998.

"The Power of Horses." In *Earth Power Coming: Short Fiction in Native American Literature.* Ed. Simon J. Ortiz. 1983.

"A Visit from Reverend Tileston." In *Talking Leaves: Contemporary Native American Short Stories.* Ed. Craig Lesley. 1983.

Reading about Elizabeth Cook-Lynn

Bruchac, Joseph, ed. "As a Dakotah Woman: An Interview with Elizabeth Cook-Lynn." *Survival This Way: Interviews with American Indian Poets.* Tucson: University of Arizona Press, 1987. 57–71.

Danker, Kathleen. "The Violation of the Earth: Elizabeth Cook-Lynn's *From the River's Edge.*" *Wicazo Sa Review* 12.2 (fall 1997): 85–94.

Matchie, Thomas. "Spirituality in Literature: Fiction, History and Criticism." *Midwest Quarterly* 39.4 (summer 1998): 373–90.

Morris, Gregory L. "Elizabeth Cook-Lynn." *Talking Up a Storm: Voices of the New West.* Lincoln: University of Nebraska Press, 1994: 33–46.

Ruppert, James. "Elizabeth Cook-Lynn." *Handbook of Native American Literature.* Ed. Andrew Wiget. New York: Garland, 1996: 407–11.

Linda Hogan

In the 1920s the Oklahoma Osage Indians were among the richest people in the United States. Their land rights covered immense deposits of oil on the southern plains, and countless greedy entrepreneurs devised many schemes to deprive the Osage people of those rights and revenues. The novel *Mean Spirit* follows the schemes and violence inflicted on the people and the land. This introductory section establishes the matrilocal focus on the Indian characters and the living character of the land itself.

For the biography of and further reading about Linda Hogan see pages 307 and 313.

Oklahoma, 1922 (1990)

That summer a water diviner named Michael Horse forecast a two-week dry spell.

Until then, Horse's predictions were known to be reliable, and since it was a scorching hot summer, a good number of Indians moved their beds outdoors in hopes a chance breeze would pass over and provide relief from the hot nights. They set them up far from the houses that held the sun's heat long after dark. Cots were unfolded in kitchen gardens. White iron beds sat in horse pastures. Four-posters rested in cornfields that were lying fallow.

What a silent bedchamber the world was, just before morning when even the locusts were still. In that darkness, the white beds were ghostly. They rose up from the black rolling hills and farmlands. Here, a lonely bed sat next to a barbed wire fence, and there, beneath the protection of an oak tree, a man's lantern burned beside his sleeping form. Near the marshland, tents of gauzy mosquito netting sloped down over the bony shoulders and hips of dreamers. A hand hung over the edge of a bed, fingers reaching down toward bluegrass that grew upward in fields. Given half a chance, the vines and leaves would have crept up the beds and overgrown the sleeping bodies of people.

In one yard, a nervy chicken wanted to roost on a bedframe and was shooed away.

"Go on. Scat!" an old woman cried out, raising herself half up in bed to push the clucking hen back down to the ground.

That would be Belle Graycloud. She was a light-skinned Indian woman, the grandmother of her family. She wore a meteorite on a leather thong around her neck. It had been passed on to her by a man named Osage Star-Looking who'd seen it fall from the sky and smolder in a field. It was her prized possession, although she also had a hand-written book by the old healer, Severance.

Belle slept alone in the herb garden. The rest of her family believed, in varying degrees, that they were modern, so they remained inside the oven-hot walls of the house. Belle's grown daughters drowsed off and on throughout the night. The men tossed. The two young people were red-faced and sweating, tangled in their bed linens on sagging mattresses.

Belle frightened away the hen, then turned on her side and settled back into the feather pillow. Her silver hair spread over the pillow. Even resting outside in the iron bed surrounded by night's terrain, she was a commanding woman with the first morning light on her strong-boned face.

A little ways down the road toward Watona, Indian Territory, a forest of burned trees was just becoming visible in morning's red firelight. Not far from there, at the oil fields, the pumps rose and fell, pulling black oil up through layers of rock. Across the way was a greenwood forest. And not even a full mile away from where Belle slept, just a short walk down the dirt road, Grace Blanket and her daughter Nola slept in a bed that was thoughtfully placed in their flower garden. Half covered in white sheets, they were dark-skinned angels dreaming their way through heaven. A dim lantern burned on a small table beside Grace. Its light fell across the shocking red blooms of roses.

Grace Blanket sat up in bed and put out the lamp. It smoked a little, and she smelled the kerosene. She climbed out from between her damp sheets. Standing in her thin nightdress, buried up to her dark ankles in the wild iris leaves that year after year invaded her garden, Grace bent over her sleeping daughter and shook the girl's shoulder. Grace smiled down at Nola, who had a widow's peak identical to her own, and even before the sleeping girl opened her eyes, Grace began to straighten the sheets on her side of the bed. "Make your bed every morning," they used to say, "and you'll never want for a husband." Grace was a woman who took such sayings to heart and she still wanted a husband. She decided to let Nola sleep a few minutes longer.

Lifting the hem of her nightgown, she walked across the yard, and went inside the screen door to the house.

Indoors, Grace pulled a navy blue dress over her head and zipped it. She fastened a strand of pearls around her neck, then brushed her hair in front of the mirror.

It was a strange house for a Hill Indian, as her people had come to be called. And sometimes, even to herself, Grace looked like an apparition from the past walking through the rooms she'd decorated with heavy, carved furniture and glass chandeliers. It seemed odd, too, that the European furniture was so staunch and upright when Grace was known to be lax at times in her own judgments.

She went to the open window and leaned out, "Nola! Come on now." She could see the girl in the growing daylight. She looked like an insect in its cocoon.

Nola turned over.

The Hill Indians were a peaceful group who had gone away from the changing world some sixty years earlier, in the 1860s. Their survival depended on returning to a simpler way of life, so they left behind them everything they could not carry and moved up into the hills and bluffs far above the town of Watona. Grace Blanket had been born of these, and she was the first to go down out of the hills and enter into the quick and wobbly world of mixed-blood Indians, white loggers, cattle ranchers, and most recently, the oil barons. The Hill Indians were known for their runners, a mystical group whose peculiar running discipline and austere habits earned them a special place in both the human world and the world of spirits.

But there were reasons why Grace had left the hills and moved down to Watona. Her mother, Lila Blanket, was a river prophet, which meant that she was a listener to the voice of water, a woman who interpreted the river's story for her people. A river never lied. Unlike humans, it had no need to distort the truth, and she heard the river's voice unfolding like its water across the earth. One day the Blue River told Lila that the white world was going to infringe on the peaceful Hill People. She listened, then she went back to her tribe and told them, "It is probable that we're going to lose everything. Even our cornfields."

The people were quiet and listened.

Lila continued, "Some of our children have to learn about the white world if we're going to ward off our downfall."

The Hill Indians respected the Blue River and Lila's words, but not one of them wanted to give their children up to that limbo between the worlds, that town named Watona, and finally Lila, who had heard the Blue directly, selected her own beautiful daughter, Grace, for the task. She could not say if it was a good thing or bad thing; it was only what had to be done.

Lila was a trader. That was her job at the Hill settlement. She went down to Watona often to trade sweet potatoes for corn, or sometimes corn for sweet potatoes. On her journeys, she was a frequent visitor at the Grayclouds'. Moses Graycloud, the man of the house, was Lila's second cousin. She liked him. He was a good Indian man; a rancher who kept a pasture and barn lot full of cattle and a number of good-looking horses. One day, when she mustered up enough strength, Lila took cornmeal and apples down to the small town, stopped by the Graycloud house, and knocked on the door.

As always, Belle was happy to see Lila Blanket. She opened the door for her. "Come in. Welcome." She held Lila's hand and smiled at her. But when she saw Lila's grief, her expression changed to one of concern. "I see you didn't come to trade food," she said. "What is it?"

Lila covered her face with her hands for a moment, then she took a deep breath and looked at Belle Graycloud. "I need to send my daughter to live near town. We've got too far away from the Americans to know how their laws are cutting into our life."

Belle nodded. She knew that a dam was going to be built at the mouth of the Blue River. The water must have told Lila this, about the army engineers and the surveyors with their red flags.

Lila was so overcome with sadness that she could hardly speak, but she asked Belle, "Can Grace stay with you?"

"Yes. I want her here." Belle put her hand on Lila's arm. "You come too, as often as you want. There's always an extra plate at our table."

On the day Lila took Grace to the Grayclouds, she kissed the girl, embraced her, and left immediately, before she could change her mind. She loved her daughter. She cried loudly all the way home, no matter who passed by or heard her. In fact, an old Osage hermit named John Stink heard the woman's wailing and he came down from his campsite, took Lila's hand, and walked much of the way home with her.

Grace Blanket had a ready smile and a good strong way with Belle's wayward chickens, but she paid little attention to the Indian ways. She hardly seemed like the salvation of the Hill Indians. And she was not at all interested in the white laws that affected her own people. After she finished school, Grace took a job at Palmer's store in town, and put aside her money. It wasn't any time at all before Grace bought a small, grassy parcel of land. She rented it out as a pasture for cattlemen, and one day, while Grace was daydreaming a house onto her land—her dream house had large rooms and a cupid fountain—Lila Blanket arrived in Watona, Indian Territory, with Grace's younger sisters. They were twins, ten years old, and the older woman wanted them to live with Grace and go to school. Their American names were Sara and Molene. And they had the same widow's peak that every Blanket woman had. They were wide-eyed girls, looking around at the world of automobiles and blond people. The longer they were there, the more they liked Watona. And the more Lila visited them, the more she hated the shabby little town with its red stone buildings and flat roofs. It was a magnet of evil that attracted and held her good daughters.

But the girls were the last of the Hill Indians ever to move down to Watona. Molene died several summers later, of an illness spread by white men who worked on the railroad. Sara caught the same paralyzing illness and was forced to remain in bed, motionless for over a year while Grace took care of her. By the time Sara was healthy enough to sit up in a wheelchair, both she and Grace wanted to remain in Watona. It was easier to wash clothing in the wringer washers, she reasoned, than to stir hot water tubs at home, and it was a most amazing thing to go for a ride in an automobile, and to turn on electric lights with the flick of a fingertip. And the delicate white women made such beautiful music on their pianos that Grace wanted one desperately and put away some of her earnings in a sugar bowl toward that cause.

There also were more important reasons why they remained; in the early 1900s each Indian had been given their choice of any parcel of land not already claimed by the white Americans. Those pieces of land were called allotments. They consisted of 160 acres a person to farm, sell, or use in any way they desired. The act that offered allotments to the Indians, the Dawes Act, seems generous at first glance so only a very few people realized how much they were being tricked, since numerous tracts of unclaimed land became open property for white settlers, homesteaders, and ranchers. Grace and Sara, in total ignorance, selected dried-up acreages that no one else wanted. No one guessed that black undercurrents of oil moved beneath that earth's surface.

When Belle Graycloud saw the land Grace selected, and that it was stony and dry, she shook her head in dismay and said to Grace, "It's barren land. What barren, useless land." But Grace wasn't discouraged. With good humor, she named her property "The Barren Land." Later, after oil was found there, she called it "The Baron Land," for the oil moguls.

It was Michael Horse, the small-boned diviner who'd predicted the two-week dry spell, who had been the first person to discover oil on the Indian wasteland, and he found it on Grace's parched allotment.

With his cottonwood dowsing rod, he'd felt a strong underground pull, followed it straight through the dry prairie grass, turned a bit to the left, and said, "Drill here. I feel water." Then he smiled and showed off his three gold teeth. The men put down an auger, bored deep into the earth, and struck oil on Grace Blanket's land.

Michael Horse fingered one of his long gray braids that hung down his chest. "I'll be damned," he said. He was worried. He didn't know how he had gone wrong. He had 363 wells to his credit. There was no water on Grace Blanket's land, just the thick black fluid that had no use at all for growing corn or tomatoes. Not even zucchini squash would grow there. He took off his glasses and he put them in his shirt pocket. He didn't want to see what happened next.

When Grace Blanket's first lease check came in from the oil company, she forgot the cupid fountain and moved into a house with Roman columns. She bought a grand piano, but to her disappointment she was without talent for music. No mater how she pressed down the ivory keys, she couldn't play the songs she'd heard and loved when white women sang them. After several months, she gave up and moved the piano outside to a chicken coop where it sat neglected, out of tune, and swelling up from the humidity. When a neighboring chicken built a nest on the keys, Grace didn't bother to remove the straw and feathers.

After that, she only bought items she could put to good use. She bought crystal champagne glasses that rang like bells when a finger was run over the rim, a tiny typewriter that tapped out the English words she'd learned in school, and a white fur cape that brought out the rich chestnut brown in her dark skin. She wore the cape throughout her pregnancy, even on warmer days, so much that Belle Graycloud poked fun at her. "When that baby comes, it's going to be born with a fan in its tiny hands."

"That's all right," said Grace, flashing a smile. "Just so long as it's electric."

"Say, who is the father, anyway?" Belle asked. But Grace just looked away like she hadn't heard.

After Nola was born, Grace took the child back a few times each year to the world of the Hill society, and while Nola had a stubborn streak, even as an infant, she was peaceful and serene in the midst of her mother's people. As much as the child took to the quieter ways of the Hill Indians, they likewise took to her, and while Grace continued to make her way in life, enjoying the easy pleasures money could buy, not one of those luxuries mattered a whit to Nola. By the time she was five years old, it was apparent to everyone that Nola was ill suited for town life. She was a gentle child who would wander into the greenwood forest and talk to the animals. She understood their ways. Lila thought that perhaps her granddaughter was going to be the one to return to the people. Nola, not Grace, was the river's godchild.

But what Lila didn't know, even up to the day she died, was that her daughter's oil had forestalled the damming of the Blue River, and that without anyone realizing it, the sacrifice of Grace to the town of Watona had indeed been the salvation of the Hill Indians. The dam would not go in until all the dark wealth was removed from inside the land.

That morning, as the sun rose up the sky, and Nola was still asleep, Grace went to the window and called out again, "Nola. Get up!"

Nola was dark and slender. Even with her eyes swollen from sleep, she was an uncommonly beautiful girl. She sat up like a small queen in her bed, with already elegant brown skin stretched over her thirteen-year-old bones. She climbed out of the bed, still sleepy, and went indoors. She slipped out of her nightgown, washed herself, and put on a Sunday white dress, and after Grace tied the bow behind Nola's thin waist, they walked together up the road to where Belle Graycloud slept in the middle of her herb garden with a stubborn golden chicken roosting on the foot of the bed, a calico cat by the old woman's side, a fat spotted dog snoring on the ground, and a white horse standing as close to Belle as the fence permitted, looking at her with wide, reverent eyes.

It was such a sight, Grace laughed out loud, and the laughter woke Belle.

Belle was indignant. "I knew someone was looking at me. I felt it. There ought to be a law against sneaking up on people like that. You gave me a fright."

Nola had slipped away to the house even while Belle talked. She was looking for her friend, Rena.

"Especially old people," Belle grumbled, rising from the bed. "Shoo!" She pushed the hen away from her bed.

Grace moved the cat. "Here, let me help you make the bed." She began to smooth Belle's sheets.

"Leave it," said Belle. "You know the saying. Maybe if I leave it in a mess, the young men will stop chasing me all the time." She pushed her dark silver hair back from her face. It hung like an ancient waterfall. Then she headed for the house, Grace alongside her. Behind them, the cat stretched and followed.

In the house, Belle's granddaughter, Rena, was already dressed. Rena had gold skin, the color of ochre, like a high yellow mulatto. It gave her, at first glance, a look of mystery. Her eyes, also, were gold-colored, and her hair. But she was still a child and she was impatient that morning as she walked around the creaky floor of the farmhouse, impatient to go with Nola and Grace to cut willow branches, impatient also for Grace to teach her how to weave the willow baskets, how to be that kind of an Indian woman.

In the kitchen, Belle's unmarried daughter, Leticia, took the perking coffeepot off the woodstove and set it on the table. "You sure you don't want some?" she asked Grace.

The girls passed by her in a hurry, and again the screen door slammed. Lettie opened the door behind them and called out, "Do you girls swear you won't soil your good church dresses?" She looked sharply at Rena. "You hear?"

"Cross my heart," said Rena, but she was already halfway down the walk. She looked back at Lettie who was dressed in a house dress and apron, but who nevertheless wore an expensive felted wool hat on her head. It was blue and a net was stitched to it.

"That goes for you, too," Lettie called out to Grace as Grace tried to catch up with the girls.

Grace turned and took a few steps backward before she blew a kiss to Lettie. Then she caught up with the girls. The sun lit her arms. For a change, she was in a hurry and the girls fell behind. Grace wanted to gather water willows and be done in time to put in a rare appearance at church, an appearance prompted only by the presence of a new, handsome man in town, and the only thing Grace knew about him was that he was a Baptist, so she knew where to find him.

5. The Great Plains Community

The Great Plains Community

A perennial topic among Great Plains residents is the future of the region. Like Nebraska writer Wright Morris, many residents left, agreeing with him that the Great Plains is a good place to be *from*. But many others have stayed. They are the ones who keep the post offices open, hope for a good year, and educate the children who leave for places with hills and oceans, landscapes of variation and boundaries.

Those who stay continue to worry. Environmentalists wonder if the land, much of it cultivated, fertilized, and irrigated, can continue to be productive. Some researchers worry about the continuing viability of plants and animals bred for specific qualities such as disease resistance, higher yield, or particular characteristics that consumers want in the products they buy. These practices, they fear, will lessen the resistance of crops and animals to new diseases or result in unimagined environmental damage. Others worry that as the older farmers die and young people move away, the small towns will fade to a few ghostly buildings and a cemetery hidden in prairie grasses.

Plains residents acknowledge that establishing and maintaining a place on the Great Plains takes more than modern technology and an influx of cash. Hard work, intuition, and pure luck are among the necessities for successful farmers and ranchers. On the Great Plains many people have overcome the hardships early settlers endured using modern machines, farm mortgages that they can repay in a good year, and crop subsidies to fill the gap between production costs and market value. Contemporary writers often use weather or the threat of corporate invasion—rather than physical isolation—as their metaphors for the continuing struggle to survive. Some favor the metaphor of the protracted, shriveling drought to convey a sense of the imperceptible destruction of life on the Great Plains. The end comes not with cold, sudden swiftness, but in the gradual loss of resources, energy, and optimism.

Contemporary American Indian writers have unique challenges living in a modern and new existence while clinging to traditions and histories that shape their identities. At the heart of cultural survival is the ongoing struggle for land rights and for language preservation. Tribal peoples have managed to stay close to the land and persevere when many others have given up.

These stories reflect events, hardly noted when they occur, that change the nature of society and community on the Great Plains. Farms and businesses fail; people move away. Financial resources for the remaining farmers dry up when the bank closes. Railways are abandoned which means the local elevator no longer stores the grain. Farmers must truck their crops to elevators farther away. The library closes, the local church must share a minister or priest with other small churches, and then even the church is abandoned. Women's social clubs fade because the members have died, moved away, or are simply worn out. People who stay in the sparsely populated regions of the high plains adapt, as earlier residents did, to these changes. They know why they live in these places: it is a conscious choice. For American Indian peoples, the place continues to define who they are, as it has for ages.

Taken as a whole these stories reflect Wright Morris's observation that the people and places of the Great Plains provide a rich field of stories for the writers who continue to conjure them up.

Reading about Contemporary Life on the Great Plains

JONIS AGEE
Strange Angels. New York: Ticknor & Fields, 1993.
The Weight of Dreams. New York: Viking, 1999.

BRUCE BAIR
Good Land: My Life as a Farm Boy. South Royalton VT: Steerforth Press, 1997.

JULENE BAIR
One Degree West: Reflections of a Plainsdaughter. Minneapolis: Mid-list Press, 2000.

SANDRA DALLAS
The Persian Pickle Club. New York: St. Martin's Press, 1995.

ROBERT DAY
The Last Cattle Drive. New York: Putnam, 1977.

JAMES DICKENSON
Home on the Range: A Century on the High Plains. New York: Scribner, 1995.

KENT HARUF
Plainsong. New York: Knopf, 1999.
The Tie that Binds. New York: Holt, 1984.
Where You Once Belonged. New York: Summit Books, 1990.

PHILIP KIMBALL
Harvesting Ballads. New York: Dutton, 1984.
Liar's Moon: A Long Story. New York: Holt, 1999.

TOM MCNEAL
Goodnight, Nebraska. New York: Random House, 1998.

William Allen White

William Allen White's story from his collection *In Our Town* illustrates his gift for humor, a cherished talent on the Great Plains. The newspaper office is White's forum for these stories. Various reporters, with their own points of view, comment on small town life. In this story White pokes fun at the pretensions of people—women, mostly—who attempt to impose hills and valleys on the flat, democratic social plain. White's tone is light: he creates a mock war between the "Old Money" and the "Self-Made Upstart," sustaining the metaphor throughout the story. Moreover, he is thoroughly acquainted with the details. Women in the plains towns did indeed read papers on exotic topics and entertain with linens, China, and silver.* Of course, White and the reader know that social pretension, at least in 1906, was an absurdity in a small prairie town where everyone's family trees were ordinary elms, non-native interlopers.

White dislikes all forms of pretension. Like most good satirists, he aims some of his barbs at himself. White's Emporia hospitality was known across the country. He and his wife, Sallie, entertained presidents and other men and women of political and cultural note, and in his editorials he wages various battles to educate the people of Emporia on the finer things of life, including a thirty-year struggle against bad cooking, declaring, finally, that the practice of parboiling turkey before roasting "was discontinued among the best cooks in these latitudes."†

For the biography and bibliography of White see pages 333 and 337–38.

The Passing of Priscilla Winthrop (1906)

What a dreary waste life in our office must have been before Miss Larrabee came to us to edit a society page for the paper! To be sure we had known in a vague way that there were lines of social cleavage in the town; that there were whist clubs and dancing clubs and women's clubs, and in a general way that the women who

---

*One of the editors grew up in a Kansas town that had a Domestic Science Club, as home economics or human ecology was called, and a TPM Club, which, as its name indicates, met on Tuesday afternoons. The programs were only slightly less ridiculous than the titles White concocts. See also the women's club records that Wes Jackson discovers in "Matfield Green," pages 713–21 in this volume.

†William Allen White, *The Editor and His People* (New York: Macmillan, 1924), 65.

composed these clubs made up our best society, and that those benighted souls beyond the pale of these clubs were out of the caste. We knew that certain persons whose names were always handed in on the lists of guests at parties were what we called "howling swells." But it remained for Miss Larrabee to sort out ten or a dozen of these "howling swells" who belonged to the strictest social caste in town, and call them "howling dervishes." Incidentally it may be said that both Miss Larrabee and her mother were dervishes, but that did not prevent her from making sport of them. From Miss Larrabee we learned that the high priestess of the howling dervishes of our society was Mrs. Mortimer Conklin, known by the sisterhood of the mosque as Priscilla Winthrop. We in our office had never heard her called by that name, but Miss Larrabee explained, rather elaborately, that unless one was permitted to speak of Mrs. Conklin thus, one was quite beyond the hope of a social heaven.

In the first place, Priscilla Winthrop was Mrs. Conklin's maiden name; in the second place, it links her with the Colonial Puritan stock of which she is so justly proud—being scornful of mere Daughters of the Revolution—and finally, though Mrs. Conklin is a grandmother, her maiden name seems to preserve the sweet, vague illusion of girlhood which Mrs. Conklin always carries about her like the shadow of a dream. And Miss Larrabee punctuated this with a wink which we took to be a quotation mark, and she went on with her work. So we knew we had been listening to the language used in the temple.

Our town was organised fifty years ago by Abolitionists from New England, and twenty years ago, when Alphabetical Morrison was getting out one of the numerous boom editions of his real estate circular, he printed an historical article therein in which he said that Priscilla Winthrop was the first white child born on the town site.[1] Her father was territorial judge, afterward member of the State Senate, and after ten years spent in mining in the far West, died in the seventies, the richest man in the State. It was known that he left Priscilla, his only child, half a million dollars in government bonds.

She was the first girl in our town to go away to school. Naturally, she went to Oberlin, famous in those days for admitting coloured students. But she finished her education at Vassar, and came back so much of a young lady that the town could hardly contain her. She married Mortimer Conklin, took him to the Centennial on a wedding trip,[2] came home, rebuilt her father's house, covering it with towers and minarets and steeples, and scroll-saw fretwork, and christened it Winthrop Hall. She erected a store building on Main Street, that Mortimer might have a luxurious office on the second floor, and then settled down to the serious business of life, which was building up a titled aristocracy in a Kansas town.

The Conklin children were never sent to the public schools, but had a governess, yet Mortimer Conklin, who was always alert for the call, could not understand why the people never summoned him to any office of honour or trust. He kept his brass signboard polished, went to his office punctually every morning at ten o'clock, and returned home to dinner at five, and made clients wait ten minutes in the outer office before they could see him—at least so both of them say, and there were no others in all the years. He shaved every day, wore a frock-coat and a high hat to church—where for ten years he was the only male member of the Episcopalian flock—and Mrs. Conklin told the women that altogether he was a credit to his sex and his family—a remark which was passed about ribaldly in town for a dozen years, though Mortimer Conklin never knew that he was the subject of a town joke. Once he rebuked a man in the barber shop for speaking of feminine extravagance, and told the shop that he did not stint his wife, that when she asked him for money he always gave it to her without question, and that if she wanted a dress he told her to buy it and send the bill to him. And we are such a polite people that no one in the crowded shop laughed—until Mortimer Conklin went out.

Of course at the office we have known for twenty-five years what the men thought of Mortimer, but not until Miss Larrabee joined the force did we know that among the women Mrs. Conklin was considered an oracle. Miss Larrabee said that her mother has a legend that when Priscilla Winthrop brought home from Boston the first sealskin sacque ever worn in town she gave a party for it,[3] and it lay in its box on the big walnut bureau in the spare room of the Conklin mansion in solemn state, while seventy-five women salaamed to it. After that Priscilla Winthrop was the town authority on sealskins. When any member of the town nobility had a new sealskin, she took it humbly to Priscilla Winthrop to pass judgment upon it. If Priscilla said it was London-dyed, its owner pranced away on clouds of glory; but if she said it was American-dyed, its owner crawled away in shame, and when one admired the disgraced garment, the martyred owner smiled with resigned sweetness and said humbly: "Yes—but it's only American-dyed, you know."

No dervish ever questioned the curse of the priestess. The only time a revolt was imminent was in the autumn of 1884 when the Conklins returned from their season at Duxbury, Massachusetts, and Mrs. Conklin took up the carpets in her house, heroically sold all of them at the second-hand store, put in new waxed floors and spread down rugs. The town uprose and hooted; the outcasts and barbarians in the Methodist and Baptist Missionary Societies rocked the Conklin home with their merriment, and ten dervishes with set faces bravely met the onslaughts of the savages; but among themselves in hushed whispers, behind locked doors, the faithful wondered if there was not a mistake some place. However, when Priscilla Winthrop assured them that in all the best homes in Boston rugs were replacing carpets, their souls were at peace.

All this time we at the office knew nothing of what was going on. We knew that the Conklins devoted considerable time to society; but Alphabetical Morrison explained that by calling attention to the fact that Mrs. Conklin had prematurely grey hair. He said a woman with prematurely grey hair was as sure to be a social leader as a spotted horse is to join a circus. But now we know that Colonel Morrison's view was a superficial one, for he was probably deterred from going deeper into the subject by his dislike for Mortimer Conklin, who invested a quarter of a million dollars of the Winthrop fortune in the Wichita boom, and lost it. Colonel Morrison naturally thought as long as Conklin was going to lose that money he could have lost it just as well at home in the "Queen City of the Prairies," giving the Colonel a chance to win. And when Conklin, protecting his equities in Wichita, sent a hundred thousand dollars of good money after the quarter million of bad money, Colonel Morrison's grief could find no words; though he did find language for his wrath. When the Conklins draped their Oriental rugs for airing every Saturday over the veranda and portico railings of the house front, Colonel Morrison accused the Conklins of hanging out their stamp collection to let the neighbours see it. This was the only side of the rug question we ever heard in our office until Miss Larrabee came; then she told us that one of the first requirements of a howling dervish was to be able to quote from Priscilla Winthrop's Rug book from memory. The Rug book, the China book and the Old Furniture book were the three sacred scrolls of the sect.

All this was news to us. However, through Colonel Morrison, we had received many years ago another sidelight on the social status of the Conklins. It came out in this way: Time honored custom in our town allows the children of a home where there is an outbreak of social revelry, whether a church festival or a meeting of the Cold-Nosed Whist Club, to line up with the neighbour children on the back stoop or in the kitchen, like human vultures, waiting to lick the ice-cream freezer and to devour the bits of cake and chicken salad that are left over. Colonel Morrison told us that no child was ever known to adorn the back yard of the Conklin home while a social cataclysm was going on, but that when Mrs. Morrison entertained the Ladies' Literary League, children from the holy Conklin family went home from his back porch with their faces smeared with chicken croquettes and their hands sticky with jellycake.

This story never gained general circulation in town, but even if it had been known of all men it would not have shaken the faith of the devotees. For they did not smile when Priscilla Winthrop began to refer to old Frank Hagan, who came to milk the Conklin cow and curry the Conklin horse, as "François, the man," or to call the girl who did the cooking and general housework "Cosette, the maid," though every one of the dozen other women in town whom "Cosette, the maid" had worked for knew that her name was Fanny Ropes. And shortly after that the homes of the rich and the great over on the hill above Main Street began to fill with Lisettes and Nanons and Fanchons, and Mrs. Julia Neal Worthington called her girl "Grisette," explaining that they had always had a Grisette about the house since her mother first went to housekeeping in Peoria, Illinois, and it sounded so natural to hear the name that they always gave it to a new servant. This story came to the office through the Young Prince, who chuckled over it during the whole hour he consumed in writing Ezra Worthington's obituary.

Miss Larrabee says that the death of Ezra Worthington marks such a distinct epoch in the social life of the town that we must set down here—even if the narrative of the Conklins halts for a moment—how the Worthingtons rose and flourished. Julia Neal, eldest daughter of Thomas Neal—who lost the "O" before his name somewhere between the docks of Dublin and the west bank of the Missouri River—was for ten years principal of the ward school in that part of our town known as "Arkansaw," where her term of service is still remembered as the "reign of terror." It was said of her then that she could whip any man in the ward— and would do it if he gave her a chance. The same manner which made the neighbours complain that Julia Neal carried her head too high, later in life, when she had money to back it, gave her what the women of the State Federation called a "regal air." In her early thirties she married Ezra Worthington, bachelor, twenty year her senior. Ezra Worthington was at that time, had been for twenty years before, and continued to be until his death, proprietor of the Worthington Poultry and Produce Commission Company. He was owner of the stockyards, president of the Worthington State Bank, vice-president, treasurer and general manager of the Worthington Mercantile Company, and owner of five brick buildings on Main Street. He bought one suit of clothes every five years whether he needed it or not, never let go of a dollar until the Goddess of Liberty on it was black in the face, and died rated "Aa $350,000" by all the commercial agencies in the country. And the first thing Mrs. Worthington did after the funeral was to telephone to the bank and ask them to send her a hundred dollars.

The next important thing she did was to put a heavy, immovable granite monument over the deceased so that he would not be restless, and then she built what is known in our town as the Worthington Palace. It makes the Markley mansion which cost $25,000 look like a barn. The Worthingtons in the lifetime of Ezra had ventured no further into the social whirl of the town than to entertain the new Presbyterian preacher at tea, and to lend their lawn to the King's Daughters for a social, sending a bill in to the society for the eggs used in the coffee and the gasoline used in heating it.

To the howling dervishes who surrounded Priscilla Winthrop the Worthingtons were as mere Christian dogs. It was not until three years after Ezra Worthington's death that the glow of the rising Worthington sun began to be seen in the Winthrop mosque. During those three years Mrs. Worthington had bought and read four different sets of the best hundred books, had consumed the Chautauqua course, had prepared and delivered for the Social Science Club, which she organised, five papers ranging in subject from the home life of Rameses I., through a Survey of the Forces Dominating Michael Angelo, to the Influence of Esoteric Buddhism on Modern Political Tendencies. More than that, she had been elected president of the City Federation of Clubs, and, being a delegate to the National Federation from the State, was talked of for the State Federation Presidency. When the State Federation met in our town, Mrs. Worthington gave a reception for the delegates in the Worthington Palace, a feature of which was a concert by a Kansas City organist on the new pipe-organ which she had erected in the music-room of her house, and despite the fact that the devotees of the Priscilla shrine said that the crowd was distinctly mixed and not at all representative of our best social grace and elegance, there is no question but that Mrs. Worthington's reception made a strong impression upon the best local society. The fact that, as Miss Larrabee said, "Priscilla Winthrop was so nice about it," also may be regarded as ominous. But the women who lent Mrs. Worthington the spoons and forks for the occasion were delighted, and formed a phalanx about her, which made up in numbers what it might have lacked in distinction. Yet while Mrs. Worthington was in Europe the faithful routed the phalanx, and Mrs. Conklin returned from her summer in Duxbury with half a carload of old furniture from Harrison Sampson's shop and gave a talk to the priestesses of the inner temple on "Heppelwhite in New England."

Miss Larrabee reported the affair for our paper, giving the small list of guests and the long line of refreshments—which included alligator-pear salad, right out of the Smart Set Cook Book. Moreover, when Jefferson appeared in Topeka that fall, Priscilla Winthrop, who had met him through some of her Duxbury friends in Boston, invited him to run down for a luncheon with her and the members of the royal family who surrounded her. It was the proud boast of the defenders of the Winthrop faith in town that week, that though twenty-four people sat down to the table, not only did all the men wear frock-coats—not only did Uncle Charlie Haskins of String Town wear the old Winthrop butler's livery without a wrinkle in it, and with only the faint odour of mothballs to mingle with the perfume of the roses—but (and here the voices of the followers of the prophet dropped in awe) not a single knife or fork or spoon or napkin was borrowed! After that, when any of the sisterhood had occasion to speak of the absent Mrs. Worthington, whose house was filled with new mahogany and brass furniture, they referred to her as the Duchess of Grand Rapids, which gave them much comfort.

But joy is short-lived. When Mrs. Worthington came back from Europe and opened her house to the City Federation, and gave a coloured lantern-slide lecture on "An evening with the Old Masters," serving punch from her own cut-glass punch bowl instead of renting the hand-painted crockery bowl of the queensware store, the old dull pain came back into the hearts of the dwellers in the inner circle. Then just in the nick of time Mrs. Conklin went to Kansas City and was operated on for appendicitis. She came back pale and interesting, and gave her club a paper called "Hospital Days," fragrant with iodoform[4] and Henley's poems.[5] Miss Larrabee told us that it was almost as pleasant as an operation on one's self to hear Mrs. Conklin tell about hers. And they thought it was rather brutal—so Miss Larrabee afterward told us—when Mrs. Worthington went to the hospital one month, and gave her famous Delsarte lecture course the next month, and explained to the women that if she wasn't as heavy as she used to be it was because she had had everything cut out of her below the windpipe. It seemed to the temple priestesses that, considering what a serious time poor dear Priscilla Winthrop had gone through, Mrs. Worthington was making light of serious things.

There is no doubt that the formal rebellion of Mrs. Worthington, Duchess of Grand Rapids, and known of the town's nobility as the Pretender, began with the hospital contest. The Pretender planted her siege-guns before the walls of the temple of the priestess, and prepared for business. The first manœuvre made by the beleaguered one was to give a luncheon in the mosque, at which, though it was midwinter, fresh tomatoes and fresh strawberries were served, and a real authoress from Boston talked upon John Fiske's philosophy and, in the presence of the admiring guests, made a new kind of salad dressing for the fresh lettuce and tomatoes. Thirty women who watched her forgot what John Fiske's theory of the cosmos is, and thirty husbands who afterward ate that salad dressing have learned to suffer and be strong. But that salad dressing undermined the faith of thirty mere men—raw outlanders to be sure—in the social omniscience of Priscilla Winthrop. Of course they did not see it made; the spell of the enchantress was not over them; but in their homes they maintained that if Priscilla Winthrop didn't know any more about cosmic philosophy than to pay a woman forty dollars to make a salad dressing like that—and the whole town knows that was the price—the vaunted town of Duxbury, Massachusetts, with its old furniture and new culture, which Priscilla spoke of in such repressed ecstasy, is probably no better than Manitou, Colorado, where they get their Indian goods from Buffalo, New York.

Such is the perverse reasoning of man. And Mrs. Worthington, having lived with considerable of a man for fifteen years, hearing echoes of this sedition, attacked the fortification of the faithful on its weakest side. She invited the thirty seditious husbands with their wives to a beefsteak dinner, where she heaped their plates with planked sirloin, garnished the sirloin with big, fat, fresh mushrooms, and topped off the meal with a mince pie of her own concoction, which would make a man leave home to follow it. She passed cigars at the table, and after the guests went into the music-room ten old men with ten old fiddles appeared and contested with old-fashioned tunes for a prize, after which the company danced four quadrilles and a Virginia reel. The men threw down their arms going home and went over in a body to the Pretender. But in a social conflict men are mere non-combatants, and their surrender did not seriously injure the cause that they deserted.

The war went on without abatement. During the spring that followed the winter of the beefsteak dinner many skirmishes, minor engagements, ambushes and midnight raids occurred. But the contest was not decisive. For purposes of military drill, the defenders of the Winthrop faith formed themselves into a Whist Club. *The* Whist Club they called it, just as they spoke of Priscilla Winthrop's gowns as "the black and white one," "the blue brocade," "the white china silk," as if no other black and white or blue brocade or white china silk gowns had been created in the world before and could not be made again by human hands. So, in the language of the inner sanctuary, there was "The Whist Club," to the exclusion of all other possible human Whist Clubs under the stars. When summer came the Whist Club fled as birds to the mountains—save Priscilla Winthrop, who went to Duxbury, and came home with a brass warming-pan and a set of Royal Copenhagen china that were set up as holy objects in the temple.

But Mrs. Worthington went to the National Federation of Women's Clubs, made the acquaintance of the women there who wore clothes from Paris, began tracing her ancestry back to the Maryland Calverts—on her mother's side of the house—brought home a membership in the Daughters of the Revolution, the Colonial Dames and a society which referred to Charles I. as "Charles Martyr," claimed a Stuart as the rightful king of England, affecting to scorn the impudence of King Edward in sitting on another's throne. More than this, Mrs. Worthington had secured the promise of Mrs. Ellen Vail Montgomery, Vice-President of the National Federation, to visit Cliff Crest, as Mrs. Worthington called the Worthington mansion, and she turned up her nose at those who worshipped under the towers, turrets and minarets of the Conklin mosque, and played the hose of her ridicule on their outer wall that she might have it spotless for a target when she got ready to raze it with her big gun.

The week that Ellen Vail Montgomery came to town was a busy one for Miss Larrabee. We turned over the whole fourth page of the paper to her for a daily society page, and charged the Bee Hive and the White Front Dry Goods store people double rates to put their special sale advertisements on that page while the "National Vice," as the Young Prince called her, was in town. For the "National Vice" brought the State President and two State Vices down, also four District Presidents and six District Vices, who, as Miss Larrabee said, were monsters "of so frightful a mien, that to be hated need but to be seen." The entire delegation of visiting stateswomen—Vices and Virtues and Beatitudes as we called them—were entertained by Mrs. Worthington at Cliff Crest, and there was so much Federation politics going on in our town that the New York *Sun* took five hundred words about it by wire, and Colonel Alphabetical Morrison said that with all those dressed-up women about he felt as though he was living in a Sunday supplement.

The third day of the ghost-dance at Cliff Crest was to be the day of the big event—as the office parlance had it. The ceremonies began at sunrise with a breakfast to which half a dozen of the captains and kings of the besieging host of the Pretender were bidden. It seems to have been a modest orgy, with nothing more astonishing than a new gold-band china set to dishearten the enemy. By ten o'clock Priscilla Winthrop and the Whist Club had recovered from that; but they had been asked to the luncheon—the star feature of the week's round of gayety. It is just as well to be frank, and say that they went with fear and trembling. Panic and terror were in their ranks, for they knew a crisis was at hand. It came when they were "ushered into the dining-hall," as our paper so grandly put it, and saw in the great oak-beamed room a table laid on the polished bare wood—a table laid for forty-eight guests, with a doily for every plate, and every glass, and every salt-cellar, and—here the mosque fell on the heads of the howling dervishes—forty-eight soup-spoons, forty-eight silver-handled knives and forks; forty-eight butter-spreaders, forty-eight spoons, forty-eight salad forks, forty-eight ice-cream spoons, forty-eight coffee spoons. Little did it avail the beleaguered party to peep slyly under the spoon-handles—the word "Sterling" was there, and, more than that, a large, severely plain "W" with a crest glared up at them from every piece of silver. The service had not been rented. They knew their case was hopeless. And so they ate in peace.

When the meal was over it was Mrs. Ellen Vail Montgomery, in her thousand-dollar gown, worshipped by the eyes of forty-eight women, who put her arm about Priscilla Winthrop and led her into the conservatory, where they had "a dear, sweet quarter of an hour," as Mrs. Montgomery afterward told her hostess. In that dear, sweet quarter of an hour Priscilla Winthrop Conklin unbuckled her social sword and handed it to the conquerer, in that she agreed absolutely with Mrs. Montgomery that Mrs. Worthington was "perfectly lovely," that she was "delighted to be of any service" to Mrs. Worthington; that Mrs. Conklin "was sure no one else in our town was so admirably qualified for "National Vice" as Mrs. Worthington, and that "it would be such a privilege" for Mrs. Conklin to suggest Mrs. Worthington's name for the office. And then Mrs. Montgomery, "National Vice" and former State Secretary for Vermont of the Colonial Dames, kissed Priscilla Winthrop and they came forth wet-eyed and radiant, holding each other's hands. When the company had been hushed by the magic of a State Vice and two District Virtues, Priscilla Winthrop rose and in the sweetest Kansas Bostonese told the ladies that she thought this an eminently fitting place to let the visiting ladies know how dearly our town esteems its most distinguished townswoman, Mrs. Julia Neal Worthington, and that entirely without her solicitation, indeed quite without her knowledge, the women of our town—and she hoped of our beloved State—were ready now to announce that they were unanimous in their wish that Mrs. Worthington should be National Vice-President of the Federation of Women's Clubs, and that she, the speaker, had entered the contest with her whole soul to bring this end to pass. Then there was hand-clapping and handkerchief waving and some tears, and a little good, honest Irish hugging, and in the twilight two score of women filed down through the formal garden of Cliff Crest and walked by twos and threes into the town.

There was the usual clatter of home-going wagons; lights winked out of kitchen windows; the tinkle of distant cow-bells was in the air; on Main Street the commerce of the town was gently ebbing, and man and nature seemed utterly oblivious of the great event that had happened. The course of human events was not changed; the great world rolled on, while Priscilla Winthrop went home to a broken shrine to sit among the potsherds.

Notes

1. Alphabetical Morrison is a recurring character in White's stories, so called because his initials are A. B. C. He was one of the original settlers and an inveterate town booster.—Eds.
2. The Centennial: the International Centennial Exhibition, held May through November 1876 in Philadelphia. The Conklins were not alone: almost ten million people visited this fair. The first of many world's fairs held in the United States, it became the model for extravagant buildings and exhibits.—Eds.
3. Sealskin sacque: a loose-fitting, waistless dress popular in the early twentieth century and again in the early 1960s.—Eds.
4. Iodoform: a yellowish iodine antiseptic.—Eds.
5. Henley's poems: William Ernest Henley, 1849–1930. English poet known for bravado and a spirit of defiance. His best-known poems include "Invictus," which concludes:

   I am the master of my fate,
   I am the captain of my soul.—Eds.

Langston Hughes *(1902–1967)*

Langston Hughes came of age during the Harlem Renaissance in the 1920s. His 1926 essay "The Negro Artist and the Racial Mountain" is a widely acclaimed declaration of literary independence. He wrote poetry, essays, novels, short stories, plays, a memoir-autobiography, and translations of other writers' works. In several volumes of stories his creation, the character Simple, relates his troubles as a black man in a racist society. Hughes also edited volumes of works by other writers that helped to establish a place for blacks in the American literary canon.

Hughes was born in Joplin, Missouri, but until he was thirteen he lived with his grandmother in Lawrence, Kansas. Both of his grandmothers' husbands had been prominent during the battles over slavery in Kansas. Although his family enjoyed a better social situation than the characters in *Not Without Laughter*, his grandmother was poor and elderly by the time Langston came to live with her. She made a modest living renting rooms in her house to students attending the University of Kansas.

Hughes's novel reflects his experiences growing up in a restless family in a plains community. His parents divorced when Hughes was a child and his mother left Lawrence to look for work. Later Hughes lived with his mother and stepfather, and attended high school in Cleveland, Ohio, and college at Columbia University, but was more interested in the increasingly lively cultural life of blacks in New York City than he was in engineering, his stepfather's choice for him. He left college to travel in Europe and Africa, then received an associate business degree from Pennsylvania's Lincoln University in 1929. He had already begun publishing his poetry and was gaining recognition as a part of the black arts community in New York.

In *Not Without Laughter* Hughes recounts the lives of Aunt Hager, a washerwoman and community caregiver, and her grandson, Sandy. The family represents some of the options available to poor blacks in a small Kansas town in the early twentieth century. Hager's daughter, Anjee, cook and maid to Mrs. J. J. Rice, is married to Jimboy, who is frequently away looking for work. Eventually Anjee joins him, leaving Sandy with his grandmother. Hager's daughter Tempy has married a postal worker and established herself as a member of the black middle class, an Episcopalian determined to emulate the town's white society. Hughes contrasts Tempy's assimilation goals with Hager's commitment to the black community.

In the chapters from *Not Without Laughter* included here, Sandy's youngest aunt, Harriet, introduces the boy to new experiences. In "Dance" Hughes presents a vivid portrait of the blues that so deeply influenced his own art, and in

"Carnival" he recounts the lure of a life beyond the restrictions that family and society impose on young people. It appeals to both Harriet and her young nephew, Sandy, as it attracted and held Hughes.

Dance (1930)

Mrs. J. J. Rice and family usually spent ten days during the August heat at Lake Dale, and thither they had gone now, giving Annjee a forced vacation with no pay. Jimboy was not working, and so his wife found ten days of rest without income not especially agreeable. Nevertheless, she decided that she might as well enjoy the time; so she and Jimboy went to the country for a week with Cousin Jessie, who had married one of the colored farmers of the district. Besides, Annjee thought that Jimboy might help on the farm and so make a little money. Anyway, they would get plenty to eat, because Jessie kept a good table. And since Jessie had eight children of her own, they did not take Sandy with them—eight were enough for a woman to be worried with at one time!

Aunt Hager had been ironing all day on the Reinharts' clothes—it was Friday. At seven o'clock Harriett came home, but she had already eaten her supper at the restaurant where she worked.

"Hello, mama! Hy, Sandy!" she said, but that was all, because she and her mother were not on the best of terms. Aunt Hager was attempting to punish her youngest daughter by not allowing her to leave the house after dark, since Harriett, on Tuesday night, had been out until one o'clock in the morning with no better excuse than a party at Maudel's. Aunt Hager had threatened to whip her then and there that night.

"You ain't had a switch on yo' hide fo' three years, but don't think you's gettin' too big fo' me not to fan yo' behind, madam. 'Spare de rod an' spoil de chile,' that's what de Bible say, an' Lawd knows you sho is spoiled! De idee of a young gal yo' age stayin' out till one o'clock in de mawnin', an' me not knowed where you's at. . . . Don't you talk back to me! . . . You rests in this house ever' night this week an' don't put yo' foot out o' this yard after you comes from work, that's what you do. Lawd knows I don't know what I's gonna do with you. I works fo' you an' I prays fo' you, an' if you don't mind, I's sho gonna whip you, even if you is goin' on seventeen years old!"

Tonight as soon as she came from work Harriett went into her mother's room and lay across the bed. It was very warm in the little four-room house, and all the windows and doors were open.

"We's got some watermelon here, daughter," Hager called from the kitchen. "Don't you want a nice cool slice?"

"No," the girl replied. She was fanning herself with a palm-leaf fan, her legs in their cheap silk stockings hanging over the side of the bed, and her heels kicking the floor. Benbow's Band played tonight for the dance at Chaver's Hall, and everybody was going—but her. Gee, it was hard to have a Christian mother! Harriet kicked her slippers off with a bang and rolled over on her stomach, burying her powdery face in the pillows. . . . Somebody knocked at the back door.

A boy's voice was speaking excitedly to Hager: "Hemorrhages . . . and papa can't stop 'em . . . she's coughin' something terrible . . . says can't you please come over and help him"—frightened and out of breath.

"Do, Jesus!" cried Hager. "I'll be with you right away, chile. Don't worry." She rushed into the bedroom to change her apron. "You, Harriett, listen; Sister Lane's taken awful sick an' Jimmy says she's bleedin' from de mouth. If I ain't back by nine o'clock, see that that chile Sandy's in de bed. An' you know you ain't to leave this yard under no circumstances. . . . Po' Mis' Lane! She sho do have it hard." In a whisper: "I 'spects she's got de T. B., that what I 'spects!" And the old woman hustled out to join the waiting youngster. Jimmy was leaning against the door, looking at Sandy, and neither of the boys knew what to say. Jimmy Lane wore his mother's cast-off shoes to school, and Sandy used to tease him, but tonight he didn't tease his friend about his shoes.

"You go to bed 'fore it gets late," said his grandmother, starting down the alley with Jimmy.

"Yes'm," Sandy called after her. "So long, Jim!" He stood under the apple-tree and watched them disappear.

Aunt Hager had scarcely gotten out of sight when there was a loud knock at the front door, and Sandy ran around the house to see Harriett's boy friend, Mingo, standing in the dusk outside the screen-door, waiting to be let in.

Mingo was a patent-leather black boy with wide, alive nostrils and a mouth that split into a lighthouse smile on the least provocation. His body was heavy and muscular, resting on bowed legs that curved backward as though the better to brace his chunky torso; and his hands were hard from mixing concrete and digging ditches for the city's new water-mains.

"I know it's tonight, but I can't go," Sandy heard his aunt say at the door. They were speaking of Benbow's dance. "And his band don't come here often, neither. I'm heart-sick having to stay home, dog-gone it all, especially this evening!"

"Aw, come on and go anyway," pleaded Mingo. "After I been savin' up my dough for two weeks to take you, and got my suit cleaned and pressed and all. Heck! If you couldn't go and knew it yesterday, why didn't you tell me? That's a swell way to treat a fellow!"

"Because I wanted to go," said Harriett; "and still want to go. . . . Don't make so much difference about mama, because she's mad anyhow . . . but what could we do with this kid? We can't leave him by himself." She looked at Sandy, who was standing behind Mingo listening to everything.

"You can take me," the child offered anxiously, his eyes dancing at the delight-ful prospect. "I'll behave, Harrie, if you take me, and I won't tell on you either. . . . Please lemme go, Mingo. I ain't never seen a big dance in my life. I wanta go."

"Should we?" asked Harriett doubtfully, looking at her boy friend standing firmly on his curved legs.

"Sure, if we got to have him . . . damn 'im!" Mingo replied. "Better the kid than no dance. Go git dressed." So Harriett made a dash for the clothes-closet, while Sandy ran to get a clean waist from one of his mother's dresser-drawers, and Mingo helped him put it on, cussing softly to himself all the while. "But it ain't your fault, pal, is it?" he said to the little boy.

"Sure not," Sandy replied. "I didn't tell Aunt Hager to make Harrie stay home. I tried to 'suade grandma to let her go," the child lied, because he liked Mingo. "I guess she won't care about her goin' to just one dance." He wanted to make everything all right so the young man wouldn't be worried. Besides, Sandy very much wanted to go himself.

"Let's beat it," Harriett shrilled excitedly before her dress was fastened, anx-ious to be gone lest her mother come home. She was powdering her face and neck in the next room, nervous, happy, and afraid all at once. The perfume, the voice, and the pat, pat, pat of the powder-puff came out to the waiting gentleman.

"Yo' car's here, madam," mocked Mingo. "Step right this way and let's be going!"

> *Wonder where ma easy rider's gone—*
> *He done left me, put ma new gold watch in pawn!*

Like a blare from hell the second encore of *Easy Rider* filled every cubic inch of the little hall with hip-rocking notes. Benbow himself was leading and the crowd moved like jelly-fish dancing on individual sea-shells, with Mingo and Harriett somewhere among the shakers. But they were not of them, since each couple shook in a world of its own, as, with a weary wail, the music abruptly ceased.

Then, after scarcely a breath of intermission, the band struck up again with a lazy one-step. A tall brown boy in a light tan suit walked his partner straight down the whole length of the floor and, when he reached the corner, turned leisurely in one spot, body riding his hips, eyes on the ceiling, and his girl shaking her full breasts against his pink silk shirt. Then they recrossed the width of the room, turned slowly, repeating themselves, and began again to walk rhythmically down the hall, while the music was like a lazy river flowing between mountains, carving a canyon coolly, calmly, and without insistence. The *Lazy River One-Step* they might have called what the band was playing as the large crowd moved with the greatest ease about the hall. To drum-beats barely audible, the tall boy in the tan suit walked his partner round and round time after time, revolving at each corner with eyes uplifted, while the piano was the water flowing, and the high, thin chords of the banjo were the mountains floating in the clouds. But in sultry tones, alone and always, the brass cornet spoke harshly about the earth.

Sandy sat against the wall in a hard wooden folding chair. There were other children scattered lonesomely about on chairs, too, watching the dancers, but he didn't
seem to know any of them. When the music stopped, all the chairs quickly filled
with loud-talking women and girls in brightly colored dresses who fanned themselves with handkerchiefs and wiped their sweating brows. Sandy thought maybe
he should give his seat to one of the women when he saw Maudel approaching.

"Here, honey," she said. "Take this dime and buy yourself a bottle of something
cold to drink. I know Harriett ain't got you on her mind out there dancin'. This
music is certainly righteous, chile!" She laughed as she handed Sandy a coin and
closed her pocketbook. He liked Maudel, although he knew his grandmother
didn't. She was a large good-natured brown-skinned girl who walked hippishly
and used too much rouge on her lips. But she always gave Sandy a dime, and she
was always laughing.

He went through the crowd towards the soft-drink stand at the end of the hall.
"Gimme a bottle o' cream soda," he said to the fat orange-colored man there, who
had his sleeves rolled up and a white butcher's apron covering his barrel-like belly.
The man put his hairy arms down into a zinc tub full of ice and water and began
pulling out bottles, looking at their caps, and then dropping them back into the
cold liquid.

"Don't seem like we got no cream, sonny. How'd a lemon do you?" he asked
above the bedlam of talking voices.

"Naw," said Sandy. "It's too sour."

On the improvised counter of boards the wares displayed consisted of cracker-
jacks, salted peanuts, a box of gum, and Sen Sens, while behind the counter was a
lighted oil-stove holding a tin pan full of spareribs, sausage, and fish; and near it an
ice-cream freezer covered with a brown sack. Some cases of soda were on the floor
beside the zinc tub filled with bottles, in which the man was still searching.

"Nope, no cream," said the fat man.

"Well, gimme a fish sandwich then," Sandy replied, feeling very proud because
some kids were standing near, looking at him as he made his purchase like a grown
man.

"Buy me one, too," suggested a biscuit-colored little girl in a frilly dirty-white
dress.

"I only got a dime," Sandy said. "But you can have half of mine." And he
gallantly broke in two parts the double square of thick bread, with its hunk of
greasy fish between, and gravely handed a portion to the grinning little girl.

"Thanks," she said, running away with the bread and fish in her hands.

"Shame on you!" teased a small boy, rubbing his forefingers at Sandy. "You got
a girl! You got a girl!"

"Go chase yourself!" Sandy replied casually, as he picked out the bones and
smacked his lips on the sweet fried fish. The orchestra was playing another one-
step, with the dancers going like shuttles across the floor. Sandy saw his Aunt
Harriett and a slender yellow boy named Billy Sanderlee doing a series of lazy,

intricate steps as they wound through the crowd from one end of the hall to the other. Certain less accomplished couples were watching them with admiration.

Sandy, when he had finished eating, decided to look for the wash-room, where he could rinse his hands, because they were greasy and smelled fishy. It was at the far corner of the hall. As he pushed open the door marked GENTS, a thick grey cloud of cigarette-smoke drifted out. The stench of urine and gin and a crowd of men talking, swearing, and drinking licker surrounded the little boy as he elbowed his way towards the wash-bowls. All the fellows were shouting loudly to one another and making fleshy remarks about the women they had danced with.

"Boy, you ought to try Velma," a mahogany-brown boy yelled. "She sure can go."

"Hell," answered a whisky voice somewhere in the smoke. "That nappy-headed black woman? Gimme a high yaller for mine all de time. I can't use no coal!"

"Well, de blacker de berry, de sweeter de juice," protested a slick-haired ebony youth in the center of the place. . . . "Ain't that right, sport?" he demanded of Sandy, grabbing him jokingly by the neck and picking him up.

"I guess it is," said the child, scared, and the men laughed.

"Here, kid, buy yourself a drink," the slick-headed boy said, slipping Sandy a nickel as he set him down gently at the door. "And be sure it's pop—not gin."

Outside, the youngster dried his wet hands on a handkerchief, blinked his smoky eyes, and immediately bought the soda, a red strawberry liquid in a long, thick bottle.

Suddenly and without warning the cornet blared at the other end of the hall in an ear-splitting wail: "Whaw! . . . Whaw! . . . Whaw! . . . Whaw!" and the snare-drum rolled in answer. A pause . . . then the loud brassy notes were repeated and the banjo came in, "Plinka, plink, plink," like timid drops of rain after a terrific crash of thunder. Then quite casually, as though nothing had happened, the piano lazied into a slow drag, with all the other instruments following. And with the utmost nonchalance the drummer struck into time.

"Ever'body shake!" cried Benbow, as a ribbon of laughter swirled round the hall.

Couples began to sway languidly, melting together like candy in the sun as hips rotated effortlessly to the music. Girls snuggled pomaded heads on men's chests, or rested powdered chins on men's shoulders, while wild young boys put both arms tightly around their partners' waists and let their hands hang down carelessly over female haunches. Bodies moved ever so easily together—ever so easily, as Benbow turned towards his musicians and cried through cupped hands: "Aw, screech it, boys!"

A long, tall, gangling gal stepped back from her partner, adjusted her hips, and did a few easy, gliding steps all her own before her man grabbed her again.

"Eu-o-oo-ooo-oooo!" moaned the cornet titillating with pain, as the banjo cried in stop-time, and the piano sobbed aloud with a rhythmical, secret passion. But the drums kept up their hard steady laughter—like somebody who don't care.

"I see you plowin', Uncle Walt," called a little autumn-leaf brown with switching skirts to a dark-purple man grinding down the center of the floor with a yellow woman. Two short prancing blacks stopped in their tracks to quiver violently. A bushy-headed girl threw out her arms, snapped her fingers, and began to holler: "Hey! . . . Hey!" while her perspiring partner held doggedly to each hip in an effort to keep up with her. All over the hall, people danced their own individual movements to the scream and moan of the music.

"Get low . . . low down . . . down!" cried the drummer, bouncing like a rubber ball in his chair. The banjo scolded in diabolic glee, and the cornet panted as though it were out of breath, and Benbow himself left the band and came out on the floor to dance slowly and ecstatically with a large Indian-brown woman covered with diamonds.

"Aw, do it, Mister Benbow!" one of his admirers shouted frenziedly as the hall itself seemed to tremble.

"High yallers, draw nigh! Brown-skins, come near!" somebody squalled. "But black gals, stay where you are!"

"Whaw! Whaw! Whaw!" mocked the cornet—but the steady tomtom of the drums was no longer laughter now, no longer even pleasant: the drumbeats had become sharp with surly sound, like heavy waves that beat angrily on a granite rock. And under the dissolute spell of its own rhythm the music had got quite beyond itself. The four black men in Benbow's wandering band were exploring depths to which mere sound had no business to go. Cruel, desolate, unadorned was their music now, like the body of a ravished woman on the sun-baked earth; violent and hard, like a giant standing over his bleeding mate in the blazing sun. The odors of bodies, the stings of flesh, and the utter emptiness of soul when all is done—these things the piano and the drums, the cornet and the twanging banjo insisted on hoarsely to a beat that made the dancers move, in that little hall, like pawns on a frenetic checker-board.

"Aw, play it, Mister Benbow!" somebody cried.

The earth rolls relentlessly, and the sun blazes for ever on the earth, breeding, breeding. But why do you insist like the earth, music? Rolling and breeding, earth and sun for ever, relentlessly. But why do you insist like the sun? Like the lips of women? Like the bodies of men, relentlessly?

"Aw, play it, Mister Benbow!"

But why do you insist, music?

Who understands the earth? Do you, Mingo? Who understands the sun? Do you, Harriett? Does anybody know—among you high yallers, you jelly-beans, you pinks and pretty daddies, among you sealskin browns, smooth blacks, and chocolates-to-the-bone—does anybody know the answer?

"Aw, play it, Benbow!"

"It's midnight. De clock is strikin' twelve, an' . . ."
"Aw, play it, Mister Benbow!"

During intermission, when the members of the band stopped making music to drink gin and talk to women, Harriett and Mingo bought Sandy a box of cracker-jacks and another bottle of soda and left him standing in the middle of the floor holding both. His young aunt had forgotten time, so Sandy decided to go upstairs to the narrow unused balcony that ran the length of one side of the place. It was dusty up there, but a few broken chairs stood near the railing and he sat on one of them. He leaned his arms on the banister, rested his chin in his hands, and when the music started, he looked down on the mass of moving couples crowding the floor. He had a clear view of the energetic little black drummer eagle-rocking with staccato regularity in his chair as his long, thin sticks descended upon the tightly drawn skin of his small drum, while his foot patted the pedal of his big bass-drum, on which was painted in large red letters: "BENBOW'S FAMOUS KANSAS CITY BAND."

As the slow shuffle gained in intensity (and his cracker-jacks gave out), Sandy looked down drowsily on the men and women, the boys and girls, circling and turning beneath him. Dresses and suits of all shades and colors, and a vast confusion of bushy heads on swaying bodies. Faces gleaming like circus balloons—lemon-yellow, coal-black, powder-grey, ebony-black, blue-black faces; chocolate, brown, orange, tan, creamy-gold faces—the room full of floating balloon faces—Sandy's eyes were beginning to blur with sleep—colored balloons with strings, and the music pulling the strings. No! Girls pulling the strings—each boy a balloon by a string. Each face a balloon.

Sandy put his head down on the dusty railing of the gallery. An odor of hair-oil and fish, of women and sweat came up to him as he sat there alone, tired and a little sick. It was very warm and close, and the room was full of chatter during the intervals. Sandy struggled against sleep, but his eyes were just about to close when, with a burst of hopeless sadness, the *St. Louis Blues* spread itself like a bitter syrup over the hall. For a moment the boy opened his eyes to the drowsy flow of sound, long enough to pull two chairs together; then he lay down on them and closed his eyes again. Somebody was singing:

St. Louis woman with her diamond rings . . .

as the band said very weary things in a loud and brassy manner and the dancers moved in a dream that seemed to have forgotten itself:

Got ma man tied to her apron-strings . . .

Wah! Wah! Wah! . . . The cornet laughed with terrible rudeness. Then the drums began to giggle and the banjo whined an insulting leer. The piano said, over and over again: "St. Louis! That big old dirty town where the Mississippi's deep and wide, deep and wide . . ." and the hips of the dancers rolled.

Man's got a heart like a rock cast in de sea . . .

while the cynical banjo covered unplumbable depths with a plinking surface of staccato gaiety, like the sparkling bubbles that rise on deep water over a man who has just drowned himself:

Or else he never would a gone so far from me . . .

then the band stopped with a long-drawn-out wail from the cornet and a flippant little laugh from the drums.

A great burst of applause swept over the room, and the musicians immediately began to play again. This time just blues, not the *St. Louis,* nor the *Memphis,* nor the *Yellow Dog*—but just the plain old familiar blues, heart-breaking and extravagant, ma-baby's-gone-from-me blues.

Nobody thought about anyone else then. Bodies sweatily close, arms locked, cheek to cheek, breast to breast, couples rocked to the pulse-like beat of the rhythm, yet quite oblivious each person of the other. It was true that men and women were dancing together, but their feet had gone down through the floor into the earth, each dancer's alone—down into the center of things—and their minds had gone off to the heart of loneliness, where they didn't even hear the words, the sometimes lying, sometimes laughing words that Benbow, leaning on the piano, was singing against this background of utterly despondent music:

When de blues is got you,
Ain't no use to run away.
When de blue-blues got you,
Ain't no use to run away,
'Cause de blues is like a woman
That can turn yo' good hair grey.

Umn-ump! . . . Umn! . . . Umn-ump!

Well, I tole ma baby,
Says baby, baby, babe, be mine,
But ma baby was deceitful.
She must a thought that I was blind.

De-da! De-da! . . . De da! De da! Dee!

O, Lawdy, Lawdy, Lawdy,
Lawdy, Lawdy, Lawd . . . Lawd . . . Lawd!
She quit me fo' a Texas gambler,
So I had to git another broad.

Whaw-whaw! . . . Whaw-whaw-whaw! As though the laughter of a cornet could reach the heart of loneliness.

These mean old weary blues coming from a little orchestra of four men who needed no written music because they couldn't have read it. Four men and a leader—Rattle Benbow from Galveston; Benbow's buddy, the drummer, from Houston; his banjoist from Birmingham; his cornetist from Atlanta; and the pianist, long-fingered, sissyfied, a coal-black lad from New Orleans who had brought with him an exaggerated rag-time which he called jazz.

"I'm jazzin' it, creepers!" he sometimes yelled as he rolled his eyes towards the dancers and let his fingers beat the keys to a frenzy. . . . But now the piano was cryin' the blues!

Four homeless, plug-ugly niggers, that's all they were, playing mean old loveless blues in a hot, crowded little dance-hall in a Kansas town on Friday night. Playing the heart out of loneliness with a wide-mouthed leader, who sang everybody's troubles until they became his own. The improvising piano, the whanging banjo, the throbbing bass-drum, the hard-hearted little snare-drum, the brassy cornet that laughed, "Whaw-whaw-whaw. . . . Whaw!" were the waves in this lonesome sea of harmony from which Benbow's melancholy voice rose:

> *You gonna wake up some mawnin'*
> *An' turn yo' smilin' face.*
> *Wake up some early mawnin',*
> *Says turn yo' smilin' face,*
> *Look at yo' sweetie's pillow—*
> *An' find an' empty place!*

Then the music whipped itself into a slow fury, an awkward, elemental, foot-stamping fury, with the banjo running terrifiedly away in a windy moan and then coming back again, with the cornet wailing like a woman who don't know what it's all about:

> *Then you gonna call yo' baby,*
> *Call yo' lovin' baby dear—*
> *But you can keep on callin',*
> *'Cause I won't be here!*

And for a moment nothing was heard save the shuf-shuf-shuffle of feet and the immense booming of the bass-drum like a living vein pulsing at the heart of loneliness.

"Sandy! . . . Sandy! . . . My stars! Where is that child? . . . Has anybody seen my little nephew?" All over the hall. . . . "Sandy! . . . Oh-o-o, Lord!" Finally, with a sigh of relief: "You little brat, darn you, hiding up here in the balcony where nobody could find you! . . . Sandy, wake up! It's past four o'clock and I'll get killed."

Harriett vigorously shook the sleeping child, who lay stretched on the dusty chairs; then she began to drag him down the narrow steps before he was scarcely awake. The hall was almost empty and the chubby little black drummer was waddling across the floor carrying his drums in canvas cases. Someone was switching off the lights one by one. A mustard-colored man stood near the door quarrelling with a black woman. She began to cry and he slapped her full in the mouth, then turned his back and left with another girl of maple-sugar brown. Harriett jerked Sandy past this linked couple and pulled the boy down the long flight of stairs into the street, where Mingo stood waiting, with a lighted cigarette making a white line against his black skin.

"You getter git a move on," he said. "Daylight ain't holdin' itself back for you!" And he told the truth, for the night had already begun to pale.

Sandy felt sick at the stomach. To be awakened precipitately made him cross and ill-humored, but the fresh, cool air soon caused him to feel less sleepy and not quite so ill. He took a deep breath as he trotted rapidly along on the sidewalk beside his striding aunt and her boy friend. He watched the blue-grey dawn blot out the night in the sky; and then pearl-grey blot out the blue, while the stars faded to points of dying fire. And he listened to the birds chirping and trilling in the trees as though they were calling the sun. Then, as he became fully awake, the child began to feel very proud of himself, for this was the first time he had ever been away from home all night.

Harriett was fussing with Mingo. "You shouldn't've kept me out like that," she said. "Why didn't you tell me what time it was? . . . I didn't know."

And Mingo came back: "Hey, didn't I try to drag you away at midnight and you wouldn't come? And ain't I called you at one o'clock and you said: 'Wait a minute'—dancin' with some yaller P. I. from St. Joe, with your arms round his neck like a life-preserver? . . . Don't tell me I didn't want to leave, and me got to go to work at eight o'clock this mornin' with a pick and shovel when the whistle blows! What de hell?"

But Harriett did not care to quarrel now when there would be no time to finish it properly. She was out of breath from hurrying and almost in tears. She was afraid to go home.

"Mingo, I'm scared."

"Well, you know what you can do if your ma puts you out," her escort said quickly, forgetting his anger. "I can take care of you. We could get married."

"Could we, Mingo?"

"Sure!"

She slipped her hand in his. "Aw, daddy!" and the pace became much less hurried.

When they reached the corner near which Harriett lived, she lifted her dark little purple-powdered face for a not very lingering kiss and sent Mingo on his way. Then she frowned anxiously and ran on. The sky was a pale pearly color, waiting for the warm gold of the rising sun.

"I'm scared to death!" said Harriett. "Lord, Sandy, I hope ma ain't up! I hope she didn't come home last night from Mis' Lane's. We shouldn't've gone, Sandy . . . I guess we shouldn't've gone." She was breathing hard and Sandy had to run fast to keep up with her. "Gee, I'm scared!"

The grass was diamond-like with dew, and the red bricks of the sidewalk were damp, as the small boy and his young aunt hurried under the leafy elms along the walk. They passed Madam de Carter's house and cut through the wet grass into their own yard as the first rays of the morning sun sifted through the trees. Quietly they tiptoed towards the porch; quickly and quietly they crossed it; and softly, ever so softly, they opened the parlor door.

In the early dusk the oil-lamp still burned on the front-room table, and in an old arm-chair, with the open Bible on her lap, sat Aunt Hager Williams, a bundle of switches on the floor at her feet.

Carnival (1930)

Between the tent of Christ and the tents of sin there stretched scarcely a half-mile. Rivalry reigned: the revival and the carnival held sway in Stanton at the same time. Both were at the south edge of town, and both were loud and musical in their activities. In a dirty white tent in the Hickory Woods the Reverend Duke Braswell conducted the services of the Lord for the annual summer tent-meeting of the First Ethiopian Baptist Church. And in Jed Galoway's meadow lots Swank's Combined Shows, the World's Greatest Midway Carnival, had spread canvas for seven days of bunko games and cheap attractions. The old Negroes went to the revival, and the young Negroes went to the carnival, and after sundown these August evenings the mourning songs of the Christians could be heard rising from the Hickory Woods while the profound syncopation of the minstrel band blared from Galoway's Lots, strangely intermingling their notes of praise and joy.

Aunt Hager with Annjee and Sandy went to the revival every night (Sandy unwillingly), while Jimboy, Harriett, and Maudel went to the carnival. Aunt Hager prayed for her youngest daughter at the meetings, but Harriett had not spoken to her mother, if she could avoid it, since the morning after the dance, when she had been whipped. Since their return from the country Annjee and Jimboy were not so loving towards each other, either, as they had been before. Jimboy tired of Jessie's farm, so he came back to town three days before his wife returned. And now the revival and the carnival widened the breach between the Christians and the sinners in Aunt Hager's little household. And Sandy would rather have been with the sinners—Jimboy and Harriett—but he wasn't old enough; so he had to go to meetings until, on Thursday morning, when he and Buster were climbing over the coal-shed in the back yard, Sandy accidentally jumped down on a rusty nail, which penetrated the heel of his bare foot. He set up a wail, cried until noon over the pain, and refused to eat any dinner; so finally Jimboy said that if he would only hush hollering he'd take him to the carnival that evening.

"Yes, take de rascal," said Aunt Hager. "He ain't doin' no good at de services, wiggling and squirming so's we can't hardly hear de sermon. He ain't got religion in his heart, that chile!"

"I hope he ain't," said his father, yawning.

"All you wants him to be is a good-fo'-nothin' rounder like you is," retorted Hager. And she and Jimboy began their daily quarrel, which lasted for hours, each of them enjoying it immensely. But Sandy kept pulling at his father and saying: "Hurry up and let's go," although he knew well that nothing really started at the carnival until sundown. Nevertheless, about four o'clock, Jimboy said: "All right, come on," and they started out in the hot sun towards Galoway's Lots, the man walking tall and easy while the boy hobbled along on his sore foot, a rag tied about his heel.

At the old cross-bar gate on the edge of town, through which Jed Galoway drove his cows to pasture, there had been erected a portable arch strung with electric lights spelling out "SWANK'S SHOWS" in red and yellow letters, but it was not very impressive in the day-time, with the sun blazing on it, and no people about. And from this gate, extending the whole length of the meadow on either side, like a roadway, were the tents and booths of the carnival: the Galatea illusion, the seal and sea-lion circus, the Broadway musical-comedy show, the freaks, the games of chance, the pop-corn- and lemonade-stands, the colored minstrels, the merry-go-round, the fun house, the hoochie-coochie, the Ferris wheel, and, at the far end, a canvas tank under a tiny platform high in the air from which the World's Most Dangerous and Spectacular High Dive took place nightly at ten-thirty.

"We gonna stay to see that, ain't we, papa?" Sandy asked.

"Sure," said Jimboy. "But didn't I tell you there wouldn't be nothin' runnin' this early in the afternoon? See! Not even the band playin', and ain't a thing open but the freak-show and I'll bet all the freaks asleep." But he bought Sandy a bag of peanuts and planked down twenty cents for two tickets into the sultry tent where a perspiring fat woman and a tame-looking wild-man were the only attractions to be found on the platforms. The sword-swallower was not yet at work, nor the electric marvel, nor the human glass-eater. The terrific sun beat fiercely through the canvas on this exhibit of two lone human abnormalities, and the few spectators in the tent kept wiping their faces with their handkerchiefs.

Jimboy struck up a conversation with the Fat Woman, a pink and white creature who said she lived in Columbus, Ohio; and when Jimboy said he'd been there, she was interested. She said she had always lived right next door to colored people at home, and she gave Sandy a postcard picture of herself for nothing, although it had "10¢" marked on the back. She kept saying she didn't see how anybody could stay in Kansas and it a dry state where a soul couldn't even get beer except from a bootlegger.

When Sandy and his father came out, they left the row of tents and went across the meadow to a clump of big shade-trees beneath which several colored men who worked with the show were sitting. A blanket had been spread on the grass, and a crap game was going on to the accompaniment of much arguing and good-natured cussing. But most of the men were just sitting around not playing, and one or two were stretched flat on their faces, asleep. Jimboy seemed to know several of the fellows, so he joined in their talk while Sandy watched the dice roll for a while, but since the boy didn't understand the game, he decided to go back to the tents.

"All right, go ahead," said his father. "I'll pick you up later when the lights are lit and things get started; then we can go in the shows."

Sandy limped off, walking on the toe of his injured foot. In front of the sea-lion circus he found Earl James, a little white boy in his grade at school; the two of them went around together for a while, looking at the large painted canvas pictures in front of the shows or else lying on their stomachs on the ground to peep under the tents. When they reached the minstrel-show tent near the end of the midway, they heard a piano tinkling within and the sound of hands clapping as though someone was dancing.

"Jeezus! Let's see this," Earl cried, so the two boys got down on their bellies, wriggled under the flap of the tent on one side, and looked in.

A battered upright piano stood on the ground in front of the stage, and a fat, bald-headed Negro was beating out a rag. A big white man in a checkered vest was leaning against the piano, derby on head, and a long cigar stuck in his mouth. He was watching a slim black girl, with skirts held high and head thrown back, prancing in a mad circle of crazy steps. Two big colored boys in red uniforms were patting time, while another girl sat on a box, her back towards the peeping youngsters staring up from under the edge of the tent. As the girl who was dancing whirled about, Sandy saw that it was Harriett.

"Pretty good, ain't she, boss?" yelled the wrinkle-necked Negro at the piano as he pounded away.

The white man nodded and kept his eyes on Harriett's legs. The two black boys patting time were grinning from ear to ear.

"Do it, Miss Mama!" one of them shouted as Harriett began to sashay gracefully.

Finally she stopped, panting and perspiring, with her lips smiling and her eyes sparkling gaily. Then she went with the white man and the colored piano-player behind the canvas curtains to the stage. One of the show-boys put his arms around the girl sitting on the box and began tentatively to feel her breasts.

"Don't be so fresh, hot papa," she said. And Sandy recognized Maudel's voice, and saw her brown face as she leaned back to look at the show-man. The boy in the red suit bent over and kissed her several times, while the other fellow kept imitating the steps he had just seen Harriett performing.

"Let's go," Earl said to Sandy, rolling over on the ground. The two small boys went on to the next tent, where one of the carnival men caught them, kicked their behinds soundly, and sent them away.

The sun was setting in a pink haze, and the show-grounds began to take on an air of activity. The steam calliope gave a few trial hoots, and the merry-go-round circled slowly without passengers, the paddle-wheels and the get-'em-hot men, the lemonade-sellers and the souvenir-vendors were opening their booths to the evening trade. A barker began to ballyhoo in front of the freak-show. By and by there would be a crowd. The lights came on along the Midway, the Ferris wheel swept languidly up into the air, and when Sandy found his father, the colored band had begun to play in front of the minstrel show.

"I want to ride on the merry-go-round," Sandy insisted. "And go in the Crazy House." So they did both; then they bought hamburger sandwiches with thick slices of white onion and drank strawberry soda and ate pop-corn with butter on it. They went to the sea-lion circus, tried to win a Kewpie doll at the paddle-wheel booth, and watched men losing money on the hidden pea, then trying to win it back at four-card monte behind the Galatea attraction. And all the while Sandy said nothing to his father about having seen Harriett dancing in the minstrel tent that afternoon.

Sandy had lived too long with three women not to have learned to hold his tongue about the private doings of each of them. When Annjee paid two dollars a week on a blue silk shirt for his father at Cohn's cut-rate credit store, and Sandy saw her make the payments, he knew without being told that the matter was never to be mentioned to Aunt Hager. And if his grandmother sometimes threw Harriett's rouge out in the alley, Sandy saw it with his eyes, but not with his mouth. Because he loved all three of them—Harriett and Annjee and Hager—he didn't carry tales on any one of them to the others. Nobody would know he had watched his Aunt Harrie dancing on the carnival lot today in front of a big fat white man in a checkered vest while a Negro in a red suit played the piano.

"We got a half-dollar left for the minstrel show," said Jimboy. "Come on, let's go." And he pulled his son through the crowd that jammed the long Midway between the booths.

All the bright lights of the carnival were on now, and everything was running full blast. The merry-go-round whirled to the ear-splitting hoots of the calliope; bands blared; the canvas paintings of snakes and dancing-girls, human skeletons, fire-eaters, billowed in the evening breeze; pennants flapped, barkers shouted, acrobats twirled in front of a tent; a huge paddle-wheel clicked out numbers. Folks pushed and shoved and women called to their children not to get lost. In the air one smelled the scent of trampled grass, peanuts, and hot dogs, animals and human bodies.

The large white man in the checkered vest was making the ballyhoo in front of the minstrel show, his expansive belly turned towards the crowd that had been attracted by the band. One hand pointed towards a tawdry group of hard-looking Negro performers standing on the platform.

"Here we have, ladies and gents, Madam Caledonia Watson, the Dixie songbird; Dancing Jenkins, the dark strutter from Jacksonville; little Lizzie Roach, champeen coon-shouter of Georgia; and last, but not least, Sambo and Rastus, the world's funniest comedians. Last performance this evening! . . . Strike her up, perfesser! . . . Come along, now, folks!"

The band burst into sound, Madam Watson and Lizzie Roach opened their brass-lined throats, the men dropped into a momentary clog-dance, and then the whole crowd of performers disappeared into the tent. The ticket-purchasing townspeople followed through the public opening beneath a gaudily painted sign picturing a Mississippi steamboat in the moonlight, and two black bucks shooting gigantic dice on a street-corner.

Jimboy and Sandy followed the band inside and took seats, and soon the frayed curtain rose, showing a plantation scene in the South, where three men, blackened up, and two women in bandannas sang longingly about Dixie. Then Sambo and Rastus came out with long wooden razors and began to argue and shoot dice, but presently the lights went out and a ghost appeared and frightened the two men away, causing them to leave all the money on the stage. (The audience thought it screamingly funny—and just like niggers.) After that one of the women sang a ragtime song and did the eagle-rock. Then a man with a banjo in his hands began to play, but until then the show had been lifeless.

"Listen to him," Jimboy said, punching Sandy. "He's good!"

The piece he was picking was full of intricate runs and trills long drawn out, then suddenly slipping into tantalizing rhythms. It ended with a vibrant whang!—and the audience yelled for more. As an encore he played a blues and sang innumerable verses, always ending:

An' Ah can't be satisfied,
'Cause all Ah love has
Done laid down an' died.

And to Sandy it seemed like the saddest music in the world—but the white people around him laughed.

Then the stage lights went on, the band blared, and all the black actors came trooping back, clapping their hands before the cotton-field curtain as each one in turn danced like fury, vigorously distorting agile limbs into the most amazing positions, while the scene ended with the fattest mammy and the oldest uncle shaking jazzily together.

The booths were all putting out their lights as the people poured through the gate towards town. Sandy hobbled down the road beside his father, his sore heel, which had been forgotten all evening, paining him terribly until Jimboy picked him up and carried him on his shoulder. Automobiles and buggies whirled past them in clouds of gritty dust, and young boys calling vulgar words hurried after tittering girls. When Sandy and his father reached home, Aunt Hager and Annjee had not yet returned from the revival. Jimboy said he thought maybe they had stopped at Mrs. Lane's to sit up all night with the sick woman, so Sandy spread his pallet on the floor at the foot of his grandmother's bed and went to sleep. He did not hear his Aunt Harriett when she came home, but late in the night he woke up with his heel throbbing painfully, his throat dry, and his skin burning, and when he tried to bend his leg, it hurt him so that he began to cry.

Harriett, awakened by his moans, called drowsily: "What's the matter, honey?"

"My foot," said Sandy tearfully.

So his young aunt got out of bed, lit the lamp, and helped him to the kitchen, where she heated a kettle of water, bathed his heel, and covered the nail-wound with vaseline. Then she bound it with a fresh white rag.

"Now that ought to feel better," she said as she led him back to his pallet, and soon they were both asleep again.

The next morning when Hager came from the sick-bed of her friend, she sent to the butcher-shop for a bacon rind, cut from it a piece of fat meat, and bound it to Sandy's heel as a cure.

"Don't want you havin' de blood-pisen here," she said. "An' don't you run round an' play on that heel. Set out on de porch an' study yo' reader, 'cause school'll be startin' next month." Then she began Mrs. Reinhart's ironing.

The next day, Saturday, the last day of the carnival, Jimboy carried the Reinharts' clothes home for Hager, since Sandy was crippled and Jimmy Lane's mother was down in bed. But after delivering the clothes Jimboy did not come home for supper. When Annjee and Hager wanted to leave for the revival in the early evening, they asked Harriett if she would stay home with the little boy, for Sandy's heel had swollen purple where the rusty nail had penetrated and he could hardly walk at all.

"You been gone ever' night this week," Hager said to the girl. "An' you ain't been anear de holy tents where de Lawd's word is preached; so you ought to be willin' to stay home one night with a po' little sick boy."

"Yes'm," Harriett muttered in a noncommittal tone. But shortly after her mother and Annjee had gone, she said to her nephew: "You aren't afraid to stay home by yourself, are you?"

And Sandy answered: "Course not, Aunt Harrie."

She gave him a hot bath and put a new piece of fat meat on his festering heel. Then she told him to climb into Annjee's bed and go to sleep, but instead he lay for a long time looking out the window that was beside the bed. He thought about the carnival—the Ferris wheel sweeping up into the air, and the minstrel show. Then he remembered Benbow's dance a few weeks ago and how his Aunt Harriett had stood sullenly the next morning while Hager whipped her—and hadn't cried at all, until the welts came under her silk stockings. . . . Then he wondered what Jimmy Lane would do if his sick mother died from the т. в. and he were left with nobody to take care of him, because Jimmy's step-father was no good. . . . Eu-uuu! His heel hurt! . . . When school began again, he would be in the fifth grade, but he wished he'd hurry up and get to high school, like Harriet was. . . . When he got to be a man, he was going to be a railroad engineer. . . . Gee, he wasn't sleepy—and his heel throbbed painfully.

In the next room Harriett had lighted the oil-lamp and was moving swiftly about taking clothes from the dresser-drawers and spreading them on the bed. She thought Sandy was asleep, he knew—but he couldn't go to sleep the way his foot hurt him. He could see her through the doorway folding her dresses in little piles and he wondered why she was doing that. Then she took an old suit-case from the closet and began to pack it, and when it was full, she pulled a new bag from under the bed, and into it she dumped her toilet-articles, powder, vaseline, nail-polish, straightening comb, and several pairs of old stockings rolled in balls. Then she sat down on the bed between the two closed suit-cases for a long time with her hands in her lap and her eyes staring ahead of her.

Finally she rose and closed the bureau-drawers, tidied up the confusion she had created, and gathered together the discarded things she had thrown on the floor. Then Sandy heard her go out into the back yard towards the trash-pile. When she returned, she put on a tight little hat and went into the kitchen to wash her hands, throwing the water through the back door. Then she tip-toed into the room where Sandy was lying and kissed him gently on the head. Sandy knew that she thought he was asleep, but in spite of himself he suddenly threw his arms tightly around her neck. He couldn't help it.

"Where you going, Aunt Harriett?" he said, sitting up in bed, clutching the girl.

"Honey, you won't tell on me, will you?" Harriett asked.

"No," he answered, and she knew he wouldn't. "But where are you going, Aunt Harrie?"

"You won't be afraid to stay here until grandma comes?"

"No," burying his face on her breast. "I won't be afraid."

"And you won't forget Aunt Harrie?"

"Course not."

"I'm leaving with the carnival," she told him.

For a moment they sat close together on the bed. Then she kissed him, went into the other room and picked up her suit-cases—and the door closed.

Further Reading

The Best of Simple. 1961.

The Big Sea: An Autobiography. 1940.

The Collected Poems of Langston Hughes. 1996.

Fine Clothes for the Jew. 1927.

Langston Hughes and the Chicago Defender: Essays on Race, Politics and Culture, 1942–1962.
    1995.

The Langston Hughes Reader. 1958.
Laughing to Keep from Crying. 1952.
Selected Poems of Langston Hughes. 1958.
Tambourines to Glory. 1958.
The Ways of White Folks. 1934.
The Weary Blues. 1925.

Reading about Langston Hughes

Berry, Faith. *Langston Hughes, Before and Beyond Harlem.* Westport CT: L. Hill, 1983.

Emmanuel, James A. *Langston Hughes.* New York: Twayne, 1967.

Gates, Henry Louis Jr., and K. A. Appiah, eds. *Langston Hughes: Perspective Past and Present.* New York: Penguin, 1993.

Rampersad, Arnold. *The Life of Langston Hughes.* 2 vols. New York: Oxford University Press, 1986–88.

Trotman, C. James, and Emery Wimbish, eds. *Langston Hughes: The Man, His Art and His Continuing Influence.* New York: Garland, 1995.

Walker, Alice. *Langston Hughes, An American Poet.* New York: Crowell, 1974.

Larry Woiwode (b. 1941)

This story is about the accumulations of place and time: after so many generations have existed in a place and each new inhabitant has piled on overlays of other histories, the origins of a place—a house—are lost unless someone finds a link, some *thing* to reconnect past time with place. And then, the past may overwhelm the present.

Larry Woiwode is a contemporary chronicler of Great Plains family life. In *Beyond the Bedroom Wall* he traces Martin Neumiller's family in their eastward migration from North Dakota to Illinois, then follows Martin's sons Jerome and Charles into adulthood in *Born Brothers*. Martin's wife, Alpha, like Rølvaag's Beret, becomes more and more detached from her family and the present with each move. In all of these works, including *The Neumiller Stories*, Woiwode suggests that without a firm attachment to a *home* place we become mere migrants without identity. It is this rootlessness that eventually defeats Alpha and her sons.

Woiwode was born in North Dakota and, like the Neumiller clan, moved to Illinois where he attended the University of Illinois. His career centers on his writing. He has been a professor, a writer in residence, and a workshop director. His work has gained a number of awards. Place, Woiwode has pointed out, is especially important to his writing. "I see nature, I see into it, and I see details of it. . . . And it's those details that seem to me to make up the substantiality of the world that my people move within." In "The Old Halvorson Place" this sense of place is evident in a house that, Woiwode explains, is "nature substantiated that each of us is always moving through."*

The Old Halvorson Place (1989)

A family of fourteen had lived in the house before the Neumillers. Their name was Russell. Mr. Russell, who was the sexton of St. Mary Margaret's Catholic Church and the janitor of the parochial school, had seven sons and five daughters ranging in age from eleven to thirty-six. Two of the sons were ordained into the priesthood and three of the daughters became nuns. One daughter was said to be an

---

*Larry Woiwode, "Interview," *Contemporary Authors: New Revision Series* vol. 16 (Detroit), 458.

accomplished musician and another had literary leanings, and together they composed the music and lyrics of the school song that is still sung in Hyatt, North Dakota.

Martin Neumiller, the principal of the high school, had been annoyed for years by the stilted words of the old song (sung to the tune of "On, Wisconsin!") and he persuaded the Russell girls to write the new one. It begins

We'll raise a lofty, mighty cheer for you,
Straight from the hearts of students fond and true

and its concluding lines are

Deep as the ocean, our love and devotion
For the Hy—! Hy—! Hyatt High School!

The parish owned the Russell house and everybody in the parish had expected the Russells to live out their lives in it, a monument to the faith. But one day old Mr. Russell went to Father Schimmelpfennig and said that he was giving up both jobs and moving out of town.

What?

He was grateful for all the parish had done for him, but he felt there were better opportunities in South Dakota for him and the children who remained at home.

Father Schimmelpfennig offered him the house rent-free.

Mr. Russell said he couldn't accept charity. Hyatt wasn't growing and would never grow, he felt, and he wanted to take advantage of the boom down at Rapid City, maybe even go into business for himself, and hoped the younger kids could attend bigger schools.

Two months later the Russells were gone. They were a cloistered, close-knit family, and other than the song, they left little trace of themselves behind when they moved. Father Schimmelpfennig let their house stand vacant for a year, as if he found it impossible to admit their absence, and then the Neumillers needed a place.

Martin Neumiller, who was devoted to home life and ambitious for his family, but without guile, nearly biblical in his purity of motive and character, was Father Schimmelpfennig's friend and confidant, and Martin had three bright, promising young sons.

The Neumillers had lived in several other houses in Hyatt, none of them satisfactory. One they rented from a widow, who continued to live on in a separate wing and promised to make herself "so scarce you won't know I'm here," but didn't. In another, the furnace never worked properly, and a smell that originated in one of the kitchen walls was amazing in its rankness. Rather than break into the wall of a house that didn't belong to them, they kept wondering, What could it be?

In their present house, the basement flooded to the floor joists in the spring (bringing up buried salamanders that went floating out into the yard), and the foundation eroded so badly several walls began to part from the ceiling. And all of these places had contained noisy populations of mice and rats, driven indoors by the bitter, drawn-out winters, and none of the houses had been large enough. At this time, the Neumillers' three sons—Jerome, Charles, and Timothy—were sharing the same room to sleep and play in, and although Jerome, the oldest, was only five, Alpha Neumiller was pregnant again.

There were ten rooms in the old Russell house—three bedrooms upstairs, plus a large attic, and three more bedrooms downstairs; a living room, with a big bay window, and a dining room; a kitchen; a pantry as large as the kitchen; a basement with vegetable bins and rows of shelves for canned food; an indoor bathroom (a rarity in Hyatt—there was no running water in the village and only the drains were plumbed in) with all of the fixtures; a front porch, with turned posts and gingerbread trim; an enclosed porch on the south side; and, attached to the rear of the house, a lean-to porch which had once been used to stable a pony and was now a coal shed. The rent was twenty-five dollars a month.

Alpha Neumiller was ecstatic. She pirouetted through the rooms of the empty house, saying, "The space, the space, the space!" And several months later, on Charles's fifth birthday, she leaned against a wall with her arms folded, smiling as she watched a dozen birthday guests play Red Rover—*Red Rover!*—in her living room. The room was so large that her upright piano, which had always been in the way, seemed to have shrunk three sizes. Her piano! She sat down and began playing "Clair de Lune," and all the children stopped their game and stared at her as she played.

Martin could appreciate the depth of her satisfaction; there were articles close to her heart, family heirlooms and wedding presents, that they hadn't unpacked since their marriage, and some of their furniture—a dining-room set with inlays of bird's-eye maple, a handmade gateleg table—had never been used. But around town and at the Friday-night pinochle games at Father Schimmelpfennig's, Martin was heard to say, "Sometimes I can't understand that woman. She loves the place, sure, how could she help it? But it's always been like this. The happiest times of her life are when we move."

Martin's father, who had settled in Illinois several years ago, was in North Dakota visiting relatives and friends, and he drove up to Hyatt to help them move. Somehow he got stuck with the job of bringing in the basement things, and toward the end of the day he turned to Alpha with a solemn face and said, "I've carried nine hundred and ninety-nine empty fruit jars down these stairs." He was a building contractor. He made minor repairs around the house, and persuaded Martin to pour a concrete slab that began at the outside wall of the lean-to, went in a curve around the corner of the house, past the enclosed porch, and abutted against the bay window. It was a full day's work for five men, excluding Martin and his father, and when the slab was finally poured, and Martin's father had finished troweling it by the light of a floor lamp Martin held above him, he said, "There. Now the boys have a place to ride their tricycles."

While they were still getting settled into the house, Martin took Jerome and Charles upstairs and led them into a room overlooking the street corner. Against one wall was an enormous rolltop desk of oak. "Look!" Martin said, and turned to them as though offering a gift. The boys looked at one another with questioning frowns, and Jerome shrugged. "Well, don't you see what's happened here?" Martin asked.

They didn't see.

"First of all, you can tell by looking that it couldn't have come up by the stairs. They're too narrow. The door to this room is even narrower than the stairway, and the windows are narrower yet."

He squatted at the desk and rapped on it with a knuckle. "That's solid oak, you hear? The corners have been dovetailed and then trimmed over. You can feel the dovetailing here in the back. Right here. Now, nobody could take this apart, once it was built, without damaging the wood somewhere—especially where it's dovetailed—and they certainly would have left a mark on the finish. But the finish is practically perfect—the original, I'd guess. Isn't it beautiful?"

They nodded, impatient to get their own hands on that feathery dovetail stuff.

"There's only one possibility," Martin said, and smiled at them in conclusion. "When this place was built, an elderly cabinetmaker came to the house, carried his hand tools and materials up to this room, and built this desk on the spot where we're standing. But why? Why would anybody want to build a desk way up here?"

Mysteries, for Martin, were a source of delight; there was nothing unnatural about them, as he saw it. They were a major ingredient of life, meant to be explored and marveled at, but never feared, and seldom explained. Where others overlooked mystery, he could find it, and this kept him in a state of childlike wonder, exuberance, and joy.

Alpha was surprised that the interior of the house wasn't more beat up. From the outside it appeared that it would be; paint was flaking from the second story, the roof of the lean-to was beginning to sag, and the hedge that bordered the yard on three sides had been allowed to grow to a height of seven feet. But Martin's father said that the house was structurally sound, surprisingly so, and the interior was in excellent condition, even though fourteen people had lived in the place for a decade.

The hardwood floors didn't need refinishing. The baseboards at toe level were battered, but otherwise the original oak woodwork, the sliding oak doors to the master bedroom, the turned posts beneath the oak banister leading upstairs, the bookshelves around the bottom of the bay window, also of oak, had hardly a scratch on them. And there were no ink stains or adolescent carvings on the rolltop desk.

The Russells had even left a new-looking chair at the desk. The Neumillers couldn't understand why, unless it had been standing there when the Russells moved in, because the Russells left nothing else behind to provide a clue to their life in the house—no old receipts, letters, or notes, not one stray sock in the bottom of a closet, not even a drawing or a set of initials on the walls, or, as Alpha put it, "not a speck of themselves or their dirt."

The attic, however, was packed with valuables, so layered with dust it looked as though the Russells had never touched them. Was it because they belonged to the family that had built the house and lived there originally, the Halvorsons? Their name was everywhere in the attic, on the backs of daguerreotypes and photographs, in the flyleaves of books, underneath chair seats; even written, along with a set of measurements, across the bosom of an old dress form.

In a large and decaying leather-bound volume, *A Century End History and Biography of North Dakota*, Martin found an engraving of a daguerreotype of Mrs. Halvorson, a twin to another picture of him in the attic, along with this information:

ALVARD J. HALVORSON. This gentleman, of whom a portrait will be found on the opposite page, occupies a prominent position as a real-estate dealer in Hyatt, Leeds County. To his influence is due much of the solid prosperity of Leeds and Ecklund Counties.

Our subject was born in Hamlin Township, Michigan, Aug. 1, 1839, and was the only son of Selmer and Dora (Waldorf) Halvorson, the former of Scandinavian and the latter of German descent. Mr. Halvorson was raised on his father's farm and attended country schools and at the age of nineteen went to Indianapolis, Indiana, in company with his father and later was engaged in business and also in farming with his father in Indiana for about twenty years.

Our subject moved to Valley City, North Dakota, in the fall of 1879 and became interested in Leeds County lands in 1881, since which time A. J. HALVORSON CO. has added as much as perhaps any other firm in the development of the possibilities of the agricultural and stock-raising interests of North Dakota, and he now conducts an extensive real-estate business in Hyatt, where the family located in 1895, two years after the founding of Hyatt.

Our subject was married at Indianapolis, Indiana, in 1865, to Miss Catherine Maxwell, who is of Scottish descent. Mr. and Mrs. Halvorson are the parents of three children, who bear the following names: Olivia C., Alice N., and Lydia. The two older children were born in Indiana and the last named in North Dakota. Politically, Mr. Halvorson is a Republican and has taken a highly active part in affairs pertaining to local government.

Nobody living in Hyatt at present could remember the Halvorsons, much less say why they'd moved and left so much behind. This fascinated Martin. He went to the library in the county seat, McCallister, and conducted his own research in the record books there. He didn't find many allusions to Mr. Halvorson, but he discovered how it was possible for the Halvorson family to be forgotten; the village had changed that much.

It was plotted by Richard Hyatt, an English lord, and began as a settlement of wealthy and cultivated Englishmen and Scots (one of whom constructed an artificial lake and a nine-hole golf course at the edge of town), and then it turned into a trading center for the German and Scandinavian and Irish immigrants who homesteaded in the area, and for a while was the county seat. And finally, after the county building was hauled off by the tradesmen of a neighboring town in the dead of the night, and after suffering the effects of the Crash and the Great Depression, besides being missed by the main line of the railroad, it became what it was now—a poor village, largely German and Roman Catholic, with only the lake remaining as a reminder of its past. Its present population was two hundred and thirty-two. This figure Martin knew before he began his research; he'd taken the 1940 census.

Although several other families must have lived in the Neumillers' house since the time of the Halvorsons, it appeared that no one had touched the Halvorsons' belongings in the attic, as though to tamper with them or to remove them were to tamper with the heart of the house. Or perhaps their possessions had been so numerous (wasn't the desk theirs?) that people had merely taken what they wanted without much diminishing the original store. Martin, for instance, as he walked around the attic, said that when they left, if they ever did, he was going to take those candlesticks, that teapot, the horse collar there, and a wheelbarrowful of these books.

Alpha said that just to stand in the place made her temperature drop ten degrees, and she'd rather he left everything the way it was.

"But what about these?" he said, and held up a set of copper bowls with silver medallions on their handles. "These are collector's items."

"I have more bowls than I know what to do with already."

"What about a book? Wouldn't you like to read some of these books?"

"I would if I'd bought them." She picked up Timmy, who was putting fluffs of dust into a china commode, and started out the door.

"Let's have an auction," Jerome said. "Let's sell all this stuff and make a bunch of money." He and Charles were sorting through a stack of dusty phonograph records.

"Leave those alone," Alpha Neumiller said. "They're not yours. I don't want you two playing in this attic—ever, you understand? I'm going to keep the hook at the top of this door latched. I bet that's what Mrs. Russell did. You don't belong in here."

The boys turned to their father, who was rummaging through a round-topped trunk bound with leather straps, and Jerome asked if they could move this—he

rapped on an ancient Victrola with his knuckles—and the records into their playroom. The door was plenty big, Jerome said. Martin looked up, his eyes bright and
abstracted, unaware that Alpha had spoken, and said, "Sure. Why not? Let's get it
in there and see if it works."

The Victrola sat in a corner of the second-floor room designated as the boys'
playroom, near the door that led to the attic. It was such a tall machine they had to
stand on a stool to place records on the turntable. On the underside of its cover,
beveled like a coffin lid, *Lydia* had been scratched into the wood with something
sharp, and the name, foreign to them, seemed strangely appropriate there. No
needles had survived with the machine, so their father fashioned one from the end
of a safety pin. Among the old records from the attic, they found only one they
really liked; the rest, thick Edison records with hymns on them, they sailed out a
second-story window.

They played that same record over and over, in spite of the scratches on its
surface—years of them, layers of them—that made the metallic tenor sound as
though it came out of the center of a gale, and they never tired of hearing the man
sing about Sal, his maiden fair, singing Polly Wolly Doodle all the day, with her
curly eyes and her laughing hair . . .

They stood on the stool and worked the crank, staring at the name scratched on
the lid. "Fare thee well! Fare thee well!" the tenor sang. "Fare thee well, my fairy
fey!" And no matter how many times it rose up, tinny and frail from the ancient
grooves, the image of a grasshopper sitting on a railroad track (singing Polly Wolly
Doodle all the day) always made them get down, laughing, and roll around and
slap the floor in hysterics.

They had their own library in the playroom; they had clay, blocks, marbles, and
mallets, dominoes, Lincoln Logs, an electric train, and a handmade alphabet with
wooden characters five inches high which they kept in dull-green ammunition
boxes an uncle had brought back from the war. But none of these possessions were
of the same caliber of interest as the Victrola, and when they weren't playing it,
they spent their afternoons at the rolltop desk.

Their father had appropriated the desk. Here, he said, was where he intended
to sit when he wrote his book—a project he talked about often, especially after any
unusual or moving experience, or whenever he sat down and told them a story
from his past. He referred to the book simply as "the book of my life," and if he'd
been up in the room for the evening, Jerome and Charles would go to the desk the
next day, slide its slatted cover up, and search through its drawers and cubbyholes
for evidence of the book, in which they hoped to be included.

There was always a neat pile of white paper in the center of a green blotter,
with a pen and a bottle of ink, plus a bottle of ink eradicator, standing ready.
Next to the blotter was the large, leather-bound volume their father had found in
the attic. Searching through the pigeonholes of the desk, they found old letters,
scripts of dramatic and patriotic readings their father had performed in high

school and college, a rubber stamp that reproduced his high, tilted signature, a watch fob braided from his mother's hair, a broken pocket watch, some rocks from the Badlands, and a plastic tube they could look into and see a monument of stone and the inscription *Geographical Center of North America, Rugby, North Dakota.*

In one of the drawers was a half-filled box of flaky cigars with IT'S A BOY! printed on the cellophane wrappers, and in another a metal file that contained insurance policies, birth certificates (their own and their parents', too, which was unsettling), government savings bonds in their names (money!), and their father's baby book. In the center drawer were pens and pencils and a ream of that same white paper, which never seemed to diminish.

Once, they discovered this on the top sheet:

CHAPTER I
—*My father's influence on my life*
  (Mom's too)
CHAPTER II
—*The Depression Years*
CHAPTER III
—*I meet Alpha, my wife-to-be*
CHAPTER IV
  ?

Other than some notes to himself and a Christmas-card list, they never found anything else their father had written.

They could not resist the temptation of the attic, although they knew this upset their mother. She disliked the attic, disliked even more the idea of anybody's being in it (she never entered it herself), and was so adamant and humorless in her dislike that their father teased her by calling North Dakota "the cold-storage box way up at the top, the *attic* of the United States!"

They would put their record on the Victrola, move a stool over to the attic door, unlatch the hook, ease the door open, and step inside, and sunlight, coming through a pair of windows in the far wall, fell over them with a warmth sunlight had nowhere else. Old cobwebs powdered with dust, and shining filaments that spiders had recently strung in place, sparkled in its light, imparting a summer radiance to the air. The personal effects of the Halvorsons—the dress form, a brass bedstead, the boxes and trunks of memorabilia, a wooden wardrobe with a dress sword and sash hanging from its top, chairs, books, an oval mirror that held their reflections—stood around in solid eloquence.

Charles tiptoed over to a settee, upholstered in red velvet badly damaged by moths and nesting mice, and sat down. He bounced his weight on its springs. Who had sat here? What had they talked about? Had anybody cried on it, as he had on their couch? Or done a flip on it? He looked up at Jerome, who hadn't moved since they'd stepped into the attic.

The surrounding objects were as real and as awesome as a roomful of strangers, and more compelling; they belonged to a world removed not only by time—by half a century, as their father said—but by convention and law: the world of adults. Here they could handle and examine that world in every detail (and only through touch would it give up its mystery), without interference or protest, as they could not examine the world of their parents.

Since any wholehearted examination of the property of others was forbidden, they held back, hesitant, but all of the objects seemed to strain toward them, as if to give up their secrets. Jerome and Charles were not the only ones who sensed this. Only moments after they'd unhooked the door, they would hear, coming from the foot of the stairs, "Are you two into that attic again?"

"No!" they cried at the same time, a dead giveaway.

"You stay out of there when your father's not around! You hear?"

"We're not in here," Charles said.

"Don't lie to your mother"

They looked at one another, and then Jerome went over and began to examine the object that had held his attention, and Charles picked up a wooden doll with most of its limbs missing, while the dented and tattered dress form—composed of varnished strips of paper that were lifting up in orangy translucent curls—stood above them, as unmoving and silent as a second, more permissive mother.

Jerome studied a wooden box with wires and disklike electrodes dangling from it. Its lid swung open like a little door, and from what he could understand of the instructions, which were pasted on the inside of the lid, it was a device for giving shocks to the head and feet.

"Look at this," Charles said. He took a lace dress out of a trunk and held it in front of him. "This is what they wore then. What would you think if you saw somebody wearing it? What would you think if I was a girl?" He wrinkled up his nose and giggled like one.

"Quit it," Jerome said. "Put it back." He was more cautious than Charles, more like his mother, and a dress seemed too personal to disturb.

He picked up a candlestick and pictured the dining room in a different setting, at night, deep in shadow, with candle flames lighting the faces around a table, a sound of silver scraping on plates, the rustle of skirts, and then a man's voice, gentle as the candlelight, rising from the shadows: "I have decided—"

"Hey, look at this," Charles said. He'd slipped on the rusty jacket of an old suit of tails that was many sizes too large for him.

"Take it off," Jerome said. "Put it back."

"All right. But I'm going to take this." It was a book, *Children of the Garden*, that personified the common species of flowers, giving them human features and appendages and names such as Betsy Bluebell. "We'll keep it in the playroom."

"Oh, all right. But don't leave it where Mom'll see it."

Jerome went to a box that contained daguerreotypes and old, fading, tea-colored photographs. There were pictures of rural families lined up in front of farmhouses: the farmer, bearded or with long side-whiskers, often sitting in a kitchen chair; his wife, her hair pulled back, standing beside him in a long-sleeved black dress, apparently old enough to be the children's grandmother; and all of the children, even the babies, looked big-headed and mature.

There were pictures of houses they recognized, of Main Street as it had once been, with a horse and carriage parked in front of Reiland's Tavern, and several views of their own home. Jerome motioned Charles over, and with an air of solemnity pointed to a rear view of their house, placing his fingertip on the attic window.

There were pictures of the Halvorsons, with the subject's name, the year the portrait was taken, and the person's age at the time written in an artistic hand across the back of each.

"Look at this," Jerome said, and wiped his forearm across a picture. A plump man in muttonchop whiskers stared up at them with the sparkling eyes of an unrepentant roué. Jerome frowned. "It's Mr. Halvorson. Do you like the way he looks?"

"I don't know."

"I don't." Jerome shuffled through all the pictures of Mr. Halvorson and his wife, who was broad and square-jawed and looked enough like her husband to be his brother. Two of the daughters looked exactly like her. In a portrait of the third girl, however, Jerome saw what he had hoped to see in the rest of the family. She was reclining at one end of the settee, an open book in her lap, a finger placed along her cheek, her lower lip, with a shine on it, shoved out. Light-colored hair fell to her waist, and her dark eyes were staring off at a scene, apparently a heartbreaking one, in the distance.

"See," Jerome said, pointing to the lace dress she was wearing. "That was probably hers."

"What about it?"

"You shouldn't be messing around with it like that."

"Why?"

"If it was hers— You shouldn't, that's all. Look how pretty she is."

"Not anymore."

"What do you mean?"

"She's probably old and ugly by now."

Jerome turned the picture over: "Lydia, at the age of thirteen, in the year of our Lord 1901."

"See," Charles said. "That's even before Dad was born, and look how old he is. If she—"

But the girl had Jerome in her possession. He saw her running through the downstairs hall on a day as sunlit as this one, running up the steps, her hair streaming behind, and rushing into the playroom to the Victrola. He turned. His mother stood in the doorway, flushed and out of breath from climbing the stairs in her condition.

"What did I tell you two? Get out of here! Get out, get out, get out!"

In August, Alpha Neumiller gave birth to a daughter, whom she named Marie, after Martin's mother. Jerome and Charles were envious of the attention the girl received, and embarrassed by her. They spent more and more of their time outdoors. But Tim, who was constantly left out of their projects and play, would stand at Marie's bassinet with his hands clasped behind him, sometimes for an hour, as if she were his only hope. Martin was proud of her as only the father of a daughter can be proud, and Alpha, who had always wanted a girl, associated this stroke of good luck with the move into the house. Before the baby arrived, she had decorated a downstairs bedroom in pink and frills.

It was becoming Alpha's house. Over the first winter, she had closed off the upstairs to reduce the heating bills and her own work, but now it was open and a major piece of framework in the home she was building within the house, not merely a place where the boys went to get off by themselves or make trouble. She put a sleeping cot, white organdy curtains, and glassed-in bookshelves that she'd bought at an auction, and thought she'd never use, in the room occupied by the rolltop desk, which she referred to as Martin's office. In a battered box of junk, she unearthed the shell of a painted turtle that Martin had once found, empty, along the railroad tracks and had filled with cement—a mislaid, long-forgotten talisman, which he used to use as a paperweight. She placed it on the pile of paper on his desk.

And she had her own room upstairs, a sewing room with an easy chair and a lamp for reading, when she wanted to relax and read, large closets that accommodated all their winter clothes, and so much space she was able to keep her curtain stretchers permanently set up.

She painted, with white enamel, the cupboards in the pantry and the kitchen, and Martin put down new linoleum in every room. He trimmed the hedge around the house, all of it, down to four feet, and got blisters and sores and then hands as hard as horn from the project, which took weeks. He bought and installed an oil heater in the living room, so they could keep the chill out of the downstairs on fall days without starting the furnace in the basement, and when school dismissed for the summer, he hired a neighbor, William Runyon, as a helper, and they scraped and wire-brushed and painted the outside of the house. It was the color Alpha had always wanted her house to be—warm yellow, with white trim.

She was unpacked and had found a place for everything, from the rocker she'd inherited from her grandmother to her everyday soup spoons, and all of her furniture was being used. Then Martin bought a bedroom set of solid maple she'd dreamed of owning for five years ("$210," she noted in her diary, "but so what?"), with a tall dresser for him and a vanity with a mirror big enough to satisfy her. And still the house looked underfurnished. Which to her was perfectly all right; nothing or nobody was underfoot.

She had helped Martin lay out a garden, and as vegetables came into season she canned and preserved them, along with fruits from the market, jellies and jams, berries picked from the countryside during picnics and outings, and some capons Martin bought from a neighbor. The shelves in the basement were beginning to fill up. The potato bin was full. There were parsnips, kohlrabi, turnips, and ruta-bagas, all dipped in paraffin to preserve them, in the other bins. She brought out the winter clothes and began to mend them.

One afternoon in late October, she was sitting in her rocker in the alcove formed by the bay window, absorbing the last of the season's sunlight before winter, and knitting a heavy pink cardigan for Marie, when she thought she heard a knock at the front door. She paused in her work and looked up; nobody ever used that door. The knock came again. She put her work in the seat of the chair and went to the boys' bedroom and found all three of them there, up to no mischief. She went through the living room, down the long hall to the front door, and opened it. A tall, youthful-looking priest stood on the porch.

"Hello. I'm James Russell. Just call me Father Jim."

"Oh. Hello."

"You must be Mrs. Neumiller."

"Yes."

"I used to live here."

"Well, come in."

He stepped inside, and his bright-green eyes traveled over every area of the entry and stairway, as if following a familiar course, and stopped; her sons, who had trailed after her through the living room, were standing at the end of the hall. "Ah," he said, "I see you have three fine young boys."

He strode past her, his cassock smelling of cologne and cigarette smoke, and went up to them and ruffled their hair. "Your father's a fine gentleman," he said. "He taught two of my brothers and two of my sisters, and they have nothing but praise for him. You can be proud. Have either of you—not you, little fellow—made your First Communion yet?"

"Me," Jerome said.

" 'What is God's loving care for us called?' "

" 'God's loving care for us is called Divine Providence.' "

" 'What do we mean when we say that God is almighty?' "

" 'When we say that God is almighty we mean that He can do all things.' "

" 'Is God all-wise, all-holy, all-merciful, and all-just?' "

" 'Yes. God is all-wise, all-holy, all-merciful, and all-just.' "

"You've learned your catechism well. Good, good." He turned to Alpha. "Do you have others?"

"A daughter, two and a half months."

"Is she asleep?"

"Yes."

"Ah, that's too bad. I'd like to bless the little tyke. Is your husband here?"

"No."

"Will he be back soon?"

"Later today. He's gone to McCallister."

"I'm afraid I won't even have a chance to see him, then, I'm so awfully rushed. That's a disappointment. He's meant a lot to us, you know, the younger ones especially. I haven't been in the area since I was transferred to Minneapolis, nearly three years now. I'm with the Jesuits there. I believe it was thought best that I not visit the family. We were all quite close." He rubbed and wrung his hands as if washing them as he looked around. "But the family, God bless them, is gone from the area now, and a conference came up in Bismarck that the Monsignor couldn't attend—one that might be quite important to the laity, by the way; it deals with sacramentals—so the Monsignor delegated me to go, and loaned me his car (I left the engine running; I'm already late), and since I was so close, only twenty-five miles off, I couldn't resist. I had to see the old place. Isn't it a lovely house?"

He began to pace around the living room, displacing the air in a way that Martin never did, his eyes moving with such speed and restlessness he kept changing direction, turning to look behind, staring up or to the side, turning again. "You've done very well by the old place. It's decorated with taste and is as neat as I can remember. The outside looks fine also—the new paint job, I mean—and the hedge; I think Father let that go the last years. I can't understand why he felt compelled to leave. The hardware store certainly hasn't worked out as he expected, not in that location, and he just suffered a second stroke. Edward and Jackie have left, of course, but Dennis is still at home to help. Dennis is a good lad. Enid has decided to take her vows—a surprise to us all, she seemed so involved in the arts—and Margaret graduated valedictorian this year. That makes five in the family so far." He stopped at the bay window.

"Isn't this a beautiful view? I've always liked to stand here and admire it. So did Mother. She would look out and pray the Rosary here at night, when most of us were in bed, and the whole house fell quiet. The lilac bushes there, the garden beyond, that nice oak down the road next to the Runyons'—somehow the arrangement is so pleasing and serene. I hope nobody ever builds on these lots to the corner. It would ruin the view. You can see past the state highway to that far-off Indian mound, or whatever it is. I think it's never been decided for sure, though it certainly couldn't be a hill—not in this territory. Hawk's Nest, it's called. Did you know that it stands nearly in the next county? I used to love to study it and wonder what it could be. Here's where I decided to become a priest."

He removed a white handkerchief from the sleeve of his cassock, blew his nose hard, then folded the handkerchief square, still staring out the window, and replaced it in his sleeve. Then he started to pace again, glancing into the dining room, the kitchen, the boys' bedroom, and through a gap in the sliding doors into the master bedroom.

"I'm sorry I'm in such an unneighborly rush. I'd like to sit down and visit, have dinner with you all—I can tell by your healthy boys you're a wonderful cook—and I wanted so much to see Martin." He stopped. "I'd love to run up and look at my old bedroom. But I'm afraid that would be imposing."

Alpha started to speak, but he held up his hand. "Also, I don't know if I could face it. Too emotional. Patrick and I used to share the room, and we lost him in the war." He crossed himself in a hurried way that appeared involuntary. "Well, boys, remember always to honor your father and mother, don't forget your morning and evening prayers, and keep yourself pure, for there's nothing more honorable in the eyes of God than purity. Now, come here, kneel down, and I'll give you my blessing."

Jerome and Charles knelt in front of him with their hands clasped and eyes closed, and Tim, copying them, did the same. Father Jim sketched crosses in the air above their heads and spoke the Latin in a clear voice, three times, without hurrying the familiar words. He thanked Alpha for her patience and hospitality, once again apologized for his rush, reminded her to give Martin his greetings, and then strode to the front door.

Jerome and Charles and Time stood at the end of the hall and watched while he said goodbye to their mother and, as she bowed her head, quickly gave her his blessing. Then he walked across the porch, across the lawn, and out of sight, and they heard the sound of his car engine echo off a building and grow faint.

Their mother closed the door. She stood with her forehead against it and her hand on the knob, as though examining her thoughts with an intensity that held her there, and then turned to them. She looked thinner and older than a moment ago, and her expression, distant yet resigned, was an expression they'd never seen. But they knew what she was feeling; now the Russells, as well as the Halvorsons, would always occupy a part of their house. And although their mother might resist it, they knew it would only be a matter of time before they moved.

Further Reading
Beyond the Bedroom Wall. 1975.
Born Brothers. 1988.
A Family Album. 1975.
Indian Affairs. 1992.
Poppa John. 1981.
What I'm Going to Do, I Think. 1969.
What I Think I Did: A Season of Survival in Two Acts. 2000.

Greg Kuzma

Like Larry Woiwode's Neumillers, Greg Kuzma's narrator must come to terms with the past—in his case, his own father. Kuzma's speaker sifts through the memories of his father, deciding what to discard and what the final emotional sum of this addition and subtraction will be.

For the biography and bibliography of Kuzma see pages 70 and 72.

A Person in My Life (1984)

My father ascends
and now he comes down.
My father is eating his breakfast
in peace and quiet
and then he goes out to the yard.
The yard has grown small around him.
My father is sleeping, now he awakes,
my father has dreamt of himself as a child.
My father has seen his brother gone off
to the war, his sister insist on the money.
My father is lonely, worse than before.
My father has gone to the woods
where the snow is deep.
All night it has risen against the trees.
He walks in the snow there
carrying me.
My father is glad that the dream is of snow.

Into the attic he goes, hand over hand.
Into the darkness of books
with the pages missing, books
in another language.
In the old high school yearbook
he looks for himself, for his face,
as once long ago as a boy I looked for my father.
As once in the future my son and my daughter

will come to imagine me.
He tries on all the old clothes,
he tried on all the old dreams.
And none of them fit.
He has grown and diminished in odd ways.
He has left them for decades in boxes,
in darkness, and now
when they're called on
not one will come.
Not one will slip over head and arms.
Not one will marry the present and past.
My father assumed it would happen.
My father had guessed he would lose.
My father decided and so it is so.

When I went to find you father
a long time ago
I found the glasses and the cups
you washed
stacked on the rubber mat
next to the sink
and I asked them
where you were
how they had let you get away.
They said the door might know
so I went to the basement door
down the stairs you walked
a thousand times
but I did not meet you
coming up.
I asked the stairs why they
did not hold you in your shoes
I asked the workbench
which still held your tools
what you looked like to them
to tell what they knew
that whole bench full
but not one spoke
not one hammer, not one blade or screw.
How loyal they are to you.
Not even the dust under the bench
would tell.

In a rented boat one day
with the sun a breeze upon us
we set out from the hard packed beach
over the lily padded water
over the blue lagoon
to fish. You driving,
me in the bow catching the wind head on,
watching the water slide under the boat,
and hearing the motor as if far off,
as with one arm you leaned back to it,
your face somewhere back there in the sky,
holding it like you would a woman.
I remember the day in the fall
you showed me to walk on tiptoe
through the steep ravine
with the gun cradled, shells in my pockets,
looking for grouse,
and finding instead
only the weather.
I remember us coming to rest
in a grove of trees
the coffee hot in the tin cup.
I remember the night you came home
from the clambake
drunk and the coins in your hand
to show us you'd not lost
all your money,
dropping them one at a time
into mother's reluctant palm.

It is late as you stay awake
in the old house
from which we have all set forth into the world
except yourself.
Keeper of the past
maker of half my dreams.
The streets you brought me up on
have grown furious with cars.
The neighborhood's infected by another time.
The once sheltering lilacs have grown past
their spread and now,
as slender poles, crack-barked,

they lean and bake or freeze
and will not keep your privacy.
In spring they're nearly leafless
with just a few flowers.
The dog's dead. Mom's left.
And no one calls you on the telephone.

You told me men grow sad.
If they are lucky they are old.
You told me men grow weak and tire
in spite of everything.
If they are lucky they are dead.
The world's wrong, a great no place,
no singing, no pets, no dreams.
Rubbed by the world in one right way
like wood I achieved a fine finish.
My teachers dumped the polish on
and elbow greased me clean.
Far from your house I weaned,
took on my wax, and shone.
Far from the workbench dungeon
of your self
I learned another lore.
I strove, my body like a prized loaf
buttered with a fine shellac.
Yanked from their ovens
they pronounced me done.
Brought to your table,
almost you took me back.

I see a great room
where we meet
and you are in charge.
I see how the guns are laid out
so carefully
each waxed in its oil, and glittering.
Today we will shoot each other
across the dining room table.
Today we will assemble the heavy revolvers
and load them,
and then we will sit down to eat.
We will talk and the talk will turn bad.
We will sit there and fume

as the sun goes down into snowbanks.
Mother will serve up the cupcakes in tears,
my brother will drop to the floor
on all fours,
the dog crawl out to the hallway.
Then we will shoot point blank
into each other's words.

When you came to find me father
I was less than you,
a mere vibration set in motion by your voice.
When you bid me hold the board end
where you worked
my mind went off like birds
into the dusk.
I had no hands, no posture for that job.
Pinched by a feeling I could not bear,
distracted always by myself,
foot clumsy, impetuous,
my life with you
was one long huge abstraction.
Failing, I did not hit
the nail on the head,
failing, I did not drop the log
at the proper moment.
What work I did I did alone
you came behind to finish
doubling your time.
Taking the life from mine.

A gray sky, snow deep in the driveway,
the sound of your shovel scraping the gravel
as I lie high in the room, warm
in the covers.

Not once did I help you shovel out.

That road you traveled, 15 miles,
I've learned my own way now.
It is plain, where you go,
as is my own. A few houses,
some cows in a field,
and the trees come down to the road
or held back by fences.

A left turn and a right, like mine.
And the sound of the motor
vaguely threatening,
and under us the road unsure in its ice.

I am through hating you.

With such an outlook
I was fitted.
It came down over my face
like veil or helmet.
I walked around for years
in those gray clothes.
I built it up, day into dusk,
light into night.
Grew sad as you grew old.
Grew up as the gray stone rose.

I remember that kitchen
its waxed panels of pine.
The cupboards you built endlessly
month after month
in the cellar, then
with my help lugged up the narrow
stairway, sparing them bruises,
fitting them tight to the walls,
bolting them down. On Saturdays,
a month of Sundays, you worked,
finding the dream. The floor
already laid down carefully,
the old linoleum whisked away,
that ugly dark blue rubbed and scratched,
in big sheets peeled,
replaced by little squares
of veined gray. The sink
you bought new, but not the
stainless steel, the porcelain again,
for it was weight you loved,
preferring always the heavy
over the lighter thing—built better
if it could not be lifted,
best if it never moved.
Things you installed yourself were best.

Now eighteen years beyond those days
the kitchen doors swing tight
on hard hinges, and the sink
holds water. Only the dishes
are new, new purchased when my
mother took the old.
Everything you laid your hand to
built to last except her love.

Frederick Manfred *(1912–1994)*

In this story, with a touch of humor that reveals his awareness of the historical context of the "homestead formula," Frederick Manfred encapsulates the stereotypical Great Plains tale. All the characters are here: the hardworking homesteader who cares more for his fields and his barns than he does for his wife; the wife who endures a flea-infested sod house and is as barren as the land is fertile; and the wife's sister, Delphine, the outspoken critic but also the voice of common sense. A small patch of wild land inconveniently situated across the creek is their link to the land's deep past.

Manfred named his literary territory "Siouxland," a region that corresponds with the place where Minnesota, South Dakota, and Iowa meet.* Manfred collected stories of settlement and of the struggle to survive and sometimes succeed in the West and on the Great Plains. The student of Great Plains literature would be most interested in Manfred's novels such as *The Chokecherry Tree* (1948), a novel about coming of age in a small prairie town; *The Golden Bowl* (1944), an account of the dust bowl and depression years in North Dakota; and *This Is the Year* (1947), whose main character resembles Jasper Dollarhide in "Wild Land." The title of this last novel reflects a Great Plains truism: every year *might* be the year of a good crop, a little profit, enough rain.

Wild Land (1965)

I

In the very southwest corner of Minnesota, tight against the Iowa and South Dakota borders, lived a squirrelly sort of fellow who for a long time was a puzzle to his neighbors. His name was Jasper Dollarhide and he was the last of a dying New Hampshire family.

Jasper Dollarhide came to Siouxland in the spring of 1885, just as Whitebone was growing up from a stage stop to a good-sized town on the Big Rock River. By that time most of the land around Whitebone had already been homesteaded. It took Jasper a month to discover that the only free land left lay south and west of

---

*Manfred's first books were published under his legal name, Feike Feikama, reflecting his Saxon and Freisen heritage. He claimed the title of "America's Tallest Novelist" at six feet nine inches.

town. For some reason no one had yet claimed the quarter in the fartherest south-west corner of the state. Jasper rode out on horseback, saw that the one hundred sixty acres were good, didn't ask why it hadn't been taken before, and filed on his claim.

Jasper built himself a sod shanty on a rise in the land above Blood Run Creek, turned over the required ten acres with a breaking plow, planted the ten acres to corn with an ax, dug a shallow well, built a shelter for his horses, and then eased back to see what nature's pleasure might be. Jasper was a waiter even though a strange fire was always burning in his rust-red eyes.

The first summer Jasper ate his main meal with a neighbor named Breede. Breede was a heavy square-set man with a black walrus mustache and a balding head. He had a pinchface wife named Emmy and two daughters named Lucy and Delphine. The Breedes lived in a one-room board house.

Pa Breede never had much to say. Neither did his wife. After boarding with them for about a month, Jasper gradually got the feeling that the Breedes were a defeated couple. Neither liked the country. When they did talk it was about the old days back in Syracuse, New York. Ma Breede was lonesome for her mother's old white clapboard home; Pa Breede missed his drinking companions at the black-smith shop.

The two sandy-haired daughters, Lucy and Delphine, however, favored the new country. They came as babies and in due time were graduated from the eighth grade in the country school across the section. They grew up with memories of walking to school through waving wild flowers on the virgin prairies.

Delphine often spoke of those days. "It was like an everlasting garden. Spring-time we got wild roses mostly. And then in the fall came the coneflowers."

"I liked the wild plums best," Lucy said. "They bloomed in May. And then in July we made plum jelly. Mmm. Put that on fresh baked bread and was it good."

Ma Breede shook her head. "It's because them two never knew no better. And, maybe it's just as well."

"It was all hard work to me," Pa Breede said.

It was understood from the start that Jasper Dollarhide would probably marry one of the girls.

Jasper was always the jolliest with Delphine. The two were perfect teases to each other. She liked to hide his hat; then when he got warm looking for it she'd boldly defend the hiding place with her willowy body. He liked to tuck her bonnet in his overall in back; then when she'd spot it he'd challenge her to reach for it. Sometimes they got to wrestling, rough even, falling to the floor flushed and hot-faced.

Jasper never touched Lucy. Lucy watched the two cut-ups tease each other into a fight, and then smiled to herself, quietly, as if she knew something.

Thus Pa Breede almost fell off his chair the day Jasper drew up a three-legged stool from the corner by the stove and sat his runt of a body on it and said, "Mr. Breede, Pa, if you don't mind, I'd like to take one of your girls off your hands. Lucy."

"What! Lucy?"

Jasper laughed. "What's the matter, Pa, something wrong with Lucy that I don't know about?"

"No no, Jas, boy."

"Well, Lucy and me's talked it over and Lucy says she is willin'."

"But I thought from the way you and Delphine—"

"Delphine is a fine girl. But I got my mind set on Lucy." Jasper then gave Pa Breede a head-on look. His eyes burned a hot dark brown. "Unless'n a course you got a objection."

"No no. I ain't got no objection, boy. Cuss it, I'm rightly glad Lucy is gonna get hitched. We was always afraid she'd . . . Sholy, we're right glad for Lucy. And for you too, a course."

Jasper next turned to Ma Breede. "And what do you say?"

"I don't like it," Ma Breede said, grim. "But go ahead."

"Afraid I won't make a good enough son-in-law, Ma?"

"Go ahead. But there's bound to be trouble."

"Oh, come on now, Ma. You know Lucy won't be any trouble to me."

Ma Breede shot a gray look across the room at Delphine. "Go ahead. But her is the one that'll be the trouble to you."

"Hey. I ain't marryin' her, Ma. And that's why, too."

"Go ahead. I won't stand in your way. But don't say I never told you."

Jasper last turned to Delphine. "Well? And you?"

Delphine laughed. Her light-gray eyes sparkled. She seemed to think it a good joke. "Go ahead for all of me. Though I warn you I'll be the first in line to kiss the groom."

All the while Lucy sat with knees tight together on a hardback chair. She picked at a thread in her flowered calico dress. Her soft gray eyes were half-closed.

"There'll be another'n along before long, Delphine," Pa Breede offered. "There's more than one pebble on the beach, I always say."

Delphine snapped, "Pa, I don't aim to get married. I like my freedom too much. Heck, look at poor Ma there. She's been a slave of mud and fleas for most of her life. And that's not for me."

"I'll get us a hired hand to stay here," Pa Breede offered. "My back won't take much more of this kind of work."

"Don't you fret over me." Delphine tossed her sandy hair. "I'm going to stay as free as the wind."

Jasper and Lucy were wed, then, in the old schoolhouse across the section. Afterwards Lucy moved her trunk and clothes into Jasper's sod shanty. It was late in November. Four days later the season's worst blizzard struck from the northwest. And Jasper and Lucy for all practical purposes were cut off from the Breedes for most of the winter.

2

In early April, when the very first warm moist air came up the Big Sioux Valley, Lucy dared a visit to her folks. On the way over she found a single pasqueflower on the sunny side of the road. It had just opened and she picked it.

Delphine spotted the pale purple petals the minute Lucy entered the door. In some strange way the pasqueflower resembled the single thick braid hanging down Lucy's back. There was always a mauve shadow along the roots of her sandy hair. "Don't you know you're not supposed to pick wild flowers? Look at that poor thing now. Drooping already."

Lucy looked at the limp flower. When she and Delphine were little girls going to school together they'd sworn never to pick certain flowers, especially shy pasques. She turned her head so that the limp hood of her blue bonnet hid her face. "I picked it for you," she said.

The angry look on Delphine's face changed to one of compassion and she threw her arms around her sister. "Oh, Luce, I do hope Jas has been good to you."

"He has."

"Oh, Luce, you ain't expectin' already, are you?"

"No'm."

Ma Breede spoke up from the board table where she sat peeling potatoes. "Delphine, leave off pesterin' her. The idea, such questions. There's other things in life besides that."

"I just want to make sure that that little runt treats her right." Delphine balled up a small fist. "Because if he don't, I'm going to go over and fix him right. That little devil."

Ma Breede said gently, "Sit down, Lucy. We're still kin, you know. This chair across the table from me."

Lucy's purple calico dress rustled on her black high-laced shoes as she stepped over. She sat down. She sat a bit stooped, lap open.

Ma Breede said, "Lucy, y'u ailin', girl?"

"No'm."

Ma Breede got up and came around the table and lifted Lucy's head by the chin. "Let's have a good look at you." Ma Breede unfastened the strings of the blue bonnet; took it off. "My goodness, girl, you ar' ailin'. Jas hasn't beat you up, has he?"

"No'm."

"Well, what then, girl?"

"Now you're pesterin' her," Delphine said, cattish.

At that moment a cough rose slowly, deep, in Lucy. It took hold of her innards and shook her, violently. And she continued to cough for a good minute. When the spell finally finished shaking her, she sagged in her chair, limp, exhausted. Her mauve-tinted sandy braid hung to one side.

Gaunt Ma Breede stood over her, staring. Then she snapped to. Her head crooked around. "Delphine, get the mustard. This child needs a plaster."

They plastered her; they bathed her feet in hot mustard solution; they put her to bed. They got out the camphor bottle and let her have a few whiffs. They swathed her body with hot towels.

Later in the day Delphine went to tell Jasper. Sweeping along in her best blue velvet dress, watchful of white collar and cuffs, she by odd chance came across the spot where Lucy had knelt to pick the shy pasque. Delphine clucked her tongue. Then, going on, she spied the new leaves of a violet. To have a better look at it she herself nestled down on her heels. Her fingertips hovered over the tiny buds from which in a month petals as beautiful as a baby's eyes would open. But she didn't pick it.

Jasper was breaking a new patch of virgin sod south of the house. Coming back on the home stretch of a round, he saw Delphine sitting in the grass. He stopped his team of black horses at the end and called over. "Find some gold?"

Delphine's eyes deepened to a thoughtful gray. She rose and walked toward him.

"Find some gold?" he repeated, hitching up his trousers.

"If I did, I wouldn't tell you about it."

"Hmm. I see you come through the winter pretty good."

"How would you know?"

"That gold shine in your hair."

"I didn't come here for that," Delphine said.

Jasper slipped the knotted lines off his back and tied them to the handles of the plow. The black horses puffed. It was heavy pulling through the tough root-interlaced sod. "Don't tell me the flowers are out already?"

"Some are. And that silly wife of yours picked one."

"What's the difference when there's millions?"

"There's never enough pasques."

Jasper cocked wise eyes at her. "By gum, if it don't sound like you have a soft side after all."

Delphine examined his tough runty gnarled frame. "You look as if you had a hard winter, though. What's the matter, didn't you two eat well?"

"Two?" Jasper said, flesh showing above his teeth.

"You darn fool. Lucy came over with her death o' cold."

Jasper reared back. "What? Lucy walk over?"

"Lucy is in bed at Ma's. She's coughing something awful."

"Well, I coughed all winter too."

"So that's where she got it."

"Well, what do you expect me to do, sleep with the horses when I get a bad cold?"

Delphine placed hands on hips. "Are you two getting along?"

"Toler'ble."

"I suppose you two fought most of the winter?"

"Not one cross word."

"Well, Lucy looks a fright."

Short as he was, Jasper straightened to his full height against her. "Lemme get this straight. You meanin' to boss me around?"

"No. But I'm letting you know that if you don't treat my sis good, real good, there's gonna be trouble. And plenty of it. Poor Luce, so soft."

Jasper bit off a chew. The tobacco cracked in his teeth as he worked it. "Lucy is in bed at Ma's you say?"

"Yes."

"Ha. You've come over to cook for me then."

"Not on your life. You can walk over like in the old days."

Jasper wyed his head around and looked across the wild waving prairies toward the Breede house. "Quite a ways for a man who walks all day behind a plow."

"Suit yourself," Delphine snapped, and started for home.

That night Jasper ate with the Breedes again. Pa Breede gave him an accusing look for having abused his daughter. Ma Breede had little to say to him. Delphine went around snappish.

When Jasper walked back to his own sod hut in the dark, alone, he gave the moon a mean look. "You! That's what I get for moonin' after wimmen."

Four nights later Jasper found himself at Pa Breede's bedside. Pa Breede had caught what Lucy had. It was pneumonia and it was slowly choking him to death.

There wasn't much they could do except poultice Pa Breede. There wasn't a doctor around for miles. The one in Whitebone had gone to better pastures in Sioux Falls. They all waited. Pa Breede's fine black walrus had suddenly turned gray and lay like a soaked rope across his face. The white fringe around his bald dome was so frizzed and wispy it looked more like cigar smoke than hair. Every now and then the poor man would try to mutter something through a paste of phlegm in his throat. Sometimes they could make out he was talking with the boys at the blacksmith shop in Syracuse, New York; sometimes that he was scolding Ma Breede for letting Lucy get her feet wet on the way to school across the section.

"He's out of his head," Ma Breede said, putting a fresh wet towel on his forehead.

Jasper said, "Some things sure stuck in his craw way back then."

Ma Breede said, "He always did favor Lucy."

Delphine said, "Poor Luce, how are you feeling?"

Lucy wavered beside the bed. "Pa, Pa," she cried, "please don't leave us now."

Pa Breede seemed to hear her. Slowly, like a Lazarus sitting up in his burial wraps, Pa Breede rose out of his blankets. His eyes rolled slightly until vision fell on Lucy. Then they steadied. "Emmy?"

"Here I am," Ma Breede said.

"Go back to Syracuse with the girls before something happens."

"We'll hold the thought, Pa."

Pa Breede shuddered. A cough rumbled in his bowels. It tried to work up through the paste in his chest; couldn't quite make it. Choking, face blackening, Pa Breede's body contorted, jerked, and then he fell backwards, dead.

The women swooned over him, crying his name.

Jasper got up. He coughed. He said, "Well, now," to himself. He walked over to the window and looked west toward his sod shanty.

After a while Jasper led the women from the bed and set them each on a chair on the other side of the one-room house. Then he closed Pa Breede's eyes, gently, and held Pa Breede's arms folded over his chest, firmly, until they stayed in place. Later Jasper washed the body and laid it out in Pa Breede's best clothes. All night long Jasper kept a cloth wet with vinegar on the body's face to deter the mortification. And the next morning they buried Pa Breede in the garden where Ma Breede had planted some white lilacs years before. Jasper read a few awkward words from the Bible.

Jasper expected Lucy to come home after the funeral.

But Lucy didn't.

Lucy behaved peculiar. She just sat on the chair by the window looking out at the white lilacs beside Pa Breede's grave. She sat with her lap open, shoulders drooped, soft gray eyes leaden with grief.

Once Jasper grabbed Lucy roughly by the shoulder and tried to lift her off the chair and carry her home. "C'mon, woman, the house waits for you."

"The bed, you mean," Delphine said, coming up and pushing Jasper aside. "Leave her alone. She'll come home when she's good and ready to. You darn men."

"By gum, woman, I'm getting mighty hungry. Running over the farm all day behind them fast-stepping blacks of mine and then comin' in at night with nothin' on the table. I can't do both."

"Get out," Delphine said. "We'll call you when we're good and ready."

Jasper turned to Ma Breede. "Please, won't you tell my wife to come home?"

Ma Breede said, "I wonder who'll do the farm work around here now?"

Jasper almost jumped straight up into the air. "By gum, don't look at me. A quarter alone is more than enough for one man."

One day Ma Breede made up her mind. "I've had enough," she said. "I can't farm the place myself. I'm going back to Syracuse."

Delphine and Lucy fell into a stupor at the announcement.

Jasper had himself a long chew.

Ma Breede said, "I know Pa would want me to go."

The girls stared white-faced at her.

At last Jasper decided it was just as well. And he wound up urging Ma Breede to go. "Can't say as how I blame you none, Ma. You'll find in nature when a dam sees the end coming she always returns to where she had her babies."

"Dam?" Delphine cried. "You brute, how dare you speak like that of our mother?"

"Well, old lady then. But I seen it."

Delphine smoldered. "Yes, and I know why you want her to go too."

"Why?"

"You know dargone well we girls won't leave here."

"I'd like my wife back," Jasper said. "After all, either we're married or we ain't. This is no way."

Lucy looked up from staring at her lap long enough to say, "When are you going, Ma?"

"As soon as I sell the place. I've got to raise the money for the train ticket somehow."

Jasper got to his feet. "I'm busy spring plantin' and all just now, Ma, but if you want me to I'll ride into Whitebone and have the bill of sale made for you."

"Thanks," Ma Breede said, curt. "But I can still ride a horse. Besides, there's another matter I have to attend to too."

"What's that?" Delphine asked.

"Never you mind."

Four weeks later, the place was sold to some people named Peterson. Also, Ma Breede had her husband dug up by a Blue Wing embalmer and put in a special sealed crate and together she and the crate were put aboard the train at the end of the line at Blue Wing.

Lucy returned to Jasper.

And Delphine moved in with them.

For a while Lucy went about even more crushed, if that was possible.

Delphine tried to console her. Delphine went over to the old homestead with a spade and dug up the white lilacs and brought them to Jasper's place. Delphine also found Lucy some new flowers. The best ones she found in a piece of wild land across the creek which Jasper owned.

Gradually Lucy got over her sick spell.

By late July when the wild plums were ripe she sometimes had a shy smile for Jasper again.

3

Jasper had a good summer. He planted wheat on the forty acres he'd sodbusted so far and the price that August was good. He came back from hauling the last load of wheat to Blue Wing with the announcement that some lumber and a carpenter were on the way. Also, behind his wagon were tied two new horses and two cows, and inside the wagon were four pigs and a dozen chickens—all bought at a sale.

The womenfolk greeted the news each in their fashion: Lucy picked at the tablecloth and said nothing; Delphine gave Jasper a waiting look.

The carpenter first built a large barn. It had eight cow stanchions, four big horse stalls, a large calf pen, a large fattener pen, and a pigpen. Neighbors traveled from some distance to have a look at it. They came because in the building of it Jasper and the carpenter had worked out an original idea. The barn was round, not rectangular, with the haymow in the middle, from floor to ceiling, and with the animals facing a circular alley around the hay. Everyone agreed it was a real labor-saver as well as a warm shelter. Jasper painted it red, with white trim on the windows and doors.

The carpenter next built a small henhouse and a smokehouse. These Jasper painted red with white trim too.

The carpenter last put up a high board fence on three sides of the barnyard, west, north, east, making a warm windbreak. On sunny days in the winter the animals could be outside for an hour or two at noon even if it was twenty below.

After the carpenter left, Delphine asked at supper, "Where's Lucy's new house?"

Jasper looked up from his plate of cornbread and sorghum molasses. "What whose new house?"

"Lucy's new house."

"What's wrong with this one?"

"This . . . pigpen?"

"Pigpen?"

"Yes. Pigpen. Mud from the roof dribbling into your hair even after the littlest shower. Puddles on the dirt floor. Mice in the food no matter how one stores it. Fleas in the sod walls. Flies everywhere in the food and in the milk and waking us early in the morning. You call that a home for your wife? Why, ever since I moved in with you I've had to sleep on the floor."

Jasper laughed out of the side of his mouth. "Ha. I slept that way for two years afore I got married. It didn't seem to hurt me none."

"Jas, listen. I'm glad you and Luce got a bed. Such as it is. Stuck into the wall like it might be a feedrack. I don't begrudge it to you. But when I got to make up my own bed with a hoe, soften up the dirt floor so I don't get a crick in my back, that's the last straw!"

"Good practice for when you start our big garden next year."

"Jasper Dollarhide!"

Jasper clicked his fork and knife together. "Woman, I hope you don't think I married Lucy to have you underfoot for the rest of my life. Squeakin' at me all day long like it might be some pig's tail I stepped on."

"Are you chasing me out?"

"How come the yard ain't thick with buggies? With young bucks come to spark you?"

Delphine smoldered.

Lucy held out a pan. "More cornbread, Jasper?"

"Yeh. Don't mind if I do. And I'll have some more of that sorghum too. Thanks." Jasper sat on a box and every time he lifted fork to mouth it creaked.

A stove against the north wall grumbled with burning box elder logs. It was chilly October outdoors and the fire felt good.

Lucy said after a while, "Jasper, sleeping on the dirt floor isn't healthful."

"Huh. I notice you're the one coughin'. Not Delphine. And you've got the bed."

Lucy looked down at her plate. She picked at her cornbread. "You have to admit, though, Jasper, that with all the sweeping we do the floor is gradually wearing pretty deep into the ground."

Delphine snickered. "Another winter of sweeping and it'll be worn down to where the cellar should be."

Jasper gave both women a crabbed sideways look. "Are you two wimmen working me for a new house yet this year? I ain't got the money."

Delphine muttered to herself. "He thinks more of his blessed cows and pigs than he does of his wife."

Jasper cracked knife and fork on the plank table. "I said, I ain't got the money."

Delphine switched to another sore point. "The past summer, when I started hearing cozy noises in your straw tick, it was all right by me that I had to get up and take a look at the wild flowers in the moonlight. But don't expect me to get up and take a look at the snowbanks this coming winter."

"Put some cotton plugs in your ears," Jasper said.

Delphine picked up her calico needlework and began jabbing into it. "Jas, there's no talking to you. I can see that now."

Lucy looked down at the cold cornbread and molasses still left in her plate. "The Lord willin', maybe next year we can break some more sod. Maybe we can afford it then, Jasper."

"Maybe."

Delphine said, "Jas, I'll help with the yard work if you really will bust some more sod."

"You chorse on the yard? With them lily-pickin' hands of yours? That'll be the day."

"Name the job and I'll do it!" Again Delphine jabbed her needle angrily into the calico. "Just name it."

"All right. Manure out the calf barn tomorrow."

"You would pick the worst. You darn men."

Lucy said, "I'll do the yard work. Delphine can keep house."

Jasper said, short, "We'll see come next spring."

The winter turned out to be a hard one. One December blizzard came howling in so fiercely, choused across the open prairies with such driving force, that Jasper found snowbanks in the barn. Fine powdery snow had sifted in especially on the north side where the horses were stalled. The blacks at the end stood so high on packed snow that their heads, still tied to the manger, hung down even with their knees. On the last night of the storm the snow came so blinding thick Jasper didn't dare try to make it back to the house for fear of getting lost in his own yard. He drank the milk he'd milked and slept with the animals.

When the weather cleared for a few days, Jasper hustled up food. He took a load of wheat to the Klondike mill on the Big Sioux River and had flour ground for the house and grist ground for the chickens. When yet another December storm closed them in, he had to grind corn in the coffee mill for his cornbread.

In the depths of the winter in January, to pass the time away, he got out a wood gouge and made some household utensils: plates, spoons, ladles, bowls. He next got out the saw and plane and built three stools. He fashioned a cabinet of sorts for spices and condiments. And finally, because he couldn't think of anything else to do, he cut some slender willows along Blood Run Creek and made Delphine a bed.

Delphine gave him grudging thanks. "Well, at last I'm off the floor."

"When you get married you can take the durn bed with you," Jasper said. "I give it to you as a wedding present."

Delphine went on as if she hadn't heard. "Now if you could only build us a partition. So I could sleep once."

"Don't you want us to have us a family?"

"Best night I had was the night you had to sleep with your blessed cows. It was like in the old days to sleep with my sis again."

"What you need is a bedwarmer. A live one with two legs and a automatic damper. Ha"

"If Lucy doesn't get a new house next fall," Delphine said, "we'll just see."

"Just see what?"

Lucy spoke up from contemplating her hands in her lap. "Jasper, put some more wood in the stove. My feet are getting cold."

4

Spring came at last, and with it the shy pasques and the tender violets. Delphine forgot her grudges and pitched in with the yard work. With an ax she broke up some sod east of the shanty and spaded it and planted it to lettuce, radish, carrots, beans, squash, pumpkins, peas, and cabbage. She made good nests for the layers in the henhouse. She milked the two cows the nights Jasper worked late in the field.

The same day Jasper got his wheat in, he rolled out the breaking plow. Working like a Turk, he managed to bust another twenty acres of virgin sod and plant it to corn before the end of May. Then plenty of rain fell, and a hot sun came, and by great good luck the grasshoppers stayed away.

Lucy, despite her cough, gradually toughened. Perhaps it helped that she wasn't plagued with children. She always had the meals ready on time. She kept the sodhouse neat. She kept Jasper's overalls and shirts and socks mended. She found sweetgrass beside Blood Run Creek and hung bunches of it along the ceiling to give the place a wholesome smell. She even managed to find time to embroider bedcovers for the two beds.

All three got along tolerable that summer. The days were lived each for itself, from dawn to dusk, work work, eat eat, and sunsets enjoyed. There were no flies, hardly any mosquitoes, and no cutworms to destroy the garden.

The wheat crop came in so heavy it was almost too much for Jasper to handle. The distant neighbors were busy with their own crops, so Jasper had to ask Delphine and Lucy to help him. "Now that we're this close to a bumper, it'd be a shame to lose it."

Delphine smiled. "Sure we'll help, Jas. Won't we, Luce?"

Lucy held her leathery face to one side. "Guess so."

"Just tell us what to do," Delphine said.

"Just let us get this crop in," Jasper said, "and I promise you wimmen you'll have you a palace to match my barn."

They helped him shock and thresh the wheat. And in late August, when Jasper began hauling the wheat away by wagon to the elevator in Blue Wing, they did all the chores. The price was right, again, and so on the return trips Jasper hauled home lumber. On the last trip he returned with another carpenter, this time a first class woodworker.

With the women still doing his yard work for him, Jasper helped the carpenter put up the house, a frame affair, one story with an attic. They built it in the shape of an L, with a porch in the crook facing the south. They got the outside shell built before the first frost came. They had it painted white before Jasper had to break off to pick his corn. The carpenter finished the inside of the house alone, doing the doorhanging and plastering and woodwork. The women cleaned up the rooms as they were finished, washing, wallpapering, varnishing, and making the curtains. When the first blizzard hit in early December, the corn was cribbed, the carpenter had gone home, and the house was done.

"Well, what've you got to say now?" Jasper said. Sitting in the big kitchen warm by the stove, Jasper leaned back on two legs of his chair and surveyed it all: the clean white curtains, the yellow oilcloth-covered table, the new cast-iron range, the cabinet for spices and such, the big pantry for canned vegetables and meats, the bright rag-rugs on the floor. "Pretty nice, ain't it?"

"We live decent again," Delphine said.

"Now you won't have to soften up your bed with a hoe anymore," Jasper said with a side laugh. "Ha."

"And good riddance too."

"Maybe we can have a housewarming," Lucy said. "With fiddles."

"Say, that's an idee," Jasper said. "Invite all the young bucks from Whitebone over. That way Delphine can take her pick."

"Not on your tin-type," Delphine said. "I've got me a nice home at last, with a

room of my own, and I mean to enjoy it a while first. I'm not going through a
sodhut time with another honyocker again."

Jasper laughed. "I thought I married the other Breede girl."

"Maybe we can invite the new reverend from Whitebone over some night,"
Lucy said. "For supper."

"And I'm not marrying him either," Delphine said. "Even if he is God's
anointed, or whatever it is they do to his head. An old maid I was meant to be and
an old maid I will remain."

Lucy coughed and looked down at where the two legs of Jasper's chair touched
the floor.

Delphine caught the look. "Tipping back on two legs digs holes, Jas."

"That's right. I forgot." Jasper dropped his chair back on all four. He shook his
head. "Have to learn a whole new set of manners to go with the new house, I
guess."

Delphine said, "Well, maybe we all do."

"One thing, though. It's gonna take a lot of chopping to keep this palace warm.
At least you had to say that for the old sod shanty. It was always half-warm on the
earth side." Jasper watched snow streak past the green windowpanes in swirls.
"Hmm. We still got some money left over. When this storm lets up, I'm going to
get us a hard-coal burner. That'll burn slow. One load of hard-coal should last us
the whole winter."

Lucy said, "I think we would do better to get us some coats. For when we go
visiting."

Delphine said, "Where would we go? Me, I plan to stay home, cozy in my
room."

Jasper laughed. "You sure ain't much on society, are you, Delphine? When the
funny thing is, of us three, you're the one with the looks for it."

Lucy said, with a throw of sly tapioca eyes at Delphine, "Just a homebody."

"I'm complete unto myself," Delphine said, snappish. Then she gave Lucy a
hard look. "And seeing how you two animals get along, I don't lack for examples
on how not to live."

5

The next few years Jasper continued to sodbust his land. And except for a piece of
four acres of wild land across Blood Run Creek, and the yard, he finally got the sod
all turned under.

Almost the entire quarter turned out to have black fertile land. There was just
enough sand in it to keep it from packing down. When he plowed in the fall the
humus curled off the moldboard with a glossy satiny finish, almost as shiny as the
share point itself. Wheat and corn grew fast on it, so that in one week the whole
quarter seemed to lift like bread dough on the rise. When the wind touched it the
land moved like a sea. It was alive with tides of growth.

Jasper put up good fences of cedar post and barbwire all around. He dug up willow shoots along the creek and planted a windbreak around the yard. From Sioux Falls, where he went on a trip to get new harnesses, he brought little fruit trees and planted them inside the windbreak. Within three years they had crab apples and cherries and raspberries. Within five years they had greenings to munch on during the long winter evenings. He found some black walnut seedlings along the Big Sioux and set them out too. In seven years Lucy was flavoring her cakes with nuts.

6

It was after supper, the dishes were washed, it was greening out, and they were sitting in the living room each in a rocker by the big bay window.

Jasper said, "You know, there's one thing I've never been able to understand. How come this land was the last to be homesteaded? Why some folks'd been in the county twenty years before I filed on it. I sure was lucky they overlooked it."

"Pa once thought of filing on it," Lucy said. "For us girls. But then he heard something about it and he didn't."

"I remember that," Delphine said. She was busy tatting a delicate piece of lace.

"What?" Jasper stopped rocking to fill his corncob pipe. "What did he hear about it?"

"I forget just what it was he heard about it," Delphine said. "Had something to do with an Indian battle. Between the Omaha and the Yankton Sioux, I believe. But I forget."

Jasper fell into a study. "That's funny. I've never turned up no arrowheads. Nor Indian bones."

Delphine rocked. "Maybe the battle was fought over on our little piece of wild land there."

"You mean them four acres of wasteland across the crick?"

"I think that's where I heard it was."

"Hmm. This summer when I plow it up I'll keep an eye out for arrowheads then."

Delphine shook her head. "I don't know as I would plow that up. There's a superstition about that place."

"What superstition?"

"Some chief, I think it was Yellow Smoke, the friendly Indian, some chief said that if them bones was disturbed, the spirits of the dead would come back to haunt us."

"Talk." Jasper's rocker creaked again. "Just talk."

"No, it ain't just talk."

Jasper rocked faster. "Then you did know there was a battle on our wasteland. You wasn't just guessin'."

"Yes. No. Them nights when you two was restless, and I went out for a walk, I saw what looked like hants moving over our wild land."

"Well, why didn't you say so in the first place? Instead of playing like you didn't know."

Delphine bit off a thread with her teeth. Then with the deft whirl of a fingertip she retied the two ends. "Thinking on it just now it all came back. Memory comes and goes, you know."

"Hmm."

The next morning, after chores, Jasper went over to have a look at the four acres of wasteland.

Because of the way Blood Run Creek meandered, and because the entire creek bottom was treacherous, the four acres were hard to get at with the horses and machines. The only way in was to drive around to the bridge a mile west and then come in on the Iowa side.

Jasper leaped across the creek at its narrowest part, where the black banks were high. He scuffed through the tall grass. He kept his eyes peeled for arrowheads and bones. The sod was still thick and springy. The thought that it was still unplowed excited him. Virgin prairie had always stirred him. It was like being given the Garden of Eden free and ready to live in. No trees to cut down, no stumps to clear away. Thousands of men throughout all ages had dreamt of getting such a prize piece of land, rich as cream. And here it was. He had it. All to himself. A whole quarter of it.

Tiny flowers were beginning to show between last year's faded stalks of bluestem, wrestling for growing room. New grass had just begun to spear up. Fresh shiny brown beetles, chased by red ants, bumbled through the undergrowth. Mice scurried away into the low shadows. Ahead a gopher popped up out of the grass like a suddenly erect pony phallus. A wild prairie chicken raced away, vanishing in a clump of wolfberries.

It reminded Jasper of his first days on the quarter, when he was still single, while walking through the waving wild grasses on his way to eat at the Breedes. It reminded him of the days when he and Delphine teased each other, faces flushed. It also reminded him of his first nights with Lucy. He and Lucy had both been green ones together, exploring the dark track of love, so worked up with their own wild flaming sensations they had little left with which to think of the other.

He looked down at the untouched wild sod, then said, aloud, "There's still Delphine."

That night, when he sat down to supper, he hadn't yet made up his mind what to do with those last four unbroken acres. On the one hand it seemed like a good thing to keep untouched at least one small piece as she once was, a memento of the old times. Yet on the other hand it bothered him that, like an unbred heifer, good land wasn't being used.

Sipping the last of his coffee, he said, "Took me a walk over that piece of wasteland today."

"Oh?" Delphine said. Delphine still looked young. She had only a few wrinkles around the eyes and they showed only when she smiled or threw one a shrewd look.

"Yeh. Kicked all around through it. But nary an arrowhead did I see. Nor any Indian bones."

"Oh, well, them, they'd be covered up by grass by now. That was supposed to have happened a hundred years ago. At least."

"When I plow it up this summer we'll keep an eye on the furrow and then we'll see what we'll see."

Delphine spooned up some coffee. "My advice to you is to leave that piece alone. No good will come of it."

Lucy looked down at her coffee. The streak of gray over her temples had spread, making her hair look coarse. She almost looked old enough to be Delphine's mother.

Jasper played some sugared coffee between his teeth; then swallowed it. "Well, at that I kind of hate to touch it. We could make it into a kind of park."

Delphine nodded. "That'd be a good thing. Set aside some of God's land in commemoration of what it once was. A sort of a Garden of Eden."

"Well, we'll see," Jasper said.

7

A few days later they were sitting in their rockers looking out of the bay window toward Blood Run Creek.

Delphine said, "Took a walk today."

Jasper grunted, puffing on his corncob.

"Out to our piece of wild land there. The wasteland."

"Oh."

"Full of flowers this time of the year. Wild roses. Buffalo beans. Violets."

"Hmm."

"Sure lovely now."

Lucy's rocker stilled. "You never told me."

"Never told you what?" Delphine snapped.

"Didn't bring any home either," Lucy went on.

"I don't pick wild flowers," Delphine said, short.

Lucy started up her rocking again.

A long silence followed.

Presently Delphine lay aside her fancywork. She sighed. "So lovely. Yes. But I'm afraid Satan has crept into our little Eden."

Jasper spoke with pipe still in mouth. "Come again?"

"I said, I'm afraid Satan has crept into our little Eden."

"Crept? Oh. Well, there's always been a few garter snakes around."

"I don't mean garter snakes."

"You don't happen to mean rattlers?"

"No, not rattlers either. I mean gophers."

"Oh. Them." Jasper lipped his pipestem. "Well, there's always been plenty of them around."

"Not that many."

"In the old days I used to shoot a dozen a day every spring."

Delphine shook her head. "All the gophers left in the state of Minnesota seem to be making a last stand in that last bit of wild land. Like Indians pushed tight together on a reservation. I counted up to fifty and then I lost track. Gophers poking up everywhere out of little holes. Everywhere. The place was so full of holes it looked like a honeycomb. I kept stumbling around like my shoes had lost their heels."

Silence.

A creaking of rockers.

The sun began to set outside. Night misted in slowly from the east.

"Gophers kept whistling at me from all sides," Delphine went on.

"Hmm."

"Holes, holes. Everywhere holes."

"Oh, for catsakes," Lucy cried, "shut up about them gophers and their holes once, will you? I'm sick and tired of hearing about them."

Jasper clapped out his pipe and put it away in the bib pocket of his overall. "You do sound like you got holes on the brain a little, Delphine." He got to his feet and stretched. He groaned pleasantly. "Well, anyways, it's time to hit the hay. Comin', Luce?"

The next night Delphine was at it again. "Took another walk this afternoon."

"Mmm."

"Just to see if I really had holes on the brain."

"Mmm."

"Those holes are in the ground all right. I made a special point of counting them. Just walking across it once, in a straight line, I counted forty-nine."

Jasper's rust-red eyes opened slightly.

"On the whole piece there must be at least seven times seven that many more."

"Oh, come now."

"Yes, come now, that many."

Three rockers creaked.

Jasper clapped out his pipe. "Well, and I still say you got gophers on the brain a little, Delphine." He got to his feet and groaned pleasantly in a long stretch. "Well, Luce, c'mon, it's time to feed the bedbugs."

Delphine just couldn't let go of it. The following night she said, "That piece of wild land now."

"Don't tell me you took another walk over it!" Lucy cried.

Delphine nodded, grim. "Yes. Last night. When you two was asleep."

"Don't tell me we kept you awake again!" Jasper cried.

"No. Yes. The moon was out last night and what I saw was enough to scare me into old age."

"Naw."

"Guess what I saw."

"What."

Delphine's head shot forward. "Hant gophers . . . I mean, hant Indians!"

"Naw."

"All right. If you don't want to hear about it, just say so. Just say so."

"Go ahead. We're listening."

Rockers creaked.

"Go ahead, we're listening, I said."

Delphine tatted away. Holding silver shuttle between right thumb and forefinger, precisely, she kept pecking into a web of linen thread held outspread on the fingertips of her left hand, over and over knotting intricate little ties, gradually working out a lovely lace pattern.

"Go ahead, we're listening, I said."

"Well, I saw them. Hants rising out of the ground. Human. With silverish bodies. They rose out of the earth and then drifted away to the west. They looked at me from under their hands, then moved away across the tall grass."

Jasper asked quietly, "About how many would you say?"

"As many as the gopher holes I counted the other day. At least."

Jasper studied the dark outdoors. "Maybe they had a big battle there at that."

"It's land rich with the blood of the Indian dead."

Lucy clapped a hand to her forehead. "Oh, for catsakes, will you two ever shut up about them gopher holes?"

Then another thought struck Jasper. "Hey. Which way did you say they drifted to?"

"West," Delphine said.

"Hmm. The wind was east last night. And it was as cold as a well-driller's butt out."

"What's your mind, Jasper."

"Well, the wind was east. And it was a cold wind. More than likely they was only little bits of mist rising out of all them gopher holes, the earth bein' warm like it was. The sun was hot on it all day yesterday and then in the evening it all of a sudden got cold from the east."

Lucy got up from her rocker so quick she almost pitched it against a potted fern. Her mouth ridged squarish. "Please, for catsakes, will you two ever shut up about them darn gopher holes once? Or else, please, for catsakes, let's plow the piece up and be shut of it. I'm going crazy listening to you two always talking about them gopher holes. Please!" And with that, Lucy ran outdoors and disappeared into the privy.

8

Jasper was one of those who always awoke with a little snort, sat up in bed with a start, and then, with a bunching of shoulder muscles, swung out of bed and into his clothes. Often he was whistling by the time he hit the kitchen.

But one spring morning Jasper wouldn't get up when the alarm went off.

The alarm clock clattered and drummed on the chair beside the bed, until at last, like a death rattle in an old throat, it ran down and stopped.

Lucy gave Jasper a bump with her butt. "Jasper." Lucy liked to stay in bed. She always waited until the last minute to get up, sometimes just barely managing to have the coffee poured when Jasper came in from getting up the cows from the pasture.

"Jasper."

Jasper lay like a squirrel curled up for the winter, knees tight against his chin.

"Jasper. Get up. The alarm's already run down."

Jasper didn't move.

Lucy sat up on her elbows. She stared down at the knobby ball of a man beside her. Her eyes were like oval knots in old gray wood. "Jasper, you sick?"

Jasper didn't move.

She touched the back of his neck where it showed above his gray underwear. "You're not feverish. What's the matter with you?"

Jasper didn't move.

Again she bumped him. "Get up. The alarm's rung off. It's five past five already."

"Mmm."

"What's the matter with you?"

"Mmmmm."

"You sick?"

"Mmm."

"Well, if you're not going to worry about getting up, I ain't either." And with that she sank back into her pillow, hooking into the bedcovers on her side with an elbow and nuzzling under.

Outdoors a robin sang of the joy of a new day born. A meadowlark whistled, "Hello-there-you-in-there." Sparrows cukked on the henhouse roof.

She lay still. Her long lashes made soft brushing noises against the pillowcase each time her eyes moved. What ailed the crazy man now? After fifteen years of married life, never a miss in the morning being up with the first ding of day, he now suddenly pulled this stunt.

She sat up on her elbows again. "Jasper?"

No answer.

"Jas?" It was what Delphine often called him. "Jas?"

Jasper didn't move.

"Jas! It's a good five-thirty already. The alarm's long run off."

"Mmm."

She gave him another hard bump. "Wake up. You die in the night or something?"

"Mmmmm."

"Get up. I think I hear Delphine moving already. And you know she always favors herself with that extra wink in the morning."

"Mmm."

She stared at the back of his head, noting the whorls of graying brown on either side of his turkey-cock neck and then the wild brush on top. She saw too the dried half-pear ear with its curdle of wax dirt. What was working in that funny nut head anyway?

"Well," she said finally, "I don't know about you, but me, I'm gonna get up. I can't stand this." And up she got, slipping on her black bloomers under her nightgown, and then, with a look at him to make sure he wasn't sneaking a peek, quick whipped off the nightgown and got into her underskirt and dress. With still another look, this time huffy, she marched off to the kitchen.

Some ten minutes later, just as the coffee began to simmer, Delphine came downstairs.

"Jasper's still in bed." Lucy announced. "Good morning."

It took a moment for Delphine to get this. "Good morning. In bed?"

"Yes. I don't know what's got into that crazy nut today. He won't answer me. Nor nothin'. The alarm rang off but he wouldn't move."

Delphine blinked. She looked out through the window over the yard. "He isn't out milking then?"

"I said he was still in bed. The crazy coot."

Delphine went to the washstand and splashed her face with cold rain water. She dried herself briskly. "You say he's still in bed?"

"Go look for yourself if you don't believe me."

Delphine poured herself some coffee.

"You go and try to get him up if you think you can." Then Lucy added, a little bitterly, "Maybe at that he'll listen to you. You always seem to have more luck with him than I do. Getting him to do something."

Delphine sipped some more coffee standing up, then did go and look for herself.

Delphine entered the bedroom firmly and went over and shook Jasper. "Well well, Jas, playing games now, are you?"

Jasper still lay with his knees curled up under his chin.

"Jas?"

No movement in bed.

"Jas, get up! You're already late with the milking. And you know what happens if you skip milking."

The alarm clock ticked on the chair beside the bed.

"The cows'll get bealed bags if you don't milk them on time."

"Mmm."

"What seems to be the matter with you, Jas? You haven't given up, have you?"

"Mmmmm."

She touched him, gently. "What's the matter, Jas? Tell sis."

Jasper slowly unclamped his legs, slowly straightened out under the covers, slowly rolled over on his back. His knees cracked.

"Tell me. The door's closed in case it's something you don't want poor Luce to hear."

Jasper's eyes opened and he threw Delphine a slow lustreless glass-brown look. Then he stared up at the ceiling. "It's no use," he said at last.

He sounded so low, so beaten, Delphine started. Her eyes opened, wide.

"It's no use," he said. "No use. Work work work. And what for? For nothing. You just get older and rundown with nothing to show for it."

"Oh, come now, Jas, you know that's not it. Tell sis."

"Sure we make a little money each year. Sure we put some into the place to improve it. Sure we save some in the bank. But what for? For who? We're all going to die in the end anyway."

"Jas, something's eating you and you're not telling me."

"I quit."

He spoke so hollowly, spoke so finally, that Delphine decided to let him be for a while.

She went back to the kitchen and told Lucy she would do the chores that morning, the milking, the feeding, and so on.

"That lazy bum," Lucy said. "He could easy do it."

Delphine looked down at the floor. "I think we better humor him along today."

"Humor him? Him?"

"After all, Luce, the poor man's worked for nigh onto fifteen years now with nary a rest. Hasn't he? No time off for play. Pretty good for a little runt, I'd say. And never no hired man either in all that time."

"How about all the times we helped him?" Lucy snorted, poker in hand as she was about to stir up the coals under the oatmeal.

"We really didn't help him much. Except in emergencies."

"Well! So you finally see some good in him after all."

After chores, after breakfast, Delphine took a cup of hot coffee in to Jasper. She found him still curled up under the covers. She sat beside him on the bed and lifted the corner of the colored quilt and let steam from the hot beverage drift slowly past his nose.

Jasper's breathing didn't vary in the least.

Delphine's eyes opened. That looked bad. Jasper was more of a coffee hound than she was. After a bit, she got up and left, taking the coffee with her.

Back in the kitchen, Lucy asked, "Well?"

Delphine showed her the still full cup.

Lucy plumped down in her chair. She folded her hands in her lap. "There is something wrong with him then. Really."

"Yes."

Lucy sat a while, thinking to herself. "What do you think it is?"

"I hate to think what it is."

"He ain't crazy or nothing like that, is he?"

"No, not that."

"Well I never."

"I think we ought to just leave him be. Stay out of there all day."

Lucy said, "Maybe when he gets hungry enough he'll get up."

"I don't think so," Delphine said slowly.

Presently Lucy got to her feet and with a sidelong glance at Delphine went outdoors and disappeared into the privy.

9

Jasper didn't get up all day. He didn't eat either. Nor did he use the big white throne under the bed with its fancy crochet-covered lid.

The two women were as baffled as a pair of hens caught in a summer whirlwind. They didn't know which way to turn to right things.

Lucy was so scared she wouldn't go to bed with him that night. She slept on the hard leather sofa in the sitting room. She lay awake most of the night waiting for him to make a noise in the bedroom, any kind of stirring at all, which would show he was coming out of whatever it was he was in. But wait as she would she didn't hear a peep from him.

The next morning both women faced each other bleary-eyed over the breakfast table. A pot of fresh coffee steamed between them.

"I think we better call a doctor," Lucy said.

"No," Delphine said.

"I think we better."

"No. I think I know what's wrong."

"What, then?"

"Wait."

After a while Delphine took a cup of hot coffee into the bedroom. She found Jasper still curled up into his furry ball. His beard had grown and his hair was wilder. She pulled the covers back and again let steam from the hot coffee drift slowly past his nose.

His lips moved. "That's a dirty trick," he said hoarsely.

"Get up, Jasper."

"No."

"Why not?"

"I quit."

Delphine touched the side of the hot cup against the bony hump of his nose.

"That's a dirty trick."

"Get up, Jas."

"I quit."

Delphine set the coffee down and pulled the white owl from under the bed. She lifted the crocheted cover and peered in with fine womanly delicacy. The pot was as dry as a bone. Softly she let down the cover again. Dispite her care the chamber pot made a sound like that of a distant cannon booming.

"Jas, you'll poison yourself if you don't at least use this."

"That's my plan."

"You better get up."

"I quit."

Again they let him alone for the day.

Delphine did the chores. She also climbed up into the haymow and had a look around at the neighborhood to see how far along everybody was with their field work. Jasper usually was ahead of the neighbors by at least a day or two. So a day or two he could miss and still be up with them. But she had to make sure.

Lucy began to act quite raddled. She'd work hard ten minutes; then sit down staring at the floor ten minutes. She drank quarts of coffee. Then right in the middle of work, as she was dusting a chair, or sweeping the porch, she'd drop her rag or broom, and run for the privy.

The following morning Delphine tried once more.

She brought in the usual steaming cup of coffee and held it under Jasper's nose. His beard by now had grown out considerable. He looked more than ever like a gray squirrel curled up for a long winter's sleep.

"Dirty trick," Jasper muttered, eyes tight shut.

"Get up, Jasper."

"I quit."

Delphine looked in the pot. Dry.

"Jas, you fool you, get up or you'll poison yourself with your own castings. Your lye and wax."

"That's my plan."

"Jas, I was up in the haymow."

No answer.

"Looked out of the cupola."

No move.

"Guess what. Peterson is just about done planting his corn."

"Mmm."

"That puts you behind a day, don't it?"

"Mmmm."

"And Jim Styles across the border is cutting his alfalfa."

"Mmmmm."

"Have some coffee, Jasper."

"I quit."

Delphine set the cup down. Then, grim, she grabbed him by the neck and shook him and set him up in bed. She held onto his cock neck until his eyes popped open, part-crossed. "Now I want you to tell me what's wrong. Right now. We've had enough of this silly business."

"Nothing's wrong. I've just quit, is all."

"Tell me." She let him go when she saw he'd sit up.

Jasper threw her a sidelong look; then stared straight ahead at the bedpost. "Well, for one thing, what good does it do me to raise all them bumper crops? There still ain't no kids in the house. The land produces but the woman don't."

"Well, at least you've had a living. Just think of all the poor duffers who've starved and lost and gone into debt and who also hain't had no children either."

"They was licked all around and that makes it different."

"And you've had Lucy for a wife all this time."

"Ha. Just a clothespin. Can't produce."

"My goodness, Jasper Dollarhide."

"No, there's nothing to live for."

"Not even for God?"

"Not hardly."

"Not even for me?"

Jasper threw her a look, intent, rust-red. "You ain't expectin', are you?"

"Nor even for yourself then? Just to be pure and simple selfish?"

"I tried that. It don't work. All you get is a echo. And that's worse than nothing."

"I see."

"Do it for myself? Woman, don't make me laugh. I'm the last of the Dollarhides. Our line was about to die out back in New Hampshire. So I came west. To a new land. But if I don't get kids soon, we're done."

"Well," Delphine said, slowly, at last getting to her feet. "I'm going to leave the coffee with you. And you better use your white friend under the bed pretty soon now or else us girls are going to have to put you on it. Like a ma might her naughty boy."

Jasper drank the coffee. He even ate some eggs and apples. He also talked some more with Delphine. But except for using the white friend he didn't get up.

10

Jasper wouldn't talk to Lucy.

The result was Lucy became more and more nervous. Also more and more suspicious.

Then one morning, nine days after Jasper took to bed, Lucy took matters in her own hands.

She put on one of Jasper's old overalls and a pair of his old yard shoes. She next got up Jasper's new team of bays from the pasture, harnessed them, got out the old sod-breaking plow, and hitched the horses to it. She drove the team a mile west, crossed the bridge over Blood Run Creek into Iowa, came back and entered the four-acre piece of wild land from the Iowa side. She set the plow in, point first, tied a knot in the black leather lines and caught them around her shoulders, grabbed both handles, and clucked up the horses.

The plow dug in, too deep. The next thing she knew the handles had reared up, she with them, throwing her onto the back of the right hand horse. Her spine popped.

"Whoa!" she hollered, and dropped to the ground.

She stared around wildly. Then, a terrible grimace cutting across her face, she pulled the handles down, re-aimed the plow point, and started up again.

This time she set the point too shallow and it sheared up out of the tough sod, almost leaping onto the horses.

"Whoa!" she yelled, and yanked back on the lines.

She sat down on the handles. She cried. Her wrists ached. Her spine burned. Her right hip felt cracked. She cried. She decided to give it up as a bad try.

Squirrels from all around popped out of their holes, astounded at the intrusion upon their old Eden. They whistled at her. There were so many squirrels the place looked like a suddenly popped out asparagus patch.

The squirrels peering at her made Lucy mad again. She got to her feet once more.

"If it's the last thing I ever do, I'm going to chase them dargone gophers across the border. All of them. Let Iowa worry about them pests."

After a while Lucy got the hang of it, and by the time the sun went down the piece of wild land was no more.

II

The terrible effort of holding down the leaping old breaking-plow did something to Lucy. In rapid succession her bad cough came back, then came a fever, and finally one morning, at five, just seven days after she'd sodbusted the wasteland, she hemorrhaged in a gush and choked to death.

That got Jasper out of bed.

Where before he had lain curled up in dull melancholy, he now was active in wildest grief. He literally flew over the yard. He made funeral arrangements, planted corn, cut alfalfa, wept bitterly, seemingly all at the same time. He hardly slept. And the day of the funeral he was up at three, did the chores, got the last of the corn in by noon, at one was listening to the reverend conducting house services, at two was in church crying over Lucy's gaunt chinaware face, at four heard dirt clodding on her casket in the Whitebone cemetery, and at six was out raking up the down alfalfa. He went around with his face fearfully wrinkled up and drawn. His rust-red eyes burned. His lips moved in soundless talk.

During all the burial commotion, Mrs. Peterson, the neighbor's wife, stayed at the house. But right after the funeral she went back to her own family. Thus when Jasper came home late from work that night, he was a little startled to find a big trunk and a fat suitcase in the kitchen and Delphine sitting on them. She still had on the mourning clothes she'd worn at the funeral.

He came down out of his soul's rage long enough to ask, "Where you goin'?"

"I quit," she said.

"What's that you say?"

"Think I'm gonna go on staying here? Alone with you? Now?"

"Why not?"

"And be a sweet potato in the mouth of every fool gossip in the county before morning?"

"I don't get you, woman."

"Well, you and I are here alone now, you know."

"Oh." He blinked. "Oh."

"So get out the buggy and bring me across the border into Iowa. Mrs. Styles says she can use a housekeeper. She's ailed all her life too, as you've probably heard."

"Who's gonna cook for me? And keep house?"

"I don't know. I haven't given it a thought."

"There ain't nobody I can walk over to for my meals. Mrs. Peterson has already done enough for us. Don't want to be any more beholden to her."

"Anyway, I quit."

His whole face let down, and he slumped into a chair by the door. "Now I am bad off." He covered his walnut face with gnarly hands. "Oh, Lucy, Lucy, what did I do?"

Delphine looked at him for a few moments; finally said, "I'll walk over. Jim Styles can get my trunk and suitcase later on."

12

It was Jim Styles who brought the news to Delphine. He came stumping in with it in his red rubber boots. "I think you better go back and help Jasper, Delphine."

"Oh? How so?"

"I heard cows bellerin' in his yard this morning. So I tied up the horses on the line fence and stepped over to see what the heck was going on. Well, I found him in bed."

"Ohhh." Delphine sat down on the edge of the kitchen table.

"I'll be glad to drive you over."

"What about Mrs. Styles?"

"Oh, we'll manage. We did before. Besides, maybe we can advertise for a girl."

"He was in bed, you say?"

Styles coughed apologetically. "I first knocked on the door. You know. But when nobody answered, I poked my head in, slow, and then . . ."

"All curled up in a ball? Under the covers?"

"Yeh."

"That foxy little devil!"

Jim Styles fell silent.

"All right," she said. "All right. Take me over."

13

Delphine didn't go in to see Jasper right away. She set her fat suitcase beside the trunk where Jim had set it and then went out and milked the bellering cows to take them out of their misery. The milk was so clotted and bloody she had to throw it all to the pigs.

"That foxy little devil."

She next cleaned up the house, all except the bedroom. She left Jasper strictly alone, letting him figure out who it might be that was tromping around in his house while he lay abed.

Again in the evening she milked the bellering cows. The milk was somewhat clotty still, but by straining it through a piece of cheesecloth she managed to save some of it for creaming. She ate alone in the kitchen, still ignoring Jasper in the bedroom.

Afterwards she rocked awhile in front of the bay window. She watched a rooster and a hen climb the boardwalk into the henhouse. She watched a primrose sunset flower and fade. She watched night whelm in from the east.

Then, quiet, determined, she lit a lamp and marched into Jasper's bedroom. She set the lamp on the commode, slipped into a silk nightgown, the one she'd saved all these years in her hope chest, blew out the lamp, and slid under the quilts beside him.

Jasper leaped out of bed. "Lucy!" he cried. "Are you a hant?"

Delphine smiled in the dark. "Yes," she said, sweetly. "I am a hant. From out of your piece of wild land there."

"Delphine!" he cried. "So soon after?"

"Get back into bed," she said. "We might as well make come true what really was true all along."

"No."

"Get back into bed! The next time we go to town we'll get ourselves married in the eyes of the law."

14

They had just six years left in which to do it. And they did it. They had five children, four of whom survived. There was something wrong with the fifth child and it was just as well that it died.

Jasper was overjoyed that the Dollarhide line was saved. While Delphine suffered it all.

Delphine battled Jasper for the children's sake; she battled him for the house's sake. Her children were models and she was the first woman in the county to have running water in the house.

Further Reading

Conquering Horse. 1959.

King of Spades. 1966.

Lord Grizzly. 1954.

No Fun on Sunday. 1990.

Riders of Judgment. 1957.

Scarlet Plume. 1964.

The Selected Letters of Frederick Manfred, 1932–1954. Ed. Arthur R. Huseboe and Nancy Owen Nelson. 1988.

Reading about Frederick Manfred

Conversations with Frederick Manfred. John R. Milton, moderator. Salt Lake City: University of Utah Press, 1974.

Flora, Joseph. *Frederick Manfred*. Western Writers Series. Boise ID: Boise State University, 1974.

Nelson, Nancy Owen. "Frederick Manfred." *Updating the Literary West*. Fort Worth: Texas Christian University Press, 1997. 693–700.

Wright, Robert C. "Frederick Manfred." *Literary History of the American West*. Fort Worth: Texas Christian University Press, 1987. 792–805.

Wright Morris *(1910–1998)*

In the 1930s and 1940s Wright Morris was a photographer. *The Inhabitants* (1946) and *God's Country and My People* (1968) explore the ways we use visual images and words to perceive our surroundings. In *God's Country* Morris juxtaposes prose paragraphs with photographs. Although there are no people in the stark photos of abandoned structures in *The Inhabitants,* the title does not seem ironic to Morris. In this work, as in most of Morris's photos, the absence of people is intentional: "[T]he presence of people in the houses and barns was enhanced by their absence in the photographs."* Commenting on the contrast between his approach to photography and that of other photographers who captured vivid images of the people affected by poverty and suffering during the 1930s and 1940s, Morris explains, "I wanted the *persona* behind the social abuses, one that would prove to be the same with or without them."† Morris's success with this subtle kind of symbolism is clearly evident in all of his work.

Morris published his first novel, *My Uncle Dudley,* in 1940, and for the next forty years he published a new book every two or three years. A complete bibliography of his work is several pages long. Although his prose often seems fragmented, it is grounded in metaphors and clichés rich with layers of implied meanings that, like his photographic images, become icons of things there but not immediately apparent. At the same time, Morris is vividly specific: his verbal images are as stark as his black and white photos of uninhabited buildings. As critic Joe Wydeven has said, Morris's readers must "grapple with subtly suggestive images saturated with conceptual meaning."

Morris repeatedly suggests in his novels and essays that on the Great Plains the sky is literally the limit, that an unlimited horizon frees the plains dweller to imagine not only political, social, or economic freedom but corporeal freedom as well. He chronicles the lives of average men and women who are trying to make sense of a world of confusing changes, inexplicable violence, and frustrating limitations.

The Home Place is Wright Morris's effort to combine photos and words in a novel, a technique he applied in his photo-essays. In the novel, photos face each page of text. In both media Morris uses complementary techniques: closely viewed details that obliquely suggest broader themes that the reader or viewer must learn to recognize.

---

*Wright Morris, *Time Pieces: Photographs, Writing and Memory* (New York: Aperture, 1989), 114.
†Morris, *Time Pieces,* 115.

In this early novel Morris explores one of his most persistent themes: the mix of stubborn commitment, nostalgia, and aversion to change that holds the plains inhabitant anchored in place. It is a theme that he explores in other novels, most notably in *Ceremony in Lone Tree*. In *The Home Place* Morris considers the implications of "home": what gains might be realized in a barren landscape if one remains firmly anchored and what losses the plains resident incurs if he casts off to be adrift in America's placeless society. Both options demand sacrifices and commitment.

The opening pages of this novel, included here, illustrate one of Morris's most familiar fictional techniques: people in his stories very seldom speak directly to each other, but rather they communicate through motion, gesture, and cryptic comments. The result is a tension between the scene and the action of the story that can be both humorous and ironic. The apparent conflicts encapsulate the novel's principal theme: the search for a home place. What Clyde Muncy, a struggling young writer, wants is a home place for his own family, natives of New York City and now cross-country transients. He has come to the Nebraska farm of his Aunt Clara and Uncle Harry hoping that this can be his home place. But the plains people are typical Morris characters: Clyde Muncy, his Uncle Harry, and his Aunt Clara are incapable of acknowledging the Muncys' situation. Clyde tries to find ways to let his aunt and uncle know the purpose of his family's visit without *telling* them. Of course, Uncle Harry and Aunt Clara know that purpose, but there's no reason for them to tell Clyde: obviously, he knows, too.

Clyde Muncy is a lifelong migrant, the son of a restless railroad man. The only *place* Clyde feels any connection to is the farm of his aunt and uncle where he spent relatively long periods of time as a boy. His attempt to attach his own past to the farm and thereby to connect his migrant family to his fictional version of his past is unraveling even during the first hours of their arrival. Finally Clyde realizes that he cannot assume possession of his Uncle Ed's house: his imagined past is not a strong enough link to someone else's home place. He cannot impose his family on his uncle's home place where Uncle Ed's life is visible in the patterns worn into the carpets and the old man's things.

Morris was born in Central City, Nebraska. His mother died a week after he was born. He spent his boyhood in the small towns of Nebraska with his father, the prototype for many of Morris's unsettled, neglectful fathers and husbands. This pattern continued through high school, and various colleges and jobs after that. He spent time in Europe with the Lost Generation. Like many plains residents, he migrated to California, where he settled in to teach for years at San Francisco State University. He was awarded the National Book Award in 1957 for *Field of Vision* and the American Book Award for *Plains Song* in 1980. In his last decade Morris's photography was honored with a 1983 traveling exhibition organized by the Corcoran Gallery of Washington DC, and he published his three-part memoir, *Will's*

Boy (1981), *Solo: An American Dreamer in Europe* (1983), and *A Cloak of Light* (1985). In his last published book, *Time Pieces: Photographs, Writing and Memory* (1989), Morris presents various essays and lectures that articulate his theories about the relationship between the visual world and the mind's eye.

Excerpt from *The Home Place* (1948)

What's the old man doing?" I said, and I looked down the trail, beyond the ragged box elder, where the old man stood in the door of the barn, fooling with an inner tube. In town I used to take the old man's hand and lead him across the tracks where horses and men, little girls, and sometimes little boys were killed. Why was that? They didn't stop, look and listen. We did.

"Is he planting melons?" Clara said.

"No, he isn't planting melons," I said. Clara put her hand over her glass eye, drew down the lid.

"If he isn't planting melons it would be nothing useful," she said.

"He's fixing his inner tube," said the boy.

"Thanks son," I said, and put my hand on his head. After the girl I wanted a boy so I could stand with my hand on his head, or his shoulder. But you can't. Try it sometime. I took my hand off his head and put it on the cool handle of the dipper, pressed on the handle, and skimmed off three drowned flies. I showed them to the boy and said, "Sprinkle them with salt and they'll be as good as new ones."

"How's that?" said Clara.

"I was just telling the boy to feed flies like that to the chickens." I opened the screen, and tossed the water into the yard. Four or five seedy leghorns ran through the shadows, scratched for them. "You see that, son?" I said.

"I told him to bring fresh water," she said, "but I don't think he's got around to it. He's eighty-one. He don't get around too much."

"You're not so young yourself," I said.

"I'm a farmer's wife," she said, and pulled a green stocking cap low on her head. My Aunt Clara is a raw-boned woman, a little over six feet tall, flat as a lath, and with the stalking gait of a whooping crane. In the early morning she wears a bright green stocking cap. She's been doing that for at least thirty years—against the night air, as she calls it—the tassel dangling over the ear that once troubled her. It gives her a certain rakish look. "I'm a farmer's wife," she repeated, and picked up a small tin bucket, with a blue Karo label, and started across the yard. She seemed to wade through the soft, pitted chicken mounds. "There's not a square inch of this yard," she said, without turning to look at me, "them chickens haven't scratched from one place to another one." She walked behind the hedge fencing the drive, where I could see the bright glint of her cap, like a whip tassel, jogging along toward the barn.

"What you looking at, son?" I said.

He was out in the yard, his head between his knees. He picked up something, smelled it, put it down again.

"What you got there?" I said.

"Nothing—" he said, and stood up.

"Suppose we take these pails," I said, "and get Grandma some nice fresh water?" I took two pails from the table on the porch, gave the boy the short one, with the blue and white stripes. I took the milk pail with the wooden handle, the tall straight sides. "When I was your age," I said, "I used to fetch fresh water every morning," using the word *fetch* advisedly. I nodded my head toward the pump, where the old man was standing, fooling with his tube, before I noticed how close to the house it seemed. The last time I fetched water that pump was a block away.

"What's this?" the boy said, and kicked at a bump he saw in the yard. He kicked it loose, and it rolled across the yard into the weeds.

"That's a croquet ball," I said, and looked around the yard for the wickets. When I was a boy I tripped over those wickets all the time.

"Cro-kay?" said the boy, "what's cro-kay?" He was standing with the ball, scratching off the layers of dirt. Under the dirt was a faded orange band, he sniffed at it.

"It smells like the subway," he said.

There you have it. There you have it in a nutshell. Two thousand miles from New York a city boy turns up something in a farm yard, it smells damp and earthy, like a storm cave, so he calls it the subway smell.

"You think its smells like the subway?" I said.

"It's smelly," he said.

"Put it down," I said, "before your sister has to sniff at it." He put it down, wiped his fingers on his clean city pants. Peggy is worse than the boy in the sense that she can't see, feel, or smell anything, without comparing it with something else. God knows what she would think that ball smelled like.

"What's cro-kay?" said the boy.

"Let's get that water," I said, then seeing the old man I added, "suppose you ask your Grandpa. He's the man to answer questions like that." We picked up our pails and walked down the trail toward the old man.

"Thinks I—" the old man said, "tube as heavy as that'll last forever. Well, says he, would if it was rubber, but it ain't rubber. What is it, says I? Airsuds, says he. What's that, says I? That's what it is if it ain't rubber, says he."

"Where's the handle to the pump?" I said.

"Airsuds, says he. That's what it is if it ain't rubber." The old man hung the tube around his neck and put the boy's bucket on the pump nozzle. He pulled on a piece of taped wire that went into the pump house. A motor started. "Hole in it as big as my head," he said, and squeezed his finger into the nail tear.

"This new rubber is not so good," I said.

"It ain't rubber," said the old man. "It's airsuds." He liked that word. He spit and watched the water spill into the pail.

"What's cro-kay?" said the boy.

The old man took the small pail off the nozzle, hung on the milk pail.

"This boy pullin' my leg?" he said, but without looking at him. He gazed across the yard at the hay rick, the break in the trees.

"You've got to remember," I said, "this is the first time he's been out in the country. In the city you don't have yards like this. You don't play croquet."

"I didn't play it much," the old man said, "but I knew what it was."

"You had it right here in the yard," I said. "The boy's never had a yard. If he had a yard like this he would play croquet."

"Seems to me somebody might've told him what it was."

"He never asked before," I said. "There's two or three hundred thousand boys in the city who never heard of croquet. They don't know what it is. What's more," I said, "they don't want to know." Was he listening? He had turned his back to me to spit.

"Viola's kids were born and raised in Lone Tree," he said, "but they know what croquet is."

"Lone Tree—" I said, my voice a little high, "is not New York. There is no grass in New York, no yards, no trees, no lawn swings—and for thousands of kids not very much sky. They live in cages," I said, "it's like a big zoo of kids. A cage with windows and bars."

"Seems to me a man with any sense, or any kids, would live some place else."

I managed to keep control of myself by picking up the pail. I put it down again and said—"You may not know it, but there's several million people, Americans—" I added, "without a decent place to live. They live in trailers, tents, and four or five people to one room." I stopped. My voice came back at me from across the yard.

"Two empty houses—" the old man said, his voice flat, and wheeled to point at them. He pointed east, then directly across the road. My hands were shaking so bad I didn't want to risk spilling the water. I put my left hand on the pump nozzle. It was cool. "One across the road," he said, "be empty in a week or two."

I wet my lips and said, "I thought Ed lived across the road."

"Ed's sick—" he said.

"He's sick?"

"Be dead in a week or two." The old man spit, stepped on the quid like it was a bug. "Didn't see him for ten or twelve days, so Clara thought I'd better look over. He was in bed. Lyin' there. Well, says I, ain't it about time you was gettin' up? Well, says he, it's in my legs. What, says I? I can't move, says he." The old man felt in his pocket for his pipe, tapped the bowl on his palm. He took out a ten-penny nail and scratched the ashes off the top. "Couldn't twitch his toes. Been lyin' there eight or nine days."

"God almighty," I said.

"First thing I did was give him somethin' to get a little movement. Set him on the potty. Held him like a kid. Guess he hadn't been to the outbilly for ten or twelve days."

"Where's he at now?"

"Bed in town with a lady to watch him. Day and night. Well, says I, ain't you a little old for this kind of tinkerin'? Says he, I ain't too old to enjoy it."

I put my hand out toward the boy, but he ducked. "You want to help your Grandma look for eggs?" I said.

"I want to know what cro-kay is," he said.

"Ask your daddy later," I said, "run along now and look for some eggs."

"How'd he know where to look for eggs?"

"Well, I've told him a thing or two," I said. "After all, his daddy was born on a farm."

The old man looked at me. He twanged his nose between his thumb and forefinger—"I thought you was born in Lone Tree?"

"Lone Tree is a small town," I said, "and I was born on the edge of Lone Tree. We had a horse and some chickens. We had a cow—for a while," I said.

"I didn't think you was born on a farm," the old man said. He picked up the smaller pail and started for the house.

As my boy was eyeing me, I said, "I could walk right from here and put my hands on some eggs. I used to do that all the time. All summer," I said.

"I'd think about it first," the old man said, "as them old hens are gettin' pretty touchy. They catch you foolin' with them eggs an' they'll cackle half the night." Alongside the corn planter he came to a halt, put down the pail. He took the inner tube from his neck and looped it around the seat post of the planter. "Come to think of it," he said, "used to wonder why them chickens was so fretful in the summer, and in the winter was just as nice an' quiet as you please." He gazed across the yard, toward the shade elm and the house, where the croquet court used to be. "My, them Plymouth Rocks was sharp—let it get a little dark an' they come in along the drive. Them fool leghorns get tangled in them wickets, every time."

"You know where an egg is?" the boy said.

"There's your sister," I said, and pointed at Peggy standing in the door of the barn. She's a good deal like her mother, so I said— "What have you been into?"

"Nothing—" she said.

I put the pail down and walked toward her across the yard. She was holding her new apron like she had made a muss in it, but instead of running she waited for me. I came up and looked at the white egg in her lap.

"That belongs to the chickie," I said, in her mother's best manner. "It's the chickie's egg. It isn't our egg. We'll put it back."

"The chickie gave it to me," she said.

"All right," I said, "go find Grandma and show her what the chickie did." She started off. "Take your brother long," I said.

"I've got my hands full *now*," she said, and sighed like her mother.

"What's cro-kay?" said the boy.

"There's your mother at the screen," I said. "She's been helping Grandma. Canning. Let's both take your mother a nice cool drink." I went back to the pump for my pail, but when I looked around the boy was gone. The barn door was swinging, and two swallows were noisy on the wires.

"See those birds?" I called to me wife. "They're barn swallows. They live in the barn."

"Not a bad idea," my wife said.

That could be taken several ways, but not right at the moment.

"How's my little dove?" I said, and smilingly walked toward her. But I seemed to have forgotten how to carry those milk pails. I put it down and looked at the water on my white buck shoes.

"Parboiled—" she said, in answer to my question, then—"If you're going to play at being Old McDonald you can first come in here and change your clothes."

"When I was a boy—" I said, biding my time, "there was a fine clipped lawn right where I'm standing. I used to mow it. Play croquet every afternoon."

"Where are my babies?" she said.

"They went off to find some eggs," I said, and left the pail where it was till I had changed my shoes.

My wife opened the screen, then let it slam and followed me into the kitchen. Clara's beets were cooking on the cob range. There were newspapers spread on the table and over the lid of the water bin, with lapping red beet rings from the dripping mason jars.

"Boy!" I said, "Pickled beets!" and took a deep breath.

"Suppose you stand right there and inhale it," my wife said.

"Now look here—" I said.

"I didn't come out here," she said, "to be parboiled in another woman's kitchen."

"I don't know as she asked you to," I said.

"What do you expect me to do?" she said. "Sit in the front room in the rocker while she's out here parboiling?"

"That's a good word," I said, "so long as you don't overdo it. You keep telling me you were born on a farm, so I just took it for granted you could live one day where the old lady's lived all of her life."

"I *can* carry a bucket of water," she said.

"If you think you can control yourself," I said, "it might interest you to know that I've located a house. Right here in the neighborhood." That calmed her.

"We can't furnish a house right now," she said.

"This house is all furnished, all ready," I said. She looked at me. "You don't *have* to pickle beets," I said, "there are other things you can pickle, and I suppose you've noticed how your babies like the farm." She had. "But a good deal depends on your being able to control yourself. If they thought that one afternoon in the kitchen was more than you could stand—"

"Suppose you walk over there and lean over that stove," she said.

"You seem to forget," I said, "that I was born and raised out here."

"I've often tried to," she said, "but I can't."

"If that's the way you feel," I said, "suppose you call the kids and tell them we're leaving." I went to the screen, cleared my throat, and called, "Oh Peggy!"

"Are you absolutely crazy?" my wife said.

"Don't worry," I said. "She won't come."

"The least you might do," she said, "is try to understand how I'm feeling. I wasn't born out here." She looked at the stove. "And I don't like pickled beets."

"You've never tasted a real pickled beet," I said, and walked into the front room, where it was cooler.

"If it's like her *real* fried egg," said my wife—"Why it was vulcanized. I couldn't cut it."

"That will be enough of *that*," I said.

"What makes me so sick," my wife said, "is that you can't take it as well as I can. I'm at least polite. I don't yell at them like a fishwife."

"I was not yelling at him," I said.

"Well, you raised your voice," she said.

"He always makes me raise my voice," I said, "but I was not yelling at him. He's not very well informed, and you can't tell him anything."

"You ought to try and tell *her* something," she said.

"I'll tell you what it is I can't stand," she said. "It's *all right* for you to share their lives. That's fine. But they don't give a dam about yours."

I walked through the dining room to the front door that Aunt Clara had always kept locked. It was still locked, as they had never put a porch at the front of the house. If she left it unlocked, the old man, or some stranger, might have killed himself. The old man was forgetful, and sometimes gave the door a try.

My wife came in and said, "I'm just all nerves from this housing situation. It's all I can do to just try to be nice—"

"I'm a little touchy, too," I said, "but I am trying to do something about it. For one thing," I said, "I have just driven your babies two thousand miles."

"You're very sweet."

"These people think we're crazy," I said "—if they think about us at all, but it doesn't keep them from sharing their own house. They'll share what they got, including their vulcanized eggs."

"I didn't mean that—" she said, "but I couldn't cut it—either."

"The old man thinks I'm a total loss, but you notice how he offered me what he smokes?"

"What *is* it?" said my wife.

"Airsuds—" I said. "That's what it is if it isn't tobacco." I walked into the small room at the side, where my wife slept with Peggy, and looked at my face in the bureau mirror.

"You're sunburned—" she said, and looked at me in the mirror. "Does it have to be so dark in here?"

"She's trying to keep it cool," I said, "for people like yourself. She used to have a lot of trees, nice big shade trees, but they died in the drouth."

We stood there and I could hear the chickens cackling.

"What about this house?" she said.

"If you can just keep your mouth shut," I said, "I think I've got my hands on a house." My wife took out some pins, put them in her mouth, and let down her hair. She ran her fingers through the braid and said—

"What house?"

"If I remember correctly," I said, "Ed's house has a john and running water. He put it in for his mother. I don't think he married anyone."

"Ed who?" she said.

"Uncle Ed—" I said. "On Clara's side."

"What's the matter with him?"

"He's sick," I said. Then I cleared my throat and said, "The old man says he's a goner. In a week or two."

"I didn't come two thousand miles," my wife said, "to do what they're doing in New York."

"No—?" I said.

"Well, not exactly," she said. "I'm not going to budge until he's really dead."

"That's being really thoughtful," I said. She didn't pick that up, so I said, "It's a small-type house, one floor and an attic," and I raised the blind a foot or so and looked at the road. There were still a few trees, mulberry and catalpa, but I could see the front of Uncle Ed's house. I remembered him as the owner of an Edison Gramophone. I liked the horn and the felt-lined case of black cylinders. "Pretty nice for the kids," I said, "they could spend a noisy day over here, then come home and spend a quiet night with us."

My wife came to the window and said, "So it's come to this."

"You can be dam thankful it has," I said.

"I wonder what it's like inside?"

"There's just one floor," I said. "That window opens on the attic. The thing to remember is the running water and the inside john."

"That's important," she said, "seeing as how you can't carry a pail of water."

I ignored that and said, "You can't judge the place on how it looks now. This was some farm," I said, "thirty years ago. The old man had a five acre orchard with the finest apples in the state; he's got a trunk full of the ribbons he won at the fair." That reminded me of something and I said, "I wish you could have seen the old lady. She won all of the jelly and quilting prizes they had around here."

"What happened?" she said.

"You wear out," I said. "Out here is where people and things wear out. You keep winding it up till one day the ticker stops."

"Can't they get any help?"

"You can't get farm help any more," I said. "Men will do anything rather than work on a farm."

"Women, too," she said.

"Sure," I said, "women too."

"It makes you wonder, doesn't it?"

"The old man's an awful dam fool," I said. "You can't tell him a thing—but there's something about him."

"There's always something about an old fool," my wife said.

I left her there and walked through the house to the back porch. Aunt Clara and Peggy were coming in from the barn; Clara was tipped away from the bucket I had left near the pump, and Peggy was carrying the Karo can, full of white eggs. I walked back to the folding doors and said, "Well, here she comes."

"Do you have to shout?"

"If she left you here with her beets, all I've got to say is you better be here."

"Hmmm—" she said.

"If you can just control yourself," I said, "I'll have you a nice little place in the country. But you leave it to me. Just try and control yourself." I took a quick look at the stove, to see if anything was burning, then I went upstairs to change my clothes.

The stairs are right behind the range, in something like a steep chute—one of the reasons you can't live up there in the summer time. I could feel the heat right through the plaster wall. As a boy I had the room at the head of the stairs, where the ceiling slopes down over the bed, but on hot summer nights I slept on the floor. The windows were low, and there was sometimes a breeze down there. As my own boy is about that age—eight next October—I had an odd feeling when I got to the top of the stairs. Put it this way—for a moment I wondered who I was. Since we left New York, a week ago, I'd been trying to tell my boy, whenever he'd listen, what it was like to live on a farm. You can't do it. You can't tell a city kid anything. But I had talked a good deal to myself, and lay awake thinking about it, which might account for the feeling I had. I was Spud Muncy, sometimes known as "the little fart."

Whoever I was, I was facing Viola's room with its flower-cluttered wallpaper, and the handcolored photo of her skinny brother, Ivy. Ivy had been seven that summer, but he was not a little fart, in any respect, so he had been able to wear my clothes. That's my fauntleroy he's wearing on the wall. He was also wearing my high button shoes, and my pink Omaha garters, which showed all right, but not in the photograph. I sat in the buggy and thumbed my nose at him. I was wearing his cast-off rompers, with the drop-seat and the dark brown stains, and while thumbling my nose I was smoking licorice cigarettes. A good deal of my spit was there on the buckboard, beside the old man's.

I was facing Viola's room, and Ivy, but when I turned on the stairs the door to the old man's room—their room, that is—stood open. All of the upstairs rooms are dark, as the windows are low, floor level, and the blinds are usually drawn against the heat. All the light was on the floor—I used to lie there and read. Midsummer nights I would lie near the window and read the Monkey Ward catalogue, the descriptions of watches, long after the old folks had gone to bed. As my father always talked a good deal, in bed, I used to wonder why these people, who went to bed so early, never said a word. Their shoes would drop on the floor, that was all. I would hear the old man puff at the lamp—sometimes he had to whooosh at it— then the dry rattle as he settled back on the cornshuck mattress. Some nights, for quite a little while, he would yawn and burp. Thirty years ago he often complained of what he called a weight in his stomach—a stone at the pit of it, he said. When- ever he complained at supper, he burped at night. My father always said no human could live on a diet of potatoes and pork gravy, but the old man is alive, and my father is dead, now, ten years. I lay awake the night before, thinking of that.

I suppose after fifty years of marriage there may be things to keep you awake, but not much for you to lie bed and talk about. If you pile out of bed around a quarter past five, single plow a foot deep with a team of deaf mares, at a quarter past eight the odds are you'll be ready for sleep. Sometimes I'd hear the old man sit up, and use the potty, or hear Clara tell him, in her high private voice, that it was storming and he had better put the windows down. That was one thing he could do. Would do, that is.

I went to the window and raised the blind so I could look at the seedy elm, the leaning cob house, and along the untrimmed hedge toward the barn. The chickens had made a spongy pit of the yard. That accounted for a good deal of the worm- neck, and the stumbling gait I had seen among the hens, as you can't let chickens mess around in their own dirt. But you couldn't tell the old lady that. After a little more than twenty years, four of them at the state Aggie college, Ivy managed to tell the old man a little bit about hybrid corn. Not much, but a little bit. But he could never tell him to move his machines in out of the rain. Or to vaccinate his cows, or his pigs, against the cholera. No, you couldn't tell him anything. Years ago, when I was in school, I sent the old man a pound can of tobacco, a fine blend I couldn't afford to smoke myself. I also sent him a French brier, a small bottle of pipe sweetener, and an English-made cleaning tool. He sent everything but the tool back to me. "I thank you for the tool," he said, "which I got right here in my pocket, but Granger's the only cut I get any satisfaction from." No, you couldn't tell them, show them, or give them anything. They were like the single plow below my window—when the old man had a piece of plowing to do he hitched up his team of mares, and that was what he used. A foot deep and a yard wide, stopping at the end of the furrow to sit on the crossbar and spit on the white grubs at his feet.

"It's men like him," Ivy had said, "who made this goddam dust bowl."

True enough—but it was men like him who were still around when the dust blew away. As my wife said, there's always something about an old fool.

"Oh, Dearie—!" my wife called.

"Coming—" I said, and sat down on the edge of the bed to change my shoes.

Further Reading

Ceremony in Lone Tree. 1960.
Field of Vision. 1956.
Fire Sermon. 1971.
The Fork River Space Project. 1977.
The Home Place. 1948.
Man and Boy. 1951.
My Uncle Dudley. 1942.
Plains Song: For Female Voices. 1980.
The Works of Love. 1952.
The World in the Attic. 1949.

Reading about Wright Morris

Bird, Roy K. *Wright Morris: Memory and Imagination.* New York: Peter Land, 1985.

Crump, G. B. *The Novels of Wright Morris.* Lincoln: University of Nebraska Press, 1978.

——. "Wright Morris." *Literary History of the American West.* Fort Worth: Texas Christian University Press, 1987.

Howard, Leon. *Wright Morris.* Minneapolis: University of Minnesota Press, 1968.

Knoll, Robert, ed. *Conversations with Wright Morris: Critical Views and Responses.* Lincoln: University of Nebraska Press, 1977.

Wydeven, Joe. *Wright Morris Revised.* Boston: Twayne, 1998.

——. "Wright Morris: Update." *Updating the Literary West.* Fort Worth: Texas Christian University Press, 1997. 685–92.

Robert Kroetsch (b. 1927)

Robert Kroetsch is a postmodernist who creates novels that rework the usual literary conventions. Kroetsch has said that he wants to force the reader to interact with the story, so he likes to "uninvent" or "uncreate" his stories, to try to make an old story work in new ways. His themes of dispossession, exile, and the quest for new identities are especially appropriate to the postmodern form and to the dry, empty prairie setting.

Kroetsch was born in Heisler, Alberta. He worked in the Canadian north for six years before earning a bachelor's degree at the University of Alberta, a master's degree at Middlebury College in Vermont, and a Ph.D. at Iowa University. He has taught at the State University of New York at Binghamton and at the University of Manitoba, where he was named a distinguished professor in 1985. His novel *The Studhorse Man* (1969) received the Governor General's Award, Canada's most prestigious literary prize.

In *Badlands* Kroetsch explores the prehistoric past revealed in the eroded canyons of the Red Deer River in the dry regions of eastern Alberta. Many of the dinosaurs reconstructed in museums around the world were dug out of these valleys and ravines, where erosion has exposed the ancient sea floor layered beneath the western reaches of the Great Plains. The egotistical William Dawe pursues bones with the intensity and determination of earlier hunters who trapped the beaver and killed the buffalo. In 1916, however, he is too late to make his name with a major find. Dawe's odd party includes his assistant, Web, the Chinese cook, Grizzly, and Tune, a piano-playing boy found deep in a mine and brought to the surface by Dawe. They are shadowed by the tribally unidentified Indian Anna Yellowbird, whose husband has vanished in the Europe of World War I, a place and event she cannot imagine. She believes that Dawe can take her to the world of the dead where she will find her absent husband.

Literally and metaphorically Dawe's expedition floats down the river, through layers of geologic time, far beyond the normal routines of life that continue on the table land above the river's deep cut. The disfiguring hump that distorts Dawe's physical self mirrors the psychic deformities that have turned him from the present to search for dry bones far beyond time and human history. He pries deep into the landscape where he believes he will find the bones that will make his reputation. Searching for these ancient specimens in the most inhospitable landscape enables him to avoid his wife and domestic obligations: he wants nothing less than to realize the Western myth of absolute independence.

Kroetsch disturbs his narrative even more by having Dawe's daughter, Anna, retrace her father's route fifty-six years later, using his field notes as her guide. Anna's commentary and the notes serve as interchapters, or breaks in the narrative. Anna Dawe encounters Anna Yellowhair, and the two women create their own ironic parody of Dawe's effort to slip through time. At the novel's end they encounter a huge male bear dangling helplessly from a helicopter, being unceremoniously dumped in the wilderness where he can do no harm—the postmodern alternative to Dawe's narcissistic expedition.

This selection opens with forty-five-year-old Anna's meditation on her father's field notes at the site of the party's excavations. Dawe has his first direct encounter with the shadowy Anna Yellowhair and her house of the dead, made from the very bones Dawe is searching for. Dawe's expedition into the past is only slightly more absurd than many of the treks across the region made by explorers who had their own visions of opportunities, both mythical and economic, on the Great Plains.

Excerpt from *Badlands* (1975)

Anna Dawe

Just as my name was determined in that season eleven years before I was born, so were my character, my fate. For in that summer of his glory my father became not only what he had always implicitly been, but what he explicitly wanted to be. After that he was a man without a history, for in that season he became the man that twenty-six more seasons, in the bonebeds of the world, would only confirm. Failure might have ruined him back into history; but failure was never to be his good fortune. It is true that success never made him wealthy. But my mother's sense of guilt, or pride, or perhaps her need to keep him in the field, provided him with the means to live beyond his income. And beyond us as well.

It was in my fate to dream a father, in my character to wait. And I waited for ten years after his death, as if he must bring himself back from his own bonebed.

Surely, yes, I worked at the waiting; as he had worked at his starting out. I studied the documents. I read of the bitter feuds of Marsh and Cope, those first great collectors of dinosaur bones; and from that lesson I learned mostly that my father had been born one generation too late. But he was not to be deterred by a mere error in chronology. My mother and I read his field notes, and then I read them alone. And we—I—read of his ventures into deserts and jungles, into Africa and Texas and Patagonia, into the Arctic islands. I read of his brave and absurd and (needless to say) successful expeditions into Mongolia—in search of dinosaur eggs. But while he went on, annually if not endlessly, collecting evidence of Cretaceous and then Jurassic and then Triassic life; while he persisted as if he must one happy morning get back to the source itself, the root moment when the glory of reptiles, destined to dominate the world magnificently for one hundred million years, was focussed in one bony creature, one Adam-seed burrowing in the green slime—

But I was left always with the mystery of his own first season. For in his summer of 1916, in the Badlands of the Red Deer River, discovering the Mesozoic era, with all of Europe filling its earth with the bones of its own young—he removed himself from time.

Whatever the desperate reason that had taken him into that far place, he came back delivered of most of the impulses we like to think of as human. He could survive any weather, any diet, any deprivation. And that was necessary to a man whose back bore on it a hump larger than any of us could see. But somewhere in the course of that first journey that was his own—somewhere, somehow, he shook himself free of any need to share even his sufferings with another human being. His field notes, after that summer, were less and less concerned with his crew, his dangers, his days of futile prospecting, his moments of discovery, his weariness, his ambitions, his frustrations. They became scientific descriptions of the size and location of bones, of the composition of the matrix, of the methods of extraction and preservation . . .

And I had to visit those badlands where his success began. Because, there, in that beautiful and nightmare season—he ceased to dare to love.

26. Deadlodge Canyon at Last

Dawe writing: *Wednesday, July 5. Into Oldman formation. Moved downriver at dawn. Hot by 9 A.M. Herons wading in the shallows. A mule deer watching from a cliff. The landscape dusty and dry and brown beyond the green at the river's edge. Making shore-camp now, below the mouth of Little Sandhill Creek. Eight miles from rimrock to farthest rimrock, the canyon itself extending downriver, how many miles I won't guess. Web, as we landed, looking up at the endless buttes and coulees: "Where did you say you dropped that needle?"*

"Where's the pickaxe?" Tune said.

"Woops," Web said. "Knew we forgot something."

They were setting up a second tent, for the cook; Grizzly insisted that the cook's tent be well up on dry land, on the sagebrush flat above the cutbank, with cottonwoods and poplars nearby, a huge patch of thorny buffalo berries outside the tent flaps. They would leave the main tent on the boat, where they might sleep at night in a breeze, free from mosquitoes and the heat.

"What should I do?" Tune said. "Can't drive a stake in this ground."

I could have hit Web with an axe. But he's right. Now that we're here: where do I begin—

And Dawe, then, telling his crew: "Unload the lumber and the plaster of paris. Get a decent table built. Lay in a supply of firewood for Grizzly." And Dawe himself bent over his open steamer trunk, locating a specimen bag, a small pick, a brush, a compass. Dawe striking out: alone, hurrying, he walked out across the flat, finding a path through the sagebrush, the blue-grey hairs of the sage, the twisted, upthrust branches blurring his figure, only his strange back, his black hat, clear in motion. He turned off the flat, away from the river and up onto a ridge, went over and down, into a dry creek bed where not the slightest breeze stirred; and moving up the wall of a butte he found no relief, the sun glaring off the layered clay, off the rust-colored ironstone, the grey bentonite.

He was breathing too hard and he sat down on a boulder to rest; he must learn to move more slowly in the heat. Must. Wrong time to commence. Dizzy from hunger and heat and thirst. Precipitous. High noon the wrong time.

He started back towards the boat—towards camp: Grizzly's stove should be ashore, the fire lit. Time for dinner. Eat a square meal. Look for that canteen and down to the river and fill it. Dehydration can kill a man. After too damned much water for too long.

He almost fell into a deserted quarry.

The hole in the side of the butte had been hacked out, gouged out, by men working in this heat. Dawe thinking, hazily, bitterly: Brown and his five skilled assistants. Sternberg and his three sons and their trained crew. Dawe, down over the crest of the butte, staring into the empty niche. Already the sudden, harsh rains of three seasons, four seasons, had softened the broken edges of clay. But the hole was there, gaping, huge, reminding Dawe that his was only the latest, not the first, expedition. And if nothing new, nothing of importance was to be found, then not only the latest but the last. Skunked. The booby prize.

He walked into camp and found Tune and Web wrestling the stove up the cutbank. Dawe trying the cook's tent and finding it stuffy hot, going down to the river, back to the flatboat from which he had thought himself freed. Dawe, pretending he was busy, pretending he wasn't afraid: *The hole is empty. Redundant. Be careful of the sun. Redundant. A hunchback will, easily, if exerting himself beyond the natural, suffer from anoxia.* He looked at what he had written. He felt safer. *Redundant,* he dared to add.

Web and Tune, sweating, came up the gangplank to begin to unload the lumber, the wood for the packing boxes. Dawe, putting away his stub of pencil:

"Where did Grizzly get to?"

Tune, mopping his forehead with the tail of his shirt. "Went somewhere with a fishing pole."

Web groaned aloud. "Can't be another goddamned goldeye in this river. I absolutely refuse to choke on, spit out or swallow another fishbone."

Grizzly, small, silent, hurrying, came out of the cottonwoods that bordered the water; he was carrying his fishing rod and three goldeyes.

27. Looking for Fossils

Next morning Dawe took Tune and Web with him into the coulees, showed Tune, showed Web again, how to recognize a fossil if there chanced to be a fossil to be recognized. Without a fragment to look at he tried to tell them of creatures no one had ever seen, explained how to watch for the brown concretion that wasn't quite brown, the texture that wasn't merely rock, the shape that couldn't be expected to have been bone but wasn't quite anything else. And on the morning of the day after that day he elaborated further, unwilling to believe they had learned their lesson, believing they had not learned, for if they had they would not have failed so miserably as had he; he who could (blindfolded, he explained to Tune) without fail recognize a gastrolith or a horn cone in the rubble at the base of a cliff, a vertebra in a concretion in a sandstone outcrop. And that day, too, they learned again how to move slowly, the thermometer in the tent's shade reading 105 degrees by 2 P.M., how to make a canteen of water last, how not to drink too much when they returned to camp and fell down flat on the bank and dipped their faces into the river. And on the evening of that (third) day Dawe wrote something on page 39, Book A, of his field notes for 1916, then tore off the bottom half of the page and, presumably, destroyed it: Dawe, at last, come to doubt.

28. House of Bone

Smoke, as they commenced the fourth day of their prospecting, billowed down into and filled the long canyon. Somewhere to the west a prairie fire burned unchecked, the drifting clouds of smoke blurring the buttes with a veil that in its diffusion of light produced a blue-grey glare. The three men, out prospecting, kept their eyes to the ground, learned quickly they could lose each other from sight, learned quickly to listen. And it was Dawe's intense listening, not his sight, that led him to his first discovery.

He was little more than a mile below camp, returning from the day's vain search, when he heard a voice that he took to be Tune's. The voice lifting into song. He was so exhausted he had passed it by, had passed by the singing, before he understood it was in a language that neither he nor Tune might know.

Dawe turned off the sagebrush flat, turned back, entered a clump of old cotton-woods.

The singing resumed.

He took another thirty paces, forty paces, broke through the circle of trees and into a dry gulch.

The heap of dinosaur bones at first appeared to him to be just that: he recognized at a glance the fragments of ribs and vertebrae, of the shells of turtles, of skulls, of long bones. He believed for a moment he was losing his mind, in the aimless light, was fantasying the bones he had not been able to find in four days of searching. Without a pause he began to walk in a circle around the heaped and apparently singing bones, vaguely aware as he did so that the fragments were arranged in some sort of pattern.

Then, on the river side, he came to the opening, two five-foot femurs, crossed against each other, tied to make an inverted vee.

He did not have to step inside.

Anna Yellowbird came to the low doorway, stooped from her dugout, her cabin of bones, her fossil tipi.

"Come in," she said.

She was as tall as the silent man who confronted her. It was his speechlessness, his absolute loss for words, that made him obey. He stooped after her into the tipi, straightened in the small and conical room. Saw, in looking about him in the subdued light, an axe that was from his boat, a blanket that was from his boat, a tarpaulin from his boat, food from his boat.

He might have reached up, had he been able, might have brought the bones crashing down upon their heads. And even as he confronted the futility of that proposal, he recognized that the girl, the child, the woman, had had help in building her strange house: from one or more or all of the men who were supposedly helping him seek these rare and precious specimens.

Dawe did not speak. It was the sheer domesticity of the scene that broke him away and back to the doorway. It was not the heaped and mysterious bones themselves, not the grotesque doorway of the joined thighbones of a hadrosaur nor the stacked and interlocked fragments of fish and turtles and petrified wood; not the broken and fragmented limbs and hips, the bony shields, the huge pelvic bones, the teeth, the jaws, but the fire in the middle of the small room, the pot by the fire, the knife and fork by the pot.

"Soon," the woman said, Anna Yellowbird said, "we will find them."

Dawe stepped out of the tipi, out into the failing day, turned, found the path into the crooked trees and through them, stumbled out onto the sagebrush flat, followed what to him looked like a path, a new, worn path through the sagebrush and the buffaloberry bushes.

He stepped into the cook's tent.

Grizzly and Tune were kneeling on the ground in front of Web; Web sat on a bench, the legs of his trousers pulled up above his dirty knees.

"Fucking cactus," Web said. "Thought I saw a genuine dinosaur sticking its ass out of the clay and I got so excited I knelt right down on my knees in some fucking cactus. Found more ironstone."

Tune was dabbing iodine onto Web's knees, painting them brown.

"So she's here," Dawe said.

Tune began to put the cap on the bottle of iodine, as if he recognized at that instant they were all of them, Dawe, Web, Grizzly, himself, all past all healing.

"Did you hear me?"

Not one of the three listening men stirred. They held him off, excluded Dawe, ignored him, denied him his confrontation and his moral outrage at whatever it was he felt a right to be outraged about, refused him even the invited deceit of surprise or feigned refutation. A housefly buzzed in the stuffy air in the tent; Grizzly picked up the fly swatter he'd made from a willow stick and a square of canvas.

"I want to tell you men something," Dawe said. He feigned his self-discipline, as well as the others feigned their not feigning anything, let himself back towards the flaps of the tent; then he stood hunched and hesitating, like a bear that had entered a tent for bacon and found instead the stench of men.

"One of you gentlemen goes near that squaw, I'll fire you. Fire all of you. You can *walk* out of here, you can goddamned *crawl* out of here, all the way out in the stinking heat and the smoke and the flies."

He stopped.

"Like she did to get here," Web said. "And beat us on top of it."

Dawe, turning away, limping away; he went down to the river to soak his swollen feet so they, again, in the morning, would fit his boots.

Anna Dawe

It was another of the ironies of that season that the wars of Europe had sent the Indian girl into the canyon of my father's dreams. She was fourteen years old when she married, fifteen when she became a widow. At fifteen, newly a widow, having learned that her husband was vanished and gone, with an iron ship bound for something called England, for something called the World War, she had wandered blindly towards the east, knowing that England lay to the east, the war raged to the east; she had listened for the guns, watched for the strange ocean on which an iron ship might float; she wandered disconsolate, desolate, on those western prairies that were taken from her family before her husband too was taken: and vaguely, desperately, despite the Anglican if not Christian missionaries who taught her husband submission and love, she recalled a shaman whose whereabouts she did not know but whose sacred and recollected words she knew she must heed. And she found, was found by, three strange white men and a chinaman. And she knew, had known, watching the four of them leave Tail Creek in their hurry to be away from her necessary if imitation grave, it was the hunchbacked man, not the others, who could find the way to the place of the dead. Even as she vaguely knew, vaguely and yet vividly remembered, what the shaman had said: do not eat, lie in your grave, wait for the guide.

And she had followed her guide so bravely she had preceded him to his own goal.

Further Reading

Alibi. 1983.
But We Are Exiles. 1960.
Gone Indian. 1973.
A Likely Story: the Writing Life. 1996.
The Lovely Treachery of Words: Essays New and Selected. 1989.
The Man from the Creeks. 1998.
What the Crow Said. 1978.
The Words of My Roaring. 1966.

Reading about Robert Kroetsch

Lecker, Robert. *Robert Kroetsch*. Boston: Twayne, 1986.

Neuman, Shirley, and Robert R. Wilson. *Labyrinths of Voice: Conversation with Robert Kroetsch*. Edmonton: NeWest Press, 1982.

Thomas, Peter. *Robert Kroetsch*. Vancouver: Douglas and McIntyre, 1980.

Douglas Unger *(b. 1952)*

Douglas Unger's novel *Leaving the Land* is a decidedly ironic take on the myths of the garden and the democratic utopia. Set in the high plains of western South Dakota, Unger's novel follows the life of Marge Hogan Vogel, her son, Kurt, her parents, Ben and Vera—who homesteaded their meager farm in the last land rush of the early twentieth century—and her husband, Jim Vogel, a lawyer for the Nowell-Safebuy Company who pressures area landowners to become a part of his company's monopolistic, vertically integrated turkey operation.

The title is ironic: people cannot make a living on the land and cannot leave it. They are trapped not only by economic failure but also by the pull of the wasted land itself. The central character in this dilemma, Marge, dreams of leaving the land but stays to care for those who cannot leave. Kurt joins the navy but returns after eight years, drawn by obligations and emotions he cannot fully explain.

Unger was born in Moscow, Idaho. He attended the Colegio San Miguel in Argentina, and holds a bachelor's degree from the University of Chicago and a master of fine arts degree from the Iowa Writers Workshop. He taught theater and dance at Western Washington University in Bellingham, Washington, and creative writing at Syracuse University. Since 1991 he has been on the faculty at the University of Nevada at Las Vegas. He has been an essayist for the MacNeil-Lehrer News Hour and a screenwriter.

Unger revisits the South Dakota setting in another novel, *The Turkey War* (1988), an account of German prisoners of war working in a turkey processing plant. His other novels are set in Argentina, a region he came to know as a college student and during Fulbright appointments in Argentina, Uruguay, and Chile.

In this chapter from *Leaving the Land*, narrated by Kurt Vogel, Unger contrasts the story of Ben Reary, who succumbed to Jim Vogel's high pressure tactics and traded farming for turkeys, with the story of Ben Hogan, who resisted the corporation and scraped out a living on his own land. It is an account of the homesteading boom in reverse, the predictable end of an economy that values land only as commodity.

Excerpt from *Leaving the Land* (1984)

The turkey plant shut down. It didn't happen in a single day or month but over a period of two years, with steadily increasing expenses combined with low prices and declining volumes. The Nowell-Safebuy completely restructured its system of farms. The logical extreme of vertical integration was direct ownership of the land. When the smoke finally cleared from the N.F.O. protests and the violent upheavals in local farm credit during hard times for farmers, the Nowell-Safebuy began to buy land. It was a slow process. For example, the Reary farm was overextended. Ben Reary couldn't get the First Bank of Belle Fourche to extend his loans or to refinance, couldn't get president David Whitcomb to give him what farmers called the guts and hide loan, "the loan it takes the banker a barrowload of guts to give and everyone involved stands to lose his hide."

Sam Carlson made a personal visit to Ben Reary's farm. He inspected the long steel outbuildings in which Ben housed ten thousand White Holland hybrid turkeys in tier upon tier of wire cages. He watched Ben push the buttons on his new Harvestore silo, like a huge thermos bottle standing between his turkey barns, which let loose its measured doses of dry, vacuum-packed feed with a powerful inrush of air. The feed moved out along mechanical troughs, corn spilling like yellow rain down long gutterways. At the first loud *whoosh* of the silo and the humming of the electric augers that moved their feed, ten thousand turkeys stood up in their cages. They pranced a little, shook out their wings. A call rose among them, a single gobbling cry quickly joined by another and another until as if by that one lone command, the entire flock joined in with a deafening shriek. Turkeys rushed forward in their tiny cells, some in excitement slamming hard against the wire. Clouds of white feathers drifted across the barn like an exotic snow. Beaks clattering in the metal troughs, ten thousand bald red heads reached out and stuffed themselves.

Ben Reary showed off his cornfields—four hundred acres of level gumbo that produced more than enough to pack his silo, more than enough even to sell locally to smaller growers. He showed off his tractor, as big as a small house, his discs and harrows and seeders as wide as a two-lane highway, which were costing him thousands of dollars per quarter just in interest. Sam Carlson produced a sheaf of papers, dozens of forms, prospectuses, statistical graphs, even a health insurance plan. He made an offer to Ben Reary to pay off all his loans, buy his turkeys and his barns, his silo, his tractor, everything. Ben would get several thousand for himself to count as equity for the work of two generations. And he could still live on in his new house, could still work the land, still wake up every morning to punch the buttons on his Harvestore silo controls and feed his birds. Sam would hire him as "unit farm manager" to work turkeys for the Nowell-Safebuy on a steady salary, just like the plant workers in town. The Nowell-Safebuy would take over all obligations. It would also assume direct ownership of the land.

The Reary family didn't know what to do. Ben Reary placed frantic ads in newspapers clear to Cheyenne and listed his place for sale with a half dozen realtors. But in such hard times, no one wanted to invest in raising turkeys. He finally had to accept Sam Carlson's offer. He sold his farm. So did Jake Ballock, the

Bosserds, the Hinkles too, eventually. Even Pearly Green and his kids finally sold out to the Nowell-Safebuy, though they didn't agree to work for them.

That next harvest, Ben Reary and many other small farmers raised turkeys for wages. It was one of the smallest harvests many could remember; slightly less than eight hundred thousand turkeys were hatched, stuffed with grain, trucked to town, butchered, packed, frozen, shipped out of town again. Ben Reary climbed back into his empty Nowell-Safebuy stock truck, which still echoed with the sound of turkeys. He leaned forward over the wheel, sweating, silent. His wife, Connie, sat next to him. He reached into his shirt pocket and handed her the check. She slowly unfolded that check with a tired glance. She pressed her lips with the same determination she had always had, would have as long as she lived—the same ability to forget her dreams for now and make her man as proud as she could of what little was there. In prior hard years, they did their best to hang on to the land; that was most important. They paid what bills they could and made plans for the coming year, that better year they all expected, had to expect in order to raise spirit enough to keep working through snowbound winter months overhauling in preparation for spring. But Sam Carlson's program was working. They didn't own the land anymore.

Sam Carlson should have known. He should have been aware of the Bates Rubber Company's fiasco in northwest Colorado. Bates bought up hundreds of thousands of acres of wheat and grazing land, pumping millions of investment dollars into the most modern cattle feeders, into a fleet of tractors powerful enough to level mountains and into a new crossbreed of cattle that could grow to weights of up to two thousand pounds in eighteen months with the aid of growth hormones. Everything was beautifully described in color brochures printed by the thousands for stockbrokerage firms in the East, including graphed projections of vast profits symbolically represented to the potential investor by line drawings of a series of ever fatter steers growing across the page.

But Bates couldn't find enough workers willing to sacrifice for the land. It had to hire one and a half times as many unit farm managers as there had once been family farmers, with production remaining just about the same. Bates discovered after intensive sociological research that family farmers are willing to work eighteen hours a day if need be and not just for money, but to hold on to the land. There is an immortality given to the earth, a sense of expansive dream passed from immigrant homesteader through generation after generation of his children in a self-perpetuating vision of the meaning of freedom and wealth. Unit farm managers punched their time clocks after eight hours and drove home. Production dropped. It wasn't long before the Bates Land & Cattle Company began losing millions.

Leading agrieconomists in the East, most of them men who had never so much as once experienced the realities of scraping barnyard manure off their boots, suddenly stopped talking about the benefits of vertical integration. They sat discoursing around a brand-new topic called "farm unit management problems." And the same thing happened here. Or almost the same. It wasn't long before even the Nowell-Safebuy began losing money.

The turkey plant slowed down, laying off two hundred workers. People hung on through the winter, optimistically talking of future recovery. Times grew harder. It was the year my mother's divorce papers finally came, her settlement being the house and everything in it, the second car, and a small monthly check for my support. She made plans to sell the house. A half dozen real estate agents poked at the rafters with screwdrivers, clucked their tongues at the patchwork and spackling on the floor and ceiling of my mother's bedroom. She had plans to sell the house and move us both to California where her childhood friend Rae Ott lived, granddaughter to the Reverend and Beatrice Ott. It was a place near the ocean. My mother had never seen an ocean. But times were hard and the offers that came in for the house weren't half of what she expected. She decided to hold out for better times. And as a year passed, she might have grown wise enough to sell the house for any offer she could get before the turkey plant completely shut down. We might have lived in California. But then my grandfather died.

Grandpa Ben died suddenly one night. He simply fell back gasping. He called for his wife, his voice slurred, his tongue thick. They had just come home from an annual celebration—that one night each year when they unfailingly left whatever kids and problems behind for a dinner out to commemorate the first time Ben had carried a lariat rope ten miles across the snow-covered plains from his homestead to the Norman place. As the story goes, the Norman family house was small, constructed so that if the five Norman girls had in mind to do some proper courting, they had to lower themselves through a trapdoor, climb down a rickety ladder into the living room, then sneak out past their parents sleeping there. Old man Norman sometimes scattered crumpled newspapers on the floor to make sure there would be enough noise to wake him.

Grandpa Ben used a soft lariat rope to get his Vera down out of her high window, sometime after the moon had paled. He crept around out there a long time in the fierce winter winds. He carried lumps of meat to bait the dogs. It wasn't long before Ben and Vera had a small fire going in the Norman harness shop, way off behind the barn. This went on night after night for several weeks before they were married. They had a proper wedding in a church. But they always celebrated their anniversary according to the date of that first cold winter night when Ben had stood in the backyard, the dogs whining and simpering as he jumped around half frozen, lariat rope in hand. On that anniversary, Ben and Vera left the farm, drove to Cheyenne, had a dinner out and spent the night at a motel. The afternoon after their last anniversary, Ben and Vera pulled in at home with Ben grumbling for some unknown petty reason or, as Vera thought, because he had such a hangover from the night before. Ben went on about his chores, taking care of a few chickens, his two horses, the few beef cattle he kept for family use, mending a stretch of fence between the house and old hayfield that was now being rented out for pasture. At supper, Vera noticed Ben had a fierce headache and that he was so thick-tongued it was hard for him to eat or speak. But she thought he must have been drinking a little to chase his hangover away. Later that evening, he fell back dead of stroke in the living room.

"Don't tell me nothing," my grandmother said after we arrived late that evening. There were no tears, no evident signs of grief. Only the harshness in her voice let on how pierced she was by death. "No. Don't tell me nothing," she said. "He did what he could. He worked like the hammers of hell. After we lost the boys, he just did what he could to get by. He left this place. That's what he left. And there won't be much left of that once the neighbors finish. That new pump in the barn'll likely be gone before morning. Somebody'll just drive on up in an hour or so and take it. Oh, they'll offer me something. A few dollars. But if we wasn't sitting in this house right now, you can bet they'd be going over the very chair I'm sitting on. . . ."

"Don't let 'em, Mama," my mother said. "You don't have to let them."

"You hush up now," said Grandma Vera. "You're the one who's going off to Florida."

"California," my mother said.

"One of them sunshine states," said Grandma Vera. "It don't matter much which one."

"But, Mama . . ."

"Don't you tell me nothing," Grandma said. "Ben and me used to do it too. I remember when Simon Lisky died. Never knew the news of a death to move so fast. Almost everybody beat us to it. But Ben still picked himself up a rifle and some horse harness at the funeral. He paid the widow a couple of dollars. Then when it came to me going through that dead man's house, no matter what I knew about the pretty lamps Simon had, no matter how much Ben kept telling me to get in there and bring us out something, I just stood there and watched them other women. They jumped on widow Lisky's personal belongings like a flock of crows. I never seen nothing like it. That old woman just sitting there letting them do it because she knew the farm would be sold for a song and she was too feeble to go anywhere but a rest home. So she just gave her house away. There was a lot of things in there I could have had, too. But all I took was one of Simon's dogs. Simon always liked his dogs. So I fed that one better than the rest."

My mother was sitting on the floor in front of Grandma Vera's chair. My mother leaned her head on Grandma's lap. Grandma stroked my mother's hair. After a few pets like that from Grandma's hand it was as if an inner strength my mother had kept balled up inside suddenly weakened. She broke down crying in Grandma's lap. "Now I ain't saying I blame anybody," Grandma said. "The men can come take anything they please, pay me anything they want. Just don't you let them touch this house. Just because your papa's gone, that don't mean they can have what belongs to me. I plan to stay on here. That's what I decided. Your papa would have liked me to turn the farm over to you right now. But, honey, I don't see why I should. You'd likely sell it out from under me or worse. Worse is you might want to move out here yourself. And I just don't want to see you with that kind of hard work and endless days. So I'm going to stay on here until the barn blows down. Nobody's going to farm this place. Nobody's going to put a hand to it until I'm gone. I'll put affairs in order, then just sit right here until I can watch out the window and see this place look just like it did when Ben first gave it to me. This place is mine until I'm gone. Then you'll get your chance," Grandma Vera said, still stroking my mother's hair, a gentle bitterness in her voice that made my mother raise her head and look. "You can come take anything you get a hold on," Grandma said, "when that happens."

My mother looked at me as if I could help somehow. I didn't know what to say. The expression on my mother's face suddenly changed. She returned Grandma Vera's bitter tone of voice. "Just don't you dare let the neighbors see him," she said. "I don't care what your side's tradition is. You know he didn't want a viewing. He told me once that if you tried to give him a viewing, he'd sit up howling drunk in his coffin."

"He's my husband," Grandma Vera said. "I can do whatever I want with him."

"We'll see about that," my mother said.

"It's already been seen to," Grandma answered. "It's done by now."

We buried my grandfather two days later, embalmed and in a fancy blue metal casket that cost every dime in Grandma's savings account. "He never would have stood for this," my mother said even as she helped Grandma clean Grandpa's brown wool suit. My contribution was to polish Grandpa's good black stovepipe boots with embroidery from Mexico. Then I waited in the car parked in front of the Millis mortuary as the two of them went into what Darwin Millis called his "slumber room" to dress Grandpa for his funeral. There was a last-minute argument with Darwin about whether he was legally allowed to bury Grandpa in the old-fashioned way—on his own land instead of in a licensed cemetery. My mother spent the next day driving back and forth from one county office to another to get all the new paperwork done, mountains of forms to sign indicating exactly where the private plot would be in relation to future county development plans, hundreds of dollars in fees required even then. With the exception of a few others, including my Grandma Vera's, it was one of the last such burials ever permitted in this state. The upshot was that even if a man owned ten thousand acres of the remotest wilderness, he could do anything he wanted or could afford to do but have himself buried on it.

The funeral was on Grandpa's farm. There was some last-minute tension about whether all the necessary forms were done in time, but finally the maroon hearse from the Millis mortuary in town drove Grandpa back home in his coffin. Pearly Cyrus Green, Will Hartley, Jim Fuller, Charlie Gooch and his son Dan, friends of my Grandpa's even though they were both mostly Indian, and Jim

Claypool served as pallbearers. They carried Grandpa's coffin into the living room and set it up on painted sawhorses. Then they opened the lid.

Grandpa Ben looked dipped in wax. Someone had drawn dark lines around his eyes. His cheeks and lips were red. His hands were twisted around a cluster of red and white carnations, with one finger rudely projecting out of control, pointing toward his viewers. The expression on his face looked angry. He looked to me like he wanted to sit up and cuss out everyone in the room. A crowd gathered in front of him, dark suits and white shirts making them look like magpies among the colorful funeral wreaths, hands still compulsively brushing snow off clothes and hats as if to be neat and dry was a form of security against death. My mother stood on with a fragile sense of time and place, looking shocked, uprooted but for the support she gave her mother, who leaned against her arm. There came a moment when Reverend Ott in his white robes stood in front of us. He spread his arms like wings. Even the sound of weeping fell back across the room like a soft diminishing wind until it became a sound so frail and piercing it was almost inhuman, a sound like foxes whistling in the distance. We knelt down on Reverend Ott's signal. He surveyed us with an evident sense of personal importance, as if he was pleased somehow despite this death by his stewardship of a tribe again confronted by the higher realities. He slowly found a passage in the notes for his service and began to read the words as if they were in the prayerbook: "Lord, we shall return to greet each other without our burdens. We shall greet each other without our problems, our cares, our sins. Even without the guiding hand of the church, there is a place for all good men in heaven. . . ."

The Reverend Ott looked out over us as he prayed. Almost everyone prayed with him. And everyone knew what he was saying, knew that my Grandpa Ben hadn't set foot in a church since my mother's wedding.

Reverend Ott finished his prayer. Everyone stood. People began to file by Grandpa in his coffin. Grandma Vera reached out and touched two fingers to his lips. My mother was crying. I was crying too, and I didn't want to look at Grandpa again. I went into the bathroom and locked the door. I sat on the stool and cried for the times I wouldn't see him, for the times I had had the chance to please him and did not.

Will, Jim, Pearly, Charlie Gooch and the others picked up Grandpa's coffin. Pearly passed a pint bottle of something to keep them warm. Then they carried the coffin out and down the porch steps, straining under its weight nearly two hundred yards through a fresh dusting of snow to a lone cottonwood behind the barn. Reverend Ott walked close behind them, in front of my mother, my Grandma and me, the crowd following. The pallbearers set the coffin down beside a deep grave they had dug the day before by the cottonwood, using pickaxes to break through the first layer of frozen ground.

Reverend Ott read the funeral service from the Bible. Everyone rose. They watched Pearly and the others lower the coffin into the ground. And even as my

Grandma Vera threw handfuls of earth over her husband, even as we waited there a minute in silence while she said goodbye, the looting had begun. The homeplace suddenly became the scene of a kind of joyous farm auction with very little money and Pearly acting as a kind of auctioneer, taking haphazard bids, not letting things go for nothing but not bidding them up too high, either, Eunice Fuller following along behind him writing prices down in a notebook. Men scrambled this way and that through the sheds and coops, pawing through the barn and shop to pick up whatever they could find—old harness, plowblades, mower and rake teeth, buckets, tools, car and tractor parts. An old man fell to the ground with two huge tires over his shoulders. Women and children chased after random chickens for a quarter apiece, stuffing them in old grain sacks and cardboard boxes. Jim Fuller, quickly away from the gravesite, was already trying to get Grandpa Ben's old stubborn goat around the neck with a rope. In the corral, a group of range boys was laughing and hooting, one of them beating on a pan with a spoon, taunting Grandpa Ben's two hard-mouthed geldings, which were smart enough to kick around devilishly to discourage any easy approach. After a while, whoever could stay on them would take them home for forty dollars a head. As I walked toward the house with my mother and Grandma Vera, everyone was busy around us, everyone with an armload of something: Ben Hogan's fishing poles, his milking stools, his shotgun, even the old, worn-out pad from his tractor seat. Bits and pieces of everything my grandfather had ever built or worked on in his life were soon piled in front of the cars and pickups parked haphazardly in front of the house.

My grandmother went into the house to join the women setting out a buffet. My mother and I stayed outside, watching.

"Why are they taking everything?" I asked.

"If your grandpa were here today, he'd probably join them," my mother said. "He was always one for looting funerals. He was the kind who made a party out of the occasion."

"But, Mom," I said. "Don't you want any of Grandpa's stuff?"

"It's not mine to take," my mother said. "It's Grandma's now."

"But why, Mom?"

"Look. When Grandma dies, God forbid, this farm will be ours. We'll probably sell it. That's what everyone else is doing. So when the neighbors see a place that's going to be sold after a funeral, or one that's bound to sit idle, they come for things. That's the way they do it. And it's better this way. It's better than letting all this stuff sit around and rot. It's better the neighbors, your Grandpa's friends, end up with something."

As my mother was walking, she was suddenly knocked into by a man with a heavy load. She lost her footing and fell in the snow.

"Hey!" I shouted after the man. I helped my mother to her feet. I watched the man struggling to get from the barn door to his pickup with a load of tack and harness. He carried so much of it over his arms, head and shoulders that he looked about two feet taller than he should, a kind of weird giant with a bale of tangled leather for his head. He must hardly have been able to see in front of him.

"Damn you, Don Hinkle!" my mother shouted. Don Hinkle didn't turn to look in our direction. He kept right on going, a tangle of old leather traces dragging through the snow behind him.

My mother might have left him go at that, left that old man alone with his treasures if she hadn't seen it: "My bridle," she said. She turned to me. "He has my bridle! Don!" she called out to him. Don Hinkle didn't even break his stride. "Just you wait here a minute," she said. "Don!" she shouted again, louder. She had to run to catch up with him.

"Don, you've got something of mine in there," she said.

Don Hinkle turned. He nearly dropped his load, buckling under the weight, his face sweating, steaming.

"Oh, what a terrible thing," he said, "a terrible, terrible thing." He made an effort to shake his head in condolence under a heavy horse collar. "It's just plain grieving to me," he said. "A terrible, terrible thing now, Marge. . . ."

"Don, you've got something that belongs to me in there."

The man appeared to understand well enough. He smiled, showing the few broken teeth left in his mouth.

"Well, I don't know as I do," he said. "Ben already give all this here to me. Why, just last week it was! We was sitting in his shop. Just last week he said Don, Don, he said, when I'm gone, you go on and take all that old harness in there. Give Vera twenty bucks."

"I don't care about the harness," she said. "You can have all the harness you want and you know it. But you can't go taking my bridle."

Don Hinkle looked nervously away, out across the frozen meadows. He was staggering, some determined force still drawing him a few steps closer to his pickup truck.

"Marge, just last week it was," he said. "He said Don, Don, when I'm gone, you go on and take all that old harness *and* that bridle in there. Ain't much good left to it anyhow."

"You're lying," my mother said. "You've got my bridle and you know it's mine. I didn't ride with it much. I was never much of one for horses. But as I recall, the times I did ride it was over to your place to visit Carol and you used to admire that bridle. Now, Don, no hard feelings. I'll be grateful you found it for me."

"Well, I did find it in there," said the man with finality. He looked as if he was going to make a fight of this at best. "Ben gave that bridle to me just last week!"

Don Hinkle nodded his head once as if that was the end of it for him. He turned and started back up the lane, walking faster now despite his burden. I looked around somewhat bewildered, as if there would be anyone disposed to help us. The looting was on. A whirlwind of scavengers was busy pulling my family's homeplace apart with amazing efficiency. Men tottered in and out of the ram-shackle buildings as if they owned them, arms loaded, bags and pockets bulging. A group was teamed up and straining at an old orange tractor with starting prob-lems. Another, larger group was perched like a covey of gnarled old doves on the corral fence. There was a kind of rodeo in the corral, each of those old boys making his turn with one of Grandpa's cut-proud geldings out there, stamping, panicked, the white showing around his eyes at every approach. Pearly Green sat with the others up there and watched, passing a bottle.

Near the corral, I saw the rusted end of a piece of pipe sticking up out of the snow. I ran over to it. I wrenched it up, the snow crust breaking like white glass. I was out of my head. But the pipe was too long to swing when I pulled it up.

"Hey!" I shouted to the men on the corral fence. I waved a hand toward Don Hinkle. "Somebody help me stop him!"

No one knew what I meant. Pearly Green raised his pint bottle at me like he was offering a drink.

"Help me!" I shouted.

"It's all right, Kurt!" my mother called out. "It's all right now."

I looked at her. Her face was severe, something showing in it that I had never seen before—like the faces of old tintypes of my family where the inflexible cast to the mouth, the deep lines around harsh, distant eyes tell of hardship, scant food, the deaths of children.

Don Hinkle's boots scuffed through the snow. One of his large brown hands slowly began to work its way into the tangled heap of harness he carried, a good deal of it dragging behind him in the snow, horse bells and buckles jangling like a childhood promise of a sleighride. Strap by strap, rein by rein, I watched that hand shaking something free. A dark hash of bridle dropped off into the snow. He kept right on going, not looking back, not even once.

My mother picked up her bridle. She straightened it out in her hands, dried it tenderly on her coat. It was a work of remarkable beauty, brown and white horse-hair braided into a diamond pattern, the reins at least six feet long, fluted Spanish silver bells woven into the cheek straps and two large, dark green onyx jewels set into silver dollars where the headband joined that part that fastened behind a horse's ears. Suddenly, my mother turned and hugged me, squeezing so tight I couldn't breathe. I held her back, held her up, helpless to her grief.

Don Hinkle unloaded the harness in his truck. When he was finished, he looked toward us quickly once, then quickly away. He climbed into his truck and started the engine. He backed around in a neat circle, truck chains whistling on the ice. He stopped in front of the house. He honked his horn several times. His wife soon came out and traded words with him. He said something to her with an ugly expression on his face. She nodded at him once. She hurried back into the house for her things. Then she climbed into the truck with him and they drove off up the lane.

I helped my mother through the yard gate, stepping carefully along the slick, icy path. Inside the house, the women had already laid out buffet dishes, candles glowing over the food, the windows filled with warm blue abstractions of steam.

"You all O.K. there?" Pearly Green called out behind us. I nodded in answer to him and he grinned, red-faced, filled with a kind of celebration I would never understand. We waited for him. We joined him up the steps and into the house.

All that afternoon, through the slow movement of a kind of disordered wake, that gathering of cowboys, I couldn't keep from thinking of Don Hinkle. My mother wrapped up her bridle and tucked it neatly away in her suitcase. She held a kind of humble court in the living room, relaxed more now and greeting each guest, really visiting with many of them for the first time since she had married and moved to town. She did a lot of talking with Dan Gooch, a tall, young-looking Indian. I didn't like the way she was talking with him. I mixed through the crowd, a small stranger shaking hands and explaining who I was when asked. Most men stepped back from me a little when I told them my name, or at least the ones who didn't know the family history. There was something in the way they looked at me. They hadn't forgotten what my father had done or whom he had worked for. Then everyone began moving down the buffet line and dishing up a plate.

I wasn't hungry anyway. I went outside. The short winter day was almost gone, an aura of violet over the horizon. I walked out toward the barn, all the doors left open wide and creaking in the light breeze. In the barn, everything was overturned, everything was stripped from the rusty spikes driven into the beams as hangers. I looked out the half gate into the corral. There was a horse there, all alone. He pawed with one front hoof at the frozen ground. He sagged a little, hung his head low. No one had been able to stay on him. Or no one wanted to take him home.

I found the hay bales in the loft. I pushed a bale out the loft door and it fell to the earth in the corral, bounced once and broke open. My grandfather's gelding smelled it and nickered, breath steaming out his nostrils. He looked tired. His hooves lifted slowly in the muddy, frozen ground. He looked up at me, then looked at the hay. He didn't know what to make of me. He took a short step closer. Then he threw his head up suddenly, pawing at the ground. He lifted his head and snorted at me. I stepped back into the darkness. I crouched there quietly in the hay and listened to the dry rustle of his eating.

I wondered what Don Hinkle would do with all the harness he'd taken. He didn't have a team anymore. Then I imagined him hanging it around his farmhouse as decoration, bits and pieces of a full six-horse hitch in the living room, part of a sulky rig complete with scattered implements in one corner of the dining room as there were antique implements arranged around my grandfather's house, displayed like so many exhibits in a museum. I imagined a set of horse collars and hames hung over the heating stove. I thought of bell straps hung up so they would jangle in a summer breeze. In my mind, I heard an old man's voice spinning tales and outright lies about that harness, stories of just how it was when he was a young man out there horse farming, *gee hawing* and slogging through sod-covered earth sowing homestead wheat with that very same tack hanging right there on his walls. And sometime that evening, with the fatiguing release of consciousness brought on by the presence of death, I thought I found the sense. Ownership was not to be confused with heritage. That harness would hang for years as decoration, until Don Hinkle eventually sold his farm or died. Then it would all be stolen back again from him.

Further Reading
El Yanqui. 1986.
Voices from Silence. 1995.

Sharon Butala

In her novels and short stories Sharon Butala has chronicled the struggles of ranchers, their families, and the unprepared visitors who endure the numbing cold of winter on the isolated ranches of Saskatchewan, either willingly or reluctantly. In many of her stories there is an element of redemption. There are stories of loss and isolation in *Queen of the Headaches* and *Fever,* Butala's two short story collections, but in her novels, set on the Saskatchewan plains, these forces reach a kind of equilibrium, balancing preservation, loss, and gain.

This story, "A Tropical Holiday," is a break from the usual contemporary Great Plains stories by Butala and other writers. It shares a plot and gentle humor with stories such as Hamlin Garland's "Mrs. Ripley's Trip" or William Allen White's "The Homecoming of Colonel Hucks." In these stories, Great Plains residents, after years of poverty and hard work, find renewal in a trip and satisfaction on their return to the familiar.

The theme of escape, renewal, and return recurs in Great Plains literature often enough that we can note is as a countertheme to the grimmer stories of entrapment and defeat. Leaving or staying put are familiar choices on the Great Plains.

For the biography of and further reading about Butala see pages 24 and 35–36.

A Tropical Holiday (1985)

Mrs. Hackett had pulled the last of the corn stalks and the cucumber vines. She had canned or pickled or frozen everything else in her garden and breathed a sigh of relief to have that over for another year. There was now only herself and Mr. Hackett to eat her garden produce, so that at the end of one season there remained a jar or two of pickled beets from the season before and several quarts of raspberries. They sat on their shelf in her cellar next to the unopened quarts of dills and peaches with dates on them going back four or five years. She could not bring herself to throw out perfectly good food.

At noon Mr. Hackett came into the kitchen and wordlessly tossed the mail on the table. He sat down and began to eat the lunch Mrs. Hackett had prepared and set on the table for him.

"Finished the garden this morning," she said, sitting down and sighing heavily.

He was thumbing through the *Country Guide* and didn't answer. "Soon be time to start my quilts. I'm going to make a "Trip Around the World' in blues and greens, I think, for the fair. Elvira Maxwell wants me to teach her to quilt. She'll never learn." Mr. Hackett didn't say anything. She fanned out the mail with her left hand, holding her fork with her right, while she carried on her one-sided conversation. "Now old Mrs. Maxwell, there was a quilter. Made the most beautiful quilts. I didn't always care for her colours myself."

'Vacation in Bermuda,' the travel brochure under her outspread hand said, and a slim young woman in a skimpy bathing suit ran through shallow, turquoise water at the end of a sandy beach. In the background, a ring of tall palms swayed gently. Mrs. Hackett picked it up and saw that there were three more brochures in the pile, one suggesting a Caribbean cruise on a floating hotel, one about Jamaica, and another titled 'Fabulous Fiji.' Her husband raised his head to see why she had stopped talking.

"I can't imagine who'd send us this stuff," she said.

"Let me see." He shuffled through them. "Junk! It must be for them Mitchells." He tossed them down. "Always on the go," he said. "Don't milk a cow, or keep chickens or even plant a decent garden. Where the hell's Jamaica?" He pronounced it 'Jamaisa.' He went back to his magazine.

"She doesn't know how to quilt either," Mrs. Hackett said, studying the Jamaica brochure absently. "Course she's a city girl, and young. Runs him a merry chase with her dresses and her trips." She got up to serve the dessert.

Sometime in the night she woke up, bewildered, and tried to get her bearings. She had been somewhere warm, where the air was gentle on her arms and face and the sunlight limpid and golden. It soothed her forehead and her cheeks, it bathed her whole body. She felt as though her limbs would melt with the ease of it. She said to her companion, or tried to say, or only thought, "The prairie sun is harsh, like a knife. It pierces you." And then she wakened in her dark bedroom beside Mr. Hackett who lay gently blowing air through his lips, while the glow of the tropical sun still warmed her arms and legs.

She didn't remember her dream the next day. Mr. Hackett decided to help a neighbour bale his straw and Mrs. Hackett went along to keep the neighbour's wife company. They spent the day talking about the fowl supper which was coming up and how glad they were to have finished the canning.

Mrs. Hackett had taken along her bag of cotton scraps and started cutting the pieces for her quilt.

"What's the matter, Ellen?" Mrs. McDonald, who was crocheting an afghan, asked after a long silence.

"Why, I meant to make it in blue and green and all these oranges crept in. I don't remember cutting them."

"It looks pretty," Mrs. McDonald said.

"I guess so," Mrs. Hackett answered, and decided to leave them.

That night she dreamt again. This time she was on an airplane, a small one, just she and the pilot, and they swooped low over an island set in a clear blue sea, so low that she could see the driftwood on the beach and the wavy ridges in the sand left by the tide. The tops of the palms almost grazed the belly of the little plane and she wanted to land, but the pilot kept on going past the island out over a transparent, glittering sea.

She did not like her dreams. They upset her and confused the boundary between sleep and wakefulness. She tried to tell Mr. Hackett, in the evening when the last program on television had ended and the eleven o'clock news had not yet begun.

"Last night I had the strangest dream. I dreamt I was. . . ." She stopped, for she didn't know where she had been, and Mr. Hackett was rattling his newspaper and not listening.

Sometimes when she was making their bed, or standing at the sink washing dishes, she would suddenly feel again the heat of the tropical sun warming her back, or catch a strange, clean scent in the air.

During the day she spaded up her annuals flower bed, pulling out the dead, dried stalks, remembering with regret the rich purple of the pansies, and the orange and gold of the zinnias that had been there. She went to church, or drove to town with Mr. Hackett to buy groceries. One day she ran into young Mrs. Mitchell in the Co-op.

"Some of your mail came to us by mistake," she said. "Some things about a tropical holiday."

"Oh?" Mrs. Mitchell said. "We didn't order any travel brochures. They couldn't have been meant for us."

"But who would send them to me?" Mrs. Hackett wondered, and puzzled over it during the rest of their conversation. "How's your garden?" she asked. "All taken care of?" and, "Quite a wind we had last night," and, "Get your crop off all right?"

That night she woke again with a sense of having been near water. She could feel a light touch on her cheeks, and a faint scent of salt still lingered in the air. But she was at home in their bedroom, and Mr. Hackett lay sleeping beside her. She got out of bed very quietly, and went in to the spare bedroom where she opened the closet and searched through some cardboard boxes piled in the back. After a moment she emerged carrying a box of books. She set the box on the bed and began to look through it till she found the child's school atlas she had been looking for. She turned the pages quietly and then stopped at a map of the islands in the Caribbean. Jamaica, yes. She liked the look of Jamaica. She didn't want to go to an island as big as Cuba, where she wouldn't know she was on an island at all, and some of the others were too small. She would be afraid she would fall off. Jamaica was just the right size. She didn't notice she had decided to go.

"I'd like a holiday," she said to Mr. Hackett, sitting beside him in the pick-up on the way to town.

"I've been thinking I should go up to Medicine Hat," he replied. "I need some new boots and I'm going to start dealing on a new baler." Mrs. Hackett rode along in silence for another mile. Every fall they went to Medicine Hat, never Calgary, never Great Falls, and only once in every six or seven years, to Regina.

"I'd like to go somewhere different," she said. Mr. Hackett didn't answer. Very well, she thought, and didn't mention it again.

She didn't think actively how she would pay for her trip, or how she would get there, but every once in a while, a new detail would pop into her mind complete, as though deep down some part of her was mulling over the practical problems, while the rest of her cooked the meals and vacuumed. She had six hundred dollars of egg and cream money saved. She could sell five or six quilts for a profit of at least a hundred dollars each. One year at the fair, a lady from Regina who had come to see the quilts had asked to buy Mrs. Hackett's. When Mrs. Hackett had said that they were all promised, the woman had given her the address of the store she owned in Regina, and begged her to send some to her as soon as she could make more. Now Mrs. Hackett packed up her stored-away quilts and mailed them to Regina. In two weeks she had six hundred and fifty dollars for them, having told the woman in her letter that she wanted immediate payment, or she wanted the quilts back. Every time she thought of it she could feel the colour rise in her cheeks. She didn't know how she had managed to be so daring.

She puzzled over how a person would get to Jamaica. She thought of asking Mrs. Mitchell. Several times she had her hand on the telephone to call her, but each time, she couldn't bring herself to do it. What if Mrs. Mitchell laughed at her? And then, she thought, she could just go to Regina and buy a plane ticket. It couldn't be that hard. On television they were always trying to persuade you to go to places like Jamaica, and to fly with this airline or that. Surely they would make it easy for a person. She decided that when the time came, she would go to Regina.

She and Mr. Hackett went to Medicine Hat. She found two nice cotton dresses on sale in Simpson's, one white with blue flowers, and the other, a red and white check with white collar and cuffs. She bought them for her trip. She lingered with Mr. Hackett in front of a travel agent's window (it didn't occur to her to go in), but he was impatient and didn't pay any attention. There was a lifesize cardboard cutout of a girl in a bathing suit waving beside a palm tree and she said to Mr. Hackett, "I wonder if that's a date palm or a coconut tree." Mr. Hackett grunted. "I'd like to go there sometime," she said very quickly. She waited, staring hard at the girl in the window.

"What the hell for?" he asked, already walking away, looking at his pocket watch. Mrs. Hackett felt much stronger. She would go in January. She had always hated January on the farm.

At breakfast on the morning of January first Mrs. Hackett said, "I'm going to take a holiday." Mr. Hackett was laying honey thickly on his toast and did not reply. After a while he said, "Where are you going?" as though amused but willing to humour her.

"To Jamaica," she said, with force. He laughed, turning the page of his newspaper.

"How are you going to pay for that?" he asked, not looking at her, acknowledging that he knew she wasn't joking. "Don't think I'll give you any money. It's foolishness." He looked directly at her when he said this.

"Don't need your money," she replied. "I'm going on the fifteenth." They looked at one another silently for a moment. Then Mr. Hackett went back to his newspaper. Mrs. Hackett stood up suddenly, banging her chair out of the way. She began to wash the dishes.

Mrs. Hackett did not know how she would get to Regina. It was no use to ask Mr. Hackett to take her, and although she could drive the tractor, she had never driven the car, which they seldom used. She was afraid to try. Meanwhile, she readied her wardrobe and withdrew her money from the credit union.

"I'm taking a holiday," she said to the Dingwall girl who was the teller. The announcement had burst out unexpectedly. It struck her what she was about to do, and her hand, picking up the money, shook.

"Where are you going?" the teller asked.

"To Jamaica," she replied, and then, "I'm taking the bus to Regina." So that decision was made.

The morning of the fifteenth while Mr. Hackett was shaving, she called to him, "I'm going now. I'll be back on the thirtieth. Good-bye." Mr. Hackett didn't answer. He'll get over it, she thought. Then she drove away with a neighbour woman whom she had called for a ride to town to catch the bus. The neighbour seemed to think she was going to Regina for medical tests. Mrs. Hackett didn't both to correct her.

By the time she had arrived in Regina, she knew what her next step would be. She would take a taxi to the airport.

She was very nervous when she approached the Air Canada desk. The young girl behind the counter was wearing so much makeup that Mrs. Hackett couldn't tell what she looked like.

"A ticket to Jamaica, please," she said. The girl's eyes flickered from Mrs. Hackett's tight grey hair to her worn wool coat. She looked as though she wanted to laugh.

"You can't . . ." she began, then after glancing at the man next to her who was weighing people's suitcases, she said in an annoyed voice, "There are no direct flights from Regina." She tapped her pencil rapidly.

"How do I get there?" Mrs. Hackett whispered and then cleared her throat. She couldn't go home now. Mr. Hackett would never let her forget it.

"You fly to Toronto. Maybe they can get you on a flight fairly soon." Mrs. Hackett must have looked uncertain. "In the winter everyone wants to go south. Most people make reservations months in advance." Her voice was filled with irritation. "They don't just arrive here and expect to get a ticket." Snippy young thing, Mrs. Hackett thought.

"Just a minute," the girl said, sighing. "I'll see what I can do." She began punching the buttons of a machine that looked like a typewriter. After a moment she said, "You can take the two P.M. flight to Toronto, but you'll have to wait once you get there to see if any seats open up. It looks as though they're all taken for the next few days. I can put you on standby though." This was incomprehensible. Mrs. Hackett's feet were beginning to hurt, and a line was forming behind her. Why did I ever leave home? she asked herself, then remembered the frost on the kitchen window, and how grouchy Mr. Hackett was on the really cold days. Again the glow of tropical heat settled on the back of her neck, just below her knot of hair. Her determination renewed itself.

"That will be fine," she said, as though she had understood perfectly. She was given an envelope which the girl said contained her ticket and her boarding pass. The man who was weighing suitcases next to the ticket counter said, "Over here, Ma'am." He weighed her suitcase and slapped some tags on it. "Be sure to collect it when you get off the plane in Toronto," he warned her. "If you don't, you'll wind up in Jamaica without it."

He pointed out Gate Two. She was surprised to find there wasn't a gate there at all. A voice on the loudspeaker called out something about Flight 391 leaving for Toronto. All the people stood up and crowded toward the door, so she went along too, walking through the security system in bewilderment. She followed the crowd onto the plane. With the help of a stewardess, she managed to find the right seat and to do up her seatbelt. When the plane left the ground, and she was forced back into her seat by the momentum of the takeoff, she thought she was having a heart attack she was so frightened, but this passed, and she was flying!

The sky was high and clear and a pale blue. Down below she could see the city receding to dirty smudges on the glistening plain of snow. They climbed and climbed. Far below she could see the blackened squares of land which she finally recognized must be summerfallow with the snow blown off. Beside them were yellow and white squares which would be the fields of stubble. Sometimes she could pick out elevators and clusters of black dots that must be towns. She had no fear of crashing. She had no fear of anything. She was flying!

When she arrived in Toronto, she went right to where the stewardess had told her to go. The man at the desk said, "Ma'am, are you in luck. There's one empty seat on the flight tomorrow at six. Somebody actually called in and cancelled." Shaking his head at her good fortune, he went about preparing her ticket. Mrs. Hackett wasn't surprised. It was only right. She had not questioned that there would be a seat for her, as she had not been afraid that they would crash. Such things didn't happen to people like her.

She stood with her ticket in her hand wondering what to do. Finally she went over to a woman who looked to be her own age and asked her if she knew where there was a hotel where she could spend the night since her flight didn't leave till the morning. The woman, who was wearing an expensive beige suit the same shade as her hair, looked Mrs. Hackett over quickly.

"The airport hotel would be best," she said. "You can't get lost if you stay there. They'll wake you in the morning so you don't miss your flight. Just go through that door there, and there is a bus that will take you over. The bus is free." Mrs. Hackett thought, now there's a sensible woman.

She slept little, worrying about the expense, afraid she would miss her flight. When the phone rang in the early morning to call her, she nearly fainted from the shock. She answered it hurriedly for fear someone else would be wakened by the noise.

They arrived in Kingston in the morning. It was eighty degrees, but Mrs. Hackett didn't mind. She had known from her dreams what the air would feel like. As she stepped down off the plane, she sighed deeply and stopped on the steps smiling, as though she were a visiting ambassadress waiting for the welcoming committee to recognize her.

Then, as she stood waiting to collect her suitcase at the baggage pick-up, she saw others from her flight drifting to various vans and buses with the name of hotels written on the sides. She realized that she hadn't a place to stay. Confused, she turned her head this way and that, watching all the people dispersing.

"Can we help you?" a loud voice asked. She spun around. "You look puzzled. Was somebody supposed to meet you?" A big, grey-haired man with a red face stood behind her, a suitcase in each hand. Touching his arm was a tiny woman in a cotton sundress. They both peered solicitously at Mrs. Hackett. "Maybe we can give you a lift to your hotel? We've rented a car," the man said. Mrs. Hackett wished he wouldn't talk so loud. Everybody was looking at them.

"Do let us help," the woman said.

"Now come along," the man boomed. "I insist on driving you."

"I . . . I haven't got a room," Mrs. Hackett said weakly. She expected him to laugh. She expected the whole airport to laugh. But he only said, "No room? Well, I'll take care of that. Come along now."

"Yes, do come along," the lady said. "My name is Mary Dalrymple and this is my husband, Steve."

"Mrs. Harold Hackett," she said, "from Saskatchewan." She picked up her suitcase and followed them across to the exit, torn between relief at having her problem solved, and her need to see the island at once.

Mr. Dalrymple found her a room in the same hotel they were staying in by insisting and bullying till Mrs. Hackett was embarrassed. Mrs. Dalrymple suggested that they go to their rooms, change and 'freshen up,' and meet for lunch. Mrs. Hackett said, "Thank you, but I'm not hungry. I want to see the beach first, and the ocean." So they left her with promises to have dinner with her that evening.

She found the beach without difficulty. It stretched out in front of her hotel for a quarter mile in each direction. When she realized that in a short moment's time, if she kept going in the direction she was walking, she would wet her feet in the Caribbean Ocean, she felt suddenly that that would be more than she could bear at once, so she turned and began to walk along the beach parallel to the water. She had trembled, but not so that anybody would notice. A light breeze was blowing in off the water. It ruffled the brim of her straw sun hat which she had bought in the lobby of her hotel. It plastered the skirt of her dress against her heavy legs, and then released it. After a moment, she sat down on the sand, first placing her purse on it and sitting on that, and carefully took off her shoes. After glancing around to see that nobody was watching her, she lifted her skirt slightly over one leg and began to unroll her knee-high stockings. In a minute she was barefoot. She stood, picked up her purse, collected her shoes and began to walk down the beach once more. The sand was a delicate beige and very warm. It gave slightly, sliding sideways under her soles and slithering up between her toes. After the first few steps, taken gingerly, she began to like the gritty, sliding feeling, and so, any stranger on the beach might have seen Mrs. Hackett strolling happily back and forth along the sand, looking first out to the ocean, and then across to the big pink hotels, her purse under one arm and her shoes under the other.

The Dalrymples had not forgotten her. Together, they criss-crossed the island in their rented car with Mrs. Hackett in the back seat clinging to the door handles as they bumped and bounced along the narrow roads. They rolled past black-skinned women in red dresses carrying baskets of fruit on their heads, and men in torn white shirts and khaki shorts riding by on rickety bicycles. Evenings they sat by the pool at their hotel and watched the puzzling, fiery dancing under the limbo bar. Mrs. Hackett sat with her hands folded neatly on her plump lap and watched the pink palms of the drummers winking at her.

Every night she dreamt about her quilts. She quilted all night long, little brown islands dotted with palms, perched on an ocean alive with silver fish, long beaches covered with black people in yellow and red bathing suits, and blonde tourists in white dresses and big straw hats huddling together in the market while black shopkeepers pirouetted around them.

She was waking each morning confused and exhausted, unable to separate her dreams from the reality of the world she traversed each day. As the days passed she grew more agitated and more distracted. She found she couldn't sit by the pool, but she no longer wanted to go out in the car, or go shopping or to entertainments organized for the guests. On her last afternoon she went to the beach and began to pace up and down its length. Now and then her lips moved silently. Every once in a while she would stop and turn as though to go back to the hotel. Then she would hesitate in mid-step and look over to the ocean as if she intended to go wading. She would hesitate again, and then continue her pacing. After almost two hours of this, she realized she was very tired and she thought she would nap.

In her room Mrs. Hackett lay down. Her knot of grey hair had come loose and rested on one shoulder. She closed her eyes, clasped her fingers over her stomach, and immediately dropped like a stone into a bottomless sleep. Beads of sweat appeared on her forehead. Now and then her hands jerked.

She saw the jungles and the vast, glistening turquoise sea. She saw the beaches again, peopled with blacks in scarlet bathing suits, she saw the city teeming with black people wearing lime, and purple, and lemon dresses, and all the guests at the hotels in their garish costumes weaving through the palm trees. Miraculously they danced in her hands, they whirled off her fingertips onto rectangles of cloth and froze there in dazzling postures, their hands up in surprise, their bodies bent at wonderful angles, their faces alive with amazement and joy. Her fingers stitched them this way and that. She created the long beaches and peopled them, she built the city stitch by stitch. Under her fingers jungles grew and flowers blossomed. Then the figures changed and she found herself stitching the farm. Behind her needle the caragana hedges grew and bloomed with little yellow flowers. Crops sprang from the ground and waved, sighing in the heat from the great orange sun she had created. Cattle came to the dugout she had filled with water and gave birth to their calves beside the sage on the hillside she had brought into being. She created Mr. Hackett, and then their children, one by one. Her needle sang them to life and their beauty was blinding.

She woke enveloped in the dense, perfumed darkness of the tropical evening. A soft white light filled her and as she rose from the bed, she felt as though she could walk on air if she chose. She bathed, put on her blue and white dress, and went down to join the Dalrymples for dinner.

"Your last evening, eh Ellen?" Mr. Dalrymple shouted as he came to his feet.

"You look . . . rested," Mrs. Dalrymple said. "I was worried about you, and here you look wonderful!"

"I feel very well," Mrs. Hackett replied serenely as she picked up her menu. All the diners bending over their food in the shadowed dining room formed a tableau for her and she smiled graciously at it.

In the morning the Dalrymples drove her to the airport. Mr. Dalrymple had made reservations for her and explained three times what she should do in Toronto. Mrs. Dalrymple hugged her and made her promise that she would come and visit them in Winnipeg.

When Mrs. Hackett reached the door of the airplane, she stopped and turned for one last look at the island. Then she went to her seat, strapped herself in, and closed her eyes. A satisfied smile appeared on her lips.

Mr. Hackett was waiting for her when she stepped off the bus. She was pleased to see him. She could tell by the way he picked up her suitcase and nudged her to show her where the truck was, that he had gotten over it, and was glad to see her.

In the truck he said, "Well, you satisfied? Ready to stay home?" Mrs. Hackett did not reply for a moment.

"It was the country of my dreams," she said. They rode another mile or two without speaking. Then Mrs. Hackett said, "I found what I went for." Mr. Hackett turned the wheel taking them round the curve that led into their farmyard. The collie ran out from under the porch and barked. They climbed out of the truck and walked up the steps. Mrs. Hackett paused at the kitchen door. "Yes," she said. "I believe I am ready to stay home."

Garrison Keillor (b. 1942)

In his *A Prairie Home Companion* radio show Garrison Keillor has introduced America to his own particular distillation of the Great Plains myths and motifs. Although his prairie is geographically a bit east of the Great Plains, metaphorically it is familiar terrain for Great Plains residents. In Lake Wobegon struggling immigrants have become contented Norwegian bachelor farmers. Work has become good works at Our Lady of Perpetual Responsibility Catholic Church and the Norwegian Lutheran Church. The symbol of abundance and community is no longer the harvest hands' meal, but rather the inevitable tuna hot dish that housewives contribute to the church dinners.

Keillor has created his own community that, rather like Brigadoon, has slipped into a kind of geographical time warp. It clearly exists in the minds of Keillor and his listeners. The characters are as carefully described and as tightly interrelated as Faulkner's characters of Yoknapatawpha County or the Kashpaws and Lamartines in Louise Erdrich's novels. Over the years, in his weekly news reports from Lake Wobegon, Keillor has created personal histories for the town's people and recounted their quiet successes and embarrassing failures. The local celebrations he reports have a kind of 1950s nostalgia about them, since they are based in large part on memories of his own childhood in a town very like Lake Wobegon.

Keillor has refined the art of oral storytelling. The news from Lake Wobegon often seems to have as much structure as stream of consciousness but, like Mark Twain's tales of the jumping frog and grandfather's ram, Keillor usually returns to the story's point of origin.

Keillor was born in Anoka, Minnesota. He graduated from the University of Minnesota and went to work for Minnesota Public Radio. *A Prairie Home Companion* began in 1974 as a live variety show broadcast from Macalaster College in Minneapolis. By 1980, when national broadcasts of the show began, it had become the familiar mix of vernacular music—folk songs, jazz, and international groups, both amateur and professional—skits, commercials for Lake Wobegon businesses such as Bertha's Kitty Boutique or Ralph's Pretty Good Grocery, and, of course, the news from Lake Wobegon. Keillor had his first farewell program in 1987, but he resumed the show from New York City in 1989 as *the American Radio Company of the Air*. In 1993 PHC returned to St. Paul, Minnesota, on "the edge of the prairie."

Dozens of audio cassettes are available for Keillor fans. Keillor has compiled and published some of his broadcasts of Lake Wobegon news, but he has also written books for children and for quite different audiences in both the *New Yorker* and *Time*. He says that writing is "simply something I do every day," like other people garden. Thousands of listeners and readers are glad he does such a good job of identifying the foibles and habits of their neighbors.

Collection (1987)

It has been a quiet week in Lake Wobegon. Sunday morning Clarence Bunsen stepped into the shower and turned on the water—which was cold, but he's Norwegian, he knows you have to take what you get—and stood until it got warm, and was reaching for the soap when he thought for sure he was having a heart attack. He'd read a *Reader's Digest* story about a man's heart attack ("My Most Unforgettable Experience") and this felt like the one in the story—chest pain like a steel band tightening. Clarence grabbed the nozzle as the rest of the story flashed before his eyes: the ride in the ambulance, the dash to the emergency room, unconsciousness as the heart team worked over him, the long slow recovery and the discovery of a new set of values. But as he imagined what was about to happen, the heart attack petered out on him. The story said it felt like an elephant stepping on you. This felt more like a big dog, and then somebody whistled and the dog left. So it wasn't a heart attack, there was no story, and Clarence felt better.

(The storyteller is disappointed, of course. A full-blown heart attack would be a reasonable test of his ability, perhaps leading to death itself, a narration of the last moments, the ascent of the soul through the clouds, an exclusive report.)

It wasn't a heart attack, but for ten or fifteen seconds it could have been one, and in the depths of his heart he thought it was—so in a way it was. When you believe you're dying, ten or fifteen seconds is like a lifetime, and when the false attack was over, he nonetheless felt he sort of had a new set of values. For one thing, he wasn't sure he should waste time taking a shower, life being so short, having come so close to death in the sense that when death comes it might come exactly like this. It was Sunday morning, but he wasn't sure he wanted to go to church and sit through a sermon, life being so short. If you knew you had twenty minutes left to live, why, then, church would be the place you'd head first; you'd turn yourself in, no more fooling around, no kidding, pour the sacred oil on me, Jack, say the words, and pluck your magic twanger—I don't have all day.

He thought instead of going to church he'd like to go for a walk (good for your heart) and worship God in the singing of birds, the sunshine, green grass, and flowers, which, this being Minnesota, we don't have yet. He thought: Life is short, so you should do something different. He dried his old body off and put on underwear—maybe, life being short, you ought to get new underwear, but what can an old man wear except boxer shorts? Can't go around in those bikini things you see in stores. What if a robber with a gun forced you to strip down to your underwear ("Hey you—old guy!—hear me? I said, *strip*"), and there you be, an old geezer in tiny purplish briefs, robber'd take one look ("Hey, man, you are ridiculous"), *bam,* you're dead. Dead because you did things different because life is short. He stood at the dresser, shopping for socks (black, brown, gray, gray-black, Argyle). Arlene called up the stairs, "It's almost nine-thirty!"

He wanted to yell back that he was feeling delicate from what he'd thought at the time was a heart attack, but it was hard to yell something so vague, so he yelled, "Be there in a minute," and in not many minutes he appeared in the kitchen in full Sunday regalia: brown suit, black shoes, white shirt, and one flash of color, the tiny red flecks in his dark blue tie. He appeared through the door in a cloud of bay rum, poured himself a cup of coffee, drank some, then kissed his wife (in that order—he is Norwegian), and looked in the frying pan on the stove and saw food that whenever you read about cardiovascular disease you read about that stuff.

He put a pan of water on to boil, for oatmeal. Arlene watched, spatula in hand. "What's the matter? Breakfast is ready. I got your eggs." Hard to explain: a semi–heart-attack. A heart that wasn't attacked but heard footsteps in the weeds. Maybe it was only a twig, maybe the whole aorta about to fall off.

"I don't feel like bacon and eggs this morning."

"Well, I guess I'll have to throw them out, then."

"Yeah . . ."

"Are you feeling all right? Are you sick?"

He's Norwegian; he said, "No. I'm just fine." A Norwegian's dying words: "I'm just fine." On the field of battle, torn to a red pulp except for your mouth: "I'm just fine." Wreckage of a car, smashed to smithereens, a bloody hand reaches out the window and writes in the dust: "O.K."

It was warm out, and on the way to church they smelled mud, a sweet smell of rot and decay, and a whiff of exhaust as the Tolleruds cruised by with their carload of kids. Clarence used to walk to Sunday school with his four little kids. Now, having almost had a heart attack, he misses their sweaty little hands for one heart-breaking instant and misses how, before going in to worship the Lord, he ran a quick bladder check and a nose check to see where blowing was needed. The kids always cured him of the sort of morbid mood he felt this morning—he never had these long grim thoughts about death when the kids were little, but then he was younger, of course.

Church was half full and restless. Pastor Ingqvist's Lenten sermons have gotten longer. Val Tollefson has been after him to liven up his preaching. Sunday morning before church, Val tunes in "Power for Tomorrow" on TV from the Turquoise Temple in Anaheim, and there is a gleam in Reverend La Coste's eye that Val wishes Pastor Ingqvist would emulate and also use more dramatic inflection, rising, falling inflection, cry out sometimes, use long pauses to give solemnity to the sermon.

Clarence checked out of Pastor Ingqvist's sermon early. It was about the parable of the laborers in the vineyard, the ones who came late getting the same wage as those who came early and stayed all day, a parable that suggests you need not listen carefully to the whole sermon from the beginning but can come in for maybe the last sentence or two and get the whole point. Besides, the pastor's long pauses were hypnotic. Clarence's mind drifted away to other things, until suddenly he was startled by his own heavy breathing: he opened his eyes; the sermon wasn't over, it was only a long pause. The pastor's inflection suggested he was coming toward the end and the offering was next. Clarence eased his wallet out and saw he had no cash. He got out a pen and hid the checkbook in his Bible (next to Psalm 101) and quietly scratched out a check for thirty dollars, more than usual, because he had almost had a heart attack and also because his offering was personalized. He wrote surreptitiously, trying to keep his eyes up and ahead—knowing you're not supposed to write checks in church, it isn't a grocery store.

He glanced to his right, and Mrs. Val Tollefson was glaring at him. She thought he was writing in the Bible. (In the old Norwegian synod you didn't write in a Bible, not even little comments in the margin like "Good verse" or "You can say that again," because every word in the Bible is true and you shouldn't add any that might not be true, not even in pencil, because it undermines the authority of Scripture.) Meanwhile, the sermon ended and Pastor Ingqvist launched into prayer. Clarence tried to tear the check quietly out of the checkbook. There's no worse sound in the sanctuary than a check ripping. His check wouldn't come quietly, the first half-inch rip sounded like plywood being torn from a wall, so he waited for the pastor to launch into a strong sentence of fervent prayer to cover up the check removal, but Pastor Ingqvist was pausing at odd points, so Clarence couldn't tell when it was safe or when suddenly he would be ripping in the middle of pure holy silence. Clarence folded the check back and forth until it almost fell off. Mrs. Tollefson was about to get up and snatch Scripture out of his hands. At prayers' end, as they said the Lord's Prayer, he eased the check out ("And lead us not into temptation, but deliver us from evil: For thine is the kingdom, and the power, and the glory, for ever. Amen"), and when Elmer passed the basket, Clarence laid down the check folded neatly in half in the basket and bowed his head and suddenly realized he had written it for three hundred dollars.

He had written with his eyes averted and he knew he had written three-zero-zero on the short line and three-zero-zero on the long line. Could a man sneak downstairs after church and find the deacons counting the collection and say, "Fellows, there's been a mistake. I gave more than I really wanted to"? He now felt fully alive for the first time all day. He felt terrifically awake. He had given all he had in the checking account and a little more. What would they do until the end of the month to keep body and soul together? Maybe they would have to eat beans and oatmeal. What's a man gonna do? A man's got to live.

Life Is Good (1987)

It has been a quiet week in Lake Wobegon. Lightning struck the Tollerud farm Tuesday, about six o'clock in the evening. Daryl and his dad were walking the corn rows, talking, and the clouds were dark and strange but it wasn't storming yet, and Daryl said, "If I were you, I'd take Mother out to Seattle tomorrow and enjoy the trip and not worry about this." Right then it hit, up by the house: a burst of light and a slam and a sizzle like bacon. They ran for the house to find her in the kitchen, sitting on the floor. She was okay but it was close. It hit a crab apple tree thirty feet from the kitchen window.

Some people in town were reminded of Benny Barnes, who was hit by lightning six times. After three, he was nervous when a storm approached, and got in his car and drove fast, but it got him the fourth time, and the fifth time it was sunny with just one little cloud in the sky and, *bam*, lightning again. He had burn scars down his legs and his ears had been ringing for years. After the fifth, he quit running. The sixth one got him sitting in the yard on an aluminum lawn chair. After that he more or less gave up. When the next thunderstorm came through, he took a long steel pipe and stood out on the hill, holding it straight up. He had lost the will to live. But just the same it took him fifteen more years to die. It wasn't from lightning: he caught cold from the rain and died of pneumonia.

Daryl wished the bolt had come closer to his dad. His dad has a character flaw that drives Daryl crazy: he hates plans. The trip to Seattle was planned before Thanksgiving, letters were written to relatives, calls were made; June 30th was the date set to go, but the old man gets uneasy when plans are made and feels trapped and cornered, even if the plans are his own, so one night after chores he said, "Well, I don't know about that trip to Seattle, I might be too busy, we'll have to see about that," which made everybody else want to shoot him.

Daryl jumped up. "How can you say that? Are you crazy?" No, just nervous about plans. Always was. To agree to do something and have people expect you to do it: it bothers him. When his kids were little, he'd tell them, "Now, I'm not promising anything, but maybe next week sometime I could take you swimming, up to your uncle Carl's, but don't count on it, it all depends." As next week came around, he'd say, "I don't know about that swimming, we're going to have to see about that. Maybe Thursday." Thursday the kids would get their bathing suits out and he'd say, "We'll see how it goes this morning, if I get my work done we'll go." Right up to when they got in the car, he was saying, "I don't know. I really ought to get to work on that drain pipe," and even when he stuck the key in the ignition, he'd hesitate. "Gosh, I'm not sure, maybe it'd be better if we went tomorrow." He couldn't bring himself to say, "Thursday we swim," and stick to it. Daryl and his brothers and sisters learned not to look forward to things because Dad might change his mind.

The old man is the same with his grandkids. He says, "Well, we'll see. Maybe. If I can." But the Seattle trip beats all. Ruby got the train tickets and had the suitcase packed three weeks ago, then he said, "I don't know how I can leave with the corn like it is." Ruby put her head in her hands. He said, "You know, the Grand Canyon is a place I always wanted to see, maybe we should go there." She sighed, and he said, "You know, I never agreed to this Seattle trip, this was your idea from day one." And then Ruby went to Daryl's to talk to Daryl and Marilyn. They sat drinking coffee and getting madder and Ruby said, "Oh well, you have to understand Dad." Marilyn stood up and said, "I do not have to understand him. He's crazy. He doesn't just have a screw loose, the whole top has come off."

She is reading a book, *Get Down and Garden,* about getting tough with plants. She has yanked a bunch of slow movers out of her flower garden, the dullards and the dim bulbs, and it's improved her confidence. Now she often begins sentences with "Look," as in "Look. It's obvious." She used to begin with "Well," as in "Well, I don't know," but now she says, "Look. This is not that hard to understand."

She said to Ruby, "Look. It's obvious what he's doing. He wants to be the Grand Exalted Ruler and come down in the morning and hear his subjects say, 'What is your pleasure, sire?' and he'll say, 'Seattle,' so they head for the luggage and then he says, 'No, we'll stay home,' so they sit down, and then 'Grand Canyon' and they all jump up. As long as you keep jumping, he'll keep holding the hoop up there."

Not only does Old Man Tollerud hate to commit himself to trips, he also likes to stay loose in regard to drawing up a will or some other legal paper that gives Daryl and Marilyn some right to the farm that they've worked on for fifteen years. When Daryl mentions it, his dad says, "Well, we'll have to see. We'll talk about it in a few months." Daryl is forty-two years old and he's got no more ownership of this farm than if he'd gone off and been a drunk like his brother Gunnar. Sometimes he gets so mad at the old man, he screams at him. But always when he's on the tractor in the middle of the field with the motor running. Once he left a rake in the yard with the tines up, hoping his dad would step on it and brain himself.

Last April he saw a skunk waddling toward the barn and got a can of catfood and lured the skunk into the tractor shed, hoping his dad would start up the John Deere the next morning and get a snootful. He fed the skunk day after day, waiting for it to do the job for him. Sweet justice. Blast the old bastard with skunk sauce at close range so nobody would care to see him for about a year. Then the skunk started following Daryl, who fed him such rich food, so Daryl quit and the skunk disappeared.

Daryl got some satisfaction at the Syttende Mai dinner at the Lutheran church in May, Norwegian Independence Day, where his dad went through the buffet and loaded up and was heading for a table when his paper plate started to collapse on him. He balanced his coffee cup on his wrist to get his other hand under the plate, and it was *hot*—the meatballs had sat in a chafing dish over a candle. The old man winced and looked for a place to dump the load; then the hot gravy burned right through the paper plate and he did a little tango and everything sloshed down the front of his pants. Daryl watched this with warm satisfaction.

But that was months ago, the satisfaction has worn off. The day after the lightning strike, Daryl drove up to the house to have it out once and for all. He practiced his speech in the pickup. "You don't treat me like I'm your son at all, you've never treated me like a son." He got to the house and found a note on the door: "Gone to Saint Cloud for windowshades. Back soon. Clean the haybarn."

Clean the haybarn! He ripped the note off and wadded it up and drop-kicked it into the peonies. He stalked to the end of the porch and back and stood and yelled at the door: "You don't treat me like I was your son, you bastard, you treat me like I was a—" And then the terrible truth dawned on him. His mother had said, "If anything happens to us in Seattle, I left you a letter in my dresser drawer. I've been meaning to give it to you for years." So he wasn't their son. He was adopted. That's why his dad wouldn't make out the will.

Daryl had wondered about this before, if he was his father's son. He thought, "I'm forty-two, it's time to find out." He walked in and climbed the stairs, step by deep purple step, and turned and entered his parents' bedroom, the forbidden chamber, and walked to the dresser and heard something move on the bed. He turned—it was their old tabby cat, Lulu, on the bed—his hand hit a bottle and it crashed on the floor. She didn't jump at the crash, she sat up and gave him a long look that said: "You're not supposed to be in here and you know it. You ought to be ashamed of yourself. You're no good, and you know it. Shame on you." He clapped his hands—*Ha! Git!*—and she climbed down and walked away, stopped, looked over her shoulder, and said: You'll suffer for this, you just wait.

He picked up the shards of perfume bottle and opened both dormer windows to air out the room. Unbelievable that his mother would ever smell like this, it smelled like old fruit salads. He dug down into the dresser drawer where he'd seen her stick old pictures, under her stockings and underwear. There was a book, *Sexual Aspects of Christian Marriage: A Meditation* by Reverend E. M. Mintner, that he'd read when he was twelve, and he dug beneath it to a packet of envelopes tied with a thick rubber binder, *tight*. He slipped it off: they were his dad's pay slips from the Co-op; each envelope held a year's worth; there were more than thirty envelopes.

He sat on the bed, feeling weak. Of all his parents' secrets, this was the darkest: how much money did they make? They would no more talk about that than discuss sexual aspects of marriage. One Sunday little Daryl piped up at dinner and asked, "Dad, how much money do you make?"

His dad has several different voices, a regular one ("So how come you went down there when I told you I needed you? I don't get it") and a prayer voice ("Our Father, we do come before Thee with hearts filled with thanksgiving, remembering Thy many blessings to us, and we do ask Thee now . . ."). When he discussed money he used the second voice and he said, "I don't care to discuss that and I don't want you to discuss it with anyone else. Is that clear?"

Oh yes. We don't talk about money, that is very clear. Except to say, "I got this window fan for four dollars; it's brand-new except for this scratch, and you know those things run ten, twelve dollars." Bargains yes, but salaries no.

So here was the secret. He opened the first envelope, 1956. Forty-five dollars. That was for a whole week. Not much for a good mechanic. Forty-five dollars and five kids: it explained all that scrimping, his mother darning socks and canning tomatoes. When the old man forked over their allowance, he counted the two quarters twice to make sure he wasn't overpaying. It explained why he was such a pack rat, saving tinfoil, string, paper, rags—once Daryl looked around for string and found a box full of corks, another of bits of wire, and one box with hundreds of odd jigsaw-puzzle pieces, labeled "Puzzle: Misc."

It dawned on him that he wasn't adopted, he was their boy all right. He'd inherited their frugality and stoicism. If his paper plate fell apart, he'd try to save it, even if his hand was burning. Same as his dad. They raised him to bear up under hardship and sadness and disappointment and disaster, but what if you're brought up to be stoic and your life turns out lucky—you're in love with your wife, you're lucky in your children, and life is lovely to you—what then? You're ready to endure trouble and pain, and instead God sends you love—what do you do? He'd been worried about inheriting the farm, meanwhile God had given him six beautiful children. What happens if you expect the worst and you get the best? *Thank you, Lord,* he thought. Thank you for sending me up here to the bedroom. It was wrong to come, but thank you for sending me.

He heard Lulu tiptoe in, and when she brushed against his leg he was sorry for chasing her out. He scratched her head. It didn't feel catlike. He looked down and saw the white stripes down its back.

The skunk sniffed his hand, wondering where the catfood was. Then it raised its head and sniffed the spilled perfume. It raised its tail, sensing an adversary. It walked toward the window. It seemed edgy.

"Easy, easy," he said. If he opened the window wider, it might go out on the roof and find a route down the oak tree to the ground. He was opening the window wider when he heard the feet padding up the stairs. He hollered, "No, Shep, no!" and raised his leg to climb out the window as the dog burst into the room, barking. The skunk turned and attacked. Daryl went out the window, but not quite fast enough. He tore off all his clothes and threw them down to the ground, and climbed back in. The bedroom smelled so strong he couldn't bear it. The skunk was under the bed. He ran down and got the shotgun and loaded it. Daryl was almost dying of the smell, but he crept into the bedroom. He heard the skunk grunt, trying to squeeze out more juice. Daryl aimed and fired. Feathers exploded and the skunk dropped down dead.

He carried it out on a shovel and buried it, but that didn't help very much: the deceased was still very much a part of the Tollerud house when his parents arrived home a little while later. Daryl sat on the porch steps, bare naked except for a newspaper. He smelled so bad, he didn't care about modesty. Ruby said, "Oh dear. Are you all right?" She stopped, twenty feet away. She thought he looked naked, but he smelled so bad she didn't care to come closer.

His dad said, "You know, Daryl, I think you were right about Seattle."

And they left. They didn't take clothes with them. They went straight out the driveway.

That was Tuesday. Daryl has been living at his parents' house all week. But life is good. I'm sure he still believes this. Life is good, friends. It's even better if you stay away from Daryl, but basically life is good.

Further Reading

The Book of Guys. 1994.
Cat, You Better Come Home. 1992.
Happy to Be Here. 1981.
Lake Wobegon Days. 1985.
Lake Wobegon Summer, 1956. 2001.
The Sandy Bottom Orchestra. 1996.
We Are Still Married. 1989.
WLT: *A Radio Romance.* 1991.

John Janovy Jr. *(b. 1937)*

Back in Keith County is one of a series of books that chronicle John Janovy Jr.'s travels, studies, and acquaintances in the Sandhills region of northwest Nebraska. In this selection Janovy talks to the Corfields and the Petersons, owners of one and eighteen square miles of the Sandhills, respectively. He wants to know *why*, not *how*, they live in such a remote area. The town of Arthur, population 135, is the only one in Arthur County in the southern Sandhills. The county's population is a mere five hundred. It is the county just north of the more populous Keith County, which is dissected by Interstate 80 and the Platte River. Ogallala, population six thousand, is the largest town in Keith County.

Janovy, a biologist, is Varner Professor at the School of Biological Sciences at the University of Nebraska in Lincoln. He was born in Louisiana. He received degrees from the University of Oklahoma and did postdoctoral work at Rutgers University. His nature essays are in the tradition of Lewis Thomas and Ann Zwinger, who are fascinated by details and find meaning in careful scientific examinations of nature ranging from the smallest form to entire ecosystems. For example, Janovy's book *Yellowlegs* (1980) follows the life of a single sandpiper. Janovy finds writing a natural extension of his work as a teacher who tries to enable the average observer to understand the natural world in a complex technological age.

Home on the Range (1981)

Millie Corfield lives up south of Arthur in one of the more interesting homes in the Sandhills. I had stopped at the Corfield's three years earlier, asking permission to look in their well tank for snails. On that day three years ago I was pretty hesitant. The Corfield place did not advertise for visitors and the isolation of the Sandhills, an isolation that must be felt for it cannot be described, combined with my stupid snail mission, a fancy state-owned four-wheel-drive truck, and my city-slicker camera, gave me a sense of real physical danger. I could not have been more wrong about anything than I was about that sense of danger three years ago. That was my conclusion as I sat in Millie's living room and listened to her tell of their life on the prairies, watched Erle and Jim look at her as she talked, and finally turned to answer "No" to Erle's question:

"Ever hunt coyotes?"

It is obvious why I was sitting in that living room. The Corfield place was the origin of my strongest impressions of the isolation, the estrangement, the brazen self-reliance, that very pluck of the coyotes they hunt, the audacity to confront the elements that sweep down out of the north, which must characterize a family that would make a home on such range. My search for snail had, those earlier years, taken me throughout several quadrangles, over several hills that looked out only over more trackless hills as far as could be seen. I had stood so many times looking forward into that horizon, then turned to make sure I could see a landmark behind, could locate tire tracks from a different angle, before stepping high again into that cab for a windmill a map said was a mile away. But of all the places I'd seen, of all the permission I'd asked and not asked, of all my contact with the dry dunes and those that live upon them, none had been remembered with the force of the Corfield place. Back in Keith County, driven to write of intellectual freedom by those experiences in search of tropical health, there was, of course, only one place I could start to get the human answers I wanted. I'd like to think some of that Sandhills mettle has rubbed off after a few years of working out there. For in search of Sandhills mettle, I never considered any first stop other than the one that had already given me such apprehension. The Corfield place hadn't changed much, and neither had son Jim. He was still interested in the "sallymanders" in that well tank and could still speculate on how they got there.

Erle and Millie were out for groceries, so Jim and I talked for a while. The world goes away when you drive into the Corfield place, and it goes away even further when you sit down with Jim to talk about one-room schoolhouses. There was a time when I was out on the Sandhills right before sunrise, on a windless cloudless morning, and watched the special light diffuse out over the land. I could look east and see only one human mark upon that land: a one-room schoolhouse and a hint of a road leading to it. There was another time when a visitor from the East came to the Sandhills and we took him up south of Arthur to see some prairie. There was a one-room schoolhouse on the way to the prairie. We'd passed it dozens of times in the last three years, but the visitor wanted to stop. The schoolhouse was unlocked and we went in. The place was clean, immaculate, organized, with an irrigation company calendar, a curtained shelf with their little dried biology projects of a past year: quart jars with seeds planted. On the shelf with the biology projects was the library: a stack of National Geographics from the Mesozoic. The whole thing was absolutely wrenching, and the strongest feelings of empathy, the strongest desire for success for these unknown children, welled up inside. The others felt the same, and the visitor from the East, a most sensitive man and teacher, expressed those feelings for us all. Back in the Corfield living room, you know what I had to ask Jim: what was it like going to one of those one-room schoolhouses? He answered without much hesitation:

"It was kind of boring."

I wondered then, and we wondered together, what kind of person would come to teach at one of those schools. That's when he told me all their names, every teacher he'd had down through the years, how long they'd stayed, which ones were the good ones, and how he got to school. There was an element of American grit in his descriptions of his teachers. A person might think, believing what we're often told is the American dream of higher, faster, more, that an ambitious person might not come to a one-room schoolhouse to teach. Furthermore, a teacher with ambitions might truly see one of those schoolhouses as the end of the world and wonder about the choice of a profession that started in a small white building with only the wind for company. At least those were my thoughts about teaching in one-room schools until Jim said something of the turnover rates of one-room schoolhouse teachers:

"Most of them stayed a year, then moved on. The better ones, they stayed about three years."

Right then I re-defined "ambitious" as applied to teachers.

We talked about social life, about girls, games, cars, jobs, his parents and what they could do in the future if they had to, or wanted to, or ever considered any life other than the one they were living. But always through such conversation ran a track of isolation, a track of sparseness, a track of closeness to the prairie. And at the end of that sheltered time, I came away feeling that maybe I'd met just another creature whose life was inextricably pounded into that econiche known as the Sandhills. He saw nothing strange, nothing unusual, about his life. Erle was the one who later would underscore the values that I could sense in Jim but couldn't quite get out, couldn't quite identify. Yes, Erle was the one, later, when he turned the questions back on me. It was the father, who told me through his questions what I was seeing in his son, when from the corner of a table he came out with:

"You live right *in* town, do you?"

I'd asked about the number of kids that go to those one-room schools and Jim had responded by telling me of the tragedy—the auto accident I'd read about at the other end of the state. That accident reduced their school's population to two, maybe only one. Later on, when Erle and Millie returned, we talked a little while of the administration of a one-room school with one student and one teacher. There were four in Jim's school, when he went there years ago, three girls and Jim. Years ago, Jim was in the eighth grade and the oldest girl was in the third grade. He told me that, then he made the comment about it being "kind of boring."

"It was kind of boring," he said. "We were supposed to play a certain game at recess, but I used to go play with the horses."

Jim works in Ogallala, too, as a "sanitation specialist."

"Not much to make a living on up here," he said. "People tell me I'm crazy to work in Ogallala, drive every day. Fifty miles an hour saves a lot of gas, but still, the gas prices has really hurt, and that job's not really what it ought to be." For the historical record, this conversation took place on July 2, 1979. Gas was pumped in

Ogallala at under 90¢ a gallon in July, 1979. The sentence was written on January 13, 1980, and for the historical record, gas was then pumped for $1.07 a gallon. That's an average, estimated, for leaded regular. I'm sure Jim's Ford pickup, parked outside their home on the range, burned regular. None of those kinds of pickups ever burned premium.

"I've been to Cheyenne, Sioux City, Texas, and Chickasha, Oklahoma. Not much to make a living on up here, but if I had my choice, I'd make enough money to live right here and be the happiest man in the world. The folks own one section. Went to college one semester, but even if I'd had four years of business, I'd still have come back to live right here. Oh, folks could sell this section, move into town, buy a house, make nine, ten thousand a year off inflation and interest on what they'd get for the land. They'd never do that. We're not money hungry, just prefer the horses and cattle. They leased the place in 1948; bought it in 1962." Jim looked around his living room, then he said "Nobody ever so much as give Dad a nickel."

"I'd like to get a picture, Jim."

"Let me get my hat and boots; wouldn't really be a picture of me without my hat and boots." Nor without his can of Skoal, although he didn't say that. Back out in the Sandhills brightness, a car moved through the distance along a road I knew was there but couldn't see. "That's them comin' now." I asked one last question before Erle and Millie pulled into the yard. It was a question I had to ask, standing in the July heat.

"What's it like out here in the winter, Jim? What was last winter like?"

He reacted almost as if I'd kicked him in the foot.

"*It's a bitch!*"

I took a couple of pictures of Jim in front of their home on the range as Millie and Erle drove in. I introduced myself.

"This fella's a writer," said Jim. "Wants to talk to us about what it's like living out here."

Erle didn't say much, shook hands, then kind of turned away watching me out of the side of his eye. His name was across the back of his belt, and as he turned away I memorized its spelling. Millie had other concerns, I suppose from having survived in the Sandhills.

"Let's get these groceries inside," she said. Inside she offered iced tea, sized me up, and was way ahead of my question. "If I had it to do all over again, I wouldn't do a single thing different," she said.

Erle smiled from the corner of the kitchen table and rolled a cigarette, the first of several he went through while we talked, but it was Millie who was ready to tell of life in a home on the range: "When I was younger I worked in Omaha for about six months then came out here for a vacation. I had every intention of going back, but stayed. I would never do a single thing differently. We are free, we have our health and our land, our kids are on their own, we've done it on our own." My pride at being a part of this nation where a person can say those things almost brought those emotional tears, and as I write those emotional tears come back. Yes, Millie, you are free, you have a freedom that so few others know, that three billion people do not even understand, and best of all, *you* know it! Awareness, is that not the essence of human, an awareness of self, an awareness of life, of death, of joy and pain, of status? An awareness of *freedom,* of *independence,* is that not the ultimate essence also of being a human, of realizing all the potential contained in that word "human"? Yes, it is. Of course Erle knows it too, and that one section of Sandhills dunes that he and Millie bought in 1962 has worked wonders on his perspective.

"What's California got that we don't?" he said in a voice that could have belonged to some Senator—deep, polished, confident and secure, at the corner of his own kitchen table, rolling his own cigarette. "What's California got that we don't?"

Nothing, Erle, California's got nothing that you don't have. You own your own land and you are free, an independent man. You fit my definition of a cowboy. There is nothing California can add to that.

"I'm a teacher," said Millie, "in Arthur. I teach six, seventh, and eighth grades." That brought the discussion back to one-room schools, of children who go to them, of their ambitions, their performances, and of the teachers who teach in them. Millie was one of those teachers once. "They rotate teachers in and out of those schools. You teach all the subjects, all in one room, but sometimes the art and music teachers come in just for that." We talked for a while about her students, the ones in Arthur, then in general about school kids in Arthur. "Math is easiest to teach," she said. "I like it the best and I do the best job at it."

"Where'd you get your college education, Millie, your teaching certificate?"

"I never finished high school," said Millie Corfield. "It was the Depression. I couldn't finish high school."

Seems Erle had found a matchbook not too long after they were married; probably picked it up somewhere to fire up one of those rolled cigarettes, rolled while he contemplated some piece of land or some coyote out ghosting across it. The matchbook had an advertisement: HIGHSCHOOL BY CORRESPONDENCE. Millie took the matchbook up to her friend, Annie Mae at the courthouse, sought another opinion on whether the advertisement was legitimate. Annie Mae wasn't too impressed with the matchbook. Instead, she told Millie she ought to take the GED exams, General Educational Development exams. If you passed, you got a high school equivalency certificate. They threw the matchbook away; wasn't much question in *her* mind that she'd acquired the General Educational Development equivalent of a high school education. She passed, went to Kearney State, got her twelve hours and certification, and came back to the Sandhills. Kearney is still Nebraska, it's still on the border of 20,000 square miles of Sandhills, but it's not actually *in* the dunes. Millie came back west with her certification and now she teaches middle grades in Arthur. Math—that's her favorite, the one she feels she does the best. They still print those matchbooks—HIGHSCHOOL BY CORRESPON-DENCE. The last one I saw was in the Denver airport. It reminded me, as they always will, of how Millie Corfield became a math teacher in Arthur.

My notes, my scribbled ideas, hasty observations and things I must remember, tend to be kept on any handy scrap of paper. I clean out my pockets every once and a while and put those notes in my briefcase. Then about every six months I clean out my briefcase and put those notes in a file. You wouldn't believe that file. Actually there are several such files. One of these days I'll take all those files and put them together in a file cabinet, and on and on. So a couple of years ago I bought this little red vinyl covered notebook with the seal of the University of Nebraska on the front. It was quite a joke when I first bought it. There wasn't a single thing on any of the pages, and I used to tell people it contained all there was of significance about the state of Nebraska. That's no joke any more; my notes taken that day on the Corfield place are in that red notebook, but I'm wondering why I remember so much more about that day than is written in my notes. There is a message to me in the medium of those pages, and the message is this: where those notes dribble out, where there are only a couple of sentences to remind me of an hour's conversation, those are the times the conversation hypnotized me so I could no longer concentrate on the notes.

I wish I could convey Erle's voice, his way of telling about hunting, but not really telling at all, just having that certain look on his face when the subject came up. You could tell by that look something of the hunting of *Canis latrans* upon the dunes of western Nebraska—or at least you could *imagine* it, but your image might not even be close to reality. Then we talked about town, about Ogallala. Too much of an urban influence to move their kids into Ogallala, said Millie, and Erle agreed. That's when he asked me if I lived "right *in* town, right *in* Lincoln?" I don't think he'd ever been that close to a person who lived right *in* a town of 160,000. I said my good-byes and they said their come-on-backs. Even then I wondered why I'd come, what right I had to simply drive up to the Corfield place, ask them about their lives, then write it in some kind of a book. Maybe it's not a right, but a responsibility instead. Maybe I have this responsibility to put down for someone somewhere my impressions of a couple of hour's conversation with people who *know* they are free, independent, have their own land, and who refused to move into town when their kids were small. Maybe that's a responsibility we all have.

If you don't remember what late 1979, early 1980, were like, then I can remind you. Americans were being held hostage in the embassy in Iran. Russia invaded neighboring Afghanistan. OPEC's biggest internal squabble was over how much to raise crude oil prices, how much the United States could afford, the upper limit that would sustain the apparent American addiction to energy but not generate true backlash from the American citizens. The concept of a nation so free that its own citizens, its own press, could express their opinions without fear of reprisal, was a concept so foreign to the world of 1980 that it resulted in ridicule of my land.

Maybe this is only my outlaw approach to life coming to the surface, but I no longer feel any qualms about saying the things said all through these pages: there are, out in Arthur County, Nebraska, a lot of cowboys who *know* they are independent, free, a lot of people whose *awareness* of their freedom is a lesson in higher civilization itself. I left Millie, Erle, and Jim, turning out onto the blacktop west, back toward the highway south of Arthur.

A mile down that road toward highway 61 is another gravel drive, this one leading up to the Packard Ranch house. On that same trip three years ago after snail, that same trip where I'd first met the Corfields—without really meeting them—I'd also tried the Packard Ranch. No one had been home, then, but the dogs were home. You should know there's a reason strangers are wary of ranch dogs. We'd been able to raise no one at the Packard Ranch house three years ago, and I was very disappointed. There were a number of wells on their property that I wanted to check for snails, and that fact alone, once you've looked at a Sandhills map, tells you something about the Packard Ranch. I remember thinking at the time that by getting permission from the Packards, we could visit four or five, maybe ten wells. Sandhills water wells are surprisingly evenly distributed. Throughout northern Keith and southern Arthur Counties, Nebraska, there is an average of 1.2 water wells per square mile.

Shirley Packard was making salad, Gerry was gone somewhere, and one of the Packard girls was mowing the lawn, when I pulled into that gravel drive to talk about a home on the range. The Packard home on the range is fairly well known outside of cowboy country, and in fact the words "Packard Ranch" are on file with the federal government: there is a U.S. Geological Survey topographic map, 1:24,000, rolled in my map file, marked with numbers on water wells, worn from being out on the dunes. That map is officially titled the "Packard Ranch Quadrangle." The Packard Ranch quadrangle is bordered by others with equally romantic names: Bear Hill, Glinn Ranch, Martin, Lemoyne, Spotted Horse Valley, each name identifying the major geographical or sociological feature of that section of America. There is nothing like a U.S. Geological Survey topographic map to give you the wanderlust; mostly even the name of some quadrangle will do it. Often there's a special feature of some kind that you can see on a 1:24,000 map—a geographical feature, a long canyon, a steep canyon, maybe a marsh. A 1:24,000 map is large enough to show even the numbers and placements of buildings. On the Packard Ranch quadrangle you can see the Packard Ranch buildings, their relative sizes, their placements, and you can see another special feature of the Packard Ranch quadrangle. A small airplane indicates an airstrip. You can also see the wind sock from that blacktop road east of highway 61.

"Gerald H.—that's Gerry's dad—he flies," said Shirley Packard as she handed me her copy of *Keith County Journal* to autograph.

Shirley Packard, like Jim Corfield, had some comments about the winter past.

As I type these words it is also winter, mid-January, and ten after five in the morning. There is a gentle rain falling, the first in many weeks. It was in the fifties yesterday, and the day before that, and even back through the weekend, when I spent a day of the prairie winter doing what people normally do in April: soccer with John III, a minor tune-up for a balky vehicle, an hour sitting on the front step with a beer watching America go by. For some stupid reason I was watching television late last evening. There was a smell of spring, a false smell, of course, in the night air, and the weather girl was on. Television is not one of my major forms of entertainment, but when it's spring on the prairies in January, it sometimes makes you curious enough to watch the late evening weather. A year ago almost to the day, the high was 0°F.; yes, zero was the high. Now I understand there are colder places in the world. But I also understand that when the high is zero and the wind comes ripping down over the dunes from North Dakota, then it's time to take shelter in a home on the range. My notebook doesn't indicate what my question was; somehow I assumed I'd remember it. But it must have concerned winter, since my notebook does indicate Mrs. Packard's answer:

"After *last* winter that's a hard question to ask. Last winter was tough." The question must have had something to do with the nature of Packard Ranch operations. I must have asked what their major business operation was, which of their activities provided most of their income, occupied most of their time, and how they did those things in the winter.

"Gerry's grandparents homesteaded here in the early 1900s," she said. "There are eighteen sections total. We have cattle, of course, and hay, corn, rye, alfalfa, and sorghum. We do all our own mechanical work. The horses are mainly for personal use. We've put in some center pivots, the first one about ten years ago, primarily because of the shortage of hay in the dry years. But we've also had to diversify because of the cattle prices. Corn made more than cattle last year." We talked on for a while about her kids and their plans, about Gerry's stint as a Marine in San Diego, Florida, Texas, about *Keith County Journal,* until the talk inevitably—because I'm a teacher, probably—got around to the one-room schoolhouse, especially a certain one on the Packard Ranch quadrangle.

"Petersen's hired man's little girl will be the only student in there until Christmas. Petersen's hired man and his wife, they'd be the ones to ask about one-room schools right now. Their little girl will be the only one in there unless someone else moves in. Another kid is supposed to start kindergarten there after Christmas. *That* school is a result of the consolidation." She paused as I wrote the words faithfully in the red vinyl notebook containing all there is of significance about the state of Nebraska. Those were evidently her exact words, for they are written so legibly: "That school is the result of the consolidation."

"All three of ours went to the one-room school. Both Gerry and his brother went there. There's nothing wrong with a one-room school; it's great if you have enough kids."

"How many is enough?"

"Enough kids is as many as it takes to instill some competition."

"Do you remember their teachers?"

"All three had Millie Corfield as a teacher."

I finished with the question I was after that day, July 2, 1979, two days before the 203rd anniversary of the signing of the American Declaration of Independence. And Shirley Packard answered with the only answer I've gotten from anybody in that country, the same answer that has come in form after form, from person after person, in medium after medium, in place after place, wherever boots slip a little bit in the sand and wherever the needlegrass tries to work its way into a pair of jeans.

"Some folks stay for sentimental reasons," she said, "and a lot of them won't admit it, but they're staying for independence, for dependable neighbors, for the freedom of owning their own place, being their own boss, that's why they stay, for independence."

The Nebraska Sandhills, Cowboy Country, U.S.A., covers approximately twenty thousand square miles. The Corfields own one of these. The Packards own eighteen. There are those who live there in the midst of the dunes and own none. There are others who cannot see the ends of their properties. Out across those twenty thousand square miles people have chosen not to leave. They'll tell you where a burrowing owl nest is, for they've seen it from horseback. They'll tell you about the deer and they'll tell you what's in their well tanks. They leave their foreman in charge while they go off to rodeo. They drive pickups, put that pinch of Skoal between their teeth and gums, and stick a rifle up in the rack across the back window. They fight the north wind that roars down upon them in the dark and when it's all over they're out there in the late spring a year older. There are more kangaroo rats, voles, wild roses, earless lizards, lark buntings, deer flies, and swallows out there in those twenty thousand square miles than they can imagine, much less count. They're uncomfortable in town; at least they *look* uncomfortable in town. Some folks would say they live in the wilderness, out there in the middle of all those dunes.

But other folks know better, know things about wilderness that not all of us know. These other folks know that when you can look around at the dunes, say you own some, say that nobody so much as ever give you a nickel, say that there are more kangaroo rats, voles, lark buntings, wild roses, and earless lizards than you can imagine, that you've made a home on the range with them, then these other folks knew you are free and independent. And these other folks know *you know* you are free and independent. Some city people might call you a cowboy, then, when it's obvious you know you are free and independent.

The Nebraska Sandhills is a recreation area. Hunters come, and fishermen, all with much equipment, boats and the like. Game and Parks tries to supervise Big

Mac, the biggest lake in cowboy country. The Fourth of July weekend is big business around Big Mac. I came out of the Sandhills that weekend in my white Merc with the black stripe, tape deck blaring Waylon Jennings, red vinyl notebook straining with the individuality of the Corfields and Packards, into the rush of holiday sunburn, campers, ice, fish, boats, motorcycles, sand, and blue water twenty-two miles to Lewellen. I stopped at Sportsman's Complex for a beer. Some guy was buying bait.

"Got any shiners?"

Right away that reminded me of a kid named Mark Safarik. "Shiners" had taken on a new meaning over the past few weeks. The new meaning reminded me that the unyielding individuality I'd found that afternoon up south of Arthur could be found in other places, places such as the brains of students. "Shiners" was one of four existing types of fish, said Mark, and off went his brain into a flight of fancy. He also wrote songs; some of the better ones were about worms. You must know that when a person writes songs about worms and reduces the world to four categories of fish, then there is in that person a creative individuality worthy of study. Maybe that person lives in his own home on the range, his own home of his own creation out on that range of unfettered thought that stretches to infinity, that rises in marching dunes through history. And maybe when that person has homesteaded his own home on such a range, then that person is also a cowboy of sorts.

Further Reading

Dunwoody Pond: Reflections on the High Plains Wetlands and the Cultivation of Naturalists.
    1994.
Keith County Journal. 1978.

Ron Hansen

Ron Hansen's character Cecil lives his life of quiet boredom in Mari Sandoz's Sandhills. In this region of hard winters and scattered population the early settlers, whose hardships were chronicled by Sandoz, and the contemporary ranchers visited by John Janovy are equally committed to their places. Hansen recounts the life of a man with nothing to do. In a region where, as Janovy reports, winter is a bitch, Cecil talks to telephone solicitors, watches his wife wrap pennies, and worries about his friend's illnesses and when the mail will arrive, all with equal attention. As Wright Morris has pointed out, the Great Plains are tipped toward the southeast: the weather and the population tend to slip down to the cities along the eastern borders of Kansas, Nebraska, and the Dakotas. In the rest of the Great Plains people like Cecil are trying to survive on their own terms.

For the biography and bibliography of Hansen see pages 413 and 425.

Red-Letter Days (1989)

Jan 25. Etta still poorly but up and around. Hard winds all day. Hawk was talking. Helped with kitchen cleanup then shop work on Squeegee's fairway woods. Still playing the Haigs I talked him into in 1963. Worth plenty now. Walked up to post office for Etta's stamps. $11.00! Went to library for William Rhenquist's book on Court and Ben Hogan's *Five Lessons*. Finest golf instructions ever written. Will go over with Wild Bill, one lesson per week. Weary upon return. Skin raw. Etta said to put some cream on. Didn't. We sat in the parlor until nine, Etta with her crossword puzzles, me with snapshots of Wild Bill at junior invitational. Will point out his shoe plant and slot at the top.

Feb 2. Will be an early spring, according to the groundhog. Went ice fishing on Niobrara with Henry. Weren't close as boys but everybody else dying off. Extreme cold. Snaggle hooks and stink bait. Felix W on heart and lung machines and going downhill in a handcart. Dwight's boy DWI in Lincoln. Sam Cornish handling trial. Would've been my choice too. Aches and pains discussed. Agriculture and commodities market and Senior Pro /Am in August. Toughed it out till noon—no luck with catfish—then hot coffee at Why Not? Upbraided for my snide comments about *The People's Court*. Everyone talking about Judge Wapner the way they used to gush about FDR. Wild Bill's poppa slipped into the booth and hemmed and hawed before asking had *William* said anything to me about colleges. You know how boys are. Won't talk to the old man. Writing to Ohio State coach soon re: sixth place in Midwestern Junior following runner-up in Nebraska championship. And still a sophomore! Etta tried for the umpteenth time to feed me haddock this evening. Went where it usually does.

Feb 9. Hardly twenty degrees last night. Felix W's funeral today. Walked to Holy Sepulchre for the Mass, then to cemetery; taking a second to look at our plots. Hate to think about it, but I'll have my three score and ten soon. Felix two years younger. Estate papers now with Donlan & Upshaw. (?!) Widow will have to count her fingers after the settlement. Etta stacked her pennies in wrappers while watching soaps on television. Annoying to hear that pap, but happy for her company. And just when I was wishing that kids and grandkids would have been part of the bargain, Wild Bill showed up! And with his poppa's company car, so he took us out to the golf club and we practiced his one and two irons from the Sandhills patio, hitting water balls I raked up from the hazards in September. Wild Bill in golf shoes and quarterback sweats and Colorado ski sweaters, me in my gray parka and rubber overboots. You talking *cold?* Wow! Wild Bill getting more and more like Jack Nicklaus at sixteen. Lankier but just as long. His one irons reaching the green at #2! And with a good tight pattern in the snow, like shotgun pellets puncturing white paper. Homer and Crisp stopped by to hoot and golly, say how amazing the kid is, but I wouldn't let em open their traps. The goofs. W. B.'s hands got to stinging—like hitting rocks, he said—so we quit. Have spent the night perusing *Reader's Digest.* Our president making the right decisions. Feet still aching. Hope it's not frostbite.

Feb 20. Helped Etta with laundry. Hung up sheets by myself. Brrr! Heard Etta yelling "Cecil!" over and over again, nagging me with instructions. Would not look back to house. We're on the outs today. Walked the six blocks to Main for the groceries ($34.17!) and got caught out in the snow right next to liquor store. Woman I knew from a Chapter Eleven took me home. Embarrassing because I couldn't get her name right. Verna? Vivian? Another widow. Says she still misses husband, night and day. Has the screaming meemies now and again. Was going to invite her inside but thought better of it. In mailbox the *Creighton Law Review* and *Golf Digest,* plus a jolly letter from Vance and Dorothy in Yuma, saying the Winnebago was increasing their "togetherness." A chilling prospect for most couples I know. Worked in shop putting new handgrips on Henry's irons. Eighteen-year-old MacGregors. Wrong club for a guy his age, but Henry's too proud to play Lites. Work will pay for groceries, just about. Half pint of whiskey behind paint cans. Looked and looked and looked at it; took it up to Etta. Ate tunafish casserole—we appear to be shying away from red meat—and sat in parlor with magazines. Tom Watson's instructions good as always but plays too recklessly. Heard he's a Democrat. Shows. Etta's been watching her programs since seven. Will turn set off soon and put out our water glasses as the night is on the wane and we are getting tired.

Mar 4. Four inches last night and another batch during the day. Old Man Winter back with a vengeance. Woke up to harsh scrape of county snowplows. Worried the mail would not get through, but right on the button, including Social Security checks! Helped Etta put her Notary Sojack on, then trudged up to the Farmer's National. Whew! Kept a sawbuck for the week's pocket money. Hamburger and coffee at the Why Not? Happy to see Tish so chipper after all her ordeals. Checked out Phil Rodger's instruction book from library—great short game for Wild Bill to look at, although Lew Worsham and Paul Runyan still tops in that category. Helped Etta tidy up. Wearing my Turnberry sweater inside with it so cold, but Etta likes the windows open a crack. Shoes need polishing. Will do tomorrow or next day. Early to bed.

Mar 12. Etta has been scheming with Henry's wife about retirement communities in Arizona. And where would our friends be? Nebraska. We put a halt to that litigation in September, I thought. Expect it will be an annual thing now. Dishes. Vacuumed. Emptied trash. Hint of spring in the air but no robins yet. Wild Bill lying low, sad to say. Girlfriend? Took a straw broom into rooms and swatted down cobwebs. Etta looking at me the whole time without saying a word. Haircut, just to pass the time. Dwight snipping the air these days, just to keep me in his chair. We avoided talk of his boy and jail. Seniors potluck meeting in Sandhills clubhouse at six. Shots of me with Dow Finsterwald, Mike Souchak, Jerry Barber still up in the pro shop. Worried new management would change things. (Pete Torrance still my idea of a great club professional.) And speaking of, a good deal of talk about our own Harlan "Butch" Polivka skunking out at Doral Ryder Open and the Honda Classic. Enjoyed saying I told you so. We'll plant spruce trees on right side of #11 teebox, hoping to make it a true par five. Alas, greens fees to go to six dollars (up from 50¢ in 1940) and Senior Pro/Am will have to go by the way this year. Hours of donnybrook and hurt feelings on that score, but Eugene late in getting commitments. Everybody regretting August vote now. Would likes of Bob Toski or Orville Moody say no soap to a $1,000 appearance fee? We'll never know. Betsy said it best at Xmas party. Eugene looks very bad, by the by. Chemotherapy took his hair, and a yellow cast to his eyes now. Wearing sunglasses even indoors. Zack much improved after operation. Wilma just not all there anymore. Etta tried to make coherent conversation but got nowhere. Sigh. Upon getting home, wrote out checks to water and sewer and Nebraska power and so on, but couldn't get checkbook to zero out with latest Farmer's National statement. Frustrating. Sign of old age, I guess. Will try again tomorrow.

Mar 17. Looked up Wild Bill's high-school transcript. Would appear he's been getting plenty of sleep. We'll have to forget about Stanford and the Eastern schools and plug away at the Big Eight and Big Ten. Etta wearing green all day in honor of old Eire. Was surprised when I pointed out that Saint Patrick was English. Told her that *Erin go bragh* joke. She immediately telephoned Betsy. Late in the day I got on the horn to Wild Bill, but Cal said he was at some party. Kept me on the line in order to explore my opinions on whether Wild Bill ought to get some coaching from the Butcher, acquire some college-player techniques. Well, I counted to ten and took a deep breath and then patiently, patiently told old Cal that golf techniques have changed not one iota in sixty years and that Harlan "Butch" Polivka is a "handsy" player. Lanny Wadkins type. Hits at the golf ball like he was playing squash. Whereas I've taught Wild Bill like Jack Grout taught Nicklaus. Hands hardly there. And did Cal really want his boy around a guy known to have worn knickers? Well, old Cal soothed my pin feathers some by saying it was only a stray notion off the top of his head, and it was Cecil says this and Cecil says that since his son was ten years old. Told *him* that *Erin go bragh* joke. Heard it, he said. From Marie.

Mar 20. Took a morning telephone call for Etta, one of those magazine-subscription people. Enjoyed the conversation. Signed up for *Good Housekeeping.* Weather warming up at last, so went out for constitutional. Wrangled some at the Why Not? Squeegee getting heart pains but don't you dare talk to him about his cigarettes! Lucky thing Tish got between us. She says Squeegee still doesn't know what to do with his time; just handwashes his Rambler every day and looks out at the yard. Encouraged her talk about a birthday party for Etta with the girls from the Altar Sodality and the old "Roman Hruska for Senator" campaign. Ate grilled cheese sandwich in Etta's room. Did not blow it and broach party subject. Etta's hair in disarray. We sang "The Bells of St. Mary's" and "Sweet Adeline" while I gave it a hundred strokes. Etta still beautiful in spite of illness. Expressed my sentiments.

Mar 25. Worked out compromise with insurance company. Have been feeling rotten the past few days. Weak, achy, sort of tipsy when I stand up. Hope no one stops by. Especially Wild Bill. Sandhills' one and only PGA golf professional is again favoring us with his presence in the clubhouse. Will play dumb and ask *Harlan* about his sickly day at the Hertz Bay Hill Classic. Etta's temperature gauge says it's fifty-two degrees outside; March again going out like a lamb. Ike biography petered out toward the end. Haven't been able to sleep, so I took a putter from the closet and have been hitting balls across the parlor carpet and into my upended water glass. *Tock, rum, rum, plonk.*

Apr 1. Hard rains but mail came like clockwork. Nice chat with carrier. (Woman!) Quick on the uptake. April Fool's jokes, etc. Letters to occupant, assorted bills, and then, lo and behold, government checks. Wadded up junk mail and dropped it in circular file, then Etta walked with me to Farmer's. Enjoys rain as much as ever, but arthritis acting up some. Hefty balance in savings account thanx to Uncle Sam, but no pup anymore. One hospital stay could wipe us out. Have that to think about every day now as 70 looms on the horizon. Will be playing nine tomorrow with Zack, Mel, and Dr. Gerald S. Bergstrom, P.C. Hoping for another Nassau with old P.C. Lousy when "pressed," and the simoleons will come in handy. Evening supper with *Reader's Digest* open under milk glass and salad bowl. National Defense called to task. Entire Navy sitting ducks. Worrisome.

Apr 4. Have put new spikes in six pairs of shoes now; at $15 a crack. Wrist is sore but easy money. Dull day otherwise. Walked over to Eugene's and played cribbage until five. Eugene is painting his house again. Etta and I have been counting and think this is the sixth time since Eugene put the kibosh on his housepainting business. You know he's retired because he will *not* do anyone else's house. Have given up trying to figure Eugene. Walked past Ben's Bar & Grill on the way home. Just waved.

Apr 10. Wonderful golf day. Timothy grass getting high in the roughs, but songbirds out, womanly shapes to the sandhills up north, cattails swaying under the zephyrs, great white clouds arranging themselves in the sky like sofas in the Montgomery Ward. Homer and Crisp played nine with me and zigzagged along in their putt-putt. Hijinks, of course. Exploding golf ball, Mulligans, naughty tees. (Hate to see cowboy hats on the links. We ought to have a rule.) Even par after six, then the 153-yard par three. Hit it fat! Chopped up a divot the size of Sinatra's toupee and squirted the pill all of twenty yards. Sheesh! Examined position. Easy lie and uphill approach. Eight iron would have got me there ten years ago, but I have given in to my age. Went over my five swing keys and thought "Oily," just like Sam Snead. Hard seven iron with just enough cut to tail right and quit. Kicked backwards on the green and then trickled down the swale to wind up two feet from the cup. Homer and Crisp three-putted as per usual—paid no attention to my teaching—and I took my sweet time tapping in. *Quod erat demonstrandum.* Crisp says Butch has been claiming he shot a 62 here last July but, conveniently, with some Wake Forest pals who were visiting. Funny he never gets up a game with me. Tax returns in. Have overpaid $212, according to my pencil. Early supper, then helped Etta strip paint from doorjambs. Hard job but getting to be duck soup with practice. Will be sore tomorrow.

Apr 15. Squeegee passed away just about sunup. Heart attack. Etta with Mildred as I write this. The guy had been complaining of soreness in his back but no other signs of ill health other than his hacking and coughing. Looking at yesterday's diary entry, I spot my comment on his "hitching," and it peeves me that I could not have written down some remarks about how much his friendship meant to me over these past sixty-five years. Honest, hardworking, proud, letter-of-the-law sort of guy. Teetotaler. Excellent putter under pressure. Would not give up the cigarettes. Will keep pleasant memories of him from yesterday, say a few words at the service. Weather nippy. Wanted booze all day.

Apr 17. S. Quentin German consigned to his grave. Especially liked the reading from Isaiah: "Justice shall be the band around his waist, and faithfulness a belt upon his hips. Then the wolf shall be a guest of the lamb, and the leopard shall lie down with the kid; the calf and the young lion shall browse together, with a little child to guide them." And then something about a lion eating hay like the ox. Excellent applications to old age/erosion of powers/nature's winnowing process. Following, there was a nice reception at the Why Not? Haven't seen Greta since she had her little girl. Mildred wisely giving Squeegee's Haigs to the golf team at William Jennings Bryan. Etta and I took short constitutional at nightfall. Warm. Heather and sagebrush in the air. Have begun Herbert Hoover biography. Iowa boy. Engineer. History will judge him more kindly than contemporaries did. Low today; no pep.

Apr 20. Etta sixty-seven. Took a lovely little breakfast to her in bed, with one yellow rose in the vase. Nightgown and slippers just perfect, she says. Foursome with Sam Cornish, Henry, and Zack. Shot pitiful. Kept getting the Katzenjammers up on the teebox. Hooked into the Arkwright rangeland on #3. Angus cattle just stared at me: Who's the nitwit? And then skulled a nine iron approach on #17 and my brand-spanking-new Titleist skipped into the water hazard. *Kerplunk.* Hate the expense more than the penalty stroke. And to top it off, Cornish approached me in pro shop with a problem on the Waikowski codicil. Hadn't the slightest idea what he was talking about. Sam has always loved those *ipse dixits* and *sic passims,* but that wasn't the problem. The problem is me. I just can't listen fast enough. Everything gets scrambled. I say to him, "What's your opinion?" And when he tells me, I pretend complete agreement, Sam pretends I helped out. Humiliating. Roosevelt at Yalta. Etta had her party today. She hadn't predicted it, so apparently I managed to keep the cat in the bag for once. Had a real nice time; plenty of chat and canasta. She needed the pick-me-up.

Apr 25. Walked a slow nine with Henry and Eugene. No birdies, two bogeys, holed out once from a sand trap. Eugene and Henry getting straighter from the tees. Haven't pointed out to them that their mechanics haven't improved—they're just too weak to put spin on the golf ball these days. Lunched at Sandhills and shot the breeze until four, then walked by the practice range. Wild Bill out there with you know who. And Wild Bill slicing! shanking! Everything going right. Lunging at the ball like Walter Hagen. Butch dumbfounded. Addled. Looked at hands, stance, angle of club face, completely overlooking the problem. Head. Yours truly walked up without a word, put a golf ball on the tee, took a hard hold of Wild Bill's girl-killer locks and said, "You go ahead and swing." Hurt him like crazy. About twenty hairs yanked out in my hand. I said, "You keep that head in place and you won't get so onion-eyed." I just kept holding on and pretty soon those little white pills were riding along the telegraph wire, and rising up for extra yardage just when you thought they'd hang on the wind and drop. Walked away with Wild Bill winking his thanx and our kid pro at last working up the gumption to say, "Good lesson." Will sleep happy tonight.

Apr 30. I puttered around the house until ten when Wild Bill invited me to a round with Wilbur Gustafson's middle boy, Keith. We've let bygones by bygones. Keith also on golf team. Ugly swing—hodgepodge of Lee Trevino and Charlie Owens— but gets it out okay. Keith says he hasn't got *William*'s (!) touch from forty yards and in, but scored some great sand saves. Was surprised to hear I lawyered. And Wild Bill says, "What? You think he was a *caddy?*" Was asked how come I gave up my practice, but pretended I didn't hear. Was asked again and replied that a perfectionist cannot put up with mistakes. Especially his own. Hit every green in regulation on the front nine, but the back jumped up and bit me. Old Sol nice and bright until one P.M., and then a mackerel sky got things sort of fuzzy. (Cataracts? Hope not.) Well: on #12, Wild Bill couldn't get the yardage right, so without thinking I told him, "Just get out your mashie." You guessed it: "What's a mashie?" And then we were going through the whole bag from brassie to niblick. Kids got a big kick out of it. Hung around and ate a hot dog with Etta, Roberta, and Betsy, then jawed with Crisp on the putting green. Watched as a greenskeeper strolled from the machine shed, tucking his shirt in his pants. Woman walked out about two minutes later. Won't mention any names.

May 6. Weather getting hotter. Will pay Wild Bill to mow yard. ($5 enough?) Endorsed government check and sent to Farmer's with deposit slip. Helped Etta wash and tidy up. Have been bumping into things. Match play with Zack, a one-stroke handicap per hole. Halved the par threes, but his game fell apart otherwise. Would have taken $14 bucks from him but urged Zack to go double or nothing on a six-footer at #18 and yanked it just enough. Zack's scraping by just like we all are. AA meeting, then Etta's noodles and meat sauce for dinner. (According to dictionary, P. Stroganoff a 19th century Russian count and diplomat. Must be a good story there.) Early sleep.

May 15. Nice day. Shot a 76. Every fairway and fourteen greens in regulation. Four three-putts spelled the difference. Took four Andrew Jacksons from Dr. Bergstrom, but ol P.C. probably makes that in twenty minutes. Will stop playing me for cash pretty soon. Tish got a hole-in-one at the 125-yard par three! Have telephoned the *Press-Citizen*. Her snapshot now in pro shop. Oozy rain in the afternoon. Worked on Pete Upshaw's irons until four P.M. His temper hasn't improved. Went to Concord Inn—Etta driving—for the prime-rib special. Half price before six. And then out to Sandhills for Seniors meeting. We *finally* gave out prizes for achievements at Amelia Island tournament. (Marie sorry for tardiness, but no excuse.) Joke gifts and reach-me-downs, but some great things too. Expected our "golf professional" to give me a chipper or yardage finder, something fuddy-duddy and rank amateur, but the guy came through with a seven wood, one of those nifty presents you don't know you want until you actually get it. We have no agreement, only a truce. Zack got a funny Norman Rockwell print of some skinny kids with hickory sticks arguing golf rules on a green. Looked exactly like Zack and Felix and Squeegee and me way back in the twenties. Talked about old times. We're thinking Pinehurst for next winter trip. Have suggested we open it up to get some *mannerly* high-school golfers to join us. (Would be a nice graduation present for Wild Bill.) Everybody home by nine.

May 22. Early Mass and then put in an hour mixing up flapjack batter at the Men's Club pancake breakfast. Heard Wilma has Alzheimer's. Earl Yonnert having thyroid out. Whole town getting old. Went out to links at noon. Wild Bill there by the green with his shag bag, chipping range balls into a snug group that looked just like a honeycomb. Etta asked him to join us. Have to shut my eyes when she gets up to the ball, but she skitters it along the fairway okay. Wild Bill patient, as always. Has been getting great feelers from Ohio State, thanx to my aggressive letter campaign and his Nebraska state championship. Everything may depend upon his ranking on the Rolex All-American team. Says he hopes I'll visit him in Ohio, maybe play Muirfield Village, look at videotapes of his swing now and then. Has also politely let me know that he now prefers the name William. Wonder what Frank Urban "Fuzzy" Zoeller would have to say about that? But of course the kid never heard of Wild Bill Mehlhorn and his cowboy hat at the 1925 PGA. Well: Went nine with him and got skinned. His drives now a sand wedge longer than mine, so I'm hitting my seven wood versus his nine iron or my sixty-yard pitch versus his putt. Waited on the teebox at #7 while some guys in Osh Kosh overalls and seed-company caps yipped their way across the green. Etta laughed and said she just had a recollection of Squeegee saying, Even a really bad day of golf is better than a good day of work. We all grinned like fools. Especially Wild Bill. Hit me that my lame old jokes have always seemed funny and fresh to him. One facet of youth's attractiveness for tiresome gaffers like me. Tried a knock-down five iron to the green, but it whunked into the sand trap. Easy out to within four feet, and then a one-putt for par. Wild Bill missed an opportunity. Etta got lost in the rough with her spoon and scored what the Pro/Am caddies used to say was a "newspaper 8." Walked to the next tee in a garden stroll under an enormous blue sky, just taking everything in, Wild Bill up ahead and my wife next to me and golf the only thing on my mind. And I was everywhere I have ever been: on the public course at age nine with Dad's sawed-down midiron, and again when I was thirteen and parred three in a row, and on my practice round with Tommy Armour and Byron Nelson in 1947, or playing St. Andrews, Oakmont, Winged Foot, Pebble Beach, or here at Sandhills years ago, just hacking around with the guys. Every one was a red-letter day. Etta said, "You're smiling" "Second childhood," said I. Wild Bill played scratch golf after that and then went over to the practice range. Has the passion now. Etta and I went out to the Ponderosa for steak and potatoes on their senior-citizen discount. Have been reading up on Columbus, Ohio, since then. Home of the university, capital of the state, population of 540,000 in 1970, the year that her own Jack Nicklaus won his second British Open.

May 30. Went to Holy Sepulchre Cemetery with Etta and put peonies out for the many people we know now interred there. Etta drove me to the course—getting license back Wednesday. Eugene was there, trying out putters, stinking like turpentine, getting cranky. Went eighteen with me, but only half-decent shot he could manage was a four-wood rouser that Gene Sarazen would have envied. Were joined by a spiffy sales rep from Wilson Sports and Eugene just kept needling him. And a lot of that raunchy talk I don't like. Then hot coffee in the clubhouse. Was asked how long I have been playing the game and said sixty years. Eugene worked out the arithmetic on a paper napkin and the comeuppance was I have spent at least five years of my life on a golf course. "Five years, Cecil! You can't have 'em back. You could've accomplished something important. Ever feel guilty about that?" I sipped from my cup and said, "We're put here for pleasure too." And then we were quiet. Eugene crumpled up the napkin and pitched it across the room. Looking for a topic, I asked how his chemotherapy was playing out, and Eugene said he'd stopped going. Enjoyed my surprise. Said, "What's the point? Huh? You gotta die of somethin'." And I had a picture of Eugene at forty, painting my window sashes, and headstrong and ornery and brimming with vim and vigor. Saddening. Hitched a ride home with him, and Eugene just sat behind the wheel in the driveway, his big hands in his lap, looking at the yard and house paint. "We have all this technology," he said. "Education. High-speed travel. Medical advances. And the twentieth century is still unacceptable." "Well," I said, "at least you've had yourself an adventure." Eugene laughed. Went inside and repaired the hosel on Butch's Cleveland Classic. ($15.) Watched TV. Looked at Nebraska Bar Association mailing about judges under consideration. Have no opinion on the matter. Etta sleeping as I write this. Hope to play nine tomorrow.

Louise Erdrich

In 1993 Louise Erdrich issued a "new and revised edition" of her award-winning novel *Love Medicine* (1984). This daring act reminded readers of the mutability of oral traditions and storytelling. The materials she added helped tie together the saga of her North Dakota novels by fleshing out characters and backgrounds. One of the added chapters is "The Tomahawk Factory."

Lyman Lamartine has inherited his father Nector Kashpaw's sense of business survival. Lyman tries to bring together the tribal community through a factory that will manufacture and market museum-quality artifacts. Traditional clan rivalries, modern factions, and an old-fashioned love triangle erupt into a battle that parodies Indian battle clichés and rubber tomahawks.

For the biography of and further reading about Erdrich see pages 179 and 191.

The Tomahawk Factory (1983)

Lyman Lamartine

As I walked back from the river that filled my brother's boots, I could feel change coming onto me, riding me hard. I knew, from the first moment I got back to the house, I was not the same Lyman Lamartine who had left—that boy was gone. I saw my talent for money was useless with the deeper problems. Worse than useless. If I bobbed to the surface, others went down.

For weeks after Henry Junior's death, I still couldn't take in the fact. I sat in his chair before the television, fit my hands over the raw spots where his had gripped, shut my eyes to get the sense. The old ones say a Chippewa won't ever rest if he's drowned, a rumor that both scared me and kept me up at night. But I decided if I talked to Henry Junior as a wandering ghost, I would explain once and for all that he owned the damn convertible.

You thought you'd win our little argument by killing yourself, I said out loud to the blackened screen. *But you just bought out my share.*

I suppose I was trying to get him to take issue and argue back, but it never worked. He stayed gone, dead, and I never saw him again except in old pictures. The best I could do was imagine him down there at the bottom of the current, cruising, driving the red hulk north.

I went lower, maybe lower than he ever went, until I sank to a place I didn't move from. In the meantime my business fled, my stocks crashed, my money dwindled, accounts failed, and tax information and credit notices showed up in the mail, piling high, higher, high as the springtime river until they overflowed and littered the kitchen floor. Quite a few months had gone by then, almost a year, in which I stayed drunk or messed up on whatever came through the reservation.

I don't like to say this, nobody can believe it, but here's the way it is with us Indians—Uncle Sam taketh away and Uncle Sam giveth. He took Henry. But then he went and gave life back to me. I was sitting in my chair—broke-down, busted of money—when a breeze from a punched-out window flipped a paper over on the floor. It was a 1099 from the Department of the Treasury. Copy B. I read the notice and threw it aside, but then I picked it up again. You want to know why? I couldn't get the small-type warning phrase, the IRS penalty for negligence, out of my head. I had lost my own brother, who was a father to me too. You wouldn't think the government could get to me with numbers—and yet, right after that, I went rummaging for a paper clip. I intended to attach the form to something, anything, it didn't matter. I'd had fits of responsibility in the past year, but always, they died on me. If I found a paper clip, I knew this one would pass.

I couldn't find a clip, though, nowhere in the shambles. I looked around—bare walls, empty sockets—the light bulbs stolen out by partygoers, nothing but a three-legged couch and a shifting rug of papers. And in the whole junk pile, not a fucking paper clip. Not one. Not a stapler. Not a stamp. No way to report. No clean envelope.

I strayed into a mad calm. I walked around and around, a tax form in my fist, and that strange current of motivation soon built up to a rapid churning and frothing in me, until I grabbed whatever I could reach, lifted my arms like King Kong. My hands balled up Bureau of Indian Affairs recommendations, reports, newsletters. Then I threw it all down and stomped on it. I would have punched the walls, but the Sheetrock already was destroyed. I wound myself up to shout, to roar, but no sound came. And if it did, who would hear? Anyone who might have cared had long ago left me in disgust. I was forgotten. My mother was now heavy into politics. My phone was ripped out. My jeans almost slithered off my skinny hips. I looked down at my caved-in stomach. I was useless for sex, had no interest, no desires like I always did in the days I was a money-maker.

Here, to my surprise, I had ended up a nobody. I could die now and leave no ripple. Why not! I considered, but then I came up with the fact that my death would leave a gap in the BIA records, my IRS account would be labeled incomplete until it closed. There would be minor confusion. These thoughts gave me a warm jolt. In cabinets of files, anyway, I still maintained existence. The government knew me though the wind and the earth did not. I was alive, at least on paper. I was someone. I owed cash.

Or *was* owed, perhaps. The thought that I could have overpaid my taxes in the year I was solvent made me so thirsty I grabbed armfuls of paper from the floor. I began to stack things, one letter onto another, to categorize. Wedged into a crack in the floor, I found a pen that still worked. I began to label. On the very same day,

I filed. Once I filed, I knew I was on my way back. I was gathering myself. Identity was taking shape. I was becoming legitimate, rising from the heap. The ironic thing was that when I finally got around to the 1099 I saw that someone had typed my box number onto a form that belonged to someone else—the whole thing was a mistake.

Out of a typo, I was formed. Out of papers, I came to be. By the end of the week, I'd signed on with the BIA.

I hit my stride without warming up, acted as though my year as a soak had been a kind of unpaid vacation. I ignored my mother's jabs on the subject of selling out, and I went up so fast the trees blurred. In a matter of years, I rose through the ranks, adding on a GS number every time I cleared out my equipment, until I had acquired one secretary, two, and then four. By the time I worked myself over to Aberdeen, home of the Fischer Quintuplets and BIA area office, I was a slick-looking eyesore, built square as my desk. I gave up trying to look like Henry and turned into myself—short like my mother, but with a Kashpaw mug, bold and unredeemed, eyes narrowed for the bottom line. I repaired my confidence, learned how to benefit from complex tribal development projects. In my office—a bunker with no-see-in slots for windows and fluorescent lighting overhead—former doubts vanished. With a sweep of my pen I signed off on go-aheads, freed moneys, or, on the other hand, blocked plans I had no use for by consigning them to my personal limbo—"pending," or I sent them slogging through "other channels," "other agencies," and worst, if I really hated what I saw, slipped the whole proposal off to Washington where it would be finally and hopelessly snarled.

If my comeback sounds simple, it was—much too easy to last for long. One day, as I was dictating a slew of memos, I got a call from my boss, the BIA superintendent, Edgar "Dizzy" Lightninghoop.

"Your mother has occupied my office."

I gripped the phone hard. "What's she doing?"

"She's sitting at my desk," he said. "I'm standing right across from her." His voice was slow, almost shaking. "In one hand she has the draft of that project I was due to present to Washington." He paused a long moment. "Just finished it this morning. My only copy."

"Put her on, Dizzy."

"Wait a minute. Now she's taking something from her purse. She's holding it up, showing me. It's a cigarette lighter."

"I see."

I considered, collected my thoughts before I spoke. "Better handle things yourself."

I quietly hung up. My mother did wild things to exasperate me sometimes, as if she was anxious to regain my whole attention. You know Lulu Lamartine if you know life is made up of three kinds of people—those who live it, those afraid to, those in between. My mother is the first. She has no fear, and that's what's wrong with her. She lives hard and devil-may-care, especially in her age, and lets the worry and the consequences land on me.

For instance, in my absence from the reservation, she had become a sometime ally of my late father's wife, Marie Kashpaw. What was I—the flesh-and-blood proof of Nector Kashpaw's teepee-creeping—supposed to think? In youth, Marie and Lulu were both terrors, cutting a wide unholy swath. In marriage they fiercely raised their children. It was in age that they came into their own. With Nector Kashpaw gone, the two of them were now free to concentrate their powers, and once they got together they developed strong and hotheaded followings among our local agitating group of hard-eyes, a determined bunch who grew out their hair in braids or ponytails and dressed in ribbon shirts and calico to make their point. Traditionals. Back-to-the-buffalo types.

Marie had dressed that way right along—never caught up with the present. But when they tried to get my mother to go calico, Lulu Lamartine sniffed down her nose at the length and bagginess of old-time skirts. She led her gang of radicals in black spike heels and tight, low-cut dresses blooming with pink flowers. She wore her makeup, her lipstick, and what I used to call her "Dear Abby" wig, a coal-black contraption of curls.

As it happened, on the day I refused to reason with her over the phone, I was up to my neck in the very same project that she had in mind to torch. It was a proposal to take up where Nector Kashpaw had left off, to set into motion a tribal souvenir factory, a facility that would produce fake arrows and plastic bows, dyed-chicken-feather headdresses for children, dress-up stuff. Years before, when the factory concept was first introduced, the product was aimed to be competitive with low-priced Taiwanese goods. By the time my mother and the traditionals, old-time and new, finished their equal opportunity–mandated consulting, the game plan had altered. The product now was "museum-quality" artifacts, and the price had gone up, in keeping.

By then Mom was on the planning board as the official community input. She put in all right. Dizzy Lightninghoop leaned on me to chair a meeting not long after the occupation. Supposedly, I would talk some sense into my own mother as well as her coconspirator, Marie Kashpaw. As it turned out there was a wild jack in the bunch too. There always is. Usually, though, you don't have to take him personally.

Lipsha Morrissey bugged me from the first moment I stepped into the meeting. Slouched in a corner chair away from the table, feet big in unlaced shoes shapeless as plaster, skinny otherwise, wearing a jean jacket cuffed too short for his knobby wrists, he looked puzzled. People treated him special, as though he were important somehow, but I couldn't see it. A found child, a throwaway is what he was, and yet there was talk he had a medicine skill. His hair was tied in a tail. His smooth brown face was clever and contriving as a fox, and there was no mistaking the family resemblance to the wanted poster of my fugitive brother, hanging in the post office. Yet, at the same time, he acted bashful and bewildered, rarely spoke. Of course, he didn't have to. My mother, his great admirer, held the floor.

"They're natural artists, our people," she was asserting.

The rest of the planning board nodded their approval, but the generalization irritated me.

"*I* can't draw," I said, as I walked to the front of the room. "Neither can you, Mom. You're no artist."

She turned, slow, theatrical, and regarded me with a look of surprise that she shifted before my eyes to fond amusement.

"There's lots of arts besides the pictorial," she finally countered, speaking in a too-gentle voice.

"For instance, what?"

I never knew when to quit with her. The rest of the planning board leaned alertly toward out little argument, and Lulu Lamartine gloried in the suspense.

"You," she said. "You're a work of art. You're my baby."

She licked her bowed lips and tapped her passion-pink fingernails. Heat rose up my neck and flooded my face. I was, as I said, the child of her wild grass widowhood and everybody knew it. I looked at Marie Kashpaw, who did not smile at me but only sat there composed and unyielding. To me, it seemed unfair that I should be taking on public blame for my own existence, standing guilt-struck before the wronged wife of my father, sheep-faced, when my mother was the one responsible. Right there, I thought to break their little game.

"You call it art, I call it old-fashioned whoopee," I said to shock her.

Silence. A quiet current of embarrassment rippled all around the table. My mother inclined her head when it lapped against her, against Marie. Still they sat, steadfast, showing me up, and right after that Lulu took her eyeglasses from her purse, steel-blue ovals of plastic. When she perched them on her nose I knew I was in for it. There was always trouble when my mother put the world in focus.

The transfer was a shock. Two months later, shipped from Aberdeen back up to my reservation to run the factory, I pulled into the drive beside a new tan govern-ment prefab that had been set down on cinder blocks only hours before. Standing in my empty new front room, looking out on the endless blue space of sudden grazing land, I thought things I couldn't have imagined anywhere else.

This house is a toy, appeared in my mind. Whereas before, you should have heard me on the subject of HUD. For a minute, I pictured some five-year-old's enormous chubby paw descending from nowhere with this squat, tan-and-blue windowed box, setting it right down on a gooseberry patch or cow flops, haphaz-ard, without consideration. Soon it would be connected to the maze of plastic sewage pipes and concrete water mains under the earth of the reservation town. That would, at least, make it part of the ebb and flow of something.

In the meantime, I did have electricity, a mattress on the floor, and a six-pack of cold Bud in the narrow refrigerator. U-Haul rental vans generally did not come onto Indian land, for the same reasons that banks refuse loans within reservation boundaries. Risk. So the government would move me sometime this week. Until that time, with what I had packed in the car, I was comfortable enough. I'd brought a patio chair of webbed plastic and aluminum bars. I set it up right outside the front door, and then I occupied it just like any longtime homeowner.

It was late spring. The sky was clear, the ground so dry that ruts made months ago in clay gumbo by the wheels of cranes and trucks were molded permanently into the earth. The sun reflected off the clouds in bronze streaks, almost tigerish. The animals moving through the wide spread of brown pasture below me were shaggy and humped, massive through the head and shoulders, with graceful legs and hindquarters. Buffalo. My mother's work, of course. She was part of an effort to bring back these old-time stubborn animals. Watching them move through the dust haze, the winter silt caught in the broken grass, rising like smoke, I felt a pang of longing, though I didn't know for what. Maybe some buried hunter's mentality, the need to ride out there and shoot myself dinner. Carve off the hide. Chop the carcass into chunks. Dry it. Freeze it. Tan the skin with the beast's dull brains and live inside it as a shelter. These thoughts left me with appreciation for my instant house, so I turned to look at it—right there, so solid, the darkening vista reflected in its windows of insulated glass.

I finished that beer, had another, was into can three when my mother pulled up. For all her insistence on returning to the old ways, she regularly traded in so that her car was the latest Chevy, new and shiny. This current model was a mink-brown Citation with cherry dingle-dice hanging from the rearview.

It was her bingo night at the church, and she wore a red sweater with linebacker shoulder pads and flashy flowers on the front sewn of sequins and beads. Tight black stretch pants showed off her good legs. Long earrings of porcupine quills hung to her shoulders, and pointed black boots twinkled on her feet. I offered her my chair, stood behind her, breathing traces of the perfume she wore—a shaft of smoky crystal in the cool spring air. As a boy, I'd pressed my face to that fragrance, a web of excitement caught in the material of coats and dresses. It wasn't just man-made perfume that hung about her, it was sweetgrass and baby powder, a dish-soapy musk, and then, I suppose, the throbbing cinnamon undertones of Lulu Lamartine herself. She took in the same view I did now, and it made her reflective.

"The four-legged people. Once they helped us two-leggeds."

This was the way her AIM bunch talked, as though they were translating their ideas from the original earth-based language. Of course, I knew very well they grew up speaking English. It drove me nuts.

She went on, musing, and I tried to listen. "Creation was all connected in the olden times."

"It's pretty much connected now," I said. "As soon as my plumbing's hooked in I'll be part of the great circle of life.

"Make fun," she said pleasantly. "But you're just a two-legged creature, no better than the four-legged, even the no-legged."

"What are those?"

"The fish people."

"Get off it. I'd like to see a fish drive a car."

"Or you live underwater."

There was no arguing with my mother, and besides we lapsed to silence in the sudden and mutual thought of Henry Junior. When she spoke again, it was clear that she had visited for a whole other purpose than simple welcome or pronouncement or sentiment: she was here in her official capacity, to tell me who to hire.

"You can't do that," I protested.

She set her lips, folded her arms across her chest, and got that project-burning look on her face. From her purse, she drew a paper and smoothed it out before me.

"What's this?"

"I've got your job applicants broken down to clans and families. Hire ten from each column and you'll be all right."

This was an important moment. My mother held my gaze, poker-straight. I looked right back at her, and with that look, I lied. I didn't use words to fool her, I just smiled as if I was delighted to accept her considerations, nodded to indicate that I would gladly put them into effect. Her eyes glazed slightly. She did not believe me, but suddenly I had a minor vision: she was getting wound up for something bigger than the dreamstuff, and so was I.

I would be the bureaucratic opposition by which she measured her success, the quo that gave her status. She was the kind of person who fell over unless she had a wall to bang head against. As we sat there together, our smiles twin, false, polite, I knew that in coming back here I was doing unexpected duty as a son. I had tried to fill my brother's shoes until the river took my place. Now it was my turn to walk in the tracks that Kashpaw had left. By becoming the worthy adversary my mother now missed, by taking over his factory, I was keeping her instinct to control a man alive, giving her strength.

I ran things the way I thought Nector Kashpaw would have. I posted my system first, then hired. I knew how once upon a time my mother had stood and blocked his plans with paternity threats. Now I took pleasure in carrying out old ideas that surfaced in the dusty file trunks of the tribal offices.

1) Billy Nanapush inserts precut rectangle into punch press. Trips press. Press inserts grommet into leather. Drops leather into pile at next station.

2) Agnes Deer picks up leather rectangle right hand, pinewood dowel left hand. Draws leather thong through grommet. Ties thong loose knot. Passes dowel handle next station.

3) Mary Fred Toose picks out assortment of feathers. Inserts quill ends into knot. Draws thong tight. Passes handle.

4) Felix Pukwan, glue-dripper, drips one drop glue on end dowel handle. Piles handles at next station.
5) Lipsha Morrissey, Billy Nanapush, Norris Buny secure heads with rawhide and more glue.
6) Bertha Ironcloud inspects assembled war clubs. Heads reinforced with black suede strips. Bertha strings colorful beads on strip and lays war club on short conveyer belt.
7) At the receiving station backboards are assembled and spray-painted. Kyle Morrissey.
8) Eno Grassman. End man. Swabs industrial-strength glue on heads, bases, war clubs, and lays each within the backboard's spray-painted shadow.
   End product:
   An attractively framed symbol of America's past. Perfect for the home or office. A great addition to the sportsman's den. All authentic designs and child-safe materials. Crafted under the auspices of the U.S. Department of the Interior, Anishinabe Enterprises, Inc. Hand produced by Tribal Members.

Tobacco pouches, roach spreader, hair ties, makuks, deer calls and cradle boards were slated for work systems analysis, and by the third month I put into production two other traditional Ojibwa items: moccasins, and my favorite: patterned birch bark. In the past, women bit the shapes of snowflakes and stars into pieces of birch bark and hung these against the light. I had wanted to manufacture these pretty toys from the first, but systematizing was a challenge. I could not have my workers sit around nibbling, dental benefits wouldn't cover it. In the end I went over to the tooling plant and worked up a machine fitted with champers, iron slugs shaped like molars and incisors. One worker operating this machine could produce, in a day, the winter's work of a hundred Chippewa grandmothers.

The real life grandmothers gave me more problems, not to mention the mothers. My scheme was to hire both Lulu and Marie—at first as consultants, then as instructors in basic beadwork. I planned to phase them out of the picture altogether, very gradually of course, over the next few months. Still, the physical placement of the two in the factory was a delicate decision. Their statures had to be completely equal. I could show no preference. Their positions, at the beading table, which overlooked the entire workplace, had to be precisely measured. They each needed territory to control.

Their friendship, if that's what you'd call it, was hard to figure. Set free by Nector's death, they couldn't get enough of their own differences. They argued unceasingly about the past, and didn't agree on the present either. Whenever I was caught, they drew me in as a referee, and so I tried to avoid them, walked quickly past their table, which always seemed to be in motion, set awhirl by history's complications.

"Lyman," my mother called, grabbing my sleeve one of those times I didn't move fast enough, "wasn't it too a Lazarre who cracked a Nanapush on the head with a plow coulter!"

I knew, of course, that since Marie was a Lazarre before marrying a Kashpaw, my mother was angling for a dispute.

"I couldn't say."

"It was a Pillager who sent the twisted-mouth!" Marie said. "Don't deny it!"

She set her jaw into a grim rock, her mouth in an arrow line, and waited for me to take my mother's side. But I just shrugged.

"A Lazarre stole old Rushes Bear and shaved her head! Who could forget that one?"

"A Morrissey. It was a Morrissey." Marie Kashpaw firmly stated, her hands steady at their work. "Like the one you married," she added under her breath.

"Young and hot." My mother sighed and leaned sideways in her chair, confidingly. "I used to like them fresh. Now I go for day-old bread."

They burst into laughter so complete and sudden that it took me by surprise. Their wildness irritated and confused me, for I couldn't tell anymore what they took seriously and what really aggravated them. Men, it seemed, from their long-lived height, had been the pawns in their lives by which they worked out large destinies. They teased like girls, flirted like house cats, made bold jokes, whispered behind my back, made tongue-in-cheek show of respecting my position and then undercut me.

The one thing they didn't do, I noticed, the one area they left alone and never made into a joke, was my origin. Nector's fatherhood. That subject remained untouched.

At least Lipsha Morrissey was too young for anything but a three-day-a-week work-study job. He put plastic rocks onto the ends of the tomahawks on those afternoons, and if he showed up after school I let him sweep, box scraps, pack orders once in a while, just to placate the two women. He made me uneasy for two reasons. Number one, Kashpaw had claimed him—*him*, not me—and he wasn't even blood. Number two, Lipsha Morrissey was a combination of the two age-old factions that had torn apart our band. His mother was a Morrissey, but I was his half uncle, and that gave the two of us the same descent, the Pillager background. The Pillagers had been the holdouts, the ones who wouldn't sign the treaties, the keepers of the birch bark scroll and practitioners of medicines so dark and helpful that the more devout Catholic Indians crossed their breasts when a Pillager happened to look straight at them.

At loose ends, I sometimes wound up talking to Lipsha after quitting time. As his relative, I felt the obligation to keep him out of trouble and sometimes we went and shot pool for a couple of hours. He drank sodas, propped himself against the table, and beat me with effortless strokes. I tried to pretend I was losing for his benefit. His shit-eating smile made me fantasize pouring a can of beer on his head, but I controlled myself. After all, I was the boss.

For the time being anyway. To tell the truth, I was treading quicksand only weeks after shipping off the first orders. I had trouble finding outlets, new places to sell, but I still looked good on paper. Fall began with days so cold that the weather solved a lot of problems. The building Kashpaw had raised was vast, cold, with overhead lighting that turned the workers' faces dead and green. I planned skylights, kept the thermostat turned high. People showed up to work, if only to get warm. To counter friction and make myself seem friendlier, I ordered in free doughnuts and had hot coffee available by the time clocks.

One day, my mother snagged me there. We were alone for a change. She was sitting in one of the plastic chairs near the coffee urn. "You don't realize," she informed me straight out, as if she'd been waiting for this moment, "but Marie and me are keeping your workers from each other's throats."

"I'm turning down new applicants, haven't had a complaint." I was bluffing, but her superior ways were wearing on me. Avoiding the beading table was getting to be a nuisance and their whispers dogged my turned back.

"Mother," I said in my most ingratiating grade school voice. "I never thanked you for pushing my idea that one step farther." I sat down close to her, had a sweep of inspiration. "So I'm thanking you. *Megwitch.* Now you're fired."

I'd meant to say it kindly, but her conniving had stripped my patience. When she heard the revealed tone of my voice my mother made big eyes, then turned her mouth down in an expression of underhanded sweetness.

"If I walk out that door," she pointed with her lips, "your workers walk with me."

"They need jobs," I said indulgently.

"Not this kind of job!" Her body stiffened to a shield. She trembled and sat upright, her face hard, her glare spinning cut-glass light.

"Open your eyes, Lyman," she cried out. "People were desperate for work in the beginning, but now they're caught up on their car payments. Pretty soon they'll look at the junk they're making. They'll look at what's in their hands."

"I'm proud of our product," I said.

"*Ka-ka! It's nothing but ka-ka!*"

Her mouth stayed open as if stuck at the hinges, and the image froze in my gaze. I still see her in that flash, her brows and eyeglasses pointed, her hair jutting at a steep pitch, anger pinching her neck tight. Lulu Lamartine was usually controlled as a cat, and got her way through coaxing, cajoling, rubbing against your leg. An old woman who remained infuriatingly pretty, she bent others to her will before they knew what was happening. That day, for once, she didn't care how she looked. She let her face sag, teeth show, and raged at me until she was rehired.

Lay-offs. By mid-January, we had only received a few new orders. I had done such an efficient job of fulfilling the demands of suppliers that they couldn't sell their stock. I'd hired on too many people in the first place, produced more than I could ship. We'd start a catalog, I decided one night, and mail it out to millions of

American homes. That required research and the purchase, from our local missionaries, of likely lists of customers. By February, we were neck-deep in promotional copy and packed snow. By March we were not unthawed. April arrived and the stubborn cold deepened. More white stuff came down and there was confusion. Spring blew hot, then clamped down cold again. Birch trees put out their leaves in a sudden warm spell and froze dead. Oak held in their buds and stayed bare till June. Cows didn't calve right, and horses and dogs grew thicker fur instead of shedding. People, too, were affected. I was sick of making layoffs, took too bare a return on mail orders, and our warehouse was stuffed. I felt like the weather: uncertain, a little wild.

I began to find doughnuts stuffed into corners, not a single bite gone.

"Waste," I complained to my mother.

"Stale bait," she answered.

And then, one afternoon in late June, I walked into the employee lounge in the middle of working hours and found Marie Kashpaw sitting alone. She was staring at one of those damn doughnuts, thinking, smooth and solid as a dun stone. She did not so much as glance at me as she ate the doughnut, breaking it up first, putting it by quarters into her mouth, chewing with maddening concentration. I can't say why, exactly, but my nerves suddenly twanged like a banjo.

"Why the hell aren't you on the line?"

Shame followed my words. No matter how she and my mother gossiped and planned, she was a grandmother, my elder. That under-the-rug connection to her Kashpaw, whose thick hair and business sense I was losing day by day, probably had weighed on me. I didn't like to look at her and be reminded of him so often. Still, at that moment she showed pity. She could have taken me down, embarrassed me, but Marie remained composed, eyes clouded. Weary, knowing, she took a little napkin and patted her lips, then stared at me for an endless moment.

"Your mother went and snapped her eyes at me. For no reason. None," she told me in a tone of low outrage.

I knew that I'd added to my mother's insult, then, and as in one slow, grand movement Marie Kashpaw rose and surged out of the overheated room, I felt the balance of the whole operation totter with her, away from me. The factory was both light and momentous now, a house of twigs.

One slight tap, I realized.

The tap came, and it was no glancing blow, but a direct hit. It came suddenly. I had actually sought out the two women, stood behind their table, waiting to apologize to Marie Kashpaw. I wanted to tell her in private that I was sorry, but my mother's eyes beamed on me. I didn't move, and expected that, as usual, the two would catch me up in some old wordy dispute. Perhaps the lack of talk between them should have been my clue.

Marie was busy complaining to herself about the weather. I held back. She pulled her hair, tossed aside a rosette she was finishing.

"You shouldn't pull on your hair, Marie," my mother observed. Her voice was pleasant, cagey.

"Why not?" Marie was a parked truck idling in low gear, and I couldn't believe my mother wouldn't have the sense to step aside. But, although she allowed a beat of silence to collect, my mother then produced a fake, elaborate sigh.

"You could lose your hair."

"I doubt I'll go bald." Marie's voice dropped sarcastically.

"*Bald?*" I could see my mother's wig settle and her mind leap. "No surprise you should talk about making bald. It's an old Lazarre trick!"

Marie had been restringing a needle, and now she jabbed it into one of the pincushions my mother sewed in her spare time, a little blue Victorian lace-up shoe.

"Look at you! Bald old witch. Don't blame that on the Lazarres! Morrisseys shaved the head of Old Rushes Bear. I took care of that woman until her last days. I should know."

My own mother, then, brought up the forbidden topic.

"You took care of Rushes Bear, that's for damn sure. You managed to turn her against her own son!"

Marie seemed to increase in size, to gather more life. Her dress puffed large around her, beige, sprigged with tiny white crosses. Her heavy arms unfolded and her voice, when it came, barged through the room.

"Her son. Who would that be? The man who balded you by burning down your house!"

"Nector never meant to."

Marie closed her eyes slowly, opened them. She knew what she knew.

There. His name was out in the air and I breathed deeply, as if to take it in, hold it until I turned purple. In the unsteady silence there was only one more name to speak. Mine. I didn't think they would go that far, and I turned partly away, almost breathed, but then Marie's voice, a metal blade, scraped bare ground.

"You think I don't know you married Hat Lamartine to hide your head! You think I don't remember? Your bigshot Lyman was two years old by the wedding!"

At the mention of my own name, the crack of my parentage, I twisted to the factory at large. Some workers were watching, and their heads had craned to my mother's side of the table. I whirled to see as she picked up her bowl, all yellow beads, in one hand. In the other, she took her butter tub of blue. With a single motion she reached across the table and dumped the blue and yellow into Marie's green.

Marie Kashpaw's eyes darkened with disbelief, then fury. The blue and the green were nearly indistinguishable mixed together in the bowl, a day's headache work to re-sort. A striking repose gripped her, then she rose magnificently to her feet. From deep in her body she began to gather breath until she'd swelled, powerfully, all eyes on her, into the sound of her own private war cry, a *windigo* yell that at once paralyzed and mobilized every worker on the line.

Machines stopped champing, biting, and grommeting. It was as if a hand of ice had gripped every man and woman, freezing them in watchfulness. Everyone knew what the scream itself meant. Having long since chosen one side or the other, each worker's mind clicked with decisions: go for a personal enemy? Defend a puny nephew? Duck under the table until it blew over? An eerie slow-motion minute of speculation lazed over the group, a minute in which I stepped forward and put up my arms, vainly, as a person does before an avalanche, and then I stopped too, and for some reason, perhaps because he was the hinge of bloods, along with everyone in the room I looked at Lipsha Morrissey.

He was staring at what might have been the millionth imitation rock he'd caught automatically on the end of his glued stick. He nodded at the end of the stick, then he turned and looked questioningly at the beading table. Whatever he saw there decided his next action. I know it was my mother, I know it in my heart. For when he showed the grin that made the Catholics kiss their scapulars, the grin I had seen at the pool table, a look he would fix at the end of his cue when anticipating a shot of banks and ricochets that would put three balls away and take the game, it was her wolf smile, the Pillager grin. It was an expression of mathematical certainty, a grin that foresaw the end of Anishinabe Enterprises. My stomach clenched. Then Lipsha assumed a judge's solemnity and brought the fake tomahawk down on the table with the crack of a sentencing gavel.

The next instant, havoc. The factory blew up. Order popped like a bubble. Kyle Morrissey whacked a friend of the Pillagers, Billy Nanapush, with an authentic reproduction of a Plains coup stick and, worse yet to a Chippewa, called him a puppy-eating Sioux. Billy responded by pushing his press over on Kyle's girlfriend, Mary Fred, who threw her feathers aside, rolled out from under the machine, and came up swinging one of the light bone war clubs Felix Pukwan had put together. The head flew off, and Mary Fred gouged, whacked, and thrust at all in her path with the bared stick. She was terrible when aroused, and infected others with her fury so that in a few seconds the room was chaos.

Rubber hatchets, dowels, leather pouches, flew through the air. I saw my own mother fling stinging handfuls of seed beads like sand at Marie's eyes. They butted past me, crashed together like buffalo, and I went down, trampled under knife-sharp heels and rubber treads. In clock time, the actual battle did not last long and people soon began to leap through doors and even crash through shut windows. If the whole thing had ended there and everyone had gone home, I might have understood it—just another episode in a small and vicious hundred years' war. However, after the fighting tapered off, those who were still in condition to do so, Nanapushes and Morrisseys and Lazarres alike, methodically demolished, scattered, smashed to bits, and carried off what was left of the factory. And as they did so, walking around me as if I were just another expensive and obsolete government-inspired mechanism, there was a kind of organized joy to it that I would recognize only many drinks later as the factory running backward.

It ran like a film sucked back into the projector. It ran like a machine made to disassemble itself. Standing among the rapid disintegrations, in a dream, I felt myself rewinding, too, and made no move to stop anyone or save myself. I just stood, awed, until it was done and everybody gone. Then my knees gave. I went down on all fours and crawled into the wreckage, scraped through the litter, knelt beside the fractured, dislocated machines, and unplugged the birch bark biter, which was gnashing its iron teeth in the twilight.

I pulled myself up on the legs of a table, closed the door on the work area, sat down at my desk, and after an hour or two pulled a bottle from the bottom file drawer. Zenith, crudely labeled but of indisputable potency, was a local brand of one-hundred-eighty-proof grain alcohol. Most people used it in winter to unclog frozen gas lines in their cars. DO NOT OPEN NEAR FLAME, a cautionary line advised. In the glare of my fluorescent lamp, I tipped the bottle ceilingward every few minutes, igniting my surprise bit by bit with each swallow until it flared so bright I could not contain it. I threw the bottle. The door opened while glass was still falling.

Lipsha Morrissey.

I was too far gone to speak.

"I saw your light," Lipsha explained.

My mouth opened and I felt, I saw, flame lick out and crackle in the air. I opened my mouth wider and it was like opening the vent in a furnace. Air rushed in and the fire licked my ears.

I looked at Lipsha, and Lipsha doubled. Then he doubled again and six Lipshas were standing quietly. Again Lipsha doubled and made an even dozen. I watched the twelve Lipshas who would not meet my eyes, then got up to thrust myself into their line of vision. Each of the Lipsha Morrisseys cocked their heads. I waved my burning, shaking hands before their faces and then the Lipshas broke with politeness and gazed straight at me.

Their look was the charge that blew me apart.

I grabbed my padded steel chair, brought it over my head and down on the desk and then, with an elbow rest, lambasted the Lipsha Morrisseys right and left, chasing them down one by one as they stood quietly before me. I whipped a bunch before my blaze diminished, and then I began beating methodically on the few that were left, working them into the floor with the wood, until I came to the last Lipsha, who grabbed my hands and held them still.

"Uncle," this Lipsha begged.

I sagged. Furious self-pity rose in me. I tried to keep my head above it, but I failed in that, too.

Outside, I allowed myself to be led like a child. I breathed in the sweet, dry air of June, waved to passing carloads of teenagers. My drunken thoughts were the dusky clattering of a high breeze in the cottonwoods. By the time I passed through the battered door and into the downtown bar, I was filled with a great, sad, lapping warmth. I pulled some bills out of my pocket.

"Take them!" I threw the money into a pile before the bartender. I wheeled wide and then I entered the crush of people. Things went upside down after that, for a while events got strange. It was a night of hugging loss and talking quickly and far too much, until I found myself in quiet at the same table with Marie Kashpaw, who was drinking a glass of fizzy sweet orange pop.

"Allow me to apologize for my rude remark."

I got formal when I drank too much, my voice thin, slow, morose.

Marie answered with a downward glance shy as a girl's, until her eyes strayed up and met mine. At their jolt, I looked away. She was all by herself, out of place in this bar, but she didn't care. I saw that my mother, estranged, still furious with her, was now speaking with intensity to a group hunched together at a distant table. She was planning, plotting, running the reservation, or so she thought. I looked again at Marie and in that moment, I recognized my ally. Whether I figured into their war, admitted, unadmitted, just plain invisible or not, I couldn't tell. I used to have a dream where I hung by one arm from a tree branch over a deep black pit that went down forever, so far I couldn't see how far, so dim in the air and babble. In the dream, my arm trembled. The other arm cast about me, desperate for another branch—my father, I used to think. It had never occurred to me that maybe what I needed to hold on to with both hands was a mother.

Marie inclined her head toward me and allowed a careful smile to cross her face, which was very deep, I suddenly saw now, and intelligent. Her eyes went through me like the eyes of a saint carved into the wood of a broad wall. An unquiet light from the dance floor cast a blue shadow on her forehead. Her hair stood out on each side, white and winged, and I felt suddenly as though very powerfully and quietly she was straining at a half-snapped leash.

Automatically, I withdrew my hand.

"Did he talk about me?" I got the nerve up to whisper, staring at her from what seemed like far below.

I thought her lips formed around the word yes, but instead she frowned into the wavering air between us. She was going to say that her husband, my father, would have been proud or, better yet, jealous of what I'd attempted, that he would have understood the failure of this worthwhile project. She was going to tell me that change came about in slow measure and although my pain was bitter, it was not unnatural and therefore I could absorb it the way earth drinks in rain. She was going to tell me that the drowned could stop wandering, go home. Marie Kashpaw was going to say that I was of the outer and the inner, and though I whirled in the homeless suites and catered luncheons of convention life I could come back, make my way down the narrow roads. She was going to tell me that I had a place. But, before she could speak, I noticed she was holding out her hands and in reflex I held out my own hands to her.

We rose together.

The jukebox voices groaned, the noise churned around us. Our gazes held through the stupid mist of alcohol and she stared at me. They say I look like Nector, but I myself can't tell. Maybe, for that night, I did. Taking her tough hand in mine I saw that her fingers were swollen and tender. I looked closely, and even in the smoky light I could make out a few little raised marks that formed regular patterns—stars, snowflakes, lucky spiderwebs.

Fearful, yet cradling her fingers, I stood and waited.

"When things got going," she laughed, showing her teeth, "I ran my hands into the birch bark machine."

Of all the things that went wrong it hit me worst that Marie Kashpaw's hands were hurt. Her hands had held babies and dragged grown men from sloughs, her hands fed and walloped, her hands were rope burned, worked raw, kissed by Nector. Her hands, now stiff, still powerful, should have been protected. I bent my head to look closer. In one palm there was a raised white scar, an old wound that twisted like a small tough twig.

"I'm sorry," I mumbled.

It was the first apology that ever made me feel forgiven too, but she didn't hear it. Marie Kashpaw was listening to the music. As though her whole life she had been pulling something very heavy and all of a sudden the trace had snapped, she straightened with such easy grace that she seemed to lift into the air. Motioning slowly, she tipped sideways, two-stepped, and then we danced to the center of the floor.

Linda Hasselstrom

Linda Hasselstrom provides another narrative of the daily routine that keeps people connected on the sparsely populated high plains. Like John Janovy, Hasselstrom focuses on the ways people make places for themselves on the land and in the towns on the Great Plains.

For the biography and bibliography on Hasselstrom see pages 95 and 99.

Going to the Post Office (1991)

Going to the post office is a social occasion as well as a major undertaking on the South Dakota plains. I live only six miles from my symbol of the federal government's attempt to guarantee mail delivery, but it's still not a trip one makes in house slippers and bathrobe. In winter I often go in the coveralls in which I've just fed cattle—splashed with some of the less pleasant by-products, noisy in my five-buckle overshoes, with my stocking cap pulled down to my muffler. I always hope no one will recognize me, an absurd idea, since every neighbor for twenty miles knows my pickup, my walk, and the coveralls I've been wearing for the last eight years, except in periods of major weight gain, when I wear a size larger with no stripes.

The first stop is at the mailbox itself, located at the end of our half-mile ranch road, leaning gently against three other mailboxes. My parents' box is perched on the axle from a 1920s vintage car, set in concrete badly chipped when the road grader hit it one winter. My mailbox is larger, newer, with a patched bullet hole, and several dents caused when our second-nearest neighbors took the corner a little short with a stack of hay. They considerately set the box upright and repaired it; neighbors in the country are like that. We speak of "neighboring" with nearby ranchers, as in, "Do you know the Smiths?" "Yes, we neighbor with them." That doesn't simply mean that our land lies next to theirs, but that we help each other out in times of trouble, physical or mental.

Next is the box shared by that neighbor and his son, who has helped us in several major crises; this is a large box topped by the silhouette of a buffalo. The buffalo disappears every now and then, and we speculate on who has taken considerable risk, given ranchers' reputations for being quick on the draw, to saw through the heavy metal legs for the privilege of displaying this art object. Next to that box is the whitewashed one belonging to my closest neighbor and friend Margaret, who first pointed out to me that the word "neighbor" is a verb, and her husband Bill. She is the sister of the man who patiently makes the buffalo, and thus daughter of our second-nearest neighbor.

Today I tuck a Christmas gift in the back, hoping this week's carrier will leave it there. Last time I left magazines for her, tightly banded and labeled, the carrier carefully unwrapped them, read the address, and placed them in my box. People who live fifty miles from postal service used to conduct business through their mailboxes. They'd leave unstamped mail and several dollars when they were out of stamps, or a note requesting the carrier to bring a loaf of bread and milk the next day. Some postal carriers delivered medicine, tractor parts, or anything else they were asked to carry. In today's world of specialization, where the postal carrier is no longer a neighbor but the lowest bidder for the route and maybe a stickler for regulations, such friendly help is rare.

As I top the hill on the highway, headed toward the little town where the post office is, I note that our neighbor to the north has taken his cattle home. He left them longer than usual this year, because we've had no snow, and grass is everywhere scarce. But now he'll have to feed hay, and this pasture is too far from his home ranch to do it conveniently. In the next few days, he'll bring his bulls down, and they'll lean through our fences all winter, making eyes at the too-young female calves in our corral. The little pine tree Margaret and I watch has scarcely grown this year, and the cows have rubbed it ragged; I hope it will survive.

A derelict car is parked in the next turnoff; I slow to look, but no one is visible. For three days, I've debated looking inside for an injured or frozen driver, but I don't have the nerve, and the Highway Patrol surely has. I note a new pile of beer cans and a mattress in the ditch; this turnout is especially wide, and seems to have become a favorite dumping spot. To be fair, it also serves as a parking place for joggers who leave nothing but a little sweat.

Out of habit, I watch the tops of fenceposts and electric poles for the teardrop silhouette of a hawk or eagle; as they migrate sought, we often see non-native species, including snowy and barn owls, peregrine falcons, and whooping cranes. Once a tiny merlin shot between me and an approaching car to snatch a meadowlark out of the air. The driver of the other car didn't react, but I nearly drove into the ditch, shocked at the swift ferocity of the strike.

The next neighbor is out in his yard, leaning against the door of a pickup with its engine idling, the preferred visiting method in all weather but a blizzard. He's ready for winter: haystacks are neatly aligned next to the barn, not too close together in case one of them catches fire; the tractor stands in front of the garage where he's been checking oil and antifreeze.

Just up the road, a pickup is parked next to a pile of broken railroad ties. Two men are pitching chunks into the pickup box, presumably for firewood—a dangerous practice, because ties are soaked in creosote, which builds up inside chimneys. But we're due for snow any day, and fire danger was so high in the woods during most of the summer that use of chainsaws was prohibited; if they can't afford to buy wood, this may be the next best alternative. The railroad has piled the ties in readiness for winter, when a crew will spend days pouring gasoline over them and setting them afire; columns of black smoke will rise a hundred feet straight up as all that wood turns to ash. I can't stand the waste; I pick up all I can lift and turn them into snow-catching fences. Our hilltop now looks like a fortified redoubt; I only half-jokingly call it Fort Snell, in honor of George. He likes to live high up, his view unobscured by trees and with, as he puts it, "a good field of fire." He denies being paranoid; "it's not paranoia if they really are after you," he says.

At the next place, a cow is licking a newborn calf, while others look on with what appears to be approval. Calving in December is a calculated risk; if the calves get a month of good weather, they'll be four to five months larger than calves born in spring, and probably bring more money at sale time. But if we have snow tonight or tomorrow, this calf, and others, may die.

The next house intrigues me; it was built on a single high sidehill acre at the edge of a rancher's land. The single-story, shed-roofed house came first, then a greenhouse nearly as large. Because winter was upon them, they erected a sheep barn out of bales of hay, supported inside by a meager framework of two-by-fours. By spring, the sheep had eaten nearly through the inside walls; they polished off the structure during lambing. That summer, the father and three sons built a wood barn, while the wife planted a huge garden, for which she won prizes at the county fair. Together, they planted several rows of sheltering trees, now head-high to a tall cowboy—on a horse. From a bare hillside and three years of sustained work that family made a home, just as pioneers did a hundred years ago. Overhead, rolling clouds indicate those trees may be catching snow by nightfall; water is scarce on their hilltop, and the snow will percolate down and reduce the amount of irrigating needed next summer.

The cemetery is cold and barren today, the wind whipping fragments of plastic flowers into the lilac bushes, scouring the old headstones. The county's history is here, from the victims of the diphtheria epidemic and the women who nursed them to the newer graves of youngsters lost to speed and alcohol since the highway became a major truck route. Just below the hill of the dead is the store, surrounded by pickups as folks stop by for groceries, a newspaper, or other items they suddenly need before a storm rolls in. I've always been comfortable there, even with the small amount of its history that I know.

I'm not the only one in coveralls in the post office. We wait for our mail, steaming gently, our faces red from the wind, noses dripping discreetly into red cotton handkerchiefs, silk neckscarves twisted around our bare throats. We talk about who's in the hospital, who's gone south, the likelihood of a storm, how much we need moisture but that we'd just as soon get it as rain in the spring. One by one we collect our letters, discard the junk folders in the trash, clomp back to our pickups. I wipe the windshield with a greasy glove, and head for home and more feeding. We feel a little more in touch with the world now that we've used our voices in friendly greetings to our neighbors, maybe for the first time in several days. The precious rolls of mail we carry will keep us busy for hours later tonight— after the outside work is finished—as we warm the chill out of our joints, and perhaps stare at the square screen where we never will see lives like ours. The post office is our real link to other worlds.

William Stafford

This poem recalls for William Stafford and his reader a time and place "where little happened and much was understood," a kind of complement to Wright Morris's stories of unspoken meaning. Stafford's family, like Morris and his father, lived typically itinerant lives on the Great Plains, moving here and there looking for work or a better life. Stafford rescues one of those years by transposing it into poetry so "that the year did not escape me"—or the reader.

For the biography of and further reading about Stafford see pages 68–69.

The Rescued Year (1998)

Take a model of the world so big
it is the world again, pass your hand,
press back that area in the west where no one lived,
the place only your mind explores. On your thumb
that smudge becomes my ignorance, a badge
the size of Colorado: toward that state by train
we crossed our state like birds and lodged—
the year my sister gracefully
grew up—against the western boundary
where my father had a job.

Time should go the way it went
that year: we weren't at war; we had
each day a treasured unimportance;
the sky existed, so did our town;
the library had books we hadn't read;
every day at school we learned and sang,
or at least hummed and walked in the hall.

In church I heard the preacher; he said
"Honor!" with a sound like empty silos
repeating the lesson. For a minute I held
Kansas Christian all along the Santa Fe.
My father's mean attention, though, was busy—this
I knew—and going home his wonderfully level gaze

would hold the state I liked, where little happened
and much was understood. I watched my father's finger
mark off huge eye-scans of what happened in the creed.

Like him, I tried. I still try,
send my sight like a million pickpockets
up rich people's drives; it is time
when I pass for every place I go to be alive.
Around any corner my sight is a river,
and I let it arrive: rich by those brooks
his thought poured for hours
into my hand. His creed: the greatest ownership
of all is to glance around and understand.

That Christmas Mother made paper
presents; we colored them with crayons
and hung up a tumbleweed for a tree.
A man from Hugoton brought my sister
a present (his farm was tilted near oil
wells; his car ignored the little
bumps along our drive: nothing
came of all this—it was just part of the year).

I walked out where a girl I knew would be;
we crossed the plank over the ditch
to her house. There was popcorn on the stove,
and her mother recalled the old days, inviting me back.
When I walked home in the cold evening,
snow that blessed the wheat had roved
along the highway seeking furrows,
and all the houses had their lights—
oh, that year did not escape me: I rubbed
the wonderful old lamp of our dull town.

That spring we crossed the state again,
my father soothing us with stories:
the river lost in Utah, underground—
"They've explored only the ones they've found!"—
and that old man who spent his life knowing,
unable to tell how he knew—
"I've been sure by smoke, persuaded
by mist, or a cloud, or a name:
once the truth was ready"—my father smiled
at this—"it didn't care how it came."

In all his ways I hold that rescued year—
comes that smoke like love into the broken
coal, that forms to chunks again and lies
in the earth again in its dim folds, and comes a sound,
then shapes to make a whistle fade,
and in the quiet I hold no need, no hurry:
any day the dust will move, maybe settle;
the train that left will roll back into our station,
the name carved on the platform unfill with rain,
and the sound that followed the couplings back
will ripple forward and hold the train.

Epilogue

Sustaining America's Grasslands

Not much has changed since the first settlers crossed the Missouri, although Indian peoples made many adjustments to survive. Great Plains residents know that they give up certain amenities by staying put, but they may gain something as well. Still, sometimes the inhabitants dream of flight—up or away.

For a while in the 1980s and into the 1990s attention was being paid to the Great Plains. There was yet another farm crisis that resulted in Farm Aid rallies and concerts, and a few movies about hard work and its rewards down on the farm. Legal cases reasserted tribal sovereignty. In the early 1990s geographers Frank and Deborah Popper, professors at New Jersey's Rutgers University, suggested that the sparsely populated regions of the high plains could become a buffalo commons, a region of grassland populated not by people but by the region's original flora and fauna. The notion got residents riled up enough to attend the meetings that the Poppers held across the high plains. In plain words, these residents of the high plains voiced their objections to the region's abandonment and offered countersuggestions. Ten years later the metaphor has become a cliché that identifies, among other things, a chamber music society and a birding safari group. Buffalo ranches dot the Great Plains from Saskatchewan to southern Kansas, and the depopulation that originally drew the Poppers' attention to the region has accelerated: over a third of Great Plains counties have fewer than six people per square mile, and in half of those there are fewer than two people per square mile.[1]

Not much came of the attention, which may be a good thing. Towns still lose population and farms sales mark the end of more farmers' time on the land. Some marginal land has been reclaimed by grasses, thanks to neglect or the federal Crop Reduction Program. There are some countersigns of persistence and prosperity. Some farmers have developed value-added products: hay turned into neatly packaged hamster food or chemical-free beef that is marketed to health-conscious city dwellers. Indian communities showed revitalizing population growth in the 2000 census. In the coming years even more studies will be made and innovation will bring new prosperity to some rural areas, but the battles with capricious weather, the realities of loans that are due, crop and cattle prices that are too low for the producer to make a profit, and the disappearing water table will, inevitably, persist. Unfortunately, Native peoples continue to suffer from racism through ignorance or invisibility.

In the epilogue's two essays, Kathleen Norris and Wes Jackson offer ways to evaluate the place of humans on the Great Plains. Norris describes a parallel life in the Benedictine monastic order, a routine she finds particularly appropriate in western South Dakota: in either place one must consciously assess the reasons for leaving, for returning, or for staying put. There are few casual monks or accidental residents on the high plains. Inhabitants of both places know the rewards of a life apart from the mainstream and the dangers of taking one's place too lightly. Similarly, Jackson asks the reader to reassess our use of the land. He wants us to imagine a "polyculture" of mixed perennial grasses crossbred with cereal grains, and to imagine communities that are similarly radical. These are concepts that Jackson believes might be capable of indefinitely sustaining both the land and the people.

The Great Plains envisioned by Norris and Jackson is not a promised garden. Both of them challenge the reader to consider the possibility that radical change might be necessary. Perhaps the future will be somewhere along the continuum between their radical conceptions of the region. The possibilities deserve our attention.

Notes

1. Florence Williams, "Plains Sense: Frank and Deborah Poppers' 'Buffalo Commons' Is Creeping toward Reality," *High Country News,* 15 January 2001.

Reading about the Future of the Great Plains

Matthews, Ann. *The Buffalo Commons: The Storm over the Revolutionary Plan to Restore America's Great Plains.* New York: Grove Weidenfeld, 1992.

Williams, Florence. "Plains Sense: Frank and Deborah Poppers' 'Buffalo Commons' Is Creeping toward Reality." *High Country News.* 15 January 2001. *www.hcn.org.*

Kathleen Norris *(b. 1947)*

Dakota: A Spiritual Geography is Kathleen Norris's account of her move to her maternal grandmother's house in Lemmon, South Dakota, after years living in New York City. At first this is merely a duty for her and her husband, both poets. They are to oversee her family's legacy of farms after the death of her grand-parents. But their stay quickly becomes a quest for community and self on the Great Plains. *Dakota* is the account of Norris's "settling into" the town and, more important, into her Grandmother Totten's life, memorialized in the simple rou-tines of Lemmon and the local Presbyterian church.

For Norris, a purely practical act becomes a deeply spiritual quest, initiated by her sense of her maternal family past and her growing awareness of not only the physical but also the spiritual nature of the high plains landscape. In the midst of her effort to come to terms with the emotions stirring in her, Norris discovers the Benedictine abbeys that invite lay persons to share their rituals and routine. In time spent among the monks Norris finds a place to contemplate and affirm herself as a poet and as a resident of a small Dakota town. The monks' asceticism provides a map for learning to live in Lemmon.

In this selection, "Sea Change," she explains how these halves of her life com-plement each other in a place that is geographically and spiritually isolated—and how the rewards come from such a life in such a place. In her account of the traveler's journey from east to west, she describes the sea change, that radical, visible change in the landscape—and in herself—at the one-hundredth meridian, between prairie and high plains.

Norris's "geography" is not an exercise in nostalgia but rather a hard-edged examination of a place struggling to maintain an identity in a time of dwindling population and economic hardship. It is a place that the writer has come to value for both its landscape and community. Geographically Lemmon is just south of the North Dakota border in western South Dakota.

Norris was born in Washington DC, went to high school in Hawaii, and gradu-ated from Bennington College in Vermont. In New York City she worked as an arts administrator at the Academy of American Poets.

Sea Change (1993)

*Calenture: a disease incident to sailors within the tropics, characterized by
delirium in which the patient, it is said, fancies the sea to be green fields and
desire to leap into it.*
—Oxford English Dictionary

The atmosphere of the sea persists in Perkins County.
—*David J. Holden,* Dakota Visions

My move from New York City to western South Dakota changed my sense of time
and space so radically I might as well have gone to sea. In journeying on the inland
ocean of the Plains, the great void at the heart of North America, I've discovered
that time and distance, those inconveniences that modern life with its increasingly
sophisticated computer technologies seeks to erase, have a reality and a terrifying
beauty all their own.

Like all who choose life in the slow lane—sailors, monks, farmers—I partake of
a contemplative reality. Living close to such an expanse of land I find I have little
incentive to move fast, little need of instant information. I have learned to trust the
processes that take time, to value change that is not sudden or ill-considered but
grows out of the ground of experience. Such change is properly defined as conversion, a word that at its root connotes not a change of essence but of perspective, as
turning round; turning back to or returning; turning one's attention to.

Both monasteries and the rural communities on the Plains are places where
nothing much happens. Paradoxically, they are also places where being open to
conversion is most necessary if community is to survive. The inner impulse toward conversion, a change of heart, may be muted in a city, where outward
change is fast, noisy, ever-present. But in the small town, in the quiet arena, a
refusal to grow (which is one way Gregory of Nyssa defined sin) makes any
constructive change impossible. Both monasteries and small towns lose their ability to be truly hospitable to the stranger when people use them as a place to hide
out, a place to escape from the demands of life.

Because of the monotony of the monastic life, the bad thought of boredom (or
acedia, the noonday demon) has traditionally been thought to apply particularly
to monks, but I think most people have endured a day or two along the lines of this
fourth-century description by the monk Evagrius:

> It makes it seem that the sun barely moves, if at all, and the day is fifty hours
> long. Then it constrains the monk to look constantly out the window, to walk
> outside the cell to gaze carefully at the sun and determine how far it stands
> from the dinner hour, to look now this way and that to see if perhaps one of
> the brethren appears from his cell.

Anyone living in isolated or deprived circumstances, whether in a monastery or a quiet little town on the Great Plains, is susceptible to the noonday demon. It may appear as an innocuous question; "Isn't the mail here yet?" But, as monks have always known, such restlessness can lead to profound despair that makes a person despise his or her neighbors, work, and even life itself. Perhaps the noonday demon helps explain the high rate of alcoholism found in underpopulated steppes, whether in Siberia or the American West.

Ever since moving to western Dakota, I've wondered if the version of the demon we experience here isn't a kind of calenture, a prairie version of the sea fever that afflicted sailors several centuries ago. The vast stretch of undulating land before us can make us forget ourselves, make us do foolish things.

I almost think that to be a good citizen of the Plains one must choose the life consciously, as one chooses the monastery. One must make an informed rejection of any other way of life and also undergo a period of formation. Some of the ranch families I know in Dakota are raising their children in the way Benedict asks monasteries to treat would-be monks, warning, "Do not grant newcomers to the monastic life an easy entry."

These parents do not encourage their children to take up the hard and economically uncertain life of farming and ranching. Instead, they provide them with the opportunity to see what is available in other careers, in other places. And most of the young people move on. But, as one couple recently told me of their daughter, "She's traveled, she's seen the outside world. And it's not that she's afraid of it or couldn't live there, she's decided she doesn't need it. She wants to come back here."

They're hoping she will find a teaching job in the area, not a great prospect in the current economic environment, when many Dakota schools are consolidating or closing. But what interests me about her parents' remark is how like monastic formation directors they sound. They, too, want people who have lived a little, who have seen the world, and, in the words of one monk, "know exactly what it is they're giving up." He added, "The hard part is that this has to become all they need. The monastery has to become their home."

Making the Plains a home means accepting its limitations and not, as so many townspeople do even in drought years, watering a lawn to country club perfection. Making this all we need means accepting that we are living in the arid plains of western South Dakota, not in Connecticut (which has the rainfall to sustain such greenery) or Palm Springs (which doesn't but has the money to pretend otherwise). Once the water runs out, the money won't be worth much.

I wonder if the calentures don't explain why, from the first days of white settlement, Dakotans of the West River have tried to recreate the land before them in the image of the rain-blessed places they knew, the rich farmland back East in New York or Virginia, or the old country farmland of Sweden, or Scotland. Encouraged by the railroads and the government to pretend that the land could support families on homestead allotments of 160 acres, they believed the rural economy could maintain small towns nine or ten miles apart, the distance a steam locomotive could go before needing more water. But, in trying to make this place like the places they had known, they would not allow it to be itself.

Eastern North and South Dakota have enough rainfall and population density to hang on at the western fringes of the Midwest, having more in common with Minnesota and Iowa than with Montana. But in western Dakota, the harsh climate and the vast expanse of the land have forced people, through a painful process of attrition, to adjust to this country on its own terms and live accordingly: ranches of several thousand acres, towns that serve as economic centers forty or sixty miles apart. Taking the slow boat to Dakota, driving in from the East, the reality of the land asserts itself and you begin to understand how the dreams of early settlers were worn away.

Heading west out of Minneapolis on Highway 12, you pass through 150 miles of rich Minnesota farmland, through towns that look like New England villages with tall trees well over a hundred years old. These are sizeable towns by Dakota standards: Litchfield (pop. 5,900), Willmar (15,900), Benson (3,600). South Dakota is visible, a high ridge on the horizon, long before the crossing a few miles past Ortonville (pop. 2,550, elev. 1,094).

Your first town in South Dakota is Big Stone City (pop. 630, elev. 977) at the southern edge of Big Stone Lake, named for huge granite outcroppings in the area. Here you begin your climb from the broad Minnesota River Valley to what French trappers termed the "Coteau des Prairies" or prairie hills of eastern South Dakota. This is the beginning of the drift prairie of eastern North and South Dakota, named for the glacial deposits, or drift, that make up its topsoil. The road narrows, twisting around small hills and shallow coulees. You pass by several small, spring-fed lakes formed by glaciers and several good-size towns: Milbank (pop. 3,800), Webster (2,000), Groton (1,100).

After Groton you cross the James River Valley, its soil rich with glacial loam deposits. By the time you reach the city of Aberdeen, South Dakota (pop. 25,000, elev. 1,304), one hundred miles from the Minnesota border, you are in open farm country with more of a gentle roll to it than eastern Kansas, but basically flat and treeless except for shelterbelts around farmhouses and trees planted and carefully tended in the towns.

Driving west from Aberdeen you find that the towns are fewer and smaller, with more distance between them: Ipswich (pop. 965), Roscoe (362), Bowdle (590), Selby (707). One hundred miles west of Aberdeen you come to Mobridge (pop. 3,768, elev. 1,676), on the banks of the Missouri River.

What John Steinbeck said in *Travels with Charley* about the Missouri River crossing 120 miles to the north is true of the Mobridge crossing as well. He wrote: "Here's the boundary between east and west. On the Bismarck side it is eastern landscape, eastern grass, with the look and smell of eastern America. Across the Missouri on the Mandan side it is pure west with brown grass and water scorings and small outcrops. The two sides of the river might well be a thousand miles apart."

The boundary is an ancient one. The deep gorge of the Missouri marks the western edge of the Wisconsin ice sheet that once covered most of north central America. Passing through Mobridge and crossing the river you take a steep climb through rugged hills onto the high plateau that extends west all the way to the Rockies. Lewis and Clark marked this border by noting that the tallgrass to the east (bluestem, switch grass, Indian grass) grew six to eight feet high, while the shortgrass in the west (needle-and-thread, western wheat grass, blue grama grass, and upland sedges) topped at about four feet. You have left the glacial drift prairie for a land whose soil is the residue of prehistoric seas that have come and gone, weathered shale and limestone that is far less fertile than the land to the east but good for grazing sheep and cattle. Here you set your watch to Mountain time.

Here, also, you may have to combat disorientation and an overwhelming sense of loneliness. Plunged into the pale expanse of shortgrass country, you either get your sea legs or want to bail out. As the road twists and turns through open but hilly country, climbing 325 feet in twenty-two miles to the town of McLaughlin (pop. 780), you begin to realize you have left civilization behind. You are on the high plains, where there are almost no trees, let alone other people. You find that the towns reassuringly listed every ten miles or so on your map (Walker, McIntosh, Watauga, Morristown, Keldron, Thunder Hawk) offer very little in the way of services. All but McIntosh (pop. 300) have populations well under a hundred. You climb imperceptibly through rolling hayfields and pasture land punctuated by wheat or sunflower fields for another eighty miles or so before you reach another town of any size—Lemmon (pop. 1,616, elev. 2,577).

You should have filled your gas tank in Aberdeen, especially if you're planning to travel after dark. For many years there was no gasoline available at night (except in the summer) between Aberdeen and Miles City, Montana, a distance of nearly four hundred miles. Currently there are two 24-hour stations in towns nearly 200 miles apart. On the last stretch, the 78 miles from Baker, Montana, to Miles City, there are no towns at all, just a spectacularly desolate moonscape of sagebrush. Farmers will usually give or sell a little gas to stranded travelers, and small-town police forces often have keys to the local service stations so they can sell you enough to get you on your way. But the message is clear: you're in the West now. Pay attention to your gas gauge. Pay attention, period.

But it's hard to pay attention when there is so much nothing to take in, so much open land that evokes in many people a panicked desire to get through it as quickly as possible. A writer whose name I have forgotten once remarked, "Driving through eastern Montana is like waiting for Godot." I know this only because a Lemmon Public Library patron brought me the quote, wanting to know who or what Godot was. It struck me that the writer may as well have been talking about the landscape of Dakota from Mobridge or Mandan west. And it seemed appropriate that the good citizen of the region wanted to know if her homeland was being praised or put down. Had he lived here, I wonder if Beckett would have found it necessary to write the play.

But people do live here, and many of them will tell you in all honesty that they wouldn't live anyplace else. Monks often say the same thing about their monasteries, and get the same looks of incomprehension. People who can't imagine not having more stimulation in their lives will ask, "How can you do it?" or, "Why do it?" If those questions are answerable for either a monk or a Plains resident, they can't be answered in a few quick words but in the slow example of a lifetime. The questioner must take the process of endless waiting into account, as well as the pull of the sea change, of conversion.

Often, when I'm sitting in a monastery choir stall, I wonder how I got there. I could trace it back, as I can trace the route from back East to western South Dakota. But I'm having too much fun. The words of Psalms, spoken aloud and left to resonate in the air around me, push me into new time and space. I think of it as the quantum effect: here time flows back and forth, in and out of both past and future, and I, too, am changed.

Being continually open to change, to conversion, is a Benedictine ideal: in fact, it's a vow unique to those who follow Benedict's *Rule*. This might seem like a paradox, as monks, like farmers, stay in one place and have a daily routine that can seem monotonous even to them. But the words spark like a welder's flame; they keep flowing, like a current carrying me farther than I had intended to go. At noon prayer we hear the scripture about "sharing the lot of the saints in light," and in the afternoon I read in a book about quantum physics that some scientists believe that one day everything will exist in the form of light. At vespers the text is from I John: "Beloved, we are God's children now; what we will be has not yet been revealed."

The sun is setting and a nearly full, fat-faced moon is rising above the prairie. We have time on our hands here, in our hearts, and it makes us strange. I barely passed elementary algebra, but somehow the vast space before me makes perfectly comprehensible the words of a mathematician I encountered today: it is easy to "demonstrate that there are no more minutes in all of eternity than there are in say, one minute."

The vespers hymn reads: "May God ever dress our days / in peace and starlight order," and I think of old Father Stanley, who said not long before he died: "I wish to see the Alpha and the Omega." He'd been a monk for over fifty years, a Dakotan for more than eighty. It's a dangerous place, this vast ocean of prairie. Something happens to us here.

Further Reading

Amazing Grace: A Vocabulary of Faith. 1998.
The Cloister Walk. 1996.

Falling Off. 1971.
Little Girls in Church. 1995.
The Middle of the World. 1981.
On the Plains. 1999. Introduction to a photographic essay by Peter Brown.

Reading about Kathleen Norris

Kelleher, Ray. "Kathleen Norris." *Poets and Writers* 25 (May–June 1997): 62–72.

Wes Jackson *(b. 1936)*

Wes Jackson strays outside the boundaries that constrain most of the people who think about the future of the Great Plains: he wants us to imagine a very different kind of plains community. At the Land Institute outside of Salina, Kansas, he has been imagining his ideas into reality by applying his knowledge of genetics to the problems of renewable grain production, extractive energy sources, and responsible management of the land. His efforts to crossbreed native grasses with grains has received widespread interest. Jackson points out that the current practice of planting monocultures of corn, wheat, and soybeans so that they can be replanted the next year depletes top soil, pollutes streams with chemical fertilizers and pesticides, and reduces our supplies of oil and other extractive energy sources.

Instead, the scientist Jackson envisions a polyculture, that is, a mix of native grasses combined with cereal grains. The result would be a sustainable system that would produce food crops with a minimum of soil disturbance. Fossil fuels would be replaced with renewable biodegradable and solar fuel sources, and the supporting community would be composed of people who have "become native to the place."

This is not a circumstance that Jackson expects to realize in his lifetime. Although academics and researchers are increasingly open to his ideas, Jackson himself often admits that "we're where the Wright brothers were at Kitty Hawk in 1903." Just as the brothers couldn't imagine the stealth fighter or the jumbo jet, we can't imagine what agriculture practices will be routine in another one hundred years.

In this essay Jackson explains his attempt to apply to a human community his principles of sustainability. Since the essay was written, the Matfield Green post office has indeed been closed and the village officially abandoned. As Jackson points out, his portrait of Matfield Green could be redrawn thousands of times across the Great Plains. His description of the town's past, discovered in the women's club programs he finds in the detritus of abandoned houses, echoes the small-town society created by William Allen White and by John Janovy's portraits of residents in Arthur County, Nebraska.

Matfield Green is on the edge of the Kansas Flint Hills, just a few miles off of the Kansas Turnpike along the highway that leads to the Tallgrass Prairie Preserve, the nation's only national park devoted to the grasslands. The preserve draws an increasing number of visitors each year. Twenty-five years from now, who knows what the visitors will see at Matfield Green, or in the rich creek-bottom fields along the highway, or on the upland prairie itself. Jackson wants us to imagine that the grass, the crops, the cattle, and the people will still be there, living lightly, sustaining the land and their communities on the tallgrass prairie.

Jackson was born in northeast Kansas. He earned a bachelor of arts degree in biology from Kansas Wesleyan University in 1958, a master's degree at the University of Kansas, and a Ph.D. in genetics from North Carolina University in 1960. He founded the Environmental Studies program at California State University at Sacramento. In 1976 he established the Land Institute. He was named a Pew Conservation Scholar in 1990, and was the recipient of a MacArthur genius award in 1992.

Jackson has written for various magazines and journals, including *The Atlantic Monthly* and *Audubon*. His work has been featured in numerous popular and specialized magazines and journals as well, such as *Life Magazine* and *The MacNeil-Lehrer News Hour*.

Matfield Green (1994)

I am writing in what is left of Matfield Green, a Kansas town of some fifty people situated in a county of a few more than three thousand in an area with thirty-three inches of annual precipitation. It is typical of countless towns throughout the Midwest and Great Plains. People have left, people are leaving, buildings are falling down, buildings are burning down. Fourteen of the houses here that do still have people have only one person, usually a widow or widower. I purchased seven rundown houses in town for less than four thousand dollars. Four friends and I purchased, for five thousand dollars, the beautiful brick elementary school that was built in 1938. It has ten thousand square feet, including a stage and gymnasium. The Land Institute has purchased the high school gymnasium (four thousand dollars) and twelve acres south of town (for six thousand). A friend and I have purchased thirty-eight acres north of town from the Santa Fe Railroad for three hundred thirty dollars an acre. On this property are a bunkhouse, some large corrals to handle cattle, and about twenty-five acres of never-plowed tallgrass prairie.

South of town is an abandoned natural gas booster station with its numerous buildings and facilities. Situated on eighty acres, it was part of the first long-distance pipelines that delivered natural gas from the large Hugoton field near Amarillo to Kansas City. A neighbor in his late seventies told me that in about 1929 his father had helped dig the basement, using a team of horses and a scoop (contemporary sunlight used to leverage extraction of anciently stored energy). Owned by a major pipeline company, the booster station stands as a silent monument to the extractive economy, foreshadowing what is to come. A small area has been contaminated with PCBs. Think of the possible practicality and symbolism if this facility, formerly devoted to transporting the high energy demanded by an extractive economy while at the same time dumping a major environmental pollutant, could be taken over by a community and converted to a facility that would sponsor such renewable technologies as photovoltaic panels or wind machines.

Imagine this human community as an ecosystem, as a locus or primary object of study. We know that public policy, allegedly implemented in the public interest, is partly responsible for the demise of this community. The question then becomes, How can this human community, like a natural ecosystem community, be protected from that abstraction called the public? How can both kinds of communities be built back and also protected?

The effort begins, I think, with the sort of inventory and accounting that ecologists have done for natural ecosystems, a kind of accounting seldom if ever performed for human-dominated ecosystems. How do we start thinking about what is involved in setting up the books for ecological community accounting that will feature humans? I emphasize accounting because our goal is renewability, sustainability.

About 85 percent of the county in which this small town is situated is never-plowed native prairie. Over the millennia it has featured recycling and has run on sunlight just as a forest or a marsh does. Though the prairie is fenced and is now called pasture and grass, aside from the wilderness areas of our country it is about as close to an original relationship as we will find in any human-managed system. Even though the people left in town seem to have a profound affection for the place and for one another, they are as susceptible to the world as anyone else—to shopping mall living, to secular materialism in general.

Nevertheless, I have imagined this as a place that could grow bison for meat, as a place where photovoltaic panels could be assembled at the old booster station, where the school could become a gathering place that would be a partial answer to the mall, a place that might attract a few retired people, including professor types, who could bring their pensions, their libraries, and their social security checks to help support themselves and take on the task of setting up the books for ecological community accounting. Essentially all academic disciplines would be an asset in such an effort, but only if confronted with a broad spectrum of ecological necessities in the face of small-town reality. Much of what must be done will be in conflict with human desires, if not human needs.

Let us allow our imaginations to wander. What if bison (or even cattle) could be slaughtered in the little towns on a small scale and become the answer to the massive industrialized Iowa Beef Packers plant at Emporia, a plant to which some area residents drive fifty miles and more in order to earn modest wages and risk carpal tunnel syndrome. What if the manufacture of photovoltaic panels could happen before the eyes of the children of the workers? What if the processing of livestock could take place with those children present? What if those children were allowed to exercise their strong urge to help—to work? What, finally, if shopping malls and Little League were to become less interesting than playing "make-believe" with all ages?

One of our principal tasks as educators is to expand the imagination about our possibilities. When I walk through the abandoned school with its leaky gym roof and see the solid structure of a beautiful 1938 building, with stage curtains rotting away and paint peeling off the walls, where one blackboard after another has been carried away as though the building were a slate mine, I am forced to think that the demise of this school has resulted in part from a failure of imagination, but more from the tyranny of disregard by something we call the economy.

I am in that town at this moment, typing in a house that in its history of some seventy-five years has been abandoned more times than anyone can recall. First it was home to a family in a now-abandoned oil field a few miles southeast of here. Then it was hauled intact on a wagon into town in the 1930s, set on a native stone foundation which, when I bought it recently, was crumbling and falling away. Three ceilings supported as much as three inches of dirt, much of it from back in the Dust Bowl era. The expanding side walls had traveled so far off the floor joist in the middle that the ceiling was suspended. They had to be pulled back onto the floor joist and held permanently with large screws and plates. Three major holes in the roof had allowed serious water damage to flooring and studs. An opossum had died under the bathtub long enough ago that only its bones were displayed, lying at rest in an arc over the equivalent of half a bale of hay. Two of my seven houses, one empty for nearly twenty years and the other for fifteen, had been walked away from with their refrigerators full. Who knows when the electric meters were pulled—probably a month or two after the houses were vacated and the bill hadn't been paid. To view the contents—eggs and ham, Miracle Whip and pickles, mustard and catsup, milk, cheese, and whatnot—was more like viewing an archaeological find than a repulsive mess.

Where I sit today at my typewriter in that oil field house that relatives and friends have helped remodel, I can see an abandoned lumberyard across the street next to the abandoned hardware store. Out another window, but from the same chair, is the back of the old creamery that now stores junk (on its way to becoming antiques?). With Clara Jo's retirement, the half-time post office across the street is threatened with closure. From a different window, but the same seat, I can see the bank, which closed in 1929 and paid off ten cents on the dollar. (My nephew recently bought it for five hundred dollars.) I can see the bank now only because I can look across the vacant lot where the cafe stood before the natural gas booster station shut down. If my front door were open, given the angle at which I sit, I would be looking right at the Hitchin' Post, the only business left—a bar that accommodates local residents and the cowhands who pull up with their pickups and horse trailers and some of the finest saddle mounts anywhere. These horses will quiver and stomp while waiting patiently as their riders stop for lunch or after work to indulge in beer, nuts, and microwave sandwiches and to shoot pool. (The Hitchin' Post lacks running water, so no dishes can be washed. The outhouse is out back.) Around the corner is an abandoned service station. There were once four! Across the street is the former barbershop.

I know that this town and the surrounding farms and ranches did not sponsor perfect people. I keep finding whiskey bottles in old outhouses and garages, stashed between inner and outer walls here and there, the local version of a drug culture. I hear the familiar stories of infidelities fifty years back—the overalls on the clothesline hung upside down, the flowerpot one day on the left side of the step, the next day on the right—signals to lovers even at the height of the Great Depression, when austerity should have tightened the family unit and maybe did. There were the shootings, the failures of justice, the story of the father of a young married woman who shot and killed his son-in-law for hitting his daughter and how charges were never filed. Third-generation bitterness is common. The human drama goes on. This place still doesn't have a lifestyle, never had a lifestyle, but rather livelihoods with ordinary human foibles. Nevertheless, the graveyard contains the remains of both the cuckolder and the cuckoldee, the shooter and the shot, the drunk and the sober.

This story can be repeated thousands of times across our land, and no telling will deviate even 10 percent. I am not sure what should be done here by way of community development. I do believe, however, that community development can begin with putting roofs on buildings that are leaking, and scabbing in two-by-fours at the bottom of studs that have rotted out around their anchoring nails. I doubt, on the other hand, that a sustainable society can start with a program sent down from Washington or from a Rural Sociology Department in some land-grant university, or for that matter as a celebration of Columbus Day.

Locals and most rural sociologists alike believe the answer lies in jobs, *any* jobs so long as they don't pollute too much. Though I am in sympathy with every urgent impulse toward human welfare, rural America—America!—does *not* need jobs that depend on the extractive economy. We need a way to arrest consumerism. We need a different form of accounting so that both sufficiency and efficiency have *standing* in our minds.

The poets and scientists who counseled that we consult nature would have understood, I think, that we might begin by looking at that old prairie, by remembering who we are as mammals, as primates, as humanoids, as animals struggling to become human by controlling the destructive and unlovely side of our animal nature even as we set out to change parts of our still-unlovely human mind. The mindscape of the future must have some memory of the ecological arrangements that shaped us and of the social structures that served us well. So many surprises await us, even in the next quarter-century. My worry is that our context then will be so remote from the ways we survived through the ages that our organizing paradigm will become chaos theory rather than ecology.

At work on my houses in Matfield Green, I've had great fun tearing off the porches and cleaning up the yards. But it has been sad as well, going through the abandoned belongings of families who lived out their lives in this beautiful, well-watered, fertile setting. In an upstairs bedroom I came across a dusty but beautiful blue padded box labeled "Old Programs—New Century Club." Most of the programs from 1923 to 1964 were there. Each listed the officers, the club flower (sweet pea), the club colors (pink and white), and the club motto ("just be glad"). The programs for each year were gathered under one cover and nearly always dedicated to some local woman who was special in one way or another.

Each month the women were to comment on such subjects as canning, jokes, memory gems, a magazine article, guest poems, flower culture, misused words, birds, and so on. The May 1936 program was a debate: "Resolved that movies are detrimental to the young generation." The August 1936 program was dedicated to coping with the heat. Roll call was "Hot Weather Drinks"; next came "Suggestions for Hot Weather Lunches"; a Mrs. Rogler offered "Ways of Keeping Cool."

The June roll call in 1929 was "The Disease I Fear Most." That was eleven years after the great flu epidemic. Children were still dying in those days of diphtheria, whooping cough, scarlet fever, pneumonia. On August 20, the roll call question was "What do you consider the most essential to good citizenship?" In September that year it was "Birds of Our Country." The program was on the mourning dove.

What became of it all?

From 1923 to 1930, the program covers were beautiful, done at a print shop. From 1930 until 1937, the effects of the Depression were apparent; programs were either typed or mimeographed and had no cover. The programs for two years are missing. In 1940, the covers reappeared, this time typed on construction paper. The print-shop printing never came back.

The last program in the box dates from 1964. I don't know the last year Mrs. Florence Johnson attended the club. I do know that Mrs. Johnson and her husband, Turk, celebrated their fiftieth wedding anniversary, for in the same box are some beautiful white fiftieth anniversary napkins, with golden bells and the names "Florence" and "Turk" between the years "1920" and "1970." A neighbor told me that Mrs. Johnson died in 1981. The high school had closed in 1967. The lumberyard and hardware store closed about the same time, but no one knows for sure when. The last gas station went after that.

Back to those programs. The motto never changed. The sweet pea kept its standing. So did the pink and white club colors. The club collect that follows persisted month after month, year after year:

A Collect for Club Women
Keep us, O God, from pettiness; Let us be large in thought, in word, in deed.
Let us be done with fault-finding and leave off self-seeking.
May we put away all pretense and meet each other face to face, without self-pity and without prejudice.

May we never be hasty in judgment and always generous.

Let us take time for all things; make us grow calm, serene, gentle.

Teach us to put in to action our better impulses; straightforward and
    unafraid.

Grant that we may realize it is the little things that create differences; that in
    the big things of life we are as one.

And may we strive to touch and to know the great common woman's heart
    of us all, and oh, Lord God, let us not forget to be kind.

                                                          —Mary Stewart

By modern standards these people were poor. There was a kind of naivete
among these relatively unschooled women. Some of their poetry was not good.
Some of their ideas about the way the world works seem silly. Some of their club
programs don't sound very interesting. Some sound tedious. But their monthly
agendas were filled with decency, with efforts to learn about everything from birds
to our government, and with coping with their problems, the weather, diseases.
Here is the irony: they were living up to a far broader spectrum of their potential
than most of us do today!

I am not suggesting that we go back to 1923 or even to 1964. But I will say that
those people in that particular generation, in places like Matfield Green, were
farther along in the necessary journey to becoming native to their places, even as
they were losing ground, than we are.

Why was their way of life so vulnerable to the industrial economy? What can we
do to protect such attempts to be good and decent, to live out modest lives respon-
sibly? I don't know. This is the discussion we need to have, for it is particularly
problematic. Even most intellectuals who have come out of places such as Matfield Green have not felt that their early lives prepared them adequately for the
"official" culture.

Let me quote from two writers. The first is Paul Gruchow, who grew up on a
farm in southern Minnesota:

> I was born at mid-century. My parents, who were poor and rural, had never
> amounted to anything, and never would, and never expected to. They were
> rather glad for the inconsequence of their lives. They got up with the sun
> and retired with it. Their routines were dictated by the seasons. In summer
> they tended; in fall they harvested; in winter they repaired; in spring they
> planted. It had always been so; so it would always be.
>
>   The farmstead we occupied was on a hilltop overlooking a marshy river
> bottom that stretched from horizon to horizon. It was half a mile from any
> road and an eternity from any connection with the rest of the culture. There
> were no books there; there was no music; there was no television; for a long
> time, no telephone. Only on the rarest of occasions—a time or two a year—
> was there a social visitor other than the pastor. There was no conversation in
> that house. (Gruchow 1991, 20)

Similarly, Wallace Stegner, the great historian and novelist, confesses to his feeling of inadequacy in coming from a small prairie town in the Cypress Hills of Saskatchewan. In *Wolf Willow* he writes:

Once, in a self-pitying frame of mind, I was comparing my background with that of an English novelist friend. Where he had been brought up in London, taken from the age of four onward to the Tate and the National Gallery, sent traveling on the Continent in every school holiday, taught French and German and Italian, given access to bookstores, libraries, and British Museums, made familiar from infancy on with the conversation of the eloquent and the great, I had grown up in this dung-heeled sagebrush town on the disappearing edge of nowhere, utterly without painting, without sculpture, without architecture, almost without music or theater, without conversation or languages or travel or stimulating instruction, without libraries or museums or bookstores, almost without books. I was charged with getting in a single lifetime, from scratch, what some people inherit as naturally as they breath air.

How, I asked this Englishman, could anyone from so deprived a background ever catch up? How was one expected to compete, as a cultivated man, with people like himself? He looked at me and said dryly, "Perhaps you got something else in place of all that."

He meant, I suppose, that there are certain advantages to growing up a sensuous little savage, and to tell the truth I am not sure I would trade my childhood of freedom and the outdoors and the senses for a childhood of being led by the hand past all the Turners in the National Gallery. And also, he may have meant that anyone starting from deprivation is spared getting bored. You may not get a good start, but you may get up a considerable head of steam.

Countless writers and artists have been vulnerable to the so-called official culture, as vulnerable as the people of Matfield Green. Stegner goes on to say:

I am reminded of Willa Cather, that bright girl from Nebraska, memorizing long passages from the *Aeneid* and spurning the dust of Red Cloud and Lincoln with her culture-bound feet. She tried, and her education encouraged her, to be a good European. Nevertheless she was a first-rate novelist only when she dealt with what she knew from Red Cloud and the things she had "in place of all that." Nebraska was what she was born to write; the rest of it was got up. Eventually, when education had won and nurture had conquered nature and she had recognized Red Cloud as a vulgar little hold, she embraced the foreign tradition totally and ended by being neither quite a good American nor quite a true European nor quite a whole artist. (Stegner 1962, 24–25)

It seems that we still blunt our sensitivities about our local places by the likes of learning long passages from the *Aeneid* while wanting to shake from us the dust of

Red Cloud or Matfield Green. The extractive economy cares for neither Virgil nor Mary Stewart. It lures just about all of us to its shopping centers on the edges of major cities. And yet, for us, the *Aenid* is as essential to becoming native to the Matfield Greens as the spear was to the paleolithic Asians who walked here across the Bering land bridge of the Pleistocene.

Our task is to build cultural fortresses to protect our emerging nativeness. They must be strong enough to hold at bay the powers of consumerism, the powers of greed and envy and pride. One of the most effective ways for this to come about would be for our universities to assume the awesome responsibility for both validating and educating those who want to be homecomers—not that they necessarily want to go home, but rather to go someplace and dig in and begin the long search and experiment to become native.

It will be a struggle, but a worthy one. The homecomer will not learn Virgil to adorn his or her talk to show off, but will study Virgil for insight, for utility, as well as for pleasure.

We can then hope for a resurrection like that of Mrs. Florence Johnson and her women friends, who took their collect seriously. Unless we can validate and promote the sort of cultural information in the making that the New Century Club featured, we are doomed. An entire club program devoted to coping with the heat of August is becoming native to a place. That club was more than a support group; it was cultural information in the making, keyed to place. The alternative, one might suggest, is mere air-conditioning—not only yielding greenhouse gases but contributing to global warming and the ozone hole as well, and, if driven by nuclear power, to future Chernobyls.

Becoming native to this place means that the creatures we bring with us—our domesticated creatures—must become native too. Long ago they were removed from the original relationships they had with their ecosystems and pressed into our service. Our interdependency has become so complete that, if proprietorship is the subject, we must acknowledge that in some respects they own us. We humans honor knowledge of where we came from, counting that as baseline information, essential to our journey toward nativeness. Similarly, we must acknowledge that our domesticated creatures are descendants of wild things that were shaped in an ecological context *not* of our making when we found them. The fence we built to keep their relatively tame and curious wild ancestors out of our Early Neolithic gardens eventually became the barbed wire that would contain them.

At the moment of first containment, those fences must have enlarged our idea of property and property lines. When we brought that notion of property lines with us to this distant and magnificent continent, it was a short step to the invisible grid that in turn created the tens of thousands of hard and alien lines that dominate our thoughts today. Those lines will probably be with us forever. But we can soften them. We'll have to, for the hardness of those lines is proportional to our sense of the extent to which we own what we use. Our becoming native will depend on our emerging consciousness of how we are to use the gifts of the creation. We must think in terms of different relationships. Perhaps we *will* come to think of the chicken as fundamentally a jungle fowl. The hog will once again be regarded as a descendant of a roaming and rooting forest animal. Bovines will be seen as savanna grazers.

An extractive economic system to a large degree is derivative of our perceptions and values. But it also controls our behavior. We have to loosen its hard grip on us, finger by finger. I am hopeful that a new economic system can emerge from the homecomer's effort—as a derivative of right livelihood rather than of purposeful design. It will result from our becoming better ecological accountants at the community level. If we must as a future necessity recycle essentially all materials and run on sunlight, then our future will depend on accounting as the most important and interesting discipline. Because accountants are students of boundaries, we are talking about educating a generation of students who will know how to set up the books for their ecological community accounting, to use three-dimensional spreadsheets.

Still, classroom work alone won't do. These students will need a lifetime of field experience besides, and the sacrifices they must make, by our modern standards, will be huge. They won't be regarded as heroic, at least not in the short run. Nevertheless, that will be their real work. Despite the daily decency of the women in the Matfield Greens, decency could not stand up against the economic imperialism that swiftly and ruthlessly plowed them and their communities under.

The agenda of our homecoming majors is already beyond comprehensive vision. They will have to be prepared to think about such problems as balances between efficiency and sufficiency. This will require informed judgment across our entire ecological mosaic. These graduates in homecoming will be unable to hide in bureaucratic niches within the major program initiatives of public policy that big government likes to sponsor. Those grand solutions are inherently antinative because they are unable to vary across the mosaic of our ecosystems, from the cold deserts of eastern Washington to the deciduous forests of the East, with the Nebraska prairie in between. The need is for each community to be coherent. Knowing this, we must offer our homecomers the most rigorous curriculum and the best possible faculty, the most demanding faculty of all time.

Further Reading

Altars of Unhewn Stone. 1987.
Becoming Native to This Place. 1994.
Meeting the Expectations of the Land. 1984. With Wendall Barry and Bruce Colman.
New Roots for Agriculture. 1980.

Reading about Wes Jackson

"The Genius of Place: The Land Institute Founder, on Tapping the Genius of the Prairie in the Design of Agriculture." An interview with Wes Jackson by Kathryn True. In *Context: A Quarterly of Human Sustainable Culture. www.context.org.* From *A Good Harvest* 42 (fall 1995): 40.

Jones, Lisa. "The Gospel According to Wes Jackson." *High Country News* 27.8 (1 May 1995). *www.hcn.org*

"Mainstreaming Sustainable Agriculture: Strategies for Putting Our Biological Knowledge to Work." An interview with Wes Jackson by Robert Gilman. In *Context: A Quarterly of Humane Sustainable Culture. www.context.org.* From *Sustainable Habitat* 14 (autumn 1986): 33.

Source Acknowledgments

Part 1. The Lay of the Land

THE NATURE OF THE PLAINS: IMPRESSIONS

N. Scott Momaday, excerpt from *The Names: A Memoir* (Tucson: University of Arizona Press, 1976), 42–57. Reprinted by permission of the University of Arizona Press.

Ian Frazier, chapter 1 in *Great Plains* (New York: Farrar, 1989), 3–16. Reprinted by permission of Farrar, Straus, and Giroux, LLC. Copyright © 1989 by Ian Frazier.

Sharon Butala, "The Subtlety of Land," in *The Perfection of the Morning: An Apprenticeship in Nature* (Toronto: Harper Collins, 1994), 76–92. A Phyllis Bruce Book, published by Harper Collins Publishers Ltd., Toronto. Copyright 1994 by Sharon Butala. All rights reserved.

Loren Eiseley, "The Flow of the River," in *The Immense Journey* (New York: Random House, 1957), 15–27. Copyright 1946, 1950, 1951, 1953, 1955, 1956, 1957 by Loren Eiseley. Used by permission of Random House, Inc.

William Least Heat-Moon, "Atop the Mound," in *PrairyErth* (Boston: Houghton Mifflin, 1991), 81–84. Copyright © 1991 by William Least Heat-Moon. Reprinted by permission of Houghton Mifflin Company. All rights reserved.

PLAINS NATURE: NATURAL HISTORIES

John Madson, "The Lawns of God," in *Where the Sky Began: Land of the Tallgrass Prairie* (San Francisco: Sierra Club Books, 1982), 51–79. Used by permission of Dycie J. Madson.

William Stafford, "In Response to a Question," in *The Way It Is: New and Selected Poems* (Saint Paul MN: Graywolf, 1998), 86. Copyright 1959, 1962, 1966, 1998 by the Estate of William Stafford. Reprinted with the permission of Graywolf Press, Saint Paul, Minnesota.

Greg Kuzma, "Songs," in *Of China and Greece* (New York: Sun, 1984), 61–62. Used by permission.

Dan O'Brien, excerpt from *The Rites of Autumn: A Falconer's Journey* (New York: Doubleday, 1988), 90–103. Reprinted by permission of the Lyons Press.

Paul A. Johnsgard, "Seasons of the Sandhill Crane: A Sandhills Spring," in *Crane Music: A Natural History of Cranes* (1991; rpt. Lincoln: University of Nebraska Press, 1998), 37–44. Copyright © 1991 by the Smithsonian Institution. Used by permission.

Paul Gruchow, "Spring 4," in *Journal of a Prairie Year* (Minneapolis: University of Minnesota Press, 1985), 37–40. Copyright © 1985 by the University of Minnesota.

Bruce Cutler, "From a Naturalist's Notebook: Smoke," in *The Year of the Green Wave* (Lincoln: University of Nebraska Press, 1960), 56–57. Copyright © 1960 by Bruce Cutler. Used by permission of David Cutler.

Linda Hasselstrom, "Coffee Cup Cafe" and "Red Glow in the Western Sky," in *Land Circle: Writings Collected from the Land* (Golden CO: Fulcrum Press, 1991), 26–30. Used by permission.

Part 2. Natives and Newcomers on the Great Plains

FIRST STORIES: NATIVE AMERICAN ACCOUNTS

STORIES OF EXPLORATION AND TRAVEL: NEWCOMERS' ACCOUNTS

Meriwether Lewis, William Clark, and Members of the Corps of Discovery, excerpt from *The Lewis and Clark Journals: An American Epic of Discovery,* abridged ed., ed. Gary E. Moulton (Lincoln: University of Nebraska Press, 2003). Reprinted by permission of the University of Nebraska Press. Copyright © 2003 by the University of Nebraska Press.

Edwin James, chapter 9 of *From Pittsburgh to the Rocky Mountains: Major Stephen Long's Expedition, 1819–1820,* ed. Maxine Benson (Golden CO: Fulcrum, 1988), 287–300. Used by permission.

Josiah Gregg, text of "On the Trail," in *Commerce of the Prairies: A Selection,* ed. David Freeman Hawke (1844; rpt. Indianapolis: Bobbs-Merril, 1970), 13–24.

Diane Glancy, "October\From the Back Screen Country," in *Claiming Breath* (Lincoln: University of Nebraska Press, 1992), 66–68. Reprinted by permission of the University of Nebraska Press. © 1992 by the University of Nebraska Press.

Susan Shelby Magoffin, excerpt from *Down the Santa Fe Trail and into Mexico: The Diary of Susan Shelby Magoffin, 1846–1847,* ed. Stella M. Drumm (1926; rpt. Lincoln: University of Nebraska Press, 1982), 31–44. Copyright © 1926, 1962 by Yale University Press. Used by permission.

Washington Irving, "The Grand Prairie—A Buffalo Hunt," in *A Tour on the Prairies* (1835; rpt. Alexandria VA: Time-Life Books, 1983), 263–79.

Francis Parkman, "The Platte and the Desert," preface to the 4th ed., and preface to the illustrated ed., in *The Oregon Trail: Sketches of Prairie and Rocky Mountain Life* (1847; rpt. Boston: Little, Brown, and Company, 1906), 51–64, ix–xi, and vii–viii.

Kenneth Porter, "Land of the Crippled Snake," in *No Rain in These Clouds: Poems, 1927–1945* (New York: John Day and Company, 1946), 125–28. Copyright 1946 by Kenneth Porter.

Mark Twain, chapter 3 and "Bemis and the Buffalo," in *Roughing It,* ed. Franklin R. Rogers (Berkeley: Published for the Iowa Center for Textual Studies by the University of California Press, 1972), 50–81. Copyright © 1972. Mark Twain Company.

Part 3. Arriving and Settling In

PIONEERS

James Fenimore Cooper, "Ishmael Bush's Camp," chap. 2 in *The Prairie: A Tale* (1827; rpt. Albany: SUNY Press, 1985), 18–28. Reprinted by permission of the State University of New York Press © 1985, State University of New York. All rights reserved.

Robert J. C. Stead, "Prairie Land," chap. 3 in *The Homesteaders* (1916; rpt. Toronto: University of Toronto Press, 1973), 39–53.

SETTLERS

Linda Hogan, "Calling Myself Home," "Red Clay," and "Heritage," in *Red Clay* (Greenfield Center NY: Greenfield Review Press, 1991), 8–9, 7, and 20–21; and "Return: Buffalo" and "Crossings," in *The Book of Medicines* (Minneapolis: Coffee House Press, 1993), 20–21 and 28–29. Used by permission.

Hamlin Garland, "Among the Corn Rows," in *Main-Travelled Roads* (1891; rpt. Lincoln: University of Nebraska Press, 1995), 98–121.

William Allen White, "A Story of the Highlands," in *The Real Issue: A Book of Kansas Stories* (Chicago: Way and Williams, 1897), 75–86.

Diane Glancy. "September\Peru, Kansas," in *Claiming Breath* (Lincoln: University of Nebraska Press, 1992), 55–56. Reprinted by permission of the University of Nebraska Press. © 1992 by the University of Nebraska Press.

O. E. Rølvaag, "Home-founding," in *Giants in the Earth* (New York: Harper & Row, 1927), 22–61. Copyright 1927 by Harper & Row, Publishers, Inc. Renewed 1955 by Jennie Marie Berdahl Rølvaag. Reprinted by permission of HarperCollins Publishers, Inc.

John Ise, "A New Homestead," in *Sod and Stubble,* ed. Von Rothenberger (Lawrence: University Press of Kansas, 1996), 30–36.

William Stafford, "The Farm on the Great Plains," in *The Way It Is: New and Selected Poems* (Saint Paul MN: Graywolf, 1988), 64. Copyright 1959, 1962, 1966, 1998 by the Estate of William Stafford. Reprinted with the permission of Graywolf Press, Saint Paul, Minnesota.

Era Bell Thompson, "God's Country," in *American Daughter* (Chicago: University of Chicago Press, 1946), 23–40. Copyright 1946 by the University of Chicago Press.

James Welch, with Paul Stekler, chapter 1 of *Killing Custer: The Battle of the Little Big Horn and the Fate of the Plains Indians* (New York: W. W. Norton, 1994), 25–47. Copyright © 1994 by James Welch and Paul Stekler. Used by permission of W. W. Norton & Company, Inc.

Louise Erdrich, "Dear John Wayne," in *Jacklight* (New York: Henry Holt, 1984), 12–13. Copyright © 1984 by Louise Erdrich. Reprinted by permission of Henry Holt and Company, LLC.

Part 4. Adapting to a New Country

SURVIVING NATURE'S STORMS

Ron Hansen, "Wickedness," in *Nebraska* (New York: Atlantic Monthly Press, 1989), 3–22. Used by permission of Grove/Atlantic, Inc. Copyright © 1989 by Ron Hansen.

Sinclair Ross, "A Field of Wheat," in *The Lamp at Noon and Other Stories* (Toronto: McClelland and Stewart, 1968), 67–76. Used by permission, McClelland & Stewart. *The Canadian Publishers.*

May Williams Ward, "Dust Bowl (A Sequence)," in *Wheatlands: Poems and Black Prints* © 1954 (self-published in Wellington KS), 48. Wichita State University Libraries, Department of Special Collections. Used with permission.

Lois Phillips Hudson, "Water Witch," in *Reapers of the Dust: A Prairie Chronicle* (New York: Little, Brown and Company, 1965; rpt. St. Paul: Minnesota Historical Society Press, Borealis Books, 1984), 73–83. Used with permission.

CREATING COMMUNITIES IN AMERICA

Willa Cather, "Neighbour Rosicky," in *Obscure Destinies* (Lincoln: University of Nebraska Press, 1998), 7–61. Reprinted by permission of the University of Nebraska Press. © 1998 by the University of Nebraska Press.

O. E. Rølvaag, excerpt from *Peder Victorious: A Tale of the Pioneers Twenty Years Later,* by Ole Rølvaag and trans. Nora D. Solum and the author (1929; rpt. New York: Harper & Row, 1966), 186–98. Copyright 1929 by Harper & Brothers, renewed © 1956 by Jennie Marie Berdahl Rølvaag. Introduction and biographical note by Gudrun Hovde Gvale copyright © 1966 by Harper & Row, Publishers, Incorporated. Reprinted by permission of HarperCollins Publishers, Inc.

Mari Sandoz, "The Christmas of the Phonograph Records," in *The Christmas of the Phonograph Records* (Lincoln: University of Nebraska Press, 1966), 3–27. Reprinted by permission of the University of Nebraska Press. © 1966 by the Estate of Mari Sandoz.

Will Weaver, "A Gravestone Made of Wheat," in *A Gravestone Made of Wheat* (New York: Simon and Schuster, 1989), 13–28. Reprinted with the permission of Simon & Schuster. Copyright © 1989 by Will Weaver.

Luther Standing Bear, "What the Indian Means to America," in *Land of the Spotted Eagle by Luther* (Lincoln: University of Nebraska Press, 1978), 247–50. Reprinted by permission of the University of Nebraska Press. Copyright 1933 by Luther Standing Bear. Copyright © renewed 1960 by May M. Jones.

Zitkala-Ša, "Americanize the First American." The Gertrude and Raymond Bonnin Collection, 2881.B75 G47x 1998. Used by permission of the L. Tom Perry Special Collection, Harold B. Lee Library, Brigham Young University, Provo, Utah.

Elizabeth Cook-Lynn, "End of the Failed Metaphor," chapter 13 in *Why I Can't Read Wallace Stegner: A Tribal Voice* (Madison: University of Wisconsin Press, 1996), 142–49. © 1996. Reprinted by permission of the University of Wisconsin Press.

Linda Hogan, "Oklahoma, 1922," in *Mean Spirit* (New York: Ivy Books, 1990), 3–11. Used with permission.

Part 5. The Great Plains Community

William Allen White, "The Passing of Pricilla Winthrop," in *In Our Town* (New York: McClure, Phillips, 1906), 217–40.

Langston Hughes, "Dance" and "Carnival," in *Not Without Laughter* (New York: Macmillan, 1969), 79–98 and 99–112, respectively. Copyright 1930 by Alfred A. Knopf, a division of Random House, Inc. Used by permission of Alfred A. Knopf, a division of Random House, Inc.

Larry Woiwode, "The Old Halvorson Place," in *The Neumiller Stories* (New York: Farrar, 1989), 97–119. Reprinted by permission of Farrar, Straus, and Giroux, LLC. Copyright © 1989 by Larry Woiwode.

Greg Kuzma, "A Person in My Life," in *Of China and Greece* (New York: Sun, 1984). Used by permission of Greg Kuzma.

Frederick Manfred, "Wild Land," in *Apples of Paradise* (New York: Trident Press, 1965), 101–37. Used by permission.

Wright Morris, excerpt from *The Home Place* (Lincoln: University of Nebraska Press, 1998), 1–25. Reprinted by permission of the University of Nebraska Press. Copyright 1948 by Wright Morris.

Robert Kroestch, excerpt from *Badlands* (Canada: New Press Trendsetter, 1975), 138–47. Used by permission.

Douglas Unger, excerpt from *Leaving the Land* (1984; rpt. Lincoln: University of Nebraska Press, 1995), 177–92. Reprinted by permission of the University of Nebraska Press. © Copyright 1984 by Douglas Unger.

Sharon Butala, "A Tropical Holiday," in *Queen of the Headaches* (Regina, Saskatchewan: Coteau Books, 1985), 131–45. Reprinted by permission of the publisher.

Epilogue

SUSTAINING AMERICA'S GRASSLANDS

Index of Works by Author

Butala, Sharon: "The Subtlety of Land,"
24; "A Tropical Holiday," 641

Cather, Willa: "Neighbour Rosicky," 447
Cook-Lynn, Elizabeth: "End of the Failed
Metaphor," 512
Cooper, James Fenimore: "Ishmael Bush's
Camp," 288
Cutler, Bruce: "From a Naturalist's Note-
book," 93

de Castaneda, Pedro: excerpt from "The
Narrative of the Expedition of Coronado," 202
Deloria, Ella Cara: excerpt from *Waterlily*,
154

Eastman, Charles: "A Legend of Devil's
Lake," 130
Eiseley, Loren: "The Flow of the River," 37
Erdrich, Louise: "Dear John Wayne," 407;
"Father's Milk," 179; "The Tomahawk
Factory," 678

Frazier, Ian: excerpt from *Great Plains*, 15

Garland, Hamlin: "Among the Corn
Rows," 315
Glancy, Diane: "October," 241; "Septem-
ber," 339
Gregg, Josiah: "On the Trail," 231
Gruchow, Paul: "Spring," 88

Hansen, Ron: "Red-Letter Days," 669;
"Wickedness," 413
Harjo, Joy: "Deer Dancer," 194; "Deer
Ghost," 197; "For Anna Mae Pictou
Aquash . . . ," 196; "Grace," 193
Hasselstrom, Linda: "Coffee Cup Cafe,"
95; "Going to the Post Office," 694;
"Red Glow in the Western Sky," 97

Heat-Moon, William Least: "Atop the
Mound," 44; "Under Old Nell's Skirt,"
101
Hogan, Linda: "Calling Myself Home,"
307; "Crossings," 312; "Heritage," 309;
"Oklahoma, 1922," 520; "Red Clay,"
308; "Return: Buffalo," 310
Hudson, Lois Phillips: "The Water Witch,"
437
Hughes, Langston: "Dance," 542; "Carnival," 552

Irving, Washington: "The Grand Prairie—
A Buffalo Hunt," 251
Ise, John: "A New Homestead," 369

Jackson, Wes: "Matfield Green," 713
James, Edwin: excerpt from *From Pittsburgh to the Rocky Mountains*, 218
Janovy, John, Jr.: "Home on the Range,"
659
Johnsgard, Paul A.: "Seasons of the Sandhill Crane," 82

Keillor, Garrison: "Collection," 651; "Life
Is Good," 654
Kroetsch, Robert: excerpt from *Badlands*,
622
Kuzma, Greg: "A Person in My Life," 574;
"Songs," 70

Lewis, Meriwether, and William Clark: ex-
cerpt from *The Lewis and Clark Journals*,
207
Low, Denise: "Another Tornado Dream,"
105
Madson, John: "The Lawns of God," 50
Magoffin, Susan Shelby: excerpt from
Down the Santa Fe Trail, 244
Manfred, Frederick: "Wild Land," 581
Momaday, N. Scott: excerpt from *The*

Names, 4

Morris, Wright: excerpt from *The Home Place,* 611

Neihardt, John G.: "The Great Vision," 136
Norris, Kathleen: "Sea Change," 706

O'Brien, Dan: excerpt from *The Rites of Autumn,* 73

Parkman, Francis: "The Platte and the Desert," 258; preface to *The Oregon Trail,* 4th ed., 266; —, illustrated ed., 268
Porter, Kenneth: "Land of the Crippled Snake," 270

Rølvaag, O. E.: "Home-founding," 342; excerpt from *Peder Victorious,* 471
Ross, Sinclair: "A Field of Wheat," 426

Sandoz, Mari: "The Christmas of the Phonograph Records," 481
Stafford, William: "The Farm on the Great Plains," 374; "In Response to a Question," 68; "The Rescued Year," 698
Standing Bear, Luther: "Crow Butte," 151; "The Holy Dog," 152; "What the Indian Means to America," 504

Stead, Robert J. C.: "Prairie Land," 297
Stegner, Wallace: "The Question Mark in the Circle," 107

Thompson, Era Bell: "God's Country," 376
Twain, Mark: excerpts from *Roughing It,* 273

Unger, Douglas: excerpt from *Leaving the Land,* 629

Ward, May Williams: "Dust Bowl," 434
Weaver, Will: "A Gravestone Made of Wheat," 491
Welch, James: excerpt from *Killing Custer,* 389
White, William Allen: "The Passing of Priscilla Winthrop," 531; "A Story of the Highlands," 334
Woiwode, Larry: "The Old Halvorson Place," 560

Zitkala-Ša: "Americanize the First American," 507; "Impressions of an Indian Childhood," 166; "When the Buffalo Herd Went West," 125